D0847914

Harvard East Asian Series 40

ASIAN IDEAS OF EAST AND WEST

The East Asian Research Center at Harvard University administers research projects designed to further scholarly understanding of China, Japan, Korea, Vietnam, and adjacent areas.

ASIAN IDEAS OF EAST AND WEST

Tagore and His Critics in Japan, China, and India

STEPHEN N. HAY

Harvard University Press

Cambridge, Massachusetts

1970

Distributed in Great Britain by Oxford University Press, London

Preparation of this volume has been aided by a grant
from the Ford Foundation

Library of Congress Catalog Card Number 73–89972

SBN 674–04975–6

Printed in the United States of America

This book is dedicated to all those, regardless of
nationality or vocation, who seek
"to imbue the effective leadership of the day
with a deeper understanding of modern world history."

PREFACE

My primary purpose in writing this book has been to study the intellectual leaders of India (now India and Pakistan) in the first half of the twentieth century alongside their contemporaries in China and Japan. Its most important parts, as I see it, are therefore Chapters Three, Six, Seven, and the Epilogue. The Bengali poet and philosopher Rabindranath Tagore figures prominently in the other chapters because by his great popularity in India after receiving the Nobel Prize for Literature in 1913, and by lecturing in Japan in 1916 and China in 1924, he stimulated writers, philosophers, and religious and political leaders in all three countries to publish more or less simultaneously their own views on the questions of common concern he posed: How could the most precious traditions inherited from their ancestors be preserved and strengthened in a time of rapid technological change and increasing influences from abroad? Could a pan-Asian front be established which would help each country defend its cultural heritage against the baneful effects of "Western" influence? Should selected European and American ideas and organizational methods be welcomed and adapted to suit local needs and, if so, which?

Answers to these questions, covering an enormous range of opinion, constitute a well-defined body of evidence related to a single catalytic agent. I have sought to interpret this evidence from four different perspectives. Looking at it as a whole, I have noted striking similarities in the lives and ideas of particular individuals in all three countries, often as the result of exposure to similar Western influences. Considering the leading thinkers of each society as a separate community, I have tried to reconstruct what I have variously called their common intellectual landscape, their thought-world, or the structure, spectrum, movement, currents, or universe of their ideas. Indian (both Hindu and Muslim) attitudes toward China, Japan, and "Asia" and Chinese and Japanese attitudes toward India and "Asia" provide a third set of perspectives on each society and its cultural traditions.

By far the most difficult and important part of my work has been to see each individual thinker as a study in himself, as an independent agent with a unique life history and world view. This has involved, first, sketching his biography, then allowing him to speak for himself in his own words, much as I did some years ago for those nineteenth- and twentieth-century Indian intellectuals included in the anthology *Sources of Indian Tradition* (New York, 1958). The chapters devoted to Tagore (especially One and Four) may be regarded as a case study of the method by which I have endeavored to plumb the depths of each man's psyche — correlating the historical and contemporary development of his family, region, and country in the political and the cultural realms, on the one hand, and his own psychological development and impact on his society and culture, on the other. In brief, I assume that an individual thinker is not merely a "reflection" or "product" of his society but develops his own ideas in reciprocal interaction with his contemporaries, as well as through studying the writings of his predecessors in the domain of his intellectual activity.

This last point deserves special emphasis in this age of simplistic theorizing about historical "forces" or "movements" such as "nationalism," "imperialism," "Westernization," "modernization," or "revolution." To a limited extent such broad concepts are useful and necessary, and I have had recourse to them here, I hope sparingly. The danger inherent in their overuse is that they can conceal the incalculable diversity of human experience behind a facade of plausible half-truths, and by conveying a brilliant illusion of certainty can discourage that tentative but persistent groping for more reliable generalizations about the real world which is the heart and soul of scientific work. Hypotheses we must have, lest our data amount to no more than an accumulation of trivia; but we must be ever alert to modify or discard them when they fail to fit the facts. To this end I ask that my readers approach with caution the concept of "revitalization" of cultural traditions on which I have placed some emphasis. The phenomenon to which it refers is not the operation of some abstract and impersonal "historical force" but the free activity of unique human beings living in specific environments and personal circumstances, thinking about the present in the light of the past and searching among the words and lives of previous generations for ideas and examples which will help them to make wise decisions in their own lifetimes, both for themselves and for their fellow men.

S.N.H.

University of California, Santa Barbara
July 5, 1969

ACKNOWLEDGMENTS

MANY PERSONS HAVE ASSISTED ME in one way or another to bring this book to its present form. My greatest debt is to my beloved wife, Eloise Knapp Hay. Cold print is inadequate to convey my gratitude for her faithful companionship, inspiring example as a scholar and teacher, and excellent advice. She has contributed stylistic improvements to most of the draft versions of the manuscript. I also greatly appreciate the interest and suggestions of the following persons who have read parts or all of the manuscript: Margaret H. Case, Chow Tse-tsung, Albert M. Craig, Sudhindranath Datta, Edward C. Dimock, Jr., John K. Fairbank, Wilma Fairbank, Pratulchandra Gupta, Marshall G. S. Hodgson, John F. Howes, Immanuel C. Y. Hsü, Daniel H. H. Ingalls, Ann Louise McLaughlin, Susanne Hoeber Rudolph, Benjamin I. Schwartz, Milton Singer, and Arthur F. Wright. The men and women who granted me personal interviews (only some of whom are named in the "Interviews" entry in the Bibliography) provided invaluable aid in getting the "feel" of the cultural and political life of India, Japan, and China during their lifetimes. I am especially grateful to L. K. Elmhirst, Mrs. Kora Tomiko, and Kalidas Nag for their reminiscences of Tagore's Asian travels and for reading to me excerpts from their private diaries.

Without the help of excellent language teachers and assistants I would not have been able to scan and translate so readily the Asian-language sources used. My procedure has been to learn the scripts, grammatical principles, and basic vocabularies of Bengali, Chinese, Gujarati, and Japanese, then to work with a cotranslator whose mother tongue is the language in question. First the passage to be translated is read aloud. One of us then makes a rough sight-translation orally, which I write down. We discuss alternative ways of conveying in English the nuances of meaning in the original, referring to two-language dictionaries especially for light on key terms with several possible translations. To minimize the distortions that might arise from our imperfect knowledge of each other's language, I have worked on most of the Chinese and Japanese passages quoted in this book with a second cotranslator, comparing the two versions and returning to dictionaries to iron out discrepancies. I wish to thank all those who joined me in this pleasant work, and especially the following: for Bengali — as teachers Somdev Bhattacharji, Edward C. Dimock, Jr., and Sakuntala Rao Sastri, and as cotranslators principally Hirendranath Goshal, also Amitava Chaudhuri and Ajit Datta; for Chinese — my teachers at the United Nations Secretariat, the Asian Institute in New York, Los Angeles City College, and, at Harvard, Francis W. Cleaves and Rulan Chao Pian, and as cotranslators principally Ch'en Ching-mei, also Ch'eng Chung-ying, Winston Hsieh, Hsü Cho-yun, Lin Yu-sheng, P'eng Tse-chou, and Yang Mei-huei; for Gujarati — as cotranslators Nandini Joshi and P. J. Mistry; for Japanese — my teachers at Yale University's Summer Language Program in Japanese, and as cotranslators principally Hagihara Nobutoshi, also Gail Bernstein, Nobuyuki Horie, and Martha Shinohara. Unless otherwise noted, the original text of all quoted material is in the language of the source cited in the corresponding note.

I am grateful to many librarians and booksellers for assistance in finding the materials used here, especially the staffs of the National Diet Library, Tokyo, the Ueno Public Library, the Tōyō Bunko, the Tōyō Bunka Kenkyujō, the Meiji Zasshi Shimbun Bunko and the Library of Tokyo University, the National Library, Taipei, the Union Research Institute, Hong Kong, the Feng P'ing-shan Library and the Library of the University of Hong Kong, the National Library, Calcutta, the Bangiya Sahitya Parishat Library, Rabindra Sadan Archives, Santiniketan, the National Archives of India, New Delhi, the Bibliothèque Nationale, the India Office Library of the Commonwealth Relations Office, London, the British Museum Library, the Library of the School of Oriental and African Studies, University of London, the New York Public Library, the Library of Congress, Washington, Chinese-Japanese Library of the Harvard-Yenching Institute, Lamont, and Widener Libraries of Harvard University, the Sterling Memorial Library, Yale University, the University of Chicago Libraries, and the libraries of the University of California at Berkeley, Los Angeles, and Santa Barbara.

I am also indebted to the following foundations and committees without whose financial support this book could not have been undertaken: the Ford Foundation through its Foreign Area Fellowship Program,

1953–1956, the University of Chicago through its Social Science Research and Southern Asian Studies Committees, 1956–1964, the United States Educational Foundation in India, 1959–1960, the East Asian Research Center at Harvard University, 1961 and 1964–1965, the American Council of Learned Societies, 1965–1966, the Asia Society, 1966–1968, the Center for South Asia Studies, University of California, Berkeley, 1966–1969, and the Faculty Research Committee, University of California, Santa Barbara, 1966–1969.

For permission to quote from Tagore's unpublished letters I wish to thank his literary heir, Srimati Pratima Tagore. Upacharya Kalidas Bhattacharya has kindly given permission on behalf of Visva-Bharati to quote from those of Tagore's poems published by them. Kipling's "Ballad of East and West" is quoted by permission of Mrs. George Bambridge and Macmillan Co., and of Doubleday & Company.

I thank Elizabeth M. Matheson and her staff at the East Asian Research Center, Harvard, for editing the Notes, Bibliography, and Select Glossary, Doris D. Hay for helping with proofreading and indexing, and Pramita Ghosh for assisting with the Index. All the research assistants, typists, and printers who have wrestled with various phases of this work have my lasting appreciation.

Finally, I wish to acknowledge my deep sense of gratitude to five men (the first four my professors at Harvard Graduate School in 1952–1954 and my friends since that time) whose teaching, published writings, and personal advice have been of immeasurable help in achieving the results embodied in this book. Daniel H. H. Ingalls first led me into the scholarly study of South Asian history and culture, and baptized me in the study of Sanskrit. Benjamin I. Schwartz introduced me to the discipline of intellectual history, especially that of modern China, and by his writings and conversations has stimulated me to rethink many problems of interpretation. (The title of the concluding "Postscript on 'Modernization' and Its Ambiguities" is borrowed from one of his unpublished essays.) John K. Fairbank has encouraged and supported my work at every stage and as editor of the Harvard East Asian Series has challenged me to meet standards without which this book would have appeared sooner, in an inferior version. William L. Langer gave me in two seminars on the history of international relations a superlative training in the craft of systematic historical research and analysis. Dialogues with the late Martin Buber showed me how to answer some critical questions on the religious and ethical dimensions of human experience, and what I have tried to do here may be regarded as an extension of his basic teaching that "all real life is meeting" into the realm of personal encounters between individuals living in different countries, cultures, and periods of history.

CONTENTS

CHAPTER FIVE. "THE REPRESENTATIVE OF ASIA" VISITS CHINA

MAPS (cartography by George McCann)

ILLUSTRATIONS

following page 110:

Welcome reception for Tagore at Kaneiji Temple, Ueno Park, Tokyo, 1916 (courtesy of Mrs. Kora Tomiko)

"On Oriental Culture and Japan's Mission," Tokyo, 1929 (courtesy of Mrs. Kora Tomiko)

Tagore, Hsü Chih-mo, and Miss Lin in Peking, 1924 (courtesy of Rabindra Sadan Archives, Santiniketan)

following page 142:

Tagore and Gandhi, Santiniketan, 1940 (courtesy of Bhakat Bhai and Co., Bolpur, West Bengal)

Tagore and Tōyama Mitsuru, 1924 (courtesy of Mrs. Kora Tomiko)

ASIAN IDEAS OF EAST AND WEST

INTRODUCTION

When we talk about European civilization, we use a term which is real in its meaning, it is an undoubted fact. But when they [Europeans] talk glibly of the Oriental mind and culture, they do not realize that we have not yet been able to develop a universal mind, a great background of Oriental cultures. Our cultures are too scattered.

— Tagore, in Tokyo, 1929

THERE IS NO EAST — NO ORIENT — in the cultural sense. The classical civilizations of China and India differ from each other as radically as each does from the European. Despite their fundamental differences — obvious from the very scripts and languages in which their classics are written — the idea that they (along with the disparate civilizations of Japan, Southeast Asia, and the Islamic world) are mere variants of a single "Oriental culture" or "Eastern civilization" has spread in recent centuries and continues to be widely held.

Five hundred years ago this simplistic belief was confined to the inhabitants of the far western flank of the Eurasian continent. Looking eastward to the lands of the Turk, the Arab, the Hindu, and the Mongol, Europeans grouped them all together as "Oriental." This vague consciousness of the other inhabitants of the earth's largest landmass as belonging to a single "Orient" was inherited from the Romans and sharpened by the medieval conflicts between the world of Christendom and the worlds of the Mongols and Islam. But non-Christians living on Eurasia's southwestern, southern, and eastern subcontinents had quite different ideas about the globe and their place on it. To Muslims it was self-evident that their civilization was centrally located, with unbelievers ranged around its fringes on the southwest (tropical Africa), northwest (Europe), northeast (China), and southeast (Hindu and Buddhist India and Southeast Asia). The Muslim community itself spanned the then known world, from its westernmost lands in Morocco (so named from Arabic *maghrib*, "the West") to the spice islands ten thousand miles to the east — with Mecca, the spiritual capital of the Islamic world, lying close to its geographical center.

Brahman pandits meanwhile considered their subcontinent as the southernmost (and best) part of a disc-shaped continent on which human beings lived. From their viewpoint, the rest of the inhabited world lay mainly to the north, with portions slightly to the northeast and northwest. History seemed to confirm their view, for outsiders had for centuries been pouring down onto the Indo-Gangetic plain from the northwest. What impressed the outsiders, however, about the southern subcontinent were its great rivers. And so, slightly mispronouncing the Sanskrit word *sindhu*, "river," they named it Ind or Hind and its people Hindus.

Oblivious of these western, southwestern, and southern traditions, the massive population of the fertile eastern flank of the Eurasian continent regarded *their* society as the only civilized one on the earth's surface. Thus the men of Han (or the Chinese, as others dubbed them, after the explosive conquests of the Ch'in emperor in 221–210 B.C.) contentedly named their country *Chung-kuo* "the Middle Kingdom," relegating the tribes to the north, east, south, and west to the status of outlying barbarians. The only society in all Eurasia to think of itself as "eastern" was that peopling the islands 450 to 1000 miles off the east coast of China. Accepting the Chinese writing system (later combining with it their own syllabic script), these islanders also adopted the Chinese custom of calling their country "the land of the sun's origin" (*Jih-pen* in Chinese pronunciation, hence "Japan" in English).

The great voyages of discovery which ended the fifteenth century like a burst of fireworks — Diaz' around Africa's southern tip in 1486, Columbus' magnificent failure to reach the Indies in 1492, and Da Gama's success in this aim in 1498 — set in motion the expansion of European power, European techniques and artifacts, and European ideas into all parts of the globe. Inevitably, the ideas of Europeans themselves were vastly changed in the course of this triple expansion.[1] By degrees, their conception of Europe as "the West" grew grander with their westward-moving conquest and settlement into the two sparsely populated continents across the Atlantic. So likewise the idea

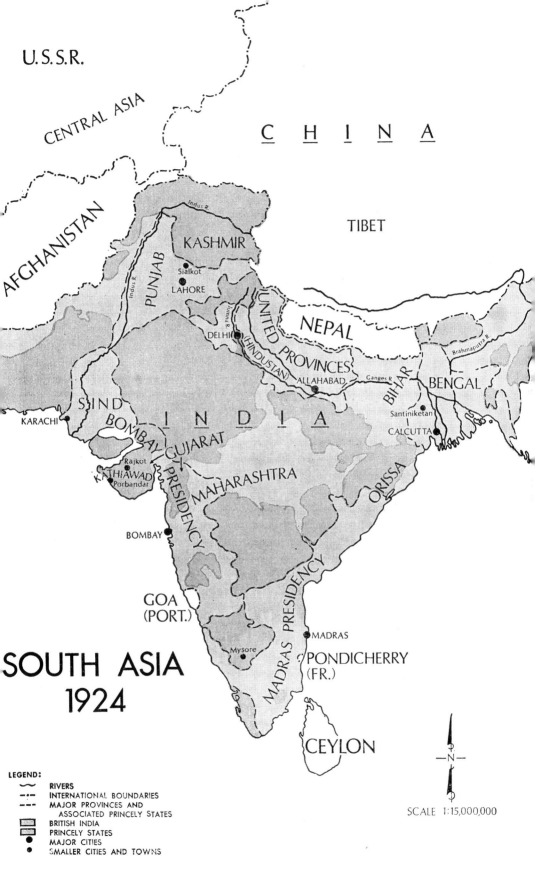

U.S.S.R.

CENTRAL ASIA

C H I N A

AFGHANISTAN

TIBET

Indus R.

KASHMIR

PUNJAB

Indus R.

Sialkot

LAHORE

Jumna R.

DELHI

UNITED PROVINCES

NEPAL

HINDUSTAN

Brahmaputra R.

ALLAHABAD

Ganges R.

BIHAR

BENGAL

SIND

KARACHI

BOMBAY

GUJARAT

I N D I A

Santiniketan

CALCUTTA

Rajkot

KATHIAWAD

Porbandar

PRESIDENCY

MAHARASHTRA

ORISSA

BOMBAY

GOA
(PORT.)

MADRAS PRESIDENCY

MADRAS

Mysore

PONDICHERRY
(FR.)

SOUTH ASIA
1924

CEYLON

LEGEND:

~~ RIVERS
–·– INTERNATIONAL BOUNDARIES
– – – MAJOR PROVINCES AND
     ASSOCIATED PRINCELY STATES
▨ BRITISH INDIA
▤ PRINCELY STATES
● MAJOR CITIES
• SMALLER CITIES AND TOWNS

SCALE 1:15,000,000

N

of "the East" swelled and grew as European — and, by the late eighteenth century, American — ships sailed with equal ease the waters off the coasts of India, Southeast Asia, China, and Japan, trading as they went (and sometimes fighting where they could not trade) with "Orientals" at Calcutta, Canton, and dozens of other ports of call.

One result of the overseas expansion of European ideas was that as scholars in India, Japan, and China learned European languages and studied European maps they came to think of themselves as being what the "Westerners" told them they were: "Eastern" and "Oriental." But this new idea of belonging to "the East" spread in quite different ways, and was associated with distinctive local traditions. Nineteenth century Hindu intellectuals took directly from their English conquerors the idea that India was, not the southern continent as their forefathers had believed, but the quintessential "East," the home of lofty religions and therefore the land par excellence of "spirituality."

In Japan, too, the idea of being part of "the East" caught on in the nineteenth century, but within a quite different geographical, political, and cultural situation. Since they already thought of themselves as Easterners with reference to the Chinese, the Japanese readily accepted the designation when it was applied to them by the Europeans and their American cousins. Indeed the prospect of assuming the leading role in a rising Oriental civilization held a strong attraction for some of Japan's intellectuals.[2]

In China, however, the weight of custom and the physical remoteness of the "southern barbarians" (as the Europeans and Americans were first called) kept the scholar-official class largely indifferent to the new terminology. The slogan, "Eastern ethics and Western science," coined in the 1840's by Japan's Sakuma Shōzan, did not become popular in China until the 1890's, and even then it was rephrased sinocentrically by the reformer-general Chang Chih-tung: "Chinese learning to provide the [moral] basis, Western learning to provide the [technical] means."[3] But gradually the European and American characterization of their world as "the West" and all Asia (or at least Eastern Asia) as "the East" permeated Chinese writings, under considerable influence from Japan, to which many young Chinese looked for the new learning in the decades after China's defeat by Japan in 1895.

All this while, the victorious advance of European arms, trade, and

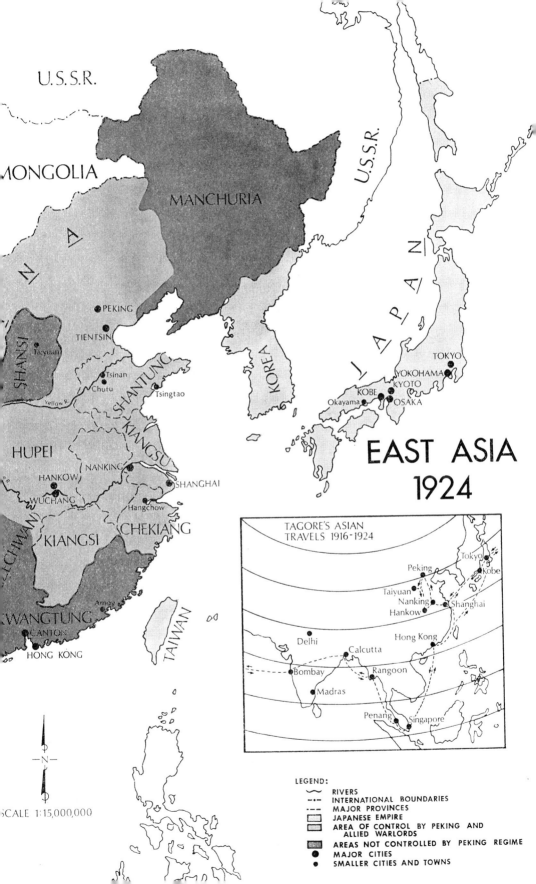

U.S.S.R.

MONGOLIA

MANCHURIA

U.S.S.R.

J A P A N

KOREA

TOKYO
YOKOHAMA
KYOTO
KOBE
Okayama OSAKA

PEKING

TIENTSIN

SHANSI
Taiyuan

Tsinan
Chutu
Tsingtao
SHANTUNG

Yellow R.

KIANGSU

HUPEI

HANKOW NANKING

WUCHANG SHANGHAI

Hangchow

KIANGSI CHEKIANG

SZECHWAN

AMOY

KWANGTUNG
CANTON
HONG KONG

TAIWAN

EAST ASIA
1924

TAGORE'S ASIAN
TRAVELS 1916-1924

Tokyo
Kobe
Peking
Taiyuan
Nanking
Hankow
Shanghai

Delhi
Hong Kong

Calcutta
Bombay Rangoon
Madras

Penang Singapore

N

SCALE 1:15,000,000

LEGEND:
~ RIVERS
-··-··- INTERNATIONAL BOUNDARIES
-··- MAJOR PROVINCES
☐ JAPANESE EMPIRE
☐ AREA OF CONTROL BY PEKING AND
    ALLIED WARLORDS
▨ AREAS NOT CONTROLLED BY PEKING REGIME
● MAJOR CITIES
• SMALLER CITIES AND TOWNS

ideas in Asia was stimulating European and American intellectuals to believe ever more firmly in the existence of a global dichotomy between "Eastern" and "Western" civilization. England's men of letters were strongly attracted to this twofold concept, particularly after the disturbing outbreak and suppression of the 1857 rebellion in northern India. Matthew Arnold distilled the comforting idea of the unwarlike, purely spiritual East in his 1862 lines on the Roman conquest of Palestine:

> The East bow'd low before the blast
> In patient, deep disdain;
> She let the legions thunder past,
> And plunged in thought again.[4]

Rudyard Kipling summed up the idea in 1889 in a jingle that soon became a slogan chanted even by children: "Oh, East is East and West is West, and never the twain shall meet." [5] Wherever English cultural influence extended among Asian intellectuals, especially in the Anglicized cities and universities of British-ruled India, the Arnold-Kipling idea of "the East" continued to spread.

By 1900 the stage was set for leading intellectuals in the two most Western-influenced societies in Asia, India and Japan, to give new impetus and meaning to this vagabond concept of a single Eastern civilization. Men in each society had accepted the East-West dichotomy from Westerners; now the modern Westerners' conquest of space through steamships, railroads, and telegraphs made it easy for Indian and Japanese intellectuals to meet in Calcutta or Tokyo, in London or Boston, to join forces for the strengthening of what they assumed was their common Oriental culture. The Bengali religious leaders Mozoomdar and Vivekananda had already visited Japan in the 1880's and 1890's. The Japanese art historian Okakura came to India for a year's stay in 1901–2, and the fruits of his discussions (in English, necessarily) with Bengal's cultural leaders appeared in London in 1903 in the form of a book, *The Ideals of the East*. Kipling's challenge had been accepted: men of "the East," informed of being radically different from men of "the West," had taken their first step toward realizing in practice the unity ascribed to them by their Western contemporaries.

The next major thrust toward Asian unity was taken by India's leading poet, Rabindranath Tagore, who visited Japan in 1916 with the express purpose of propagating the idea of a renascent Eastern civilization. He was welcomed enthusiastically by Japan's educated class, not because of his friendship with their own Okakura, but because he had been awarded in 1913 one of Europe's highest accolades, the Nobel Prize for Literature. In three public lectures, "India and Japan," "The Message of India to Japan," and "The Spirit of Japan," Tagore presented his view of the Oriental civilization to which he assumed both countries belonged. Each Japanese intellectual reacted to Tagore's message in his own way, but when all their comments were published it was clear that most of them disagreed with the Indian poet's concept of a spiritual East standing aloof from, and undefiled by, a materialistic West.

Tagore was sadly disappointed with Japan and blamed the intense nationalism and militarism he saw there on insidious Western influences. But his faith in Eastern civilization was soon strengthened by the repeated assurances of British, French, German, and American friends (themselves disillusioned with "Christian" Europe in consequence of the holocaust of the 1914–1918 war), that the West needed the healing power of Oriental religion and philosophy to save it from its own self-destructive folly. These assurances encouraged him to make one more attempt to link Asia's intellectual leaders in a common front for the revitalization of their common heritage of peace-giving light and love. This time China was his target. The year was 1924. But most of China's intellectuals, caught in the throes of revolution and civil war, turned a deaf ear to his message. Communist-led attacks on his lectures so wounded the sensitive poet that he canceled all but one final appearance in Peking and left for Japan and home.

Tagore's failure to win the support of China's educated class for his ideal of the East is one of the most poignant incidents in the intellectual history of modern Asia. Its significance, however, and that of his politer but only slightly less galling rejection in Japan, reaches far beyond the realm of personal tragedy. For the Indian poet, by his forthright and eloquent declaration of an Indian (and, in fact, Indo-Western) idea of Eastern spiritual civilization, succeeded in evoking from well over a hundred of his Japanese, Chinese, and Indian contemporaries equally forthright statements as to what they believed to be the nature and proper relation of "East" and "West."

An enormous variety of ideas and attitudes can be found in these writings, probably for three main reasons. In the first place, the intrusions into Asia of European and American military, political, and economic power began at different times, proceeded at different speeds, and resulted in different political relationships between Asian societies and the nation-states of the West. Clive's 1757 conquest of Bengal, Commodore Perry's 1854 overpowering of the Tokugawa Shogunate, and the 1900 suppression of the Boxers at Peking by an international expedition marked successive stages in the growth of Western power in Asia. It was strongest along the continent's southern rim, in the tropical and subtropical zones closest to Europe. India was by far the largest of Europe's dependencies, and her subjection to the benevolent despotism of her British administrators was well-nigh complete. Western power was weakest in Japan, the furthest part of Asia from Europe, and the nearest from the United States.

The facts of geography greatly conditioned the development of these political relationships: relative distance from Europe, accessibility of the hinterland from the seacoast, and the magnitude and nature of the economic resources of each country presented natural opportunities or obstacles to European expansion. So also did the aims and capabilities of the different European powers, Britain's primary aim being expanding trade by sea, Russia's expanding territorial control by land, and so on. Another factor was the strength and resilience of the political system of each Asian country: India's weaknesses in this respect invited the British to secure their trade by making her a colony; Japan's relatively centralized system, tightened from the 1860's onward, enabled her leaders to keep her independent. China's system of government by Confucian-trained scholar-officials proved too rigid to change and had begun to be abandoned even before the 1911 revolution, but no alternative form of centralized polity was found to take its place until the Russians suggested Marxism-Leninism.

A second major reason why Asia's intellectuals expressed such a great variety of ideas and attitudes in their writings on "East" and "West" is rooted in the diverse cultural traditions with which they were familiar — the principles and ideas, indigenous to each society and recorded in its ancient and medieval "classics" or scriptures. Through centuries of historical development, by a process akin to the survival of the fittest in biological evolution, in each society certain of these traditions had achieved greater authority than others, and this paramountcy was directly related to the high social position of the élite group which educated itself in those traditions. In India, we find Brahmans occupying this paramount position in Hindu society at the time of the Western intrusion; in China, the Confucian scholar-officials; in Japan, the Samurai. Confronted with the challenge of Western power, these intellectual leaders naturally responded to it in ways shaped by their positions in society and by the kinds of education they had received as boys and young men. The Brahman and Samurai élites, being born to their high status, were freer to experiment with new ideas, to reinterpret indigenous ones, or to borrow Western ones, without risking a drastic decline in social and economic well-being. Members of the Confucian-educated class, however, had to be much more cautious, for they owed their socioeconomic position not to ancestry but to rigid examinations testing mastery of the ideas and phraseology of the Confucian classics. When that examination system was discarded in 1906, China's literati were deprived of both intellectual certitude and job security. A Pandora's box of possibilities, most of them dismal, opened before their bewildered eyes.

A third reason why intellectuals in India, Japan, and China were of such different minds was that as they learned more about the technology, the institutions, and the ideas emanating from the expanding Western peoples, they became increasingly aware of the possibilities for choice among the many strands comprising the civilization of the Europeans and Americans. Often their first reaction was to study most intently those aspects of Western civilization that corresponded most closely to the kinds of activities they had come to value as a result of their early educations. They could also look to different Western countries for different models to follow. Japan's Samurai leaders, traditionally entrusted with military and political responsibilities, drew on the English model for their navy, the German example for their army and their monarchical constitution, the French prototype for their legal system. India's English-using educated class had little choice but to follow the British model in those aspects of Western civilization their British-supervised school system required them to absorb. Brahman intellectuals took little interest in military or economic affairs in any case; their traditional concern with religion, philosophy, and literature encouraged them to concentrate their attention on these fields. Far more Indian than

Japanese or Chinese scholars learned the English language — the key to the storehouse of Western culture as represented by its British variant. There is much truth in an Indian writer's comment that "India has absorbed most of the theoretical knowledge and the philosophical ideas of the West but did not to that extent imbibe the techniques and the know-how of the West. Japan in contrast took on most of the latter." [6]

China's thinkers began their foreign studies in earnest only after Japan's 1895 victory over their country, and they flocked to Japan to learn the secrets of her success. This meant that in many cases "Western" influences entered their minds initially through a Japanese screen. Ideas from the United States and England proved popular during World War I, but as China's political helplessness deepened after that war, the sons of her old Confucian scholar-official class turned increasingly to Bolshevik Russia as their model in the task of overhauling a large and decayed empire.

These differences in political status and cultural heritage meant that even the same ideas and institutions, borrowed from the same Western source, could take very different forms and meanings within the political framework and cultural environment of each Asian society. The idea of nationalism, for example, could blend in India with religious revivalism, in Japan with military expansionism, and in China with social and political revolution. Another central idea was that of continuing historical "progress," "civilization," or the more recently popular term, "modernization." But definitions of what constituted progress varied tremendously: what seemed forward-looking and "modern" to one Asian intellectual could appear retrogressive and baneful to another. Communism, for example, so much admired by China's young intellectuals, was dismissed by Tagore as outmoded in its adherence to the materialist philosophy of the nineteenth century, and condemned by Gandhi as dangerous because of its violent methods.

Within the particular political, geographical, social, and cultural environment in which he found himself, each individual philosopher, writer, religious or political leader in Asia was able to select and combine from two main sources — the diverse traditions and models within his own heritage, and the multiplicity of ideas and modes of action available for importation from Europe and North America. As transportation and communication speeded up interactions within and among Asian societies, their intellectual leaders could also borrow and learn from one another — as Japan had previously learned from China and China from India in the first millenium of our era. In the years during and following World War I contacts among these three thought-worlds grew apace, and introduced an added, pan-Asian dimension to the debates in each one concerning the relative merits of indigenous and Western cultural traditions. In this time of lively controversy over the nature of "East" and "West" and their civilizations, Tagore's ideas on this problem were widely known and warmly debated.

What Tagore sometimes called the "message" of India, sometimes the "voice" of Asia, is therefore significant, both in its own right, and because the dramatic way he presented it stimulated educated men in Japan, China, and India to articulate their own views on the major issues he raised. As a prism diffracts a single ray of light into the separate bands of color which comprise it, so Tagore's ideas provoked leading thinkers to make clear just where they stood along the intellectual spectra of their societies. By studying eighty-seven of these men — forty-eight Japanese, twenty-four Chinese, and fifteen Indian — and analyzing the positions they took in relation to the central questions raised by Tagore we may be able to gain considerable insight into the structure and movements of thought in the three major countries of Asia during the first half of the twentieth century.

CHAPTER ONE

THE MAKING OF A MODERN PROPHET

I, the world's poet,
Play its tunes on my flute,
But as I improvise,
Many notes I leave apart.

Yet in so many silent hours,
Helped by imagination's powers,
This whole globe's great symphony
Fills my heart.

— Translated from
Tagore, "Oikatān" (Symphony)

THE NEWS THAT THE INDIAN POET and Nobel laureate Rabindranath Tagore was to arrive that evening brought over twenty thousand Japanese thronging to Tokyo's Central Station on June 5, 1916. Eight years later a much smaller but equally excited crowd greeted the bearded poet at Peking's Ch'ien Men station with flowers and exploding firecrackers. No mere tourist, Tagore came bearing a distinctive message to the intellectuals and students of both Japan and China, a message which he summed up in 1924 on his return to a hero's welcome in his native Calcutta:

I feel that Asia must find her own voice. Simply because she has remained silent so long the whole world is suffering. The West has got no voice. She has given us nothing that could save us — that which gives immortality. She has given us science — a great gift no doubt — which has its special value, but nothing that can give us life beyond death. Her cult of power is based on pride and greed and the deliberate cultivation of contempt for other races. . . . I do feel that if Asia does not find her own voice, humanity will not be saved. That was my message to China and Japan and they listened to me and I do hope that some good will come out of it.[1]

That Asia had a voice, a message, which could grant humanity salvation, life beyond death, immortality — this was an extraordinary idea, and Tagore as its prophet cut an extraordinary figure on the lecture platforms of Japan, China, India, Europe, and America in the 1910's and 1920's. How far he succeeded in propagating this message is a story worth telling. It begins with the genesis of the idea itself, and its ripening in the mind of India's most gifted poet in modern times.

The word "Asia" may be of Asian origin, derived possibly from the Babylonian *asu,* meaning "to rise" and indicating the direction from which the sun rises.[2] The Greeks knew little of Asia, as they called the lands lying eastward from Hellas, until Alexander's conquests brought them direct reports of India. In Roman times, more was learned of Hindu and Buddhist metaphysical thought, transmitted principally through Alexandria; and the image of India and the East as the home of religious wisdom gained in substance, as the Latin tag *ex oriente lux,* "light comes from the East," suggests. For the Christian citizen of medieval Europe the geographical source of his religious revelation lay eastward in Palestine, but he also pictured the Garden of Eden as lying beyond it still farther in the east, somewhere in the vicinity of India. The more precise knowledge of Asia acquired by Europeans during the age of discoveries dispelled this fanciful notion. By the eighteenth century, French rationalist philosophers were holding up as a model for Europe an idealized empire of China, a secular state where all religions were thought to be regarded, as in Gibbon's Rome: "by the people as equally true; by the philosopher as equally false; and by the magistrate as equally useful."[3]

The older image of the East in general, and of India in particular, as the fountainhead of higher wisdom came back into vogue in the nineteenth century through a combination of circumstances. Of first importance was the British conquest of the Indian subcontinent. Displacing the predominantly Muslim heirs to the ruins of the Mughal Empire, the British found the Hindu commercial and administrative classes firm supporters of their rule, particularly in the rich and strategically placed Bengal delta. Desiring to stabilize their position as governors of a vast and alien population, British officials worked with local pandits to codify the customary law by which their Hindu subjects considered themselves bound. These researches, conducted chiefly in Calcutta by members of the Asiatic Society (founded in 1784) and the

College of Fort William (founded in 1800), stimulated the discovery, translation, and publication of Sanskrit texts, not only on law, but on philosophy and religion as well.[4]

In Europe the arrival from India of translations of such works as the *Bhagavad Gītā,* Kalidasa's *Shakuntalā,* and the Upanishads produced an exhilarating effect on thinkers for whom Christian doctrines had lost their appeal. Schopenhauer, for example, predicted in 1818 on the basis of his study of the Upanishads that "the influence of Sanskrit literature will penetrate into Europe not less deeply than did the revival of the Greek classics in the fifteenth century," and that "Indian wisdom will flow once more over Europe and will transform from top to bottom our science and our thought." [5]

In the United States, Emerson and Thoreau and other Transcendentalists found the *Bhagavad Gītā* a revelation. In France, Edgar Quinet announced in 1841: "The pantheism of the Orient, transformed by Germany, corresponds to the Oriental Renaissance, just as the idealism of Plato, corrected by Descartes, crowned in the seventeenth century the Greek and Latin Renaissance." But the enthusiasm for Indian culture reached its greatest heights in Germany, where a succession of writers and poets in the Romantic movement developed an idealized, mythical image of that distant eastern land.[6]

IDEAS OF EAST AND WEST IN NINETEENTH-CENTURY BENGAL

The discovery by Western savants of the grandeur of ancient Indian thought and the glories of its literature probably had its greatest effects, not in the West, but in India itself. Most of the ancient texts, embedded in the labyrinthine structure of Sanskrit grammar and preserved in privately held manuscripts, were known only to a small number of Brahman specialists, and the Upanishads in particular were considered esoteric teachings to be confided only to disciples. Once these texts were translated, printed, and published for all the world to read, literate Hindus of every caste could assimilate the teachings they contained. The application of modern methods of scholarship and publication to the corpus of Sanskrit writings thus produced a transformation in the way high-caste Hindus regarded their ancestral religion. We can date this process precisely: in 1805, England's greatest Sanskritist, Henry

Colebrooke, published his essay, "On the Vedas, Or the Sacred Writings of the Hindus," containing translated portions of the Upanishads, and noted that the worship of deified heroes such as Rama and Krishna was a later historical development not sanctioned in the Vedas; ten years later, the Bengali Brahman Rammohun Roy made this finding a key point in his campaign against the prevailing Hindu system of idol-worship. From 1816 to 1820, Rammohun published the Sanskrit texts and their Bengali, Hindustani, and English translations of several Upanishads manifesting what he asserted to be "the real spirit of the Hindoo Scriptures, which is but the declaration of the unity of God." [7] From these beginnings we can trace most of the subsequent attempts by Hindus themselves to reform their society and religion from within — and eventually to reform the rest of the world as well.

Bengal provided an exceptionally fertile soil for this movement of religious reformation. Accustomed for centuries to serving their Afghan and Mughal rulers as subordinate officials, the three literate high-caste groups — Brahmans, Kayasthas, and Vaidyas (significantly, the Kshatriya, or warrior caste had by the nineteenth century become virtually nonexistent in Bengali Hindu society) — continued in these roles under the British, and by the 1820's were demanding that English be substituted for Persian as the language of administration and higher education. The smaller group of educated Bengali Muslims protested against this change, but in vain, and when the substitution came in the 1830's they held back from English education, with the result that their influence declined as rapidly as that of the Hindus increased.[8] Throughout the nineteenth century, as the British extended their military and political control into the interior of the subcontinent, setting up army cantonments, administrative offices, courts, schools, and hospitals, the English-speaking Bengali babus went with them to fill positions in the expanding cadre of subordinate officials and professional men. A genuine symbiosis thus developed between Britisher and upper-caste Bengali Hindu which was reinforced by the fact that the capital of British India remained in Bengal, at Calcutta, right through the century and was shifted to Delhi only after 1912. In Bengal itself, Hindus who had prospered in commerce or administration purchased large estates, or *zemindaris,* from which they derived increasing income as the production of cash crops increased and the land tax remained fixed at 1793 rates under the Permanent Settlement.

This close partnership with the British had one great drawback: it exposed Bengali Hindus to alien cultural influences that threatened to deracinate them and to undermine their high status in their own society. Conversion to Christianity, which some English-educated Hindus embraced out of admiration for its ethical and spiritual content, nevertheless seemed to most a betrayal of their own heritage. The solution to this dilemma was now presented by Rammohun Roy: reform Hinduism from within by going back to the lofty philosophy of the Upanishads, and at the same time accept the ethical principles taught by Jesus, without subscribing to the doctrines of Christ's divinity or saviorhood. Rammohun's dual reinterpretation of Hinduism and Christianity — essentially a new faith combining what seemed the best features in both religions without requiring a conversion from one to the other — became the starting point from which Bengali Hindu reformers in succeeding generations were to develop their own religious ideas.[9]

With Rammohun Roy the British-Hindu symbiosis in Bengal, begun in the seventeenth century in the field of commerce and extended in the eighteenth to the field of government, in the nineteenth century entered the realm of philosophy and religion as well. The Hindu-Christian synthesis he proposed at once caught the attention of those Western intellectuals who felt constricted within the confines of Judeo-Christian and Greco-Roman thought. His writings on religion, phrased in fluent English, were quickly reprinted in England, America, and continental Europe. When Rammohun broke the customary Hindu ban on overseas travel to visit England and France in 1831, he was welcomed by the young Unitarian movement (which claimed him as one of their leaders), sought out by the aging Jeremy Bentham, and otherwise honored in London, Paris, and Bristol (where he died in 1833). His interpretation of the Vedas as enjoining "spiritual devotion . . . benevolence, and self-control, as the only means of securing bliss," [10] and his sympathetic attitude toward Christianity (he even recommended it to the skeptical Robert Owen) made an excellent impression in Britain and prepared the way for the later visits of other Bengali Hindu religious leaders: Keshub Chunder Sen in 1869–70, P. C. Mozoomdar in 1883, Vivekananda in 1893–1896, and finally Rabindranath Tagore in 1912–13.

The reformed Hindu faith formulated by Rammohun was slow to attract converts until it was adopted by a young Brahman who as a boy had known and admired Rammohun and attended one of the schools he had founded. This young man was Debendranath Tagore (1818–1905), father of the more famous Rabindranath. The Tagores were an important Calcutta family and in fact were among the city's founding fathers, for they had settled there about the time Job Charnock planted a trading post on the east bank of the Hooghly in 1690. "My own family came floating to Calcutta upon the earliest tide of the fluctuating fortune of the East India Company," Rabindranath once wrote. Considered outcaste Brahmans because a remote ancestor was supposed to have smelled the odor of cooked beef at the court of his Muslim ruler, the Tagores had little to lose and much to gain by associating with the British traders. As Rabindranath put it, "the unconventional code of life for our family has been a confluence of three cultures, the Hindu, Mohammedan and British." Their unconventionality and adaptability were well rewarded in the eighteenth century: Rabindranath's great-great-grandfather amassed a considerable fortune while serving as a collector of revenue for the Company.[11] Rabindranath's grandfather Dwarkanath (1794–1846) became one of the wealthiest men in Calcutta through his astute management of this fortune, which he invested in coal mines, indigo, and sugar plantations. His import-export firm, Carr, Tagore and Company was the first business partnership to be formed between an Indian and an Englishman. Dubbed "Prince" Dwarkanath because of his lavish spending, he twice broke the Hindu prohibition against overseas travel by sailing to England, where he dined with Queen Victoria and was banqueted by the Lord Mayor of London. "A lively sympathy with the spirit of modern progress," wrote an English admirer in summing up Dwarkanath's career, "made the participation of his fellow countrymen . . . in the blessings of Western civilization the great object of his efforts." [12]

Debendranath Tagore, Dwarkanath's eldest son, turned his energies in a quite different direction, one which was to make a decisive impression on his own youngest son, Rabindranath. Debendranath's mother had separated from his father because he violated Hindu custom by eating meat with Europeans, and so Debendranath was left to be raised by his paternal grandmother, a woman of intense and not entirely orthodox faith. This beloved grandmother died when he was eighteen, and the shock of losing her brought on a religious experience which set the course he was to follow throughout his life. "A strong aversion to wealth arose within me," he recalled; "in my mind was awakened a joy unfelt before." Although Dwarkanath was ambitious that his eldest son "should follow his example, and reach the topmost heights of rank and fame and worldly honours," Debendranath's aspirations were directed toward spiritual rather than material rewards:

> To renounce everything and wander about alone, this was the desire that reigned in my heart. Imbued with His love I would roam in such lonely places that none would know; I would see His glory on land and water, would witness His mercy in different climes, would feel His protective power in foreign countries, in danger and in peril; in the enthusiasm of this desire I could no longer stay at home.[13]

Debendranath did become a great traveler, and his many journeys up the Ganges Valley and into the Himalayas, as well as his sea voyage to Singapore, Hong Kong, and Canton, must have stimulated in Rabindranath's mind a strong desire to emulate his father's example. The religious ideas that Debendranath developed both before and during these wanderings also formed the theological basis of Rabindranath's own declared faith. Rejecting both the polytheism of popular Hinduism and the absolute monism of the Advaita Vedanta philosophy, Debendranath worshiped a personal God whom he believed to be present both in the individual soul and in the universe. This was essentially the theistic position adopted by Rammohun Roy. The personal friendship and intellectual link between the two men became an institutional one as well in 1843 when Debendranath joined the Brahmo Samaj (Society of Worshipers of the One God), founded earlier by Rammohun, and built it into a large and vigorous organization.[14]

Rabindranath, born in 1861, Debendranath's fourteenth child, and the youngest of the twelve offspring who survived infancy, tremendously admired his father. But Debendranath was constantly traveling, and even on the rare occasions when he was at home, the children had to talk in whispers and could not even peep into his room.[15] It appears from his reminiscences that Rabindranath felt somewhat neglected as a child. "I was very lonely — that was the chief feature of my childhood — I was very lonely," he told an English friend. "I saw my father seldom; he was away a great deal, but his presence pervaded the whole house and was one of the deepest influences on my life." [16] Rabindranath also saw little of his mother, for she was ill and left her infant son in the care of her eldest daughter. When he reached boyhood, Rabindranath was put in the hands of the servants (or the "servocracy," as he later termed their strict collective rule), who did not let him leave the house, cuffed him when he was naughty, and fed him on a Spartan diet. Forbidden to step outside the chalk circle which was drawn around him, he used to stand on the balcony of the many-roomed family mansion and look out longingly at the distant houses, trees, and clouds. This prolonged experience of confinement at a sensitive age imbued the outside world with an irresistible allure, and contributed to that love of travel which expressed itself so fully in the latter part of his life. "Caged in the house as we were," he wrote of himself and his cousins, "anything savouring of foreign parts had a peculiar charm for me." [17]

Suddenly Debendranath opened the cage and took the eleven-year-old Rabindranath on a four months' journey to the Punjab and the Himalayas. Debendranath gave his gifted youngest son predawn lessons in Sanskrit declensions, chanted verses from the Upanishads for him, and instructed him in English and astronomy. Rabindranath not only enjoyed at last immediate access to the father he had up to this time worshiped from afar, he was also liberated from the shackles of the senseless discipline which had been imposed by servants and schoolteachers. "As he allowed me to wander about the mountains at my will," Rabindranath noted of his father, "so in the quest for truth he left me free to select my path. . . . He held up a standard, not a disciplinary rod." [18]

The special attention Debendranath had paid to his youngest son and the wonderful tales Rabindranath told of their trip raised him to a new status in the eyes of his family. "The chains of the rigorous regime which had bound me snapped for good when I set out from home," he wrote in his *Reminiscences*. "On my return I gained an access of rights." [19] His mother was impressed by his recitations of the *Ramayana* epic, and gave him the seat of honor when the womenfolk would gather in her room. The pleasurable memory of sudden recognition consequent to a glamorous journey may have remained for the rest of Rabindranath's life a stimulus to re-enact this archetypal experience.

After his miraculous transformation from ugly duckling into much-admired swan, Rabindranath began to share in the bright cultural world which his elder brothers, sisters-in-law, and cousins were creating in the 1870's. The expanding family of the Tagores occupied several adjoining mansions in North Calcutta. Already cut off from orthodox Hindu society by their status as degraded Brahmans, they had become even further isolated by Debendranath's combination of iconoclastic religious ideas and conservative social customs. Enclosed in their self-sufficient family compound, the talented members of the family created a subculture of their own, within which young Rabindranath was free to experiment while discovering his own identity as a poet.

Experimentation with new forms of artistic expression came easily to the members of this self-contained social group. The eldest brother, Dvijendranath, philosophized in prose and verse; his magnum opus, much admired by Rabindranath, was a long poem entitled "The Dream Journey." The fifth eldest, Jyotirindranath, "would spend days at his piano engrossed in the creation of new tunes." [20] Rabindranath's cousin Gunendranath was an accomplished dramatist whose sons Gaganendranath and Abanindranath were to become two of India's foremost painters. His sister Svarnakumari Devi, Bengal's first woman novelist, also edited the monthly literary magazine *Bhāratī* (a name for the goddess of speech) which Jyotirindranath and Dvijendranath had started, and to which Rabindranath began contributing at the age of sixteen. Frequent soirees brought other men of culture to the house, and the impressionable boy Rabindranath would eavesdrop on their discussions, listen to their songs, and watch the plays they staged. When he was only eight, a second cousin induced him to begin writing verses, and his elder brothers encouraged him to continue these experiments.

During these years of precocious adolescence Rabindranath was absorbing the basic ideas about Hinduism and India, and about East and West which he later elaborated in his lectures in many lands. One of his early poems, read in 1875 at the Hindu Fair organized by his brother Jyotirindranath and other cultural nationalists in Calcutta, expressed pride in the ancient civilization of India, coupled with sorrow at its decline in more recent times. Three years later, when he was seventeen, his elder brother Satyendranath (the first Indian to be admitted to the élite Indian Civil Service) took him with him on an extended trip to England. Delighted with this opportunity to see the Western world at first hand, Rabindranath wrote a Bengali essay for the family's monthly, *Bhāratī*, which contained in embryo the concept he later made his message to Japan, China, and the West:

If the remnants of Indian civilization were to become the foundation on which European civilization is to be built, what a most beautiful sight that would be! The European idea in which freedom predominates, and the Indian idea in which welfare predominates; the profound thought of the Eastern countries and the active thought of the Western countries; European acquisitiveness and Indian conservatism; the imagination of the Eastern countries and the practical intelligence of the West — what a fullness will emerge from a synthesis of these two.[21]

These three related ideas — that India and the East were synonymous, that Eastern civilization was distinguished by spiritual profundity, and that the East and the West complemented each other perfectly — did not originate with Rabindranath. In one sense they were the natural expression in an idealized form of the symbiosis between upper-caste Hindus and their British rulers in nineteenth-century Bengal, and accordingly were articulated, either singly or jointly, by intellectuals on both sides of the partnership. As early as 1802 one of the young Englishmen at the Company's orientalist college in Calcutta had equated India with Asia and claimed that "literature, taste and science originated in Asia and by a general diffusion, in the course of time, spread themselves over Greece and Italy."[22] In 1823 Rammohun Roy had sought to deflate a Christian critic of Hinduism by arguing:

If by the "Ray of Intelligence" for which the Christian says we are indebted to the English, he means the introduction of useful mechanical arts, I am ready to express my assent and also my gratitude; but with respect to *Science, Literature,* or *Religion,* I do not acknowledge that we are placed under any obligation. For by a reference to history it may be proved that the World was indebted to *our ancestors* for the first dawn of knowledge, which sprang up in the East.[23]

Rammohun also buttressed his case for the religious superiority of Asia with an argument which was to gain wider currency as the nineteenth century progressed: "Almost all the ancient prophets and patriarchs venerated by Christians, nay even Jesus Christ himself . . . were Asiatics, so that if a Christian thinks it degrading to be born or to reside in *Asia,* he directly reflects upon them."[24]

The same ideas were frequently voiced by the magnetic orator Keshub Chunder Sen (1838–1884), who was first Debendranath's assistant, and then his successor as leader of the Brahmo Samaj. "And was not Jesus Christ an Asiatic?" he asked in his 1866 lecture, "Jesus Christ: Europe and Asia." "To us Asiatics, therefore, Christ is doubly interesting, and his religion is entitled to our peculiar regard as an altogether Oriental affair." [25] In his first lecture in India after returning from England in 1870, Keshub suggested the complementarity of Indian religiosity and English ethics: "Let, then, India learn from England practical righteousness; let England learn from India, devotion, faith, and prayer," and called India, "the noble representative of the East." Seven years later he told a Calcutta audience which included the viceroy, Lord Lytton: "Let modern England teach hard science and fact; let ancient India teach sweet poetry and sentiment. Let modern England give us her fabrics; but let the gorgeous East lend her charming colors." [26]

In "Asia's Message to Europe," delivered in Calcutta in 1883, Keshub wove together the four themes of India as the essence of Asia, of Asia as spirituality incarnate, of himself as Asia's representative, and of the complementarity of Asian and European civilization — the exact themes which Rabindranath Tagore was to propound in his own lectures in the 1910's and 1920's, also in beautifully phrased English. "Thy civilization has proved a blessing," Keshub declared to Europe, "but inasmuch as it utterly exterminates our nationality, and seeks to destroy and Europeanize all that is in the East, it is a curse. Therefore will I vindicate Asia. . . . These lips shall plead for Asia." "I am called to represent the interests and minister to the wants of a whole continent. In standing forward as Asia's servant and spokesman I feel proud of my exalted position. As an Asiatic, representing a vast constituency, I feel as I never did feel, never can feel as a mere Indian." Keshub then dilated on the qualities which he felt distinguished Asia: "The East is emphatically the Holy Land." "The Spirit of Asia" was tolerant and comprehensive. "Asia boasts of a higher unity. It is the unity of kinship and brotherhood." The genius of Asia was religious: "Asia is the fountainhead whence have gone forth streams of various creeds and diverse movements . . . to the uttermost parts of the world." "It is un-Asiatic not to know God." "Verily there is nothing secular in Asia." Keshub concluded that Europe and Asia should learn from each other: "Europe, the Lord has blessed thee with scholarship and science and philosophy, and with these thou art great among the nations of the earth. Add to these the faith and intuition and spirituality of Asia, and thou shalt be far greater still." [27]

How deeply Keshub Chunder Sen's ideas influenced Rabindranath's thinking is difficult to say, but the virtual identity of their idea that Asia had a message for the West can scarcely be a coincidence. Keshub was living in the Tagore home when Rabindranath was born, and the poet later wrote, "I was fortunate enough to receive his affectionate caresses at the moment when he was cherishing his dream of a great future of spiritual illumination." [28] Rabindranath's elder brothers Satyendranath and Hemendranath were especially devoted to the magnetic Keshub at the time, and their admiration probably survived the split between him and their father on the question of social reform in 1865. Keshub was lecturing in Calcutta throughout the formative years of Rabindranath's life, and the audience at his enthusiastic 1883 lecture on "Asia's Message to Europe" may have included the sensitive thirteen-year-old.

The idea of India's spiritual greatness seems to have remained popular, and even to have increased its hold on the imaginations of Indian and Western intellectuals alike in the last quarter of the nineteenth century. The Russian Madame Blavatsky and the American Colonel Olcott, who founded the Theosophical Society in New York in 1875, made much of reincarnation and other Hindu and Buddhist ideas. They came to India in 1879 and within six years had made enough converts among educated Indians and British officials to establish over one hundred branches throughout the country. (One prominent Theosophist, A. O. Hume, was the chief organizer of the Indian National Congress, which began its annual meetings in 1885.) In Britain the publication in 1879 of *The Light of Asia,* retelling the life of Gautama Buddha in epic poetry, created a literary sensation and more than half a million copies were sold during its seventy-odd reprintings. Its author, Edwin Arnold, had served in Poona as principal of the Deccan College and learned some Sanskrit there. Arnold's preface praised Buddhism as "this great faith of Asia," and described the Buddha's "spiritual dominions" as extending over "the whole Eastern Peninsula," including India itself, for "the mark of Gautama's sublime teaching is stamped ineffaceably upon modern Brahmanism." A great enthusiast for empires (he owed his subsequent knighthood in part to his jingoistic editorials in the *Daily Telegraph*), Arnold spoke of the Buddha's "magnificent empire of belief," and took obvious pride in claiming that "more than a third of mankind, therefore, owe their moral and religious ideas to this illustrious prince." [29] Yet another influential Indophile of the period was Oxford's professor of Sanskrit and the editor of *The Sacred Books of the East*, F. Max Müller, whose collection of essays entitled *India: What Can It Teach Us?* was much appreciated by his friend Keshub Chunder Sen. One passage in particular has been frequently cited by Hindus as proof of the greatness of their religious heritage:

> If I were asked under what sky the human mind has most deeply pondered on the greatest problems of life, and has found solutions of some of them which well deserve the attention of those who have studied Plato and Kant — I should point to India. And if I were to ask myself from what literature we, here in Europe . . . may draw that corrective which is most wanted in order to make our inner life more perfect, more comprehensive, more universal, in fact more truly human, a life, not for this life only, but a transfigured and eternal life — again I should point to India.[30]

English-speaking Hindus readily accepted these words of praise, and often were led by them to study their own scriptures in the translations provided by Western savants. (Such was the case with a young man from Gujarat studying law in London in 1890, Mohandas K. Gandhi, who was introduced by two English Theosophists first to the *Bhagavad Gītā* in Sir Edwin Arnold's verse rendering, and then to *The Light of Asia*.[31]) Their mastery of English also enabled Hindu intellectuals to expound to British and American audiences the greatness of these texts, which Western scholars were helping them to interpret, and Bengalis were particularly active in this effort. In effect, a Hindu missionary movement now arose, owing much of its impetus to the example and the challenge of the Christian missionaries, who were steadily intensifying their educational and conversion efforts in the closing decades of the century. Keshub Chunder Sen had spoken more in Christian than in Hindu terms during his 1870 speaking tour in England, but his disciple, P. C. Mozoomdar (1840–1905) placed greater emphasis on India's contribution to a universal theistic faith while lecturing in England, the United States, and Japan in 1873, 1883, 1893, and 1900.[32]

India's most successful missionary to the West in the nineteenth century, Swami Vivekananda (1862–1902), was also a Bengali Hindu, but his interpretation of Hinduism was based on its medieval form, which embraced worship before idols, as well as the ancient Upanishadic ideas stressed by Rammohun and Debendranath. Inspired by his teacher, the Brahman mystic Sri Ramakrishna (1837–1886), Vivekananda advanced Hinduism's claim to world-wide acceptance during his five years of lecturing and teaching in the United States and England in 1893–1896 and 1898–1900. Both he and P. C. Mozoomdar appeared in Chicago in 1893 at the World Parliament of Religions, and the enthusiastic American response to Vivekananda's eloquent exposition of Hinduism earned him immediate fame in his own country. His success in the West then emboldened him to command his admiring countrymen when he returned to them: "Up, India, and conquer the world with your spirituality! . . . The world wants it; without it the world will be destroyed. . . . Now is the time to work so that India's spiritual ideas may penetrate deep into the West." Like Keshub and countless other Indian and Western intellectuals in the nineteenth and twentieth centuries, Vivekananda equated India's spirituality with the essence of Eastern or Asian civilization. "The voice of Asia has been the voice of religion. The voice of Europe is the voice of politics. Each is great in its own sphere," he told a Los Angeles audience in 1900.[33] And in New York he declared: "When the Oriental wants to learn about machine-making, he should sit at the feet of the Occidental and learn from him. When the Occident[al] wants to learn about the spirit, about God, about the soul, about the meaning and mystery of this universe, he must sit at the feet of the Orient[al] to learn." [34]

This concept of a synthesis between Indo-Asian spirituality and Western practicality was exactly the "message" which Rabindranath Tagore was to deliver to his audiences in Japan and China, in the United States and Europe in the years between 1916 and 1930. For Rabindranath to accept this concept seems perfectly natural, considering how widely it was held in India and in England in the late nineteenth century. What seems more difficult to explain is his persistence and zeal in preaching this idea abroad; for Keshub, Mozoomdar, and Vivekananda were avowedly leaders of religious movements seeking converts to their faiths, while Rabindranath was known primarily as a poet and a man of letters. To understand his motives for assuming the role of prophet we must study his psychological and intellectual development from the time of his first trip to England in 1877 to his third in 1912, which heralded the beginning of his missionary career.

FROM POETRY TO PROPHECY

Tagore himself considered the most important event in his religious life to be the mystical experience which overwhelmed him one morning as he stood watching the sun rise from the veranda of the house where he was living with his favorite brother Jyotirindranath and his beloved sister-in-law Kadambari Devi. "A sudden spring breeze of religious experience for the first time came to my life and passed away, leaving in my memory a direct message of spiritual reality," a message of cosmic unity.

> When of a sudden, from some innermost depth of my being, a ray of light found its way out, it spread over and illuminated for me the whole universe, which then no longer appeared like heaps of things and happenings, but was disclosed to my sight as one whole. This experience seemed to tell me of the stream of melody issuing from the very heart of the universe and spreading over space and time, re-echoing thence as waves of joy which flow right back to the source.[35]

Even the passers-by on the street were transformed by this divine light and sound from within; they "seemed to me all so extraordinarily wonderful as they flowed past — waves on the sea of the universe." For four days young Rabindranath remained in this "self-forgetful state of bliss," but the vision of the unity of his consciousness with the whole of creation — exactly the experience described in classical Hindu terms as the union of the individual soul (ātman) with the Universal Soul (brahman) — remained with him for the remainder of his life.[36]

At this point in his life Rabindranath had no worldly responsibilities to worry him. He was twenty-one, and an income from the tenants of the family's large estates was assured him for life. He had been allowed to discontinue at thirteen the formal schooling whose meaningless discipline he loathed. Seeing that he was an able youth, his elder brothers had suggested that he prepare himself for a profession, perhaps the law, and with this in mind Satyendranath had taken him to England when he was seventeen. There he attended lectures at London University, was taken in by the family of a London doctor, and wrote letters home praising the freedom with which men and women could meet each other in English society. His father became anxious about the possibility that he was falling in love with the doctor's daughter, a girl of his own age, and summoned him home just as he was settling down to serious studies.[37] Rabindranath obeyed Debendranath's command quite willingly, but a year after his return to Calcutta asked for and received permission to go to London once more to study law, only to change his mind on the ship. "In fear and trembling," he came back to explain himself to his father, but was surprised to find that Debendranath, "showed no sign of irritation, he seemed rather pleased. He must have seen in this return of mine the blessing of Divine Providence." [38] Debendranath himself had turned away from a worldly career in his late teens and apparently he approved Rabindranath's decision to do the same.

Free to do as he liked, Rabindranath settled down to a comfortable existence with his favorite brother and sister-in-law, wrapped in the cocoon of their love. The poet tells us that his sister-in-law Kadambari Devi (who was ten years younger than her husband but only two years older than Rabindranath) had long "lavished on me a wealth of affection and regard," and "a profusion of womanly affection." Under her care he lived a life of "right royal laziness" and "utter disorderliness" for the next three years, and it was early in this period that he underwent the mystical experience of at-oneness with the world which left its indelible stamp on his memory. These years also opened the way for him to continue his experiments in creative writing, and to establish his reputation as an outstanding, albeit "lisping," lyric poet in Bengali.[39]

Two sudden changes brought to an end this idyllic period. First his father, very much the patriarch, arranged to have him marry an eleven-year-old girl, the virtually uneducated daughter of an employee on the family's East Bengal estates. Then, five months later, his beloved sister-in-law, apparently despondent over her husband's self-indulgent life away from home, and possibly because Rabindranath was no longer as close to her as he had been before his marriage, took her life by swallowing an overdose of opium. This tragedy shocked and wounded Rabindranath more deeply than any other event in his life:

I was utterly bewildered. All around, the trees, the soil, the water, the sun, the moon, the stars, remained as immovably true as before; and yet the person who was as truly there, who, through a thousand points of contact with life, mind and heart, was ever so much more true for me, had vanished in a moment like a dream. . . . Alone on the terrace in the darkness of night I groped all over like a blind man trying to find upon the black stone gate of death some device or sign.[40]

In his grief Rabindranath went through a period of revolt against the conventions of society. He wandered about in fashionable bookshops with a coarse sheet as his only upper garment. "To be called upon to submit to the customs and fashions of the day, as if they were something soberly and genuinely real, made me want to laugh. I *could* not take them seriously," he later wrote. As one of his friends recalled, "For some months he would not wear a shirt and would often visit our house wearing only a dhoti and covering himself with a chadar of long-cloth. He wore shoes very rarely, and mostly went about in slippers, which the quainter they were the better he liked." [41]

Rabindranath's bereavement seemed to quicken rather than to check the flow of his poetry, which he came to consider his lifelong homage to the memory of the friend who had guided him through adolescence to the discovery of his identity as a poet. This was his thought in a poem he addressed to Kadambari Devi some thirty years later, after unexpectedly discovering her photograph:

> You dwell at the root of my life . . .
> All that I am
> Has found in you its innermost harmony.
> Unknown to me, unknown to any,
> Your melody sounds in my songs;
> You are the Poet in the heart of the poet . . .[42]

In this same poem Rabindranath suggests that a connection existed between his comradeship with his sister-in-law and his subsequent love of continual travel.

> Once you came on the path walking by our side,
> There was heaving in your breast,
> There was life in your limbs

Creating forms with rhythm ever-new,
In songs and dances,
Beating time with the universal rhythm.
. . . In our journey together,
The night came,
And under its screen
You stopped still.
Since then
I have moved on, day and night,
. . . An unknown tune
Has thus led me farther and farther away,
I have been intoxicated by the urge of the road.[43]

Rabindranath's child-bride, Mrinalini Devi, offered him a loving heart and bore him four children, but his favorite niece, Indira Devi (who was about the same age as his wife) gradually came to fill the role of intellectual companion vacated by Kadambari Devi's departure. Despite the satisfaction gained from continuing to improve and win recognition as a poet and writer, Rabindranath grew increasingly restless. He reminisced: "I was torn by a furious impatience, an intolerable dissatisfaction with myself and all around me." [44] A striking poem of 1888, "Wild Hopes," seethes with this restlessness: ". . . O that I might be an Arab Bedouin! Beneath my feet the boundless desert, melting into the horizon! My horse gallops, the sand flies! Pouring my stream of life into the sky, day and night I go with fire burning in my heart! My spear in my hand, courage in my heart, always homeless!" [45]

As his restlessness increased, he had a painful sense of being excluded from the world of men. He felt like "an outsider" and was "simply fretting for want of an invitation to the place where the festival of world-life was being held." When his brother Satyendranath and a friend set out for a holiday in England in 1890, Rabindranath decided to go with them. As he explained, "From some far-away sky came to me a call of pilgrimage reminding me that we are all born pilgrims — pilgrims of this green earth. A voice questioned me: 'Have you been to the sacred shrine where Divinity reveals itself in the thoughts and dreams and deeds of Man?' I thought possbly it was in Europe where I must seek it and know the full meaning of my birth as a human being in this world." [46] These hopes seem to echo the optimistic note sounded in his 1878 essay on the feasibility of blending Eastern and Western civilizations. Here a lifelong pattern becomes clear: each time he set out on a voyage overseas he idealized the purpose of his trip, hoping to find through it the answer to some great problem.

Rabindranath's second visit to England did give him an answer to his search for meaning, but it was an almost wholly negative one. He could not trace the family in which he had found such an affectionate welcome twelve years earlier. A disturbing flirtation with an English singing teacher and reproachful letters from Indira Devi combined to accentuate the dissatisfaction he had hoped to relieve by coming to London. "My mind is very restless. I'm fed up," he wrote in his diary on his thirteenth day in London after reading a letter from his niece. Two weeks later his state of mind was no better, as this entry shows:

> Monday. Last night I had a terrible dream the whole night long — I've seen just this kind of dream so many times that I've lost count — I think that some day it will come true — in this one night I felt as if I were suffering intolerable pain for a whole month. — Today is mail day. I won't get a letter from Babi [Indira Devi, whose previous letter had informed him she was not going to write him any more letters]. I've decided to return home. I can't stand it any more.[47]

Three days later he sailed for India on board the S.S. *Thames.*

Rabindranath's diary indicates that his principal reason for shortening his stay in London was a purely personal one. In the year following his return, however, he published *Yurop yātrīr-dāyārī* (The diary of a traveler to Europe), not the original diary at all but a new work, in which he blamed his sudden departure on the unsettling effects produced in his mind by the hurly-burly of Western urban life:

> Huge buildings, huge factories, all kinds of entertainment places, people coming and going to and fro as in a great festival. No matter how dazzling and wonderful this may be, it tires the onlooker. One's consciousness cannot be satisfied merely by wonder and excitement; on the contrary, they always perplex the mind.
> Finally these words come to mind: "All right, sir, well and good. Agreed that you are a great city, a great country, whose wealth and power know no limits. I need no more proof. Now I will be relieved if I can go back home. There I know everyone, understand everyone; there I can pierce through all outer appearances and can easily savor the humanity in people. There I can enjoy with ease, think with ease, love with ease." [48]

The difference between the original and the published diaries suggests that, having failed to resolve his inner restlessness, Rabindranath projected it onto an external reality, Western civilization itself. This hypothesis seems confirmed by another passage in the published Diary, which takes a much more pessimistic view than his 1878 essay does regarding the possibility of synthesizing Eastern and Western civilizations. The contrast between Indian and English cultures reminded him in 1891 of the fable about the difficulties the crane and the fox had in dining together — the crane could eat only from a tall jar, the fox from a shallow plate. Creative writing alone offered a common substance for all men: "Each people has its own past history and external ways and customs which are useful to it, but a barrier to other people. . . . An international feast is only possible in the realm of literature. There he who has a long beak is not deprived of food, and he who has a greedy tongue is also satisfied." [49] Over two decades later this belief in the international feast of literature was to encourage him to translate some of his Bengali poems into English, while preparing for his third and far more successful visit to London — with results which were to restore his earlier faith in intercultural synthesis, and to extend it to painting and music. In the intervening twenty years, however, he searched in his own land and its traditions for that sense of purpose he had failed to discover in the West during his disappointing 1890 visit.

Among the external influences helping him to move in this Indo-centric direction the most important were his father, his close contact with rural Bengal, and the rise of patriotic feeling in India. When Rabindranath returned from his second trip to England, Debendranath intervened once more in his youngest son's life, insisting he take charge of the management of the family's landed property in the remote up-country districts of East Bengal, northern Bengal, and Orissa. For the next ten years, Rabindranath spent most of his time on these estates, supervising the planting, irrigating, and harvesting of crops and collecting rent and taxes from his sharecropping tenant farmers, and reporting in person once a month to Debendranath, who "would remember every figure, and ask awkward questions whilst the report was being read." Rabindranath's son Rathindranath recalled that "Father used to be afraid of this day of trial, like a school-boy going up for his examination. We children would wonder why *our* father was so afraid of *his* father." [50] Just how deeply Debendranath influenced his son's inner life during this period is difficult to estimate; the poet's deepening religiosity, which eventually produced the poems known in English translation as *Gītān-jali,* was surely encouraged by the example and advice of his stern but saintly father, whom educated Indians honored as the Maharshi, or "great sage." Rabindranath's most able biographer attributes to his father's influence both his preoccupation at this time with ancient Indian legends and medieval Hindu chivalry, and the fact that in 1901 he followed family custom and arranged the marriages of his eleven- and fourteen-year-old daughters — an action which contradicted the satirical attacks on the evils of child marriage he had delivered in the late 1880's.[51]

Rabindranath's daily contacts with the simple sharecropping peasants on his family's estates also led him to value Indian traditions more highly than he had in his more rebellious youth. Separated most of the year from his wife and children, he spent much of his time on the houseboat with which he navigated the many rivers of East Bengal. As his boat was carried by the current or poled upstream by his boatmen the constant change of scene soothed his restless spirit. "There is no effort on my part, no labour, and yet a tireless movement outside pervades the mind with a tender calm," he wrote at the time.[52] In more active moods, he found an outlet for his energies in a "pouring abundance" of creative writing.[53] Many of his short stories deal with the lives of villagers, and his poems show a deepening love of his natural surroundings. Indeed, the beauty, simplicity, and harmony with nature of rural life grew so congenial to him during the 1890's that he henceforth idealized this life as the true foundation of Indian culture. Against it he came to counterpoise the ugliness, overactivity, and organized selfishness he saw in city life, whether in London or in Calcutta.

By the time he reached his fortieth birthday, Rabindranath had expanded this dichotomy between ruralism and urbanism into a full-blown opposition between the peaceful village-centered society of India and the aggressive nation-states of the West. In the spring of 1901 he devoted an entire essay to a discussion of the difference between Hindu civilization and European civilization. European civilization, he declared, was essentially political in nature, dedicated to strengthening the nation-state and its sovereign independence. Hindu civilization, by contrast, he saw as dedicated to spiritual rather than political freedom, and its goal was the religious liberation of the individual. The word "nation" did not exist in any Indian language, he noted, nor did India's history or its religious, social, or domestic life show any evidence of emphasis on nation-building activities. "The foundation of our Hindu civilization is the society, while the foundation of European civilization is politics," he concluded.

> Man can achieve greatness through the society, or he can achieve it through politics. But we are mistaken if we believe that the building up of a nation on the European pattern is the only type of civilization and the only goal of man.

Accepting the terminology then current in the English-speaking world, Rabindranath entitled this important essay "Eastern and Western Civilization." [54]

The contrast between India and Europe, the East and the West, became even sharper in Rabindranath's mind as he contemplated the rapid expansion of Western empires and spheres of influence in Africa and Asia in this heyday of imperialism. Britain's aggression against the Boer Republic seemed to him the epitome of evil, and on December 31, 1900, the last day of the century, he wrote a group of sonnets on the contrast between the West and East. One opened:

> The last sun of the century sets amidst the blood-
>   red clouds of the West and the whirlwind of hatred,
> The crimson flow of light on the horizon is not the
>   light of thy dawn of peace, my Motherland,
> It is the glimmer of the funeral pyre burning to ashes
>   the vast flesh — the self-love of the Nation —
> dead under its own excess . . .

The nineteenth century had been the century of the West, he seemed to say, but the twentieth would be the century of the East. He therefore advised India to remain true to her spiritual civilization:

> Thy morning waits behind the patient dark of the East,
>   meek and silent, meek and silent . . .
> Be not ashamed, my brothers, to stand before the proud
>   and powerful with your white robe of simpleness.

Let your crown be of humility, your freedom the freedom of the soul.
Build God's throne daily upon the ample bareness of
your poverty
And know that what is huge is not great and pride is
not everlasting.[55]

China, too, was suffering under the intensified rivalry of the European imperialist powers, and from 1897 onward was being sliced up
into different spheres of foreign influence. News of the Boxer uprising
in 1900 and of the cruelties inflicted by foreign troops during its suppression caused the Bengali weekly *Hitavādī* (Adviser), of which Rabindranath was once literary editor, to bemoan China's fate: "The last of
the Asiatic empires is going to disappear. Is that not a matter for sorrow
to the people of Asia?"[56] Some two years later Rabindranath read with
excitement a slender volume entitled *Letters from John Chinaman*, the
first sentence of which spoke significantly of "the fundamental antagonism between Eastern and Western civilization." The anonymous author,
apparently a Chinese official, indicted the people of the West for their
harsh treatment of China during the Boxer troubles, and eloquently
argued the moral superiority of Chinese over Western civilization.

Rabindranath at once wrote a review of the book, describing the
"peculiar joy and strength" he had derived from reading it. "I have
seen from it that there is a deep and vast unity among the various peoples
of Asia," he declared. This discovery was a real source of strength for
India, he continued, for it not only showed that "Indian civilization is
one with Asian civilization," but that the very longevity of Asian civilization was also evidence of its sheltering an immortal truth. European
civilization has demonstrated its greatness by spreading itself over large
areas of the globe, but up to this point India could only prove the greatness of her civilization by the words of her scriptures. Now a new proof
was at hand:

If we can see that our ancient civilization has spread to China and
Japan then we can understand that it has a great place as an expression
of human nature, that it is not merely the words of manuscripts. If we
can see that China and Japan have experienced success within this
civilization, then our own inglorious and impoverished condition dis-
appears, and we can see where our real treasure lies.[57]

Even though the European flood was covering the earth, "Eastern civilization will defend itself," Rabindranath proclaimed, for "Asia is ready to search for and strengthen her ancient dams." The life of Europe was in trade and politics, he repeated, but Asia's life lay in religion and in social organization. "Asia is growing ever more eager to defend this life. In this we [of India] are not alone; we remain linked with the whole of Asia." [58]

It must have unsettled Rabindranath when he learned that the anonymous author of *Letters from John Chinaman* was not a Chinese official but an Englishman, G. Lowes Dickinson, a fellow at King's College, Cambridge.[59] Neither Dickinson nor Tagore knew China or its civilization at first hand; both men were projecting onto it an ideal image, accenting its moral or spiritual virtues as a foil against which to depict the greed and brutality of Western imperialism in Asia. Just at this point in Rabindranath's life he came to know an English-speaking Japanese intellectual who did know something about China and was now touring India. With Okakura Kakuzō's visit to Calcutta in 1901–2, two streams of thought on Asian civilization met for the first time — one Hindu-British, and the other Japanese-American — and powerfully reinforced each other.

A Gentleman from Japan and a Lady from Ulster

Okakura Kakuzō (1862–1914) was in many ways the Japanese counterpart of Rabindranath Tagore. The son of a samurai who had gone into the silk trade at Yokohama (as Tagore was the son of a Brahman family which had prospered in the commercial city of Calcutta), he studied English at the mission school of the Rev. James Hepburn, but also learned some Chinese, the classical language of East Asia (as Tagore studied both English and Sanskrit in addition to his mother-tongue).[60] But the essential similarity between the two men lay in their efforts to revitalize their countries' cultural traditions at a time when Western influences seemed to threaten their very existence. Tagore had chosen to become a Bengali poet with the approval of most of his family; the principal influence on Okakura's decision to become a leader in the development of Japanese Art was his American professor at Tokyo University, Ernest Fenollosa. Just as Tagore's ideas on Asian civilization cannot be understood apart from the effects of European Orientalist scholarship and Indophilia on nineteenth-century Hindu thought, so to understand Okakura's idealized image of Asia we must know more about the ideas of his American teacher.

Four years after his graduation from Harvard at the head of the class of 1874, Ernest Fenollosa (1853–1908) arrived in Tokyo to teach philosophy.[61] Fascinated with the aesthetic traditions of Japan, he began to study Japanese art. His student Okakura Kakuzō, already a member of a Bohemian art group, proved a willing helper and interpreter. With two other American admirers of Japan, William Sturgis Bigelow and Edward S. Morse, Fenollosa and Okakura traveled to Kyoto and Osaka in 1882 to inspect ancient temples and buy old art objects, then held in low esteem because of the craze for things Western in Japan. At the Miidera Temple above Lake Biwas the Americans had an interview with the Buddhist Abbot Sakurai Keitoku which led to Fenollosa's and Bigelow's conversion to Buddhism. (Both later asked that their ashes be buried at Miidera, where they lie today.) From Keitoku, Fenollosa imbibed the grand idea that "the Western spirit was nearly ripe to receive the lofty doctrine which Eastern guardians have preserved for its precious legacy." [62]

During Fenollosa's remaining eight years in Japan, he succeeded in arousing the interest of the government in the task of preserving the country's art treasures, and in 1886 he and Okakura, now his younger colleague, were sent on a mission to Europe to study the most advanced methods of art research. Partly at Fenollosa's urging, the Japanese government established a national art school, of which Okakura, then only twenty-eight, became the principal in 1890. Fenollosa returned to the United States the same year, and three years later published a book-length poem entitled *East and West*, whose preface stated the very ideal which Rabindranath was to proclaim to the world in his lectures: "In 'East and West' I have endeavored to condense my experiences of two hemispheres, and my study of their history. The synthesis of two continental civilizations, matured apart through fifteen hundred years, will mark this close of our century as an unique dramatic epoch in human affairs. At the end of a great cycle the two halves of the world come together for the final creation of man." [63] Fenollosa's characterization of Eastern and Western civilizations also parallels the contrast which Rabindranath was setting forth in his essays and poems. "Eastern culture, slowly elaborated," wrote Fenollosa, "has held to ideals whose refinement seems markedly feminine. For it social institutions are the positive harmonies of a life of brotherhood. Western culture, on the contrary, has held to ideals whose strength seems markedly masculine." Fenollosa, fascinated with Hegel's dialectic at this time, laid more stress on the idea of synthesis between East and West than Rabindranath was doing, and in 1898 expounded this idea in an essay in *Harper's Monthly* under the title "The Coming Fusion of East and West," arguing, "it is necessary to regard the fusion of East and West as indeed a sacred issue for which Time has waited. Each was doomed to failure in its isolation. . . . Each has the privilege to supply what the other lacks." [64]

Okakura meanwhile pursued the mission which Fenollosa had helped him to conceive by endeavoring to develop a school of Japanese art which would conserve the artistic traditions of the past while using the most modern techniques. In 1893 he traveled for six months in China, in search of paintings, sculptures, and pottery which would show his students the great heritage of Buddhistic art. Five years later he was forced to resign his government post and with his disciples founded an art school of his own; like Rabindranath he preferred the independent and creative life of the artist to a career as a bureaucratic functionary.[65]

In 1901 Okakura was able to visit India, a plan he must have cherished for some time. He arrived in Calcutta in December, accompanied by Prince Oda, a high-ranking Buddhist priest. Apparently one purpose of their trip was to arrange for a conference of Asian Buddhists to meet either in India or in Japan — a project which did not materialize, but which does indicate Okakura's interest in Asian cultural unity. He had traveled from Japan in the company of two Western devotees of Swami Vivekananda, the wealthy American, Mrs. Ole Bull (who probably paid his passage), and Miss Josephine MacLeod, who took him to see their master at his monastery near Calcutta. Vivekananda told Miss MacLeod that Okakura no longer "belonged" to her, but to him, and added: "We are two brothers who have found each other again after coming from the opposite ends of the earth." Another source tells us that Vivekananda was filled with joy when Okakura invited him to attend "a Congress of Religions" in Japan. Despite his failing health, Vivekananda joined Okakura and Oda on their pilgrimage to Bodh Gaya and Sarnath, the sites of the Buddha's illumination and of his first sermon. During this trip by train and horse-carriage the two men must have shared the ideas on Indo-Asian spirituality which Vivekananda had already expressed in his lectures and which Okakura was soon to put into writing.[66]

Rabindranath probably did not meet Okakura until some time after the latter's arrival, for he had been busy since December 1901, starting a boy's school at his rural retreat at Santiniketan, ninety miles north of Calcutta. His duties as estate manager had ended shortly before, when two branches of the Tagore family had divided their landed properties; his elder son needed more formal education than he had been getting in their East Bengal home; and Rabindranath, in keeping with the ruralistic philosophy he had evolved during the preceding decade, did not wish to return to the family mansion at Calcutta. His father had purchased some land and built a house at Santiniketan, on the arid plains of West Bengal, and had used it occasionally as a retreat. Rabindranath had loved this spot since his first visit during his boyhood trip with his father. Now he decided to make it his home, and secured Debendranath's permission to settle his family there. Gathering around him a few Brahman boys and five teachers, among them being Brahmabandhab Upadhyay, a boyhood friend of Vivekananda who was trying to be a good Roman Catholic and a Hindu religious mendicant at the same time, Rabindranath tried to model his school on the hermitages in which the sages of ancient India had taught their pupils.[67]

News of Okakura's presence in Calcutta must have reached Rabindranath through his relatives in Calcutta, for his cousin, the painter Abanindranath Thakur, had met the Japanese art historian at a garden party given by the American consul general, and Okakura had also been introduced to Surendranath Tagore, the elder brother of the poet's niece Indira Devi. Surendranath acted as Okakura's guide on a tour of architectural monuments in northern and western India during the hot spring months of 1902, a tour which ended in a "remote Bengal village" which may have been Rabindranath's Santiniketan, for both Surendranath and Rabindranath later commented on Okakura's delight in the handicrafts they showed him at village fairs in rural Bengal. They could also have met in Calcutta, for Okakura lived in the rambling Tagore mansion as Surendranath's guest and worked there on the book he was writing on Asian art history.[68]

We have no record of what the poet and the art historian said to one another, but on his second visit to Japan, Rabindranath told a Japanese audience, "from him we first came to know that there was such a thing as an Asiatic mind." And on his third visit, in 1929, he opened his Tokyo lecture "On Oriental Culture and Japan's Mission" with a fuller statement of his debt to Okakura:

> Some years ago I had the real meeting with Japan when a great original mind from these shores came in our midst. He was our guest for a long time and he had immense inspiration for the young generation of Bengal in those days which immediately preceded a period of a sudden ebullition of national self-assertion in our country. The voice of the East came from him to our young men. That was a significant fact, a memorable one in my own life. And he asked them to make it their mission in life to give some great expression of the human spirit worthy of the East. . . . He said that if they could maintain a simple attitude of worshipful mind towards a great eternal idea which is the East, they would be able to summon up the strength to suffer martyrdom in their aspiration for a glorious future.[69]

By the end of his eleven-month stay in India, Okakura had finished the manuscript of a book, *The Ideals of the East,* and sent it to London to be published. When copies reached India it created a sensation among the English-speaking intelligentsia. It called for a pan-Asian revival based on a return to the religious and cultural unity ascribed to the period when Indian influence spread to China and Japan. "Asia is one," declared the book's opening sentence:

> The Himalayas divide, only to accentuate, two mighty civilisations, the Chinese with its communism of Confucius, and the Indian with its individualism of the Vedas. But not even the snowy barriers can interrupt for one moment that broad expanse of love for the Ultimate and Universal, which is the common thought-inheritance of every Asiatic race, enabling them to produce all the great religions of the world, and distinguishing them from those maritime peoples of the Mediterranean and the Baltic, who love to dwell on the Particular, and to search out the means, not the end, of life.[70]

Most of *The Ideals of the East* extolled the artistic heritage of Japan, but the opening and closing portions of the book stressed the cultural unity of all Asia and the need to rediscover and revive this traditional unity: "Not only to return to our own past ideals, but also to feel and revivify the dormant life of the old Asiatic unity, becomes our mission. The sad problems of Western society turn us to seek a higher solution in Indian religion and Chinese ethics." "However its form may change, only at a great loss can Asia permit its spirit to die. . . . The task of Asia today, then, becomes that of protecting and restoring Asiatic modes. . . . It must be a renewal of self-consciousness that shall build up Asia again into her ancient steadfastness and strength. . . . But it must be from Asia herself, along the ancient roadways of the race, that the great voice shall be heard." [71]

Such stirring words must have been music to Rabindranath's ears, and we shall hear their echoes in his lectures to audiences in Japan and China. There are good reasons, however, for believing that these were not Okakura's words, but those of a British woman from Northern Ireland who is known to have collaborated with him on this manuscript. This was Margaret Noble, a schoolteacher interested in Theosophy who heard the magnetic Vivekananda lecture in London and decided to become his disciple, taking the name of Sister Nivedita (the dedicated one). Nivedita followed Vivekananda to Calcutta in 1899, and when he introduced to a Calcutta audience her lecture on "The Influence of Indian Spiritual Thought in England," he took the occasion to give his impressions of "the prevalence of Indian spiritual thought in Eastern Asiatic countries" on the basis of his brief stops in Hong Kong and Japan on his last trip to the United States. He had noticed what he thought were Sanskrit mantras (actually Buddhist sutras) inscribed in Bengali (actually Tibetan script) on the walls of Chinese and Japanese temples, and from this concluded: "India dies not. China dies not. Japan dies not. Therefore, we must always remember that our backbone is spirituality." It could well be that Vivekananda first entertained the idea of the pan-Asian aspect of Indian spirituality on meeting Ernest Fenollosa in Boston at a symposium organized by Mrs. Ole Bull in 1894. [72]

Passed from Vivekananda to Nivedita, from Fenollosa to Okakura, and then between Vivekananda and Okakura and between Nivedita and Okakura, the idea of resurgent Asian spirituality counterbalancing Western practicality grew more and more exciting. And what environment could be more conducive to molding this idea into flowing English prose than the home of the Tagore family in Calcutta? The collaboration of the Japanese art critic and the British schoolteacher in the midst of their enthusiastic Bengali friends was an international undertaking worthy of the grand scale on which they were all thinking. Young

Surendranath Tagore recalls "wildly exhilarating evenings" sitting around the table in Okakura's room, "listening to his glowing passages deploring the White Disaster spreading over the East, in its intellectual and spiritual surrender to the Western cult of Mammon." [73] Some of the more militant passages had to be suppressed, it appears, for Okakura took back to Japan a manuscript which he never published. This was "The Awakening of Asia," which began with a paraphrase of Vivekananda's famous appeal, "Brothers and Sisters of America!" (which had won him such applause at the World Parliament of Religions in 1893):

> Brothers and sisters of Asia! A vast suffering is on the land of our ancestors. The oriental has become a symbol for the effeminate, the native is an epithet for the slave. Our lauded gentleness is the irony which alien courtesy owes to cowardice. In the name of commerce we have welcomed the militant, in the name of civilization we have embraced the imperial, in the name of Christianity we have prostrated before the merciless. [74]

Sister Nivedita not only helped Okakura to rewrite part or all of his *Ideals of the East*, [75] she also contributed a lengthy introduction, arguing that Hinduism was the source of the underlying unity of Asia. "The thing we call Buddhism cannot in itself have been a defined and formulated creed," she asserted. "Rather we must regard it as the name given to the vast synthesis known as Hinduism, when received by a foreign consciousness." "Not only the Buddhaising, but the *Indianising* of the Mongolian mind, was the process actually at work." Without successive "waves of Indian spirituality," the art of China and Japan would have "remained at the level of a great and beautiful scheme of peasant decoration." Now a new wave of spirituality was moving outward from India: "Hinduism has again become aggressive, as in the Asokan period," with the work of Swami Vivekananda, "the great Indian thinker," who had predicted that Hinduism "may yet dominate the world." This might come about rather quickly, Nivedita concluded, for "the process that took a thousand years at the beginning of our era [the spread of Buddhism and Indian culture to East Asia] may now, with the aid of steam and electricity, repeat itself in a few decades and the world may again witness the Indianising of the East." [76]

Rabindranath, who was to become the chief exponent of the revival of Indo-Asian spirituality, never met Vivekananda (who died, exhausted

at thirty-nine, shortly after Okakura's arrival), but he did know Nivedita and felt the influence of her powerful personality. They met for the
first time in 1898, when both organized relief for the victims of the
plague which broke out in Calcutta that year. They then corresponded
about raising funds to support the research of their mutual friend, the
biophysicist Jagdishchandra Bose. Rabindranath solicited funds for Nivedita's girls' school in north Calcutta, and the two were again in contact
as leaders in the nationalist agitation of 1905. In 1907 Nivedita visited
Tagore on his East Bengal estate, and it is said that he conceived the
plot for his novel *Gora* (Paleface) when she asked him one evening to
tell her a story. Adapting the plot of Kipling's *Kim,* Rabindranath has
the novel's hero, the most orthodox and xenophobic of Hindus, discover
that he is an adopted foundling of Irish descent, a revelation which
makes him a more tolerant patriot. It is clear from the essay he wrote
at the time of her death in 1911 that Rabindranath was both attracted to
Nivedita and disapproved of her naiveté in accepting uncritically everything Hindu, for he remarked: "I felt a great barrier between us . . .
[but] despite the way her ideas repelled me, I received more help from
her than I think I have had from anyone else." [77] Given his admiration
for educated and strong-minded women, and the basic similarity of their
interests in the revival of ancient Indian ideals, Tagore must have been
even more strongly influenced in his Asian idea by Nivedita than by
Okakura.

Okakura's visit left Rabindranath a confirmed Japanophile, and
throughout the next decade he welcomed a stream of Japanese visitors,
most of them recommended by Okakura. First a young man named
Hori came to study Sanskrit at Santiniketan. Then Okakura's protégés,
Yokoyama Taikan and Hishida Shunsō, arrived in 1903 to exchange
ideas and techniques with Rabindranath's artist cousins Gaganendranath
and Abanindranath, and from 1905 to 1908 a third artist, Katsuda
Shokin, underwent a similar experience. In 1905 Rabindranath sent to
Japan for a teacher of judo and the Japanese language; Sano Jinnosuke
answered the call and remained at Santiniketan for several years.[78] 1905
was the year in which Japan defeated Russia on land and sea — the first
time in modern history that an Asian power had forced a European one
to sue for peace after a major war. Rabindranath was enthusiastic about
this news, and is said to have led a group of his Santiniketan students in
a triumphal march. The poet even wrote three short verses in terse Haiku

style praising the Japanese warriors — incongruous as this may seem in one who believed so strongly in spiritual as opposed to material force. His first poem spoke of the blood-red clouds which marked the ending of the night and of the birds in the eastern sky who sing of victory to the greatness of the East. Another extolled "the daring heroes — I have seen how many foes they have conquered." The third contrasted the monks who brought the teachings of Buddhism from India to Japan with the new lesson which Japan was teaching India:

> Wearing saffron robes, the Masters of religion [dharma]
> Went to your country to teach.
> Today we come to your door as disciples,
> To learn the teachings of action [karma].[79]

Concurrently with their excitement over the Russo-Japanese war, Bengal's intellectuals were growing increasingly agitated in 1905 over the impending partition of their native province into two smaller provinces, one (East Bengal and Assam) with a Muslim majority, the other (West Bengal, Bihar, and Orissa) with a Hindu majority. Rabindranath played a leading role in the public demonstrations in Calcutta protesting this measure, which was interpreted as a British plot to weaken the Bengalis, India's most vocal nationalists, by dividing them along religious lines. His patriotic song, "Sonār Bāmlā" (Golden Bengal), a hymn to the land shared by both Hindus and Muslims, was soon on every lip. At his suggestion, the medieval Rajput ceremony of tying a thread on the wrist of warriors to remind them of those they protect by their valor was revived on the day of the partition. He also sought to harness the popular excitement to constructive projects, notably the development of an indigenous school system.[80]

At one point in a lengthy public speech delivered at an early stage in both the Russo-Japanese war and the Bengal anti-partition agitation, Rabindranath sought to relate the two events to each other and to his ideal of an India-centered Asian spiritual civilization. After asserting that "India's main endeavour" had always been "to establish a personal relationship between man and man," he called this "the way of the East" and cited the example of the Japanese soldiers who "remained related to their Mikado and their country in a reverential self-dedication." "The Japanese by not neglecting their pristine magnificience

[sic], while making efficient modern war, won the admiration of East and West alike." India, too, had once been "wonderfully strong," and had inspired all of Asia with her ideals. "China, Japan and Tibet, who are so careful to bar their windows against the advances of Europe, welcomed India with open arms as their *guru,* for she had never sent out armies for plunder and pillage, but only her messages of peace and good will. This glory, which India had earned as the fruit of her self-discipline, was greater than that of the widest of Empires." [81] Considering how "miserably weak" their country had become in recent centuries, Rabindranath concluded that Indians must use their "inherent powers," not only in their own self-defense, but also because "to-day the world stands sorely in need of the priceless fruits of the discipline of our ancient Rishis [sages]." [82] The missionary note in this last passage is both reminiscent of some of Vivekananda's proclamations and prefigures many of Rabindranath's remarks during his years as a lecturing traveler.

THE CROWN FROM THE WEST

Although he played an important role in the *swadeshi* (patriotic self-help) movement in Bengal, Rabindranath's distaste for politics soon reasserted itself. In 1906 and 1907, the pronouncements of other leaders, among them his friend Brahmabandhab Upadhyay, grew more narrowly chauvinistic, and bickering between the Moderate and Extremist wings of the Indian National Congress led to their split after a disgraceful scuffle at the annual session in December 1907. Meanwhile a band of young terrorists had launched a series of assassinations, which culminated in the killing of the wife and daughter of an English barrister on April 30, 1908. Disgusted at these developments, Rabindranath severed his connections with the nationalist organizations of which he was a member and withdrew entirely from political affairs.[83]

Rabindranath's last public speech before this retirement, delivered in Calcutta in June–July 1908, was a plea for tolerance and for acceptance of the positive contributions which the West could make in India. "In India," he declared, "the history of humanity is seeking to elaborate a specific ideal, to give to general perfection a special form which shall be the gain of all humanity — nothing less than this is its end and aim." This ideal was the synthesis of races, religions, and cultures, in which the Englishman must be allowed to take part. "The India to which the Englishman has come with his message, is the India which is shooting up towards the future from within the bursting seed of the past. This new India belongs to humanity." Rabindranath cited Rammohun Roy as laying the foundation for this great synthesis: "With a wonderful breadth of heart and intellect he accepted the West without betraying the East," and led India "out into the freedom of Space and Time, and built for her a bridge between the East and the West." Ranade in Western India had also "spent his life in the making of this same bridge," and in Bengal, both Bankimchandra and Vivekananda had worked for the realization of this ideal. But a weak India was not fit to enter a partnership with the West, and "neither tall talk nor violence, but only sacrifice and service are the true tests of strength." In an almost mystical peroration, Rabindranath concluded: "Only when she [India] can meet him [the Englishman] as his equal, will all reason for antagonism, and with it all conflict, disappear. Then will East and West unite in India — country with country, race with race, knowledge with knowledge, endeavour with endeavour. Then will the History of India come to an end, merged in the History of the World which will begin." [84]

Rabindranath's disengagement from the popular agitation in which he had played so prominent a role naturally exposed him to the charge that he had betrayed the national cause. "Patriotism cannot be the final refuge for my soul," he wrote in explaining his action. "I have embraced humanity — I will not buy glass at the price of diamonds — I will not permit patriotism to take precedence over humanity in my life — I took two steps down this path and saw that I could go no further — if I cannot see religion and all mankind as superior to my country, if God is obscured by attachment to the country, then I am deprived of the food of my soul." [85] One of his first biographers, and his close colleague at Santiniketan, later gave essentially the same explanation for Rabindranath's abrupt abandonment of the antipartition cause: "the narrow and aggressive lines on which the whole movement was worked out . . . grew discordant to the poet's growing spiritual life. He suddenly cut himself away from the movement. He sought the solitude of spirit, he sought the universal joy of nature, he sought the hidden springs of spiritual life." [86]

This decision to retire from public activity marks an important turning point in Rabindranath's life for it had the effect of excluding him from the world of Indian politics and therefore of closing to him a field of activity in which he might otherwise have expended a considerable part of his energies. From 1908 to 1912, from his forty-eighth to his fifty-second year, he underwent a period of deliberate withdrawal, from which he was to emerge into activity in a much wider world than the one which had engaged him theretofore. As one Bengali biographer puts it, "a great spiritual longing possessed him from within. He was trying to see everything, to understand everything, only by concentrating within himself." [87] Death had struck down one member of his family after another in the previous six years: his wife in 1902; his daughter Renuka in 1903; his father in 1905; and his most gifted child, his younger son Samindranath, in 1907. Rabindranath himself was suffering pain and bleeding from hemorrhoids, and thoughts of his own possible death began to occur to him. But his impulse to write was stimulated rather than checked by his mood of sober self-concentration, and he produced in this period some of his finest religious poems, the Bengali collection entitled *Gītānjali* (An offering of songs). The longing of the lover for the beloved, of the soul for the Divine, is a frequent theme in these poems.[88]

Now in his fifth decade, Rabindranath had reached full maturity as a poet. The richness and variety of his Bengali style — the sonorous rhythms, the alliterations and internal rhymes, the supple use of intricate meters — are impossible to translate. One short fragment may convey something of the music of the original. Notice the swinging beat (indicated by acute accent marks), and the repeated sounds "a" (as in English "but"), ā (as in "bar"), "g," and "sh":

Agádh bāshoná,	With infinite desire,
Ashím āshá,	With limitless hope,
Jágat dékhite chái.[89]	I long to see the world.

The mood of longing suffusing many of the *Gītānjali* poems again appears in the drama Rabindranath wrote at this time, *The Post Office*. Asked why he chose as his hero a dying boy longing to leave his sickbed to go outside, he commented: "I was very restless . . . That gave me the idea of a child pining for freedom, and the world anxious to keep it in its bounds. . . . I was anxious to know the world. At that time, I thought that it was in the West that the spirit of humanity was experimenting and working. My restlessness became intolerable." [90] Rabindranath had often found traveling soothing. Why not, then, make a third trip to the West, to England? His first visit there had been intellectually stimulating, and he noted in his *Reminiscences,* which he now began to write, "I received no shock calculated to shatter the original framework of my life. Rather East and West met in friendship in my person." [91] His second trip in 1890 had been a failure, but perhaps that was because he had nothing to offer and could establish no meaningful contact with English people. Recently he had sensed a heightened interest in Indian culture among European intellectuals: in succession, the Russo-German philosopher Hermann Keyserling, the English artist William Rothenstein, the Socialist leader Ramsay MacDonald, and Prince William of Sweden had passed through Calcutta and sought out the Tagore family because of their reputation as men of culture. [92] His friend Okakura Kakuzō, an equally restless spirit, had revisited India in 1911 on his way back to Boston, where he had been working since 1905 as a curator at the Museum of Fine Arts. The fact that Okakura had found more active support for his ideas in the United States than in Japan possibly suggested to Rabindranath that he, too, might find a sympathetic public in the West. [93] Bengali friends in London, prompted by Rothenstein, prodded him with letters assuring him that if he came there he would meet "men after his heart." Finally, his painful illness was growing worse, and England or the United States was more likely than Calcutta to have the doctor who could cure him. [94]

This third visit to the West more than fulfilled his expectations. Before and during his sea voyage Rabindranath experimented in rendering some of his recent poems into English prose. Arriving in London in June 1912, he showed these translations to his friend Rothenstein, who passed them on to the poet William Butler Yeats. Even though the music and rhythm of the Bengali originals were lost in these prose versions, their devotional spirit moved Yeats, who declared they "have stirred my blood as nothing has for years. . . . We are . . . moved . . . because we have met our own image, as though we had walked in Rossetti's willow wood or heard, perhaps for the first time in literature, our voice as in a dream." [95] First in a reading by Yeats at a gathering of friends at Rothenstein's house, then in a private printing of five hundred copies, then in regular editions, and finally in translations (into French by young André Gide), the *Gītānjali* poems reached an ever-widening circle of appreciative readers in Europe and America.

The England to which Rabindranath brought his translated religious verse in 1912 proved extraordinarily receptive to his modernized Hindu outlook. Yeats's response typified that of intellectuals groping for some metaphysical framework to replace the Christian beliefs they and their parents had abandoned during the nineteenth century. The menacing rumbles of the war that was soon to erupt in Europe quickened their quest for a meaning to life and a path to peace. Did India hold the key? Annie Besant and others in the Theosophical Society, which she headed after making her home in India in 1893, believed it did. Yeats had already dabbled in Theosophy before moving on to spiritualism. Shortly before Tagore's arrival he had been persuaded by an American medium that his mind was being guided by his astral counterpart, the dark-skinned medieval Moorish poet Leo Africanus.[96] Small wonder that the arrival in the flesh of an exotic and mystical poet from India should have so elated the susceptible Yeats. But the spark struck between the minds of the Irish and the Bengali poets was more than merely a personal rapport: it also symbolized the climax of a century-long interchange of ideas between English-speaking Indians and the Westernmost inhabitants of the English-speaking world.

From England, Rabindranath made his first journey to the United States, hoping to find in the Midwest, then a great center of homeopathic medicine, a cure for his hemorrhoids without undergoing an operation. In February 1913 he visited Okakura Kakuzō at the Museum of Fine Arts in Boston and their conversation reminded him of the concept of Asia's spiritual greatness in which he had not ceased to believe. Okakura particularly asked Rabindranath to visit China, and promised to be his guide to show him "the real China," so that he would come to know "the genius which her past history revealed," and which "still lived in the heart of the people." Rabindranath recalled the effect on his mind of Okakura's advice:

> It at once strengthened my interest for the ancient land, my faith in her future, because I could trust him when he expressed his admiration for those people . . . who were, according to him, waiting for another opportunity to have the fulness of illumination, shedding fresh glory upon the history of Asia. When I first met him I neither knew Japan nor had I any experience of China. I came to know both of these countries from the personal relationship with this great man whom I had the good fortune to meet and accept as one of my intimate friends.[97]

After Rabindranath's departure Okakura felt "a sudden loneliness." A few weeks later he returned to Japan for the last time and within a few months died of Bright's disease.[98] Rabindranath was soon cured of his worrisome ailment by surgery in London on his way home from the United States.

A stupendous event in his life resulted from Rabindranath's third voyage to the Western world. The publication of his poems in English and their retranslation into other European languages brought his work to the attention of the Nobel Prize Committee, who found that it satisfied the clause in the explosive expert's will requiring them to honor "the most distinguished work of an idealistic tendency in the field of literature." The award gave Tagore at one stroke an enormous popularity within India (where few non-Bengalis had previously known his name) and an unparalleled opportunity to present Indian ideals to the people of other countries. Rabindranath was quick to realize that the prize would change the course of his life and is said to have exclaimed, "I shall never get any peace again. I shall be worried with appeals, all kinds of people will be writing to me." [99] He knew well that he was the first Asian writer ever to receive the world's most coveted literary honor, and he deduced that he would be considered as a living symbol of Asia's cultural and spiritual achievements — "the representative of Asia," as he was to call himself during his lecture tour in China eleven years later.

At Santiniketan in November 1913 Rabindranath received the news of the Nobel award with mixed emotions. On the one hand he feared the erosion of the solitude, so necessary for his creative writing, which he had maintained for the past few years. On the other hand, he saw in the prize a confirmation of the ideal of East-West synthesis which he had been writing and talking about for many years. Though the crown weighed heavily on his head, he wrote his American friend and publisher (the founder of *Poetry*), Harriet Monroe, "still I must bear it proudly, rejoicing in the fact that the East and the West ever touch each other like twin gems in the circlet of humanity, that they had met long before Kipling was born and will meet long after his name is forgotten." [100]

Except for a meeting honoring him on his fiftieth birthday, Rabindranath had been generally ignored in India since parting company with the antipartition movement. Suddenly he was acclaimed as a hero, and a group of five hundred admirers traveled the ninety miles from Calcutta by special train to felicitate him. His response to their flowery congratulations took them by surprise. "What brings you gentlemen here today?," he asked. "You, whom I had failed to please so long, what have I done, pray, now to please you so mightily? It is not my worth, but the recognition of the foreigner, that has evidently worked up this outburst of appreciation. I thank you for your generosity," he is said to have concluded sarcastically, "but excuse me please, if I refuse to get drunk with you over this gilded cup of foreign wine." [101]

This outburst, for which Rabindranath was immediately rebuked in the Calcutta press, illuminates the distance he felt between himself and most of his fellow countrymen. The shallow chauvinism motivating their sudden hero-worship seems to have contrasted painfully in his mind with the spirit of internationalism he had so recently found among his Western admirers. The irony of his position lay in the fact that he was upholding an ideal — that of cultural synthesis between Eastern spirituality and Western practicality — which had been vigorously championed by nineteenth-century Bengali intellectuals; moreover, just at the moment when Western intellectuals seemed most receptive to this message, Indians were betraying it by becoming increasingly nationalistic, anti-Western, and unspiritual. The passage of time did not help Rabindranath to resolve this dilemma; on the contrary, it was to become even more acute in the following decade, when Gandhi's Non-cooperation Movement further intensified the xenophobic strain in Indian nationalism.

The history of Rabindranath's family and of his psychological and intellectual development from childhood to middle age gives a number of clues to the origins of that driving restlessness and missionary zeal which carried him abroad on twelve tours between 1916 and 1934. The desire simply to see the world had been evident since the physical confinement he had suffered in boyhood. In adolescence, family environment gave him leisure and freedom to develop his literary gifts; then his sister-in-law's suicide shocked him into a permanent restlessness. His patriarchal father's intervention at four decisive points — and above all his saintly example — deeply influenced Rabindranath's emotional and intellectual life. An abortive second visit to London initiated a long period of Indocentricity, which was broadened to Asia-centricity by contacts with Okakura and others. The rise of nationalism in Bengal attracted him until its narrowness and violence drove him into retirement, from which he emerged only to travel abroad for the third time. The enthusiastic response of English and American intellectuals to his spiritual viewpoint, followed by the award of the Nobel Prize, seemed to confirm the hope, which he had expressed as early as 1878, that the spiritual ideals of ancient India could become the foundation of a new world civilization incorporating the best qualities of both East and West. This was the vision Rabindranath was to spend so much of his energy in the next two decades in explaining to audiences in India and elsewhere. Working in combination, the love of travel he had known since his boyhood, the restlessness that had possessed him since his twenties, the isolation from his society that had become habitual by his forties, and the opportunities for overseas lecturing opened up by the international reputation he acquired at fifty-two, transformed Rabindranath from modern India's greatest poet into a tireless prophet bringing to the world at large a grand design for the reconstruction of civilization.

Paradoxically, the idea that Asia possessed a uniquely spiritual civilization was essentially a Western idea, ancient in origin but transmitted in modern times to English-speaking intellectuals in the Westernized city-ports of the coasts of Southern and Eastern Asia — cities such as Calcutta, Tokyo-Yokohama, and Shanghai. Their very insistence on the importance of Eastern culture as a counterweight to Western civilization thus betrayed the depth to which men like Rabindranath and Okakura had been influenced by Western ideas about the Orient. In Tagore's case, as his own experiences in Japan and China were soon to show, this paradox contained the seeds of personal tragedy.

CHAPTER TWO

INDIA'S MESSENGER IN JAPAN

Of all countries in Asia, here in Japan you have the freedom to use the materials you have gathered from the West according to your genius and your need. Therefore your responsibility is all the greater, for in your voice Asia shall answer the questions that Europe has submitted to the conference of Man.

— Tagore, *The Message of India to Japan*

THE OUTBREAK OF WAR IN AUGUST 1914 suddenly darkened Rabindranath's vision of a synthesis between Eastern spirituality and Western practicality. Only a few months earlier the news that he had received the Nobel Prize encouraged him to believe that the West was ready to absorb the peace-giving influence of Indian thought. The war in Europe now convinced him that the West needed Eastern virtues more than ever, but simultaneously frustrated his growing desire to carry India's message there in person.

Meanwhile, he suffered greatly from the constant interruptions and unwelcome publicity attendant on the Nobel award. Waves of depression drove him into solitary retreat several times in the spring and summer of 1914. "I know that I am being lifted from the sphere where I was before; and it is the loneliness of the new situation and the cry of the old life that is still troubling me," he wrote to his young English friend, C. F. Andrews, as he emerged from one of these periods of seclusion.[1] Evidently he was conscious that a great responsibility had been thrust upon him, and felt more than once the need to retreat into the wilderness to prepare himself to bear its weight. As early as May 1913 the Viceroy of India had dubbed him "the Poet Laureate of Asia,"[2] and in 1915 King George V was to confer on him a knighthood. Inevitably, the shy poet Rabindranath (a name foreigners found difficult to pronounce and remember) was now reborn as Tagore, the world-famous celebrity.

THE OPEN ROAD TO THE EAST

As the months passed, Tagore felt recurrent twinges of that restlessness to which he had succumbed so many times in the past. To return to England was out of the question until the war was over. To the East, however, the road lay open, for the hostilities had not spread to the Asian continent, excepting the brief encounter between Japanese and German forces on China's Shantung Peninsula. Okakura's request that he visit Japan and China was still fresh in his mind, and even before the year 1914 closed he had decided to go eastward. He wrote his friend William Rothenstein, "when this reaches you I shall be sailing for Japan." [3] But as he was about to board a ship bound for Japan from Calcutta in February 1915, he changed his mind (perhaps because Mahatma Gandhi had just joined his band of followers at Santiniketan, where Andrews had settled them on their arrival from South Africa[4]). On February 18, Tagore wrote two letters: one was to Andrews to say he would soon leave Calcutta for Santiniketan in order to meet Gandhi for the first time; the other was to the visiting Japanese scholar at Calcutta University, Kimura Nikki:

Dear Mr. Kimura,
    Instead of starting for Japan immediately my intention is to wait a few months longer. Meanwhile sending you there to make necessary preparations. I want to know Japan in the outward manifestation of its modern life and in the spirit of its traditional past. I also want to follow the traces of ancient India in your civilization and have some idea of your literature if possible. I doubt not that you will be able to help me. I must ask you to protect me, while I am there, from pressure of invitations and receptions and formal meetings. I want to live very simply and quietly with as little [word illegible] as possible.
                                Very sincerely yours,
                                Rabindranath Tagore[5]

A few months later, Tagore received a letter from the Buddhist monk-explorer, Kawaguchi Ekkai (who had visited him in 1908), urging him to come to Japan.[6] He was certainly interested enough, but as he explained in a letter to Rothenstein, "I must give up Japan at least for the present. Not for any sudden failure of courage or enthusiasm but for the same blessed reason that brings a modern war to its halt. My finance is hopeless, mainly owing to the European complication." In another letter to Rothenstein in July, Tagore gave a further reason for postponing his trip. "Famine threatens Bengal," he began. "I was about to take a trip somewhere when the cry of misery reached me from our villages and I have come here to see what I can do to help these famished souls," he wrote of his East Bengal tenants. At the bottom of his letter Rabindranath appended his translation of what seems to have been a recent poem, in which his longing to travel is expressed through a variety of metaphors:

To move is to meet you every moment, Fellow-traveller!
It is to sing to the music of your steps.
He who is touched by your breath never seeks the sheltered bank, he
    sets his reckless sails to the wind riding the turbulent water.
He who throws his doors open stepping onwards receives your greeting.
He stops not to count his gain or to mourn his loss; his heart beats the
    drum for him to march on, for to march is to march with you every
    step, Fellow-traveller!
      .   .   .   .
Be ready for the sailing of the sea, my heart! and let those linger behind
    who must.
For your name has been called in the loud morning light! [7]

    The restlessness grew stronger as the months passed. "I have the call of the open road, though most of the roads are closed," he wrote Andrews in June, "I am in a nomadic mood, but it is becoming painful to me for want of freedom." In July he referred with mild self-deprecation to his "proposed visit to Japan," adding, "I am busy floating my dreams, as the children do their paper boats." A trip to Kashmir in October soothed him temporarily, and reconciled him to accepting and sublimating "the restlessness that has been so persistent with me." [8] But a series of criticisms by fellow-Bengalis in the winter of 1915–16 set him again thinking about a trip outside of India. First his fanciful play, *Phalguni* (*The Cycle of Spring*), was coolly received; then his latest novel *Ghare baire* (*The Home and the World*), was attacked as immoral and un-patriotic; finally even his friends criticized as pro-British his articles on a fracas at Presidency College between Bengali students and their un-popular teacher, an Englishman. "After all this effort, in such varied kinds, his mind was ready to snap," Thompson tells us. "There was bit-terness all round. The poet's mind turned longingly to thoughts of de-serting the world, and turning *sannyāsī*. Instead . . . he went to Japan." [9]

Another of Tagore's English friends, his admirer and coworker at Santiniketan, C. F. Andrews, attributed a somewhat loftier motive to the decision to visit Japan, seeing the terrible carnage of war in Europe as the principal cause of the poet's mental distress. "To the Poet, whose thoughts were always in terms of Humanity rather than in those of any lesser unit, the fratricidal war in the West revealed the dangerously un-balanced condition of the human race," he wrote. According to Andrews' interpretation, Tagore wanted to visit East Asia "in order to win the friend-ship and co-operation of the leading thinkers of China and Japan," for together they might bring about a new birth of peace-giving spiritual values. As he prepared to start for Japan:

> the Indian poet was absorbed in the contemplation of the great Buddha land of Asia, where religion, culture, literature and art had flourished for thousands of years, beginning from India and spreading to South Eastern Asia, China and Japan. The poet pictured the Renaissance of this ancient world-culture. He saw Okakura's dream fulfilled, and har-mony restored between all the countries of the Far East. This should bring back to humanity the light of a new dawn, just when the sun of the West had sunk and the horizon of the West had become dark with the darkness of night. Such was his first vision of the redemption of the world, after the War, through the rising of the East. [10]

Decisive human actions are often compounded of frustration at one's present situation, aspiration toward an ideal, and the appearance of a suitable opportunity. The third ingredient in Tagore's decision to travel to East Asia came in mid-April 1916, in the shape of an unexpected telegram from the American impresario Major James B. Pond, offering him the sum of twelve thousand dollars if he would undertake a lecture tour in the United States the following autumn and winter. Rabin-dranath noted that this trip would make a visit to Japan en route "inexpensive and easy." He set forth his rationale for his fourth foreign tour in a letter to his daughter, Mira Devi:

I was saying to myself *"Where* shall I go?" A restlessness has been rocking me much like the impatience which came over me each time before I went to England. But the road there is closed because of the disturbance of war. So when the telegram from America came, it seemed to me like an invitation had arrived from the great world. I have tested and tried again and again, and finally I have clearly understood that the Creator did not make me for the life of a householder. Probably that is why I have done nothing but roam about since childhood — I could never establish a household anywhere. The universe has embraced me, and I in turn shall embrace the universe.[11]

Two days later Tagore composed the final poem in his great series, *Balākā* (A flight of swans). He addressed it to "the wanderer," and urged him to "let the whirlwind of Movement/Taking hold of you,/ Free you from the trammels of the earth/And lead you to the ends of the world!"[12] Less than three weeks later, on May 3, 1916, he gathered up his two English disciples, C. F. Andrews and W. W. Pearson, and his young protégé, the artist Mukul Dey, and boarded the Japanese freighter *Tosa Maru* at Calcutta just as the hottest weeks of India's year were approaching.[13]

Tagore little realized how closely his movements were watched, and used, by a small and daring band of Bengali revolutionaries who were developing a worldwide network of anti-British espionage and sabotage with German support. The very ship on which he sailed for Japan had been outfitted two years earlier by members of this group in a complex plot to smuggle arms into India.[14] One revolutionary slipped out of India in 1915 by pretending to be a member of Tagore's family; using false papers, he convinced the Calcutta port authorities that the poet was sending him to Japan to prepare for his forthcoming visit. Once safely in Japan, the revolutionary, Rashbehari Bose, announced that it was he who had thrown the bomb that wounded the viceroy, Lord Hardinge, in December 1912.[15]

The only preparations Tagore made for his arrival in Japan were to work on the lecture he expected to deliver, "The Message of India to Japan," and to cable word of his impending arrival to Yokoyama Taikan, one of the three artists who had stayed with him in Calcutta. If he still expected to live "very simply and quietly" in Japan, he underestimated the amount of curiosity and excitement his visit would arouse. As his ship sailed toward East Asia, Tagore came ever closer to the clash that was to occur between his ideas and the dynamic and many-sided thought-world of Japan's best minds.

From Calcutta to Tokyo

Japan in 1916 was a nation enjoying the fruits but spared the hardships of war. She had joined the Allies shortly after the outbreak of hostilities in 1914, and had captured the German naval base at Tsingtao, China, after a brief campaign. From that point on, enriched by the incorporation of Germany's South Pacific territories and her claims in China's Shantung Province, she took little active part in the Allied war effort. The war proved a windfall to her economy as well, for her factories and mills were kept busy supplying manufactured goods to countries which could no longer obtain them from embattled Europe, and France, Britain, and Russia also turned to her for war matériel.

The general outlook of the educated Japanese at the time of Tagore's visit was understandably optimistic. Business was booming at home, and Japan's dominions were expanding abroad from decade to decade. The Ryukyu Islands in 1875, Taiwan in 1895, a sphere of influence in Southern Manchuria in 1905, Korea in 1910 and then the German possessions in 1914 had been successively added to the Japanese Empire. The great sacrifices made during the reign of the Meiji Emperor (1868–1912) seemed amply justified by this course of events, and the prestige of Japan's declining oligarchy, which in this period had directed her emergence as a modern nation, still remained considerable.

Death from old age or assassination was rapidly thinning the oligarchy's ranks, however, causing a gradual shift of political power from their hands. The demise of the Emperor himself in 1912 had an almost traumatic effect upon the populace, and dissatisfaction with the government grew as suspicions mounted that those in high places were hiding their corrupt practices behind the name of the new Taishō Emperor (who was mentally retarded and unable to direct affairs). After a period of crisis, the oligarchy (now controlled by Prince Yamagata, the founder of Japan's modern army) turned for help to Count Ōkuma

Shigenobu, who had been expelled from their ranks in 1882 because of his independent attitude but had remained a popular public figure.

As Prime Minister from April of 1914 to October of 1916, the aged Ōkuma was subject to Yamagata's veto, although his natural rambunctiousness kept asserting itself. Japan's entry into the war on the side of the democracies and Ōkuma's known preference for parliamentary as against oligarchic government stimulated the rise of a liberal spirit in politics which was to reach its zenith in the 1920's. His tenure in office is better known, however, for the infamous Twenty-one Demands presented by Japan to China in January 1915. An obvious move to take advantage of China's internal weakness at a time when the European powers were unable to check Japanese aggression, these demands, strongly urged by the ultranationalists, were tantamount to a bid for indirect control over the government of China. A compromise averted such an eventuality, but the incident was not forgotten by China's young nationalists, and indeed hastened their later advent to power.[16]

Japanese attitudes toward India in 1916 were naturally shaped by these domestic and foreign developments. There is no question that India was regarded, from a political point of view, with even greater disdain than China. Not only was she a colony completely subject to the will of a foreign power — an odious fate which Japan had escaped through diligent effort — but Japan's treaty obligations under the terms of the Anglo-Japanese alliance had bound her since 1905 to come to the aid of the British if their rule in India were ever imperiled by an invader. Probably the average educated Japanese, in looking at India, deplored her backwardness and expected her eventually to regain her political independence, while the superpatriot hoped that India's liberation from foreign rule could be hastened by assistance and leadership from Japan.

When his ship reached Singapore, Tagore began to notice signs of the eagerness with which he would be welcomed in Japan. A Japanese newspaperman boarded the *Tosa Maru* to ask for a statement, which he declined to give. Later that same day a Japanese lady repeated the request, and when it was again declined persuaded the poet and his party to join her in a drive around the island. When the ship docked at Hong Kong, the chief officer came to his cabin to tell him, "the Japanese people have been waiting to welcome you, and so a telegraphic order has come from my main office that I am not to delay in any other port. We shall unload all the cargo for Shanghai here, sending it there by another ship." Rabindranath reported this news in a letter and added that by thus honoring him the Japanese had given precedence to human over commercial considerations.[17] It is possible, however, that such an expensive change in his ship's route was dictated by governmental advice to the steamship company, perhaps to demonstrate as dramatically as possible Japanese interest in India. The change of itinerary incidentally prevented Tagore from making even a quick visit to China, but he expressed no regrets about this, and did not even get off the ship during its two-day stopover in Hong Kong. He had no personal friends in China, whereas he had several in Japan who were already making straight his way.

In his letters from Japan Tagore has given a humorous picture of the storm of excitement which greeted him when his ship reached Kobe on May 29, 1916. Four Japanese who had known him when they visited Calcutta — the artists Yokoyama and Katsuda, the explorer-monk Kawaguchi, and the gymnast Sano — had come down from the capital and were ready to whisk him off to Tokyo at once. But tugging at the poet's other sleeve was a body of local Indian merchants who had telegraphed him at Hong Kong to assure him that they would give him hospitality. The two factions argued it out for possession of the poet, and Tagore reported that he preferred the cyclone they had passed through in the Bay of Bengal to this human cyclone.[18] The Indian merchants finally prevailed, but as they were driving him to the residence of the wealthiest of them the car got stuck while turning a corner in one of the narrow lanes common to urban residential areas in Japan. Summing up his disappointment in finding Kobe so thoroughly Westernized, Tagore observed, in a remark which was widely quoted in the Japanese press: "This is the reason why I hate civilization. There is no instrument of civilization, be it tramcar, train, car or what have you, which does not disturb people's peace of mind." [19]

The poet visited nearby Osaka on June 1, and after a dinner in his honor delivered his first major address in Japan. The public meeting was sponsored by the Osaka *Asahi* (Rising Sun) newspaper, whose chief editor, Maruyama Kanji, was a close friend of Yokoyama Taikan. Kawaguchi Ekkai introduced the speaker to the audience of three thousand, which was composed entirely of men sitting on rice mats covering the floor of the large hall, and translated for him.[20] Taking "India and Japan" as the subject of his talk, Tagore began by expressing his delight at being in the country to which his thoughts had been linked since youth. But his initial impressions of the country had evidently disappointed him, for he continued: "The whirlwind of modern civilization has caught Japan as it has caught the rest of the world, and a stranger like myself cannot help feeling on landing in your country that what I see before me is the temple of [the] modern age where before the brazen images an immense amount of sacrifice is offered and an interminable round of ritualism is performed. But this is not Japan." [21] Tagore contrasted the very ease with which he had traveled to Japan with the arduous journeys of India's Buddhist monks of old and lamented, "In the days of heroic simplicity, it was easy to come near to the real man, but in modern times it is the phantasm of the giant time itself, which is everywhere and man is lost beyond recognition." "But I must not lose heart," he concluded. "I must seek and find what is true in this land, — true to the soul of the people, — what is Japan, what is unique, and not merely [the] mask of the time which is monotonously the same in all latitudes and longitudes." This sentiment seems to have touched his hearers, for the speech was reported to have "elicited cheers and acclamations." However, the Tokyo *Asahi,* the nation's most influential newspaper, displayed a more negative attitude toward his message, reporting it under the heading, "Tagore Curses Civilization." [22]

It may seem surprising that Tagore had such definite ideas about the true nature and uniqueness of Japan after spending barely two days in one of its most Westernized modern cities. This lecture, however, and the two public lectures he subsequently delivered in Tokyo, are in large part merely elaborations on a theme he had been brooding over throughout his voyage from Calcutta to Kobe: modern industrial civilization, which had created the great seaports of the world, was defiling nature. "This rebellion against the gods," he called the night-long blaze of lights surrounding the ship before it weighed anchor in Calcutta. Rangoon similarly depressed him: "wherever this machine-ridden trade has gone, it has spread a pestilence of greed throughout the world with its soot and ugliness and cruelty." At Penang he wrote: "As our ship slowly sailed up to port, and the ambitious projects of man began to loom larger than nature, and the factory chimneys kept drawing their straight lines across nature's curves — then I could see what an amount of ugliness had been created in the world through man's passions. On shore after shore, and port after port, man's greed mocks at heaven with hideous gestures." The "hideous noise" of loading and unloading the freighter in Singapore helped to convince him that "there is no uglier nightmare on earth than a ship's quay," and at Hong Kong he inveighed against "the trade monster . . . which wearies the world with its weight, deafens the world with its noise, soils the world with its refuse, and lacerates the world with its greed." [23]

Tagore had believed since the 1890's in the superiority of rural to urban life and culture, but he had never before been exposed so painfully, and for whole days at a time, to the hurly-burly of the dockside. "It has never struck me before so forcibly as now, how far man's material needs are overwhelming his finer sensibility," he wrote at the end of his sea voyage. He stepped ashore at Kobe with his mind brimful with anger at "this demon" of economic demand and supply, and his letters for the week he stayed there repeatedly express his distaste at the commercialization of life in the modern age, and his longing for unsullied natural beauty. After protesting the rule of "the office-kingdom" in Japan, with its Western hat-and-coat uniform, he described his delight that the women of Japan had not given up their traditional dress. It was they alone, he wrote, "who have taken it upon themselves to preserve the honor of Japan." He gained other glimpses of indigenous cultural traditions when he attended a tea ceremony given by a wealthy Japanese merchant, witnessed a demonstration of flower arranging, and read some haiku in translation.[24]

The ubiquitous Japanese reporters annoyed Tagore greatly. "There is no hope that I shall see anything of Japan through the spaces between them," he wrote. To travel from Kobe to Tokyo on June 5 he had to force his way "through this crowd of inquisitive men." [25] It was a long day's train journey, and at various stations along the way groups of Japanese and Indians came to greet him. The most memorable event of the trip, as he afterwards said, was at Shizuoka, where a delegation of twenty Buddhist priests gathered to burn incense in his presence as a sign of welcome. At Numazu, the next major city, Okakura's younger brother Yoshisaburō, a professor of English, got on the train to pay his respects and to accompany the poet to Tokyo. Further along, at Kozu, he was met by Soejima Yasoroku, a director of the semigovernmental Japan-India Association, and by other members of the "Tagore Welcoming Committee," including the Unitarian minister Uchigasaki Sakusaburō, and the Buddhist priest Takeda Toyoshirō.[26]

The excitement at the Tokyo Station was tremendous. A throng estimated at between twenty and fifty thousand persons crowded as close as they could to catch a glimpse of the Nobel Laureate. Yokoyama Taikan and Okakura Yoshisaburō escorted him to a two-horse carriage in which they made their way through the crowd to Yokoyama's house near Ueno Park where Mrs. Yokoyama and Okakura Kakuzō's widow were waiting to greet him. In Yokoyama's home Tagore felt for the first time that he was beginning to become familiar with the inner life of Japan. He was charmed with the simplicity of the house and the uncluttered beauty of its near-empty rooms. After the noise and tumult of his trip he was glad to rest his mind here for a day.[27]

On June 7 the poet paid a formal call on the British ambassador, who gave a luncheon in his honor. Having tendered this token of loyalty to the rulers of his country, three days later Tagore visited Japan's prime minister, Count Ōkuma Shigenobu, at his mansion on the grounds of Waseda University (which he had founded in 1882). Ōkuma was officially concerned about Tagore's arrival, for he was the president of the Indo-Japanese Association, and in any case he always enjoyed talking with distinguished visitors to Japan. Acting as interpreter was the eminent Buddhist scholar Anesaki Masaharu, who had visited India some fifteen years before and had lectured at Harvard not long after Tagore's 1913 visit there. What was said in the two-hour conversation between the prophet of Asian cultural revival and the canny politician, under whose leadership Japan had sought only a few months earlier to take control of the government of China, has not been recorded.[28] The honor of being received by the Prime Minister (an honor not granted him on his two subsequent visits to Japan) in such a lengthy interview suggests the possibility that Ōkuma or his advisers might have had some notion of using Tagore as an opening wedge for increasing Japanese influence in India. Count Ōkuma, however, was genuinely interested in talking with his visitor about his theory of Eastern and Western civilizations. Perhaps it was Tagore's influence that led him, after his retirement from office a few months later, to begin the comparative study of Greek and Chinese philosophy.[29]

That same day Tagore paid a visit to the Nihon Bijutsuin (the Japan Art Academy), founded by Okakura Kakuzō. Many pupils and collaborators of his deceased friend gathered there to meet him. Responding to their request for a speech, he propounded an Asianistic theory of art:

Only our Asians can understand that the universe has both law and spiritual content. Except for a few poets, the Europeans cannot understand this. It is the special privilege of Asian, and especially Japanese, artists, to catch the spiritual content of the universe and to describe it in a picture. In the future, if you imitate the Europeans and forget this spirituality it will be an unforgivable thing.[30]

"THE MESSAGE OF INDIA TO JAPAN"

During the few days he had been in Tokyo, Tagore had agreed to deliver a formal lecture at Tokyo Imperial University. Apparently he had finished writing the lecture by the time he reached Tokyo, for the university had sufficient time to print it before the day of the lecture, and it was from this printed copy that he read to his audience. On Sunday, June 11, 1916, the cream of the Japanese intelligentsia assembled to see and hear him. Although the lecture did not begin until four in the afternoon, by two o'clock the hall was already filled with some fifteen hundred persons, and many had to be turned away. By four the walls were lined with standing men, and an estimated two thousand listeners (including over a hundred Indians and as many Europeans and Americans) applauded as Baron Yamakawa, the president of the university, took the chair to introduce the Nobel Laureate.[31]

As Tagore rose to speak, he presented a colorful sight to this distinguished audience. Robed in white, his flowing gray beard carefully combed, wearing the tall Taoist cap which Okakura had given him (no doubt as a symbol of Asian unity), and holding a blue notebook in his hand, the poet made a splendid picture. In his high, melodious voice he began to intone his lecture, "The Message of India to Japan." He spoke as usual in English, but apparently without an interpreter. This must have added to the mystification of his audience, only a fraction of whom were able to understand his words.[32]

Although Tagore rambled from point to point in his address, his argument can be reconstructed under three main headings. The unity of Asian civilization and its spiritual character constituted his major premise, and he emphasized it repeatedly: "For centuries we did hold torches of civilization in the East when the West slumbered in darkness"; "I cannot but bring to your mind those days when the whole of Eastern

Asia from Burma to Japan was united with India in the closest tie of friendship, the only natural tie which can exist between nations"; "The lamp of ancient Greece is extinct in the land where it was first lighted. . . . But the civilization, whose basis is society and the spiritual ideal of man, is still a living thing in China and in India"; "Our civilization is not a nebulous system of abstract speculations. . . . It has evolved an inner sense — a sense of vision, the vision of the infinite reality in all finite things"; "Eastern Asia has been pursuing its own path, evolving its own civilization, which was not political but social, not predatory and mechanically efficient but spiritual and based upon all the varied and deeper relations of humanity." [33]

Tagore stated his second theme in a minor key. The political, mechanical, and commercial character of modern civilization was threatening to devour Asia's spiritual civilization: "We have seen this great stream of civilization choking itself from debris carried by its innumerable channels. We have seen that with all its vaunted love of humanity it has proved itself the greatest menace to Man"; "The political civilization which has sprung up from the soil of Europe and is overrunning the whole world, like some prolific weed . . . is cannibalistic in its tendencies, it feeds upon the resources of other peoples and tries to swallow their whole future." With special emphasis he declared: "this political civilization is scientific, not human." [34] In fairness to the continent whose intellectual leaders had made him world-famous, he paused to acknowledge the greatness of modern European civilization in tirelessly pursuing knowledge, alleviating human misery, harnessing the forces of nature, and pouring forth "an inexhaustible cascade of beauty and truth fertilizing all countries and all time." This, Europe's "deeper nature," he asserted, was based upon the spiritual strength of Christian culture. But, while "Europe is supremely good in her beneficence where her face is turned to all humanity . . . Europe is supremely evil in her maleficent aspect where her face is turned only upon her own interest, using all her power of greatness for ends which are against the infinite and the eternal in Man." [35] (Here Tagore put his finger on the equivocal character of modern civilization: the unprecedented power it generates can be used for good or for evil ends.)

The final part of his argument followed logically from the first two. If Asian civilization constituted a great reservoir of spiritual power, and if modern civilization was about to destroy humanity itself, then it must be from a regenerated Asia that man's salvation would come. Moreover, Japan was the one Asian country best able to carry out this mission, for she had already absorbed modern civilization without abandoning "her legacy of ancient culture from the East." Therefore: "Japan cannot altogether lose and merge herself in the scientific paraphernalia she has acquired from the West and be turned into a mere borrowed machine. She has her own soul, which must assert itself over all her requirements." So Tagore exhorted the Japanese: "apply your Eastern mind, your spiritual strength, your love of simplicity, your recognition of social obligation, in order to cut out a new path for this great unwieldy car of progress, shrieking out its loud discords as it runs."

Asia now feels that she must prove her life by producing living work, she must not lie passively dormant, or feebly imitate the West, in the infatuation of fear or flattery. For this we offer our thanks to this Land of the Rising Sun and solemnly ask her to remember that she has the mission of the East to fulfil. She must infuse the sap of a fuller humanity into the heart of modern civilization.[36]

In his "Message of India to Japan" Tagore set forth his master plan for mankind, and challenged Japan to take the lead in making it a reality. In Switzerland the pacifist author, Romain Rolland, on learning of the lecture from an American magazine, commented that it "marked a turning point in the history of the world." [37] In Japan itself the full text of the lecture was given in translation in the leading Tokyo dailies the following day. Tagore could not have wished for more favorable circumstances in which to deliver what he called India's message to Japan, for his coming had excited the curiosity of a nation noted for its receptivity to new ideas, and his audience at Tokyo Imperial University included many of the capital's leading men of letters.

Two days later, on June 13, some 250 dignitaries came to the Kaneiji Buddhist Temple to honor Tagore at a formal reception. The prime minister, the mayor, the president of Tokyo Imperial University, the minister of education, "all the famous people of the day" were there. The meeting was opened by Dr. Takakusu Junjirō, Japan's most eminent Buddhist scholar, after which Heki Mokusen (who like Takakusu had visited India), senior priest of the Sōtō Sect of Zen Buddhism, read an address of welcome.[38] Tagore replied in Bengali with a succinct restatement of his message to Japan:

When I landed at Kobe, I was disappointed to find materialistic civilization in Japan. But when I came to Shizuoka by train, I was welcomed
by Buddhists burning incense. I then felt for the first time that I had
come to Japan. I finally discovered that there are two currents in Japan:
the old and the new. I sincerely hope that the Japanese people will not
forget the old Japan. The new Japan is only an imitation of the West.
This will ruin Japan. Now I believe that Japanese civilization is harmonizing the West and the East. I hope that you will carry the light of
this glorious Oriental civilization to the West.[39]

Rabindranath's remarks were translated into Japanese by his friend
Kimura Nikki, and the prime minister was then called on to conclude
the meeting. Count Ōkuma, not realizing that Tagore had spoken in
Bengali, caused some amusement when he apologized for not understanding the poet because of his ignorance of the English language. He
then expressed his "sense of gratitude to the sage of India for his timely
visit and for giving a very sound warning, for Japan stood at the present
time at the parting of the ways in her inner life, and the thought of the
world faced a turning point." [40] After the meeting the participants posed
for the inevitable group photograph, and enjoyed a vegetarian dinner.

The reception at Kaneiji Temple, tendered by Tokyo's highest officials and most eminent scholars, marked the zenith of Japanese demonstrations of interest in Tagore's visit. So much attention must surely have
pleased him after the painful months of opprobrium he had been suffering in India, and that same day he wrote optimistically to his son Rathindranath: "The students have showed their enthusiasm for me. Everyone is telling me that my coming and my lectures will make a new current flow in Japan. This is what the heads of departments at Tokyo
University are hoping for. Everyone has been encouraged by my
lectures." [41]

At some point during his stay in Tokyo, Tagore made some remarkable
statements to the correspondent of the *Manchester Guardian,* who came
to see him at Yokoyama Taikan's house. Asked about his impressions of
Japan, he told the reporter that he had felt "indications of the growing
intimacy between Japan and India and of the evolution of a new Asia
awakening to a consciousness of unity." When questioned as to what
he considered "Eastern" about Japan, he replied, "Here in Japan I find
a reverence for the past, veneration for the ancestral dead, a quiet, a

stock of ideas, perhaps even a family system like those of India. Asia, perhaps, in the ideal sense extends from India to Japan." In commenting on Japanese pan-Asianism, he was reported to have said:

It does not surprise one to hear that [the] Japanese think it their country's mission to unite and lead Asia . . . Japan cannot stand alone. She would be bankrupt in competition with a united Europe and she could not expect support in Europe. It is natural that she should seek it in Asia, in association with a free China, Siam and, perhaps, in the ultimate course of things a free India. An associated Asia, even though it did not include the Semitic West, would be a powerful combination. Of course, that is to look a long way ahead and there are many obstacles in the way, notably the absence of a common language and the difficulty of communication. But from Siam to Japan there are I believe kindred stocks and from India to Japan there is much of religion and art and philosophy which is a common possession.[42]

At no time before or since this interview did Tagore venture so deeply into the muddy waters of political pan-Asianism. In subsequent speeches in Japan he was to denounce Japanese imperialism in Asia in no uncertain terms. Perhaps he was just then under the influence of his private conversations with Prime Minister Ōkuma and other Japanese statesmen, who apparently endorsed his proposal for closer cultural ties among Asian nations but drew his attention to the advantages of giving it a political backbone. Tagore did refer in this *Manchester Guardian* interview to "thoughtful men in Japan with whom I have talked," and cited their agreement with him that "the Western apparatus which Japan has borrowed is like a garment, universal and external," which "precisely for that reason . . . cannot of itself satisfy the soul of a nation." [43]

Before leaving Tokyo, Tagore paid a visit to the Tokyo Normal School and reaffirmed to its teachers and students his faith in spiritual values: "I believe that, in a little flower, there is a living power hidden in beauty which is more potent than a Maxim gun. I believe that in the bird's notes Nature expresses herself with a force which is greater than that revealed in the deafening roar of the cannonade." Conscious that he was speaking to the young, he deliberately criticized the military ethos which he felt permeated the Japanese school system.[44]

After ten days in Tokyo, Tagore exchanged its bustle for the relative quiet of suburban Yokohama on June 15. For the next two months he lived as the guest of a wealthy silk merchant, Hara Tomitarō, to whom he had been introduced by Yokoyama Taikan. Hara was a great patron of the Okakura school and showed an admiring Tagore his fine collection of Japanese art. In the quiet of Hara's seaside villa the Indian poet began to write lectures for his forthcoming American speaking tour.[45]

Here he also received an assortment of visitors, more often Indian merchants or Chinese and Korean students than Japanese nationals. The overseas students came to tell him about "the spirit of Japan" as they had experienced it in their own lands, and their tales opened his eyes to the realities of Japanese imperialism. He was particularly saddened to learn some unpleasant facts about Japan's harsh rule in Korea, which she had formally annexed to her empire six years earlier. Occasionally young Japanese ultranationalists called on him to talk about practical steps toward uniting Asia against the West, but the poet found them crude and their ideas distasteful. At least one Japanese poet, Sazaki Nobutsuna, came to pay his respects and later recounted a minor incident which held symbolic meaning for Tagore. As they were conversing, the electric power failed and the lights went out. "The spirit of old Japan has come and extinguished the new civilization," Tagore said merrily in a voice Sazaki described as "the voice of dreamland." [46]

"The Spirit of Japan"

For two weeks Tagore disappeared from public view. At the time he left Tokyo the country's leading British-owned newspaper had assumed that he would soon be presented to the emperor. The presentation never came about. Perhaps the oligarchy considered Tagore's ideas unsound and did not wish to countenance them any further; perhaps the Taishō emperor was subject to one of his periods of incapacity. In various ways during this fortnight's interval — from newspaper comments read to him by his young interpreter, the art student Yashiro Yukio, but also from the fact that the flood of invitations to lecture suddenly dropped to a trickle — Tagore came to realize that his major speech in Tokyo had not been well received by many of his hearers.[47]

At this juncture two private colleges in the Tokyo area showed their sympathy. Japan Women's University invited him to dinner on July 2, and in the afternoon of that same day, Keiō University, founded by the great liberal reformer Fukuzawa Yukichi, was host to the students of the various private colleges of the Tokyo area, who came to hear Tagore deliver a formal lecture on the topic, "The Spirit of Japan." [48]

Seeing nothing odd in the fact that he, an Indian, was lecturing the Japanese on the spirit of their own country, Tagore placed even greater emphasis than before on the essentially spiritual character of Japanese civilization, contrasting it with "the genius of Europe," which "has given her people the power of organization, which has specially made itself manifest in politics and commerce and in co-ordinating scientific knowledge." In contrast, "The genius of Japan has given you the vision of beauty in nature and the power of realizing it in your life. . . . This experience of your soul, in meeting a personality in the heart of the world, has been embodied in your civilization. It is a civilization of human relationship." [49]

Tagore expressed the fear that "the dignity and . . . reticent power of beauty" in Japan would be overwhelmed by "the huge heterogeneity of the modern age, whose only common bond is usefulness." The city of Kobe had reminded him of a giant dragon "with glistening scales, basking in the sun, after having devoured a large slice of the living flesh of the earth." He had only found the "true" Japan at Shizuoka, where the Buddhist priests "brought their basket of fruits to me and held their lighted incense before my face . . . wishing to pay homage to a man who had come from the land of the Buddha." It was the Buddhist ideal of *maitri* (compassion for all sentient beings) which lay "at the bottom" of Japanese culture. "True" Japan was Buddhist Japan, he implied.[50]

Taking his stand on this interpretation of Japanese culture, Tagore chastised his hosts severely for adopting nationalism, politics, and war. Rather naively, he considered these Western products, without indigenous roots in Asia. He must have seen some trophies from the Russo-Japanese War displayed in a Tokyo school, for he referred to their use in illustrating his point:

> To imbue the minds of a whole people with an abnormal vanity of its own superiority, to teach it to take pride in its moral callousness and ill-begotten wealth, to perpetuate humiliation of defeated nations by exhibiting trophies won from war, and using these in schools in order to breed in children's minds contempt for others, is imitating the West

where she has a festering sore, whose swelling is a swelling of disease
eating into its vitality.[51]

Tagore couched his condemnation of nationalism in the strongest
possible terms. It was "gigantic selfishness," "an elixir of moral death,"
"an eruptive inflammation of aggressiveness," and a "universal distrust
of humanity." The Great War then raging in Europe seemed to have
convinced him that, "the vital ambition of the present civilization of
Europe is to have exclusive possession of the devil. All her arms and
diplomacy are directed upon this one object." Forgetting his enthusiastic
reaction to Japanese victories eleven years earlier, Tagore observed that
the nations of the West felt no respect for Japan, "till she proved that
the bloodhounds of Satan are not only bred in the kennels of Europe but
can also be domesticated in Japan and fed with man's miseries." To
imitate Western nationalism would be not only unworthy, but suicidal,
he warned in a passage which seemed to prophesy the blow which was
to fall on Japan nearly three decades later: "And nations who sedulously
cultivate moral blindness as the cult of patriotism will end their existence in a sudden and violent death." [52]

His most sophisticated argument against nationalism was that it did
not constitute a useful innovation in Asia — that it was not necessarily
modern, but merely Western: "One must bear in mind that those who
have the true modern spirit need not modernize, just as those who are
truly brave are not braggarts. Modernism is not in the dress of the
Europeans; or in the hideous structures, where their children are in-
terned when they take their lessons. . . . These are not modern, but
merely European." [53] In a passage which reveals him as genuinely sympathetic with the modern spirit, Tagore reminded his hearers that Japan
could modernize without imitating the West in harmful ways: "True
modernism is freedom of mind, not slavery of taste. It is independence
of thought and action, not tutelage under European schoolmasters. It is
science, but not its wrong application in life." [54]

But true modernism by itself was not enough; if harnessed to selfish
ends it would lead to self-destruction. There were some Japanese whom
the word "modern" had so charmed that they no longer felt ashamed to
use falsehoods to gain their goals. "But if undiluted utility be modern,"
Tagore continued, "beauty is of all ages; if mean selfishness be modern,
the human ideals are no new inventions. And however modern may be

the proficiency which cripples man for the sake of methods and machines, it will never live to be old." Indeed, he charged his audience, "the lumbering structure of modern progress, riveted by the iron bolts of efficiency, which runs upon the wheels of ambition, cannot hold together for long." [55]

Quite aware that Europe's civilization enjoyed great prestige in Japan, Tagore emphasized that her ideals as well as Asia's could help to liberate mankind from the misuse of modern civilization: "Through the smoke of cannons and dust of markets the light of her moral nature has shown bright, and she has brought to us the ideal of ethical freedom, whose foundation lies deeper than social convention and whose province of activity is world-wide." [56] The "inner source" of Europe's power, Rabindranath felt, was her moral nature, expressed in the ideals of public good and liberty of thought and action. Therefore, he declared, "When we truly know the Europe which is great and good, we can effectively save ourselves from the Europe which is mean and grasping . . . we can claim Europe herself as our ally in our resistance to her temptations and to her violent encroachments." [57]

In a dramatic climax to his lecture the Indian poet painted a picture of Europe's future self-destruction, predicting that through "the unspeakable filth which has been accumulating for ages in the bottom of this civilisation" a voice will call out, "the voice which cries to our soul that the tower of national selfishness, which goes by the name of patriotism, which has raised its banner of treason against heaven, must totter and fall with a crash, weighed down by its own bulk, its flag kissing the dust, its light extinguished." [58]

The apocalyptic ring in Tagore's peroration reminds us of Lenin's gleeful writings on the imminent downfall of capitalist society, especially his *Imperialism, the Highest Stage of Capitalism,* which he was writing in Switzerland in this very year. The unending holocaust in Europe seems to have stirred similar emotions in Tagore and Lenin. Each saw the war as confirmation of his own theory of history. The parallel between the Indian and the Russian prophets ended there, however: for the new day which Tagore saw breaking was not to bring an intensely politicized union of the workers of the world, but a rebirth of the spiritual civilization of the East, possibly under the leadership of Japan. "And who knows if that day has not already dawned, and the sun not risen in the Easternmost horizon of Asia? And I offer, as did my ancestor rishis [the Hindu sages], my salutation to that sunrise of the East, which is destined once again to illumine the whole world." [59]

ISOLATION AND DEPARTURE

After the lecture Tagore was driven to the Japan Women's University to attend the supper party in his honor, and then returned quietly to Yokohama, where he stayed on at Hara's villa for the remainder of July. As the many comments published in Japanese periodicals on his lectures were read out to him in translation, he found that most of the intellectuals were critical of his ideas. Years later he explained what he thought had happened. He was at first received with ovations, but then, "the government became worried and put obstacles in the way." The youth of Japan, the poet commented, "is stifled by a crushing central power." C. F. Andrews made a similar diagnosis:

> They received him with enthusiasm at first, as one who had brought honour to Asia.
> But when he spoke out strongly against the militant imperialism which he saw on every side in Japan and set forward in contrast his ideal picture of the true meeting of East and West, with its vista of world brotherhood, the hint went abroad that such "pacifist" teaching was a danger in war-time, and that the Indian poet represented a defeated nation. Therefore, almost as rapidly as the enthusiasm had arisen, it subsided. In the end, he was almost isolated, and the object for which he had come to the Far East remained unfulfilled.[60]

The sensitive poet felt his isolation keenly. "The mental suffering which had appeared at the beginning of the war returned," said Andrews. "The Poet's whole inner nature was in revolt against the violently aggressive spirit of the age." He gave vent to his feelings through his pen, writing "at white heat" his lectures on "nationalism in the West," delivered in the United States. In one bitter passage he implied that his failure was due to the thought control exercised by the Japanese government:

> I have seen in Japan the voluntary submission of the whole people to the trimming of their minds and clipping of their freedom by their government, which through various educational agencies regulates their thoughts, manufactures their feelings, becomes suspiciously watchful

when they show signs of inclining toward the spiritual, leading them through a narrow path not toward what is true but what is necessary for the complete welding of them into one uniform mass according to its own recipe. The people accept this all-pervading mental slavery with cheerfulness and pride because of their nervous desire to turn themselves into a machine of power, called the Nation, and emulate other machines in their collective worldliness.[61]

In a more poignant mood he wrote two poems in Bengali, each expressing in a different way his sense of humiliation. Addressing Japan, he wrote:

> Oh, my guest who came to me in times of old,
> My house was then full of treasure and gold.
> Now in my house there is neither gold nor treasure,
> Only tears of sorrow — I curse myself for my guilt! [62]

In a longer poem, "The Song of the Defeated," Tagore accepted the accusation of his Japanese critics that he was "the poet of a defeated country," but made his country's subjection a cause for pride:

My Master had bid me while I stand at the roadside, to sing the
   song of Defeat, for that is the bride whom He woos in secret.
She has put on the dark veil, hiding her face from the crowd,
   but the jewel glows on her breast in the dark.
She is forsaken of the day, and God's night is waiting for her
   with its lamps lighted and flowers wet with dew.
She is silent with eyes downcast; she has left her home behind her,
   from her home has come that wailing in the wind.
But the stars are singing the love-song of the eternal
   to a face sweet with shame and suffering.
The door has been opened in the lonely chamber, the call has sounded,
   and the heart of the darkness throbs with awe because of the coming
   tryst.[63]

After the apparent failure of his third and final lecture to a large Japanese audience, Tagore spent most of the remaining two months of his stay in quiet seclusion. On July 12 he was invited to visit the Zen sect's Sojiji Temple at Tsurumi near Yokohama. In a brief speech he mentioned the place of pilgrimage in India where the Ganges and

Jumna rivers flowed together, and said: "My journey to Japan is like the journey of a pilgrim to a sacred place." [64]

While the public reception of his lectures seems to have discouraged Tagore, the private talks he had with individual Japanese had the opposite effect. After his lecture at Keiō University, several groups of students and teachers came to call on him in Yokohama. A young philosophy student from Waseda University, Takao Kenichi, came to see him five different times to ask questions, on one occasion with a group of twenty-five students. A graduate of Waseda, the playwright Akita Ujaku, the Buddhist priest Takeda Toyoshirō and several other Waseda people also paid the Indian poet a visit, looking, as Takeda observed, like the assorted pilgrims in Chaucer's *Canterbury Tales*.[65] Although Tagore received more calls from foreign visitors than from Japanese,[66] he was sufficiently encouraged by his conversations with the latter to write on July 20:

> Having turned my face toward the West, now I find it hard to give my mind to the East. Having spent my sunrise on the West, let me give my sunset to the East. In Japan quite a crowd has surrounded me. I find a great joy in talking with them because they are drawn to me wholeheartedly. It is very easy for me to bring before them whatever I really have, since they want it only because they have a real need for it.[67]

In Europe also he had rejoiced at this thirst for truth. "Ideas are the food of their life," he said of both the Japanese and Europeans. By contrast, India was "a land of indigestion," he complained. "We have no appetite for ideas — that is why we don't want ideas as food, but only as chutney. But I have no more taste for this chutney business." [68]

In a long letter, full of perceptive comments, written to William Rothenstein, his closest European friend, he summarized in painterly language his impressions of Japanese civilization:

My dearest Friend
 I have nearly come to the end of my visit to Japan. I had my idea of Japan of the bookland — the Japan which had no soul of her own [and which] therefore had no difficulty in getting into the bodies belonging to others. I fully expected to find here one monotonous mist of the modern everywhere and very little Japan behind it. But to my surprise I find that the mist is not continuous and Japan is still visible. Her features are distinct — and what [is] more, she is human. She is not a mask of mod-

ern science and organisation with no living face inside. I can see that
Japan has had all the advantage of the smallness of her area, security of
her sea and homogeneity of her inhabitants. She is like a skillful gardener
having a small piece of land, compelled to take recourse to intensive culture, making every inch of the ground yield its best. She has not been
burdened with a bulk which breeds slowness and negligence. It is wonderful to see how the mind of a whole people has been trained to love
beauty in nature and bring it out in art. It has been their conscious endeavour to make their daily life in all its details perfect in rhythm of
beauty. There is no sign of oversight or vulgar display in their houses
or their manners. The reticence in their taste shows their natural sensibility for the beautiful. Because their enjoyment is true, for them the
enough is better than the more and right proportion than profuseness.

This has been made possible because for their expression they seem
to have concentrated all their resources in the picturesque. Their genius
has taken the course of the definite — they revel in the rhythm of proportion in lines and movements. But music is lacking in them and the
deeper currents of poetry which deals with the ineffable. They have
acquired a perfect sense of the form at some cost of the sense of the
spirit. Their nature is solely aesthetic and not spiritual. Therefore it has
been easier for them to make their ideals almost universal in their peoples. For these ideals are more in the sense of the decorum and deftness
of mind and fingers than in the sense of the infinite in man — they are
more of the dress than of the health. However, it is wonderful to see
perfection achieved and made the common property of a whole race of
men.[69]

Early in August, the Tokyo *Asahi* noted Tagore's departure from
Yokohama to Hara's summer place in the scenic region of Hakone in the
foothills of Mt. Fuji. "As he is a poet, it is uncertain how long he will
stay in Japan," the *Asahi* added jokingly to its account of his itinerary.[70]
In Hakone, a meeting was arranged between Tagore and the elderly
Count Kabayama, a veteran of the Formosan expedition of 1874, the
first governor-general of Formosa, and several times a cabinet minister.
When their conversation turned to the subject of Asia's political future,
Tagore, according to the interpreter, said nothing. When the Satsuma
samurai talked of his sympathy with the Indian people, the poet merely
thanked him.[71] It may have been Count Kabayama who suggested to
the poet that he might become the president of independent India, if it
were freed with Japanese help. Tagore answered this offer with a stony
silence.[72]

While in Hakone, Hara took the poet to see a famous monument to the Soga brothers who had won fame revenging their father's murder in the twelfth century. Tagore was asked if he would like to compose a short impromptu poem after the Japanese haiku fashion. He studied the monument and once again expressed the dislike of Japanese militarism which rankled in him throughout this summer:

> They hated and killed and men praised them.
> But God in shame hastens to hide their memory with
> the green grass.[73]

On the lighter side, Tagore enjoyed talking with Japanese schoolgirls, and was always pleased when they came to see him. At the invitation of the Japan Women's University, whose Tokyo campus he had visited, the poet spent a few days in mid-August at their summer school in the mountain resort of Karuizawa. Here, to the great delight of the girls, he gave daily talks of an inspirational nature. As a token of their gratitude, they presented him with a photograph album on his departure from Japan. He little realized then that one of these girls would be chiefly responsible for arranging his second, and more successful, trip to Japan eight years later.[74]

In a symbolic parting gesture, Tagore made a special journey to the seaside villa of his departed friend, Okakura Kakuzō, at Izura, 110 miles north of Tokyo. Sitting on the seacoast facing eastward across the Pacific, he composed an elegy to his late comrade recalling his great ideas. Writing to his nephew Surendranath, who had been especially close to Okakura during both of the Japanese art historian's visits to India, Tagore reflected: "I have had conversations with many very important people — I have not found among them anyone with Okakura's genius. Their understanding is very limited. In their hands everything is reduced to the simplest level." After spending a few days as the guest of Okakura's widow and son the poet returned to Yokohama to board the ship that would take him to America.[75]

Before sailing he had one final opportunity to refute those Japanese criticisms of his ideas which had come to his attention. In an interview granted to a reporter from the Tokyo *Asahi* he argued that he had been misunderstood, "as merely cursing the material civilization of the West." This was an oversimplification, he argued. Material civilization might be compared to a sharp razor: "If you want to use it, please do so carefully. But do not be so attracted by material civilization as to forget completely your spiritual civilization. In a word, I would like to say: Use a sharp razor, but do not be used by it." In this same interview Tagore denounced as an unsound tendency the apparent uniformity of thought in Japan.[76]

AFTERTHOUGHTS

On September 3, the Indian poet boarded the S.S. *Canada Maru,* bound for the United States. Seeing him off at the ship were Yokoyama Taikan, Hara Tomitarō, an art dealer named Nomura, and many others,[77] but the crowd was evidently smaller than the "human cyclone" which had greeted him at Kobe three months earlier. During the long voyage across the Pacific, Rabindranath meditated on his first visit to Japan, and recorded his impressions in a long letter home.

He was particularly interested in comparing the Japanese and the Bengalis in their respective attitudes toward modern Western techniques, institutions, and ideas. He found the two peoples alike in their receptivity to innovations and their ability to create new things. This aptitude had facilitated the introduction of European civilization in both Japan and Bengal, but a fundamental difference of attitude separated Japan on the one hand from Bengal and from Europe on the other.

> The deep foundation on which the greatness of Europe has been built up is a spiritual one; it is not only its skill in action, but its ethical ideal. Here is the basic difference between Japan and Europe. A humanistic *sādhanā* [mental and spiritual discipline] which recognizes a more perfect world and which is moving toward it . . . goes beyond the self-interest of one's nationality and the needs of domestic life, and establishes its own goal. In this realm of *sādhanā,* India is closer to Europe than Japan.[78]

Modern Europe, however, had turned to worshiping power, he noted, and the influence of Christianity was weakening. Japan seemed to be rapidly following this new trend, and to be especially inspired by Germany, where it was strongest:

> For this reason in Japan the powers that be despise the moral intelligence of man . . . and Japan even fancies herself superior for being devoid of such intelligence — she knows that she is free from the de-

mands of the life-after-death, and therefore she will be a conqueror in this life.

The religion to which the Japanese authorities have given particular encouragement is Shinto. This is because this religion is based only on traditional institutions, not on spirituality. This religion considers the Emperor and his ancestors to be gods. Consequently these traditional institutions can be exploited to stir up intense patriotism.[79]

In a remarkable passage, Tagore summed up the reflections inspired by his visit to Japan: "But the civilization of Europe does not consist of one chamber as the Mongolian civilization does. It has an inner chamber. It has been acknowledging the Kingdom of Heaven for many days. There the meek are victorious; the stranger is raised up above one's own kin." [80] Not Japan, but Bengal, he concluded, was best qualified to enter into this inner room, where all mankind would become as one: "If we cannot be close to Europe in any other place, we can still be close to her in this great place. . . . The meeting of Man in this inner chamber is the true meeting. For many days many signs have appeared that the call has come to the Bengalis to open the door to this meeting." [81]

Tagore had originally decided to visit Japan for two rather different reasons, and in looking back on his three-month stay he evidently had mixed feelings about what he had accomplished there. On the one hand, the novelty and beauty of the land and its people must have helped to relieve the painful restlessness which had driven him to leave India. On the other hand, he was disappointed that the lofty ideals he set forth in his three public lectures seemed to have fallen on deaf ears. His friend Okakura had long before encouraged him to believe that the cultural leaders of India, Japan, and China could somehow join forces to stem the tides of materialism and commercialism pouring in from the West. The holocaust in Europe prompted him to hope also that a revived, united, and spiritual East could save the excessively nationalistic West from destroying itself. Far from reassuring him in this second belief, his visit to Japan brought him to the alarming realization that what he considered the cancerous growth of nationalism was already far advanced in this part of Asia. "Some of the newspapers praised my utterances for their poetical qualities, while adding with a leer that it was the poetry of a defeated nation," he said after leaving Japan. "I felt they were right. Japan had been taught in a modern school the lesson of how to become powerful. The schooling is done and she must enjoy the fruits of her lessons." [82] Eight years later he told an Anglo-American audience in China that in Japan he "realized for the first time the terrible suffering with which the whole world was afflicted." The proud displays of war trophies taken from China made him feel "humiliated at this primitive and brutal perpetuation of the defeat of an enemy. Nationalism, therefore, seemed to me to be pure barbarism, based on pride, greed and lust for power, with wealth dominating the disease and I shuddered when I saw the result." [83]

If Tagore was disillusioned with Japan, what was the attitude of that country's leaders toward him and his ideas? Two Englishmen resident in Japan for many years answered this question to their own satisfaction in articles written close to the time of his departure. Robert Young, the founder and editor of the respected *Japan Chronicle,* and a Kobe resident since 1888, probably wrote the unsigned editorial on "Tagore and His Critics" in the newspaper's weekly edition. Japan had rejected the poet's message, the editorial said, and it ascribed his failure to a single cause:

> Tagore's contempt for mere nationalism is naturally the bitterest pill for the Japanese to swallow, since from the cradle to the grave the importance of being Japanese is firmly impressed upon them. How can they put nationalism behind them? Surely such a doctrine can only be preached by a man whose country has lost its independence — by an inhabitant of a pale, decaying land, where all things droop to ruin.[84]

A Church of England missionary, the Rev. L. B. Cholmondeley, with nearly thirty years' service in Japan, was in a better position than Young to feel the pulse of the educated élite, for he was living not in Kobe but in Tokyo, the intellectual as well as political and economic capital of the country. In addition, as honorary chaplain to the British Embassy he may have acquired information through embassy sources. His description of the Japanese response to Tagore was colorful, if not entirely accurate:

> With the same distinguished honour that they had paid him on his arrival, the Japanese took leave of their departing guest. He had been respectfully listened to by thousands, the Press had conveyed his message from one end of Japan to the other; but, so far as I know, statesmen, professors, journalists — all who could give voice to the sentiments of Japan — alike rejected it. He had no Vici to add to that Veni and Vidi

when he took his departure. Japan's answer to Tagore was in short, that we are not blindfolded; we have entered into comity with the nations of the West — into the world's fuller life — with our eyes open and of our own free will. In our nation there is the spirit of progress; it finds its own natural outlet; our watchword is Forward. Try to frighten us as you may by the perils to be passed through, the press and the strife, the dust and din, we are persuaded that life's gains and conquests outweigh the evil of them all, and nothing shall in any wise tempt us to go back.[85]

As if to confirm these judgments, when Tagore stopped at Yokohama in early February on his return to India after his lecture tour in the United States, only Yokoyama Taikan and a lone newspaper reporter were waiting at the dock to greet him.[86] By all appearances, the great expectations which had been in the air the previous June had completely vanished.

Appearances often conceal realities, however, and the judgments of highly placed English residents of Japan were not necessarily any more objective than those of Tagore himself. For the English community had reason to be worried about possible repercussions of the Indian poet's presence in Japan. Tagore had been knighted the previous year to be sure, but was he "loyal"? Indian revolutionaries, many of them from Bengal, were known to be working with German agents to overthrow Britain's rule in India, and if the war went badly for Britain, what was to prevent Japan from shifting to the German side and going after an Indian Empire of her own? One of the Indian revolutionaries in the United States, pretending that Tagore and the Japanese government were in league with them, wrote in 1917 to a co-conspirator in Amsterdam: "Sir Rabindranath Tagore has come at our suggestion. He said he saw Count Ōkuma, former Japanese premier, and Count Terauchi, present Premier. Terauchi was favorable. Sir Rabindranath also consulted a number of minor Japanese officials." [87] The letter was intercepted, made public at the San Francisco trial of some of the Indo-German conspirators early in 1918, and printed in the newspapers. Tagore was furious when he saw the press story and fired off a telegram (never answered) to President Wilson denying complicity in the revolutionaries' activities.[88]

But how did His Britannic Majesty's Government know in 1916 what Tagore was up to in Japan? Unpublished India Office records show that the poet's trip caused considerable uneasiness in London and some embarrassment to the governor of Bengal, Lord Carmichael, who had furnished Tagore with a letter of introduction to the British ambassador in Tokyo. Carmichael, called on the carpet by his superior, the Secretary of State for India, for seeming to endorse "a party about whose purpose and conduct the Government of India were so doubtful," cleared himself by explaining that he had merely introduced Tagore.[89] What probably worried British officialdom most was the possibility that Tagore's visit might result in a Japanese-Indian understanding which could eventually take a political and anti-British form. The British ambassador in Tokyo may well have reacted to Tagore's Tokyo University lecture by reminding the Japanese government that the Anglo-Japanese Alliance was still in force, that Britain and Japan were wartime allies, and that too friendly an attitude toward an Indian celebrity critical of the war could impair the good relations which had proven so advantageous to both Powers. Such a diplomatic reminder could have been a factor in producing the official coolness which followed Rabindranath's delivery of his "Message of India to Japan."

Both Tagore and his British observers were hobbled by their emotions (of disappointment on the one hand, of fear on the other) as they tried to assess the impact he had made on Japanese public opinion. The dense barrier of language also occluded their perceptions of the Japanese intellectual scene. Only a careful study of the Japanese periodicals and newspapers of the day will yield a more accurate and comprehensive picture of the way Japan's leading men and women looked at India's spokesman and his challenging ideas about Eastern and Western civilizations.

CHAPTER THREE

JAPANESE VIEWS OF TAGORE'S MESSAGE

The civilization of the West has its origin within itself, while that of modern Japan has its origin outside the country. The new waves come one after another from the West. . . . It is as if, before we can enjoy one dish on the table, or even know what it is, another new dish is set before us. . . . I do not say, however, that this is bad, or that the introduction of Western civilization should be stopped. We cannot help it; there is nothing else we can do. Nevertheless, the result is superficial.

— Natsume Sōseki

INTELLECTUALS IN MODERN JAPAN faced essentially the same problem that Tagore and other Indian thinkers had been wrestling with: how to bring their society into meaningful relationship with the modern world, particularly with the modern West, while holding fast to those traditions and values which preserve a link with the past, give pride to the people, and make a recognized contribution to world culture. Tagore and other Bengali religious leaders had answered this question by stressing modernized traditions of Indian religious and philosophical thought, leaving the direction of political, economic, and military affairs to Westerners, many of whom readily acknowledged the superior spirituality of India's sages and seers. It was the old story of the Brahman priest and the Kshatriya warrior-administrator, translated into the nineteenth-century symbiosis between Hindu and Britisher. Such a division of labor seemed to Tagore to work so well that he visualized the whole of Asia concentrating its energies on cultural and spiritual pursuits. Encouraged by his conversations with Okakura in 1902 and 1912, he had urged his Japanese listeners in 1916 to take the lead in this great venture of Asian spiritual revival.

The Japanese intellectual world in 1916 was made up of many more schools of thought than Okakura had told Tagore about. There were those who believed in spiritual values, but not necessarily the same spiritual values Tagore subscribed to: some were Buddhists, some Christians, some superpatriots for whom Japan's national polity was invested with religious significance. Others opposed the idea that spiritual and material civilizations were separable, especially along geographic lines; still others regarded all talk of spirituality with suspicion. One indication of the variety of viewpoints from which Japan's intellectuals looked at Tagore is the fact that out of eighty-seven individuals whose opinions on him were published (most of them in the three Tokyo monthlies which conducted opinion surveys after he had lectured at Tokyo University), thirty-five disapproved of his lectures and twenty-six favored them for one reason or another, five found both good and bad in them, and twenty-one passed no judgment. These comments are worth studying in some detail, not merely to find out how far Tagore failed or succeeded in finding support for his ideas, but to see how these individual statements represent in miniature form the pluralistic thought-world of the Japanese of this period.

Main Currents of Japanese Thought, 1868–1916

Selective receptivity to foreign ideas and methods was the dominant motif of intellectual and political — indeed of all spheres of Japanese life during the half-century following the 1867 overthrow of the Tokugawa government. The samurai statesmen who directed Japan's emergence as a modern nation were well aware of a historical precedent for their work: the selective borrowing of Chinese and Indian traditions pioneered by Prince Shōtoku in the seventh century. These two great movements of "modernization" were alike directed at the achievement of both political unity and the social harmony essential to the maintenance of that unity. The leaders of the nineteenth-century coup which ended the Tokugawa Shogunate system and "restored" the emperor to sole ultimate authority looked not to China for new ideas but to the nations of the West, who posed the greatest threat to Japan's sovereignty. Their policy was enunciated by the Meiji Emperor himself in 1868: "Knowledge shall be sought throughout the world so as to strengthen the foundations of imperial rule." [1]

Encouraged by this directive, and usually supported by government funds, Japan's educated men literally scoured the globe for ideas and institutions with which to strengthen the state. In the 1870's and early 1880's the slogan "civilization and enlightenment" (*bummei kaika*) popularized the new program, and wave on wave of Western ways and ideas began to sweep into the country. On the most abstract level of thought, science and Christianity were welcomed as civilizing traditions, while both Buddhist and Confucian learning fell into disrepute as symbolic of the old feudal order which had proven itself incapable of matching the power of the modern Western nations. The leading enlightenment figure, Fukuzawa Yukichi, even argued the utility of making Christianity the national faith: "Although I am personally entirely indifferent to religion, I believe that from the point of view of statesmanship we cannot avoid adopting the most influential creed of human society, in order to give our nation an independent position among civilized countries by boldly adopting their distinguishing characteristics." [2] But the discovery that in Europe and America many intellectuals considered Christianity incompatible with science took the bloom off the spreading Christian movement, and the refusal of the Western powers in the late 1880's to give up their extraterritorial privileges dealt a still more serious blow to the general policy of uncritical self-Westernization as a means of impressing the treaty powers with Japan's right to be treated as an equal.

That a sea change had set in was clear in 1890, when the collective leadership controlling the government put into effect an autocratic constitution modeled on that of the rising German empire and promulgated the Imperial Rescript on Education, laying down Confucian principles of loyalty and filial piety as the basis for moral and civic training in all the schools. These documents firmly fixed the emperor at the apex of the political, social, and moral orders, binding all three into "the national structure" (*kokutai*, also translatable as "national essence") and mediating between it and the cosmic order by virtue of the quasi-divine character inherited from his ancestors, supposedly the Shinto deities themselves. This highly conservative theory was used in the 1890's by such German-trained philosophers as Inoue Tetsujirō to attack the waning prestige of Christianity, whose adherents were accused of disloyalty for believing in a higher Power than the emperor. Buddhism began to regain respectability as its socially and politically conservative character was once more appreciated, while its intellectual content was enriched and modernized by the same process of discovery and re-vitalization of pristine ideas that had given new life to Hinduism in nineteenth-century India.

New intellectual currents from the West acted both to reinforce and to oppose this conservative and nativistic trend. German idealism, principally Kantian and Hegelian thought, helped to systematize both Confucian ethics and Buddhist metaphysics and also strengthened the absolutist philosophy of the national polity. This was the period when the American art historian Ernest Fenellosa, himself a Hegelian, aided the movement to revive Japanese art forms. At the same time the English utilitarian and democratic traditions introduced in the 1870's and 1880's, though weakened, received support from the new pragmatist thought of James and Dewey coming from the United States. Another strain of English thought, however, Spencer's evolutionism, reinforced the grow-ing tendency to stress the authority of native institutions, and Spencer himself drew up a constitution for Japan whose central feature was an authoritarian monarchy. French social thought, at first introduced in the "civilization and enlightenment" period, combined with Christian humanist thought to prepare the way for socialism, anarchism, and Marx-ism. After the exhausting war of 1904–5 naturalism became the domi-nant literary trend, but new idealistic currents rushed in after 1910, so that, as one Japanese authority put it, "the constructive ideas and philosophies of Eucken, Bergson, Nietzsche, Tagore, Tolstoy, Dostoev-sky, Maeterlinck, Huysmans, Romain Rolland, Whitman, James and others swept into this country like a rising tide." [3]

All these currents continued to swirl in the minds of Japan's intellec-tuals, sometimes combining, sometimes clashing, and when Tagore ap-peared before them they were able to scrutinize and evaluate his ideas in a wide variety of contexts. Tagore was unknown in Japan until the award of the Nobel Prize made him world-famous; then translations from his English writings came pouring from the presses. One popular anthology ran through four editions in 1915, and three thousand copies of *Sadhana, the Realization of Life* (translated from the lectures he had given at Harvard) were sold in the first two days of its publication. Two biographies and two books on his general philosophy were quickly published, and in response to the news that he would visit Japan in 1915 several monthly magazines included in their May issues articles and symposia on different aspects of Tagore's artistic and philosophical work.[4]

Nineteen of these articles, brought together in the collection *Meishi no Tagōru kan* (How famous men regard Tagore), show in miniature the variety of viewpoints from which Japan's intellectuals first turned to watch this new comet swim into their sky. Yoshida Genjirō, a Christian and a specialist on English romanticism, was one of several who were simply interested in making Tagore's writings better known in Japan.[5] The poet Noguchi Yonejirō, who was to become Tagore's greatest admirer in Japan, was even more strongly influenced by Western models than Yoshida, for he had lived some years with the California poet Joaquin Miller and had become famous in London in 1903 with the publication of his English poems, *From an Eastern Sea*. Since he had also lectured on Japanese poetry at Oxford and had published two short books on Japanese art in "The Wisdom of the East" series, Noguchi could explain that "the reason why Tagore is received with so much respect and acclaim [in the West] is that he expresses the soul of his people with traditional feeling and religiosity. . . . He is a poet who sums up all the traditional literature of the past." [6]

Interest in different currents of Western thought led Japan's intellectuals to opposing views of Tagore's philosophy of life. To Nakazawa Rinsen, a scholar of Bergson, Nietzsche, Tolstoy, and Rolland, Tagore appeared to be "the Bergson of the East." In another article, Nakazawa characterized Tagore's thought as "the antithesis of the individualism of modern Europe," and recommended it to his countrymen as a healthy antidote to unhealthy Western influences. In short, Nakazawa appears to have been encouraged by his reading of continental European idealist thinkers to oppose the spread in Japan of the English and American emphasis on individualism.[7] Another translator of Bergson, Hirose Tetsuji, writing in English, explicitly endorsed Rabindranath's ideal of Eastern spiritual revival: "It is a matter for congratulation to the minds of thinking Japanese, who have found their way to awake from their exclusive adoration of Western civilization, and have aroused within them a spirit of love and respect [for] the old traditions of their country. In that respect, I think, our nation is greatly indebted to Tagore." [8]

Exposure to a different strain of Western thought, the pragmatism of John Dewey at the University of Chicago in the 1890's, had made Tanaka Ōdō rather critical of religious ideas and emotions; accordingly, he took a skeptical stance toward the fuss that was being made over Tagore in Japan. "To my surprise, every advertisement [for translations of Tagore's works] has said that the future will be the era of Tagore," he wrote. With mock naiveté he asked Tagore's Japanese admirers to tell him exactly why they wished to introduce his thought in Japan.[9]

Several other critics, ignoring Western schools of thought, simply denounced Tagore's ideas as unsuited to Japan's needs and national spirit. Kuroiwa Shūroku, the publisher of the important daily *Yorozu chōhō* (Universal news) commented: "Tagore's thought is a kind of resignation-ism. Such thought is not suitable for Japan, so I am not pleased that he is coming to Japan. But we must have entertainment from time to time, and Tagore's thought is like a refreshing drink," he said, adding wryly, "I suppose this is why it is so accepted by the Europeans, who are very busy." The minor novelist Katō Asadori asked Tagore's admirers to distinguish between those aspects of his thought which were useful for Japan and those which were useless, adding: "His value for me lies in the fact that he is a patriot in a ruined country." Since Tagore was a man who meditated to achieve ecstasy rather than to clarify his thinking, Katō concluded that the Japanese should welcome Tagore, not as a philosopher, but as a poet.[10]

Obviously proud of Japan's success in becoming an imperial power in East Asia, the right-wing journalist Mitsui Koshi expressed the most chauvinistic of all these viewpoints in his sharp criticism of Tagore's philosophy of life, castigating it as "an escape from reality" — the reality being the condition of Indian society under the rule of foreigners. Mitsui argued that the vitality of ancient Indian thought was based on the conquering spirit of the Aryans, and suggested that if Tagore really wished to revive that thought he should look for inspiration to nations like Japan that were repeating this experience of conquering weaker peoples. "I think that he should learn from us rather than we from him," he concluded.[11]

After Tagore had arrived and delivered his "Message of India to Japan," educated Japanese had a much more specific picture of his ideas and how they might help or hinder the solution of the problems facing their country. Their comments on his message mirror all the major schools of thought, whether of foreign or indigenous origin, which prevailed among the intellectuals in the early summer of 1916.[12]

LITERARY LEADERS

Tagore's greatness as a poet, so clear in the Bengali originals, was obscured in their English translations, and Japanese translations from the English translations reduced their vitality still further. Given these linguistic obstacles, it is understandable that Tagore's most enthusiastic admirer in Japan (as later proved the case in China as well) was an aesthete steeped in English literature who also wrote and published poems in English. Noguchi Yonejirō felt a spiritual kinship with Tagore because his own English poems had scored a literary hit in England ten years before Tagore's greater success with English renderings of his Bengali verse. Also, like the Indian poet he had been encouraged by English and American interest in Asian cultural traditions to work for the preservation of those traditions against the corroding effects of wholesale Westernization in his own country. Noguchi thus declared in *The Spirit of Japanese Art,* published in London during his second visit there in 1914: "It is the time now when we must jealously guard our spiritual insularity, and carefully sift the good and the bad, and protect ourselves." [13]

Noguchi was so excited at Tagore's arrival in Japan that he somehow managed to get into his fellow poet's train compartment to talk with him on the last part of his journey from Kobe to Tokyo. "Your coming is of great importance to us," he recalled telling Tagore, "for Japan is entering a new literary era. Those who wish to establish a new Japanism by proper means are increasing." [14] Noguchi elaborated on his concept of Japanism in his analysis of Japanese reactions to Tagore's public lectures: "While some, adherents of the so-called Western civilization in Japan, called Sir Rabindranath merely a propagandist of negativism or willful dreamer . . . others, delightfully awakened into the so-called Japanism or Orientalism endorsed by the exposed weakness of the present European war, thought that Sir Rabindranath agreed with their principle in encouraging the real individualism to assert the inner development of the nation." [15] Noguchi evidently took it for granted that Orientalism and Japanism were one and the same thing. Twenty-two years later he and Tagore were to quarrel and part over this very point; in the meantime, however, Noguchi became known as the leading interpreter of the Indian poet to the Japanese public.[16]

Familiarity with English literature predisposed other Japanese intellectuals to approve of Tagore's general outlook, although they were not always pleased by his specific message to Japan. Waseda University, founded by the pro-English Premier Count Ōkuma, was known for its strong department of English literature, and several of its graduates wrote sympathetically of the Indian poet. The playwright Akita Ujaku, after talking with him wrote:

> I must admit that I cannot say I agree with most of his ideas, but I feel a strong sympathy with him as a poet and also with the leitmotiv of his philosophy, which is that of a young prophet. For example, his idea of the harmony of matter and mind, or his judgment on contemporary civilization from the standpoint of a monistic view of the laws of the universe or of human society — these seem to me very suggestive.[17]

The young novelist Yoshida Genjirō, whose biography and articles on Tagore in 1915 may have helped earn him his appointment in 1916 to his old department at Waseda, also went to see Tagore in Yokohama, and also felt "warm sympathy with this old poet who has come from afar." Listening to Tagore answer the questions of the students from China, Taiwan, Korea, and Japan, who were also visiting the poet that day, Yoshida, a Unitarian Christian, felt as though he were in the presence of an Old Testament prophet: "He was as gentle as a dove, as strong as Paul, and sometimes he seemed like a hero. 'Nation, state — all these things are mere abstract words. Only the self is absolute.' In saying these words he hinted at a profound insight." [18]

Specialists on the romantic tradition in English literature differed among themselves in their evaluation of Tagore's ideas. Saitō Takeshi and Satō Kiyoshi were both recent graduates of the English department at Tokyo University, and each was to publish a study of Keats. Saitō had the more brilliant career of the two, joining the faculty of Tokyo University and later becoming president of the Japan Women's University. "I am one of those who are thankful for the warnings which Mr. Tagore has given us," he wrote in 1916, but noted also that the poet himself had stressed the value of contact with the best in Western civilization.

"We are deeply convinced that the East is meditative and graceful," he continued, "and at the same time we would like to recognize the progressiveness and power of the West." [19] Satō, who had left Tokyo to teach at the Kansai Gakuin in Osaka, based his comment on Tagore's speech in that city, and was quite critical of it. "When it occurred to me that he was cursing modern civilization," he wrote, "the words of the interpreter made my mind completely tired." [20]

The real giant among those Japanese writers familiar with English literature in 1916 was the great novelist Natsume Sōseki. Sōseki (as in Bengal, so in Japan, eminent literary men were referred to by their given names) had chosen to major in English at Tokyo University with the idea of becoming a writer rather than a scholar. After distinguishing himself at the university and teaching in provincial posts for a while, he was sent by the government to England, where from 1900 to 1902 he read voraciously as an independent student. His meager stipend forced him to live in poor quarters and eat at cheap restaurants, acquainting him with the Dickensian side of London in the same years when Noguchi Yonejirō was there reading his Whitmanesque poetry to aristocratic ladies who knew all "the right persons." [21] Sōseki took no interest in English poetry, but reading English fiction spurred him to try to write novels in his own language that would be characteristically Japanese. Scornful both of shallow imitation of Western models (see his comment quoted at the beginning of this chapter) and of narrow chauvinism, he saw the need for "internal enlightenment," or the development of each individual's power of independent judgment so that he could accept or reject intelligently ideas and ways regardless of whether they were originally Japanese or Western. Both in his personal life and in his writings Sōseki displayed this independence and originality. The intellectual world was startled in 1907 when he resigned his prestigious teaching post at Tokyo Imperial University to become a free-lance writer, and again in 1911 when he angrily rejected the honorary doctorate the Ministry of Education had bestowed on him without even inquiring whether or not he wanted such an honor. A master in writing both Chinese poetry and Japanese haiku, he experimented in his novels and short stories with one style and genre after another, conveying in them a poignant sense of the bewilderment created in the minds of educated Japanese by rapidly changing social and moral standards, and by modern technology itself.

Unfortunately, no one attempted to bring Sōseki and Tagore together so that they could compare their ideas on the problems posed for their respective societies and cultures by rapid modernization under strong influences from the West. Tagore was quite sure of the solution to these problems; Sōseki was not. He was also in bad health, ailing from the stomach ulcer which ended his life a few months later. When asked for his opinion of Tagore, Sōseki replied with characteristic honesty: "Unfortunately I did not have a chance to meet Tagore. Nor have I read any of his writings. My knowledge about Tagore is gained only from pictures and articles in the newspapers." Saying nothing about the newspaper articles he had read, which presumably included the translated text of Tagore's Tokyo University address, Sōseki added mildly: "I suppose from those pictures that he is more splendid in his appearance than many Japanese. Besides this, I have no other thought." [22]

Although Sōseki did not say so, he may have been put off by the way in which the visiting Indian poet had been lionized by the Tokyo public and officially feted at Ueno Park. This complaint, openly expressed by quite a few Japanese literary men, reflects their alienation from the public and political spheres of life — in marked contrast to the strong sense of involvement we find among China's literary leaders in the mid-1920's. This isolation, which one scholar has identified as the characteristic feature of Japan's intellectual in the 1910's and 1920's,[23] was especially marked in the case of the brilliant and sensitive novelist, Arishima Takeo. A graduate of the Sapporo missionary school in Hokkaido, Arishima became a Christian, and then went to Harvard, but did not complete his studies there. Like Sōseki, he gave up a teaching career to devote himself to creative writing. In his personal search for a meaningful relationship with his society, Arishima moved from Christianity to a Whitmanesque individualism (he translated Leaves of Grass into Japanese), to socialism, and finally to a state of despair which brought on his suicide in 1923. Asked for his reaction to Tagore, Arishima declared: "I dislike literary prizes and the frivolous doings of the literary world, and so I have read neither Tagore's works nor any criticisms of them." Objecting to the way Tagore had been suddenly catapulted to world-wide fame by the award of the Nobel Prize, Arishima preferred to wait for the day when the Indian poet's writings could be evaluated "with a quiet heart." [24]

The main foreign influences on Arishima's life had been American idealisms — Christian, romantic individualist, and socialist. Yet another stream of idealist thought was flowing into Japan in the 1910's from Russia, principally through the writings of Count Leo Tolstoy. Chief among the Japanese Tolstoyans was the novelist and playwright Mushakōji Saneatsu, acknowledged leader of the White Birch School of writers (Shirakaba-ha) — this cold-climate tree, found in both countries, symbolizing the spiritual bond between Japanese writers and their Russian mentor.[25] Mushakōji, like Tolstoy, was a son of the old aristocracy who felt keenly his isolation from the poor peasantry of his country. Independently wealthy, he left Tokyo University before graduating, concentrated on writing in a humanistic vein, and in 1918 was to begin a "new village" movement for rural uplift.

Mushakōji thus appears as a rather close counterpart in Japan to India's Tagore: aristocratic, independently wealthy, a "drop-out" from the modern educational system, mainly a creative writer (but also a painter of distinction, as Tagore was also to become in the 1920's), and a man with a humanitarian conscience, concerned with revivifying his nation's villages. All of these similarities make his reactions to Tagore especially significant for a more general comparison of Indian and Japanese images of "East" and "West." Mushakōji was personally sympathetic to Tagore, and called him "honest, elegant, and a real poet, who speaks what is in his heart," but he felt sorry for him, and for Japan, that he was received "in such a vulgar fashion." Showing his independent attitude toward the government, Mushakōji boldly berated Prime Minister Ōkuma for being "insincere, dishonest, and rude." When it came to evaluating Tagore's message to Japan, however, Mushakōji made clear his dissent on almost every point. "I think he is much too afraid that the ordinary things in the life of Japan are going to be lost because of the influence of the West. I think we can adopt more important things from the teachings of the West, which are hard to understand and take time to fathom, than from the teachings of the Orient, which we already know too well." Instead of giving priority to bolstering the influence of things Oriental, Mushakōji thought it would be better for Japan to first take all she could from the West, and then to turn her attention to the East.[26]

At a more fundamental level of criticism, Mushakōji sharply attacked Tagore's disdain for material civilization. Even though Tolstoy also denied the value of modern civilization, Mushakōji felt that his way of doing so was "much more humanistic" than Tagore's. While it was true that the progress of civilization produces inequalities of wealth, "Tagore doesn't even mention the possible use of material civilization for the benefit of all mankind. That is why I do not want to know any more about him. Of course I hate bad civilization, but I want the strength to raise bad civilization to good civilization. I find nothing in Tagore's writings about this strength." [27] Mushakōji's comment reflects a basic difference between the experiences of intellectuals in Japan and India in their confrontations with the power and civilization of the modern West. In India the influence of Western civilization had been so prolonged and all-pervading, especially among Bengali Hindus, that an anti-Western and nativistic reaction naturally developed after a century of foreign rule. In Japan the influence of Western ways had been self-induced, and had been underway only half a century. As a result, Westernization in Japan was less thoroughgoing and the influence of traditional culture correspondingly greater. Men like Mushakōji, who had never been abroad but who valued both the material and the intellectual benefits already derived from contact with the West, saw little to lose and much to gain by further assimilation of things Western.[28]

Writers especially interested in French literature, perhaps influenced by its stronger realist and naturalist traditions, likewise found Tagore's advice unacceptable. For example, Toyoshima Yoshio, a prolific writer, critic, and translator of Hugo and Rolland, said he was grateful to Tagore "for teaching me to look back to the humanistic, racial, and simple feelings we have carried in our hearts from ancient times," but felt a "great dissatisfaction" with Tagore's message to Japan: "He doesn't show us our future direction. . . . We must give up too many things in order to reach his world. The things he wants us to give up, I regret to say, are really the things we should retain as strong building stones for the future. My young heart respects him, but does not fear him." Naitō Arō, a second specialist on French literature, commented that Tagore's lecture had reminded him of a choir singing in a church. (Since most Japanese in the audience at Tokyo University were unable to comprehend Tagore's meaning when he spoke in English, many of them were impressed instead by the sound of his voice.) After reading the Japanese translation of the lecture, Naitō curtly rejected the poet's advice: "I cannot understand the minds of those who believe that the power which will advance our civilization may lie hidden in his words and verses." [29]

England, the United States, Russia, France — these four countries supplied the outside influences to which Japan's writers and critics in 1916 were most sensitive, but it would be a grave mistake to give too much importance to the foreign origins of the literary trends developing in Japan at this time. Many writers were not conversant with a foreign language and had not lived abroad; and even those who did go abroad were able to pick and choose among the foreign traditions to which they wished to be exposed, and to apply what they learned in the West to the concrete realities of Japanese life, often with great sensitivity to indigenous Japanese literary traditions.

The rise of naturalism and socialism in the fiction of the decade following the Russo-Japanese war, for example, while drawing on post-Christian humanitarian and scientific ideas developed in Europe and the United States, was more fundamentally a response by certain Japanese writers to their changing environment: the exhaustion and economic hardship wrought by the war, the harsh realities of life among the rapidly growing urban working class, and the growing isolation of the intellectuals themselves from the government and business communities. The honeymoon between the official and the intellectual of the "enlightenment and civilization" period was over. First the government exiled hundreds of its critics in 1889; then it promulgated the Confucian-Shinto orthodoxy of the Imperial Rescript on Education in 1890; then in the 1900's as antimilitarist, socialist, and anarchist ideas filtered into the country, the tension between official and intellectual heightened, until in 1910 the government struck a shattering blow, arresting hundreds of anarchist-socialists, subjecting them to secret trial, and executing twelve for allegedly plotting to assassinate the emperor.[30]

As in mid-nineteenth-century Russia, so in post-1910 Japan, executions and censorship banished anarchism and socialism from the field of public discussion, forcing intellectuals of these persuasions to use literature and literary criticism as vehicles for the oblique expression of their ideas. Thus Ogawa Mimei, a gifted writer who emerged as a leading socialist only in the relatively freer 1920's, criticized Tagore in 1916 in words tacitly indicating his socialist position: "He is able to meditate freely and commune with nature only because he was born into a rich family. . . . Tagore curses present-day material civilization and says it is an unnatural life, but this is the opinion of a man who does not know that organisms change their forms according to their environment. . . .

To be a true artist, one must have experienced the feelings of the poor." [31] Katō Kazuo, a minor writer, echoed this theme, openly lampooning the Indian poet for his aristocratic way of life: "Tagore may be respectable in some ways, and he never frequents prostitutes, even though he is very rich. He is also trying to harmonize his inner life. Nevertheless, his thought is too tedious for people like me. I feel as though he is living in another world; his way of life is too special." Ema Nagashi, later prominent in the Proletarian Writers League, remarked that Tagore's face was "quiet, profound, and good, but I do not feel I like him so much that I can respect him so much as I do his face." Kamitsukasa Shōken, a novelist and literary editor of the *Yomiuri* newspaper, observed that he preferred the complete asceticism of a mendicant priest to the utilitarianism he found in Tagore's lecture. And Ikuta Chōkō, a prolific novelist who had moved with many of his contemporaries from naturalism to socialism, wrote curtly: "Judging by what has been written thus far about Mr. Tagore by the Japanese who wished to introduce him to Japan, I do not recognize any need to know more about him. Of course, I haven't even read a page of his writings. However, because he is a guest who has purposely come here from a foreign country, I will refrain from the rudeness of saying more than this." [32]

Considering the ideological gap which separated the socialist writers from those advocating the strengthening of indigenous Japanese traditions, it seems remarkable that both groups agreed so completely on the uselessness to Japan of Tagore's message. Writing in the nationalistic monthly *Nippon oyobi Nipponjin* (Japan and the Japanese), the famous haiku poet Kawahigashi Hekigotō reproached Tagore for his "remoteness" and lack of philosophic depth. "Being an Indian, he evades the present age, and ignores the suffering involved in committing onself to facing and fighting against the world. In short, his philosophy is optimistic." Kawahigashi confessed that he had enjoyed "a pure and pleasant feeling" while listening to his fellow-poet lecture in Osaka, but this mood was spoiled as soon as the interpreter began his translation, and so Kawahigashi simply left the hall.[33]

Fiercest of all Tagore's critics among Japan's literary leaders was the prolific novelist, poet and playwright Iwano Hōmei, a man of passionate, almost mystical decadence who prized the life of instinct and exalted the attitude he ascribed to his ancient Shintoist ancestors, who, "deeply interested in mundane affairs, lived energetically from moment to moment with fervent love of life." [34] Iwano's instinctivism had led him from *Hamlet* (which he adapted in translation in 1894), to Whitman (whom he translated into Japanese free verse), through naturalism and symbolism to "New Japanism" (*Shin Nihonshugi*), and gave this name to the periodical he founded in 1916. Although his devotion to native Japanese characteristics was precisely what Tagore had urged, Iwano rejected the Indian poet's spiritual and nonpolitical image of Japan's civilization. Japan could never accept a philosophy which laid greater stress on the development of individualism than on the evolution of the state, he wrote in the *Yomiuri*, for such impossible idealism was an obstacle to modern progress.[35] In another article he protested vigorously the way "Count Ōkuma, popular politicians, scholars, teachers, men of religions, rich men, etc., and even newspaper men and young people crowded around him for their own advantage," meanwhile ignoring the poets and thinkers of their own country. As for Tagore's message to Japan:

> It is of course absurd for him to deny material civilization with the petrified ideas of ruined India when he comes to an independent and developed country like Japan. Moreover, he has no insight into the fact that the army and navy, railroads and shipping lines, which seem to be material civilization, are also manifestations of spiritual civilization: that is, of the ancient conquering faith of the Japanese people. . . . We should take him at his face value, but his poetry and thought are indeed "worthless," to borrow the word he uses to describe material civilization.[36]

It is clear that Tagore did not win the hearts of most of Japan's literary leaders in 1916. This was certainly not because of any opposition to his ideas which government officials may have privately voiced, for both Mushakōji Saneatsu and Iwano Hōmei had explicitly attacked the prime minister himself for welcoming the Indian poet, and other writers had grumbled about the amount of attention he had received in Tokyo, or the fact that literary men had been left out of the receptions in his honor. The greatest irony in the reception of Tagore's idea of Asian spiritual revival by his fellow writers in Japan is that those who praised his message most warmly were men like Noguchi, who had been most deeply influenced by English and American romanticisms, while those who condemned it most harshly were writers like Kawahigashi and Iwano, who were most deeply committed to the revival of Japanese cultural traditions.

Religious Leaders

Tagore had presented himself to Japan's intellectuals, not as a poet but as a prophet calling for a revival of Japanese spirituality. Quite naturally he found support among some of the country's religious leaders. A goodly number of Buddhist and Christian intellectuals commented on his message to Japan, but from a variety of viewpoints.

The Buddhists who responded most enthusiastically to Tagore's appeal were three priests. One, Kuruma Takudō, later the head of the Sōtō sect of the Zen school, wrote hopefully: "In view of the nation-wide reception given to Tagore, it seems to me that the essence of spiritual civilization has not disappeared from our midst. . . . I believe he has partially awakened the Japanese from the dream of worshiping the West. If this be so, then I am obliged to him for my country's sake." Another priest, Shimaji Daitō, a scholar of the Shinshū school who had visited Buddhist holy places in India in 1902–3, thought it "delightful that the Indian atmosphere has passed through our land for a moment." The third, Takeda Toyoshirō, had also visited India and on his return had helped introduce Indian rituals into his own temple. He was one of the priests who had welcomed the poet on his way from Kyoto to Tokyo. Takeda was so enchanted by Tagore's spiritual presence that he devoted an entire essay to this impression. "I felt that I was welcoming an old friend. His countenance was as saintly as I had expected," he wrote.[37]

These three men represent the hereditary priestly class in closest touch with the common people. Protected and sponsored by the state under the Tokugawa, this class had fallen under heavy attack in the first decades of the Meiji government, which at first exalted Shintoism as a truly national religion, disparaged Buddhism for its foreign origins, and deprived many Buddhist priests of the temples they had administered. Even before the high tide of Westernization had passed in 1889–90, however, government hostility to Buddhism subsided, while Buddhist leaders themselves started movements to reform and revivify their faith. Visits to India, the adoption of Christian missionary methods of education and social work, and the scientific study of Buddhist scriptures all helped to modernize Japanese Buddhism, spurring a return to its original spirit strikingly similar to the revitalization of Hinduism pioneered in

India by Rammohun Roy and Debendranath Tagore. This structural similarity, and the fact that his visit symbolized closer contact with the homeland of their religion, go far to explain the affinity which these Buddhist priests felt for Tagore and his message.

One of the means by which Buddhists rehabilitated their damaged position in Japanese society was by promoting harmony with Shinto, Confucian, and even Japanese Christian religious leaders. Buddhists and Christians came together at a meeting in 1896 in response to rising secular and Shinto-Confucian nationalism, and in 1912–13 the government itself, probably because it hoped to counteract the spread of socialist and anarchist ideas, convened two conferences of Buddhist, Christian, and Shinto leaders in order to promote their cooperation in education and social work. For two leading Buddhists in 1916, Tagore's visit was significant because it fostered this spirit of cooperation. The Jōdo sect scholar Watanabe Kaikyoku, who had studied in Germany and begun his great edition of the Chinese Tripitaka, declared: "To our great joy, the visit of Mr. Tagore has brought that dawn abundant with the spirit of unity and tolerance in our intellectual world." Perhaps Watanabe was influenced by Tagore's ideal of Asian spiritual revival, for he later advocated a union of all the Buddhists of Japan, China, India, Burma, and Tibet. The Shinshū reformer Itō Shōshin, inspired by Tolstoy's Christian humanism to found his own communitarian religious community, also hoped that the welcome accorded the Indian poet would hasten the reconciliation among different sectors of the intelligentsia: "I am impressed by the greatness of Tagore's personality, which has enabled him in Japan to unite Buddhists, Christians, artists, politicians, and people of other persuasions, both new and old. This should not be a momentary event in our country, but should be the starting point for undertaking the great task of achieving the harmonious consolidation of our entire intellectual world." [38]

Another source of strength for Buddhism lay in the use of modern methods of critical and historical scholarship, learned principally at universities in England and Germany. Having gained recognition by their studies in Europe and India, two outstanding scholars were given appointments at Tokyo Imperial University: Takakusu Junjirō in Sanskrit and Pali (1899) and Anesaki Masaharu in comparative religions (1903). Buddhist studies were now academically respectable and under government sponsorship, for all faculty members at the four imperial universities held civil service rank in the Ministry of Education. Takakusu, who was by this time a member of the select Imperial Academy (Japan's counterpart to the Académie française), was given the honor of presiding at the great reception for Tagore at the Kaneiji Temple on June 13, 1916. Perhaps conscious that he occupied a semiofficial position as Japan's leading Buddhist scholar, Takakusu commented with elaborate caution when asked for his opinion of Tagore's ideas. He began by noting that he could not respect Indians in general, but that he did respect Rabindranath "because he is superior to his countrymen and seems to be an ideal Indian." The poet's criticism of modern science had been misunderstood: "Tagore is only against one-sided materialism," he suggested gallantly. Aside from these remarks, Takakusu merely summarized Tagore's views without revealing his own reactions to them. In general, he seemed to walk the fine line between approving the specific message which Tagore had brought to Japan, and criticizing his country's distinguished guest, in whose public reception he himself had taken so prominent a part.[39]

Anesaki Masaharu had also been called upon to welcome Tagore, and had served as interpreter for him when he called on Prime Minister Ōkuma. His article on the Indian poet's thought was confined even more narrowly than Takakusu's to an impartial exposition of his subject. What his real thoughts probably were can best be seen from an essay published twelve years later in which he argued that the opposition between Eastern and Western civilizations (a major premise of Tagore's message to Japan) was more apparent than real. In its place he suggested using the distinction between medieval and modern civilizations, and made no secret of his sympathy with modernity, which he identified with progress, activity, freedom, utility, science, industry, and democracy. One part of Anesaki's conclusion to this essay, however, seemed almost to echo Tagore's call for a blending of Eastern and Western characteristics:

> the activity of modern civilization is not entirely contradictory to the dignified composure of medieval civilization, and similarly the progressive activity of the Occident is not an irreconcilable antithesis to the contemplative attitude of the Orient. According to our view, those two are opposites united in basic principle, that is, the rich development of life aiming at the final goal of perfecting human life towards the divine.[40]

Anesaki's emphasis on activity and repose — the basic rhythm in the ancient Chinese conception of alternation between the Yang and the Yin — shows a greater consciousness of time as an element in human life than Tagore's essentially static theory of the complementarity of Eastern spirituality and Western material civilization. Moreover, Anesaki proposed to accelerate rather than to resist the spread of modern civilization in Asia, in order that "civilization would be the common heritage of the whole of mankind." To achieve this end, he recommended that "Occidentals should not regard civilization as their monopoly, nor Orientals put obstructions to its spread and expansion." [41] All in all, Anesaki was more confident than Tagore that the best in Asia's religious heritage could survive in the modern age — perhaps because his own efforts to find eternal truths in the actual words and deeds of the Buddha had been so well received, both in Japan and at Harvard, where he had been visiting lecturer from 1913 to 1915.[42]

A third stream of Buddhist activity, along with the continuation of popular Buddhism under temple priests and the rise of scholarly Buddhism at the universities, flowed in the various heterodox reform movements led by dedicated individuals. One such leader seized the occasion of Tagore's visit to lambaste the old-style Buddhists whose influence he was combatting with his Shin Bukkyō (New Buddhist Movement). Takashima Beihō (whose activities included writing, book publishing, and leadership in such varied reforming activities as temperance, animal protection, and the use of Roman script) complained that "many Japanese do not understand his [Tagore's] thought, which is not Buddhist, but Upanishadic, and yet the Buddhists made him their guest from beginning to end. Can you give him anything worthwhile?" he challenged his more orthodox brethren.[43] The leader of an offshoot of Shinshū Buddhism, Ittō-en (The Fraternity of One Lantern), inculcating in its members piety, thrift, unselfishness, and service to others,[44] was favorably impressed by Tagore's stress on spirituality: Nishida Tenkō observed that Rabindranath's experiences were much like his own, and declared that he, too, "would like to carry out in an appropriate manner the self-examination and the way of life recommended by Tagore, the sage." [45] Nishida and his fraternity were possibly inspired by Christian as well as Buddhist traditions, for he had worked for some years in Hokkaido, where American Protestant missionaries were especially active.

Christian leaders in Japan, members of a universal church, faced a peculiar dilemma in establishing their faith among one of the world's most acutely nationalistic peoples: to adapt too little to Japanese ideas and institutions would brand Christianity as an unassimilable "foreign" religion, but to adapt too much would risk the church's subordination to the "national structure" and its non-Christian metaphysic. This problem had arisen in embryonic form in the early seventeenth century, when, after a few decades of rapid expansion under the patronage of feudal lords in western Japan, Roman Catholic Christianity had been prohibited and brutally suppressed.[46] The new Meiji government did not lift this ban until 1873. Thereafter, Protestant missionaries made numerous converts among the educated class; Roman Catholic missionaries were more active in the rural areas. The government still remained on the alert lest its own authority be undermined by the Christian movement. The refusal of Uchimura Kanzō, a converted samurai who had studied in the United States, to bow before the newly issued Imperial Rescript on Education caused a nationwide scandal and dismissal from his teaching post in 1891; his vociferous pacifism during the Sino-Japanese and Russo-Japanese wars lent further credence to the suspicion that Christians were not loyal Japanese.

Anxious to decrease their cultural dependence on Western Christian forms, many Protestant Christian leaders bent their efforts toward rooting their faith more firmly in Japanese traditions. Some of the more liberal churchmen sought points of agreement with reformed Buddhism,[47] and, when Tagore arrived, welcomed him because of the general uplift he gave to the cause of religious piety, both Buddhist and Christian. For example, the Unitarian leader Uchigasaki Sakusaburō, educated at Tokyo University and Oxford, showed his keen interest in Tagore's visit by devoting two issues of his monthly *Rikugō zasshi* (Cosmos Magazine) to discussions of the poet and his ideas. In addition to securing comments from fifty-five Japanese intellectuals for publication, in his July 1916 issue Uchigasaki joyfully declared: "A tall and long-bearded old poet made a great prediction for the intrinsic idealism of the East . . . Buddhism must put on new clothes, and Christianity must seek for its original spirit. If they fail to do so, the mind of the people will abandon religion more and more. Stop beating the drum on the street [a reference to the Salvation Army?] and wash your heart with the exquisite voice of heaven: This is Tagore's message." [48]

The Congregationalist leader Ukita Kazutami, editor of the very influential *Taiyō* (Sun) monthly, also showered praise on Tagore for his spirituality. Accepting the Indian poet's claim to represent Eastern civilization, he contrasted him with the visiting American aviator, Art Smith, whose aerial acrobatics were then exciting the Japanese public. Smith probably saw little difference between the height of Mt. Fuji and the height of the Himalayas, thought Ukita: "However, Tagore's thought contains something so lofty that even if Smith were to fly to the world of the moon or the world of the stars, he still could not attain to it. In this sense, I would say that the civilization of India possesses indestructible worth." [49] Ukita had become a Christian at Doshisha University and had later studied at Yale at a time when interest in the culture of India and in Congregationalist missionary work there was high. Whether or not his sympathy for Tagore derived from this source, it appears from his comment and Uchigasaki's that those Japanese Christians best able to appreciate Tagore's message were those whose theology, acquired in the West, was closest to the unitarian Hinduism which Tagore had imbibed from his father and his father's teacher, Rammohun Roy.[50]

Blending in with the prevailing Buddhistic piety and taking on an Asian coloring was one means of adapting Christianity to Japanese conditions. Another was to link it with the more universal elements in Confucian and Shinto thought. This path was taken by the eminent Congregationalist convert and pastor, Ebina Danjō, whose early education had been Confucian.[51] Especially sensitive to the nationalist charge that good Christians could not be loyal Japanese, Ebina tried to identify Jehovah with the Shinto god of creation in order to show that Christianity was only the natural next stage in Japan's long religious evolution. He was no narrow chauvinist, however, and he commended Tagore in 1916 for opposing aggressive behavior in modern nations. All the same, Ebina rejected Rabindranath's assertion that Eastern civilization was peace-loving, and Western civilization warlike. "Animal instincts are shared by both East and West," he rejoined, "and it is a prejudiced view to say that they are associated only with Western civilization." Directly contradicting Tagore's belief in the cultural and spiritual unity of Asia, the Christian pastor declared that Japan's history was much more like the histories of such modern European countries as Germany, France, and England than it was like the history of India or China — both very large countries with ancient civilizations. "We cannot argue this problem only from a geographical viewpoint," he contended. Following a train of thought similar to that later expressed by Anesaki, Ebina concluded that Japan's future lay with the progress of modern civilization:

> The dominant trends in the world today are determined by the influence of civilization, which is reforming the world day by day. The poet Tagore says not a word on this point. A hundred years from now we shall have a civilization containing both East and West, but we shall never see the ruin of Western civilization and the rise of Eastern civilization . . . It is accordingly incorrect to divide civilization into two parts, East and West. It is more accurate to divide civilization into the new and the old.[52]

Although most Christian leaders hoped somehow to harmonize their religion with Japanese nationalism,[53] at least one seemed prepared to go the whole way with the "national structure" and its purposes. Sugiura Sadajirō, a graduate of the Episcopal Divinity School of the University of Pennsylvania, held in 1916 a number of posts: professor at the Imperial Staff College, member of the standing committee of his church's Tokyo diocese, lecturer on philosophy at Rikkyo College, and music tutor to a princess of the imperial family. Closely identifying himself with the national Establishment, he roundly condemned Tagore's message as harmful to the Empire's rise to world power: "I do not agree with his ideas. I prefer activism. If we accept material civilization gratefully, we have nothing to fear from it. The main point is that everything depends on the spirit of the people. I think that if we follow what Tagore says, our country will be ruined. Yes, Tagore is the representative of a ruined country. Our people must resolve to try to compete in the worldwide struggle for existence." [54]

Taken as a group, these Buddhist and Christian leaders voiced three different reactions to Tagore's message. Those who praised it were Buddhist priests who had visited India and Christian pastors who admired India's spiritual outlook. The most eminent commentators in the two communities, however — Anesaki the Buddhist and Ebina the Christian — agreed in rejecting Tagore's assumption that spirituality was Asian and materialism Western, and substituted for this geographical division a global movement from medieval to modern civilization in which Japan was rightly taking part. Yet a third view, represented by the militant Sugiura, was that the Indian poet's passive spiritual attitude was unsuited to the Japanese people. These last two objections to his ideas — one being that they were too Eastern, the other that they were not sufficiently Japanese — recur among the criticisms expressed by those Japanese scholars whose main concern was with various branches of academic philosophy.

PHILOSOPHERS

Thanks to the rapid development of modern universities (the imperial ones modeled on German universities, the private ones on their English and American counterparts), Japan had by 1916 a number of highly trained and specialized academic philosophers able to consider Tagore's message from a variety of viewpoints. The study of philosophy in Japan was an honored tradition as old as Prince Shōtoku's investigations of Buddhist and Confucian texts, and soon after the Meiji leaders threw open Japan's doors to the West her scholars began scouring Europe and America for philosophical ideas. At first English utilitarianism and American pragmatism, then French social thought enjoyed the greatest popularity. Then from 1890 onward German academic philosophy gradually gained the ascendancy, its more abstract, systematic, and idealistic tendencies combining well with rejuvenated Buddhist and Confucian intellectual traditions.

The influence of German idealism proved especially strong in the study of ethics. The relation of the individual to his society seemed a critical problem to young Japanese intellectuals in a period when the growing demands of the state seemed to threaten the right of the individual to adopt an independent ethical standpoint. Natsume Sōseki had objected to this tendency in his student days: "Do we go to the toilet or wash our faces for our country?" he asked his fellow students.[55] In 1916, Sōseki held the position of literary editor of the Tokyo *Asahi*, and assisting him was a young philosopher, Abe Jirō, whose *Santarō no nikki* (Diary of Santarō), a series of reflections on the personal quest for ethical and religious truth, was then a best seller.[56] Abe had read Kant and Nietzsche while at Tokyo University, and in 1916 published a translation of Theodor Lipps's *Fundamental Problems of Ethics*. Tagore's general emphasis on moral issues appealed to him, and he commented sympathetically: "I admired the fact that, unlike other visitors, he was prepared to find something [worthwhile] in Japan, and to give something to Japan." Abe only regretted that Tagore had not yet escaped from the leading strings of the aristocracy, and hoped he would move more freely among the people in different parts of Japan.[57]

Abe had been raised in a Confucian and Christian atmosphere at home, but the younger ethical thinker Watsuji Tetsurō was more deeply influenced by Buddhist philosophy. He was to become an ethical thinker of the first rank and the foremost historian of Japanese ethical thought. Teaching at the Tokyo Higher Normal School in 1916, he had already published studies of Nietzsche and Kierkegaard. "There are many points on which I agree with him," he said of Tagore's Tokyo University lecture. "I was thankful for the kind and encouraging words he has for Japan. I find his writings spiritual, but not superficial." [58]

Behind the ethical personalism of Abe and Watsuji lay the direct inspiration of a Westerner who had taught them both philosophy at Tokyo University since 1893. This was Raphael von Koeber, a Russian of German-Swedish extraction, who had studied music under Tchaikovsky and written his doctoral thesis at Heidelberg on Schopenhauer. Although von Koeber's life has not yet found the biographer it deserves, it seems probable that his motivation for coming to teach in Japan was connected with an interest in Buddhist philosophy born of his study of Schopenhauer. "What impressed his students so greatly," writes a recent authority, himself a Westerner teaching philosophy in Japan, "was not so much his philosophy (he had no real system), nor his wide erudition, but his arresting manner. He was an artistic type of sage-philosopher, who incarnated the almost mystical ideal of a tutor." [59] Their admiration of such a teacher no doubt predisposed Abe and Watsuji to look favorably on Tagore, who also appeared in Japan as an artistic sage-philosopher with an arresting manner.

The dominant influence on philosophers of this period was neither Nietzsche nor Schopenhauer, but the more systematic and technical Kant, as interpreted by German Neo-Kantians. One of the first Japanese to earn his doctorate in philosophy in Germany, Kaneko Umaji, returned in 1894 to teach at his alma mater, Waseda University, and thereafter frequently commented on the intellectual issues of the day. It seemed natural that he should be asked to contribute to the volume *Sei Tagōru* (Tagore, the Sage), prepared in honor of the poet's visit by a group calling itself The Society for Educational and Scholarly Research. Kaneko's main contribution was to sum up the two kinds of reaction in Japan to Tagore's ideas: "On the one hand, there are those Japanese who admire Mr. Tagore without having any understanding of his thought; they regard Tagore as though he were a saint or a wise man. On the other hand, there are those who think that Tagore's thought is unoriginal and is just the same as that in the traditional Upanishads of India, and they therefore believe they have nothing to learn from him." Kaneko himself indicated that he belonged in the second camp, for he concluded: "The most important thing about him is that he is a poet par excellence." [60]

Kant's principal exponent in Japan, Kuwaki Genyoku, concentrated his attention on epistemology, insisting that the problem under discussion and the terms used in dealing with it be clearly defined. He held in 1916 the chair of philosophy at Tokyo University, the most senior position in his field, having studied in Germany and been awarded the Japanese government's honorary doctorate and Fourth Class Order of Merit. Asked for his impression of Tagore's lecture at the university, he replied succinctly: "His voice and his words were beautiful," clearly indicating that he did not care to discuss the poet's ideas.[61] A perceptive historian of modern Japanese philosophy later wrote of Kuwaki: "No philosopher can be compared with him for impartial criticism and warm sympathy for every thought and matter. He seems to be more interested in relishing the good in all ideas than in fighting for his advocacy of any particular idea." [62] Given this sympathetic temperament, the fact that he had nothing at all to say about Tagore's message suggests that he could not agree with it, for he would presumably have said so if he did, and would have preferred silence to criticism if he did not.

Kuwaki's predecessor in the chair of philosophy at Tokyo University, Inoue Tetsujirō, spoke out emphatically against Tagore's message to Japan. Inoue had studied for six years in Germany, but his early grounding in Confucianism remained the foundation of his thought, and his best work dealt with Chinese Neo-Confucianism in a manner which showed the influence of German idealism on his thinking.[63] Inoue was an enthusiastic supporter of the government's attempts to create a national morality from Confucian and Shinto ideas, and wrote the official interpretation of the 1890 Imperial Rescript on Education, led the 1892 attack on Christianity as an un-Japanese religion, and as a member of the Textbook Investigation Council worked vigorously for the compilation of patriotic school texts in the period 1908–1911. Other professors regarded Inoue as an official scholar (*goyō*) who articulated the opinions of government leaders.[64] His considerable experience as a critic of dangerous thoughts certainly qualified him to speak his mind on Tagore's message, but the fact that he wrote two separate articles on that subject does suggest that someone may have been prompting him from behind the scenes.

"His voice is like the song of a ruined country." Inoue complained, and the content of Tagore's lecture only confirmed this impression for him. "Tagore wants to reverse the current of civilization; I do not want this opinion to spread," he declared peremptorily.[65] In his second article, Inoue repeated his objection that Rabindranath was a man from a defeated country, and stated his reasons for resisting whatever influence the Indian poet might be exercising on the minds of the Japanese intellectuals. He particularly disliked the fact that Tagore seemed to be cursing science, since in Inoue's view Japan owed her position in the world to the adoption of science and European civilization, while China and India had not made equivalent progress because they had not cultivated science. There was only one point on which Inoue found Rabindranath's ideas acceptable: "Science is necessary in order to reach human goals but science is not the goal itself. So I cannot help agreeing with the great emphasis which Mr. Tagore placed on humanity." Nevertheless, he regretted that he did not find in the Indian poet's "thought any ideas which promote the welfare of society or of the nation." He therefore concluded: "We do not accept this negative attitude of Mr. Tagore. As the people of a rising nation I think we should make every effort especially to exclude the Indian tendency toward pessimism and dispiritedness." [66]

Working on the same lines as Inoue, but with a greater interest in the relevance of Hegel's thought to the philosophy of Japan's "national structure," Kihira Masayoshi developed further Inoue's stress on loyalty to the state. His rather mystical, nativistic tendency even led him to conclude one of his serious books on philosophy with the emphatic statement: "*I am a Japanese.*" [67] Lecturing in philosophy at the National Studies University (Kokugakuin) in 1916, Kihira commented tersely on Tagore: "I am exceedingly amazed at the grand welcome given him." [68]

At the opposite pole from these ultraconservative philosophers of nationalism stood the liberal professor of political history and political theory at Tokyo University, Yoshino Sakuzō, one of the country's most

ardent and effective advocates of representative government. Yoshino
had spent three years in China as tutor to the family of General (later
Prime Minister) Yüan Shih-k'ai, and another three years studying in
Europe and America. After his appointment as professor in 1913 he
published frequent articles on international politics. His manifesto, "On
the Meaning of Constitutional Government and the Methods by Which
It Can be Perfected," which appeared in the January 1916 issue of Japan's
leading monthly, had already marked him as the mentor of the liberal
movement.[69] While Inoue Tetsujirō rejected Tagore's ideas as dangerous
to the rising power of Japan, Yoshino disliked them for quite different
reasons. "It was as if one were listening to beautiful music," he wrote of
Tagore's lecture at his university. "But as for the content of his lecture, we
could not admire it very much." [70] Yoshino's deliberate use of the plural
"we" suggests that he spoke on behalf of Japan's liberals, to whom it must
have been obvious that the Indian poet's attempts to revive Asian spiritual
values and to resist the spread of modern Western forms of government
were not going to advance the cause of parliamentary democracy in Japan.

Yoshino's political philosophy derived of course from English and
American sources.[71] The influence of Anglo-American thought on Japanese thinking had waxed and waned during the half-century since the
beginning of the Meiji era. The great reformer Fukuzawa Yukichi, with
his motto of "independence and self-respect," his pioneering work in
journalism and education, and his encouragement of business as a career
did much to popularize Anglo-American utilitarian attitudes during the
"enlightenment and civilization" decade. The "counterreformation" of
1889–90 then helped shift the emphasis away from English and American and toward German thought, but in the decade after the Russo-
Japanese war the pragmatist school of William James and John Dewey
attracted wide attention, with Waseda University its central base and
the Waseda professor Tanaka Ōdo its chief spokesman.

Tanaka had studied in the United States from 1890 to 1899. Like his
mentor, John Dewey, he wrote frequently and discursively on the problems of his time, and Tagore's visit stimulated him to produce one essay
in 1915 and two in 1916 criticizing the Indian poet-philosopher. Tanaka's
general philosophy was a pragmatism tinged with what he termed "romantic utilitarianism." An ardent defender of "modern civilization," he
considered its philosophical basis to be man's consciousness of himself
as the center of all things, and its primary vehicles to be science (in the

realm of sense-experience) and democracy (in the realm of human relations). Constant "reinterpretation" in these two spheres, he believed,
would lead to the eventual unity of all minkind. "This modern civilization," Tanaka asserted, "is in fact the best in every respect of all civilizations thus far produced by men, and its intention is incomparably more
spiritual than any other." [72]

Tanaka's criticism of Tagore's message followed logically from this
position, and the similarity between his views and those of American
critics during the poet's lecture tour that same autumn revealed how
strongly Tanaka's thinking had been influenced by his long stay in the
United States. "You misunderstand Western civilization," he told the
poet in his article in the September 1916 issue of Japan's leading
monthly, Chūō kōron (The central review). "You praised the power of
love, but if we are to realize this idea, what instrument have we except
science?" Tanaka drove his point home with a sweeping generalization:
"When I compare the civilization based on science with the civilization
based on religion and art, it seems to me that the former is more spiritual
than the latter; I cannot believe that the former is more materialistic."
Tagore was therefore leading India in the wrong direction, Tanaka
charged: "I regret to say this to the propagandist of transcendentalism,
but the worst thing for India is the very existence of transcendentalism." [73]

In October, Tanaka returned to the charge with another article, satiri-
cally entitled, "Tagore Came, and then Went." As this was one of the
last comments to be published in Japanese on the Indian poet's 1916
visit, Tanaka was able to sum up its import after most other observers
had had their say. In the first place, he declared, Tagore had not properly understood either the past history or the present civilization of
Japan: "When he discussed our country's past, he overestimated the
influence of Buddhism; and when he discussed our country's present
condition, he expressed his abhorrence of European influence without
sufficient reason." [74]

In addition to his ignorance of Japan's actual condition, Tagore represented a "ruined country." Rather than learn from him, Japanese intellectuals, "as the representatives of an advanced country of modern civilization," were in a position to teach him. "It is beyond question," Tanaka
continued, "that before entering the course of modern life we have long
since given up as useless what Tagore gave us or could give us." Japan's

modern civilization was more truly spiritual than India's traditional civilization, because it satisfied more adequately man's need to grow and to cooperate with his fellow men. Thus, "From the standpoint of modern civilization or modern life, my opinion is based on deeper [human] needs than is Tagore's. . . . We are living in the midst of modern civilization, which we cannot neglect or avoid, and we are living more freely and more fully than the Indian people. Tagore's visit has been a failure because he had neither understood these things, nor did the Japanese who welcomed him help him to see the true nature of Japan's modern civilization." He concluded: "We parted from one another without any spiritual contact in the true sense of the term. We were disappointed with Mr. Tagore, but I think he was even more disappointed with the Japanese." [75]

While Tanaka was impressed with the freedom he enjoyed as a citizen of independent and modernizing Japan, another Japanese philosopher-critic was acutely aware of how limited and fragile that freedom was and feared that Tagore's advice, if accepted, would diminish his personal freedom even further. Tanimoto Tomi had made a brilliant record as professor of education at Tokyo University and had received from the government the coveted honorary Ph.D. for his successful study-tour of European and American educational institutions. Then in 1912 his career was suddenly ended. He was dismissed from his professorship for having dared to criticize the way the nation's most honored military hero, General Nogi, had lived up to the traditional samurai code of loyalty unto death by committing hara-kiri on the day of the Emperor Meiji's funeral. Living in retirement near Kyoto in 1916, Tanimoto could only follow Tagore's activities through newspaper accounts. His first reaction was that the Indian poet's advice was "only a commonplace in Japan," for it reminded him of the well-worn slogan: "Japanese spirit; Western technique," which traditionalists since the middle nineteenth century had used to limit the influence of modern Western ideas. Tanimoto's criticism of General Nogi had shown him to be stoutly opposed to traditionalist attitudes, and he was justifiably annoyed at Tagore for encouraging their revival.[76]

Picking up his morning paper on September 3, 1916, Tanimoto found that Tagore, on the eve of sailing from Yokohama for the United States, had denounced the Japanese for allowing their government to mold their ideas. Tanimoto at once noted that this criticism was inconsistent with Rabindranath's previous stress on the revival of traditional values, and

Welcome reception for Tagore at Kaneiji Temple, Ueno Park, Tokyo, 1916

"On Oriental Culture and Japan's Mission," Tokyo, 1929

Tagore, Hsü Chih-mo, and Miss Lin in Peking, 1924

that same day wrote an article on "Tagore's parting words" which penetrated to the core of the contradiction in the Indian poet's statements. To begin with, he completely agreed with Tagore that there was a tendency, especially among scholars and educationists, "to consider the government to be omnipotent and to follow it blindly." However, he strongly disagreed with Tagore's warning that the Japanese should cling to the traditional civilization inherited from their ancestors:

> In my own view, one central characteristic of the spiritual civilization which we have inherited from our ancestors is the habit of looking up to the government officials and looking down on the people. If one is independent and self-respecting in his statements, then he is accused of being insubordinate and is regarded as a criminal and a traitor. If we follow Tagore, and try henceforth to keep our spiritual civilization, then we will not be able to get rid of this traditional weakness of following the government blindly, as he accused us of doing, and must remain forever without individuality, liberty or originality. This is why I have opposed the popular trend, and cry for reforms in education, morality and religion, and this is why I cannot agree with the easy manner in which such a foreign guest as Tagore has been greeted in Japan.[77]

Speaking from his own bitter experience as a victim of Japan's military form of spirituality, Tanimoto concluded with the sincere hope that if Tagore came a second time to Japan he would live the pure and dreamlike life of a poet, and not give superficial lectures which only hindered the strenuous efforts the Japanese were making to reform their traditional customs and manners.[78]

Tagore's appeal for a revival of "spirituality" thus touched only two Japanese philosophers, Abe and Watsuji, both of whom had been strongly influenced by German idealism and by their Russo-German teacher, Raphael von Koeber. The Neo-Kantians Kaneko and Kuwaki refused to take his message seriously, while the nationalist philosopher Inoue denounced it as dangerous, just as the Christian Sugiura had. The pragmatist Tanaka rejected it as contrary to the worldwide progress of modern civilization; so did the Buddhist Anesaki and the Christian Ebina. It remained for Tanimoto to elaborate what the liberal thinker Yoshino only implied: that the revival of traditional spiritual values in Japan could lead directly to tighter state control over individual action and thought, an ominous development which Tagore himself dreaded, but nevertheless unwittingly encouraged.

JAPANESE ATTITUDES TOWARD INDIA

For many Japanese the chief significance of Tagore's arrival in Japan lay not in the message he sought to deliver but in the fact that he had brought it from India. His visit evoked expressions of sympathy for India and its culture from a few Buddhist and Christian leaders. Conversely, several Christians, as well as secular philosophers critical of Tagore's message, argued that India, a conquered country, had been ruined by the very spiritual civilization that Tagore wished Japan to adopt. A number of other intellectuals interested in increasing Japan's influence in Asia were prompted by Tagore's presence and statements to consider the prospects for closer relations with India.

Pan-Asianism was in 1916 by no means the dominant motif it was to become for Japan in the days of the East Asian Co-Prosperity Sphere a quarter of a century later, but the idea that Japan could unite and lead the rest of Asia was by no means a new one. Probably the first Japanese to dream of conquering India was the great general Hideyoshi, who wrote to his wife in 1592 at the outset of his unsuccessful Korean expedition: "All military leaders who shall render successful vanguard service in the coming campaign in China will be liberally rewarded with grants of extensive estates near India, with the privilege of conquering India and extending their domains in the vast empire." [79] For two and a half centuries Hideyoshi's successors, the Tokugawa rulers, kept Japan isolated from the outside world, but the opening of the coutnry in Meiji times saw a resurgence of the hope of carving out an empire on the Asian mainland once more, beginning with Korea. A serious rift within the oligarchy occurred over the Korean issue in the 1870's, the conservative majority of the leaders opposing overseas expansion as premature. As Japan's strength increased, however, and as China's power over her outlying tributaries declined, the temptation to conquer these neighboring areas proved irresistible. In the context of contemporary European imperialism in Africa, Southeast Asia, and China itself, Japan's annexation of Taiwan, the Liaotung Peninsula, Korea, and the German territories in Shantung and the South Seas seemed only natural, indeed, "progressive."

Within Japan a small group of ultranationalists urged still further expansion, essentially on ideological grounds. Japan's national mission, they argued, was to extend to the whole world the blessings of "the Imperial Way" (kōdō). Under the charismatic leadership of the Fukuoka samurai Tōyama Mitsuru, various patriotic societies were founded to press this aim, the most famous being the Amur River Society (Kokuryūkai, also translatable as Black Dragon Society). By threatening and assassinating moderate politicians, Tōyama's fanatic followers exerted considerable pressure on the government, whose interests they also served by sending spies to the mainland and by cultivating unofficial contacts with leaders of potential rebellions there. Tōyama's men had given aid and comfort to Sun Yat-sen before China's 1911 Revolution, and in 1915 Tōyama sheltered in his own house an Indian revolutionary, Rashbehari Bose, who claimed he had thrown the bomb that almost killed the Viceroy, Lord Hardinge, in 1912. So great was Tōyama's influence that the government had to apologize to the British Ambassador for not daring to send police into Tōyama's house to extradite Bose.[80]

At the heart of the pan-Asian ideology of these dedicated ultranationalists was a belief in the superior spirituality of Oriental civilization which on the surface appeared virtually identical with Tagore's. Consider, for example, the phraseology used by Uchida Ryōhei in 1917, while the nominal head of the Amur River Society, proposing an alliance of Japan, China, and Russia against the Western powers: "Mr. Uchida sees Oriental civilization still shackled in the bonds of materialism and observes that material civilization alone will not save a nation which is hastening towards ruin. Without the support of Japan, whose civilization is the antithesis of Western civilization, how can Russia hope to deliver herself?"[81] Uchida was particularly interested in Russia since he had studied there and had used his knowledge to advantage when the Amur River Society was pushing for war with Russia. Turning his attention to Chinese politics after the 1911 Revolution there, he framed in 1914 the "Memorandum for a Solution of the China Problem" which anticipated the Japanese government's bid to take over her larger but weaker neighbor in 1915. India, geographically more remote than Russia or China, remained a much more distant target for Japan's pan-Asianists, but they foresaw that British rule there could not last forever and so kept a watchful eye on the situation.

The arrival of Rabindranath Tagore, India's most famous citizen, presented the ultranationalist pan-Asianists with both an opportunity and a problem. His sympathetic utterances about Japan and his criticisms of European imperialism suggested him as an ideal leader of a pro-Japanese independence movement in India. The problem was that Tagore not only expressed no interest in such a collaboration, he also publicly denounced nationalism and militarism, whether European or Japanese, and upheld a nonpolitical and purely spiritual concept of Eastern civilization. It must have been a trying experience for Japan's pan-Asianists as they pondered whether or not they should take seriously the Indian poet's exhortations to their country to apply her "Eastern mind" and her "spiritual strength" to fulfilling "the mission of the East."

The *Herald of Asia*, a Tokyo weekly written in English for foreign consumption, decided to accept Tagore's message as a clear endorsement of Japan's aspirations in Asia:

> We could not, even if we wished, prove false to the ideals of Asiatic civilization — ideals which we are proud to share with the peoples of India and China and other countries of the continent. In this respect all peoples of Asia are bound together by ties that lie deep in the sub-conscious domain of their life and aspirations. . . . The spiritual solidarity of Asia is a reality full of promise for the future course of history and civilization.[82]

Zumoto Motosada, owner and director of the *Herald of Asia* and the probable author of this editorial, was a man of long experience as a public relations officer for the Japanese government. Using the masterful English he had acquired from his American missionary teachers at the Sapporo Agricultural College, he founded in 1897 the first English-language newspaper published by a Japanese. In 1906, with the encouragement of Prince Itō, Japan's de facto governor in Korea, he took over the *Seoul Press* from an English owner, and in 1909 opened the Oriental Information Bureau in New York City. The *Herald of Asia,* founded in 1916, was short-lived, but this editorial praising Tagore served its purpose, for it was quickly sent to Calcutta and reprinted in India's leading monthly newsmagazine, the *Modern Review,* creating a favorable, although misleading impression of the reception of Tagore's message in Japan.[83]

Pan-Asianists writing only for Japanese consumption were more cautious in their appraisals of Tagore's Asian ideal. The restrained hopes of those in close touch with the government were expressed in an article in the *Chūō kōron* by the director of the semiofficial Japan-India Association, a member of the Tagore Welcoming Committee:

> We deeply respect and sympathize with Tagore's motives in seeking to console himself somewhat for his inability to do anything about the downfall of his mother country, and we deeply respect and sympathize with him for admiring Japan and for seeing in it the light of his own ideals.
>
> For this reason we make bold to hope that the Japanese, inasmuch as they have already come in contact with Tagore's beautiful voice and kind face, and have responded in unison to his ideals, will arouse themselves on behalf of Eastern Asia, working to realize these ideas in Tagore's stead and in place of the Indians.
>
> At the same time, we make bold to hope that Tagore, inasmuch as he has already recognized that he must rely on Japan, and believes that the East must arise, will cooperate for years to come with the Japanese — and especially that he will become the prime mover leading the intellectual world of the future India, reaching the true intellectuals and men of vision, many of whom are still unknown to the public, and are genuinely striving for the development, leadership, and reform of the Indian people, both spiritually and materially. Finally, we hope he will dedicate himself to the progress of mankind.[84]

To say that the Japanese people had "responded in unison" to Tagore's message was a polite exaggeration. A more realistic report appeared in the most influential organ of Japan's ultranationalist thinkers, the fortnightly *Nippon oyobi Nipponjin* (Japan and the Japanese), which followed the poet's visit closely, albeit with growing disillusionment. Its May 15 issue noted: "Mr. Tagore is not coming to Japan with any political purpose, but when we contemplate the awakening of the East, we cannot help feeling that [as Confucius said], 'To have friends coming from distant places, is this not delightful?'" The June 1 issue quoted approvingly Rabindranath's statement: "Japan is the only constitutional government in the East, and the light of Japan is illuminating India. I want to know how the Japanese people have reached this advanced stage." In order not to raise his readers' hopes too high, however, the editor reminded them that "England [*sic*] has given him the Nobel Prize, and a knighthood as well." [85] The next number carried an article warning the public: "You cannot expect to find desperate struggle or effort or great activity in Tagore's thought; if you discover a profound and subtle feeling in his poems, then you must be satisfied with that." [86]

Japan and the Japanese lapsed into a significant silence after the Indian poet delivered his Tokyo University lecture, and did not resume its commentary on him until he had sailed for the United States. Then it passed a stern judgment on his visit: "Frankly speaking, his philosophical ideas and their influence during his three months' stay in Japan, have been, we regret to say, very weak. This is disappointing both to our countrymen and to him." Looking momentarily on the bright side, the ultranationalist organ noted that Tagore was indeed an Indian patriot, "and we cannot overlook the fact that he has made some contribution to the mutual understanding of Japan and India, both politically and implicitly. . . . We can never imagine the independence of India, but if India has the same important mission as Japan has in relation to the prosperity of the Orient, then the mutual understanding of our two nations will be the most important result of his three months' stay in Japan. We cannot deny that Tagore has disappointed us," the journal concluded, "but in the above respect his contribution will go down in the history of Japanese-Indian relations." [87]

Their disappointment with Tagore did not prevent several Japanese intellectuals from voicing strong support for Indian nationalist aspirations. Mitsui Koshi, the *waka* poet and right-wing journalist associated with Japan and the Japanese, commented: "Rather than simply expressing my respect for Mr. Tagore, I would like to mention my regard for Mr. Tagore as a means of sympathizing with today's India. I would like to believe that Mr. Tagore would really be pleased at this." [88] A younger *waka* poet, Tomita Saika, a translator of Whitman and Edward Carpenter into Japanese, asserted in fluent English: "To all India's disappointment our appreciation of this great neighbour is too far from her heart's desire. Though Tagore and his countrymen live under the tropical sun their hearts are always in the bitterness of [the] cutting north wind. Let them enjoy their own nature! India wants her entire liberty. . . . She must belong only to herself." Indicating his independence of the establishment and his indifference to Tagore's ideas, Tomita (later known as a socialist) added: "I prefer just a mere silence on his message to [a] thousand vacant diplomatic words poured from the lips of our crocodile-sympathetic politicians, professors, priests, bookmakers, trumpet-blowers, drum-beaters and what not." [89] A right-wing Waseda professor specializing in colonial politics, Nagai Ryutarō (who was to become Japan's ambassador to the Nanking puppet government in 1942) declared of Tagore: "his statements and lectures betray defects common to Indians and make it plain that he is not the pioneer who will be able to build up a new India. He says he loves Japan, but as yet he does not understand Japan, especially the new Japan. Those who cannot understand the new Japan will not be able to build up a new India. In a word, I think he is only a poet." [90] Finally, a Keio professor who had actually been arrested in India because he was agitating for Indian independence, Kanokogi Kazunobu, admired Tagore as an artist, but concluded sadly: "If there is anything to learn from him, it is his beautiful personality, and the beauty which his personality embodies." Tagore, he lamented, was "the beautiful flower of a ruined country." [91]

"The beautiful flower of a ruined country" — this was not Kanokogi's view alone, for nine other Japanese noted that India was *horobiru*: ruined, lost, destroyed, or, to use the most common meaning, deceased.[92] Proud of Japan's independent status and her rise to equality with the world's great powers, these intellectuals looked down on India as a pitiful country that had lost out in the struggle for survival. And yet other Japanese looked up to Tagore, and therefore to some extent to the country that had produced him, because he had won from Europe its highest cultural prize, thus vindicating the honor of the whole of Asia. One young artist, Hirasawa Tetsuo, described his excitement in 1913 when the Nobel Prize was awarded to the Indian poet, because this made it difficult for the Americans among whom he was studying at the Art Institute of Chicago to laugh at Orientals as they had been doing.[93] This same pride in Asian culture moved another intellectual to explain in a letter the basic reason for the unprecedented popular welcome Tagore had received in Japan:

> To think that among the Orientals whom the Europeans are inclined more or less to despise in matters relating to the mind there should be one who has raised himself to a worldwide fame never dreamt of by Orientals, is no doubt at once flattering and elating to the Japanese, and a large part of the enthusiasm with which Tagore is received on his present visit to us, I am inclined to attribute to this. The Japanese who thought that things Oriental are already out of date have found in Tagore an example of how even Orientals can be the subject of respect, if not worship, throughout the world, and in this sense the Japanese have reason to be grateful to Tagore.[94]

This unsigned letter articulated the purely cultural pan-Asianism which Tagore himself had sought to cultivate in Japan. In contrast, a number of intellectuals (including two professors who later rose to high positions in the government of Japanese-occupied China) judged India by a strictly political yardstick, condemned it as "ruined," and therefore rejected Tagore's message as the epitome of that disinterest in political matters which lay at the root of India's submission to British rule. Yet a third school of thought on India and Asia combined cultural and political concerns in varying proportions. In this middle area there was room for a variety of views and misunderstandings. The English-language *Herald of Asia* could cheerfully endorse Tagore's message while ignoring his criticism of Japanese nationalism, and the editor of the ultranationalist *Japan and the Japanese* could disparage Tagore's ideas and be distinctly pessimistic about India's future. Most significantly, the director of the Japan-India Association, while seeming to agree with Tagore, emphasized that he would have to "rely on Japan" to realize his ideals. Thus the spiritual ideals of Japan's most influential pan-Asianists, though clothed in a rhetoric remarkably similar to Tagore's, could and did lead to the aggressive military action on the Asian mainland from which Tagore was to recoil in horror two decades later.

Summing Up

The numerous opinions on Tagore and his message published in Japanese periodicals exhibit a kaleidoscopic variety. Writers, religious leaders, philosophers, and pan-Asianists used the appearance of the Indian poet-philosopher in their midst as an occasion for setting forth their own views on the issues he raised in their respective spheres. By no means all the leading intellectuals of the day put their reactions into print. Among the writers, for example, Mori Ōgai and Nagai Kafū; among the religious leaders, Japan's foremost Christian, Uchimura Kanzō; among the philosophers, the top-ranking Nishida Kitarō — these and others less great remained silent. They may well have felt what the famous *waka* poetess Yosano Akiko wrote with characteristic frankness: "As I have not read any of Tagore's writings, I have nothing to say." [95] But a number of acknowledged leaders in their respective fields did speak out, and the very diversity of their opinions is an index of the healthy state of intellectual life in this period of Japan's modern history.[96]

Within each of the four groups surveyed those favoring Tagore's ideas were in the minority. Among the writers, those most pleased with the Indian poet were those best acquainted with the English and American romantic traditions by which Tagore himself had been considerably influenced. For the religious leaders, the key factors seem to have been a personal knowledge of Indian religiosity or of Unitarian Christian traditions to whose development English-speaking Hindus had contributed. The two academic philosophers who admired Tagore's outlook were strongly influenced by German ethical idealism. The only pan-Asianist to praise the Indian poet without reserve was a professional propagandist (educated by American missionaries) who wrote in English. Intellectual influences from the United States, England, Germany, and India thus appear to have fostered among Japanese thinkers attitudes concordant with Tagore's. It is striking that the only "Eastern" influences producing such sympathy were Indian in origin.

Western influences also had affected those thinkers who rejected the Indian poet-philosopher's message to Japan. Naturalism and socialism from France and Christian humanism from the United States and Russia had encouraged Japan's writers to take interest in the problems of the poor and humble, and Tagore's antipathy to the material side of modern civilization condemned him in their eyes. Some American-educated Christians stressed the spiritual component behind the development of modern material civilization. As for the philosophers, both German-influenced Kantians and Anglo-American-oriented pragmatists found the Indian poet's ideas unsatisfactory.

Some of the bitterest opposition to Tagore's message came, not from the most Westernized intellectuals in Japan (Noguchi, who best fits this description, was his most enthusiastic supporter), but from those most anxious to preserve native Japanese characteristics, often with the aid of appropriate Western traditions. The haiku poet Kawahigashi and the *waka* poets Iwano Hōmei and Mitsui Koshi were particularly severe judges of their fellow poet. Japan's leading Buddhist scholar, Takakusu, only managed a few noncommittal remarks, while his colleague at Tokyo University, the Germanized Confucianist Inoue, urged his countrymen to "make every effort especially to exclude" ideas like Tagore's. (Significantly, Takakusu and Inoue were the only intellectuals commenting on Tagore appointed to the select Imperial Academy, the summit of academic prestige.) The leading ultranationalist periodicals found the

Indian poet's sole merit in the part of his message which called for a pan-Asian movement under Japanese leadership.

These were the views of the articulate intelligentsia — that fraction of the educated population which both took ideas seriously and wrote out their own for others to read. How the majority of educated Japanese reacted may be seen from what the daily newspapers had to say about Tagore. Most businessmen, government officials, and professional men looked to their newspaper for authoritative judgments on current problems about which they had no special knowledge. Tolstoy aptly describes this habit in *Anna Karenina*:

> Stepan Arkadyevitch took in and read a liberal paper, not an extreme one, but one advocating the views held by the majority. And in spite of the fact that science, art, and politics had no special interest for him, he firmly held those views on all these subjects which were held by the majority and by his paper, and he only changed them when the majority changed them — or, more strictly speaking, he did not change them, but they imperceptibly changed of themselves within him.[97]

The two Tokyo dailies which in 1916 best fitted this definition of "advocating the views held by the majority" were the *Asahi* and the *Yorozu chōhō*. After Rabindranath read his "Message of India to Japan" at Tokyo University, the *Asahi* agreed that "mere imitation of Western civilization is not good for our future," but continued noncommittally: "The ideals of Tagore are lofty and noble. But such ideas are not entirely unfamiliar. Similar ideas have been expressed in Japan also, as for example the ideas preached in Mahayana Buddhism." The *Asahi*'s only criticism was that "some Japanese, it is said, are attempting to use Tagore as a spokesman for their own ideas. Such tendencies are regrettable." In this adroitly worded statement, the *Asahi* indicated its disapproval of any influence which Tagore might exert on the Japanese intellectual world, but did not directly rebuke the Indian visitor. Three weeks later, after his Keio University lecture, its tone grew more caustic:

> "The Spirit of Japan" lasted for an hour. The content of the lecture was in general the same as that of his previous one. He attacked material civilization as before.
> His sentences are like long melodies, and contain many beautiful phrases and metaphors, but very few people can understand the meaning of his lecture.[98]

The *Yorozu chōhō,* written generally in a more popular tone than the somewhat austere *Asahi,* agreed with Tagore's desire to reconcile East and West, but rejected his proposal that by reviving "Eastern spirituality" Japan could effect this result:

Japan's mission is to amalgamate the civilizations of the Occident and the Orient, but a moral civilization not built on material foundations can only lead a country to ruin, as history well shows. Sir Rabindra's words are like jewels; and his sentences sparkle like stars; but he offers no statistics, no figures to support his theories. He is all poetry; and for his poetry we admire him; but we must not let him discourage us in the pursuit of science and wealth.[99]

These verdicts, actually more severe than the general tenor of the opinions expressed by individual intellectuals, presumably formed the basis of the pessimistic conclusions drawn by Tagore and the English and American observers who reported that his mission to Japan had failed completely. Rabindranath certainly erred in thinking that Japan's intellectuals unanimously opposed his message, but it is equally clear that those who spoke appreciatively of his message were not only fewer in number but also were for the most part expressing personal sympathy with his idealism, meditativeness, or other worthy qualities, while those who attacked his ideas were much more specific in analyzing and evaluating them. A considerable number of others avoided discussing these ideas at all, probably feeling that it would be impolite to criticize a distinguished visitor to their country.

In the light of these findings, what are we to make of Tagore's own statement, implying that he had failed because the whole Japanese people had voluntarily submitted to "the trimming of their minds and the clipping of their freedom by their government, which through various educational agencies regulates their thoughts, manufactures their feelings, becomes suspiciously watchful when they show signs of inclining toward the spiritual"? Here the Indian poet's unfamiliarity with the Japanese scene, and especially with the Japanese language, seems to have distorted his perception of the realities of the situation. There is little evidence that the opinions expressed by the intellectuals were government-inspired, and the very diversity of these opinions belies any such assumption. Only the comments of the "official scholar" Inoue and of the Japan-India Association's Soejima seem directly to reflect the views of the government. Several of the writers who criticized Tagore most sharply, in the same breath denounced Prime Minister Ōkuma. Contrariwise, the most penetrating analysis of his message came from a professor of education who had been dismissed by the government for disapproving a traditional Japanese way of asserting the superiority of spirit over matter — the custom of hara-kiri.

The causes of Tagore's failure (for such, in the main, it was) must be sought elsewhere. His own poetical manner of presenting his ideas was partly to blame, for he was vague to the point of obscurity. Nor did he seek out the leading intellectuals of the day to talk with them personally; he was content to give three formal lectures and to remain relatively secluded during the rest of his stay, granting occasional interviews to those who sought him out. In his lectures and statements to the press, the lurid contrast he drew between the materialistic civilization of the West and the spiritual civilization of the East was not only unfair to the people of both hemispheres, it conveyed the false impression that he was an archconservative, an enemy of progress. Had he chosen to recount in some detail his own experiences in India as an opponent of fanatic patriotism and unthinking obedience to degrading customs, or had he applied his ideas to the concrete realities of contemporary Japanese life, his words would have had a more convincing and constructive effect.

At a more general level, it seems clear that Tagore failed because he misconstrued the nature of Japanese society and culture at the time of his visit. Misled by Okakura's rhetoric about the unity of Asia's cultures and persuaded by hopeful Orientophiles in India and England, he envisioned Japan and India joined in a common Eastern civilization, and ignored the many real differences between their respective cultures and histories. One such difference to which his Japanese critics drew frequent attention was that India lay supine under the rule of a Western power, while Japan was an independent sovereign state with a burgeoning empire of her own. Bringing with him a preconceived notion of what constituted the essence of "the East," he tried to impose it on a country he had never seen before and of whose rich and complex culture, customs, and institutions he had very little knowledge.

Most Japanese intellectuals quite naturally refused to accept Tagore's ideas of East and West. Of the eight writers who alluded to his concept of a complementarity between Eastern spiritual and Western material civilizations, only one agreed with him that the East had chosen the better part. Two others saw the conflict as an inevitable and perhaps insoluble one for Japan, while the remaining five stood the poet's thesis on its head and argued that Western civilization was superior to the traditional culture of Japan or the East. Three other men explicitly, and a fourth implicitly, rejected the whole framework of so-called Eastern versus Western and spiritual versus material civilization and instead stated the problem in essentially evolutionary terms. One of these, the Christian Ebina, emphatically favored "new" as against "old" civilization. The pragmatist philosopher Tanaka celebrated the spiritual superiority of "modern civilization." The novelist Mushakōji called for "good civilization" as against "bad civilization." Although silent at the time, the Buddhist scholar Anesaki twelve years later called on Japan to join in building a "modern civilization" which was to be "the common heritage of the whole of mankind."

The prevailing mood among Japan's intellectuals in 1916 seems to have been an almost mellow confidence that indigenous and Western traditions were being blended successfully and harmoniously in the progressive development of a new and better society and culture. Had not Japan moved in the space of half a century from the status of a hermit kingdom to become one of the world's five great powers? And were not her intellectuals participating actively in the most modern movements in literature, religion, art, and philosophy? To be sure, there were genuine differences of opinion within the intelligentsia as to which Western and which indigenous ideas and institutions should be developed and combined: the conservative Inoue, while welcoming science and technology, wished to see German authoritarian ideas used to strengthen Japan's national structure; the liberal Yoshino wanted to move that structure in the direction of Anglo-American traditions of representative government; while the leftward-looking Ogawa and other writers, influenced by French and Russian thought, would presumably have called for socialism had the censor and the police been likely to allow such heresy to go unpunished. Tension among the many traditions penetrating from abroad was if anything more serious than the concurrent tension between foreign and indigenous traditions.[100] Small wonder, then, that after pausing for a moment to listen to Tagore's appeal for a revival of "Eastern" spiritual civilization, most of Japan's intellectuals simply shrugged and turned once more to their tasks, each one in his own way contributing to the forward thrust of civilization in Japan.

CHAPTER FOUR

WESTERN ENCOURAGEMENT FOR
"THE MESSAGE OF THE EAST"

*A new soul is awakening in Asia which will con-
tain within itself the best qualities of the various
Asiatic peoples — the sensibility of Japan, the men-
tality of China, the spirituality of India. In this
Soul of the Future will be gathered up the great
Thought of Asia.*

— Paul Richard

THE APPARENT DEFEAT OF HIS ATTEMPT to enlist Japan's intellectuals
in the cause of reviving Eastern spiritual civilization should have warned
Tagore that he might be building his grand scheme of harmonizing the
East and the West on a faulty foundation. Nevertheless, in the years
following his trip to Japan he continued to elaborate his concept of the
distinct and complementary character of Eastern and Western civilizations, even going so far as to make it the basis of a new educational institution, his "world university" at Santiniketan. Far from abandoning
his mission to rally East Asia's intellectuals to the defense of Eastern
civilization, he was to make a second and more determined try at it in
1924 by lecturing in the principal cities of both China and Japan. As
before, both inner restlessness and appeals from the world outside led
him along this missionary path, but the most striking feature of his intellectual development in the years 1917 to 1923 is that almost all the
influences affecting his thinking about Asia came from Europe, not from
those East Asian countries whose cooperation was so essential to the
success of his scheme.

Disappointment with Japan was succeeded almost immediately by a
sometimes triumphal reception in the United States in the autumn of
1916. "I felt I must come to bring the message of the East," he said in
explaining the purpose of his lecture tour.[1] The citation given him at

Yale expressed the gratitude many of his listeners and readers felt for his "message": "We welcome you as one of the great brotherhood of seekers for light and truth, we honor you as one to whom it has been given to help thousands — yea, millions — in that search." [2] The stress of constant railroad travel, however, and perhaps some of the skepticism which greeted him in the larger cities on the eastern seaboard made him cancel his remaining lecture engagements and sail for India via the Pacific.

Not long after his return to quiet Santiniketan in the spring of 1917 his chronic restlessness began to reassert itself. Characteristically, interpreting his inner unrest as a call to heal the breach between nations, he wrote to William Rothenstein in July:

> I am afraid that the West has lost its foothold of the inner life and has been hopping with one leg, revelling in the very jerkiness of its difficult movement, because that has the appearance of power. Unfortunately the East has gone to the other extreme, and instead of using the inner life as the source of all harmonious movements has used it as a retreat for its practice of hibernation. But I, who have the amphibious duality of nature in me, whose food is in the West and breathe air in the East, do not find a place where I can build my nest. I suppose I shall have to be a migratory bird and cross and recross the sea, owning two nests, one on each shore.[3]

A year passed and the wanderlust was stronger than ever. Writing again to Rothenstein (whom he addressed in this period as "my dearest friend"), he confessed in June 1918: "For some time I have been pining to go somewhere — it was like a homesickness for the far away. I planned all sorts of excursions in my mind. . . . However, I have decided to start for America next autumn — it is but to take a desperate plunge into a violent change of surroundings." [4] The American "excursion" had to be shelved, however,[5] and for a time the poet toyed with the idea of a trip to Australia; this, too, he finally abandoned. "I earnestly hope that I shall find my home everywhere in this world before I leave it," he wrote to his English friend and secretary, W. W. Pearson, who was then touring China. But the war and its afterbirth of turmoil was to keep the doors of Europe closed to him for another two years.[6]

Confined to India, Rabindranath found scope for his energies, not so much in creative writing[7] as in a sustained effort to expand his Santiniketan school for Bengali boys — at first into an all-India center of cultural life, and then into an international educational center, a "world university."

THE THREEFOLD IDEAL OF VISVA-BHARATI

The idea had first come to him in Japan, it seems. One morning during his sojourn near Yokohama, he was gazing out to sea, watching the sun rise in the east, as was his daily habit. By his side stood the French mystic and vagabond, Paul Richard, who with his wife (later "The Mother" of the Sri Aurobindo Ashram in Pondicherry, French India) often visited the poet during July 1916. "Doesn't one feel ashamed to enjoy everything here, at a moment when Europe is a hell?" asked Richard. Rabindranath did not reply, but seems to have been deeply affected by this remark, for a week later he replied: "I have thought much about what you said to me. But now you will see what I am going to do," and then and there outlined to Richard his plan for a world university.[8]

Three months later the poet wrote his son Rathindranath, whom he had left in charge of the boys studying at his school: "The Santiniketan school must be made the thread linking India with the world. We must establish there a center for humanistic research concerned with all the world's peoples. The age of narrow chauvinism is coming to an end — for the sake of the future, the first steps toward this great meeting of world humanity will be taken on those very fields of Bolpur." [9]

Shortly afterwards, Paul Richard contributed a new impetus to the poet's burgeoning internationalism by sending him a manuscript he had just written appealing to the nations of Europe to turn from "the law of the jungle . . . to that of mutual aid and fraternal co-operation." Richard summoned man to "learn to place higher than the patriotic the human interest, to love Humanity with a wider and purer love than that which he bears to the country, to sacrifice himself not to what the country is but to what she must be in Humanity." Rabindranath was obviously in sympathy with Richard's appeal, for he contributed an introduction to it which concluded: "When gigantic forces of destruction were holding their orgies of fury I saw this solitary Frenchman, unknown to fame . . . his face beaming with the lights of the new dawn and his voice vibrating with the message of new life, and I felt sure that the great To-morrow has already come though not registered in the Calendar of the statesmen." [10]

How deeply Richard influenced Tagore's thought is difficult to determine, but they were certainly thinking along converging lines, and each probably exerted some influence on the other. For example, a comparison of the books each published in 1917 on the same theme, Rabindranath's *Nationalism* and Richard's *To the Nations,* shows that at that date the Indian thinker rejected the nation as something evil in itself; whereas the Frenchman accepted it as a necessary fact but sought its transformation, declaring, "What man is in the nation, the nation is in Humanity." Just as Rabindranath's concept of the unity of Asian civilization seems subsequently to have become a part of Richard's thinking, so Richard's view of an upward progression from loyalty to country to loyalty to humanity became part of Rabindranath's view.

It required several years for this vision of an ascending series of widening loyalties to take shape in Tagore's mind. His school at Santiniketan, to which he gave much of his time in these years, was the laboratory in which he worked to give the idea practical form. Gratified that the number of non-Bengali students was increasing, he decided in 1918 to put his educational work on an all-India basis. With some financial support from Gujarati businessmen in Bengal (whose sons formed the bulk of the non-Bengali students), he was able, on December 22, 1918, the seventeenth anniversary of the school's founding, to lay the cornerstone for a new building at Santiniketan, intended as the nucleus of a novel institution, the Visva-Bharati.[11]

Rabindranath coined this name for his latest experiment from two Sanskrit words, *viśva,* meaning "all," or "universal," or "the world," and *Bhāratī,* the Hindu goddess of speech and eloquence, more generally symbolizing learning and culture. The marriage of the two terms produced a name rich in associations, particularly since *Bhāratī* was also a feminine form of *Bhārat,* the ancient Aryan name for India. In addition to its primary meaning of "universal learning," therefore, Visva-Bharati conveyed the secondary meaning of "all-India," and the tertiary one of "the world and India." The poet thus encapsulated in five syllables the three grand ideals to which his new institution was dedicated.

Expounding these ideals to audiences in south India early in 1919, Tagore laid particular emphasis on the second. The need of the hour, he declared, was for a "centre of Indian culture," a "seat of our Indian learning." Such a center would act as "a centripetal force, which will attract and group together from different parts of our land and different ages all our own materials of learning and thus create a complete and moving orb of Indian culture." As long as Indian education remained merely imitative, he warned, the power of original thought would remain stunted, and Indian students would be unable to master what was of lasting value either in their own culture or in that of the West. "Only to him who hath is given," Rabindranath argued in Biblical language: "All the elements in our own culture have to be strengthened, not to resist the Western culture, but truly to accept and assimilate it, and use it for our food and not as our burden; to get mastery over this culture, and not live at its outskirts as the hewers of texts and drawers of book-learning." [12]

A true center of Indian culture would foster the creative and the universal, first in India's many cultures, and then in those of the world at large:

> Now has come the age for co-ordination and co-operation . . . So we must prepare the grand field for the co-ordination of the cultures of the world. . . . But before we are in a position to stand a comparison with the other cultures of the world, or truly to co-operate with them, we must base our own structure on a synthesis of all the different cultures we have. When, taking our stand at such a centre, we turn towards the West, our gaze shall no longer be timid and dazed; our head shall remain erect, safe from insult. For then we shall be able to take our own views of Truth, from the standpoint of our own vantage ground, thus opening out a new vista of thought before the grateful world.[13]

Even before this whole hope became known in the West, one intellectual there declared his gratitude to Tagore for the contributions he had already made toward a meeting of Eastern and Western cultures. The French pacifist novelist Romain Rolland, having greatly admired Tagore's "Message of India to Japan," wrote in April 1919 to ask his help in bringing "the intelligence of Asia" into closer touch with European thinkers. "My dream will be that one day we may see the union of these two hemispheres of the Spirit; and I admire you for having contributed towards this more than anyone else." [14] Rolland's project, to which Rabindranath joyfully agreed, was to acquire the support of leading intellectuals in many countries to his "Declaration of the Independence of the Spirit" from all political passions and allegiances,

Rabindranath had been thinking in terms of India and the West; Rolland now spoke to him in terms of Asia and Europe, and of the East and the West as two complementary civilizations. After receiving Tagore's sympathetic reply, Rolland wrote to him once again in the same strain:

> After the disaster of this shameful world war which marked Europe's failure, it has become evident that Europe alone cannot save herself. Her thought is in need of Asia's thought, just as the latter profits from contact with European thought. These are the two hemispheres of the brain of mankind. If one is paralysed, the whole body degenerates. It is necessary to re-establish their union and their healthy development.[15]

In his second reply, Rabindranath felt it necessary to warn Rolland not to expect a concerted response from the intellectuals of Asia. Unable to comply with Rolland's request that he recruit leading thinkers and artists from China and Japan to sign the Declaration of the Independence of the Spirit, he cautioned: "You should know that in Asia today spiritual matters and all the means of expressing them remain disorganized. Our minds are divided, our thoughts dispersed." All the same, he concluded, with Europe's help a unity might be established: "We have great need of an appeal from without which would make us aware of our mission." [16]

Tagore's confession that Asia's intellectuals needed Western encouragement to develop a consciousness of their unity indicated the vital role which Western influences continued to play in his thinking about Eastern civilization in the years between his 1916 visit to Japan and his 1924 trip to China. The memory of his failure in Japan gradually faded, and his earlier vision of an Asia reunited on the basis of its underlying spiritual civilization not only reasserted itself but was sharpened by his many contacts with European thinkers in the years 1919 to 1923. It had long been difficult for Europeans to distinguish between India in particular and Asia, or the East, in general: Rolland was quite typical of his generation in using these terms interchangeably. Even so sensitive a philosopher as Martin Buber, probably the greatest religious mind of this century, could write in his commentary on the Taoist sage Chuang-tzu: "The Orient forms a natural unity, which is expressed in its values and creations . . . A communality overspreads its different peoples and separates it with utmost clarity from the fate and creativity of the West." [17] The way in which Tagore himself helped to crystallize this Western image of the East has been noted by Alex Aronson, an acute observer of his European tours:

> The East, which had been known only on account of its vague influence on Schopenhauer's philosophy and by the popularized Victorian translation of Omar Khayyam by Fitzgerald, had suddenly been "humanised" by Rabindranath. His personality — and here we use the word in the largest sense of the term — stood for everything Indian, indeed, for everything Eastern. *People started thinking of the East in terms of intellectual generalisations.* . . . Nothing was more tempting for European intellectuals than to establish comparisons between Eastern and Western ways of life as represented on the one hand by Rabindranath and, on the other, by the artists and writers in the West.[18]

Tagore's thinking in turn was powerfully affected by this Western image of the East, an image he himself was doing so much to encourage with his appearances, lectures, and statements to European and American audiences. This two-way flow of ideas, which the 1913 award of the Nobel Prize both symbolized and stimulated, was to reach its high point in the years 1920–21, during Rabindranath's fourth visit to England and the Continent. The savagery of "the Great War" had heightened the disillusionment with their own civilization which Westerners had already felt before the war, and had correspondingly increased their receptivity to the religious ideas of non-Western prophets and poets like Tagore. To cite only one of many instances, Premier Clemenceau of France, as the fateful day of November 11, 1918, drew to a close, is said to have sent for the poetess the Comtesse de Noailles to read him poems from Rabindranath's *Gītānjali*.[19] The war's end also opened the way for Tagore to travel to the Western world, and he came as soon as he was able, like the farmer who hurries to harvest his grain after a long season of waiting and watching it grow from afar.[20]

In May 1920 Rabindranath left India for a fifteen-month tour of Europe and the United States. Although in Britain Conservative opinion was cool because of his criticisms of the government and his renunciation of his knighthood after the Amritsar Massacre of 1919, on the Continent he was everywhere welcomed and honored, and the doors of the highest society were opened to him. He was received by the kings of Belgium and Sweden; he met with Bergson in France, Thomas Mann in Germany, his old friends Yeats and Rothenstein in England, with Sydney and Beatrice Webb, Keynes, Colonel Lawrence, and with many others. In May 1921 his birthday was widely celebrated in north-ern Europe.[21] In June, Count Hermann Keyserling, who had seen him in Calcutta on his world tour ten years before, prepared a special "Tagore week" at his Darmstadt School of Wisdom, and hailed the poet as "a living symbol of the eternal One personified by the man from the East . . . the light of the Eastern sun." [22] Rabindranath himself testified that "an outbreak of love has followed me and enveloped me everywhere I have been in Scandinavia and Germany." [23] To some the tall, bearded poet in his long, flowing robes must have recalled Jesus Christ himself, and a few re-enacted a familiar New Testament scene when they pressed around to touch and kiss the hem of his garment.[24]

Such overwhelming devotion (which Rabindranath interpreted as homage to India and Asia as well as to his own personality and poetic achievement) could not fail to make a deep impression on his mind, and his weekly letters to C. F. Andrews, his closest confidante at this time, show the conclusions he drew from it. Again and again he noted that the world needed India's wisdom, that India should "win freedom for all humanity," and "come to the rescue" of mankind. After the Swedish Academy had honored him in Stockholm, he wrote:

> The fact is, there is a rising tide of heart in the West rushing towards the shores of the East, following some mysterious law of attraction. . . . Europe is like a child who has been hurt in the midst of her game. She is shunning the crowd and looking out for her mother. And has not the East been the mother of spiritual humanity, giving it life from its own life? [25]

Responding to this Western enthusiasm, Tagore announced to his European and American audiences a significant enlargement of the purposes of his embryonic Visva-Bharati. Where in 1919 he had spoken of India, he now spoke of Asia, and equated the "awakening" and "re-surgence" of the one with that of the other. Thus, a key passage on India's relation to the West in his 1919 essay, "A Centre for Indian Culture," was transformed into this:

> But before Asia is in a position to co-operate with the culture of Eu-rope, she must base her own structure on a synthesis of all the different cultures which she has. When, taking her stand on such a culture, she turns toward the West, she will take, with a confident sense of freedom, her own view of truth, from her own vantage-ground, and open a new vista of thought to the world . . . In this belief, it is my desire to ex-

tend by degrees the scope of this University on simple lines, until it comprehends the whole range of Eastern cultures — the Aryan, Semitic, Mongolian and others. Its object will be to reveal the Eastern mind to the world.[26]

Before leaving Europe for India, Rabindranath received further support for this ideal in three conversations with Romain Rolland. On each occasion the poet aired his plans for Visva-Bharati, which Rolland first took to be an "Asian university," but subsequently understood as an "International University." Rolland pledged to do "all that is in my power to support your generous initiative," but confided to his diary this remark about Tagore: "Despite his charming politeness, one sees that he is perfectly convinced of the moral and intellectual superiority of Asia — above all, of India — over Europe." [27]

Although he had often pined for the quiet of his beloved Santiniketan, "the place of peace," Tagore felt a growing uneasiness as his ship approached India's shores in July 1921. The fifteen months he had been away had been ones of mounting political agitation under the leadership of M. K. Gandhi, to whom Rabindranath himself had first given the famous title of Mahatma, "the great soul." Newspaper reports of successive stages in Gandhi's campaign to withhold Indian cooperation from the British-run courts, schools, business firms, and social functions had troubled the poet during the preceding five months, for he had written Andrews on February 8, 1921: "I am afraid I shall be rejected by my own people when I go back to India. . . . In their present state of mind, my countrymen will have no patience with me, who believe God to be higher than my country." A month later he cried in anguish: "What irony of fate is this, that I should be preaching co-operation of cultures between East and West on this side of the sea just at the moment when the doctrine of non-cooperation is preached on the other side!" His triumphal procession through northern and central Europe in the spring of 1921 had raised to new heights Rabindranath's missionary zeal:

I know that there is a call for me to work towards the true union of East and West. I have unconsciously been getting ready for this mission. . . . The accident which made me translate Gitanjali and the sudden and unaccountable longing which took me over to Europe at the beginning of my fiftieth year — all combined to push me forward to a path whose destination I did not clearly know when I first took it. This, my last tour in Europe, has made it definitely known to me.[28]

But as his ship neared Bombay, Rabindranath wondered whether it was wise to return to India at a time when his message of East-West harmony was certain to be unpopular, or "whether it was not my mission to remain in Europe at least another year where I was asked to stay." It was too late to turn back, and when the poet stepped ashore anyone familiar with his state of mind could have predicted that it would not be long before he began planning his next foreign tour.[29]

The dramatic clash in 1921 between Tagore the poet-philosopher and Gandhi the politician-saint — India's two most eminent men, each championing a different ideal for his mother country — is a story to be told in a later chapter. Its immediate result for Rabindranath was the return of "the atmosphere of continual revilement"[30] he had known and suffered before. Allowing Gandhi to have the last word in their public dispute, Tagore withdrew to stoic silence in Santiniketan and concentrated on giving a practical demonstration of his educational and cultural ideals. Gathering around him a band of co-workers from India and the West, and drawing on funds raised during his recent tour, he launched his Visva-Bharati as an international university with a formal inauguration ceremony on December 23, 1921.[31]

From the start, cooperation was the keynote of the new institution. Cooperation among the various regional and religious cultures of India, the primary purpose of Visva-Bharati at its dedication three years earlier, was taken for granted. But the place of honor was now given to cooperation among the cultures of the East, with cooperation between Eastern and Western cultures appearing as a more distant goal. The statement of purpose in the new university's constitution reflected this new emphasis faithfully. "To study the mind of Man in its realisation of different aspects of truth from diverse points of view" was the institution's long-range objective, but the more immediate ones were:

[1] To bring together, as a step towards the above object, the various scattered cultures of the East, the fittest place for such endeavour being India, the heart of Asia, into which have flowed the Vedic, Buddhist, Semitic, Zoroastrian, and other cultural currents originating in different part[s] of the Orient from Judea to Japan; to bring to a realisation the fundamental unity of the tendencies of different civilisations of Asia, thereby enabling the East to gain a full consciousness of its own spiritual purpose, the obscuration of which has been the chief obstacle in the way of [2] a true co-operation of East and West, the great achievements

of these being mutually complementary and alike necessary for Universal Culture in its completeness.[32]

Paul Richard had set Rabindranath to thinking about an international university, Romain Rolland had encouraged him to conceive it as a center of Eastern civilization, and now a third French intellectual came in person to Santiniketan to help him launch his new experiment. Sylvain Lévi, Professor at the Collège de France and one of his country's most eminent Orientalists, had met the poet several times in Paris and had accepted his invitation to spend a year at Visva-Bharati establishing a department of Chinese and Tibetan Studies.[33] Commanding a knowledge of Sanskrit, Pali, Tibetan, and Chinese, Lévi had devoted a lifetime of scholarship to reconstructing the expansion of Indian civilization into central and eastern Asia. In one of his earliest writings he stated the theme he was to develop through a long series of researches:

> As Brahmanism has given unity to India, so India in turn gives a sort of unity to Asia. From Persia to the China Sea, from the icy steppes of Siberia to the sun-scorched islands of Java and Borneo, from Oceanea to Socotra . . . India has propagated her beliefs, her genius, her civilization and her literature. Throughout a long succession of centuries, she has left her indestructible imprint on one-fourth of the human race. She is entitled to reclaim in universal history the rank that ignorance has too long refused her, and to take her place among the great nations who summarize and symbolize the human spirit.[34]

Having made much this same claim in his 1901 essay on *Letters of John Chinaman,* Rabindranath must have been greatly encouraged by Sylvain Lévi's lectures and conversation at Santiniketan in the winter of 1921–22. The ancient links between India and China especially interested both men, and together they planned the retranslation into Sanskrit of texts which centuries earlier had been translated into Chinese, the originals having meanwhile perished. Testifying anew to India's influence on Chinese culture, Lévi declared in one of his lectures in India in 1922: "China, the China of Confucius and Lao-tze, was for a thousand years after Christ a field of Hindu activity; China, in spite of her grudge against foreign influences, still bears the indelible stamp of Indian arts, morals and metaphysics." By virtue of her long contacts with Asia, the Near East, and Europe, he concluded, "India, though unwilling and even reluctant, has grown fit to become the home of an Eastern humanism." [35]

The French Orientalist spoke to Rabindranath of Sino-Indian contacts in an age long past, but three Englishmen who were close to the poet at this time were interested in the China of the twentieth century. W. W. Pearson, who had acted as his secretary during the 1916 trip to Japan, had gone from there to China; his letters and reminiscences must have stimulated the poet's growing curiosity about that country.[36] C. F. Andrews did not have the advantage of first-hand experience, but he did share with Tagore a strong conviction that India and China were linked in a common spiritual civilization. "How do India and China differ from the West?" he asked a group of Indian students in 1920. "Why have they renewed their youth so often in the long course of their history?" Andrews believed "it is because her [Asia's] peoples are fundamentally religious, that they have survived while others have perished. . . . Asia has always had faith in spiritual ideals." [37]

Leonard Elmhirst was the youngest of Tagore's trio of English coworkers at this time, and his interest in China proved of most practical help to the poet. When the two men had first met, in New York in March 1921, Elmhirst was finishing a degree in agricultural economics at Cornell University. Rabindranath was looking for someone to organize rural extension work in the villages surrounding Santiniketan, and Elmhirst seemed just the man for the job. "Have you ever been to China?" the poet suddenly asked toward the end of the interview. "No, but it is one of my ambitions to go there," the young Yorkshireman replied. "Is it? I hope to go there one day myself," said Tagore and again changed the subject abruptly. Elmhirst adds to his account of this meeting that "Tagore got the impression, I was told later, that I was only really interested in travel in the East and that most of all I wanted to visit China." [38]

As his recurrent restlessness returned after the founding of Visva-Bharati, Rabindranath found in Elmhirst a valuable aide who could combine the roles of travel agent, secretary, and intellectual companion. After accompanying the poet on his three-month tour of Bombay and South India in late 1922, Elmhirst was returning to New York in the spring of 1923. At Tagore's request he took the eastern route in order to visit China, and especially Peking, since a letter had already come from there to the poet.[39]

This expression of interest from China and Elmhirst's exploratory journey on his behalf opened the prospect of a second voyage to East

Asia. Tagore had already been four times to Europe, three times to the United States, and once to Japan. Russia was still recovering from its post-revolutionary civil war and was not to reopen relations with Britain (and therefore with British India) until 1924. One other great country, India's neighbor to the northeast, now challenged the poet to turn prophet once more. There could be no better way to realize Visva-Bharati's aim of bringing together "the various scattered cultures of the East" than to link by personal contact the cultural leaders of India and China.

THE "SYNTHESIS OF EAST AND WEST" IN CHINESE THOUGHT

The China which Elmhirst visited in 1923, and which Tagore himself would tour in 1924, was a land in the throes of a prolonged and complex revolution. The military and political history of the Chinese Revolution, extending from before 1911 to 1949, is better known than the intellectual revolution which prepared the way for it and continued beyond it, much as the ideas which entered into the making of the French Revolution have remained alive to this day. China's most active period of intellectual ferment came in the years from 1917 to 1924, when the very weakness of the Peking government and the indifference to ideas of most of the provincial warlords encouraged the introduction and discussion of all kinds of new and foreign political, social, and philosophical theories. The men who led the intellectual movements and debates of this turbulent period were almost all recent returnees from study abroad; thus many of their assumptions and arguments were derived from teachers in Tokyo, New York, Paris, London, Berlin, or Moscow, and their arguments with each other were often the same as those their teachers and fellow-students abroad were conducting among themselves.[40] And yet, as had been happening in Japan over a span of several decades, the writings of these intellectual leaders showed both the continuing impress of traditional thought and the ever-present challenge of their country's problems.

The vital center of China's "new thought movement" was the National Peking University, established in 1898 in the heart of the capital city. Its chancellor after 1917, the philosopher Ts'ai Yüan-p'ei, had passed the highest examinations in the Confucian system, then studied in Germany for four years. He appointed as dean of the faculty of letters

Ch'en Tu-hsiu, likewise well-grounded in the Confucian classics, educated for some years in Japan, and particularly interested in modern French thought. Ch'en brought to the university Hu Shih, who had studied from 1910 to 1917 at Cornell and Columbia universities. These three men, all brilliant essayists, joined forces in the successful campaign against the classical Confucian system of learning within which their own studies had begun.

In the widening search for new ideas and doctrines to take the place of the old, the two younger men, Ch'en Tu-hsiu and Hu Shih, began in 1921 to follow diverging paths. For Ch'en the important thing was political action, and he seized upon the Marxist-Leninist ideas and methods just being introduced from Soviet Russia as the answer to China's need for both doctrinal certainty and political salvation. Hu Shih, more in the spirit of American pragmatism than of Ch'en's French-influenced radicalism, remained outside the arena of practical politics and advocated a more academic and gradualist approach to China's problems. While Ch'en called for a sweeping attack on Chinese tradition — in the first issue of his fabulously successful monthly *Hsin ch'ing-nien* (New youth) he had declared, "I would much rather see the past culture of our nation disappear than see our race die out now because of its unfitness for living in the modern world" — Hu Shih, by contrast, sought to discover and rejuvenate those Chinese traditions which would help to "best assimilate modern civilization in such a manner as to make it congenial and congruous and continuous with the civilization of our own making." [41]

With Ch'en Tu-hsiu's departure from Peking University in 1921 to become secretary-general in Shanghai of the newly founded Chinese Communist Party, the bifurcation between the academic and the political wings of the intellectual revolution became an open split. Within the academic wing, still centered in Peking, the relative merits of various Chinese and foreign ideas and traditions continued to be the subject of heated debates. A central figure in the controversy over Eastern and Western civilizations was the pioneer nationalist, now retired from active political life, Liang Ch'i-ch'ao. Having served as minister of justice and minister of finance in several cabinets after the 1911 Revolution, Liang had been instrumental in getting China to enter the war on the Allied side in 1918 in order to protect her interests at the peace conference. This concern, as well as his desire to learn of the latest developments in the West, took him to Europe in 1919 as an unofficial member of the Chinese delegation to the Versailles Conference. While in Europe he was surprised to find Westerners disillusioned with their own civilization as a result of the war. On his return to China he reported in his "Record of Impressions of a European Tour" the following conversation with an American journalist:

AMERICAN: What are you going to do after you return to China? Are you going to introduce some Western civilization into China?
LIANG: Of course.
AMERICAN: Oh! Alas, Western civilization is already bankrupt.
LIANG: What are you going to do when you return to America?
AMERICAN: When I go back, I shall shut the door and wait. I want to wait until you have introduced the civilization of China to save us.[42]

In Paris, where he was an official guest of the French government, Liang sought out the aging idealist philosopher Émile Boutroux, the teacher of Henri Bergson, and was again encouraged to develop the special qualities of China's traditional culture. "I have recently read some Chinese philosophers' works in translations, and have realized how profound and how broad their ideas are. Alas! I have grown old, and can no longer study the Chinese language, but I certainly hope the Chinese people will not lose these riches inherited from their ancestors." On another occasion, when he was explaining to a group of socialist leaders Confucius' saying, "Within the four seas, all men are brothers," the ancient "well-field" system of communal ownership of the land, and other collectivist ideas of ancient Chinese thinkers, the socialists all jumped to their feet and exclaimed: "You Chinese really should be ashamed of yourselves! You have such valuable things at home, and yet you hoard them up and don't share them with us!" Moved by these appeals, Liang hoped the young people of China would do four things:

1. Sincerely honor, love and protect our own culture.
2. Use the research methods of the Westerners to study Chinese culture so as to discover its true nature.
3. Synthesize our own culture, supplement it with the cultures of other peoples, then bring about a transformation so as to produce a new cultural system.
4. Spread this new cultural system abroad so that all mankind may benefit from its virtues. Our population constitutes one-fourth of the

population of the whole world. Therefore we should bear one-fourth of the responsibility for the happiness of the whole of mankind. If we do not carry out this responsibility, we shall be failing in our duty to our ancestors, toward our fellow men, and, in fact, toward ourselves.[43]

This "great responsibility of the Chinese toward world civilization," as Liang christened his program, was comparable to Tagore's Visva-Bharati plan. Both thinkers were motivated by the desire to share with the world the best in the cultural heritages passed down to them from their ancestors, and one impetus encouraging both men in this direction came from their encounters with Westerners interested in learning more about non-Western civilizations. To carry out their ideals, both wished to create a synthesis of their own cultural traditions, then to bring about a global synthesis of cultures in which their own traditions would occupy a central position. The similarities extended to the practical realm as well, for Liang, unwittingly anticipating Tagore's scheme of establishing an educational center where foreign and Indian scholars could come together, founded in 1920 the Peking Lecture Association (Chiang-hsüeh she) for the purpose of bringing foreign lecturers to China to share their knowledge with Chinese scholars.[44]

Despite these structural similarities, Liang's program and Tagore's were also unlike in important ways. For Liang, the idea of a "synthesis of East and West" was only one of many many concerns, and he was far less fully committed to it than Tagore was to his parallel scheme. Liang was of course devoted to the strengthening of Chinese culture, Tagore to the strengthening of "Eastern" civilization, with Indian culture as its core. The kinds of foreign lecturers each invited to his country betrayed a further difference. Liang began by sponsoring three Western philosophers: John Dewey, Bertrand Russell, and Hans Driesch, while Tagore began by inviting a series of European specialists on Indian culture: first, Sylvain Lévi, in 1922 the Czech Sanskritists Moritz Winternitz and V. Lesny, in 1923 the Russian Persianist L. Bogdanov, and in 1924 the Norwegian Indologist Sten Konow.[45] Finally, Tagore conceived his own lecture tours in foreign lands as part of his Visva-Bharati program, while Liang had no such plans. It was not the Chinese philosopher who went to India, but the Indian poet-philosopher who traveled to China: Liang was host to Tagore, not Tagore to Liang.

The two Western philosophers who preceded Tagore as guests of the Chinese Lecture Association, though no experts on China's culture, had encouraging words for it. Bertrand Russell, the first philosopher invited to China by the Association (Dewey's lectures in 1919-20 were mainly supported by Peking University), had set out for China from Russia in the summer of 1920 "to seek a new hope" for he was in a "mood of terrible questioning pain in which Occidental hopefulness grew pale." During and after his visit he recommended China's civilization as an antidote to Europe's ills:

> The Great War showed that something is wrong with our civilization. . . . The Chinese have discovered, and have practised for many centuries, a way of life which, if it could be adopted by all the world, would make all the world happy. We Europeans have not. Our way of life demands strife, exploitation, restless change, discontent, and destruction. Efficiency directed to destruction can only end in annihilation, and it is to this consummation that our civilization is tending, if it cannot learn some of that wisdom for which it despises the East.[46]

Like his host Liang Ch'i-ch'ao, and like Rabindranath Tagore (with whom he had talked in London and Cambridge in 1912), Russell called for a blending of the best features of Eastern and Western civilization: "Contact between East and West is likely to be fruitful to both parties. They may learn from us the indispensable minimum of practical efficiency, and we may learn from them something of that contemplative wisdom which has enabled them to persist while all the other nations of antiquity have perished." Even in his political ideas, the British philosopher sounded like the Indian poet-sage. Politics, he declared, was inspired by "a grinning devil," and bad government in China was a bulwark of individual freedom, for "nine-tenths of the activities of a modern government are harmful; therefore the worse they are performed, the better." [47]

After the departure of Dewey and Russell, the Lecture Association turned its attention from the philosophers of the Anglo-American world to those of the European continent. Its first invitation went to Henri Bergson, whose teacher Boutroux had spoken so encouragingly to Liang; but Bergson declined. An invitation was also extended to the German idealist philosopher Rudolf Eucken, a 1908 Nobel Prize winner who had made plans to visit East Asia in the fateful year 1914, and on whom Liang had paid a call in 1919. Eucken declined also, on the grounds that he was now too old to make the long voyage to China, and recommended his disciple, Hans Driesch, whereupon Liang wrote to his own young associate, Chang Chün-mai, then in Germany, to ask him to find out if Driesch were acceptable and willing.[48]

Chang was even more enthusiastic than Liang about using Western scholarly methods, and Western scholars themselves, to strengthen Chinese culture and synthesize it with Western thought. His interest in German idealism had been awakened during his student days at Waseda University in Tokyo, and was further developed during several years in England and Germany before the war. After accompanying Liang on his European tour in 1919, he had stayed on to work with his professor, Eucken, on a book ambitiously attempting to synthesize the ethical and metaphysical ideas of China and the West. "How much of the old can be retained, and how much of the culture of Europe must be accepted [in China]?" asked Chang in his preface to the volume. Eucken's answer was that German idealism was the Western tradition which could best "exert a fruitful and beneficial effect" on China, for it could strengthen the Confucian tradition of ethical idealism then being threatened by Marxism on the one hand and Anglo-American empiricism on the other.[49]

Driesch accepted the Lecture Association's invitation, and throughout his stay in China, from October 1922 to July 1923, Chang was at his side as guide and interpreter.[50] Driesch's lectures on idealist psychology aroused little public interest, but his conversations with Chang on the need to hold fast to the humanistic values of China's Buddhist and Confucian heritages appear to have strengthened Chang's resolve to warn his countrymen against what he felt to be their unjustified faith in the power of science, for it was midway through the German philosopher's stay in China that Chang delivered his famous lecture on this subject at Tsing Hua College.

Chang's attack on the prestige of science represented the introduction into China of a European philosophical tradition, most recently expounded by Boutroux, Bergson, and Eucken, which was specifically directed at defending the validity of an idealist view of life against the attacks of materialists and determinists. In China, however, this debate inevitably became intermixed with the very different controversy, then in progress, over the relative merits of Eastern and Western civilizations, in which idealism was seen as characteristic of the traditional, "Eastern" order, and materialism as the distinctive feature of modern, Western civilization. Chang increased the natural confusion between these two very different questions by praising in the conclusion to his lecture the spiritual civilization developed in China by Confucius, Mencius, and the Neo-Confucian philosophers of the Sung, Yüan, and Ming dynasties, suggesting in addition that the modern West stood in need of their wisdom.[51]

Within a few months Chang's lecture stirred up a major controversy among the Chinese intelligentsia. The country's leading scientist, Ting Wen-chiang, launched a counterattack, asserting that philosophical problems could only be solved by scientific methods, and warning that modern science had been so recently introduced into China that to disparage it would endanger its much-needed growth. Hu Shih, a disciple of John Dewey, joined in on the side of scientific method, and Ch'en Tu-hsiu, in an effort to make political capital out of the debate, challenged both Ting and Hu to choose between idealism and historical materialism. Hu refused to sit on the horns of the dilemma Ch'en had fashioned for him, and put forward an agnostic, "scientific view of life." Liang Ch'i-ch'ao, now regarded as the elder statesman among the intellectuals, at first remained above the battle, issuing a "statement of temporary neutrality" along with a set of rules for keeping the debate from straying too far afield. A few weeks later he decided to enter the fray in support of Chang Chün-mai, and argued that science and metaphysics each had its separate sphere: "In matters concerning the intellect, man absolutely must use the methods of science; in matters concerning the emotions, man absolutely must use meta-science [i.e., metaphysics]." Few of the eighteen leading intellectuals taking part in the controversy were willing to concede even this much to metaphysics, and by the end of 1923, when the tumult of charges and countercharges had died away, it was clear that the protagonists of "science" were in the majority.[52]

Rumblings of the storm of protest aroused by Chang's speech were just beginning to be heard when in April 1923 Leonard Elmhirst arrived in Peking on his "exploratory journey" on behalf of Tagore. While lecturing on Tagore and his Visva-Bharati at Yenching University, Tsing Hua College, and Peking Union Medical College, Elmhirst came to know two young men who were close to Chang and had spent considerable time with Driesch during his travels in China. One was Chang's graduate assistant, the young philosopher of education Ch'ü Shih-ying; the other was Chang's former brother-in-law, the famous poet and

Tagore and Gandhi, Santiniketan, 1940

Tagore and Tōyama Mitsuru, 1924

aesthete Hsü Chih-mo. When Elmhirst told them Tagore was interested in visiting China if his expenses could be defrayed, the two were so overjoyed that they clapped their hands and stamped their feet, then ran to see Chang and Liang to find out if a formal invitation could be sent the Indian poet-philosopher. By June 6 sufficient funds had been raised from the Lecture Association's supporters to enable its secretary to cable Tagore offering him $1000 for expenses and asking him to come as soon as he could — by July or August if possible. "In any case we are glad that you have made up your mind to visit China, and the news has proved a tremendous joy to all your admirers already," the cablegram added.[53]

When the Indian poet finally arrived, ten months later, it was Chang, Ch'ü, and Hsü who met him at the dock, Chang who held receptions for him at the beginning and end of his tour, and Hsü who interpreted for him throughout. And behind all three men, supporting them morally and financially, stood the half-hidden but widely respected figure of Liang Ch'i-ch'ao.

Toward the Meeting of East and East

Even as Tagore made ready to accept the hospitality of the Lecture Association, he found himself beset with doubts. What good could he do in China? The Chinese people had their own poets, thinkers, and teachers, their own wisdom, capacities, and ideas; they needed no support or stimulation from outsiders. As if his mind had not earlier been set on going, he asked himself: "I am only a poet. Why do they want me to go to China? And why should I go?"[54]

He found several answers when writing to his old friend Rothenstein. One was "my mission which does not allow me any rest but drives me across long distances to strange surroundings." And, as before, Rabindranath felt himself out of tune with his own countrymen:

> The time is not at all favorable in India for me to persuade our people of the importance of the reconciliation of the East and West. They all seem to think that it can wait till we are powerful enough to negotiate with the West on equal terms, till the Western people are compelled for the sake of expediency to come to a mutual understanding. It is the pride of nationalism which stands in the way of a spiritual ideal. It is very much like saying that until we are rich we need not be honest, that

first we must have material power and then we shall be in a position to seek for spiritual perfection. Unfortunately such has been the brutal lesson of facts in the history of all powerful nations in the world, and the idealists have to fight against tremendous odds when they have to assert that there are truths which transcend all facts. . . . All the same the fact is that man is man and we must keep reminding him of it by constantly appealing to his humanity. I have taken that task in my country though the time is unfavourable[,] the minds of the people being overcast with storm clouds of resentment.[55]

The task was hard, he concluded, but he could not shirk it. "I have occasional doubts in my mind as to whether I have not strayed away from my own true vocation; — if that be so I have come too far off my track to be able to retrace my steps. I must jog on to the end of my days even though I feel weary and homesick for the solitude where my dreams had their early rest." [56]

Even after the arrangements for his visit to China had been completed, Rabindranath expressed doubts about what the trip would accomplish. Would it raise his flagging spirits? he wondered in another letter to Rothenstein: "I have an invitation to China where I shall go in the beginning of March next year. I shall have to be away for about six months or more[.] I do not yet know whether the change of environment will give me rest and detachment which I need so much or whether the strain will be too much for the present state of my health." [57]

News of his puzzled state of mind reached Romain Rolland as well, at first through Pearson, who visited Rolland in September 1923, and then in a letter from the poet himself. Pearson reported that Tagore was "isolated," and "suffering from his inability to abandon himself to his sacred calling, poetry. His health is adversely affected. He dreams of fleeing. Just now he talks of leaving this winter for China." [58] Not long before his actual departure in March 1924 Rabindranath confided to Rolland in a long letter that he felt torn between two opposing inner forces:

I . . . have a kind of civil war constantly going on in my own nature between my personality as a creative artist, who necessarily must be solitary and that as an idealist who must realise himself through works of complex character needing a large field of collaboration with a large body of men. . . . I earnestly hope that I shall be rescued in time before I die — in the meantime I go to China, in what capacity, I do not know. Is it as a poet or as a bearer of good advice and sound common sense? [59]

The complex arrangements he made for the voyage leave little doubt that the restless idealist triumphed over the solitary poet on this occasion, as on so many previous ones. Wisely foreseeing that his visit to China could take on an added significance as a renewal of the ancient cultural links between India and her northeastern neighbor, Rabindranath raised funds to enable three other Indian intellectuals to accompany him.[60] The artist Nandalal Bose, the Sanskritist Kshitimohan Sen, and the historian Kalidas Nag gladly accepted his invitation to constitute a Visva-Bhrati mission to China. Speaking on their behalf the day before they sailed, Tagore told the press:

> When the invitation from China reached me I felt that it was an invitation to India herself, and as her humble son, I must accept it. . . . In the midst of strife and conflict of contending commerce and politics, of monstrous greed and hatred, of wholesale destruction, India has still her message of salvation to offer to the world. . . . She has kept her faith in the unity of man and boldly asserted that he only knows truth who knows the unity of all beings in spirit. . . . Visva-Bharati has accepted this ideal as its own and is asking the whole world to share in all that is great and true in the common heritage of man. I am hoping that our visit will reestablish the cultural and spiritual connections between China and India. We shall invite scholars from China and try to arrange an exchange of scholars. If I can accomplish this, I shall feel happy.[61]

The strands of many motives interwove in Rabindranath's mind as he set out on one of the most exciting of his many foreign journeys. There was the call of the road, the desire for a change of scene, and perhaps for a more sympathetic public than he was finding in India. There was also the attraction of seeing at first hand a great civilization from which India had been too long cut off, and the hope of renewing ancient ties with it. Beyond and above these immediate considerations there was the grander hope of influencing the course of history itself by persuading China's intellectuals to embrace once more, as their ancestors had done centuries before, India's "message of salvation," thereby strengthening the spiritual civilization of the East which the world seemed so desperately to need. Paradoxically this image of the East had been imprinted in his mind again and again through his contacts with Western intellectuals. As he was to discover to his sorrow, India's poet-philosopher was dreaming dreams of Asia's glorious past precisely at the time when China's maturing leaders were seeing visions of an altogether different future.

CHAPTER FIVE

"THE REPRESENTATIVE OF ASIA"
VISITS CHINA

You are veiled, my beloved,
In a language unknown to me,
Like a hill which seems a cloud
Behind its mask of mists.

— Tagore to Mei Lan-fang

Buoyed up by the excitement of yet another odyssey, Tagore and his party sailed from Calcutta on the Japanese passenger freighter *Atsuta Maru* on March 21, 1924. Unlike his previous trip to East Asia, this one had been carefully arranged in advance, and a formal invitation to lecture in Peking had been received and accepted. Tagore had reason to hope that his 1916 failure in Japan would not be repeated.

Overture: Rangoon and Hong Kong

Unexpectedly, a stopover at Rangoon encouraged this hope. The Chinese community there, larger and better educated than their Calcutta brethren, organized a reception for the poet at the Chinese school, whose principal welcomed him with the assurance that his mission would "mark another epoch of great spiritual influence upon the people of China, such as had been felt in the days of the Tang dynasty." The principal spokesman for the Chinese community in Burma declared: "We fervently hope that this voyage of yours to China will prove a beacon light that will guide China and her sons to peace and goodwill." In his reply, Tagore accepted the mandate, for India, of light-bearer:

At one time the messengers from India went to China with a new philosophy of life. . . . When the messengers reached China and came into contact with life there, then there was a great illumination of mind and art. . . . We in the East have believed in some fundamental reality, some great philosophy of life, and if we can keep that truth in the centre of our being, then we have the privilege to walk abroad courting disaster and death and yet attain immortality. . . . That is the message which I shall take to your country.[1]

The two-week voyage from Rangoon to Hong Kong gave Tagore time to read and write out his ideas in the form of the lectures he was to deliver in China. Elmhirst had given him an English translation of Lao-tzu's aphorisms, and he was delighted to find them filled with familiar ideas. "This thought is so thoroughly Indian, and over and over again I am reminded of our own Upanishads," he exclaimed to Elmhirst.[2] He proceeded to organize his longest lecture around what he considered to be parallel quotations from Lao-tzu and the sages of ancient India:

> It is said in our scriptures: "In greed is sin, in sin, death." Your philosopher has said: "No greater calamity than greed". . . . Our sage in India says . . . "By the help of anti-dharma [unrighteousness] men prosper, they find what they desire, they conquer enemies, but they perish at the root." . . . The same warning was also given centuries ago by your sage when he said: "Things thrive and then grow old. This is called Un-Reason. Un-Reason soon ceases." [3]

Hong Kong, a British crown colony, gave Tagore his first and only contact with South China's intellectual and political leaders. Dr. Sun Yat-sen, the father of the 1911 revolution, sent his private secretary to invite the Indian poet to visit Canton, the capital of his Kuomintang government. Sun's invitation read:

> Dear Mr. Tagore,
>   I should greatly wish to have the privilege of personally welcoming you on your arrival in China. It is an ancient way of ours to show honour to the Scholar. But in you I shall greet not only a writer who has added lustre to Indian letters but a rare worker in those fields of endeavour wherein lie the seeds of man's future welfare and spiritual triumphs.
>   May I then have the pleasure of inviting you to Canton?
>   Yours sincerely,
>   Sun Yat-sen[4]

Tagore declined, not wishing to postpone further his arrival in North China, but agreed to visit Sun on his return from Peking. During the interview, he revealed his desire to act as a peacemaker among the war-ring factions in China, and through the Kuomintang leader's private secretary he urged upon Sun Yat-sen the necessity for an end to the hostilities between North and South China.[5] Two years later the Kuomintang was to begin its Northern Campaign, which successfully unified most of China, not through a cessation of hostilities, but through their intensification.[6]

The vice-chancellor of the University of Amoy, Lim Boon Keng, came personally to ask Tagore to visit his campus, and described his plan to create a special chair of Indian culture and history at the university.[7] Tagore again excused himself, pleading his prior engagement in Peking, but the prospect of an exchange of scholars and students between China's universities and his own excited him. "There should be no delay in building the Birla Sadan [guest house] to accommodate the scholars of China," he wrote to Santiniketan. "The first scholars should be given a good welcome and everything should be done for their comfort." [8]

ACT ONE: SHANGHAI, HANGCHOW, SHANGHAI

A sizable crowd was waiting on the dock as the *Atsuta Maru* steamed into Shanghai harbor on the morning of April 12. Waiting to welcome, garland, and be photographed with the famous poet were members of the Indian community (composed mainly of Sikh policemen or bank guards and Parsi businessmen), along with representatives of various Chinese educational and literary organizations in Shanghai.[9] Newspapermen, as usual, were on hand to interview the Nobel Laureate. Asked about the purpose of his visit, Tagore replied succinctly: "My general idea is to advocate Eastern thought, the revival of traditional Asian culture, and the unity of the peoples of Asia." He was already aware that such ideas might not be popular with some of China's young people, and took the occasion to address himself to this group:

> There is one section of the youth of Asia which denies the value of ancient Asian civilization, and follows the ideas in Western civilization, trying its best to absorb them. This is a great mistake. . . . Western civilization is simply interested in material things, and has many defects in its spiritual life. This point is obvious when we look at the bankruptcy of European culture after the World War. . . . On the other

hand, Eastern civilization is the soundest and most healthy civilization, and has often enabled us Eastern peoples to achieve great things. For this reason, Europeans have already recognized the true value of Eastern civilization, and have started to study it.[10]

Slightly contradicting his assertion that Eastern civilization was sound and healthy, Tagore concluded: "If we wish to resurrect this precious, noble, lofty, and pure Eastern civilization, the peoples of China, Japan, and India . . . must unite together . . . to demonstrate to the world our Oriental culture and our special qualities, so that the true value and fame of the Asian peoples will be made known." [11]

The first Chinese intellectuals Tagore was able to talk with in Shanghai were the representatives of the Peking Lecture Association, who met him at the dock and escorted him to the Burlington Hotel, the best in the city. All three men could speak fluent English, and this made conversation easier than it had been for Tagore in Japan in 1916, where such fluency was rare. Liveliest of the group as they talked at the hotel that evening was the American- and Cambridge-educated poet Hsü Chih-mo, who was to act as Tagore's chief interpreter during his seven weeks in China. Of graver mien was Chang Chün-mai, the idealist philosopher and disciple of Rudolf Eucken, and founder-president of the National Institute of Self-Government in Shanghai. Tagore was most impressed with Chang's assistant, Ch'ü Shih-ying, a Columbia Ph.D. in education, and felt that he was less Westernized in his outlook than Hsü or Chang.[12]

Chang acted as host the following afternoon to about one hundred Chinese intellectuals and students who gathered in his garden to drink tea and sit on the grass to hear Tagore's maiden speech in China. Hsü first told the gathering that despite "the prevailing spirit of scepticism" pervading the country, "he hoped that the radiant personality, the profound philosophy and the irresistible poetry of the Great Messenger from India would dissipate all doubts, disarm scepticism and revitalise the spiritual thoughts of China." [13]

Tagore spoke without notes, and his clear English diction, his tall, stately figure, and handsomely bearded face made a striking impression on his listeners. Apologizing for his late arrival, he confessed that he had been troubled by doubts about the purpose of his trip to China, and that he had delayed his departure from India partly because he could not resolve them: "I shall make a confession. When I had your invitation I felt nervous; I had read so many conflicting opinions about your religion and your customs that I asked myself: 'What is it these people expect when they invite me to their country, and what message is it necessary for me to take for their welfare?' " [14] From his remarks one gathers that he still had not decided whether he had come to China as a poet or as a prophet. His attempt to bring a message to Japan eight years earlier had small success; he would not have wanted to repeat that failure. On the other hand, he could not relinquish the hope that his cherished ideals would receive a sympathetic response in China.

What are poets for? he asked. "They are for capturing on their instruments the secret stir of life in the air and giving it voice in the music of prophecy." "A poet's mission is . . . to inspire faith in the dream which is unfulfilled." Then he grew hesitant again, exclaiming, "Do not make use of a poet to carry messages! . . . I am not a philosopher." The prophet soon triumphed over the poet, however, as he continued: "I want to win your heart, now that I am close to you, with the faith that is in me of a great future for you, and for Asia, when your country rises and gives expression to its own spirit — a future in the joy of which we shall all share." [15]

The spirit of China and the spirit of India merged in Tagore's mind into the spirit of Asia. Reminding his first Chinese audience of "the day when India claimed you as brothers and sent you her love," he called for a renewal of this relationship, which was "hidden in the heart of all of us — the people of the East. The path to it may be overgrown with the grass of centuries, but we shall find traces of it still." Reopening "this path of friendship between India and China" could also bring together "our neighbors all over Asia." This pan-Asian revival would be purely spiritual, he insisted: "Asia is again waiting for such dreamers to come and carry on the work, not of fighting, not of profit-making, but of establishing bonds of spiritual relationship." [16]

Although he did not explicitly call for a revival of Buddhism in these closing remarks, Tagore clearly had in mind the era when Buddhism and Indian culture had been introduced into China, and throughout this trip he and his party took pride in identifying traces of this cultural influence still visible on the Chinese scene. On his very first day in Shanghai he was driven to the outskirts of the city to see an old Buddhist temple. Although its decayed state depressed him, he commented: "If a thing is dead, let it go, it only cumbers the ground." Two days later, on April 14, Hsü Chih-mo escorted him on a train trip to the nearby city of Hangchow, capital of Chekiang Province, whose famed Western Lake had earned it the reputation of being China's most beautiful city. Near a Buddhist temple three members of his party were shown a picture carved in a rock depicting an Indian monk who had preached Buddhism on that very spot centuries before.[17]

Calling attention to this ancient precedent for his own lecture tour, Tagore told several thousand students, assembled under the auspices of the Provincial Educational Society, that he was "a descendant of the same ancestors" from whom the monk came, and "some memory of that glorious time when India did send her messengers of love to this land" was still alive in their minds. "This was the great task of India in the past, the task of building paths over obstacles." Tagore announced that he had taken up that task again. "My friends," he said, "this is my mission. I have come to ask you to re-open the channel of communion which I hope is still there. . . . I shall consider myself fortunate if, through this visit, China comes nearer to India and India to China — for no political or commercial purpose, but for disinterested human love and for nothing else." His ultimate ideal was a pluralistic world, bound not by political or economic ties, but by the mutual recognition of the diverse expressions of the human spirit. "For differences can never be wiped away, and life would be so much the poorer without them. Let all human races keep their own personalities, and yet come together, not in a uniformity that is dead, but in a unity that is living." [18]

In spite of the rainy weather, so many students had come to see and hear Tagore that the hall was crowded to overflowing, and tremendous applause followed Hsü's translation of each portion of the address. Following it, Tagore and his party were invited to tea with the leading educators of Chekiang. The oldest living poet of the province, Ch'en San-li, on being introduced to his fellow-poet, "was deeply moved" and shook his hands "with affectionate awe." Tagore was in an optimistic mood; about this time he wrote home: "We are receiving great kindness from everybody here. I feel that very cordial relations will soon be established." [19]

Returning to Shanghai after this two-day excursion, Tagore delivered his major address in that city on April 18 to over twelve hundred listeners gathered in the new auditorium of the Commercial Press, China's largest publishing house. Twenty-five different civic and cultural associations sponsored the afternoon meeting. Like so many of ancient India's Buddhist scriptures, the original text of this lecture has been lost and only its Chinese translation remains. Rendering Tagore's lecture into English, we find that he again began by disclaiming any pretensions to prophecy. "I have come to China, not with the attitude of a tourist . . . or as a missionary bringing a gospel, but only as one seeking wisdom, like a pilgrim wishing to pay homage to the ancient culture of China, in an attitude of reverence and love." [20]

Despite this modest prologue, Tagore did have a message for China. What he had seen in one of her largest industrial centers made him fear for her future:

> I am a poet, not a politician nor a diplomat, and can only say what I feel most sincerely in my heart. I feel that China is now going the same way as India. I love culture, I love life. I cannot bear to see Chinese culture endangered day by day. Therefore I sincerely warn you: know that happiness is the growth of the power of the soul. Know that it is absolutely worthless to sacrifice all spiritual beauty to obtain the so-called material civilization of the West!

The poet ended with a full-throated appeal to his Chinese listeners to help India build up the civilization he felt the world so desperately needed. "Friends! The time has come! We must use all our strength to speak for humanity, to struggle against the nightmarish demon of matter. Do not surrender to his power. Bring the world to idealism, to humanism, and destroy materialism!" [21]

A demonstration of Chinese painting and a concert of classical lute music had followed the garden party at Chang Chün-mai's house. At Hangchow he had enjoyed seeing the pavilions surrounding the Western Lake and been feted with another concert of classical music. After this lecture at the Commercial Press auditorium, Shanghai's leading educators took him to dinner at the Kung Teh Lin Vegetable restaurant where Chinese music was played, and from there the party went to a traditional Chinese play at the Ti-i Tai (Number One) Theater.[22]

The time had come for the poet and his party to leave China's largest city and move on to Peking by the usual inland route. Embarking on a river steamer, they journeyed up the Yangtse toward Nanking. Watching the moon rise over the eastwardly receding water, Tagore and Hsü

Chih-mo talked far into the night, comparing notes on the poets they had enjoyed during their student days in England.[23]

ENTR'ACTE: NANKING AND TSINAN

In Nanking the first order of business on April 20 was to call on the military governor, General Ch'i Hsieh-yüan, the warlord controlling Kiangsu, Kiangsi, and Anhwei. Tagore knew enough about modern China to realize that in the chaotic years following the collapse of the Ch'ing dynasty in 1911 a variety of provincial warlords had seized power and were still contending with one another like crabs in a basket. Seeing that such civil strife both weakened China and threatened his hopes for a revival of her traditional culture, Tagore begged General Ch'i to desist from fighting, "for the sake not only of China but of Asia and of all humanity." The general, having served champagne to all present, told the poet he was in full accord with his message and blandly assured him that he, too, was "at heart a believer in peace." Five months later, General Ch'i renewed his attack on the warlord of Chekiang; not long afterward his forces were routed and he fled into exile in Japan.[24]

The warlord's subordinate, the civil governor Han Tze-sui, showed a more genuine enthusiasm for the poet's ideals, for he told Tagore that he had been reading his speeches in the daily newspapers, and especially liked his principal talk in Shanghai. The elderly governor expressed the gratitude that he and other Buddhist scholars felt to Tagore. "For seven hundred years we have waited for a message from India," he said. "And here you are. This, Dr. Tagore, is a great anniversary." Governor Han also declared himself ready to do everything possible to encourage an exchange of students between India and China. He went on to caution the poet that his message would probably be misunderstood by China's "modern generation." [25]

More than a thousand members of this "modern generation" filled the gymnasium of the National Southeastern University that afternoon to hear and see Tagore. "Though there was much confusion," a contemporary observer relates, "due to the crowds coming and going, and the speakers were hard to hear in the big hall, yet both the dramatic appearance and the words of the Indian visitor were quite impressive." So many students crowded into the balcony immediately over his head that it groaned audibly and seemed about to collapse. It was not evacuated, but the poet calmly ignored the danger and launched into his speech.[26]

Taking his cue from Governor Han's advice, he began by identifying himself with the students' point of view. "I feel highly honoured, not so much because your elders have honoured me, but because I feel the silent invitation from the young." Appealing to their romantic sense of chivalry, he continued: "Today the human soul is lying captive in the dungeon of Giant Machine, and I ask you, my young princes, to feel this enthusiasm in your hearts and be willing to rescue the human soul from the grip of greed which keeps it chained." In one of his few references to the evils of nationalism, which he had attacked so vigorously in his lectures in Japan, Tagore called this "the darkest age in human civilization," because "individual races are shut up within their own limits, calling themselves nations, which barricade themselves . . . with prohibitions of all kinds." But he saw a new age dawning, an age in which "the immense power of sacrifice" would triumph over "the malevolent intellect of brute greed and egotism." Though not elaborating on what he meant by "the power of sacrifice," he seemed to equate it broadly with individuality: "Know that no organization however big can help you, no league of prudence or of power, but only the individual with faith in the infinite, the invisible, the incorruptible, the fearless. . . . Proclaim the Spirit of Man and prove that it lies not in machine-guns and cleverness, but in a simple faith." As always, Tagore hoped that this new humanism would originate in Asia, the homeland of the world's great religions: "Let the morning of this new age dawn in the East, from which great streams of idealism have sprung in the past, making the fields of life fertile with their influence." [27]

From Nanking the poet and his party traveled northward by train, breaking their journey at Ch'ü-fu to pay homage to the tomb of Confucius. Here in Shantung Province, one of the oldest centers of Chinese civilization, Tagore also met two Buddhist leaders, one the head of a group of Buddhist women, the other a magistrate presiding over a local society for the revival of Chinese Buddhism.[28] At Tsinan, the capital of the province, the poet spent an eventful day on April 22. A crowd of several thousand students turned out to hear his talk at the Provincial Assembly Hall, a number so large that the meeting had to be moved outside to the adjoining courtyard. Tagore spoke extemporaneously on "Materialism and the Spiritual Life," observing that he was almost sure his message of idealism would not be accepted by the majority, but that this did not matter to him, since his function was to realize and to pronounce "Truth." Hearty applause followed the lecture, however, and another audience of two hundred was waiting at the Shantung Christian University to hear him explain his educational ideals.[29]

ACT TWO: PEKING

Only a day's journey now separated Tagore from Peking, for centuries the political and cultural capital of China. In the year 1924, however, the city was far from being the center of political power it had been before 1911 and has become since 1949. Disparaging Peking's status, an American-managed Shanghai newspaper wrote at the time, that if it were not for warlord Wu P'ei-fu's support of the corrupt Peking government, and the fact that for convenience's sake most of the foreign powers recognized it as the legitimate capital of the Republic of China, Peking would become "what it really is in truth — a sprawling, rundown, shabby country town half buried in the dust of the plains of Chihli — interesting for the tourist and archeologist but of no practical value as the seat of government of a great nation." [30]

A legal fiction may seem wraithlike and fragile, but when attached to a city rich in history and culture it can acquire a remarkable durability. Peking's many temples, walls, gateways, lakes, boulevards, and the imperial palace itself had been accumulating the merit of antiquity ever since the fifteenth century, when the Ming Emperor Yung Lo had rebuilt the city near the site of the older Mongol capital. In the twentieth century the creation of the National University of Peking, the National Normal University, and a dozen or so first-class colleges had increased the cultural riches of the capital and attracted thousands of able students. As in previous centuries, many of the most learned scholars in the country had chosen to make their homes in this beautiful northern city. Here, in short, were the leading intellectuals — both young and old — whose minds Tagore had to win if he was to succeed in his mission to China.[31]

General Ch'i Hsieh-yüan had attached a special private car for Tagore's use on the Blue Express luxury train running from Nanking through Tsinan to Peking. On its part, the Peking government furnished the train with a special military guard to escort the visitors from India.[32] This was no mere gesture, for bandits had held up this same train the year before, kidnaped its thirty-five European and American passengers, and held them as hostages in a mountain redoubt for over a month. For such a fate to befall so renowned a guest as Tagore would reveal to the whole world the hollowness of the Peking government's claim to control even the plains of North China, let alone the whole of the country.

In Tientsin the president of the Peking Lecture Association, Liang Ch'i-ch'ao, boarded the train to greet Tagore and traveled with him the remaining seventy-five miles to the capital. A large and enthusiastic crowd of students and intellectuals was waiting at Peking's Chien Men station as the Blue Express arrived at 7:15 on the evening of April 23. As an Indian member of the party reported the scene, there was "a tremendous ovation" as the poet left the train "amidst showering of flowers and [the] uncanny sound of [fire-]crackers — a queer form of Chinese hospitality." The most distinguished welcomers were Lin Ch'ang-min, a retired statesman and a close associate of Liang Ch'i-ch'ao, and Dr. Chiang Mon-lin, the acting vice-chancellor of Peking University. As at Shanghai, members of the Indian community came forward to greet and garland their compatriot.[33]

After resting for a day in the luxurious Hotel de Pekin, Tagore launched himself onto the turbulent stream of Peking intellectual life. Curiously enough, his first, and most widely reported, public address in the capital was delivered to the Anglo-American Association at its luncheon meeting in the Wagon Lits Hotel. In a sort of *apologia pro vita sua*, Tagore explained that during his 1912 visit to England it had been "indeed a great experience for me to know the great minds of Britain. I was enabled to make some of the truest friends in England that man ever had. . . . It was then that I learned what freedom meant, and I could live in a larger world that breathed the air of untrammelled freedom." His next visit to Europe, after World War I, had convinced him that "the nations of the West were looking for some new ideal from the East which would reconstruct their civilization on a better basis. . . . This looking to the East touched me deeply." He had therefore felt it his personal responsibility to "help bring together the two hemispheres which were drifting apart every day." By implication he was saying that his purpose in coming to China was not to create hostility to Western civilization, but to strengthen the unity of Eastern civilization as a necessary step toward achieving a complementary relationship between the two.[34]

That same afternoon some fifty of China's leading scholars and dignitaries welcomed the Indian poet at a special reception and tea fittingly held beside the Chung Hai (Middle Lake) in the impressive Throne Hall of Imperial Splendor, where the Chinese emperors had received the homage of ambassadors from outlying kingdoms.[35] Liang Ch'i-ch'ao introduced Tagore to the select group with a beautiful talk on "The brotherly relations between the cultures of India and China," in which he emphasized China's manifold debt to her "elder brother" in the realms of philosophy, religion, literature, music, the visual arts, medicine, astronomy, education, and social organization. Liang commended Tagore for his mission of friendship and remarked, "If we can avail of this occasion to renew the intimate relationship which we had with India and to establish a really constructive scheme of co-operation, then our welcome to Rabindranath Tagore will have real significance." [36]

Tagore replied with a brief but effective presentation of his message to China's intellectuals. "Great men came centuries ago from India to greet your ancestors," he began. "I have come as a representative of that same culture, yet also as a representative of the present age — a mixture which has not yet settled down to anything satisfactory — an age of transition." Even though he disclaimed having brought a message to China, he exhorted his listeners: "In Asia we must seek our strength in union, in an unwavering faith in righteousness, and never in the egoistic spirit of separateness and self-assertion. It is from the heart of the East that the utterance has sprung forth: 'The meek shall inherit the earth.'" Hearing the New Testament quoted as though it were their own heritage may have surprised the Chinese intellectuals, but the Indian poet had grown up with the idea that Jesus Christ was an Oriental whose teachings were better understood by Asians than by Westerners.[37]

The uniquely spiritual character of a united Asian civilization as Tagore presented it in this lecture seemed to blend Christian, Buddhist, and Hindu attitudes. "It would be a degradation on our part, and an insult to our ancestors," he argued, "if we forgot our own moral wealth of wisdom," especially at a time when the people of the West had "given up their faith in a spiritual perfection of life. Their doom is upon them, and when we in the East become enamoured of their success, we must know that the terrific glow we see upon the western horizon is not the glow of sunrise, or of a new birth-fire, but is a conflagration of passion." The East must "accept truth when it comes from the West," but must never forget that "the Western people also need our help, for our destinies are now intertwined." Therefore, "in Asia we must unite, not through some mechanical method of organisation, but through a spirit of true sympathy," and in that spirit must approach the West, neither hating nor slavishly imitating her civilization. He concluded: "Let us try to win the heart of the West with all that is best and not base in us, and think of her and deal with her, not in revenge or contempt, but with goodwill and understanding, in a spirit of mutual respect." [38]

Liang repeated his welcoming address the following afternoon, April 26, to a gathering of more than a thousand students of the government colleges of Peking who met in the auditorium of the National Normal University. Arriving more than an hour late, Tagore developed the theme that temporary gains achieved through violence and lies must eventually lead a nation to its destruction. "Reliance on power is the characteristic of barbarism," he declared. "It is cooperation and love, mutual trust and mutual aid which make for strength and real progress in civilization." [39]

A noticeably defensive tone runs through this address to the students, his first talk in Peking open to the Chinese public. Even before he left India, word had reached him that "some were opposed to my coming, because it might check your special modern enthusiasm for Western progress and force. True, if you want a man who will help you in these things, you have been mistaken in asking me. I have no help to give you here; you already have ten thousand able teachers, go to them." So intent was he on driving home his warning against reliance on force that he failed to make his usual appeal to the ancient spiritual links between India and China. Instead he proudly affirmed:

> I speak to you as a member of a nation that has gone under in the race for progress, and I tell you that I am ready to accept weakness and insult and oppression of the body, but I will never acknowledge the defeat, the last insult, the utter ruin, of my spirit being conquered, so that I am made to lose my faith and purpose. . . . We need to hear this again and again and never more than now in this modern world of slavery and cannibalism in decent guise: "By the help of unrighteousness men do prosper, men do gain victories over their enemies, men do attain what they desire; but they perish at the root." [40]

In contrast to this apparently skeptical audience, the several hundred young people awaiting him the following afternoon at the Fa Yüan Ssu (Temple of the origin of the [Buddhist] Law) could not have been more sympathetic. The Young Men's Buddhist Association, which arranged the meeting, had invited him in these words:

> Now You — the great Buddhist poet — come from the original country of the Buddha to our sister-country with all your milk of thought; surely as a result we realize your flowerly givings all world round where your elephant-like steps reach; and therefor[e] we are greatly glad for this. . . . You — as a star of great love, perfect gladness[,] unlimited goodness & continuous newness as well as a representative of the Buddhistic civilization — may kindly accept our request as we think.
> Hopis [hoping] your flowerly words with a reply.
> Yours respectively,
> Young Men's Buddhist Association
> (Y.M.B.A.)[41]

How could the poet resist such an appeal to visit a temple celebrated as a favorite resort of Peking's artists, especially at this season, when its gardens were alive with lilac and peony blossoms! The Temple of the origin of the Law also housed the largest Mahayana Buddhist monastery in the city, and contained many mementoes of the flourishing state of Buddhism during the T'ang period, over a thousand years earlier. In the minds of the Indian party and their Chinese Buddhist hosts the poet's visit therefore symbolized the renewal of contacts between their countries on the basis of this Buddhist tie.

Tagore was of course not a Buddhist, but he accepted without demur the role of Buddhist teacher in which his hosts were determined to cast him. "Tagore is the great philosopher proclaiming Eastern civilization (that is, Buddhist civilization)," the spokesman for his hosts declared. "Just like the child who is reunited with his mother after a long separation, so we are indescribably happy in our hearts." The poet responded with equal warmth to this welcome: "I feel as though I have come to a quiet place in ancient India. Therefore I am deeply moved. A great joy arises in my heart because I feel that the old civilization of India, which seemed to be dead, has revealed itself here today." Earlier in the day a Westerner had assured him that China was a most suitable place to prove the value of spiritual civilization. "This is absolutely correct," the poet agreed:

> My idea is to offer this mission to all mankind. I, too, wish to join my efforts with those of others in spreading this Buddhist message. . . . Mankind must have faith in spiritual life. Therefore, China and India must unite to accomplish this great task. . . . Gentlemen, you enlightened young people must share this responsibility. You cannot refuse this duty. The great spirit of Buddhism is not found in the man who would save the world but sits at home doing nothing. I hope you gentlemen will now exert yourselves.[42]

"The most sensational event of the days spent in Peking," according to one of the Indians with Tagore, was their visit to the ex-emperor of China, P'u-i, who still lived in the Forbidden City where as a tiny child he had reigned from 1908 until the Republican Revolution deposed him, with his dynasty, in 1912. The party arrived at ten o'clock Monday morning, April 27, at the Shen Wu Men (Gate of divine military genius), and were escorted by the ex-emperor's English tutor, Reginald Johnston, through courtyard after courtyard of the old imperial palace, one official after another falling behind as a gate was reached which his rank did not entitle him to enter. In keeping with the spirit of this scene of ancient but abandoned customs, the poet and the two ladies in his party were carried in sedan chairs. At length the party entered the inner apartments where the ex-emperor and his two wives graciously received them and accepted the gifts they had been advised to bring. Elmhirst presented P'u-i with a set of the poet's English works, and Tagore offered the queens some conch-shell bangles, a symbol of prosperity (a fitting choice in view of the difficulties that would face them after they fled the palace the following year to take refuge in Tientsin). Then, says an eyewitness, "The poet conveyed to the imperial party the greetings of India and gave them their blessings. He spoke of the ancient bonds of friendship between China and India and said that we wanted to re-establish old relations again."[43]

The visit was as much a novelty for the eighteen-year-old ex-emperor as for his guests, this being the first time his chamberlains had permitted him to receive foreigners and only the second time that ordinary Chinese citizens had been admitted to his presence. (In 1922 Hu Shih had set this precedent, and by addressing him as "Mr. P'u" had also expressed the irreverent attitude of the younger generation toward the Manchu house and the Confucian system which had held it in power.) With genuine pleasure the young P'u-i conducted his visitors through what one of them called "that gorgeous maze of imperial grandeur." Another noticed how Miss Lin (Lin Hui-yin), Tagore's beautiful young interpreter, like "a small bird in bright plumage, fluttered round the poet." [44]

A gay "banquet of scholars" was held in Tagore's honor that evening at the Navy Club. Present were several of the scholar-politicians surrounding Liang Ch'i-ch'ao (two of them, Lin Ch'ang-min and Fan Yüan-lien, had been cabinet ministers for a time in the shifting political scene after 1916), and some of the capital's literary men, led by Dr. Hu Shih, a founder of the literary revolution (or *pai hua*, "common speech" movement) and a prominent advocate of liberal democracy. Lin introduced the poet with a laudatory discourse: "We cannot tell him how moved and touched we are by his presence. . . . everything about him is poetic. He is in fact poetry itself." Lin politely hoped that Tagore would "reveal to us the reality of truth, the beauty of moral courage and sacrifice. I also am willing to wave my little banner behind the crowd and follow him round the whole world." [45]

Chinese civilization, said Tagore in his felicitous reply, could not have become so "deeply instinct with this spirit of hospitality," nor could it have endured so long, had it not been "full of the life of the spirit." He went on to speak for the first and only time in China about his own literary work and its roots in the popular devotional poetry of medieval India; this mystic verse was "modern," he insisted, because "all true things are ever modern and can never become obsolete." Claiming to be as much a "revolutionist" in his own language as some of his hosts were in theirs, he urged them to study Bengali in order truly to understand his poetry. "Languages are jealous," he explained. "You have to court them in person and dance attendance on them. . . . You cannot receive the smiles and glances of your sweetheart through an attorney, however diligent and dutiful he may be." At the end of this talk, Hu Shih rose to his feet and declared that Tagore's experiences in breaking away from the rigid canons of traditional literary forms exactly paralleled the struggle of China's new literary men to free themselves from the shackles of the past without losing their respect for the best in the culture of former ages. [46]

In his talks to smaller groups in Peking, Tagore showed a remarkable ability to speak on themes close to the hearts of his listeners. To the members of the Anglo-American Association he stressed the ideals of freedom and the spiritual unity of mankind; to Chinese Buddhists he spoke of the ancient days when their faith flourished both in China and in India; and to literary leaders he dwelt on his own development as a writer and poet. Faced with a large and general audience of intellectuals and students, however, he returned to the central message of Asia's spiritual civilization already expounded in his lectures in Shanghai, Hangchow, and Nanking. On April 28 he mounted the five-foot-high marble platform of the Hsien Nung-t'an (Altar of Agriculture) to address an estimated five to ten thousand listeners seated on the grass, most of them students. Looking out over the sea of upturned faces with his faithful translator Hsü at his side, Tagore asserted his claim to speak on behalf of all Asians: "You came to listen to me, but I know it is not to me, the personal man who comes from India, but you want to hear someone speak who is of Asia. You are glad that I have come to you as, in a sense, representing Asia. I feel myself that Asia has been waiting long and is still waiting to find her voice." There was a time, he declared, "when Asia saved the world from barbarism. Then came the night, I do not know how." There followed the intrusion of the West, so overwhelming Asia that she failed to recollect her own past and began to imitate foreign ways. "We are not aware of our own treasures," the poet mourned; "we must rise from our stupor, and prove that we are not beggars. . . . Search in your own homes for things that are of undying worth. Then you will be saved and will be able to save all humanity." Tagore's parting words reiterated his opening appeal to pan-Asian sentiment: "I hope, gentlemen, that you will not keep the memory of my white beard, but will remember the words of the representative of Asia who has come to you." [47]

Even as the poet talked he must have noticed young men circulating through the seated crowd handing out copies of a printed handbill. Perhaps he knew that this leaflet was a broadside attack on his message to China, for in Nanking also such handbills had been passed out, and in Shanghai, Elmhirst had noted on April 17 that there was "already opposition to the poet" on four grounds: that he was a pacifist, was against machinery, talked about the soul, and was not a Communist. His Chinese friends must have tried to minimize the critical tone of such attacks, but

Tagore may have seen an account published in the English-language press a few days later summarizing the contents of the anti-Tagore handbill distributed at the Altar of Agriculture:

> They claim that he is preaching against the systems which the Chinese hold sacred, that he opposes material civilization for China and that he favours the abolition of administration and government, which is tended [tends] to hasten China's destruction. Lastly the attack is directed against those scholars who invited Dr. Tagore to come to China to talk to the young men in an attempt to fill them with conservative and backward thoughts.[48]

INTERMISSION

In the space of four days, Tagore had put his message before the Peking public and had managed to do some sight-seeing as well. His public lectures under the auspices of the Peking Lecture Association were not scheduled to begin for another eleven days. He passed one more day in the capital, visiting two Western scholars of Asian culture and attending a meeting with a group of Chinese painters, on whom he urged the importance of closer ties between Indian and Chinese artists. He then motored to Tsing Hua College, ten miles northwest of the city, to spend the next week in retirement at a beautiful lakeside pavilion on the campus grounds.[49]

The Indian poet spoke informally at a reception in his honor on April 29, the day he arrived at Tsing Hua. Again the dissonant note of criticism was sounded as a group of students passed out opposition leaflets to the audience. Two days later he voiced concern for the survival of China's great cultural heritage at a meeting of all the students and faculty. A new age had dawned, he said, in this period, "which is one of the greatest in the whole history of man!" All cultures were coming together as the world was becoming one. "We must justify our own existence. We must show, each in our own civilisation, that which is universal," he declared. "What out of your own house can you offer in homage to this new age?" "Do you know your own mind? Your own culture? What is best and most permanent in your own history?"[50]

Answering his own questions, the poet went on to extoll the virtues of Chinese civilization, as he understood them. Some Chinese had told him that they were a pragmatic and materialistic people. "I cannot, however, bring myself to believe that any nation in this world can be great and yet be materialistic." His own idea, "superstition if you like," was that "no people in Asia can be wholly given to materialism. There is something in the blue vault of the sky, in the golden rays of the sun, in the wide expanse of the starlit night . . . which somehow gives to us an understanding of the inner music of existence." Peking itself was proof of "a marvellous beauty of human association," in sharp contrast to Shanghai, Tientsin, and other modern cities, which were "huge demons of ugliness." If the Chinese permitted the "deformity" created by "gross utility" to encroach still further on their landscape, they would be unable to contribute to the world their "genius for turning everything to beauty." "It is your mission," charged the poet, "to prove that love for the earth, and for the things of the earth, is possible without materialism — love without a stain of greed." [51]

Tsing Hua College had been founded with funds China had agreed to pay the United States for damages to American property during the Boxer uprising of 1900, and it functioned as a training center for Chinese students preparing themselves to take advanced degrees in the United States. Many of its faculty were Americans, and the syllabus was patterned on American models. The students, some of whom began their work there at the secondary level, spoke such fluent English that when Hsü Chih-mo began as usual to translate Tagore's lecture into Chinese they simply got up and left the hall. Those specializing in English literature and thought were best able to appreciate the romanticism and idealism which the Indian poet had also derived in part from the English heritage. Tagore enjoyed his informal talks with such students, who are said to have "besieged" him with questions. One afternoon he accompanied a group of them on a walk to the nearby Jade Fountain and its pagodas, not far from the grounds of the imperial summer palace, which had been destroyed by British and French troops in the 1860 occupation of Peking. On seeing these graceful monuments, Tagore delivered an improptu talk on art to his student friends. [52]

After a week's relaxation in these idyllic suburban surroundings, Tagore returned to Peking on Monday, May 5, and took up residence in a private house. Here he worked on his public lectures, scheduled to begin on May 9, and received callers. Dr. Hu Shih, the most outstanding

English-speaking scholar in Peking despite his youth, came to breakfast on May 6. Hu had interpreted for John Dewey, his former teacher at Columbia University, and had met Bertrand Russell during his lecture tour in China, and naturally was interested in learning more about the Indian philosopher-poet who succeeded them.

Hu had read the newspaper version of Tagore's Tsing Hua speech and was curious to know if the poet really meant to condemn the large cities as such and return to nature. Tagore replied that the ideal city should act as a center of culture, radiating its influence out into the countryside. He described the wandering *baul* minstrels of his native Bengal, who brought poetry, music, and story to the villager's very door, and so kept the culture of the past alive in the hearts and minds of the people. In the West, Tagore felt, interest in Shakespeare had only been kept alive with the help of committees and benefit teas.[53]

The English teachers of North China, who gave a luncheon for Tagore that same day at Yenching University Women's College, might have taken exception to this judgment, for most of them had studied English literature in American and English colleges. The poet spoke to them, not about literature, but about his dislike of formal education and the need for an "atmosphere of culture in which freedom of thought and individuality are nurtured." "Everyone must reach through education some great ideal — the ideal of the age," he asserted. The ideal of the present age was to create "a bond of relationship among men of all nations." Therefore, "Our education must aim to make every child a fulfillment of the spiritual ideal of the present age — which is sympathy, understanding and love between people." [54]

The lovely Miss Lin accompanied the poet on this occasion, and when he repeated his remarks for the benefit of the students after the luncheon he may have had her in mind in saying that his cordial reception by the women of China had been one of his finest experiences.[55] It is no secret that Tagore enjoyed the conversation and company of young women, and the prose poem he wrote for Miss Lin neatly conveys his attention to, and his correct distance from, the fair sex in the late afternoon of his life:

> The blue of the sky fell in love with the green
> of the earth.
> The breeze between them sighs "Alas!" [56]

Some of the girl students at the college showed that they entertained similar poetic sentiments toward their handsome visitor: "We look on you as we look upon the summit of a mountain. In order to show our deep reverence we want to ask you to come to our College at the time of the setting sun or after the rising moon, when we have finished our classes. . . . We wish you 'peace in all your ways' with great respect." [57]

Tagore's sixty-third birthday, the twenty-fifth of Baishakh according to the Bengali calendar, fell on May 8, and his Chinese hosts rose to the occasion with an evening of festivities. A new group calling itself the Crescent Moon Society, organized shortly before (apparently borrowing its name from the title of Tagore's book of prose poems *Crescent Moon*), arranged a birthday party. The poet Hsü Chih-mo was the moving spirit of the society, Hu Shih was active in it, and some eighty intellectuals, most of them former students in England or the United States, came to its later meetings in a spacious Peking house.[58]

The evening celebration in the auditorium of the Peking Normal University, attended by four hundred of the capital's most distinguished citizens, was the high point of Tagore's stay in China. Liang Ch'i-ch'ao presented the guest of honor with a pair of seals and a stone tablet inscribed with the Chinese characters he had chosen to form Tagore's Chinese name. Rather than take three characters imitating the mere sound of parts of the foreign name, the usual method, Liang had chosen an ancient character for India (竺 *chu*, "bamboo") and two characters used in Buddhist texts to denote China (震 *chen*, "thunder," and 旦 *tan*, "dawn"), thus capturing the significance of Tagore's visit as creating a link between India and China. Liang gave a double meaning to the last two characters, for they could be taken as translations of the Sanskrit components of the poet's first name, Rabindra: Indra being a god of the thunderstorm, and *rabi* being a Sanskrit term for the sun (in the Chinese character 旦 the sun 日 is seen rising over the horizon 一). Seen in still another dimension, the name was a kind of epithet for Tagore himself, "the Thundering Dawn of India." After explaining this linguistic tour de force, Liang expressed his hope that "our warm love for him will follow this new name," and that "the ancient love between India and China may be revived in the person of Chu Chen-tan." [59]

Hu Shih, who had translated for Liang, offered as his birthday gift a scroll on which he had penned a Chinese poem of his own composition. "Parināmana" extolled the ideal of the bodhisattva who unselfishly turns back from entering Nirvana in order to help his fellow men attain their own salvation. (The poem, written in 1922, seems to reflect Hu's personal feelings as an American-educated Doctor of Philosophy who returned to China to help his own people attain higher levels of education.) After reading his English translation of the poem, Hu added the hope that it might "serve also to remind us of the intimate historical and cultural relationship between India and China — a relationship, which, though long interrupted, is now being renewed through the present visit of our poet and his friends." [60]

After these speeches, gifts of flowers and paintings were presented and the three Indian members of the poet's party offered their compliments: Kshitimohan Sen by reciting a Sanskrit ode, Kalidas Nag a poem from Tagore's *Balākā,* and Nandalal Bose by offering a picture. Tagore himself then took the stage, "to the sound of thunderous applause," thanked his Chinese friends for baptizing him with a Chinese name, and hoped that it would be perpetuated in history alongside those of his compatriots who came to China in ages past but who were still remembered and talked about. He explained his motive in writing the English-language play which was about to be staged, and, after a brief pause, the curtain rose on an amateur performance of *Chitra,* the drama of a homely princess' successful attempt to woo a handsome prince. The play had evidently been rehearsed under Tagore's direction, for China's leading actor, Mei Lan-fang, seated next to the Indian poet, questioned him (through an interpreter) about the Indian style of the costumes and the *mise en scène,* and jotted down Tagore's replies for his own future use. Miss Lin played the heroine, and Hsü Chih-mo, much in love with her at this time, was cast as the god of love. (Hsü would have preferred the role of the sought-after prince. The play forecast his own disappointment, for Miss Lin, the daughter of Lin Ch'ang-min, later married the son of her father's close friend, Liang Ch'i-ch'ao.) Though the play was an abridged version of the original, the performance did not end until nearly midnight.[61]

ACT THREE: PEKING

Tagore mounted the lecture platform a little after eleven o'clock the following morning to begin his announced series of seven public lectures under the auspices of the Lecture Association. The True Light (Chen Kuang) Theater, the city's largest and most modern cinema, was "comfortably filled, mostly with Chinese but with some foreigners." Liang Ch'i-ch'ao, as president of the association, introduced the speaker briefly.[62]

Irritation at the criticisms which had been reaching his ears was evident now, in Tagore's opening lecture. Someone had accused him of being "altogether out of date in this modern age," the poet told his audience. "This has caused me some surprise, which I am sure will grow into amusement when I have more leisure than I have now," he continued acidly. In India he had become accustomed to the charge that he was "too crassly modern . . . newfangled and therefore obnoxious," he said. "For your people I am obsolete, and therefore useless. . . . I do not know which is true." He dubbed himself "this unfortunate being [who] has been so continually suspected to be contraband — smuggled on to the wrong shore of time — not only by his own countrymen . . . but by others to whom he could hardly have yet given any occasion for grave anxiety." [63]

To clear up the "misunderstanding" of his position which he felt existed among the Chinese, he proceeded to describe the "revolutionary" movements in religion, literature, and cultural nationalism in which he and his family had taken a leading part in nineteenth-century India. Turning to the great problem of the twentieth century, as he saw it, he denounced the concentration of power in "outside arrangements" and organizations, whether "political, commercial, educational or religious," which obstruct "the free flow of inner life of the people." "Revolution must come and men must risk revilement and misunderstanding, especially from those . . . who put their faith in materialism and convention, and who belong truly to the dead past and not to modern times. . . . The impertinence of material things is extremely old." "The revelation of spirit in man is truly modern: I am on its side, for I am modern," Tagore concluded. "If you want to reject me, you are free to do so. But I have my right as a revolutionary to carry the flag of freedom of spirit into the shrine of your idols — material power and accumulation." [64]

In this defiant speech, Tagore touched a level of impassioned self-justification which he had seldom reached in his earlier talks in China. Intent on making clear his own "revolutionary" attitude, he said nothing about restoring the ancient link between India and China, nothing about

Asia finding her own soul. Clearly he felt himself on the defensive, and in defending himself, he launched a vigorous counterattack on his critics' faith in material power and political organization.

The critics were not easily silenced, however. They must have met that evening to plan their next move, for on Saturday morning, as Tagore was about to start his second lecture, a group of young men began distributing to the audience in the True Light Theater handbills attacking him and his message. Foreseeing some such unpleasantness, Liang Ch'i-ch'ao had asked Hu Shih to act as chairman, and Hu found it necessary to rebuke the agitators for their discourtesy toward the visiting poet.[65] Tagore rose to deliver his own counteroffensive. Announcing that he was combining two lectures into one, he first inveighed against "The Rule of the Giant," which he described as nothing more than "the hugely disproportionate growth, in modern civilisation, of the not-life . . . of unbalanced bigness." The "Giant Killer," subject of the second lecture, was "Life" itself. Now the poet railed both at the "iron monster" of industrialism and at the "cloven-footed commerce" which had made it possible. Even modern democracy came in for its share of the blame, for "innumerable lives are sacrificed" at its shrine, "but only plutocrats in various disguise[s] thrive on them." In his peroration he lashed out at those Chinese who had made known their disagreement with his message. "There are those in the East who have slavishly come to believe that superstitions which are modern denote progress." Such men suspected him of being "a reactionary," a "fanatical conservative." This he denied:

> Those who know me know that I have ever fought against obedience to the unmeaning, to traditions that are dead. . . . I preach the freedom of man from the servitude of the fetish of hugeness, the non-human. I refuse to be styled an enemy of enlightenment because I do not stand on the side of the giant who swallows life, but on the side of Jack, the human, who defies the big, the gross, and wins victory at the end.[66]

After the lecture, apparently as they were leaving the hall, Tagore and his hosts discovered some leaflets in Chinese. The poet asked what they were all about. Much embarrassed, Hu replied that they criticized him for opposing modern civilization. "What did I say that is opposed to modern civilisation?" Tagore asked. "It is true you mentioned modern civilisation favorably in your speech," said Hu, "but all the rest of your talk was about spiritual civilization." Hu must have informed Tagore also that his critics were militant atheists who strongly objected to his talking of God and the soul, for the poet, wishing to reason with his opponents, requested Hu to arrange a meeting with some of them so that they could discuss these fundamental questions. This Hu Shih promised to do, but the next day sent Tagore a note postponing the meeting, which was to have been held at his house that evening: "Unfortunately I find it difficult to get enough atheist friends for this coming meeting. Some are away while others do not fully understand English," he explained. "I do not deem it right that this rare pleasure you have promised me should be exclusively enjoyed by one of [or] two persons." [67]

Still troubled by the obviously organized opposition to his ideas, and not satisfied by Hu Shih's rather general summary of the leaflet found in the theater after his second public lecture, Tagore sought a more precise translation, which his Chinese hosts were understandably reluctant to provide. It was apparently at this point that some Japanese he had come to know in Peking came forward to furnish the information he wanted.[68] The actual text of the leaflet was more virulent than he had been led to believe.

"If this old man had come as a tourist to admire the landscape of our country, we would pass over his visit in silence," one of the leaflets began. "But since he has come to indoctrinate us, we must express the displeasure his lectures create in us." The indictment which followed arraigned Tagore on five counts:

> 1. We have had enough of the ancient Chinese civilization, which crushed the people and enriched the prince, which subjected women and exalted men, which produced feudal fiefs supporting an aristocracy. We have suffered enough from these things! We want no more of them! But Mr. Tagore wants to take us back to the civilization of these bygone ages. Therefore we must protest against him.
>
> 2. Our agriculture, which hardly feeds our peasants, our industry, which is strictly household industry, our carts and our boats, which go only a few miles a day, our monosyllabic language and our ideographic writing, our printing, which has remained at the stage of carved woodblocks, our streets, which are latrines, and our deplorably dirty kitchens have made us lose our reputation throughout the world. And here Mr. Tagore comes to reproach us for our excess of material civilization! How can we fail to protest against him?
>
> 3. Wars without rhyme or reason, pillage and rapine, lying and cheat-

ing, lust and avarice, shameless prostitution, rapacious mandarins devouring the people, pious sons giving their own flesh to feed their parents, conquerors drinking from cups made of the skulls of the vanquished, women making their beauty consist in the mutilation of their feet — behold the flower of the ancient Chinese civilization, which Mr. Tagore calls spiritual, and to which he would like to make us return. Now we have a horrible dread precisely at seeing the return of such things. We therefore protest against Mr. Tagore.

4. Our present ills have been caused in large part by the indifference to public matters of too great a number of our fellow citizens. It is this apathy which has allowed our militarists and the foreign powers to dare anything and to do everything. And now Mr. Tagore finds that we torment our souls too much by worrying about such things! In the third age of the world, he says, there is no further need for nations or for governments. It suffices for each individual to seek the consolation of his soul. It suffices that each one drown himself in universal, abstract love, and in illusions of peace. . . . In a word, this doctrine is hypnotism. It evades difficulties instead of resolving them. For us Chinese, this means accelerating the speed with which our country is being ruined: this means handing us over paralyzed to our enemies.

5. We have already had our ancient theory of Yin and Yang, our Taoism and Confucianism. Recently we have had the Harmonious Virtue Society and the Spiritual Culture Association. On top of this, Christianity, a foreign doctrine, has filled the land with its preaching. And now, after the Lord on high in whose name this was already being preached us, Mr. Tagore proclaims the abode of Brahma, to which we must return our souls in order to gain salvation. Why then should we fret and struggle on this earth? If we are made for a spiritual world where we will find our rest, why should we fight to transform the world of the flesh? . . . To preach this doctrine is to preach inaction, passivity. . . . Therefore we protest, in the name of all the oppressed peoples, in the name of all the persecuted classes, against Mr. Tagore, who works to enslave them still more by preaching to them patience and apathy. We also protest against the semi-official literati who have invited Mr. Tagore to come to hypnotize and drug our Chinese youth in this way, these literati who use his talent to instill in Young China their conservative and reactionary tendencies.[69]

The effect on Tagore of this powerful tract was deeply disturbing. "These people are *determined* to misunderstand me," he declared angrily.[70] Although physically well, he became extremely nervous, and decided that he could not continue lecturing in the face of such opposition. He was expected to give lectures each morning from Monday through

Thursday, May 12 to 15, but he now insisted that he would make the Monday lecture the last, canceling the remainder of the series.[71]

Word of Tagore's decision evidently spread quickly among the students of Peking, for some two thousand young men and women filled the True Light Theater on Monday morning, a much larger audience than had appeared the previous Friday. Hsü Chih-mo opened the meeting with an impassioned defense of his fellow-poet. Hu Shih followed with a plea for tolerance and respect for the visiting lecturer. Tagore then made his final appeal to the young people of Peking. "The young generation of men in the East are everywhere attracted by what they imagine is modern," he began. "And they have convinced themselves that Western life is modern." This was a grave mistake, he warned. "The invasion of the West is laying its stony road across the soul of the East, leading most of the traffic of ideas to the gambling den of commerce and politics, to the furious competition of suicide in the arena of military lunacy." The East must resist this invasion, he urged: "We must find our voice to be able to say to the West: 'You may force your things into our homes, you may obstruct our prospects of life — but *we judge you.*'" Tagore granted that not everything in Western civilization was bad. There were individuals in the West who had set noble examples as devotees of truth; unfortunately they were few in number. Science was a great achievement of the West, of course, but the power it created could be badly misused, enabling "the inhuman to prosper, the lie to thrive, the machine to rule in the place of Dharma [righteousness]." The East was also materialistic, he conceded: "We have witnessed the grossest form of materialism and the cruellest form of inhumanity stalking abroad wearing the uniform of spiritual culture." This unfortunate fact made it even more important for Asians to hold fast to human values: "Therefore in order to save us from the anarchy of weak faith we must stand up today and judge the West," he concluded.[72]

INTERMISSION

The abrupt cancellation of the last three of the lectures which the Indian poet-philosopher had come all the way to Peking to deliver aroused considerable comment in the capital. The explanation given to the press on May 12 was that: "On the advice of his physician, Dr. Rabindranath Tagore has cancelled all his public and private engagements and after his last lecture at the Chen Kuang Theatre this morning, he left for the Western Hills. Because of his physical and mental fatigue, Dr. Tagore will remain in the Hills until next Sunday when he will return to Peking and leave the next morning." [73] The Peking Lecture Association also explained they had insisted that the poet permit them to cancel his lectures in order to protect his health. That he was not physically ill is clear from the letter written on May 15 by a member of his party: "Gurudev [our inspired teacher] is quite well. Because he has suddenly stopped lecturing, it is stated in the paper that he is ill. Don't be anxious." [74]

Nor was the poet so indisposed that he could not keep an appointment on Tuesday afternoon which seems to have been closely related to his urge to come to grips with the ideological source of the opposition ranged against him. The appointment was not with a Chinese, but with the official representative in Peking of the young revolutionary government of the Soviet Union, Leo Karakhan, who was then very popular with Peking's radically minded students. The Tagore-Karakhan conversation, as reported in the Chinese press, reads like a classic example of an encounter between two men talking past each other. Tagore began by asserting:

> Russian territory is mostly in the East, her traditional civilization is quite close to Eastern civilization, and Russia is completely different from the countries of Western Europe, who insistently advocate materialistic civilization. Therefore I very much wish to visit Soviet Russia, both for sight-seeing and to plant there the spirit of Eastern civilization.[75]

Karakhan promised to cable Moscow at once to arrange an invitation for the poet, and expressed great interest in closer relations between India and Soviet Russia, then completely cut off from contact. Threading his needle with Tagore's theme that Russia belonged to the spiritual East, Karakhan continued:

> From the political point of view my country is very willing to help and assist all the oppressed nations of the world, for in recent years my country has suffered greatly from Western material civilization and thus there is indeed a need for joint cooperation. From the intellectual point of

view Tolstoy in the nineteenth century already rejected material civilization, so that his opinion is actually in accord with the essence of Eastern
spiritual civilization.[76]

The two also discussed Tagore's educational ideals and agreed that
they were basically the same as those of the Soviet government. One
note of disharmony did creep into the conversation. When Karakhan
boasted that a decision made in Moscow would be implemented in thousands of villages, Tagore objected, "No! That's just the opposite of my
own approach to the village." Otherwise the interview seems to have
gone smoothly, and Tagore left with Karakhan's assurance that he would
arrange the visit, perhaps for the following year.[77]

The fact that Tagore sought out Karakhan before leaving Peking suggests that he correctly perceived that the campaign to vilify his ideas in
China was inspired by the aims and methods of the Bolshevik revolution
in Russia. Unflinching in the pursuit of his ideal, he seems to have decided to place his case before the people of Soviet Russia, hoping that
once they understood his message they would influence the Chinese to
accept it as well. This interpretation of the little-known Tagore-Karakhan
discussion seems borne out by the summary dispatched from Peking by
the Japanese news agency, Kokusai (International). Tagore's reasons for
wishing to visit Russia, reported Kokusai, were twofold: "to study conditions there and to further among the Russian people the study of the
civilisation of India and the East." [78]

The Western Hills, to which Tagore now withdrew, made an ideal
retreat for the overwrought lecturer. Rising from the dusty plain ten to
twenty miles west and north of the capital, and dotted with Buddhist and
Taoist temples, these hills provided a convenient summer resort for the
aristocracy and foreign residents of Peking. A new hotel had been built
at the Tangshan hot springs, a favorite resort of the seventeenth-century
Ch'ing emperor K'ang Hsi, and here the Indian poet retired to gather
strength for his homeward journey.[79] After a few days in retirement,
Tagore was visited by Lin Ch'ang-min and other members of the Lecture
Association, who were no doubt anxious about the health and state of
mind of their erstwhile lecturer. After the dinner party they gave him
at his hotel the poet spoke of the villages of India and China and his
ideas for rural reconstruction work before reverting to the theme of the
second of his three Peking lectures: "With a machine you can count

your horsepower, but life is different. . . . It is life that we are after. Life, life, life! Here is your Jack that will kill the Giant!" [80]

ACT FOUR: PEKING

As had been announced, Tagore returned to Peking on Sunday for a brief round of farewells. Speaking to a surprise gathering of students at the National Peking University, he began by asking: "What do you want from me?" doubting that his student listeners approved of his poetic vocation. "You may call me uneducated, uncultured, just a foolish poet; you may grow great as scholars and philosophers; and yet I think I would still retain the right to laugh at your pedant scholarship." Because he had left school at thirteen, he had kept alive "the sensitiveness that thrills us when we come into touch with reality." "I have lived in this great world not as a member of a society or of a group," he confessed, "but as a scamp, as a vagabond, and yet free in the heart of the world, which I have seen face to face." Because he had remained a child at heart, he claimed to stand close to the students of China, "the young hearts of a foreign country whom my heart recognizes as its fellow voyagers in the path of dreamland." [81]

After this appeal — an appeal for sympathy rather than a message of any kind — the poet was taken to a farewell tea given by the acting chancellor Chiang Mon-lin and the professors of the university's Department of Education.[82] Judging by the length and intimacy of his remarks, he probably spoke without an interpreter to a group of American- or British-educated faculty members. There was a wistful quality in his words, and from the start he confessed "a discontent, as of something not accomplished, as of my mission not completed." Compared with the hardships of travel suffered by the Indian monks who had brought Buddhism to China, and translated their ideas into Chinese, his journey had been "a picnic." "We attend parties, amuse one another, hold teas, lectures and keep engagements. Then we go back. It is all too easy." [83]

And what had he accomplished with all his lecturing? Were not his audiences "mere shadows?" How many of them could understand his English? "For three quarters of an hour I pour down a torrent of words upon their hapless heads. It is this that civilisation has made so easy." If he had failed, he protested, he was not to blame: "The present age is the great obstacle." Then again perhaps the fault was his after all: "in the depth of my heart there is a pain — I have not been serious enough. I have had no opportunity to be intensely, desperately earnest about your most serious problems." Rather unjustly, he accused himself of having been "pleasant, nice, superficial," in keeping with "the spirit of the time which is also easy and superficial." Nevertheless, he had made some close friendships: "I have never been so happy nor so closely in touch with any other people, as I have been with you. Some I feel as though I had known all my life." [84]

Now that his trip was drawing to a close, these personal contacts seemed to mean more to the poet than his grand scheme to revive and confederate the ancient cultures of "the East," for in his closing remarks he hoped that "something has been done, that some path has been opened up which others may follow. . . . I have this one satisfaction, that I am at least able to put before you the mission to which these last years of my life have been devoted." This mission was "the ideal of brotherhood." "I believe in the spiritual unity of man and therefore I ask you to accept this task from me. Unless you come and say, 'We also recognize this ideal,' I shall know that this mission has failed." [85]

In immediate response to this challenge, Hu Shih sprang to his feet and gallantly replied: "I am sure I speak for all present when I say that all of us sincerely hope Dr. Tagore and his friends will return feeling that they have not failed in the great task they have put before us today so sympathetically and so feelingly." Hu granted that there had been misunderstanding of Tagore's ideas, and "even foolish opposition" to them, but he and other Chinese intellectuals had also been misunderstood by their own people at times. Even he had been "rather unsympathetic" at first, but had soon been "converted" to "a warm admirer of the poet and his friends." For they had achieved "a renewal of our relationship with India . . . made with great grandeur. Have they not sent to us the greatest representative that any people ever sent to any nation?" Less important than the ideas they had brought were the friendships they had established, Hu concluded. "We welcome their embassy, not as the possessors of complete truth, but as the forerunners of a long series of the best representatives of the people, of an interchange of professors, of students, of men." [86]

As Tagore prepared to leave Peking never to return, he made two last attempts to win support for his ideals. When a delegation of Mahayana Buddhists, the group which had showed him the greatest sympathy, came to talk with him on May 19, his last day in the capital, he stressed the common features of Hindu and Buddhist spirituality and hoped that China and India could join together to develop Eastern civilization on the twofold basis of spiritual education and the maintenance of their traditional rural way of life.[87] That same afternoon the poet made his final speech to a Peking audience, in the same theater where one week before he had abruptly terminated his formal lecture series.

It was a sign of Tagore's frustrated relation to Peking's intelligentsia that this farewell meeting was arranged by a foreign missionary, Dr. Gilbert Reid, whose International Institute had for thirteen years been sponsoring conferences of all religions. "This has been duly caricatured," wrote Reid in his annual report for 1923–24; "still there are many new societies in which . . . religions are brought together in pleasant synthesis." As an ocular demonstration of the International Institute's work, Reid had invited representatives of nine religions to sit on the stage with Tagore, each clad in the costume of his faith. Hinduism, Zoroastrianism, Confucianism, Taoism, Mahayana Buddhism, Lamaist Buddhism, Christianity (in the person of four Chinese Christian leaders), Eastern Orthodox Christianity, and Islam shared the platform with officers of the Young Men's Buddhist Association and of four new religious groups that had sprung up after the 1911 revolution. About a thousand students, intellectuals, civic leaders, missionaries, and other foreigners made up the appropriately cosmopolitan audience. To further enhance the colorful atmosphere, a Chinese band had been hired to serenade the solemn procession before the speaker; their grand effect verged on the ridiculous, however, for they struck up the latest hit tune, "Yes, We Have No Bananas!" and many Westerners in the audience failed to restrain their smiles.[88]

The theme of Tagore's last Peking lecture, "Religious Experience," went to the heart of his problem in communicating an essentially religious message to China's intellectuals. "I have been given to understand that China never felt the need of religion. This I find hard to believe," he began. Perhaps the fault was his, he admitted, for he "had never studied carefully the intellectual basis of other religions," and if only he could have stayed longer in China he surely could have been able "to realise those deeper chords in the heart of China, whence the music of the spirit comes." A Chinese student had once asked him to justify his religious faith, but this, he claimed, was based on intuitive experience, not on logical argument. Reviewing those moments when the touch of the divine had come to him — while watching men in a market place, looking at a sunrise, listening to the human voice, suddenly seeing a bank of dark rain clouds, admiring a budding rose — he affirmed: "Gladness is the one criterion of truth and we know when we have touched Truth by the music it gives, by the joy of greeting it sends forth to the truth in us." Having thus argued that the delight of aesthetic experience proved the truth of religious insight, Tagore concluded:

> In the night we stumble over things and become acutely conscious of their individual separateness, but the day reveals the great unity which embraces them. And the man whose inner vision is bathed in an illumination of his consciousness at once realises the spiritual unity reigning over all differences of race, and his mind no longer awkwardly stumbles over individual facts of separateness in the human world, accepting them as final; he realises that peace is in the inner harmony which dwells in truth, and not in any outer adjustments.[89]

In the evening of that same day, the poet's last in Peking, a misunderstanding occurred which showed that in achieving the unity of mankind, attention to "individual facts of separateness" is at least as important as an all-encompassing faith. The actor Mei Lan-fang, who had watched Tagore's *Chitra* with such interest, invited the poet to a special performance of the Chinese play *The Goddess of the Lo River*. As dictated by custom, the main feature was preceded by several hours of preliminary theatricals, so that it was about eleven o'clock — the poet's usual bedtime — when Mei appeared on the stage. Tagore was so tired by this time that he rose to leave midway through the performance, to the great consternation of the Chinese, in whose eyes this represented a rather serious insult. After some discussion, the poet was prevailed upon to stay, despite the lateness of the hour. A meeting between the two men was arranged for the following morning, but when the time arrived Mei sent word that he was unable to come to the poet's hotel because of illness. After further negotiations the meeting finally took place, and Tagore and Mei had a good talk about the dramatic arts in India and China.[90]

FINALE: TAIYUAN, HANKOW, WUCHANG

Their four-week stay in Peking at an end, Tagore and his party took the southbound train on May 20, following the more westerly of the two railway lines connecting the capital with the Yangtse. A branch line led them westward to Taiyuan, the capital of the mountainous province of Shansi (the name itself means "Western mountains"). The Shansi Provincial Education Association had wired an invitation to Tagore, informing him that "The people of Taiyuan are awaiting your memorable visit and long to see your personality as well as to hear your exalted ideas and accept your challenge to international brotherhood of mankind, both East and West alike." The warlord who had controlled the province since 1911, General Yen Hsi-shan, had earned fame as the "Model Governor" because of his efforts to modernize without uprooting the traditional Confucian social order. Indeed, in his concern for the moral reformation of his people, his dislike of industries and large cities, and his conviction that he was a latter-day sage whose mission it was to regenerate mankind, Yen resembled Tagore.[91]

Tagore's first duty in Taiyuan was to call on Governor Yen and explain his mission to China. "I have come, Your Excellency," he was reported as saying, "to propose to you some way of blending our ideals so that some great civilisation may again be the outcome of this meeting of the ideals of India and those of China." The Model Governor replied: "The present material civilisation has developed greatly, and if once again our moral civilisation could gain control of the material it would be so much the better for all of us." To demonstrate his sympathy with the poet's ideals, Governor Yen donated a beautiful tract of land with its adjacent Taoist temple to form the nucleus of a cooperative Sino-Indian rural development center, to be directed by Elmhirst and staffed by both Indian and Chinese volunteers. This agreement aroused much enthusiasm among Tagore's party at the time (one of them referred to the interview as "a symbolic meeting between this Hindu seer and the Chinese administrator"), but unsettled military conditions on the Chinese side interfered, and the center never went into operation.[92]

By 3:30 that afternoon three thousand citizens were waiting expectantly for Tagore in the Confucian Hall of Self-Examination erected by the governor for the moral improvement of his people. F. C. Liu of the Provincial Educational Association introduced the honored guest, praising him for his spiritual attitude, which could save China's young people from moral bankruptcy and her aged from debility and despair.[93] Evidently glad to be away from the metropolis of North China and back in a rural setting not unlike that of his beloved Santiniketan, Tagore chose this occasion to denounce the modern city as exploitative of the countryside surrounding it: "Thus, unlike a living heart, these cities imprison and kill the blood and create poison centres filled with the accumulation of death. . . . The reckless waste of humanity which ambition produces, is best seen in the villages, where the light of life is being dimmed, the joy of existence dulled, the natural threads of social communion snapped every day." [94]

To honor their guests from India, members of Taiyuan's School of Foreign Languages put on a special performance of the poet's play *Sannyasi,* after which Governor Yen gave a special banquet at his palatial residence. As Tagore continued his train journey southward during the next two days, he was reported to be "quite cheerful," "full of new ideas and enthusiasm," and his whole party was said to be "delighted at the success of the trip up to date." By now the trip was virtually over, however, for the party was headed back to Shanghai and only one overnight stop remained — at Hankow, where the Kinhan railway line came to an end.

Straddling the mighty Yangtse midway in its course from the Szechwan basin to the East China Sea, the three sister-cities of Hankow, Hanyang, and Wuchang, with a combined population of three-quarters of a million, have often been dubbed "the Chicago of China." In sharp contrast to the quiet, conservative atmosphere of mountain-ringed Taiyuan, the prevailing mood of students and intellectuals in this bustling hub of river and rail transportation was aggressively radical. Here the successful revolution against Manchu rule had started on October 10, 1911. By 1924 the new Communist movement was well entrenched among its students and its large industrial force. Nevertheless, another new movement, the Buddhist revival under the leadership of Abbot T'ai Hsü, was making progress in Central China. A Buddhist college under T'ai Hsü's direction had been opened in Wuchang in 1922, and the headquarters for all China of his Young Men's Buddhist Association was located in Hankow.

With strong organizations of both leftists and Buddhists on the scene, the stage in Hankow-Wuchang was set for a final clash between Tagore and his fiercest antagonists in China.[95]

Buddhists were no doubt among those "educational circles" who arranged Tagore's one speech in Hankow, held out-of-doors next to the Supporting Virtue Middle School on Sunday morning, May 25. Tagore was always happy to speak to young people, and told his predominantly student audience that his two reasons for coming to China were to meet the youth of the country, and to learn about its ancient culture, especially because of its affinities with Indian culture. Weaving these two themes together, he urged his young listeners to balance the development of the material side of life through science with the cultivation of spiritual civilization:

> On your shoulders, my beloved young people, lies this responsibility. Like the dawning of the rising sun, you young people are full of promise. You have a great responsibility, and you should advance with determination. Do not let our Eastern civilization imitate whatever is done in Western civilization. I hope very much that more Chinese students will come to India to study the principles of Chinese and Indian culture, for these two cultures are intimately related. Young people, I urge you to exert yourselves.[96]

No sooner had the Indian poet finished speaking than a clamoring of voices began on the outskirts of his audience. Young men shouted in Chinese, "Go back, slave from a lost country!" "We don't want philosophy, we want materialism!" and waved placards with these same slogans. Kalidas Nag hurried to the scene and, when the slogans were translated for him, feared that the demonstrators might actually assault the poet. Fortunately this did not happen.[97]

Undaunted by this rude challenge, Tagore struck back that afternoon in his talk to "a hastily gathered and miscellaneous audience" of some seven hundred people on the Wuchang public athletic field. Reading the same speech he had delivered in his first talk to the students of Peking, he warned that "reliance on power is the characteristic of barbarism; nations that trusted to it have already been destroyed or have remained barbarous." To counteract the trend in this direction, "new spiritual and moral power must continually be developed to enable men to assimilate their scientific gains, to control their new weapons and machines or these will dominate, enslave, and destroy them." He admitted that he belonged to a nation that had "gone under in the race for progress," but he was willing to accept this humiliation of the body as long as his spirit remained unconquered. "Seek righteousness even though success be lost," he urged China's youth, lest through unrighteousness they "perish at the root." [98]

A newspaper correspondent on the scene tells us that "the Chinese translation which followed the whole speech was very brief and imperfect, and so the address must have had very little effect." The reporter also noted that the Indian poet had arrived in the Wu-han cities "suddenly" and "unannounced," and had left the same night by river steamer for Shanghai. Tagore seems to have been in no mood to linger in Hankow; the city lacked a university or any other convenient base of operations, and the hostility of the radical student group must have been discouraging.[99]

The down-river journey of three nights and two days gave Tagore ample time to reflect on the results of his mission to China. In less than seven weeks, he had lectured in the country's largest city (Shanghai), its nominal political capital (Peking), and in five of its twenty-four provincial capitals (Hangchow, Nanking, Tsinan, Taiyuan, and Wuchang). He had talked with students and scholars, actors and artists, generals and politicians, poets, religious leaders, and an ex-emperor. Almost everywhere the general public had received him well. The students at the Buddhist temple in Peking, at Tsing Hua and Yenching colleges, and in provincial Hangchow, Nanking, Tsinan, and Taiyuan had seemed receptive to his ideas, though he could not always be sure how much they had understood of his English, or how faithfully and fully his translators had rendered his words into Chinese. Dissident voices had made themselves heard, however, and their chorus of disapproval grew louder as the poet's tour of China progressed. Should he try once more to make them understand? He may have wondered as the S.S. *Kut Woo* steamed toward Shanghai, the last city he would visit before sailing for Japan.

ENCORE: SHANGHAI

Both his words and actions during his final two days in Shanghai suggest that he no longer hoped to convey a message to China's intellectuals.

He first decided to accept the hospitality, not of Chinese friends, but of a prominent member of the city's foreign business community, the Italian Mr. G. A. Bena.

Mrs. Bena was interested in education and, since the poet was staying at her home, persuaded him to speak on the subject to some European friends in her living room on the evening of his arrival. The following day, May 29, Tagore went to the reception in his honor at the Japanese School on Haskell Road. He had already spoken here on April 17 concerning the ideals of Eastern civilization, and had obliquely referred to the controversy over the immigration bill being debated by the United States Congress. In the meantime the bill had become law, and Japanese sentiment began a fatal swing away from America and toward some kind of combination of anti-Western Asian powers. When Tagore urged the Japanese in Shanghai to preserve their time-honored moral virtue of "heroism that was beautiful," and expressed his "deep admiration of Japanese culture and character," his speech was greeted with enthusiastic applause. During the luncheon that followed, a member of his party informs us, "many distinguished Japanese officers and professors consulted Tagore on several problems confronting modern Japan." [100]

Finally, it came the turn of the city's Chinese intellectuals to entertain the poet, and they gathered that afternoon for a farewell meeting in the same garden where they had welcomed him almost seven weeks before. Chang Chün-mai, once again the host, opened the meeting by praising his guest and requesting him to express frankly whatever criticism he might have of current trends in China.

Tagore's final talk in China conveys something of the sadness he felt at the end of his arduous trip. Absolutely refusing to comply with Chang's request that he criticize China, he explained: "We people of the Orient possess all kinds of qualities of which others do not approve — then why not let us be friends." "You shall have no criticisms from me, and please refrain from criticising me in return. I hope my friends in China will not have the heart to probe into my failings," he declared (implying that his enemies had not been so merciful). "I never posed as a philosopher, and so I think I can claim to be let alone." If he had disappointed his hosts, "if you think I have been overpaid at the very start, do not blame me: blame your own folly," he added. "You should have been more carefully circumspect and not lavished so much praise in anticipation." [101] For his own part, Tagore admitted that he might have entertained a romanticized view of China, a "vision" formed in his imagination when he was reading the *Arabian Nights,* and amplified by his impressions of the Chinese paintings he had seen in Japan. He granted that it was "difficult for a stranger to discover that hidden store of your strength and resources which will have to be worked out over a series of centuries and brought to perfection," but he believed that "it is from the ideal that we get to know the best aspects of the real, and that the complete life is given by these two seen together." [102]

These were Tagore's parting words to his Chinese listeners:

> I have done what was possible — I have made friends. I did not try to understand too much, but to accept you as you were, and now on leaving I shall bear away the memory of this friendship. But I must not delude myself with exaggerated expectations. My evil fate follows me from my own country to this distant land. It has not been all the sunshine of sympathy for me. From the corners of the horizon have come the occasional growlings of angry clouds.
>
> Some of your patriots were afraid that, carrying from India spiritual contagion, I might weaken your vigorous faith in money and materialism. I assure those who feel thus nervous that I am entirely inoffensive; I am powerless to impair their career of progress, to hold them back from rushing to the market place to sell the soul in which they do not believe. I can even assure them that I have not convinced a single sceptic that he has a soul, or that moral beauty has greater value than material power. I am certain that they will forgive me when they know the result. [103]

The poet's closest friend in China, his traveling companion and translator Hsü Chih-mo, later described the slow and doubting way in which Tagore delivered these last words:

> It seemed as though he could not express the pain in his heart. He seemed not to be able to speak freely about his feelings. His smile, unless my mind is too sensitive, was not a true smile. Sometimes we could see it was in the place of tears. "My evil fate follows me from my own country to this distant land. It has not been all sunshine of sympathy for me." He weighed these words before he spoke them. This was the only point he didn't explain clearly or completely; these words contained unlimited bitter pain, unlimited resentment. At that time I felt very sorry for him. [104]

After this final scene, played in the fading light of a sultry Shanghai afternoon, the Nobel Laureate faced the affectionate farewell party arranged by the city's Indian community: Muslims, Parsis, and Hindus expressed their sympathy for his ideals, each donating a separate purse for the work of his Visva-Bharati University.[105] Now Japan was eagerly awaiting his arrival, and the Japanese textile magnates of Shanghai chartered a special ship, the *Shanghai Maru,* to transport him there without cost. This grand gesture seemed to taunt the Chinese for not properly appreciating their distinguished visitor.

Abandoning his high hopes for China, Tagore sailed from Shanghai on May 30, 1924, in much the same mood as had clung to him eight years earlier on sailing eastward from Japan. Four weeks later, on his way back to India, his ship docked at Shanghai for a day but he refused to go ashore, saying he was indisposed. When he reached the British colony of Hong Kong, however, he did leave the ship long enough to speak to a Chinese audience gathered at the Confucian Club. In this, his only public speech in South China, he once again appealed to both pan-Asian feeling and spiritual aspiration: "I am nothing but a poet. But let my poet's verses represent the great heart of Asia brooding on immortality — that voice, silent for centuries, yet again speaking in no uncertain tones today. For I assure you, I feel the need of it in my wanderings around the world." [106]

"Asia" could find no more able spokesman than Rabindranath Tagore. In more than two dozen talks in China he had given eloquent expression to the ideal of a resurgent spiritual civilization embracing both India and China. Were the intellectual leaders of China at all affected by his appeal? Did some of them accept him as the voice, the representative, of all Asia? How like or unlike Tagore's were their own images of Asia, of Eastern and Western civilizations, and of China's place in the world?

CHAPTER SIX

CHINESE VIEWS OF TAGORE'S MESSAGE

---

*Today China's intellectual life is completely
abreast of the times. Her leaders in the sciences
and arts . . . are working jointly and to the fullest
extent on the universal problems of our time, technical, scientific, philosophical, and artistic. And this
is the reason why Tagore no longer found in China
the favorable soil for his ideas he had hoped to
find here more than elsewhere.*

— Richard Wilhelm, Peking, 1924

THE INDIAN POET AND HIS PARTY had passed across the Chinese scene
as though through a fog, able to see clearly only those people (whether
friendly or hostile) in their immediate path. Unfamiliarity with the language, the culture, and the political problems of China severely limited
their range of vision. At a distance of over forty years from the event,
drawing on contemporary sources and later studies based on them, we
can try to dispel most of this fog and see Tagore against the larger landscape of China's cultural and political situation in the spring of 1924.
The bulk of these sources are in the Chinese language; the few in
Western languages must be used with care.

WHAT FOREIGN OBSERVERS THOUGHT HAD HAPPENED

Ten foreign observers commented on the effects of Tagore's mission
to China. Four of them thought he had scored quite a victory. The poet's
English secretary, Leonard Elmhirst, enthusiastically told Romain Rolland that the trip had "succeeded marvellously and will without doubt
be fertile in its long-term results." He described how Tagore's com-
panions were struck by "the veneration that surrounded them — even as

far as the fields in the interior of China. The peasants saluted them as envoys from the land from which the word of Buddha had reached them in bygone times." Only the young intellectuals in the coastal cities were unresponsive, he added.[1] Another Englishman, a teacher at Tientsin, reported in China's foremost English-language reference annual: "The coming of Tagore from India with his 'great awakening light' was hailed with rejoicing by Government students and scholars, and though a physical breakdown compelled his premature departure homeward, this most famous of living Asiatics did not go without giving to those who heard him an inspirational message which will not soon be forgotten." [2]

The official organ of the American Protestant missionaries in China, the *Chinese Recorder,* also saw the bright side of the picture, asserting that "the visit of Dr. Rabindranath Tagore to China during the month of May called forth such a welcome as has been given to few visitors in recent years," adding with satisfaction: "Everywhere his message centered about the appeal to the spiritual values of life." [3] A Japanese scholar of modern Chinese thought received a similar impression, noting that "when Tagore lectured in several places in China the number of his sympathizers was by no means small." [4]

Observers with more intimate knowledge of China and the Chinese language presented more somber accounts of what had happened. According to an American reporter, Tagore "aroused an enthusiastic response on the part of scholars and students, just as he has drawn forth opposition." [5] A British doctor in Shanghai believed that Tagore had not "altogether appealed to some of the elements in China," because "he is too willing to recognize the good in Western institutions and too truly international to suit the present phase of acute nationalism in this country." [6] The newly founded *China Journal of Science and Arts,* edited by the British biologist Arthur Sowerby, commented sympathetically: "Tagore is an exponent of the belief that the Asiatic, be he Indian, Chinese or Japanese, should endeavour to live up to all that is best in his own rich but serene culture rather than to strive so ardently after the hectic civilization of the West with all its engines of war and restlessness," but noted that "for this reason he did not make a great impression on the youth of China on his recent visit to this country." A good half-year after the event, an anonymous writer to the leading British daily in north China analyzed the poet's reception in Peking:

Tagore's personality did make an impression when he was in Peking, but now that he is gone almost every shred of such influence has vanished with him. The reason why he got a hearing at all was due mainly to clever advertising and to the craving on the part of many Chinese intellectuals to be in the swim. . . . His relations to the Government of India interested the student element: anything anti does. His long addresses bored nine tenths of his audiences, and there was great opposition to his ideas on the part of many influential thinkers. He simply did not appeal to the pragmatical Chinese and the permanent results of his visit are practically *nil*.[7]

A German scholar and a French Jesuit, long resident in China and deeply immersed in her classical culture, produced the most circumstantial and the most pessimistic accounts of Tagore's confrontation with China's intellectuals. Richard Wilhelm, whose perceptive account of the poet's visit to Peking is easily the best on record, called the encounter "an outward failure."[8] Léon Wieger, a close student of China's radical press and compiler of an instructive series of translated excerpts from it, termed the Tagore affair "a fiasco, villainous in form, but very instructive. The event was one of those that 'reveal the latent thoughts in the hearts of men.'" Wieger found it "hard to believe that the Indian poet will ever return to this country, which in his opinion lacks that external politeness which all the world had up until now considered its national characteristic."[9]

Although a minority of these ten foreign observers thought the Indian poet's visit a success, the majority judged it a failure. A more accurate picture of how China's intellectuals responded to Tagore's message emerges from their statements on the subject. If the event was truly "one of those that reveal the latent thoughts in the hearts of men," their reactions should disclose a variety of viewpoints in the Chinese intellectual world as of 1924, and should highlight patterns and trends which remain obscure or out of focus in biographical, political, or institutional studies of this period.

Some Newspaper Comments

Newspaper editorials often reflect the opinions of their readers and for this reason can be taken as indicative of major segments of public opinion on specific issues at particular points in time. Regrettably, only a few newspapers published in China in 1924 are now available outside the

People's Republic of China. Among these few, however, a curious cleavage is evident between the viewpoints of Chinese newspapermen writing in English and those writing in their mother tongue.

The oldest English-language newspaper in China under Chinese management, the *Peking Daily News*, strongly supported Tagore's message when he arrived in the capital, declaring: "This is a moment when acute materialism needs to be supplemented by the merits of Oriental culture. It is exactly in this respect that Sir [Rabindranath] Tagore is the man of the hour." The editorial writer believed that his countrymen would appreciate their Indian guest because, like him, "they are instinctively anti-nationalistic." Somewhat contradicting himself, he closed by endorsing the nationalist struggle for a unified China:

> Let us hope that what Mr. Tagore has to say will leave a lasting impression on the young idealists in this country, for his words will be encouraging to us not only in our present struggle for a unified nation but also in our future efforts for the realization of a far greater enterprise . . . [the supranational] bond in which all human creatures are included.[10]

Two Chinese contributors to English-language newspapers controlled by foreigners were also full of praise for the poet's message. "Mr. Tagore's denunciation of the materialistic civilization of the West has been accepted by Young China without dissent," wrote a Chinese correspondent to the Japanese-owned *North China Standard*. "May his visit rally both Young China and Old China to the standard of their own civilization!"[11] And the American-owned *North China Star* proudly published an editorial, "The Great Minds of Asia," written by "one of our Chinese collaborators who has been working with us for months but has today for the first time volunteered an editorial." This unsolicited appreciation was but "one of a host of indications that Tagore is inspiring the people of China."[12]

The three available editorials from Chinese-language newspapers contain considerable skepticism concerning Tagore's ideas and their relevance to Chinese conditions. The *She-hui jih-pao* (Society Daily) in Peking discounted the idea that Tagore had any serious purpose in mind at all: "Tagore comes to China for sight-seeing, as he is an admirer of our country. He expresses his opinions, but he has no political and religious aims, nor any propaganda to be conducted here in China." Therefore, it was senseless either to praise or to oppose his ideas: "It is absurd to say that he comes to the disadvantage of our country. . . . Is it not contrary to normal citizens' diplomacy if we disgrace him at will? On the other hand, such exaggerated welcome also seems to be absurd. Therefore, handle the citizens' diplomacy more carefully." [13]

The *Ta wen pao* (Great culture) cordially welcomed the poet to Peking, but made it clear that his warning against material civilization should be rejected by the Chinese:

> This idea of Dr. Tagore, according to this paper, should properly be regarded as a luxury in the viewpoint of the Chinese people, although it is an extremely important idea of which the Westerners should take care. The reason is that in Western countries, science has been so well developed that even though millions of books were burnt and many scholars killed . . . they could not be brought back to primitive conditions, while in China, the case is just the reverse, and the idea of yielding to nature and of non-competition has long been held by many Chinese people, and may be alleged as the cause for the scanty development of science. It is understood that China has stood far behind those Western countries, as far as scientific civilization is concerned, and that the Chinese people are mild and meek enough so that such ideas . . . should not be added to what the Chinese already have.[14]

The *Ta wen pao* acknowledged Tagore's claim to speak as the representative of Asia, but flatly denied his assertion that China needed to be Easternized even more than it already was:

> It has long been said that India may represent the civilization of the East, which, in turn may be represented by Tagore, both a poet and a philosopher. . . . Tagore himself is the flower of the civilization of the East, and we should not fail to appreciate him because of the lack of need of his thought, and we should cordially welcome him from [the] beginning [of his visit] to [the] end.[15]

From Shanghai, the *Shen pao* (Chinese daily news), the most respected daily of China's largest city, at first followed the Indian poet's tour with scrupulous care and without editorial comment. But a fortnight after his arrival it vehemently rejected his message:

> We cannot live without the benefits of material civilization. To neglect them would mean that all our four hundred million people would be the victims of the material civilization of other peoples. Would this not be

terrible? If these high-flown words of Tagore and other scholars are allowed to increase, like drops of water becoming a river, I am afraid our young students will be endlessly misled.[16]

Although these six editorial comments represented only a fraction of what must have been published in China's newspapers concerning Tagore's message, they show a remarkably consistent pattern: the three editorials in English favored Tagore's emphasis on spirituality, while the three in Chinese discounted or decried it. This contrast again suggests the possibility that each of these views reflected the thinking of a different sector of the country's intelligentsia. Other Chinese sources will show how important a sector of the intelligentsia each view represented, and what further differences existed within each sector.

As in Japan in 1916, so in China in 1924, only a small proportion of the intelligentsia were sufficiently outspoken and influential to put their ideas in writing and have them printed and published. Most of those who wrote on Tagore's ideas were living in Peking at the time, with a smaller number in Shanghai and a few scattered elsewhere. The more articulate intellectuals were thus concentrated, not in one city as in Japan, but in two. Like their Japanese counterparts, most were employed in teaching or writing, but their interests in many cases seem to have been less specialized, perhaps reflecting a society less modernized, and therefore less differentiated into professional groups.

Literature, philosophy, and politics, as in eighteenth-century Europe, often compete for the attention of the same intellectual in a period when an age-old cultural and political order is passing away and a new one is painfully being born. But this diffusion and overlapping of interests was also a continuation of the multiple roles of the scholar in imperial China, who was expected to combine literary proficiency, philosophic perspective, and political skill. As poet and philosopher, Rabindranath Tagore himself combined two of these roles, and his lectures in China had political implications, whether he liked it or not. As a result, he evoked comments on his ideas in all three contexts.

LITERARY LEADERS

The natural impulse of many writers and poets in China was to welcome wholeheartedly their colleague from India. Quite a few of Tagore's writings had already been translated into Chinese by May 1923, when it was announced that he would soon arrive in China. More translations followed, along with essays on his varied literary output.[17] From the viewpoint of literary men, Tagore could not have chosen a more propitious time to visit China, for just then they were intensely interested in the modern literatures of other countries. The younger writers in particular were striving to create a new literary language, using the spoken idiom of the people rather than the archaic classical style intelligible only to scholars, and were developing a new literature depicting the real problems of the present day. Looking abroad for models, these men took special interest in the writers of Russia and of smaller and oppressed nationalities in Europe where literature had been used as a means of awakening the mass of the people to a freer social and political outlook. As India's foremost man of letters, known for liberating Bengali literature from outworn conventions, and as the first (and even today the only) Asian to receive the Nobel Prize for Literature, Tagore was assured of a sympathetic reception among his Chinese confreres.

The young editor of the *Hsiao-shuo yüeh-pao* (Short story monthly), China's most important literary magazine and the organ of the Literary Studies Association which was spearheading the new movement, made every effort to prepare the literary world to welcome Tagore with proper respect and appreciation.

Soliciting contributions for a special issue of his monthly, Cheng Chen-to received so much material that he had to christen two issues "Tagore Numbers," with a handsome photograph of the poet wreathed in a circle of flying birds decorating each cover. Cheng himself gave the keynote for the joyful atmosphere in which he expected his countrymen to welcome Tagore:

> When with his vibrant and serious voice he makes a sincere and beautiful speech we will surely applaud vigorously, sitting or standing, or standing on the window-ledges, or standing outside the window, with warm sincerity and respect, listening very carefully with new and buoyant feelings of joy and encouragement. Truly we must welcome him in this way, but even such a welcome will fail to express one percent of the admiration, love, and gratitude we feel for him. . . . The man we welcome can give our people love, light, comfort, and blessings; he is our beloved brother, a traveler who shares the same road of knowledge and spirituality. . . . He is one of the few men in the world worth welcoming.[18]

Cheng was somewhat disappointed when he learned that Tagore would not arrive in the summer or fall of 1923, but had postponed his trip till the following spring. As soon as the poet did arrive, the Short Story Monthly was again all attention. This time Cheng brought out a special booklet as a supplement to his April issue, writing the major part of it himself. Everything about Tagore seemed to delight Cheng: his appearance, his kind manner, his simple and virtuous life, and also his message to China: "His ideal is the ideal of the East, which can raise us above the materialism of today and its oppressive bondage. He is bravely developing Eastern civilization, the Eastern spirit, and is protesting against the spirit of the materialistic, realistic, and commercial civilization of the West." [19]

As Tagore went on to Peking to deliver his message to his Chinese audiences, and as the poet in him gave way to the philosopher-sage, Cheng Chen-to must have watched with growing alarm and despair. He had sympathized with Tagore's Eastern ideal in a moment of enthusiasm, perhaps, for he failed to mention this theme again. In selecting four of Tagore's talks for publication, he gave priority to "The Confession of a Literary Revolutionist," the only talk devoted to the subject of litera-ture.[20] When Tagore returned to Shanghai on his way to Japan, Cheng noted in a brief editorial comment that the Indian poet's mood had greatly changed during his seven-week tour in China. "He gave us many very earnest talks, and what, after all, have we given him in re-turn?" Cheng asked, referring evidently to the criticisms that had caused the poet to cancel his Peking lecture series. "When we think of this," he concluded, "it is truly unbearable!" [21] Nevertheless, Cheng made no effort to defend Tagore's theory of Oriental civilization against its critics.

It is a striking fact that the two Chinese literary leaders most in sym-pathy with Tagore were both men who had studied in England. Cheng Chen-to, educated in an English-speaking college at Shanghai, attended the University of London after World War One, and his liking for the Indian poet probably dated from that period.[22] But the prime case of the Chinese literary leader imbued with an English perspective was the poet Hsü Chih-mo, Tagore's guide, interpreter, friend, and from first to last his staunchest supporter in China.

The affinity between Hsü and Tagore may have been due to their similar family backgrounds, their contacts with cultured Westerners, and their development as creative artists — the same common experiences which had drawn Okakura and Tagore together over two decades earlier. Hsü's father in the Yangtse delta, like Tagore's grandfather in the Ganges delta, was a prominent industrialist in that area of his country most deeply penetrated by modern commerce as developed through local and Western initiatives. Untroubled by financial pressures, young Hsü received the best education available in China, first at Shanghai, the modern metropolis, then at the foremost center of learning in the traditional capital, the National Peking University. Embarking at twenty-two on a four-year tour of study abroad, he attended Clark and Columbia universities in the United States from 1918 to 1920, and the London School of Economics and Cambridge University from 1920 to 1922. Studying under G. Lowes Dickinson at Cambridge (the same Dickinson whose *Letters from John Chinaman* had so delighted Tagore two decades earlier), Hsü came to feel as much at home as Tagore was among the English literati. By the time he returned to China he had adopted as his ideal the life of the romantic poet. Having been absent from his native land during the turmoil of 1919 and after, he felt as detached from China's political problems as Tagore did from India's. Just as Tagore had done in Bengali, Hsü worked to create a new form of Chinese poetry in which the techniques and themes of the English romantics blended harmoniously with those of the classical poets of his native land.

Hsü was one of those who "jumped up and down for joy" [23] when they learned that Tagore had agreed to come to China, and the eager letter he wrote Tagore in September 1923 sounded the note of uncritical admiration that was to run through all his statements about the Indian poet:

> Never before has a single writer, Eastern or Western, excited so much genuine interest in the heart of our young Nation, and few, not even our ancient sages, perhaps, have gifted us with such a vivid and immense inspiration as you have done. Your presence will lend comfort and joy to this age of gloom and doubt and agitation, a presence which will further strengthen our faith and hope in the larger things of life, which you have helped to instill into our minds.[24]

Hsü stood on the dock as the freighter bringing Tagore steamed toward the Shanghai Bund, and from that day on hardly left his idol's side. "I am powerless to describe my feelings on first seeing him: the reality surpasses what we had imagined about him," he wrote a friend in Peking. During the seven-week tour the two poets at times shared the same

room, and in their private talks the romantic Hsü opened his heart to
his sympathetic friend. It seems that he was in love with Tagore's other
interpreter, Miss Lin, but even the intercession of Tagore himself failed to
win her heart.[25] In his famous poem "Ch'u pa!" (Go away!), written the
day before he and Tagore quit Peking for Shanghai, Hsü summed up
his despair at the public and private sorrows which combined to depress
him at this point:

> Go away, dreamland, go away!
> I dash to pieces the jade cup of illusions . . .[26]

No other Chinese intellectual spoke out more strongly in defense of
Tagore at the critical moment when the Indian poet canceled his lectures
in the True Light Theater. In impassioned tones Hsü justified Tagore's
sudden decision as a response to the persistent attacks of the student
pamphleteers:

> He advocates creative life, spiritual freedom, international peace, edu-
> cational progress, and the realization of universal love. But they say he is
> a spy for the imperialists, an agent of capitalism, an exile from the en-
> slaved people of a conquered country, a madman who advocates foot-
> binding! There is filth in the hearts of our politicians and bandits, but
> what has this to do with our poet? There is confusion in the brains of
> our would-be scholars and men of letters, but what has this to do with
> our poet? [27]

Quite apart from his personal attachment to the Indian poet, Hsü is
important for the clarity with which he expressed the views of those
young Chinese intellectuals who welcomed Tagore, not because he spoke
to them of Chinese or Oriental civilization, but because he seemed to
them the highest embodiment of a romantic idealism they had come to
admire through their study of Western literatures. Hsü's encomium of
his fellow poet was characteristically cosmopolitan in scope and spirit:

> His great and tender soul, I dare say, is a miracle in human history.
> His unlimited imagination and broad sympathy make us think of Whit-
> man; his gospel of universal love and zeal for spreading his ideas remind
> us of Tolstoy; his unbending will and artistic genius remind us of Michel-
> angelo, the sculptor of Moses; his sense of humor and wisdom make us
> think of Socrates and Lao-tzu; the tranquillity and beauty of his personal-

ity remind us of Goethe in his old age; the touch of his compassion and pure love, his tireless efforts in the cause of humanitarianism, his great and all-embracing message sometimes make us recall the Savior of mankind. His brilliance, his music, his grandeur, remind us of the Olympian gods. He cannot be insulted, he cannot be surpassed, he is a mysterious natural phenomenon.[28]

Hsü clearly admired Tagore more for his personal qualities than for his ideas on Eastern civilization, but this emotional tie led him to remark approvingly on the ideal of friendship between India and China. After quoting the poet as saying to his last Chinese audience: "We two peoples are laughed at by other peoples, but since we have virtues not admired by others, we must become good friends," Hsü commented: "I don't know whether these words were made up more of tears or of blood. Should we be proud or ashamed when we hear these words?" His summary of the encounter between Tagore and China's intellectuals shows that his own mood was dominated by shame and sorrow:

The sympathetic reader must understand that during the past forty days the poet has been tested by China, and that China has passed judgment on him. He is now far away. The memories he gave us will by and by be lost. Everything will pass, as the shadow of the cloud passes through the waves in the water leaving not a trace behind. There are perhaps some people who hope that the light of day will fade completely away. Then the birds and the clouds may fly freely, and in the dark surface of the water we will not even be able to see their shadows![29]

If Hsü Chih-mo praised Tagore but ignored the theory of Eastern spirituality for which he sought Chinese support, the equally brilliant poet Wen I-to denounced the Indian visitor precisely because of his spirituality. At first glance these two young Chinese poets seem to have had much in common: Wen was only four years younger than Hsü, had been exposed to Western-style education for over a decade, and during his student years in the United States had decided to become a poet, combining Chinese and Western techniques and taking Keats as his model. But there were important differences between the careers and experiences of the two men. Wen grew up in Hupeh, the heartland of China; he came from a family of scholar-officials and was thoroughly trained in the Chinese classics at home and at nearby Wuchang; not wealth won through commercial activity but the traditional method of advancement through success in examinations enabled him to study at the American-style Tsing Hua School from 1913 to 1922, and at the Art Institute of Chicago and the University of Colorado from 1922 to 1925. Unlike Hsü Chih-mo, Wen was in Peking during the May Fourth movement of 1919 and was deeply moved by the political crisis through which his native land was passing. Unlike Hsü, he did not feel at home in the West, but instead suffered the sting of racial discrimination, which he attacked in his famous "Laundryman's Song." [30]

Wen I-to was in the United States from 1922 to 1925, but the problems of his country were so much on his mind that he reacted instantly and sharply to the news that the Indian poet was about to visit China. Well-acquainted with *Gītānjali, Stray Birds,* and *Fruit Gatherer,* Wen objected strongly to their formlessness and the unreal, abstract quality he found in them. "We may say definitely that Tagore as a poet must fail, because . . . the palace of literature must be built on the foundation stone of the reality of human life." He also objected to Tagore's mixing of poetry with philosophy, and called for a more critical attitude toward both. Mocking the eerie quality of Tagore's verse, he summed up a basic difference between the Hindu and Confucian outlooks on life: "When we read his poems, we first get a feeling of strange joy, then a fear of loneliness. We look for another human being, and want to see human activity and hear human voices. We long for our home villages, in the same way that Tagore longs for his other world." [31] While emphasizing that his countrymen should give the Indian poet a hearty welcome, Wen warned them that "today our new poetry is already sufficiently empty, weak, overintellectual, and formless. If we add to these things Tagore's influence, we will only increase the disease, till the day comes when no medicine can save us. I hope our literary world will be watchful." [32]

Wen and Hsü actually became good friends in Peking and collaborated in refounding the Crescent Moon Club in 1926 and in editing and writing for the *Hsin Yüeh* (Crescent moon) monthly in Shanghai after 1928. Ironically, it was not Hsü but Wen who actively worked for the revitalization of Chinese culture that Tagore had urged. Already in 1921 Wen had declared that genuinely "new" Chinese poetry should not merely follow Western poetic traditions, but should "produce fragrant children from the marriage of Chinese and Western art." To accomplish this end, China's intellectuals should "revive our trust in ancient literature, for we cannot create the universe anew . . . we can only build a new house on the old foundation." Wen concluded his appeal by equating, as Tagore had done, his own cultural heritage with that of the whole Eastern hemisphere: "We must expound our Eastern culture clearly. Eastern culture is absolutely beautiful, harmonious and elegant. Eastern culture is mankind's most profound culture. Oh! Let's not be frightened by the Westerners' wild shouting." [33]

The contrasting reactions of Hsü and Wen thus present a paradox: one admired Tagore for his cosmopolitan outlook but ignored his hope for an Eastern spiritual revival; the other rejected his influence as baneful but championed the ideal of revitalized Eastern civilization — albeit one based on his own interpretation of China's cultural heritage. Had either known Tagore's poetry in the original Bengali, with its intricate rhythms and rhymes, its sharp images, and its evocation of India's past, he would have better understood what the Indian poet was advocating.

Their fluency in English (thanks to English-medium schooling, first in China, later in England and the United States) enabled Cheng, Hsü, and Wen to evaluate Tagore's work within the context of nineteenth- and twentieth-century Anglo-American literature and thought.[34] Many of their contemporaries, and most of the writers born a generation earlier, lacked this background, and Tagore seemed correspondingly more foreign to them. Four other outstanding writers, three of whom had studied in Japan and one who had never left China, looked at the Indian poet with less sympathetic eyes than their Anglicized colleagues.

The two eldest were the famous Chou brothers, both of whom graduated from one of China's first centers for modern technical studies, the Nanking Naval Academy, and were sent by the Chinese government to Japan in the first decade of this century to study scientific subjects. Both brothers settled in Peking after the 1911 Revolution, and there won fame through their creative writings. The crystalline essays of the one and the sardonic short stories of the other equally reflect the skeptical scientific attitude gained from their earlier studies, an attitude reinforced by the climate of realism and naturalism which prevailed in Japanese literature after 1905.

Chou Tso-jen, the essayist and the younger of the two brothers, was teaching at Peking University when Tagore visited China, and his two essays on the event show an almost clinical detachment toward the controversy it engendered. "I have repeatedly said I don't understand Tagore," he commented after the poet's second lecture at the True Light

Theater, "so I have not joined either those who welcome or those who oppose him. Since the host must show hospitality to his guest I think we should welcome him, but if this old gentleman's name is used as a signboard to sell metaphysics, this is wrong." As for those who opposed Tagore in the name of science, Chou continued, their motives were commendable but their nerves were too sensitive: "We certainly don't believe he can really make China metaphysical, for the power of thought among the masses of the people is pitifully weak; even we who don't understand the materialist conception of history can appreciate this." The only result of his visit would be that a few more articles would be published, a few noisy gatherings held, and a few more customers would come to Peking's vegetarian restaurants and foreign book shops. "But just now these enthusiasts go running around shouting as if a great disaster were at hand. I really don't know what they're afraid of, after all." [35]

The continuing agitation against Tagore provoked Chou a month later to point out that it smacked of fanaticism inconsistent with the "steady mind and quiet temperament" of the true scientist:

> Anti-Christians are themselves the followers of a religion. Anti-Confucianists are Confucianists of a sort. There are many instances of this. Take for example the recent Oppose Tagore Movement. Its followers think they are scientific thinkers and Westernizers, but they lack the spirit of scepticism and toleration. Actually they are still the kind of Orientals who persecute heretics. If Eastern civilization contains poisons of the worst kind, then this sort of authoritarian fanaticism is one.[36]

Lu Hsün (as the elder brother, Chou Shu-jen was known), now hailed by many as China's greatest modern writer, was already famous in 1924 as the author of brilliant, sardonic stories and essays satirizing the evils of traditional Chinese society. As a guest at the celebration honoring Tagore on his sixty-fourth birthday, Lu Hsün was well aware of the Indian poet's presence in Peking, but his only comment was to note in his diary that the party had started at eight o'clock and that it was midnight when he returned home.[37] What he must have thought of Tagore's appeal for a revival of Eastern spirituality can be seen from his writings before and after this event, notably in his remarks several years later under the title, "The Old Song Has Been Sung Long Enough":

Almost all of those who praise the old Chinese culture are the rich who are residing in the concessions or other safe places. They praise it because they have money and do not suffer from the civil wars. . . . Chinese culture is a culture of serving one's masters, who are triumphant at the cost of the misery of the multitude. Those who praise Chinese culture, whether they be Chinese or foreigners, conceive of themselves as belonging to the ruling class.[38]

Lu Hsün's views on the value of traditional culture were so completely opposed to those of Tagore, and were already so well known, that he presumably saw no point in publicly criticizing the Indian poet. Besides, as his younger brother had recognized, the spirit of skepticism and toleration could better be served by silence than by noisy opposition.

Two younger writers with views even further to the left than Lu Hsün spoke out sharply against Tagore, for they were afraid his ideas would retard the sweeping changes they wished to see made in China's economic, social, and political order. Significantly, neither man was economically secure, and neither was able to study in Europe or the United States. Shen Yen-ping, later famous as a major novelist writing under the name of Mao Tun, had studied at Peking University for three years before poverty forced him to abandon his studies and take a job as a proofreader at the Commercial Press in Shanghai, China's largest publishing house. He did so well there that he was made the first editor of the Literary Studies Association's Short Story Monthly. When Cheng Chen-to succeeded him in this position, he continued to write a column on literary news from abroad, taking special interest in French and Russian writers.

Sympathy and scorn intermingled in Shen's first reactions to Tagore, recorded and published the day the Indian poet stepped ashore at Shanghai. "We respect him as a poet with a pure personality, . . . as one who feels compassion for the weak, as a poet who sympathizes with the oppressed, . . . helps the peasants . . . encourages a spirit of patriotism and provokes the youth of India to oppose British imperialism," he began. However, he continued:

We are determined not to welcome the Tagore who loudly sings the praises of Eastern civilization, nor do we welcome the Tagore who creates a paradise of poetry and love, and leads our youth into it so that they may find comfort and intoxication in meditating. . . . Oppressed as we are by the militarists from within the country and by the imperialists from without, this is no time for dreaming. . . . To loudly sing the praises of Eastern civilization at such a time is like "repelling bandits by reciting the five classics." A much better slogan for this hour, in our opinion, is that of Wu Chih-hui: "Reply to our enemies' machine guns with Chinese machine guns; answer their cannons with our cannons." [39]

Shen applied his light, sardonic touch to Tagore's central concept in a second article timed apparently to coincide with the poet's final visit to Shanghai on his way to Japan. "The title, Preacher of Oriental Civilization, has been attached to this man," he noted:

> This interests me — I, an Oriental, born and grown up in China — for (shall I admit it?) I don't know what Oriental civilization is. I have searched in vain through books, Chinese and foreign, to learn what it is. I have read the works of Mr. Tagore, especially the lectures he gave in Germany. I said to myself that a man who comes to China expressly to preach Oriental civilization will inform me better than anyone else could concerning the nature of this civilization. Therefore I have carefully followed the reports of his lectures at Shanghai, Peking, and elsewhere . . . and still I don't know what Oriental civilization is. . . . Now, in all these documents I have found nothing but a poet's sleight-of-hand. Thus I am as disappointed and unhappy as can be. Just a little more of this, and I will be ready to believe that this man is a swindler.[40]

Trying to be helpful, Shen suggested that perhaps what Tagore had in mind by Oriental civilization was the picturesque in nature, for in his first Shanghai lecture he had noted that the smokestacks of modern factories were spoiling the view of China's rice-fields. This was not a satisfactory definition, Shen objected, since the picturesque could be found everywhere, in the West as well as in the East, and since many European poets expressed nostalgia for the open fields just as Tagore did. "I confess I don't see what danger Western civilization poses for Oriental civilization," he continued. "To be sure, certain Western things which have been introduced among us are not exactly picturesque. . . . But how useful and profitable they are, how much they multiply our strength and save us time! And we are supposed to renounce them, for the sake of the beauty of nature, and return to the childish ideas and coarse habits of primitive peoples? Now really!" [41]

Making one final attempt to wring meaning from Tagore's lectures, Shen thought he found it in the concept of "the third age of humanity," which the poet had borrowed from Kropotkin and used in his lecture to the students at the Temple of Agriculture.[42] This new world could only be reached, according to Tagore, through humility and self-sacrifice, the latter assuming the salvation of the soul even though the body perished.

> Thus, the third age of humanity for Mr. Tagore is a period when, after a life of servitude and after the ruin of the body, the soul achieves enlightenment. This is therefore a world for souls, which the poet builds in the clouds; or, to put it bluntly, a world for the dead. . . . But I am alive, not a dead man, and I don't belong to that world. Now Mr. Tagore claims that, with the exception of our noble neighbor Japan, all the peoples of the East already belong to this necropolis, and should only be on their guard that the Japanese, who are so agitated, and the foreigners, who are so interested, do not disturb its peace.[43]

Shen Yen-ping was obviously more worried about the political, social, and economic effects of Tagore's ideas than about his possible literary influence, and he was by no means the only young writer to feel this way. An even sharper reaction came from the equally famous Kuo Mo-jo. Kuo's case is all the more significant because he was the first Chinese intellectual to admire and imitate Tagore's writings, which he read in Japanese translations of the Indian poet's English verse. A restless and romantic youth from a well-to-do family in remote Szechwan, Kuo was studying medicine in Japan when the Nobel award first made Tagore's writings known there. In 1916, when Tagore first visited Japan, Kuo was in distant Okayama, but followed in the Japanese press the poet-philosopher's movements and his appeal for the revival of Oriental spiritual civilization. Afflicted by a severe emotional crisis in the winter of 1916–17, Kuo at first considered committing suicide or becoming a Buddhist priest, then found great solace in reading Tagore. "A strong, clear melody would flow through my body," he later wrote, and this feeling of elation gave him relief from his misery. Within a few months, when his Japanese common-law wife bore him a son, Kuo began to worry about making money and tried unsuccessfully to interest two Shanghai publishers in bringing out his translations from Tagore. In despair, he felt that "Tagore was a noble sage and I was a worthless, common man." [44]

By the autumn of 1923 Kuo had sufficiently mastered these feelings of inferiority to have made himself a powerful figure on the Chinese literary scene as the leader of the Creation Society (Ch'uang-tsao she), dedicated at that time to aestheticism and a romantic populism. Having left behind not only his Tagore phase but Whitman and Goethe phases as well, he was on the verge of ending his passionate quest for an ideal by becoming a Marxist. So complete was the change in his thinking that he felt it his duty to be the first to warn China's intellectuals against the baneful effects of Tagore's spiritual philosophy. Having finally completed his medical training, Kuo used a doctor's language as he diagnosed the ills of the world and prescribed their treatment. "We Eastern peoples have long been immersed in a deathlike stillness," he asserted, "and the medicine which will bring us back from death to life is not this, but something else." That medicine was Marx's materialism, class struggle, and revolutionary overthrow of capitalism.

> The turbulent confusion of the West is the disease produced by its defective system, and the decay of our East is a disease caused by the bondage of private property. Although the diseases are different, the reasons for them are the same. I believe that the theory of historical materialism is the only correct path to the solution of the world's problems. Until the world has undergone a radical change in its economic system . . . [Tagore's ideas] can only be the morphine and coconut-wine of those with property and leisure, while the propertyless class continues to pour out its blood and sweat. The preaching of peace is the greatest poison in today's world. Peace propaganda is the magic charm that protects the propertied class; it is the ball and chain that fetters the propertyless class.[45]

Kuo stressed that he and his friends heartily welcomed Tagore as a private visitor to China, but hoped that the poet would not dawdle in Peking and Shanghai like a puppet of those who had invited him. Instead he recommended a rest cure, a tour of China's rivers, lakes, and mountains, so rich in poetic inspiration. "I am afraid this is the only reward we can give him for coming to China from such a great distance," he concluded.[46] By the time Tagore did arrive, Kuo was back in Japan again, translating into Chinese the work which set the seal on his conversion to Marxism: Kawakami Hajime's Social Organization and Socialist Revolution. Tagore no longer interested him, except as a relic of the "literature of yesterday," one of those "privileged aristocrats" whose writings were merely "the spiritual products of their idle leisure":

Such men either belong to the nobility, or they are the protégés of noblemen. They are fortunate to have fine opportunities to develop their talents, but those who lack these opportunities can only struggle, starve and die of disease. . . . Even if Tagore in his poetry and Tolstoy in his fiction preach benevolence and love, I feel they are just administering charity to the starving.[47]

Kuo Mo-jo's bitter hostility, Shen Yen-ping's and Chou Tso-jen's playful skepticism, Lu Hsün's careless silence — all these reactions to Tagore reflect the dominant mood of realism among China's prose writers, in sharp contrast to the idealism of the Indian poet. The "literary revolution," as it was called in China, was already becoming more and more a means toward social and political revolution. Lu Hsün and Shen Yen-ping, although they never joined the Chinese Communist Party, were to found the League of Leftist Writers in 1930, while Kuo Mo-jo did become a party member and is today head of the National Academy of Sciences in the People's Republic of China, having unashamedly proclaimed and practiced his doctrine that "this is the time for propaganda, and literature is an effective propaganda weapon." [48]

Hsü Chih-mo and Wen I-to exemplify a contrasting but weaker trend toward "art for art's sake" in modern Chinese literature, especially in poetry. Hsü looked to English literature for inspiration, Wen toward Chinese traditions, and these different orientations go far to explain their markedly different reactions to Tagore. Neither Hsü nor Wen showed any interest in the literary traditions of India — nor for that matter did Tagore make much of an effort to tell them about these traditions. Only Cheng Chen-to praised the concept of Eastern spirituality, but even he failed to defend the idea after it had come under heavy attack.

Had Tagore restricted the scope of his lectures in China to the sphere of creative writing, he would probably have exerted a greater influence on the thinking of that country's literary leaders.[49] Instead, his attempt to deliver a philosophical and religious message to the intellectual world at large produced a tragic working at cross-purposes with that particular group which felt the closest kinship with him as a creative artist. They had hoped that Tagore would encourage their movement to create a new literature, free of the outworn conventions of the past, but found that he was asking them to lead a return to the ways of their forefathers. Small wonder that even those literary men who had so proudly hailed his coming only a few months before now lapsed into complete silence concerning the message he sought to bring them.

PHILOSOPHERS

As Tagore ascended from the earthbound world of literature into the higher atmosphere of philosophical and religious thought, he attracted the attention of those Chinese intellectuals whose main interests lay in these loftier realms. Coming as the fourth of a series of eminent foreign lecturers, following in the wake of John Dewey, Bertrand Russell, and Hans Driesch, he was naturally expected to speak on philosophical questions. The very ardor and elegance of his appeal for a revival of Eastern spiritual civilization showed that he wanted most of all to reach the minds of China's philosophers, rather than those of her literary leaders. In response, seven of the country's most prominent thinkers assessed his ideas, each from his own particular point of view.

The amazing heterogeneity of these viewpoints testifies to the liveliness of philosophical thought at this period and to the openness of the philosophers to alternative theories and traditions, for both Chinese and Western traditions were being discussed and championed, sometimes singly, sometimes in unexpected combinations. From the Chinese heritage Confucian, Neo-Confucian, non-Confucian, and Buddhist traditions were being revived and reinterpreted, and from the Western heritage Greek thought, German idealism, modern pragmatism, and materialism were being absorbed and applied in the study of philosophical problems.

As soon as Tagore began to speak of defending Chinese culture against corrosive influences from the West, Peking's intellectuals were reminded of one among them who had long been talking in similar terms. This was the archconservative, Ku Hung-ming, so attached to the old Confucian order that he refused to cut off his queue (the symbol of loyalty to the Ch'ing dynasty and its ethos), which everyone else had stopped wearing when the imperial system came to an end in 1912. Like Tagore, Ku upheld an essentially aristocratic ideal of personal morality and looked with disdain on the egalitarianism and materialism he found in the modern West. Again like Tagore, Ku believed that the ancient civilization of his native land, if properly appreciated, could bring salvation to a world torn by war, social conflict, and inner doubt. It seemed only natural, therefore, to bring these two sages together, and this was arranged during Tagore's stay at Tsing Hua College where they had a long talk. Their host later observed to his regret that they did not get on well with each other,[50] but Ku politely refrained from commenting publicly on Tagore's ideas until the very day the Indian poet sailed for Japan, and then let fly a stinging letter to the editor of the *Shanghai Mercury*, to which he had long been an occasional contributor.[51]

Ku Hung-ming wished to make one thing clear: Oriental civilization, as Tagore had described it, was utterly different from Chinese civilization, which was "not an Oriental civilization like the civilization of India and Persia" at all. On the contrary:

> Just as it was Christianity which destroyed the ancient civilization of Europe, so it was Buddhism, a product of the Oriental civilization of India which after the Han dynasty nearly destroyed the true ancient Chinese civilization and, after the Renaissance of the T'ang dynasty, helped to produce the Puritanism of the Sung dynasty; and it was this Puritanism of the Sung dynasty which has made the real civilization of China became stagnant and unprogress[ive]. In view of this fact, it is very curious to see this Indian poet now telling the Chinese to revive this very Oriental civilization which has been the cause of the stagnation in the Chinese civilization.[52]

In Ku's analysis, China had much more to fear from Indian than from Western influences, for, "when the modern West once gets itself free from Mediaevalism, it will have the same civilization as China . . . a civilization of rationalism and science." Indian civilization, however, was antagonistic to rationalism and science. Therefore, Ku concluded, "if we Chinese want really to make progress, instead of reviving, we must get rid of this Oriental civilization." For good measure he added: "Now if I may venture to give an advice to this great Indian poet, I want to say to him — stick to your poetry, write poetry and don't talk of Civilization."[53]

Of all the Chinese intellectuals who commented on Tagore, Ku Hung-ming was the least Chinese but the most ardently Confucian. Born in 1857 in Penang of a family which had emigrated from Fukien two generations earlier, Ku was sent to Edinburgh for his school and college education and there came under the influence of Matthew Arnold. After thirteen years in Europe, including a spell on the Continent, he arrived in China in about 1885 and only then began to study the civilization of his own country, becoming an enthusiastic Confucianist just in the last decades of the Confucian order in imperial China. In a series of eloquent English essays, studded with quotations from the Latin, German, and French and with gems from Wordsworth, Arnold, and Emerson, he glorified the Confucian principles of morality and government and condemned the aggressive actions of the Western powers in China. Secretary-interpreter for twenty years to the reforming General Chang Chih-tung, he regarded his patron's famous formula, "take Chinese learning as the fundamental principle, and use Western learning for practical matters," as a dangerous compromise. By 1910, China's swiftly moving history had left him so far behind that he plaintively declared: "I am perhaps the only one among our men who still absolutely believes in the final victory for our cause, the cause of Chinese civilization against modern European ideas of progress and the new learning. But I am now all alone." [54]

Ku's enthusiasm for Chinese civilization was essentially that of the convert, closely akin to the Sinophilia of such Westerners as Reginald Johnston, English tutor to the ex-emperor. [55] Indeed, Ku believed so passionately in the superiority of Chinese civilization that he thought it man's best hope for the emergence of a "modern moral culture" based on reason rather than on religion. Since it was Chinese civilization that would be able "to save the civilization of Europe, to save the civilization of the world," he understandably could not agree with Tagore's conviction that India's civilization could best fulfill that role. [56]

Although Ku Hung-ming was regarded by Peking's intellectuals as a harmless eccentric, other thinkers in the capital, genuinely conservative in their upbringing and intellectual training, believed as he did that Chinese civilization was potentially the world civilization of the future by virtue of its stress on reason and moderation. An outstanding example is the philosopher Liang Sou-ming, whose book on Eastern and Western Civilizations and Their Philosophies had scored an immediate success on its publication in 1922 and was still being widely read at the time of Tagore's visit. [57] Well-versed in Confucian and Buddhist thought, Liang recognized that India and China had evolved quite different civilizations and he distinguished them by identifying the search for harmony with the world as characteristic of China and the desire to withdraw from the world characteristic of India. Unlike either of these Eastern civilizations, that of the West, based on a revival of Greek civilization, was marked in his view by its will to dominate and control the world.

Many Chinese thinkers before him had attempted to reconcile the conflicting claims of Chinese and Western civilizations. The most original feature of his theory was that it neatly eliminated this conflict by projecting into the future the worldwide flourishing of Chinese civilization. The civilization of the West had been first to achieve global dominance, and China and India still needed to adopt its attitude of struggle. Liang noted, however, that the Western way already seemed a dead end to Westerners themselves, and predicted, "the coming civilization of the world will be the revival of Chinese civilization, resembling the revival of Greek civilization in the modern world." Although he predicted the eventual triumph of the Indian attitude of ascetic detachment, Liang recommended to his countrymen that for the present:

1. The Indian attitude must be rejected, and not a trace of it be allowed to remain.
2. Western civilization must be accepted in its entirety, but must be fundamentally transformed; that is, its underlying attitude must be transformed.
3. The original Chinese attitude must be re-evaluated and presented anew.[58]

Given his hostility to Indian influences, Liang Sou-ming might be expected to have opposed Tagore's ideas with as much vehemence as did Ku Hung-ming. Instead he praised Tagore's world-view as being essentially Chinese rather than Indian:

Tagore actually has the ability to harmonize antitheses and conflicts and to revive the apathetic, the tired, and the dying. Original Brahmanism was not like this. He was probably influenced by the Western philosophy of vitalism. Therefore the path he follows is not originally Indian, nor is it the original Western one. Even though his path does not seem connected with Chinese philosophy on the surface, nevertheless I say emphatically that it belongs to China, it belongs to the path of the Confucian school.[59]

At the time of Tagore's visit to China, Liang Sou-ming was one of the most popular lecturers on philosophy at Peking University and a renowned savant. He was one of the fifty-odd eminent scholars introduced to the Indian poet at the reception held at the Throne Hall of Imperial Splendor, but did not talk personally with him, nor did he comment in print on his message to China. He did tell one of Tagore's party that he welcomed the Indian poet-philosopher as a symbol of the Eastern tradition of combining philosophy with poetry, and added, concerning his writings: "What I have read has touched my spirit." [60] Not long afterward Liang resigned from teaching and devoted himself to very much the same kind of rural reconstruction and education work that Tagore was pursuing in India, settling in Shantung province at about the same distance from Peking as Tagore's school at Santiniketan was removed from Calcutta. Like Tagore, he disliked the growth of modern, Westernized cities in China, and in 1927–28 he abandoned his earlier idea that China should adopt the Western attitude of struggle, just as he had already rejected the Indian attitude of renunciation. "What did I repudiate? I repudiated the entire Western bag of tricks, and was not again to be tainted," he wrote. "What did I believe in? I believed in our own way of setting up our country and was not again to be intimidated." [61]

The remarkable similarity between Liang's ruralism and Tagore's apparently resulted from their similar reactions to the decline of village life and the decay of traditional culture in their respective countries, rather than from any influence the Indian may have exerted on the Chinese thinker. Having arrived at the conviction that wholesale Westernization would inflict irreparable harm on his society, each thinker charted his own, highly individualistic, program for revitalizing his native culture, beginning with its traditional stronghold in the rural areas. In his practical work Liang Sou-ming resembled Tagore more closely than any other Chinese intellectual; in his theory, however, he remained essentially a Confucianist, and to the extent that he approved of Tagore's outlook he did so because it seemed to him eminently Confucian and Chinese.

The more natural tendency was for China's philosophers to identify Tagore's ideas with Indian thought, which most Chinese equated with Buddhism. This tendency was certainly justified by Tagore's frequent references to the period when Buddhism had linked India and China and by his appeal to the ideals of love, faith, and self-sacrifice. Attachment to Buddhism in one form or another seems to have been on the increase in this, as in previous turbulent periods of China's history. Tagore himself noted several signs that his message was warmly received by the professed Buddhists among China's intellectuals: the civil governor in Nanking had said as much, and the members of the Young Men's Buddhist Association in Peking had hailed him as a champion of their cause.

Among those Chinese laymen who saw in Buddhist philosophy the answer to the needs of their time, none was more eminent than the reformer-journalist-politician Liang Ch'i-ch'ao, and none welcomed Tagore more cordially. The intellectuals they had met in postwar Europe had encouraged both men to believe that their cultures could supply the deficiencies in Western civilization, forming in combination with the best in the West a new and more perfect whole. From this point on, Liang (now retired from active political life) grew increasingly interested in the history of Buddhist thought. Comparing China's new thought movement to Europe's Renaissance, he looked forward to a "Buddhistic reformation" paralleling the Protestant Reformation.

> Buddhist philosophy has always been a precious legacy of our forefathers, but because of its overdevelopment errors arose in the long run and scholars of the Ch'ing period reacted violently against it. . . . It so happens that the intellectual atmosphere of the world has undergone a similar tendency: overdevelopment of material civilization has made "spiritual hunger" all the more acute. Buddhist philosophy is a good remedy for the need of the age. Our national character is especially fit for this kind of knowledge. That is why it could develop in the past; in the future this special character will undoubtedly reassert itself.[62]

Liang Ch'i-ch'ao's desire to revitalize Chinese Buddhism, like Tagore's to revive the great age of Hindu-Buddhist culture, stemmed both from his personal need for metaphysical ideas and from his reflections on the current state of his own country and of the West. These two programs were similar, though not identical, for Liang was attracted to the rational rather than the mystical elements in Buddhist thought, and in any case insisted, "Just as Buddhism of the Sui and T'ang [eras] was not Indian Buddhism, so the revived Buddhism of the future will not be the Buddhism of the Sui and T'ang kind." [63]

By the time Tagore arrived in Peking, Liang was able to say to the audience to whom he introduced the Indian poet: "You all know that I am fond of treating things from a historical point of view; you know too that I have deep faith in Buddhism. As the proverb says: 'No man can speak three words without disclosing his own craft.' So what I am going to tell you today is but my own impression as a historian and a Buddhist." [64]

Liang seems to have been genuinely pleased that Tagore had come to China, for in welcoming him he graciously acknowledged China's many cultural borrowings from "our elder brothers, the people of India," and expressed the hope that "a warm spirit of co-operation between India and China" would result from the visit. Yet he made no mention of "Eastern civilization," clearly separating the traditions of the two countries rather than lumping them together in a single civilization, as Tagore had done: "Both the civilisations represented by India and China are hoary with ancient traditions and yet I feel that there is in them the vigour of eternal youth, which shows itself to-day in India in the two great personalities of Tagore and Gandhi." [65]

While he strongly favored closer contacts between the intellectuals of India and China, Liang Ch'i-ch'ao has left no record of how he felt about Tagore's appeal for a revival of spiritual values in China. One of his oldest friends and closest associates, Hsü Fo-ssu, did write on this subject, however, and there are good reasons for believing that his opinion was also Liang's; he not only wrote in the editorial pages of K'o-hsüeh (Science), to which Liang also made frequent contributions, but his analysis of Tagore's message echoed almost word for word the argument that Liang had pressed in his statement the previous year in the great controversy over science and metaphysics. Hsü suggested that the poet's opposition to materialism be considered separately from his avowedly favorable attitude toward science. "Tagore's opinion is not at all opposed to science per se," he noted. "As he himself says: 'Science is truth, and truth ought not to be exploited; therefore science should not be exploited.'" Hsü's concluding argument, that there was no conflict between art and science, closely resembled Liang's declaration that metaphysics and science each had its proper sphere: "Whether they worship or oppose him, I hope my countrymen will criticize Tagore's views in the spirit of Tagore himself. Since poetry and science are not mutually incompatible, we should each try to make contributions in whichever field lies closer to our own temperaments." [66]

In his address of welcome Liang Ch'i-ch'ao had expressed the hope that Tagore's influence on China would not in any way be inferior to that of Kumarajiva and Jinabhadra,[67] two of the most famous Indian

Buddhist monks who went to China. Many of China's Buddhist laymen and monks must have formed an equally favorable estimate of their Indian visitor, but China's most forceful and influential Buddhist reformer, the Abbot T'ai Hsü, definitely did not. While Liang and others hoped for the revitalization of pietistic Buddhism, T'ai Hsü championed the revival of the agnostic Consciousness Only (wei shih) school, and so derided Tagore as "an old poet-sage" who had yet to see the great light of the Buddha's teaching. "Although Mr. Tagore bases himself on the Vedanta, in the same way that Chinese Neo-Confucianism has used Mahayana Buddhism to transform the old Brahmanism of India, nevertheless Tagore's Vedanta in India and Neo-Confucianism in China are today dead and decaying." Responding to Tagore's remark that India had sent to China over a thousand years ago the "good fruits" of Mahayana Buddhism, T'ai Hsü asserted that the plant bearing these fruits had died out in India, but had taken firm root in China and now could be found nowhere else in the world but there. Being an even more fervent and practiced missionary of his faith than Tagore was of his, T'ai Hsü turned the tables on the Indian poet by urging him to become a Buddhist:

> Oh, Mr. Tagore! Have you already achieved the consciousness of ultimate truth and untruth? If you have, then you should become a missionary, working with true sincerity and great courage to transform the Chinese into young Buddhists. Do not merely remain an old poet singing like a lovely bird . . . Mr. Tagore! Mr. Tagore! I pray that you will throw away the mask of an old poet and will reveal your true face as a new Buddhist youth, coming in person to cultivate the Buddhist good fruit of peace and perfection, and spreading it all over the globe, making the world a peaceful and beautiful garden and a paradise of the new Buddhist youth.[68]

Tagore's message evidently set T'ai Hsü thinking about how his own message might be couched in terms of the popular dichotomy between Eastern and Western civilizations, for in a few months' time he produced an article on this same subject which took Tagore's theory and dressed it in Buddhist attire. Western civilization was "artificial and instrumental," while "Eastern civilization is a civilization for improving human nature," he declared.

> If we can improve human nature so as to attain its ultimate perfection, then the world will be in good order, and mankind will enjoy peace and

well-being. Then the merits of Western civilization can be put to proper use. Now we have gone to the extreme in using the defects of Western civilization, and its power is expanding greatly. If we do not exert ourselves quickly to improve human nature, we cannot counterbalance these defects. If we do not use the law of the Buddha, we will not be able quickly to improve human nature.[69]

The depth of the gulf between Tagore's and T'ai's interpretations of Buddhism and of Eastern civilization emerges in dramatic form in the statement which T'ai made in mid-1924 concerning the difference between Buddhism and Communism. "Recently I heard that the Communists were quite rampant in Peking," he began, possibly referring to the agitation against Tagore there, for which Communist leaders were chiefly responsible. "If this trend continues without any change in their behavior," he continued, "even if they gain power, and were able to kill all of mankind, they would never be able to achieve their goal of sharing all property in common." T'ai Hsü seemed to agree that communism was the ideal form of society, but asserted that it could never be achieved by the violent methods of the Communist Party (which he would rename "the Human Slaughter Party"). Only Buddhism could lead mankind to perfect communism, he explained, reasoning in traditional chain-syllogistic fashion:

> When every man is able to accept the teachings of Buddhism, then he will eliminate the concept of "I." When the self is eliminated, then "my" also is eliminated, and when "my" is eliminated, then "private property" is eliminated. . . . By this path we can reach the goal of communism. I wish people would not believe superstitiously in Marx's *Capital* and theory of materialism, but [would] come along this bright and broad path.[70]

By acknowledging Communism as a goal (while disavowing its violent methods), T'ai Hsü sounded a note that still echoes in the pronouncements of some Buddhist spokesmen in China, Vietnam, and Ceylon.

Each of the four major thinkers mentioned thus far was concerned with preserving and revitalizing a major Chinese tradition or traditional attitude: Ku Hung-ming and Liang Sou-ming with their own interpretations of Confucianism, and Liang Ch'i-ch'ao and T'ai Hsü with different traditions of Chinese Buddhism. Another prominent philosopher advocating the strengthening of Chinese traditions in 1924 was Chang

Chün-mai, the chief protagonist on the side of metaphysics in the famous 1923 controversy. When the Peking Lecture Association announced that Tagore had accepted its invitation to lecture in China, the news, coming as it did at the height of the controversy, was widely interpreted as a deliberate attempt to bolster Chang's side in the great debate.[71] As noted, when Tagore landed in Shanghai, Chang was at the dock to meet him, and he arranged for the poet's first public reception in China to be held in his own spacious garden in Shanghai. But throughout Tagore's lecture tour Chang said not a word about the ideas his invited guest was preaching to the intellectuals of his country. Finally, on the very last day of Tagore's stay in China, he once again was host at a reception for the Indian poet, and after explaining that he had been sick with smallpox since Tagore arrived, Chang let fall a few casual remarks to indicate how he felt about the message of his fellow believer in metaphysics.

Chang began by declaring he felt sorry for Tagore and feared that one reason he had encountered opposition was "because there were people saying Tagore supports metaphysics and came to China especially to help me." He seemed rather worried about the possibility that Tagore's extreme advocacy of spirituality would bring his own sober ethical idealism into still greater disrepute. Whatever his motives, Chang's comments on Tagore's message to China were decidedly unenthusiastic, even obliquely disparaging:

> Actually, I had never read anything written by Mr. Tagore before he came to China, and only now that I have read the speeches he delivered in Peking and Shanghai have I come to know that his heart is full of love and beauty. This shows us that Mr. Tagore and I have no connection with each other, and that he definitely did not come to China to assist me. Furthermore, Tagore's ideas are lofty and profound; consequently he does not wish to condescend to help my metaphysics. In general, opinions vary greatly; there are some people who support material civilization, but there are also others who support spiritual civilization. Neither can avoid criticism. Now Mr. Tagore is a critic of those who support material civilization, and he emphasizes beauty and love. Is it not curious that so many people are as worried about him as they are about a big cannon? [72]

Concluding his brief introduction before the poet made his final speech in China, Chang added noncommittally: "Now Mr. Tagore is about to depart. He wishes to see Asian civilization independent and to create a new age. I wish he would tell us what China's weak points are." [73] Tagore replied rather testily to Chang's suggestion, implying that he felt Chang was not in sympathy with him.[74]

Many years later Chang, having failed to organize a "third force" in China as an alternative to the Kuomintang and the Chinese Communist Party, spent some months as an exile in India. While there he wrote a book entitled *China and Gandhian India* in which Tagore's name appears only once, his visit to China being mentioned but not the ideas he sought to convey there. Gandhi, on the other hand, received two entire chapters of praise for his virtuous private and political life, which Chang considered the perfect illustration of the Neo-Confucian precepts found in the book of Great Learning.[75] In a more recent book, Chang has stressed that "Confucianism, as a philosophy and a standard of morality, can be modernized," and has advocated "a revival of Chinese philosophy, [which] together with the Western richness of intellectual initiative and methodology should lead to a new and larger understanding between the East and the West." [76] Despite the similarity in structure between his program and Tagore's — each hoping to improve understanding between East and West by revitalizing the philosophical traditions of his own country — Chang found Tagore's revitalized Hinduism too abstract and too devoid of ethical and political content to be compatible with even the most idealized form of Neo-Confucianism. Thus China's greatest champion of metaphysics in the 1920's could not accept the metaphysical message of his Indian counterpart.[77]

Attempts to solve the problems of China and the world by reinterpreting ancient philosophic traditions was not limited to Confucianists, Buddhists, and Neo-Confucianists. The demise of the old Confucian order and the application of critical scholarship to an ever-wider range of classical texts also brought non-Confucian and non-Buddhist traditions into greater prominence. This in turn opened the way for a new "modernist" attitude toward the classical heritage, which judged earlier traditions according to their compatibility with modern ideas.

Hu Shih best exemplifies the kind of thinker who has moved into the world of modern thought without completely surrendering the revitalist's emotional attachment to the ancient traditions of his own people. In the opening pages of his Ph.D. dissertation, written under John Dewey at Columbia University in 1915–1917, he wrote first as modernist: "The revival of the non-Confucian schools is absolutely necessary because it is in these schools that we may hope to find the congenial soil in which to transplant the best products of occidental philosophy and science." But a second and rather different purpose also interested him. The study of non-Confucian philosophers would not only help his people to see that the scientific methods of the modern West "are not totally alien to the Chinese mind," but would also show them that these same methods "are the instruments by means of which and in the light of which much of the lost treasures of Chinese philosophy can be recovered." [78] In pursuing this second, revitalist, aim Hu Shih joined Liang Ch'i-ch'ao in a movement for the "reorganization of the national heritage" (cheng-li kuo-ku), which soon had the unintended effect of encouraging ultraconservative scholars in their blind worship of tradition.[79] In 1928 Hu repudiated this movement, but remained convinced that certain aspects of China's ancient heritage were quite "modern" and therefore deserved to be revitalized:

> What pessimistic observers have lamented as the collapse of Chinese civilization, is exactly the necessary undermining and erosion without which there could not have been the rejuvenation of an old civilization. Slowly, quietly, but unmistakably, the Chinese Renaissance is becoming a reality. The product of this rebirth looks suspiciously occidental. But, scratch its surface and you will find that the stuff of which it is made is essentially the Chinese bedrock which much weathering and corrosion have only made stand out more clearly — the humanistic and rationalistic China resurrected by the touch of the scientific and democratic civilization of the new world.[80]

Hu Shih firmly refrained from commenting on the message Tagore had brought to China, but just as firmly defended the poet's right to be heard. In reproaching the students passing out anti-Tagore leaflets at the True Light Theater, he declared:

> Whether you approve or disapprove of his way of teaching matters little, but what matters is to know him as a person before deciding how you will conduct yourselves toward him. . . . China is known as a country of people who act properly, and we must deserve this reputation. If we wish to live up to our traditional politeness and hospitality, we must receive Dr. Tagore with respect. . . .
> Furthermore, Tagore's personality . . . his spirit of literary revolution, his sacrifice for rural education, his movement of rural cooperation, all

deserve our respect, to say nothing of his personality, his benevolent countenance, and his humanitarian spirit.[81]

Although courtesy and personal admiration forbade public expression of his views on Eastern and Western civilizations at the time of Tagore's visit, a few years later Hu delivered a telling indictment of the notion that the East was spiritual and the West material. Blasting "the revival of such old myths as the bankruptcy of the material civilization of the West and the superiority of the spiritual civilization of the Oriental nations," he contrasted the ricksha, which enslaves men's bodies, with the automobile, which emancipates them. Hu Shih thus arrived at exactly the opposite view from the one Tagore had presented to his Chinese audiences:

> The term "materialistic civilization" . . . seems to me to be a more appropriate word for the characterization of the backward civilization of the East. For to me that civilization is materialistic which is limited by matter and incapable of transcending it. . . . Its sages and saints may do all they can to glorify contentment and hypnotize the people into a willingness to praise their gods and abide by their fate. But that very self-hypnotizing philosophy is more materialistic than the dirty houses they live in, the scanty food they eat, and the clay and wood with which they make the images of their gods.
> On the other hand, that civilization which makes the fullest possible use of human ingenuity and intelligence in search of truth in order to control nature and transform matter for the service of mankind, to liberate the human spirit from ignorance, superstition, and slavery to the forces of nature, and to reform social and political institutions for the benefit of the greatest number — such a civilization is highly idealistic and spiritual.[82]

Taking opposite sides in the controversy over science and metaphysics, Chang Chün-mai and Hu Shih both sought to revitalize selected aspects of the philosophical heritage which had come down to them from ancient times. Not so Wu Chih-hui, an older scholar whose lengthy essay disparaging metaphysical ideas of any kind won Hu Shih's praise as the most significant event in the 1923 controversy. Nor was he as polite as Hu when it came to evaluating the message of the Indian poet-philosopher. Wu is a fascinating figure, as yet little studied, whose long life spanned almost the whole modern transformation of China from a Confucian to a Communist empire, and whose own peppery essays played no little part in speeding the transformation.

Wu Chih-hui belonged to the first generation of Chinese to imbibe modern knowledge in the new Chinese schools opened in the treaty port cities. From his studies in Tientsin and Shanghai he went on to Japan and France. An early recruit to the anti-Manchu movement of his younger contemporary Sun Yat-sen, he also espoused anarchism and had considerable influence on the Chinese students among whom he conducted revolutionary work while sojourning in France, Germany, and England in the first decade of the century. A strong supporter of the new culture movement launched in 1915, he took a leading part in the campaign to discredit Confucianism, contributing the famous slogan: "Take all those old books and throw them into the privy for thirty years." [83] Made a member of the Kuomintang's Central Executive Committee in 1924, he was widely regarded as that party's leading philosopher.

Tagore's obvious indifference to the nationalist movement moved Wu Chih-hui to contempt: "Mr. Tagore, . . . a petrified fossil of India's national past, has retreated into the tearful eyes and dripping noses of the slave people of a conquered country, seeking happiness in a future life, squeaking like the hub of a wagon wheel that needs oil." Patriotism was Wu's acid test: "How is it Tagore has written so well in English, the language of his enemy, in order to win the prize given by a rich man in Scandinavia?" he asked. "Is this not like the so-called officials under the Manchus who wrote fine poetry but forgot that their country was conquered?" Ridiculing Tagore's stand against material civilization, Wu noted that in Shanghai the poet and his party had ridden in Western automobiles of the latest model, slept in the best modern hotel, used the best foreign club for meetings, and hired a foreign photographer to take their pictures. Wu particularly objected to the Indian poet's theory that Eastern civilization was spiritual:

> Please have your honorable mouth sealed up tightly. This interpretation of Eastern and Western civilization is as shallow and ridiculous as a blind man's babblings. Our great man of letters, Liang Ch'i-ch'ao, was the forerunner of this kind of talk five years ago. . . . Now Mr. Tagore has brought to China his collected poems and a handbook of prescriptions for compounding these same medicines, which India has already taken and been fatally poisoned by.[84]

As did many other Chinese and Japanese intellectuals, Wu urged Tagore to confine himself to his poetry, for "poets do not deign to speak of worldly matters." Above all, he warned: "Don't dream dreams about the East and the West." [85]

Tagore did not profit from Wu Chih-hui's advice (which probably was never brought to his attention). Arriving in Peking, the unsuspecting poet involved himself even more deeply in worldly matters by calling on the ex-emperor P'u-i in the old Imperial Palace, and by accepting the invitation to visit the "model" Confucianist governor, Yen Hsi-shan of Shansi. This roused Wu Chih-hui to accuse Tagore of meddling in Chinese politics, of supporting the reactionary cause to reinstate the Manchu imperial line, attempted unsuccessfully by General Chang Hsün in 1917 but still considered a possibility. "Tagore in the Midst of the Noise of the Monarchist Movement," read the title of his second scornful essay. Pretending to be constrained by the rules of hospitality from speaking his mind on Tagore's Peking lectures, Wu abstractly wondered: "Why should an artist use his voice like a seller of cheap medicines by the river or by the lake, worrying only about the applause of his audience?" Wu was not seriously worried about the monarchist movement, or about Tagore's "empty and worthless words," but, he observed, "nothing is too strange to happen in China." [86]

These seven major critics of Tagore's message span the whole gamut of philosophical thinkers in the China of 1924, from the archconservative Ku Hung-ming to the archradical, Wu Chih-hui. Of the seven, only Liang Ch'i-ch'ao and Liang Sou-ming found Tagore's ideas congenial to their particular blends of Confucian and Buddhist idealism. But not even these two could accept Tagore's claim that China shared with India a common, spiritual, Eastern civilization. For all these men the distinct character of Chinese civilization remained an unalterable reality. Liang Ch'i-ch'ao and T'ai Hsü welcomed the addition of Indian Buddhist elements to this civilization, but neither wished to see another wave of Indianization such as Tagore seemed to advocate for China. Even the abbot T'ai Hsü, China's most ardent champion of an original Indian tradition, remained firmly Sinocentric; far from accepting a message from Tagore, he challenged Tagore and the world to accept the message of Mahayana Buddhism which India had forgotten but China had preserved.

Even while they resisted or rejected the specific advice proffered by the Indian poet, all but one of the seven Chinese philosophers (the exception was the iconoclastic Wu Chih-hui) were already engaged in the work he favored of revitalizing earlier traditions: Ku Hung-ming and Liang Sou-ming were occupied with Confucianism; Liang Ch'i-ch'ao and T'ai Hsü with Buddhist traditions; Chang Chün-mai with Neo-Confucianism; and Hu Shih with Mo-ist and other non-Confucian traditions. "The Reconstruction of the National Heritage" was well under way. Had Tagore known more about the actual work being done by China's scholars and philosophers, he would have recognized its structural similarity to his own work in revitalizing many of India's forgotten or decayed cultural traditions. Even the cantankerous Wu Chih-hui, for all his antipathy to orthodox Confucianism, was continuing and modernizing a very ancient theme in Confucian thought — its paramount concern with the social and political spheres of human life. Indeed, the protracted and agonizing struggle in twentieth-century China to achieve a unified and powerful nation-state — an objective which the Chinese Communist Party eventually inherited — can be seen as the triumph of this political tradition in a new and more potent form.

POLITICAL LEADERS

The absence of a strong central government, the corruption of most of the warlord regimes, and their chronic warfare among themselves had produced a dismal political situation in China from 1917 onward.[87] Driven by this immediate situation and by their traditional sense of responsibility for governing the country, China's educated men agonized over ways and means to end a chaotic and worsening state of affairs. At the time Tagore made his visit, three types of political thought and organization predominated: the conservative-minded warlords wielding actual power almost everywhere were confronted by the nationalists under the personal leadership of Sun Yat-sen and by the small but swelling Chinese Communist Party. Although Tagore instinctively shied away from political involvement, his visit and his message to China carried political implications, and he was closely watched by the leaders of these three forces to see how his ideas and his influence might advance or retard their own causes and interests.

By his conduct and statements Tagore soon identified himself with the most conservative elements on the Chinese political scene. His motives were innocent enough. Like any tourist, he wished to see something of the ancient culture of China, and so visited the tomb of Confucius in Shantung and paid his respects to the Manchu ex-emperor, the symbol of the old regime and the much-discussed object of schemes for the restoration of the monarchy. A second motive, the desire to see China's civil wars ended so that the united country could concentrate on the task of preserving and reviving traditional culture, prompted him to intercede with the warlord of Anhwei and Kiangsu to desist from further hostilities, and to accept the hospitality of the warlord of Shansi, renowned for his success in governing his "model province" by Confucian principles and methods. In both cases his visits created the impression that he was sympathetic to the warlord system of personal government by military leaders. Third, in keeping with the universality of his vision for an eventual "meeting of East and West," he readily accepted invitations to lecture to Japanese and Anglo-American gatherings in Shanghai and Peking, oblivious to the sentiments of fear and loathing with which ardent nationalists regarded these foreign powers, who still guarded their extraterritorial and other privileges in enclaves on Chinese soil. In several ways, then, the poet unwittingly associated himself with all the worst enemies of the rising nationalist and Communist movements. By enjoying the pleasure of such mixed company Tagore made himself a perfect target for the ire of those intellectuals whose goal was a strong and progressive Chinese government, independent of foreign influence.

The most important of the warlord regimes, that of Ts'ao K'un in Peking, showed a cautious interest in the Indian poet-philosopher's presence. Posing as the legitimate government of China and so recognized by most foreign nations (but in fact little more than a provincial government dressed in the trappings of a bribed "national" parliament), the Peking regime was at first reported to have considered Tagore as its "semi-official guest," [88] and the special guard it provided for the last leg of the poet's trip to Peking lent credence to this report. A move was also made to show sympathy with his message of Eastern spiritual civilization, for, the day before he reached Peking, Reuters announced: "The Ministry of Education has appointed . . . a preparatory commission to deal with the development of Oriental Civilization, for which the promoters hope that a portion at least of the Japanese Boxer Indemnity will be made available." [89]

Once in Peking, Tagore seems to have had no contact with the government. President Ts'ao gave a series of receptions on May 8, 9, and 10 for members of the diplomatic corps, government officials, and newspaper representatives, and this would have been an appropriate occasion for the poet to have been received by the politician, but no such meeting occurred.[90] Probably the intellectuals in the group around Liang Ch'i-ch'ao warned Tagore that the regime was merely a corrupt facade with little popular support; on his part, Ts'ao K'un may well have decided that there was little practical gain, and perhaps some loss of prestige, to be had from cultivating the Indian visitor.

Far to the south, in Canton another political leader claiming to head the legitimate government of China weighed the advantages of reaching some kind of an understanding with Tagore. This was Sun Yat-sen, the central figure in the maelstrom of Chinese politics throughout the first quarter of the twentieth century. Sun's ideas on the relation of Eastern and Western civilizations were in many respects identical with Tagore's. The eulogy of Asian civilization with which he opened his lecture on "Pan-Asianism" at Kobe in late 1924, for example, reads like Tagore's own writings on the subject:

> Asia, in my opinion, is the cradle of the world's oldest civilization. . . . In ancient Asia we had a philosophic, religious, logical and industrial civilization. . . . It is only during the last few centuries that the countries and races of Asia have gradually deteriorated and become weak, while the European countries have gradually developed their resources and become powerful.[91]

Like Tagore, Sun disparaged the civilization of the West as materialistic and extolled that of the East: "European civilization is nothing but the rule of Might . . . Oriental civilization is one of the rule of Right. . . . Of late, a number of European and American scholars have begun to study Oriental civilization and to realize that, while materially the Orient is far behind the Occident, morally the Orient is superior to the Occident."[92]

On the basis of these remarks, the images of East and West in Sun's mind and in Tagore's seem practically identical. But, as might be expected from China's foremost protagonist of the nationalist idea, Sun was using Oriental civilization as a cover term for Chinese civilization, in this particular case as part of an attempt to persuade his old Japanese allies to cooperate in a pan-Asian movement against Western imperialism. Only a few months before, in expounding his Three People's Principles (*San-min chu-i*) to his Kuomintang colleagues at Canton, Sun had voiced these same ideas within a purely Chinese frame of reference. He noted with satisfaction that "great philosophers like Bertrand Russell, . . . as soon as they come to China, are able to discern that Chinese civilization is superior to European or American civilization," and asserted: "European superiority to China is not in political philosophy, but altogether in the field of material civilization. . . . If we want to learn from Europe we should learn what we ourselves lack — science — but not political philosophy." [93]

Just as Tagore sought the revitalization of India's religious culture, so Sun sought the revitalization of the political civilization of China. "China was once an exceedingly powerful and civilized nation, the dominant state of the world," he declared, and asked: "Why did China once occupy so exalted a place and then 'fall ten thousand feet in one drop'?" The answer was simple: "because we lost our national spirit. . . . So if we want to restore our national standing, we must first revive our national spirit." If the Chinese people would only revive their ancient moral virtues of loyalty, filial devotion, kindness, love, faithfulness, justice, harmony, and peace, "our state will naturally flourish." Not only moral values, but scholarship, especially political philosophy, must be revitalized. Summing up his program, Sun urged the members of the Kuomintang Party: "We must now revive our national spirit, recover our national standing, unify the world upon the foundation of our ancient morality and love of peace, and bring about a universal rule of equality and fraternity." Sun's final vision was of a universal state embodying the virtues, and wielding the power, of China's ancient Confucian empire:

> When we become strong and look back upon our own sufferings under the political and economic domination of the Powers and see weaker and smaller peoples undergoing similar treatment, we will rise and smite that imperialism. Then will we be truly "governing the state and pacifying the world. . . ." You, gentlemen, . . . must all shoulder this responsibility and manifest the true spirit of the nation.[94]

Ever resourceful in his search for means to achieve his ideal of a powerful Chinese nation which could lead to a pan-Asian movement against the West, Sun did not overlook the possibility that India's leading man of letters might make a useful ally. When Tagore's secretary, Leonard Elmhirst, called on Sun in Canton in 1923, Sun said he was very anxious to have Tagore come to China. It was probably no coincidence that one of Tagore's fellow passengers on the Japanese freighter carrying him from Calcutta to Shanghai was an officer in the Kuomintang army. Writing from Peking, Elmhirst reported to Tagore's son that his famous father was reciprocating Sun's interest, for "at Hong Kong he had a long talk with Dr. Sun's private secretary and another with his right-hand man at Shanghai. With both he emphasized the need for a cessation of hostilities between North and South [China] and accepted Dr. Sun's invitation to visit him in Canton on his return. Dr. Sun himself is raising a fund toward the expenses of Visva-Bharati." [95] Yet the two leaders seem to have made no effort to contact each other after Tagore's Peking lecture series ended in a fiasco. Nor did Sun make any comment on the poet's message to China: he was enough of a realist to have recognized that Tagore's pan-Asianism and his own rested on opposite conceptions of the role of force in human affairs. As if replying to Tagore, he declared in his final presentation of his pan-Asian ideal in November 1924:

> But to rely on benevolence alone to influence the Europeans in Asia to relinquish the privileges they have acquired in China would be an impossible dream. If we want to regain our rights, we must resort to force. . . . China has a population of four hundred millions, and although she needs to modernize her armament and other equipment, and her people are a peace-loving people, yet when the destiny of their country is at stake the Chinese people will also fight with courage and determination. Should all Asiatic peoples thus unite together and present a united front against the Occidentals, they will win the final victory. Compare the populations of Europe and Asia . . .[96]

Sun Yat-sen's program of political and cultural revitalization and his social conservatism were to live on as the official ideology of the Kuomintang government which came to power in 1927,[97] but he himself recognized in the last years of his life that his political aims could not be achieved without the aid of more modern methods of political organization than could be found in the Chinese classics or the traditions of the secret societies. He was particularly impressed by the discipline and fervor of the young members of the Chinese Communist Party, and arranged in 1923 to have them enter the ranks of his Kuomintang Party without having to cut their ties to their own party. This Kuomintang-Communist alliance, although it was to last only until the Kuomintang army swept northward from Canton in 1927, at once symbolized and accelerated the fusion of nationalist and leftist ideas which in retrospect stands out as the most portentous development on the Chinese scene in the mid-1920's.[98]

The appeals of Communism to the modern-minded Chinese patriot in 1924 were many. First and foremost it offered a comprehensive and "modern" ideology, one embracing all aspects of life but embodying a concrete program of political action. This combination of theory and practice appealed strongly to the younger generation of intellectuals as they searched for ideas and methods with which to save China from internal chaos and foreign intervention. The élitist character of Communist Party work also fitted naturally into the Confucian tradition of government by scholars, and many of the young leftist intellectuals were themselves the sons or grandsons of officials. The successful revolution of the Communist Party in neighboring Russia, its fierce opposition to imperialism and colonialism in Asia, and its friendly attitude toward China's nationalist movement, all contributed to heighten the prestige of the Chinese Communist Party and its ideology. The negative consequences of totalitarian government by a monolithic party — the rule of terror, the suppression of information, and the regimentation of thought and conduct — were as yet little known in China, and at this time of national weakness and anarchy could be regarded as a small price to pay for a strong and efficient central government.

The most important Communist in 1924 was the party's general secretary since its founding in 1921, Ch'en Tu-hsiu.[99] A pioneer of the new thought movement, Ch'en had been at the forefront of virtually every intellectual battle since 1915, campaigning successively against Confucianism, Japanese imperialism, Christian missions, and all religious metaphysics. The leadership of the Communist Party suited his combative temperament, even though his basic ideas were less specifically those of a Communist than those of a patriot striving by all means to strengthen and modernize his country as rapidly as possible. Operating from the safety of the international settlement of Shanghai, created and maintained by the very capitalist system he wished to overthrow, Ch'en was strategically located to indoctrinate and organize the youth of North, Central, and South China.

Ch'en was in 1924 by all odds China's most vigorous and vitriolic critic of Tagore and his message, but even as early as 1915 he had castigated him as "an escapist poet of India" in the opening manifesto of his New Youth monthly.[100] Ch'en's attitude at this time was not entirely disapproving, for he included in his next issue his own translation of four of Tagore's Gītānjali prose-poems selecting those stressing activism and patriotism. In 1923, however, soon after Tagore's visit to China was announced, Ch'en sharply criticized the Indian poet's opposition to material civilization and sarcastically observed: "Having added to the chaotic thought of Lao-tzu and Chuang-tzu the chaotic thought of Buddhism, we have suffered enough, and are more than grateful to the Indians for their gifts. Now there is no need to add Tagore to all this!" [101]

On the very day Tagore landed in Shanghai the Chinese Communist Party, with Ch'en Tu-hsiu in the lead, began a systematic campaign of detraction against his "message." The course of this campaign may be traced in the pages of the Party's two weekly publications, Chung-kuo ch'ing-nien (China's youth), the student-oriented voice of its Socialist Youth Corps, and Hsiang tao (Guide), published for the smaller circle of the Party faithful. A third outlet was the Chüeh-wu (Awakening) daily supplement to the Kuomintang-Communist Party's Min-kuo jih-pao (Republic daily).

Ch'en fired his opening shot in China's Youth with his satirical account of a reception given to Tagore immediately after he disembarked from his ship, a reception at which Ch'en himself seems to have been present. Portraying the poet as a magician who could pull God out of a hat, Ch'en reported a series of questions to Tagore from Chinese skeptical of his ideal of the contemplative life in the forest. Said one: " 'To live in such a state of abstraction would mean condemning oneself to die of starvation!' . . . 'And to catch colds!' said another . . . 'Or to be devoured by tigers!' added a third." The audience's mood changed to approval, however, when Tagore declared that the Indian people, like the Chinese, remained opposed to the British occupation of strategic points of their country, and he descended from the platform amidst a salvo of applause.[102]

The following day a long article, headed "Oppose Tagore!" appeared in the Republic Daily's supplement, *Awakening*. No name accompanied the article, but its timing, vigorous style, and trenchant arguments mark it as most probably Ch'en Tu-hsiu's work. For a man like Ch'en, who sought to influence public opinion rather than to gain personal publicity, the device of anonymity made good sense, because it focused the reader's attention on the ideas presented in the article. The author put in their strongest form three objections which China's nationalist and leftist intellectuals held against Tagore's program of reviving Eastern spiritual civilization: his indifference to the demands of the body would discourage China's material progress; his principle that only love gives meaning to life would encourage the imperialists to devour China; and his ideal of harmony with nature leads only to individual solace at the expense of society. Not only Tagore but the Chinese scholars sponsoring his visit came in for attack. The first three philosophers they had invited — Dewey, Russell, and Driesch — had exerted little influence on China's students, for their lectures had been too specialized and too deep to be widely understood. But Tagore was different: "As literature is now very popular among our students, there is some danger that Tagore will be more interesting to them. This would be a misfortune. We warn them not to let themselves be *Indianized*. Unless, that is, they want their coffins to lie one day in a land under the heel of a colonial power, as India is." [103]

Several of these points were taken up more systematically in Ch'en Tu-hsiu's lead article devoted to "Tagore and Eastern Civilization" in the next issue of *China's Youth*. Ch'en asserted that he held no brief for Western civilization as such, but found that Eastern civilization rested on three basic propositions: to exalt the prince and abase the people, or to exalt the man and abase the woman; to live contentedly in poverty and patiently in the midst of suffering; and to prize the spiritual and depreciate the material side of life. This last, Tagore's main principle, was not new in China, having been preached by the Buddhist monks and now, among others, by Liang Sou-ming, Chang Chün-mai, and various new religious sects:

If Mr. Tagore joins these people, he would have us destroy our railroads, our steamships, and our printing presses in order to return to wood-block printing, the canoe carved from a tree-trunk, the wheelbarrow, etc. That would be truly Eastern. . . . Is that what Mr. Tagore wants? Or are his talks no more than the hollow verbiage of a poet? . . . If the latter is the case, then it would perhaps be better for him to keep quiet than to sow anxiety so inconsiderately in the minds of our intellectuals.[104]

This article of April 18 and the preceding one of April 12 appear to have served as the basis for the five-point broadside attacking Tagore's ideas which was published on May 1 in Peking. The main ideas and images in the first two documents are woven together in the third, and the report of a qualified observer that the leaflets distributed to Tagore's Peking audiences came from Shanghai also link the three documents to a common source, either in the Communist Party apparatus or in the mind of its general secretary, Ch'en Tu-hsiu himself.[105]

Articles, leaflets, and student demonstrators waving placards and shouting slogans — these were the principal weapons employed in the Chinese Communist Party's anti-Tagore campaign. A lesser, but still quite damaging instrument in the Communist armory was "The Dagger," the closing section in the Party's weekly Guide in which Ch'en Tu-hsiu and other leaders delivered short jabs at their favorite targets. Between April 23 and July 16, Ch'en thrust "The Dagger" no less than thirteen times at his Indian antagonist.

The first thrust set the jibing tone for those that followed. "When Tagore came to China, some people started a Drive Away the Elephant Party to oppose him," Ch'en remarked approvingly:

> It is very appropriate to use the elephant as a symbol for the character of Oriental peoples. The elephant is so large and self-important, but actually he can do nothing. Even though he is so large, he obediently accepts the commands of the elephant boy. He kneels down, and bows subserviently without knowing any shame. When his skin is broken, when he bleeds, he still knows no pain. Among all animals, there is none other who is so large and so numb.[106]

"Drive out the elephant!" became one of the cries used in the anti-Tagore demonstrations in Peking and Hankow.[107]

Ch'en also seems to have been the originator of the taunt that Tagore came to China some thousand years too late, the great age of Chinese Buddhism being irrevocably past: "If he could have come to China when the Eastern civilization was prosperous, and could have met the female Buddha [and usurping tyrant], Empress Wu, and greeted her with palms joined together, and talked as much as he liked about love and peace; then he would not only have smiled broadly, but as compared with today would have 'enjoyed boundless ecstasy.' What a pity he came too late!" [108] Another way to lampoon the Indian poet was to ridicule the company he kept:

> When Tagore first came to China we regarded him as a poet who cherished Oriental thought. As we were afraid that China's youth, who usually enjoy empty speculation, would fall deeply under his spell, so we could not help opposing him. But in fact this was overestimating him. Thus far he has not said anything significant in Peking. He has merely played around with the Manchu Emperor, with Schurman and Aglen [the American ambassador and the British president of the Anglo-American Association], with the monks in the Fa Yüan temple, with the young Buddhist women, and with a man like Mei Lan-fang. What kind of a thing is he! [109]

Tagore is only a poet, but he has not once talked about poetry in China; he opposes material civilization but he and those Chinese who agree with him make appeals for money; he and Liang Ch'i-ch'ao are wealthy men who "forget the constant hunger and cold of the masses all over the world; indeed, they are the representatives of Oriental civilization, which has no conscience!" So "the dagger" rose and fell.[110]

On close analysis, Ch'en Tu-hsiu's criticisms of Tagore yield few ideas that can be called specifically Communist — an indication that the Chinese Communist Party under his leadership from 1921 to 1927 as yet lacked deep ideological roots, its attention being focused on eradicating the three great obstacles to China's modernization: political disunity and debility, economic backwardness, and social injustice. It is therefore interesting to contrast Ch'en's views on Tagore with those of his younger colleague Ch'ü Ch'iu-pai, already at twenty-five a member of the Party's Central Committee. Ch'ü had studied at the Russian Language School in Peking, then gone to Moscow as a correspondent of the Peking Ch'en Pao (Morning news). During his three years there he joined the Communist Party, taught at the University of the Toilers of the East, and interpreted for Ch'en Tu'hsiu when the latter was in the Soviet capital in 1923. Four years later, in 1928, Ch'ü was to replace Ch'en as general secretary, amid the denunciations of the elder leader's incompetence and high-handedness that have since become familiar features of succession crises in Communist parties. We find a clue to this denouement in Ch'ü's principal article on Tagore, which, when compared with Ch'en's, shows much the firmer grasp of Marxist-Leninist theory.

Ch'ü Ch'iu-pai's main argument was not based on Marxism, however, but on the premise, basic to Confucian as well as to Legalist thought, that government was an indispensable instrument in the achievement of the good life. Ch'ü accordingly denounced Tagore for his view that the state was an obstacle to individual freedom and to the development of moral values. "He does not realize," Ch'ü objected with a passion worthy of his Confucian forefathers, "that only after men have been organized and regulated can they really feel a sense of moral responsibility." To be sure, Ch'ü conceded, this political principle was not an end in itself: the state should eventually become expendable, as Marx had predicted. Before this stage could be reached, however, the people must oppose the capitalist class, seize power, eliminate class differences, and introduce a planned economy. "To jump over this stage . . . and directly to deny the system of the nation-state, is impossible." [111]

Tagore's vision of a universal culture shared by all peoples was a fine ideal, Ch'ü thought, but it could not be achieved by Tagore's method of reviving Oriental culture. Take, for example, the social virtues supposedly characteristic of Oriental spiritual civilization — compassion, love, loyalty, forgiveness. "These in fact are merely reflections of the mentality of the hierarchical family system in which you do not fight, because you cannot win." With one final sweep, Ch'ü dismissed Tagore's entire theory of East and West:

> Can the East and the West be harmonized? As there is no so-called East and no so-called West, therefore there is no such problem as harmonizing them! If Tagore is truly "a singer of the common people," and "a poet of slaves," then he should encourage the spirit of aggressiveness, courage, revolt, and activism among the slaves and the common people so that they will unite shoulder to shoulder to overthrow the capitalist state system, and will manage their common life in a systematic and organized way. At this stage, in order to repress the reaction of the capitalist class, we especially need to organize our own state. This is the true road leading us to a universal culture. However, Tagore is different: he merely wishes to harmonize East and West.[112]

In a second article, "Tagore the Has-Been," Ch'ü Ch'iu-pai found Tagore's ideas hopelessly out of date, not only for China but for India as well:

India has already become a part of the British industrial economy, but Tagore, living in the world of the past, still dreams that the message of "love and light" can win over the hearts of the English capitalist class. So he tries hard to ignore India's political struggle. India has already become modern India, but Tagore still seems to want to return to the abode of Brahma [*brāhmaloka*]. No wonder he and India are moving in opposite directions — he has already retrogressed several hundred years! [113]

Tagore later noted that the Communists were his harshest critics in China, but he judged them to be a "very small" section of the population, and concluded, "for all that China received my message warmly." [114] He was nettled, nevertheless, the point of canceling the last half of the special series of lectures he had come to China to deliver — a move which jeopardized the success of his larger mission in China. If the Communists were such a small group, why had their hostility wounded him so deeply? One answer might be that they were particularly influential among the students, the very sector of the educated class the Indian poet had wanted most to impress.

STUDENTS

Tagore made no secret of his desire to influence the young people of China. He chose to deliver the majority of his lectures in schools, colleges, and universities, where students made up the bulk of his listeners. In Shanghai, Hangchow, and Tsinan he allowed local educational associations to make arrangements for his visit, and at Peking he accepted the hospitality of Tsing Hua College for an important part of his stay. During his first conversation with his new Chinese friends he had said with emphasis, "I'm not interested in seeing your antiquities. I want to meet *young* China, your artists and poets. I want to find out what young China is thinking." [115]

Sympathy, skepticism, and hostility for the Indian poet-philosopher mingled in the published reactions of China's students in about the same proportions as in those of their elders, and for much the same reasons. Sympathy flowed mainly from two sources: enthusiasm for romanticism in literature among the Anglo-Americanized youth, and idealistic religiosity among the young Buddhists. Skepticism was as characteristic of students interested in academic philosophy as it was of the more senior philosophers. Hostility to Tagore came mainly from the politically conscious students strongly committed to nationalist and Communist ideas and programs. A survey of student views of Tagore can thus serve as a quick review of the diverse standpoints from which China's articulate intellectuals regarded Tagore and his message.

The close correlation between familiarity with English romantic literature and enthusiasm for Tagore, noted in the case of Hsü Chih-mo and Cheng Chen-to, holds true for students at the colleges in Peking where English was the medium of instruction. At Yenching University's College for Women, managed by American missionaries, one young lady reported that her depressed mood while reading Shakespeare and Maupassant was "blown away" by her encounter with the Indian poet. She felt nothing but admiration and love when she shook hands with him and looked up into his face. She noticed that quite a few other girl students, normally afraid to speak with strangers, went up to Tagore and conversed with him after his lecture. "Is this because of the mysterious power that Mr. Tagore exerted on us?" she asked excitedly.[116] During the week Tagore was resting near Tsing Hua College, several men students wrote him letters of appreciation and submitted written questions which showed approval of his basic ideas.[117]

The more Westernized their outlook, the better able Chinese students were to grasp Tagore's message of Eastern spirituality, rooted as it was in modern Western concern for the revival of Asian cultures, especially of Hindu-Buddhist spirituality. At Tsing Hua, where outstanding students were being prepared for advanced study in the United States, this modern Western outlook was most readily transmitted, often through American teachers whose interest in Eastern cultures had brought them to China in the first place. One young man at Tsing Hua, already exposed to this Western Orientophilia, drew on its arguments to defend Tagore's message against the criticism it had encountered elsewhere in Peking. Lu Mou-te was surprised that some of his countrymen should have attacked the Indian poet for ideas which Lao-tzu had voiced many centuries earlier, and should worship instead the materialist concepts borrowed from the Europeans and Americans. Westerners themselves, he noted (citing Tolstoy, Russell, and one of his American teachers at Tsing Hua), had pointed out the failings of Western civilization and the strengths of Eastern civilization. "The Englishmen have a saying," Lu added innocently, "which actually sums up Tagore's theory: 'What doth it profit a man if he gain the whole world but lose his own soul?' " Seeing no contradiction between his appeal to Western and Christian authorities and his advocacy of Eastern values, Lu roundly declared that Tagore's "disgust at materialistic civilization and his emphasis on spiritual civilization are cooling and purifying medicine for those who are drunk with the culture of Europe and America." [118]

On the other end of the cultural spectrum, the leaders of the Peking Young Men's Buddhist Association endorsed Tagore's message, not because Westerners agreed with it, but because it seemed eminently Buddhist and Eastern. "He has come thousands of miles to spread the Buddha's teachings," declared one, "to encourage and help us Buddhists, to help the enlightened intellectuals of our country." [119] Another enthusiastic young Buddhist gave a resounding yea to Tagore's entire program:

> The true value of our welcome to Tagore lies in awakening the highest spiritual culture of the East, while using the European and American material civilization to enjoy material things. . . . In the future we shall unify the spirituality of the East and the materialism of the West. Western materialism will come to the East, and Eastern spirituality will go to the West; each will get what it needs from the other, and each will become full and perfect. The defects of the world will be eliminated, and heaven will be built on earth. The Chinese and Indian peoples must alone take responsibility for accomplishing this mission. In cooperation with Western cultural leaders we shall achieve the third civilization in the twentieth century. Then there will be no Westernization and no Easternization; the whole world will be in universal harmony [ta-t'ung].[120]

A third source of student support for Tagore's views, in addition to the Anglo-Americanized and the Buddhist youth of Peking, centered in some of the provincial schools, colleges, and universities, where the new thought movement was weaker and the premodern cultural traditions of China stronger than at Peking and Shanghai. The students at Hangchow, Tsinan, Taiyuan, and Wuchang (the capitals of Chekiang, Shantung, Shansi, and Hupeh provinces) had come in large numbers to hear the Indian poet-philosopher, and listened to him respectfully, if not enthusiastically. One student at the National Southeastern University in Nanking, Tung Feng-ming, took special interest in Tagore as an aesthetic leader and insisted that he be treated as a poet rather than as a philosopher:

> As hosts we should receive him politely. If some metaphysical ghosts [the partisans of metaphysics in the 1923 controversy on science and metaphysics] want to make use of this old poet in order to protect themselves, this is a filthy insult. If some young people are against Tagore because they are opposed to the metaphysical ghosts who use Tagore, then this is an even filthier insult.[121]

Tung imagined that after reaching Peking, Tagore had already been driven through the streets of that "filthy-smelling" city in an imported automobile, "and, as in Nanking, has lectured to young people in the schools and evoked a great deal of misunderstanding from them, with leaflets opposing him coming down like snowflakes. When I consider this, even though I am far away, it fills me with an unlimited feeling of repressed resentment at the way this old poet is being treated!" [122] One senses a reverence for an elder person and an aesthetic sensibility in Tung's remarks which suggest the persistence of these traditional attitudes among a larger number of his contemporaries, perhaps under the influence of the faculty group at the Southeastern University which was endeavoring to prevent the new thought movement from going too far in its rejection of Chinese traditional culture. This group, headed by two former students of Harvard's Irving Babbitt, were seeking to implement Babbitt's advice to "retain the soul of truth that is contained in [China's] great traditions," by publishing the *Hsüeh heng* (Critical review) monthly, whose two chief aims were: "to interpret the spirit and to systematize the materials of Chinese culture," and "to introduce and assimilate the standard works and best ideas of Western philosophy and literature." [123]

While students of literature and religion seem to have been most in sympathy with Tagore's message, those specializing in academic philosophy proved as skeptical of his ideas as were their elders in this field. Actually the first Chinese intellectual to talk with Tagore was a student of philosophy who sought him out when they were both in New York in 1921. Fung Yu-lan, destined to become the foremost academic philosopher that China has produced in this century, was then a student at Columbia University and was trying to work out the whole question of the nature and relation of Eastern and Western civilizations. He had been puzzling over this question since his arrival in the United States, and had just been reading a newspaper report of Liang Sou-ming's lectures on the subject when he heard that Tagore was also dealing with it in some of his American lectures. At least, thought Fung to himself as he went to call on the poet in his New York hotel suite, Tagore's views would be representative of those of a large number of Orientals.

Tagore opened the interview by explaining that he had never been to China, but had been planning to return to Japan and wanted to visit China on the way. Fung assured the poet-philosopher that he would be heartily welcomed if he were to go, and turned to the question uppermost in his mind: how should China transform herself to suit the contemporary world? Tagore bridled at the suggestion that China should take the modern West as its model, and urged Fung not to listen to the advice of Westerners but to study Eastern civilization first. "Perhaps our civilization has erred," he added, "but if we don't study it, how will we know whether it has or not?" [124] The conversation continued:

> FUNG: Recently I have often asked myself in my heart: Is the difference between Eastern and Western civilizations a difference in degree of development, or a difference in kind?
> TAGORE: I can answer that question: it is a difference in kind. The aim of Western life is activity; that of Eastern life is [spiritual] realization.
> FUNG: But isn't Eastern civilization too passive? . . .
> TAGORE: It is passive, but it also has truth, which has both active and passive aspects. . . . Now the East can help the West by giving it wisdom, while the West can help the East by giving it activity.[125]

Tagore's concept of the spiritual East reminded Fung of the letter which Tolstoy had written to Ku Hung-ming in 1906 to urge the Chinese to cling to the traditions of Confucianism, Taoism, and Buddhism.[126] Now he wanted to know what advice Tagore had for China. The poet's answer was swift but strangely out of harmony with the pacific tone he had used up to this point:

> Since the West is aggressive toward us, we should also be aggressive. I have only one piece of advice for China: "Learn science quickly." What the East lacks and badly needs is science. China is now sending many students to the West; they must learn science very thoroughly. There have been many inventors in Chinese history, and this great people can, I fully believe, learn science and also make scientific dis-

coveries. The Eastern peoples cannot be exterminated, have no fear. Just look at Japan . . .[127]

Fung Yu-lan left the interview unmoved by Tagore's appeal. To study science for its practical effects was not enough; one must absorb the very spirit of scientific research. "Empty talk about ideals, with no regard for facts — this is the basic disease of the East, and is contrary to the scientific spirit," he reflected. What Fung wanted, and what he was learning in the West, was "to investigate facts and to devise theories to explain them." "This," he exclaimed, "is truly the modern spirit of the West!" [128] Like Hu Shih, who had preceded him as a graduate student of philosophy at Columbia, Fung succeeded in applying these modern methods to the study of his own country's intellectual heritage. While Hu had sought to revitalize the logic of the non-Confucian schools, Fung concentrated on revitalizing Neo-Confucian metaphysics, developing in the process a form of existentialist theory based on Chinese philosophical traditions.[129]

The other Chinese student of philosophy who published his reactions to Tagore's ideas did so after the poet had reached Peking and made himself a controversial figure. P'eng Chi-hsiang must have been a bright but not particularly original student, for, though he did go on from Peking University to the University of Paris, after returning to China he published mainly translations of Descartes, Levy-Brühl, and other European philosophers. His critique of Tagore's whole scheme of thought was sufficiently incisive to merit publication in the monthly *Hsin min-kuo* (New republic) in the same issue with articles by Sun Yat-sen, Wu Chih-hui, and the leading Communist intellectual, Li Ta-chao. In such company, it was appropriate that P'eng should open his article with a reference to the political consequences of Tagore's poetic attitude: "If everyone should become a poet, if everyone should become like T'ao Ch'ien [who resigned from his official post to enjoy rural life and write beautiful poetry], then we may say . . . 'The collapse of our nation is indeed close.' " [130]

P'eng next analyzed Tagore's cosmology, and described it as essentially pantheistic. "This kind of thought is especially appropriate for a poet . . . but when it is transferred into the field of philosophy, we cannot help attacking it severely . . . [as] a relic of the thought of ancient times." Turning to examine Tagore's philosophy of life, P'eng did not find that very reliable either. Asking capitalists and workers to resolve their differences through love seemed as useless as the conduct of the man who marked the side of his boat to show where his sword had fallen into the water. Tagore's idealistic philosophy "will not only achieve nothing, but it will actually retard the progress of humanity," P'eng maintained. Summing up, he condemned Tagore's ideas on both practical and philosophical grounds: "His cosmology and his philosophy of life can only be appreciated by poets, and cannot be put into practice in actual life; moreover, they absolutely cannot occupy an important position in philosophy." [131]

Judging Tagore's ideas by their practical and political consequences seems to have been the prevailing tendency among the students of Peking University in this period. Their situation in the nation's premier academic institution, located in the heart of the capital city (rather than outside the walls, like Yenching and Tsing Hua) stimulated them to take a keen interest in the political situation of the country, and their support was assiduously cultivated by both nationalist and Communist propagandists and organizers.

The enthusiasm of Peking University students for the Communist program is vividly conveyed in the autobiography of T'an Shih-hua, the son of a veteran Kuomintang revolutionary and a student of Russian at the university at the time of Tagore's visit. T'an does not mention Tagore at all in his recollections, but does tell of the exciting moment at the end of May 1924 when Leo Karakhan (the Soviet diplomat who negotiated the treaty by which the Soviet Union became the first foreign power to surrender the extraterritorial privileges extracted from China in the last decades of the Ch'ing Dynasty) came to speak at the university. The students, many of whom had taken to the streets to demonstrate in support of the treaty, crowded into the main auditorium and adjoining corridors to hear Karakhan, and when he had finished speaking, they shouted together:

> Ten thousand years of life for the Soviets!
> Ten thousand years of life for China!
> Long live the people's revolution! [132]

This autobiographical witness to the popularity of Communist ideas among Peking University students is corroborated by a quite different source: an opinion poll taken on the campus in the winter of 1923–24 on the occasion of the twenty-fifth anniversary of the university's founding. Of the 1007 respondents, most of them students, 725 favored "people's revolution," as the best way "to save China." [133] Three other leading questions also elicited replies indicating strong pro-Soviet and leftist sympathies, as well as considerable ignorance about who was alive and who not among leaders of the outside world:

> Which country is China's true friend?
>   Russia: 497; United States: 107; Neither of the two: 226; Both: 12; No opinion: 253.
> What political party or system do you favor?
>   Socialism: 191; Sun Yat-sen's party: 153; Democracy: 69; Federal Republic: 40; "Good government": 14; Revolutionary party: 13.
> Who is the greatest man in the world [outside of China]?
>   Lenin: 227; Wilson: 51; Bertrand Russell: 24; Tagore: 17; Einstein: 16; Trotsky: 12; Kaiser Wilhelm II: 12; Washington: 11; Harding: 10; Lincoln: 9; John Dewey: 9; Bismarck: 9; Gandhi: 9; Tolstoy: 7; Marx: 6, etc.[134]

The publication of many articles on Tagore in the September and October Short Story Monthly and the general excitement over his impending arrival probably explain his achieving fourth place in this list of great non-Chinese, but his seventeen admirers (perhaps students of English literature infected by the enthusiasm of Hsü Chih-mo) were less than one-thirteenth the number of Lenin's, and only one-sixtieth the total population polled.

The responses to two other questions in this significant survey showed how highly the students regarded Ch'en Tu-hsiu and the weeklies he and other Communists were editing. Asked whom they considered the greatest man in China, 473 chose Sun Yat-sen, 173 Ch'en, and 153 the university's chancellor, Dr. Ts'ai Yüan-p'ei, all others named trailing far behind these three favorites.[135] Asked for their favorite periodicals, the largest number mentioned the leftist ones with which Ch'en was associated.[136] The articles in these periodicals commenting on Tagore's visit thus give a good idea of what Peking University's students thought about his message.

More than any other Communist publication the weekly *Chung-kuo ch'ing-nien* (China's youth), voice of the Socialist Youth Corps, was written and distributed in order to influence the thinking of the students in secondary schools and colleges. Because Tagore also sought to win the support of this suggestible age group, contributors to China's Youth issued repeated warnings to their readers to pay no attention to the Indian poet's message. "Let our students be on their guard against the poisonous charm of the speeches of this man," wrote one I Hsiang.

> There can be nothing more pernicious for us than such speeches at this time, when we are all striving to carry out our Revolution in the most practical possible form. Let Mr. Tagore see our country as a tourist, free to wander where he will. But if he claims to be our teacher, let no one listen to him. Let no one believe a word he says! . . . Dear students, you have been warned! [137]

The comparative youth of many Communist leaders in 1924 was a considerable asset in their campaign to win the minds and hearts of China's students. Ch'ü Ch'iu-pai was twenty-five, and Han Lin-fu, a fourth leading Party member and the author of an anti-Tagore article in a Peking University weekly,[138] was also in his twenties. Another young leader, who shared with Ch'ü and Han the status of alternate member of the joint Kuomintang-Chinese Communist Party Central Executive Committee, was the thirty-year-old Mao Tse-tung, working in Shanghai in the executive bureaus of both the national Communist Party and the local Kuomintang.[139] Mao apparently wrote nothing about Tagore, but his associate Shen Tse-min, five years his junior and a leading intellectual among the Shanghai Communists, sternly warned China's students to beware of Tagore's metaphysical doctrines. Going to the heart of the Indian poet's philosophy, Shen Tse-min identified it as essentially Hindu and contrasted it with Western thought:

> Western themes of development are based on energy. . . . Conquer nature, subdue nature: this is the formula the Westerners ceaselessly repeat, and from it spring the colossal industries of the West and the brutal imperialism of Europe. For the Hindu, on the contrary, the ideal is solitary life in the forest, with meditation the only occupation. The Hindu does not conquer; he withdraws and abstracts himself in thought. He condenses the multiplicity of things into a single idea, that of the sole real Being, to which he seeks to draw near, in which he seeks to be absorbed. For him, the most intense activity is to extinguish oneself in silent meditation. . . . [From his point of view] the Europeans are deca-

dent creatures, lost in greed, utterly removed from the Spirit and from Life.[140]

Appearing totally indifferent to Chinese intellectual traditions, Shen Tse-min argued stoutly for the Western model and against the Hindu ideal. And yet his staunch patriotism was in the best Chinese tradition:

> It is the neglect of our industries which has brought about the present importation of foreign goods. We are now only half tributaries. If we were to listen to Tagore's doctrine, we would soon be completely colonized. What we need is exactly the opposite of that doctrine. Resist! Fight until we bleed! . . . We want none of Mr. Tagore's "Eastern civilization!" It is as much out-of-date in China as in India. Mr. Tagore wants us to love old bones. To conclude: If our students listen to Mr. Tagore, his coming will not benefit our country, but will be a misfortune.[141]

CHINESE ATTITUDES TOWARD INDIA

Young Shen Tse-min's critique was as much an indictment of India and its culture as of Tagore and his message. "Is it not the laziness and inactivity of the Hindus which has brought about their subjection to England?" he asked, "and are not we Chinese already headed for this same fate?" Similarly, the anonymous author of the article "Oppose Tagore!" warned against the "Indianization of China," and declared of Tagore's poems: "Frankly speaking, they express the idle fancies of a lost nation. Feeling himself too hemmed in by the miseries of India's dreary existence, Mr. Tagore has taken refuge in the spacious and serene heights of idealism. This is the last refuge of [men of] ruined countries." Deploring the fact that some Chinese litterateurs had already succumbed to the spell of Tagore's "narcotic poetry," the author predicted: "When we all become so drugged as this, the imperialists will find it easy enough to slice up our country like a melon." [142]

Not only the leftists, but Chinese intellectuals of nearly every persuasion regarded India's subjection to British rule as a disaster which China must struggle to avoid at all costs. Wu Chih-hui, on the right wing of the Kuomintang and one of the leaders in its 1927 purge of left-wing members, attacked Tagore as a member of a country of slaves and denounced his message as medicine which India had died from taking. Even Hsü Chih-mo, Tagore's closest companion and most ardent defender, had to admit that the average Chinese had little respect for India because of its colonial status: "I dare say when we look at an Indian we do not pity him, we despise him. I think Indians are the most misunderstood people there are; although they are in Asia, too, most people think of them as the same as the red-turbaned Sikh policeman in the streets." Yet he added: "China is a little more free than India, but spiritually we are like pre-revolutionary Russia, living in a dungeon, while India's spiritual life continues." [143]

Although the presence of Sikh policemen and bank guards throughout the British concessions in Shanghai, Tientsin, and other treaty ports did provoke the ricksha coolies to call them the "red-headed rascals" (*hung-t'ou ah-san*),[144] they did not necessarily identify Tagore as the Sikhs's compatriot. In Peking, when the coolie in whose ricksha Tagore was riding was asked by another, "Who's that you're pulling?" he answered gaily, "That's the Western Saviour." [145]

Behind the immediate political fear that China would follow India's example and fall victim to foreign imperialism lay the consciousness that deep differences separated the assumptions on which Indian and Chinese philosophers had for centuries developed their ideas. China's scholars, with their highly developed historical sense, were well aware of the long competition in Chinese history between Buddhist and Confucian ideas and institutions. The prestige of Buddhist thought had reached its height a millennium earlier, then had gradually declined and never recovered after the Neo-Confucian revival of the twelfth century.[146] One of Tagore's hosts, at that time acting chancellor of Peking University, has summarized a common view of the reasons for Buddhism's eclipse in China:

> The scholars befriend or tolerate it and the common people worship it as one of the religions in China. Nevertheless it remains foreign. To the practical-minded Chinese its metaphysical system is not palatable. It exists in China because there are moral teachings in it and in time of distress one could find moral refuge in it. The Chinese only wanted to absorb foreign elements into their own system of thought, to be enriched by them; they would not surrender their own system to an alien one.[147]

Other scholars in modern China expressed not just indifference, but active dislike for Buddhism. Ku Hung-ming's lucubrations on the subject were not at all complimentary, and Liang Sou-ming called for the total rejection of Indian influences in his influential book on Eastern and Western Civilizations and Their Philosophies. Dr. Hu Shih, the most influential of the country's Western-educated philosophers, welcomed Tagore's initiative in establishing closer relations between the intellectuals of China and India, but he strongly opposed the idea that these relations should be based on a revival of Buddhist or Indian spirituality. On the contrary, he was later to condemn the Buddhist outlook as "otherworldly," "antisocial," "selfish," and therefore an obstacle to China's modernization. In his view, "the best philosophical thought" in China during the past three hundred years "got farther and farther away from the Indianized tradition. With the new aids of modern science and technology, and of the new social and historical sciences," he concluded, "we are confident that we may yet achieve a rapid liberation from the two thousand years' cultural domination by India." [148]

Buddhists themselves took a kindlier view of India, but even they voiced reservations. Among the elders, Liang Ch'i-ch'ao welcomed Tagore as the bringer of an essentially Buddhistic message of spirituality, but Liang had already made clear in his other writings that he wished to see Buddhism in China develop in such a way as to "reveal the special characteristics of the Chinese people." [149] And the Abbot T'ai Hsü insisted strongly that leadership for a Buddhist revival must come from China. As he pointed out, Buddhism had long since died out in India, the land of its birth, and Tagore was in any case not a Buddhist, but a Vedantin. Only among the student leaders of the Young Men's Buddhist Association did Indian spiritual influence on China, as transmitted by Tagore, receive a wholehearted endorsement.

Tagore's great hope had been that the close cultural ties which had bound India and China together fifteen hundred to a thousand years earlier could be renewed and strengthened in the twentieth century. Such a hope rested on the assumption that China's intellectuals looked back on this period with as much fondness as he did. In effect, he was asking them to accept another wave of cultural influence from India; the possibility that China might contribute to an equal degree to the development of Indian culture was not mentioned in his public lectures in China. The process he prescribed was one-sided, not mutual, and its feasibility depended largely on the willingness of China's intellectuals to see their culture re-Indianized. From the comments they made on his lectures and from their other writings it is evident that almost none of them wanted that great epoch of Indian influence on China to be repeated.

Comparing these attitudes toward India with those expressed by Japan's intellectuals in 1916, we find the Chinese voicing considerably greater distaste both for India's ancient cultural heritage and for her modern political situation. In pre-modern Japan the rivalry between Buddhism and Confucianism had never taken so acute a form as in China, and in modern times Japan had repelled the threat of foreign conquest to which India had succumbed and which China still greatly feared. These radically different military situations also help to explain the almost total absence of pan-Asian sentiment in China, in contrast to its vigorous expression by Japan's expansion-minded ultranationalists. An exception to this rule was Sun Yat-sen, whose ideas had been molded by his contacts with his Japanese pan-Asianist supporters, but whose image of an Asia rising to overthrow Western dominance was as Sinocentric as theirs was Japan-centered. The younger nationalists, however, saw more clearly than Sun that Japan posed a greater imperialist danger to China than did the far-off nations of the West, that in any struggle with their Eastern neighbor they could expect no material help from India, and that the kind of spiritual aid Tagore tendered China would be positively harmful to their cause.

Summing Up

When China's articulate intellectuals — her literary leaders, philosophers, political leaders, and students — had finished speaking their minds in response to Tagore's "message," it was clear that very few among them accepted it: only two English-language editorial writers, one employed by a Japanese, the other by an American newspaper; one literary leader, not a creative writer but the editor of an important monthly magazine; none of the philosophers (even though two of the more conservative ones were sympathetic to his idealistic attitude); no political leader (notwithstanding a certain kinship between Sun Yat-sen's image of Asia and Tagore's); and among the students, only a few in American-oriented colleges and a brace of young Buddhists — such was the meager harvest of published Chinese approbation for the Indian poet's ideas. Many of the intellectuals who did not or could not write for publication seem to have

felt considerable personal sympathy and admiration for their illustrious
visitor; the mere fact that he attracted so many of them to his lectures
bears silent witness to a widespread and positive feeling toward him. And
yet their very silence after he was attacked in print suggests that many
educated Chinese, no matter how much they sympathized with Tagore
as a person, as an artist, and as an emissary of friendship from India,
simply could not agree with the program he presented.

On the plane of ideas, the judgments delivered by articulate intellectuals on Tagore's message of Eastern spiritual revival show a deep gulf
separating his thought-world from theirs. Their one point of contact was
Buddhist religiosity, sitting like a nearly dried-up pool in the midst of a
variegated landscape which for centuries had been reclaimed, ordered,
and cultivated in accordance with secular, Confucian ideas and assumptions. At the time of Tagore's visit, this "traditional" landscape was
everywhere in ruinous neglect, decay, and transformation; the old order
of ideas had passed away and a new one was just beginning to emerge.
Tagore, whose knowledge of Chinese thought was apparently limited to
one Taoist classic, and who seems to have known nothing of Confucianism, was ignorant of both the old and the new landscapes of secular
Chinese thought. Many Chinese intellectuals, equally ignorant of Hindu
thought, were led to the conclusion that he was a Buddhist whose ideas
belonged not even to the recent past, which they were actively repu-
diating, but to the remote and hopelessly antedeluvian world of the T'ang
dynasty.

As Tagore walked uncomprehending through this Chinese landscape,
he passed here and there a scholar patiently at work replanting a shoot
from one ancient tree or another, hoping to revitalize it with new
methods of cultivation. Liang Sou-ming with his early Confucianism,
Hu Shih with his Mohism, Chang Chün-mai and Fung Yu-lan with
their different branches of Neo-Confucianism — these and others were
diligently engaged in tasks essentially similar to Tagore's own work in
the revitalization of Hindu cultural traditions in India. Tragically, he
was unable to see what they were doing, and by his appeal for a revival
of what seemed to them outlandish Buddhist traditions he even tended to
bring the whole process of revitalizing Chinese traditions into disrepute.

Elsewhere on the landscape of intellectual life other men were
feverishly at work uprooting everything old, clearing the ground for vast
construction projects of new and foreign design. These young men

wanted nothing to do with "Eastern civilization," whether Confucian or Buddhist. They had set themselves the task of creating a new society, and above all a new political order. China's imperial polity, for centuries one of the greatest achievements of her civilization, was now in ruins. Her young men greatly feared that if they were unable to establish a viable nation-state, foreign powers — Japan from the East, a consortium of imperialist powers from the West, or all together — might come and do it for them.

The West, for these young Chinese intellectuals in 1924, was no longer one, but two: the old West of Britain, France, and the United States, and the new world of Bolshevik Russia, where revolution was said to be solving what seemed to be social, political, and military problems similar to China's. Tagore appealed to China's youth to save the spirituality of the East from the materialism of the West. They replied in effect that spirituality had so enfeebled India that she had been conquered by the old West, and that to save China from a similar fate they were importing materialist doctrines from the new West, the Soviet Union. Their political goal — a strong, united, and progressive China — was alike dictated by the age-old assumption in Chinese thought that good government was the indispensable precondition of the good life, and by the evils and perils inflicted on their country by corrupt and warring military adventurers. Nothing the Indian poet said could divert these ardent patriots from their pursuit of a new and more viable political order.

CHAPTER SEVEN

INDIAN IMAGES OF EAST AND WEST

The old culture managed to live through many a fierce storm and tempest, but, though it kept its outer form, it lost its real content. Today it is fighting silently and desperately against a new and all-powerful opponent — the bania [*merchant*] *civilization of the capitalist West. It will succumb to this newcomer, for the West brings science, and science brings food for the hungry millions. But the West also brings an antidote to the evils of this cut-throat civilization — the principles of socialism, of co-operation, and service to the community for the common good. This is not so unlike the old Brahman ideal of service, but it means the brahmanization (not in the religious sense, of course) of all classes and groups and the abolition of class distinctions.*

— Jawaharlal Nehru, *Autobiography*

THE COOLNESS OF INTELLECTUALS IN Japan and China toward Tagore's "message" contrasted sharply with his own enthusiasm for the idea of a revitalized Eastern civilization. On one point the Indian poet and his East Asian critics did agree: both he and they assumed that he spoke to them as India's cultural ambassador to the world, that his ideas were also those of his countrymen. Was he in fact justified in claiming to speak for India as a whole or even for its educated class? To what extent did other leading intellectuals share his views, and to what extent did they disagree or hold different images of India and her relation to the rest of Asia and to the West?

Answers to these questions must be sought in the writings of eminent men over a period of several decades. When Tagore arrived in East Asia he appeared as an exotic poet-philosopher whom the West had honored with its highest literary award. His lectures, delivered within a short period of weeks, provoked a spate of comments from intellectuals located at different points along the entire spectra of Japanese and Chinese thought at that particular time. No such compact and simultaneous body of evidence exists for Indian reactions to his ideas on East and West, for in his own country Tagore was a familiar rather than an exotic figure, speaking and writing on many topics for over fifty years. Source material for this chapter must therefore be gained by casting a wider net than was necessary for Japanese and Chinese publications.

THE SOUTH ASIAN CULTURAL UNIVERSE

As in Japan and China, so in India creative individuals were at work throughout Tagore's lifetime examining, selecting, and combining ideas and methods from a variety of Western and indigenous sources, ancient, medieval, and modern. One crucial fact, however, placed South Asian intellectuals in a quite different situation from their East Asian con- temporaries. This was the dominant role played by the English language in the schools and colleges, and consequently in the world of higher learning and thought, throughout the subcontinent. For example, when- ever Tagore lectured in India outside his native Bengal, he did so in English. India's most popular magazine during the twenties and thirties was the *Modern Review,* an English-language monthly published in Calcutta, which carried many articles, short stories, and poems by Tagore. Gandhi's *Young India* weekly, published from Ahmedabad in the Bom- bay Presidency, also appeared in English, as did most of the country's major newspapers. In 1921, fully 2,400,000 Indians could read and write in English, within a total literate population of 19,300,000 and a grand total of 305,000,000. By 1931, the percentage of English-users to the rest of the literate population had risen from the 1921 figure of 12.5 to 14.8 percent.[1] More than to anything else, the popularity of English was due to the economic benefits its mastery conferred, for all the better- paying jobs in government service and the professions required fluency in it.

The central role of English in Indian life has appeared strange, if not degrading, to some observers, but it is actually the continuation in a new form of the very old South Asian custom of conducting intellectual dis- course in an imported all-India language not understood by the common people of any of the subcontinent's fourteen major linguistic regions. Sanskrit (brought by the Aryan invaders and developed by their descendants) served this purpose at the courts of ancient India. In medieval times, when Muslim rulers and officials dominated the land, they introduced Persian as their pan-Indian medium of communication. The British, seeking to stabilize their regime on the ruined foundations of the Mughal Empire, actually continued the use of Persian for official purposes until the 1830's. The readiness of upper-caste Hindus to learn these imported languages was essential to their worldly advancement. Under the Mughals many Hindus mastered Persian and some rose to high office. When the British substituted their own language for Persian and decided (on Macaulay's recommendation) to sponsor higher education in English, they responded in part to a growing demand from the literate Hindu community in Bengal. (In sharp contrast to this South Asian pattern, China's bureaucrats managed to retain their language and culture and to impart them to their successive conquerors from northern Asia.)

The spread of English, like the earlier spread of Persian, was primarily a result of a military conquest and its ensuing administrative consolidation. The Muslim conquerors, like the Aryans some three thousand years earlier, had come down from the mountains and tablelands of Afghanistan and Central Asia lying to the northwest of the subcontinent, but the British, when they arrived, came from the opposite direction, moving inland and northward from the seacoasts of the east, south, and west. As a result, the regions first exposed to and most strongly affected by British cultural influences were those at the periphery of the two older cultural systems, regions like the Dravidian Tamil land in the far south, where Aryan influences were only partial and Islamic influences even slighter, or Bengal in the east, where both Hindu and Muslim orthodoxies were weaker than in the north. Correspondingly, the last parts of the subcontinent to come under the full sway of the British were precisely those northern cities where the Persian cultural world had its most flourishing centers: Lahore, Lucknow, and Delhi. The conquest of the Punjab in 1849, the annexation of Oudh in 1856, and the subjugation of Delhi after the 1857 Rebellion came almost a full century after the decisive British victories in the south and east.

As the introduction of English influence rolled back the carpet of medieval Persian culture from the edges, it gave new life to the underlying regional languages and their scripts, most of which had begun to take their present form in those same centuries when Europe's modern languages and literatures were emerging from under the shadow of Latin. Writing and publishing in these regional languages was greatly stimulated in the nineteenth century by the introduction of printing, the compilation by missionaries and Orientalists of grammars and dictionaries, and the eventual establishment of thousands of schools, hundreds of colleges, and dozens of universities. Bengali in the east, Tamil and Telugu in the south, Marathi and Gujarati in the west, and Urdu and Hindi in the north showed the most vigorous growth.[2]

With the advent of printing, publishing, and modern educational institutions, the circulation of ideas in India increased rapidly, and new combinations of old ideas became possible. Hindus, for example, could choose to draw on the monism of the Vedanta, on the more austere Shaiva traditions, on one of the schools of Vaishnava devotional worship, or on the myriad Shakta cults revolving about mother-goddesses. In north India especially, Islamic monotheism had made itself felt among Hindus as well, and interactions between Sufi and Vaishnava mysticisms had been in progress from the eleventh century onward. In western India, the ancient traditions of Jainism remained very much alive.

The superimposition of the language, literature, and intellectual traditions of modern Britain on this intricate web of classical and medieval languages and traditions produced by the twentieth century a South Asian cultural universe of extraordinary complexity. There has come into being a kind of federal system in which each region carries on its own literary life in its own language, but beyond which its bi- or trilingual literary and political leaders also participate in all-India or worldwide intellectual activity through the medium of English. Perhaps the closest historical analogy to this system would be Europe in the late Middle Ages, when Latin was the language of educated men from Sicily to Norway but poets and troubadors sang in the languages of their respective provinces. The parallel cannot be stretched too far, however, for while Latin was discarded in Europe, South Asia has retained English as its main "link" language for federal purposes — and this remains almost as true today in the independent states of India and Pakistan as it was in the undivided British India in which Tagore and his contemporaries lived.

Because the diversity in regional situations has been so much greater in India than in Japan or China, we can best acquire an over-all view of the South Asian intellectual landscape, not by proceeding from profession to profession as heretofore, but by examining in turn the ideas of leading men in each of the five major provinces of British India. Two of these five dominate the north Indian heartland: the United Provinces (also known as Hindustan) and the Punjab. The remaining three were the great coastal "presidencies" from which British power had gradually been extended inland: Bengal, Madras, and Bombay. Having been longest under British influence, the people in the coastal regions had acquired higher literacy rates and a greater knowledge of English and of Western thought than those in the hinterland. Thus in the 1920's, while the coastal provinces accounted for one-third of the population of the subcontinent, they held one-half the total number of literate persons and three-fifths the total of those literate in English.[3] The situation in Bengal showed an even deeper penetration of modern Western influences, for its population, comprising only 15 percent of India's total population, contained 22 percent of the country's literates, and 32 percent of all those literate in English.

Bengal

Over the flat plain south of the Himalaya's highest peaks, the muddy waters of the Ganges from the northwest and the Brahmaputra from the northeast have for millennia been extending the fertile delta which is Bengal. Even from prehistoric times these rivers and their many tributaries have enabled ships and barges to develop extensive water-borne trade throughout the province and beyond it both upcountry and along all the coasts of the Bay of Bengal. Here was a rich prize for such conquistadors as Robert Clive, and a secure base from which successive governors general could extend the sway and trading sphere of the East India Company. The thriving seaport of Calcutta made a logical capital for the whole of British India, and rapidly grew to become its largest city. Stimulated by the patronage of the Company and those of its officials interested in the languages and literatures of the people, a new class of Indian intellectuals came into being from the first quarter of the nineteenth century, accomplished writers in both English and Bengali, and often in Sanskrit and Persian as well. It was these men and their descendants who pioneered in studying the civilization of England and Europe, and in reinterpreting and recombining traditions inherited from the many pasts of India.

"What Bengal thinks today, all India thinks tomorrow," was true enough when the Bombay nationalist leader Gokhale voiced the idea in the first decade of this century. All through the nineteenth century, Bengal's bicultural intellectuals were setting the tone for the new outlook on religion, politics, and literature being adopted by English-knowing Indians in other parts of the subcontinent. First the writings of Rammohun Roy and Debendranath Tagore, then the personal visits and lectures of Keshub Chunder Sen and Vivekananda, brought modern interpretations of Hinduism to Madras, Bombay, Hindustan, and the Punjab. In the political sphere it was a sign of Bengal's preeminence that the first move to organize the Indian National Congress took the form of a circular letter in 1883 to all the graduates of the University of Calcutta. Even in literature, the innovations and experiments of Bengali writers were beginning to influence the vocabulary and style of writers in other north Indian languages.

The all-India influence of this "Bengal Renaissance" was due in large part to the success of Bengal's upper-caste Hindu intellectuals in resolving the fundamental problem that faced all educated Indians: what to accept from the civilization of their British rulers and teachers, and what to leave aside or reject. Bengalis were the first to confront this problem, for their province had been the first to fall under direct British rule and their chief city, Calcutta, remained the capital of Britain's vast empire of India and Burma until 1912. Upper-caste Bengali Hindus for many decades had been working in a kind of symbiosis with the British, first in commerce, then in government, and finally in the realm of culture and ideas. The idea that Indian or Eastern culture was essentially spiritual and therefore entirely complementary to British or Western "materialistic civilization," grew out of this Bengali-British symbiosis, and Tagore, Bengal's greatest poet, became this idea's most eloquent advocate.

The opening decades of the twentieth century brought major political changes to the Hindu-British relationship in Bengal, and therefore to Tagore's position in his own province. The spread of English education and consequently of English political ideals had by 1900 produced a large and vocal school of moderate nationalists. The British bureaucracy, led by the conservative Lord Curzon from 1898 to 1905, looked down on this Anglicized class as a deracinated minority, and grievously affronted it by partitioning Bengal in 1905 into Hindu and Muslim majority areas. The ensuing anti-British agitation, while it succeeded in having the

partition revoked in 1912, produced a new extremist school of nationalists who rejected both British rule and British influence on Indian
culture. Tagore parted company with the extremists, and was regarded
by them as a defector. From his viewpoint, however, it was they who
were defecting from the high ideal of partnership between a religious
India and a political Britain. From this time forward Tagore suffered
isolation in Bengal whenever he criticized political nationalism, but was
praised whenever his poetic representations of Indian culture and ideals
won friends abroad for India's nationalist movement.

One extremist leader in Bengal not only shared Tagore's ideal of India
as the leader of Asian spiritual civilization, but articulated this ideal even
more forcefully than Tagore himself in this period. Aurobindo Ghose,
like Tagore a member of a Brahmo Samaj family, was educated in England from the age of seven to twenty. After graduating from Cambridge
he almost entered the Indian Civil Service, but instead took a position in
the princely state of Baroda in 1893 and commenced seriously to study
Sanskrit and Hinduism. Like Edinburgh-educated Ku Hung-ming in
China, Aurobindo Ghose became even more ardent in his love for his
country's ancient culture than those of his countrymen who had never
gone abroad; and both proclaimed this love in fluent English. Unfortunately for Ku Hung-ming, almost none of his countrymen understood
English. Many of Aurobindo's fellow nationalists did know English, and
his powerful speeches and articles during the antipartition agitation
moved them deeply.

India as the mother of Asia, Indo-Asian spirituality as the cure for the
world's ills: these cardinal points in Tagore's Asia doctrine were also
voiced in Aurobindo's 1908 editorial "The Asiatic Role." It was self-
evident, he believed, that India was the home of Asian civilization: "In
former ages India was a sort of hermitage of thought and peace apart from
the world. . . . Her thoughts flashed out over Asia and created civilizations, her sons were the bearers of light to the peoples; philosophies
based themselves upon stray fragments of her infinite wisdom; sciences
arose from the waste of her intellectual production." Now it was time
for India and Asia to raise Europe to their lofty plane:

> the spirit of Asia, calm, contemplative, self-possessed, takes possession
> of Europe's discovery [in the natural sciences] and corrects its exaggera-
> tions, its aberrations by the intention, the spiritual light she alone can

turn upon the world. . . . It is therefore the office of Asia to take up the work of human evolution when Europe comes to a standstill and loses itself in a clash of vain speculations, barren experiments and help-less struggles to escape from the consequences of her own mistakes. Such a time has now come in the world's history.[4]

Aurobindo's image of Indo-Asian civilization was idealistic in the extreme, and like so much of the rhetoric of extremist nationalism was largely wishful thinking. So unalloyed was Aurobindo's idealism that in 1908–9 he left politics and British India to become a yogi, taking up residence in the French settlement of Pondicherry, where we shall meet him again among the South Indian exponents of the East-West differences. His importance in the intellectual history of Bengal is that his idealized nationalism represents the first stage in the politicization of the idea of Indo-Asian "spirituality." Tagore remained loyal to an earlier, nonpolitical version of this idea, but acknowledged his kinship with Aurobindo after their famous interview in 1928. "You have the Word and we are waiting to accept it from you," he wrote in a poem addressed to Aurobindo. "India will speak through your voice to the world." [5]

The second stage in Bengal's shift from religious to political Asianism is marked by the emergence of Chittaranjan Das, one of India's chief nationalist leaders from 1917 to his death in 1925. Das won fame in 1908 when he defended Aurobindo in the Alipore Bomb Conspiracy Case and succeeded in clearing him of the charge of involvement in terrorist activity. In addition to his lucrative law practice, Das edited a Bengali literary periodical in which he and others attacked Tagore's literary ideas as overly influenced by Western models, and exalted in their stead the Hindu devotionalism of medieval Bengali poetry.[6] An eloquent speaker and a sincere patriot, he quickly gained all-India stature after his entry into politics in 1917. Even in his maiden political speech he criticized Tagore, saying: "the whole of this anti-nation idea is unsubstantial — based upon a vague and nebulous conception of universal humanity. Each nation must develop its latent manhood as a nation, ere it is possible to rouse within them the sense of true amity and brotherliness. . . . You cannot create universal humanity out of [a] vacuum." Das nevertheless agreed with Tagore that India must champion "the ideal of the East." Like the proponents of Eastern spirit and Western technique in Japan and China he declared: "We must accept only what is consonant with the genius of our being and we must reject and utterly cast aside what is foreign to our soul." [7]

Elected president of the Congress in 1922, Das devoted a part of his lengthy address at its annual session to his proposal for a pan-Asian League:

> We must keep ourselves in touch with world movements and be in constant communication with the lovers of freedom all over the world. Even more important than this is participation of India in the great Asiatic Federation, which I see in the course of formation. I have hardly any doubt that the Pan-Islamic movement, which was started on a somewhat narrow basis, has given way or is about to give way to the great Federation of all Asiatic people. It is the union of the oppressed nationalities of Asia. . . . A bond of friendship and love, of sympathy and cooperation, between India and the rest of Asia, nay between India and all the liberty-loving people of the world is destined to bring about world peace. [8]

Das's mention of the pan-Islamic movement here is a measure of the distance he had traveled from the Hindu basis, implicit in Tagore's Indo-Asian idea and explicit in Aurobindo's.

When Tagore returned to Calcutta from his 1924 tour of China and Japan, Das seized the occasion to elaborate on his proposal to give political form to pan-Asian sentiment. "We have all along urged in these columns the need for Asiatic Federation," he declared in an editorial in *Forward,* his popular daily newspaper. "There was always and has been a community of culture and civilization amongst the Asiatics. We look at life from the same point of view. We have supplied the religious teachers of the world." More important than the ties of ancient culture was the "menace which threatens all alike," Western domination and racism. Tagore had declared the day he landed, "Asia must find her own voice." Two days later Das echoed his call, and recommended giving it practical shape: "Let the blacks, browns and yellows of Asia meet together from time to time. Let them begin to share one another's aspirations and sufferings. Let them unite in the search for the voice which Asia has lost. Asia must find her own voice." [9]

Tagore's message to China and its basic premises appear to have been universally approved in Hindu Bengal in 1924, usually with the added comment that they could best be realized by political means. The politicians, however, disagreed about priorities. Das showed himself ready

for some form of pan-Asian federation at once; Bengal's more militant nationalists considered this an impractical scheme until India had gained
her independence. Their viewpoint was expressed in the province's most
popular newspaper, the *Amrita Bazar Patrika,* published in English of a
somewhat less elegant style and spelling than that of Das's *Forward,*
reflecting its middle-class rather than upper-class authorship and appeal.
"We heartily welcome Dr. Rabindranath Tagore on his return to India
from a tour in China. The great consideration and respect with which
he was treated in that country will be highly appreciated by our countrymen," the *Patrika's* editorial began, quite unaware of the barrage of
criticism to which the poet had been subjected in China. It found no
fault in his message: "Asia is the birth-place of all the great prophets of
the world and the cradle of all great religious systems. . . . Asia has
thus been the spiritual guide of the world and has taught it the immortal
truth which forms the basis of the world's civilization." India, of course,
was the teacher of Asia: "There was a time when she gave China and
Japan her religion and civilization. And even in her present stage she
produces men who excite the wonder and admiration of the civilized
world. One such man is Dr. Rabindra Nath Tagore, whose message to
China and Japan has awakened the memory of their past glory." Then
the *Patrika* added its own message to Tagore's:

> The first requisite for realizing the dream of Asiatic federation is that
> the greatest of the Asiatic countries, namely India, should secure her
> Swaraj or Responsible Government. It was an independent sovereign of
> India that had sent the Buddhist missionaries to China and Japan. And
> it is self-governing India again which alone can make the ideal of a
> federation of Asiatic peoples a living reality and help the world to realize
> the grand conception of universal humanity. We must not, however, be
> understood to belittle in the least the great service that has been done to
> China and Japan by the poet. He has also enhanced their respect and
> esteem for India and has paved the way for a better understanding be-
> tween India and those Asiatic countries by his teachings. In order that
> the effect of his great work may be made permanent and enduring it is
> absolutely necessary that India should strive her utmost to take her
> legitimate place in the confederacy of the Asiatic nations so eloquently
> preached by the great poet of Asia.[10]

The contrast between Das's enthusiasm for immediate steps toward
an Asiatic federation and the *Patrika's* more militant demand for self-

government reflects the division of political sentiment among Bengali Hindus in these critical times, a division which undermined Das's political strength and may have hastened his premature death in 1925. He was after all, like Tagore and Aurobindo, a Brahmo, or reformist Hindu, by descent, and his policy of conciliation toward the political interests of Bengal's Muslims had made him unpopular with the orthodox Hindu community which the *Patrika* in general represented. With Das's death, Bengal lost not only its greatest political leader on the all-India level but also its wisest champion of Hindu-Muslim unity. Within a year an open rift sundered the leaders of these two communities, presaging their final divorce in 1947, when Muslim-majority East Bengal became the eastern wing of the new nation of Pakistan.[11]

Muslims formed more than half Bengal's population of 48,000,000 in the 1920's, but their economic and educational levels were much lower than those of the Hindu community. While 1 Bengali Hindu in 7 was literate, only 1 Muslim in 19 could read and write. The disparity was far greater in the crucial area of literacy in English — the key to entrance into government service and the professions: 1 Hindu in 34 knew English, but for Muslims the figure was 1 in 194.[12] Thus, for every Muslim in Bengal who knew English there were more than 5 Hindus similarly equipped. In Calcutta, the political, commercial, and intellectual capital of the province, the Hindu preponderance was accentuated by the fact that the city's population of 1,100,000 was approximately two-thirds Hindu and one-third Muslim. Most of the city's newspapers and periodicals were under Hindu editorship.

Bengal's Muslim intellectuals appear to have taken no special notice of Tagore's East Asian travels. Their attitude seems clear enough from the writings of their greatest modern poet, Nazrul Islam. His career alone illustrates the economic and social difficulties holding back Bengal's Muslims from the life of the mind more accessible to the wealthier Hindu community. Born in 1899 into a poor but pious Muslim family in rural West Bengal, Nazrul left home at eleven to earn his own way in the world and at eighteen joined the army. Stationed for two years at Karachi (almost halfway from Calcutta to Mecca), he studied Urdu and Persian and began to write Bengali poetry using Persian forms and vocabulary and classical Islamic themes. Settling in Calcutta after the war, he became famous with a single poem, "Bidrohī" (The rebel), which combined military and nationalist with Muslim and Hindu themes. Unorthodox in his Islamic views and a strong believer in Hindu-Muslim unity (his second wife was Hindu by birth), he nevertheless appealed most strongly to Muslim sentiment in calling for a resurgence of Islam's early passion for justice and equality — achieved by the sword if necessary.

Nazrul acknowledged the greatness of Tagore, calling him his guru and comparing himself to a comet shooting away from the radiance of the sun (*rabi,* for Rabindranath), but he continued to rebel against the great Hindu leaders of his day:

> . . . I could not keep my mind confined!
> As often as I bind it down, it snaps the chains into two.
> From constant beating, it's almost wild and loose.
> And yet the frenzied thing listens to none, not even to Rabi and Gandhi! [13]

Nazrul accordingly did not see India's role in Asia as Tagore saw it, but as a Muslim would naturally see it, in terms of the Islamic world as a whole: "Arabia and Egypt, China and Ind, nay the Muslim world at large, are peopled by my brethren in Faith. None too high, none too low; all on equal footing to grow." [14]

For the Hindus of Bengal, however, Tagore's message to China and Japan could not fail to be exciting, whether or not they attached a political significance to it. Editorial comments in Calcutta's English-language newspapers, apart from the two giants, *Forward* and *Amrita Bazar Patrika,* were uniformly enthusiastic. "India has reason to be proud that she, though shorn of the glory of her halcyon days, is trying through her illustrious son to bring new light to Asia," wrote the *New Empire.* "China wanted a new infusion of life which could not be had from a completely alien culture," explained the conservative nationalist organ, *Bengalee;* the reason China's intellectuals invited Tagore was "to give them this idealism of India which gave culture to all the great nations of the East." When the poet returned to Calcutta after his next European tour, the *New Servant* commented romantically:

> Proud is Bengal to-day. Proud as she was in her distant days. She feels the sun once more rising in the East at whose sight the stars of the world hide their diminished heads.
> Trailing clouds of glory he comes. He saw China and life burst there as it never did. He had rebuke on his lip for Japan and Japan will perhaps be chastened and behave herself. . . .

Above all he is a world-poet. . . . No wonder he conquers with his mystic glance, his gentle foot-fall, his honeyed accents, his weird pen, where others have failed with a deluge of blood.[15]

Tagore's "message" and East Asian mission thus appears to have made an almost irresistible appeal to the sentiments of educated Bengali Hindus, even to the most sophisticated among them. A prime example is the greatest historian of India in his day, Sir Jadunath Sarkar. Sarkar's scholarly work was concentrated on the empire of the Mughals and its decline, which he studied from Persian sources, but he was widely read in European history as well and a strong advocate of the secular progress of Indian society. "If we cannot modernize ourselves and become capable of competing with the outer world to the fullest extent [in economic resources and military power] . . . we are a doomed race," he said in the final lecture of his 1928 series surveying the history of India. This was the lesson of India's past:

> This study of our country's history leads irresistibly to the conclusion that we must embrace the spirit of progress with a full and unquestioning faith, we must face the unpopularity of resisting the seductive cry for going back to the undiluted wisdom of our ancestors, we must avoid eternally emphasizing the peculiar heritage of the Aryan India of the far-off past.[16]

Sir Jadunath had anticipated this conclusion earlier in this lecture by pointing out how closely the aims and concepts of Tagore's "world mission of India" resembled those of the prophets and leaders of the Slavophile movement in nineteenth-century Russia. As he noted: "This latest form of Indian thought is based entirely on a new interpretation of our ancient Upanishads under the unconscious influence of Christianity." And yet only a few months before, when presiding at a public meeting for Tagore on the eve of his departure for Southeast Asia, Sir Jadunath had said in revivalist tones: "The sages and heroes of ancient India are present with us in spirit and are blessing the great cultural Ambassador of modern India, the true spokesman of the heart of Asia, who is going forth at a patriarchal age on yet another mission of harmony and healing." [17] Even the two offices by virtue of which he presided at this meeting seemed to symbolize the Januslike duality in Sir Jadunath's outlook, for he was then the vice-chancellor of Calcutta University, the most modern and forward-looking in the country, and at the same time president of the Greater India Society, founded in 1926 to promote the study and revival of India's ancient cultural influence in Southeast Asia.

Younger Hindu intellectuals coming to the fore in this period shared this ambivalent attitude toward the ancient Hindu past, but were better able than their elders to press forward on the secular path which men like Sir Jadunath pointed out. One advantage they enjoyed was their greater freedom to travel abroad. In the nineteenth century, only the most daring young men had ventured to break the orthodox Hindu ban on overseas travel, but the opening decades of the twentieth saw a rapid rise in the number of students going to foreign lands, not only to England, but to the United States, continental Europe, and Japan as well. Tagore's own travels were only the most famous among many examples of this Bengali reaching out for direct touch with the whole of the civilized globe. Next in importance came the voyages of the endlessly curious young sociologist, Benoy Kumar Sarkar, whose encyclopedic reports on his eleven-year tour of three continents brought to Bengalis a wealth of information on the state of the overseas world.[18]

Like Tagore, Benoy Sarkar gave frequent lectures to help defray the cost of his travels abroad, but the "message" he imparted was diametrically and deliberately opposed to Tagore's. "Neither historically nor philosophically does Asiatic mentality differ from the Euro-American," he declared in the preface of his first book published outside India. Asians and Westerners were equally materialistic, equally spiritual: "It is only after the brilliant successes of a fraction of mankind subsequent to the Industrial Revolution of the last century that the alleged difference between the two mentalities has been first stated and since then grossly exaggerated." Indians themselves were partly to blame for this exaggeration, he conceded in his next book, significantly entitled *The Futurism of Young Asia.* "The success of Vivekananda's Vedanta Societies in the United States, the inroads of theosophy upon contemporary 'new thoughters,' and last but not least, the Tagore-cult which the Nobel-prize has served to establish for mankind since 1913 — all these have been tending to divert Eur-America's attention from the India of flesh and blood, the India of human interests and ambitions to the India of phantasy and romance." To correct this false picture, Benoy Sarkar asserted:

the Orientals have served mankind with the same idealism, the same energy, the same practical good sense, and the same strenuousness, as have the Greeks, Romans and Eur-Americans. . . . The Orientals have been as optimistic, active and aggressive in promoting social well-being and advancing spiritual interests as have the other races. . . . In short, the Orientals are men, their successes and failures are the successes and failures of human beings. They should therefore be judged by the same standard by which . . . Eur-American humanity are measured.[19]

Even while seeking to prove India's equivalence to the West on the plane of material civilization, Benoy Sarkar found it difficult to give up the idea of "Asian spirit," of which he considered Hindu culture the quintessence. He even went so far as to declare, in a flush of enthusiasm at discovering similarities between Chinese and Indian religions, that the Chinese and Japanese were Hindus, and that "Hindusthan first became what may truly be called the school of Asia. Kalidasa as the embodiment of Hindu nationalism is thus the spirit of Asia." "Asiatic mind is, therefore, one," he concluded. "It is this psychological groundwork that makes Asiatic Unity a psychological *necessity* in spite of ethnological and linguistic diversities." [20]

Benoy Sarkar here displays the same ambivalence toward ancient Indian culture that we noticed in Sir Jadunath Sarkar's case, but these remarks represent only a phase in his development and are not repeated in his later writings. He expressed them in 1915–16 in China under the same influence that stimulated Tagore nine years later to utter there his most extreme formulation of Asian spirituality: the impression made on his mind by his encounter with Chinese civilization. Unlike Tagore, Benoy Sarkar came to China uninvited and stayed in Peking in the servants' quarters of a third-class hotel. His lectures at the North China Branch of the Royal Asiatic Society and the International Institute passed virtually unnoticed by China's intellectuals, even though his host at the latter — the same Rev. Gilbert Reid who arranged for Tagore's final Peking lecture — translated each lecture into Chinese. An even earlier common influence on the pan-Asian thought of both Tagore and Benoy Sarkar was Sister Nivedita and her rendition of Okakura's *Ideals of the East*. Young Sarkar had been caught up in the antipartition agitation in 1905, when he was an eighteen-year-old student in Calcutta, and so had imbibed the triple ideology of resurgent Hindu culture, resurgent India, and resurgent Asia which Nivedita, Aurobindo Ghose, and others — including Tagore — were propagating in these turbulent years.[21]

By the time Sarkar had finished his travels and settled down in Calcutta as professor of economics at the university, however, he had worked out a less romantic and more secular view of India's culture and its relation to the outside world. He interpreted Tagore's global tours in the light of this secular outlook when congratulating the poet on his seventieth birthday in 1931:

> The last quarter of a century has been one of the most momentous epochs in the creative activities of the Indian people. As some of the loftiest and noblest specimens of these creations the personality, poetry, prose and paintings of Rabindranath have contributed enormously to the possibility of the Indian people utilizing the international forces, political, economic and cultural, in the interest of its own expansion. Tagore, the singer of "unruly hope," the poet of "world-maddening dance-music," the romantic wanderer among human hearts, requires thus to be appraised also as an architect of the India of "entangling alliances," of an India which by constant association with the powers great, medium and small, Asian and Eur-American, seeks to "drink of the world's life" and acquire a fresh lease of existence, free and unfettered, mighty and prosperous.[22]

A more revolutionary Bengali traveler than Sarkar or Tagore, demanding a more radical revision of India's nineteenth-century relationship with the West was M. N. Roy. Like Benoy Sarkar, Roy became active in the nationalist agitation in the antipartition days, but his deep involvement in the terrorist wing of the movement forced him to leave India secretly in 1915 to avoid arrest. Moving eastward through Java to California, he became a convert to Marxism, helped found the Communist Party of Mexico, and found his way via Germany to Soviet Russia in time to take an important part in the Second Congress of the Communist International in 1920.[23] There, specializing in the training of potential revolutionaries from Asian countries, Roy rose steadily in the ranks of the international Communist movement. In 1924 he was elected to the Comintern's Presidium. When he read the lecture Tagore first delivered at Taiyuan in that year on the problem of "City and Village," Roy was provoked to a vehement attack on the poet's social and economic views. "How eminently aristocratic would be the society of his ideal," he exclaimed sarcastically:

> His solution to the present social problem is to replace the existing form of property-relations by an earlier form, already left behind in the evolution of modern civilization. He would replace capitalism by patri-

archo-feudal aristocracy. He begrudges the working-class that relatively higher standard of living which incidentally follows an improvement in social production. He is against modern industrialism because it disrupts the class of landed aristocracy to which he belongs.[24]

All Tagore's ideas proved, Roy declared, was that the "cultural civilisation" of the East and the materialistic civilization of the West were essentially one and the same, both being based on private property.[25]

Roy's Marxist critique of Tagore's message differed little from that of Ch'ü Ch'iu-pai, whom he must have met in Moscow and was to meet again in China when he served there for six months in 1927 as the Comintern's representative. Roy's China mission was an even worse fiasco than Tagore's, but for quite different reasons. He was sent, apparently by Stalin, to direct the policy of the Chinese Communist Party at the critical point when its alliance with the Kuomintang was breaking apart. Roy found himself entangled in a complex political and military situation, failed to grasp the motives and aims of the Chinese he was attempting to direct, and as a measure of desperation showed a telegram from Stalin calling for Jacobin measures to Wang Ching-wei, the leader of the moderate nationalist forces Stalin wished to liquidate. This gaucherie brought disaster: the moderates turned against the Communists and joined with the Kuomintang right wing in rounding up and executing them. Roy was forced to flee Hankow across the Gobi Desert to Soviet Russia in a touring car especially equipped with heavy springs, extra gasoline tanks, and GPU agents. Back in Moscow, Stalin refused to see him: Roy's usefulness to the Comintern had come to an end. One Chinese Communist commented: "Comrade R was essentially an intellectual. He always supported principles on paper, but in practice he did not settle a single problem." [26] Much the same criticism had been leveled at Tagore in 1924. Evidently the Chinese were not impressed by the gratuitous advice offered by either of the Bengali Brahmans who came to them in the 1920's with ready-made solutions to their problems.

M. N. Roy survived his disgrace by slipping out of Russia in 1928 and returning secretly to India in 1930. Discovered and arrested by the British as a dangerous revolutionary, he was given five years in prison, and in these years he reflected on his and his country's past and future. Marxism, he decided, was too dogmatic to be scientific. He nevertheless remained a staunch secularist and materialist and a fierce opponent of religion. The prevalent belief in India's spirituality especially angered him, and he collected his most trenchant critiques of the idea in his book on *India's Message*. In one essay (not mentioning Tagore by name) he asserted in the 1930's: "The claim that the Indian people as a whole is morally less corrupt, emotionally purer, idealistically less worldly, in short, spiritually more elevated, than the bulk of the western society, is based upon a wanton disregard for reality." His last words on the subject, not long before his death in 1954, seemed to sound the death knell of Tagore's East-West idea:

> The belief in India's spiritual message to the materialist West is a heady wine. It is time to realise that the pleasant inebriation [it produced] offered a solace to proud intellectuals with inferiority complex[es]. The legacy of that psychological aggressiveness is not an asset, but a liability. For it prevents India from making the most of national independence.[27]

Roy was the last in the long line of Bengali intellectuals who exercised an all-India influence. In him the Bengali reach to the outside world, as also the Bengali reformulation of Indian traditions, attained their farthest point. At the end of his life he looked forward rather than back: "The past is dead; it must be buried." Still there was in the concluding appeal of *India's Message* a note of nostalgia for the great "Bengal Renaissance" which he brought to a close: "India must experience a renaissance — spiritual re-birth." [28]

Calcutta in the nineteenth century had been the metropolis of British India and the gateway through which goods and ideas passed en route to the vast hinterland of the Gangetic plain. Its upper class, assured of rising incomes from their landed property under the guarantee that their taxes would not be raised, produced a unique succession of leaders who pioneered in selecting, reinterpreting, and synthesizing traditions from both Indian and Western sources. Tagore is generally regarded as the finest fruit of what I have called the Hindu-British symbiosis in nineteenth-century Bengal. But the synthesis he proposed between Indian or Eastern spirituality and Western material civilization was criticized increasingly in the twentieth century by younger men, at first because their nationalist spirit demanded political equality with the British, and later because their secular worldview denied validity to the realm of the spiritual. As a poet Rabindranath remained as popular as ever, and whenever his foreign tours increased India's prestige abroad he was hailed at home for his "services to the nation." As a philosopher of East-West relations, however, he was left behind by succeeding generations of Bengali Hindu intellectuals. And Bengal's Muslims, while admiring his poetic genius, seem to have taken no interest in his essentially Hindu view of India as the leader of Asia.

MADRAS

After Bengal, the province most exposed to modern Western influences was Madras, stretched like an opened pair of calipers along the entire southeast coast of the subcontinent. Madras City, which gave its name to the province as a whole, had been founded by the English East India Company in 1639 — well before the Company set up similar trading posts at Bombay in 1660 and Calcutta in 1690. But Madras lacked the rich hinterland that opened up to the British as they extended their rule over the wide and populous Gangetic plain (Clive's famous 1756–57 expedition, which ended in the conquest of Bengal, was actually launched from Madras). By the nineteenth century Madras, and South India generally, had settled down to a slow, if not sleepy, pace of economic and educational development under British rule. Few tremors of the 1857 uprising in Hindustan reached the South, nor was there any excitement to compare with the Sikh, Afghan, and other wars in the north.*

Madras had always been more or less isolated from northern India, and in consequence distinctive social and cultural patterns had developed there. Its people and languages were Dravidian at the base with an Aryan overlay. Linguistically the population fell into two main groups: the 17,000,000 Tamil speakers in the southern districts, and the 16,000,000 Telugu speakers in the north. Muslim civilization, with its egalitarian emphasis, had hardly affected this region, and nowhere on the subcontinent were differences between Brahmans and other castes so wide and so strictly observed. The Brahmans, traditionally the sole educated class, were quick to learn English, and so the Hindu-British sym-

* By the century's end, one young English officer found the boredom in South India so intense that he agitated for an assignment on the Northwest Frontier: Winston Churchill got what he wanted, saw action, wrote a book about it, and so launched himself on a successful career in journalism and politics.

biosis which emerged in nineteenth-century Madras was mainly a Brahman-British affair. In 1912, for example, a royal commission looking into the caste composition of the Indians in the service of the Madras government found that in the three highest offices to which Indians had been admitted, 72 percent of the district munsiffs, 83 percent of the sub-judges, and 55 percent of the deputy collectors were Brahmans, even though all their subcastes made up only 3.2 percent of the province's total population of 42,000,000.[29] The educated class, in addition to being predominantly Brahman, was more closely tied to British rule than its Bengal counterpart, for the land revenue in Madras was generally collected by subordinate officials rather than by a semi-independent gentry. All these factors produced in nineteenth-century Madras an intellectual élite that was politically, socially, and culturally conservative.

The winds of change began to blow more strongly in the opening decades of the twentieth century, producing a shift in the direction of nationalism and secularism paralleling that in Bengal, although somewhat later in time. Bengal's intellectuals themselves contributed to this quickening by their writings and by personal appearances in Madras City. Keshub and other Brahmo missionaries had come by sea to lecture in Madras in the days before the railway network spanned India in the 1870's, and Vivekananda created great excitement on his second visit in 1897. Political leaders came to the annual Congress sessions held at Madras in 1887, 1894, 1903, 1908, and 1914, and the Bengal anti-partition agitation reached the city in 1907 with the stirring lectures by the sea of the firebrand Bepin Chandra Pal. The two Bengalis who exerted the greatest influence on Madras intellectuals, however, were not political but cultural leaders: Rabindranath Tagore and Aurobindo Ghose. Tagore in particular found a sympathetic response in South India. The reactions of four leading men—all Brahmans—gives a fair sampling of Madras intellectuals' views on Indian and modern Western civilization.

The case of K. S. Ramaswami Sastri well illustrates both the Madras Brahman élite's conservatism in social and political matters and their enthusiasm for Bengali leaders in the renaissance of Hindu culture. Ramaswami Sastri was born a Smarta Brahman, the highest ranking and most orthodox caste group among Shaiva Hindus. At fifteen he had the unusual experience of meeting with Swami Vivekananda while the latter, still an unknown Hindu monk, was a guest at his home for a week. Four years later, in 1897, when Vivekananda reached Madras after his successful lecture tour in the United States and Europe, Ramaswami Sastri and his friends rushed to the railway station to meet him. "A carriage drawn by two horses was waiting for him. We unyoked the horses and dragged the carriage ourselves to Kernan Castle on the Marina. I was with Swami like his very shadow during all the days of his stay at Madras." [30]

Obedient to his father's wishes, Ramaswami Sastri took to the law, which he could study in Madras without having to make the outcasteing trip to England. From 1907 to 1933 he was employed in government service as a district munsiff, subjudge, and district judge, but he found time to continue his interest in English, Tamil, and Sanskrit literature and to write profusely on these subjects. Tagore was his special favorite, and he wrote three books on the Bengali poet. A typical passage reads: "Tagore has been, is, and will ever be inexpressibly dear to us because in his sweet accents it is our own Bharata Mata [Mother India] that speaks to us, her beloved children; he has revealed to us the wondrous glory of the real treasures of our race; he has restored to us our lost manhood and our true divinity." [31]

Tagore's political views pleased Ramaswami Sastri, particularly his denunciation of modern nationalism: "He has kept aloof from the turmoil of actual politics so as to give to India the ideal politics which is the life-giving atmosphere surrounding the bare earth of actual political life." Enunciating what might be called a Hindu theory of democracy, Sastri continued: "The State exists for society and society exists for the individual to realise God in himself and out of himself." It followed that foreign rule was unobjectionable as long as it permitted Hindu society and culture to flourish: "Indian culture as the embodiment of the soul of India must be preserved and perfected and propagated all over the world. The military and administrative domination over India is of no moment if India preserves herself from the conquest of her culture by alien cultures." [32] Ramaswami Sastri thus fully agreed with Tagore's hope for a synthesis of Indian and Western virtues. "If we assimilate wisely modern science and democracy and yet preserve our Indianness of soul and life and literature and philosophy and religion, India shall be the morning star of the world once more." [33] These phrases once again bring to mind the doctrine of "Eastern spirit and Western techniques" voiced by Japanese and Chinese thinkers of a somewhat earlier day.

Two aspects of Tagore's thought disturbed the Tamil judge, however.

One was his criticism of the caste system, expressed in an appreciative article on Jesus Christ. "The non-acceptance of Christianity in India is due not to lack of love for Christ," Ramaswami Sastri countered, "but to our religion including and transcending his holy religion." In defense of caste he argued: "There is no doubt whatever that the great features of the true system of caste which is intimately bound up with our religion can be preserved while the great political institutions and ideals of the West are being built into our civilisation." How this mixture would work out in practice he did not explain, but the result he expected was the resurrection of the social and cultural order of ancient India, "in which order and progress, social love and social efficiency, statical and dynamic elements, harmony and energy, peace and power, will be combined till our beloved land becomes the pattern for all other lands and the wonder and glory of the world." [34] A more serious problem was Tagore's departure from orthodox Hinduism as defined by Sankara. "The modern mind in India — Tagore is no exception to it — wants to display its fondness for western realism by ridiculing Sri Sankaracharya's doctrines." Tagore depreciated asceticism and renunciation, failing to realize that "Indian renunciation is not a flying from life; it is a procession through life to reach the lotus feet of God. . . . Further, he has not a clear and strong faith in the Hindu theory of renunciation and he has denied to himself the raptures that are born of Hindu symbolism and image-worship." In brief, "Tagore's philosophy is coloured through and through by [the] pseudo-humanism of the West which can never realise Eastern spiritualism." [35]

Tagore's Tamil biographer therefore felt a reluctant ambivalence toward his Bengali hero. When viewing Tagore in world perspective he saw him as a leader of "the Indian Renaissance," his philosophy became "one of the glories of modern India," and the poet himself was "one of the perfect incarnations of the spirit of Indian culture." His message was India's message: "We have a great message to offer to the world — the message of the unity and immanence and transcendance of the spirit. . . . The unparalleled and profound influence of Tagore on the West is only the inauguration of a great period when India will shape the literary and artistic destinies of the world." [36] But, when judging Tagore's social and religious ideas against the traditions of Shaiva Hinduism in which he was raised, Ramaswami Sastri found them contaminated with Western "pseudo-humanism." He overlooked the possibility that this humanistic element might have owed as much to Islamic influences (which were strong in Bengal but practically nonexistent in the Tamil country) as to Western ones. It is interesting that a similar disagreement had arisen a century earlier between Rammohun Roy, whose theistic Hinduism owed much to his Islamic education, and a Madras pandit, Sankara Sastri.[37] Not only the stronger influence of Western thought in Bengal, but also the centuries-old presence of Islam there may account for what appeared to the two Madras Brahmans to be the heterodox ideas of the two Bengalis.

Ramaswami Sastri's criticism may be traced back to still deeper roots, in the bifurcation within Hinduism between the monistic Shaiva doctrines to which he subscribed, and the Vaishnava qualified dualism generally accepted by Tagore and most upper-caste Bengali Hindus. In the province of Madras itself, Shaivism has been the predominant school in the Tamil area south of Madras city, while Vaishnavism has dominated the Telugu-speaking area to the north.[38] A Vaishnava from the Telugu country might therefore agree with Tagore on the very point where a Shaiva from the Tamil country had disagreed with him. Such was in fact the case with the Telugu Brahman, Sarvepalli Radhakrishnan, whose *Philosophy of Rabindranath Tagore*, published in 1918, fully endorsed the poet's religious ideas, and forcefully disassociated them from Shaiva doctrines.[39]

Radhakrishnan had more than Brahman ancestry and Vaishnava heritage in common with Tagore. Each was responding to the same Christian challenge to Hinduism that Tagore's father, Debendranath, had so vigorously opposed. Radhakrishnan spent his childhood in the Hindu pilgrimage towns of Tiruttani and Tirupati, then attended Christian mission schools in Vellore and Madras. "At an impressionable period in my life," he relates, "I became familiar not only with the teaching of the New Testament, but with the criticisms levelled by Christian missionaries on Hindu beliefs and practices. My pride as a Hindu, roused by the enterprise and eloquence of Swami Vivekananda, was deeply hurt by the treatment accorded to Hinduism in missionary institutions. . . . The challenge of Christian critics impelled me to make a study of Hinduism and find out what is living and what is dead in it." Although Indian philosophy did not form a regular part of the curriculum at Madras Christian College, Radhakrishnan was able to write in 1908 an M.A. thesis which he "intended to be a reply to the charge that the Vedanta system had no room for ethics." His mastery of English and gift for clear and systematic exposition won praise from his British professor. Encouraged by this success, he went on to a brilliant career as a teacher of Indian philosophy at Madras University, then at Mysore, Calcutta, and ultimately Oxford. No other twentieth-century Indian — not even Tagore himself — has so systematically and tirelessly expounded the value of Hinduism's philosophical heritage to the modern world.[40]

In *The Philosophy of Rabindranath Tagore,* his first important book, Radhakrishnan endorsed without reservation all aspects of the poet's thought, including his East-West theory. "In interpreting the philosophy and message of Sir Rabindranath Tagore," he told his readers, "we are interpreting the Indian ideal of philosophy, religion, and art, of which his work is the outcome and expression." For Radhakrishnan, as for Ramaswami Sastri, "Indian" meant Hindu. "The familiar truths of Hindu philosophy and religion, the value of which it has become fashionable to belittle even in the land of their birth, are here handled with such rare reverence and deep feeling that they seem to be almost new." But the Telugu philosopher, perhaps because of his greater exposure to and reaction against Western and Christian thought, went on to generalize that India and Tagore were truly Eastern, a thought that did not particularly interest his Tamil contemporary, Ramaswami Sastri.

> Through the acceptance of the civilisation of the East, which is religious and not secular, it is easy for us to enter the kingdom of God. Though not exclusively, still mainly, the emphasis in the East is on life and not possession, intuition and not intellect, religion and not science, freedom and not direction. It is because India represents this ideal that Rabindranath is proud to be a son of India.[41]

The opposition between Eastern spirituality and modern Western secular and materialist civilization, Tagore's constant refrain, was also one of Radhakrishnan's favorite themes. On the one hand, he wrote, "Western civilisation is more mechanical than spiritual, more political than religious, more mindful of power than of peace." On the other hand, "The peoples of the East do not organise themselves for power but for perfection. They do not hate and kill, suspect and envy, but live and adore, love and worship." Therefore, he concluded, paraphrasing Tagore: "If Europe can reach the Eastern ideal of a people she will have a future more glorious than her past. . . . The chance for Europe after the War lies in her adoption of the ideals of the East, namely spiritual love, beauty, and freedom, which are not diminished by sharing." [42]

Radhakrishnan's concurrence with Tagore's philosophy places him in the mainstream of modern Hindu thought as it developed first in Bengal and later in other provinces with the spread of higher education in English. Bengal's intellectual leadership was still strong enough to induce Radhakrishnan to move from Mysore to Calcutta when he was offered the George V professorship at Calcutta University in 1921. Ten years later, when presiding at the festivities in Calcutta honoring Tagore on his seventieth birthday, he reaffirmed his support for the poet's message of the East. "For the whole Western tradition, man is essentially a rational being, one who can think logically and act upon utilitarian principles. In the East, spiritual understanding and sympathy are of more importance than intellectual ability." [43]

To the objection that these generalities conveniently ignored the central role of Judeo-Christian traditions in the development of Western civilization, Radhakrishnan could reply, as had Rammohun Roy, Keshub Chunder Sen, and other Bengali exponents of modern Hinduism, that Jesus was an Asian, and really belonged to the East rather than to the West. In his *Eastern Religions and Western Thought* he presented the most erudite version of this thesis yet recorded, arguing that Jesus, "in His teaching of the Kingdom of God, life eternal, ascetic emphasis, and even future life . . . breaks away from the Jewish tradition and approximates to Hindu and Buddhist thought. Though His teaching is historically continuous with Judaism, it did not develop from it in its essentials." Radhakrishnan seemed to conclude that Jesus, along with the Buddha, was at heart a Hindu.[44] In any event, writing on the eve of World War II, he prescribed for humanity exactly what Tagore had long been recommending: "We need to-day a proper orientation, literally the values the world derived from the Orient, the truths of the inner life. . . . The fate of the human race hangs on a rapid assimilation of the qualities associated with the mystic religions of the East. The stage is set for such a process." [45]

As in Bengal, so in Madras, the advocates of nonpolitical spirituality were challenged by a rising school of nationalist thinkers, and these again divided into two major lines of nationalist doctrine, the religious and the secular. South India's most famous religious nationalist was the Tamil poet, Subramania Iyer, whose eloquence won him the Sanskrit title of Bharati, after the same goddess of speech for whom one of the Tagore family's literary periodicals had been named.

Bharati was born in 1882 in an orthodox Smarta Brahman family, but he was a rebellious youth and grew disdainful of the old caste ways. At fifteen he left his home in the extreme south to travel to Benares, where an uncle managed a hostel for Tamil pilgrims. During his three years there he improved his English, learned some Hindi and Sanskrit, and came in touch with the nationalist ideas beginning to penetrate the heart-land of the subcontinent from the Bengal and Bombay coasts. Bharati returned to north India briefly in 1906 and 1907 as a reporter covering the annual Congress sessions, and saw his heroes, the extremist Hindu nationalists Tilak, Lajpat Rai, and Aurobindo, and the Irish-born disciple of Vivekananda, Sister Nivedita. In 1908 the British began to prosecute the extremists more vigorously, and Bharati took refuge in the French colony of Pondicherry, just south of Madras City. In 1910, Aurobindo also settled at Pondicherry, and at intervals during the next eight years he and Bharati discussed (in English necessarily) their ideas of reviving their country and its Hindu traditions.

Bharati's contacts with North Indian leaders broadened his outlook well beyond the parochialism of most of his Tamil contemporaries — and even, it might be said, beyond the parochialism of most of his Bengali contemporaries. For, while Bengal's leading newspaper, the *Amrita Bazar Patrika*, passed over in silence Tagore's visit to Japan in 1916, Bharati hailed the Bengali poet as *Lokaguru*, "the world-teacher," and chided the Indian press with indifference to his apparent triumph, asking: "Does it happen every day that an Indian goes to Japan and there receives the highest honour from all classes of people, from Prime Minister Okuma as well as from the simple monk of the Buddhist shrine?" Bharati went on to use Tagore's mission to Japan as an occasion to appeal to his countrymen to take more pride in India's greatness:

> The Indian ear must ring with the fame of Indian genius. The present intellectual and spiritual revival in the country will be regarded by coming generations as one of the most brilliant chapters in Indian history. I appeal to our great publicists to identify themselves more completely with the Revival. For true is the message which Vivekananda brought us, the message that we are to be born again. An individual poet is merely a symbol. We shall soon have scores and scores of them, men of thought and men of deed. . . . Karma-yoga [the yoga of action] must be easier

to learn for the children of Krishna. So let us achieve all things by throwing ourselves at the lotus feet of the Bhagavan [Lord Krishna]. So let us offer full praise to those who lead us on this great path.[46]

When Bharati praised India, he did not necessarily have in mind the whole population within the borders of British India, but was thinking essentially of its Hindu majority.[47] Aurobindo's influence may have been responsible for this, but a more general process was at work on both men, as on many other nationalists seeking indigenous foundations on which to base their claims to equality with their foreign rulers. Hindus looked first to Hindu traditions, Muslims to Muslim ones, and out of this engrafting of political nationalism onto the primal roots of religious traditions sprang the tragic splitting of independent South Asia into Hindu- and Muslim-majority states. For Tamils in particular the presence of Islam seemed very remote, for Islam had never made the impact in the south that it had in northern India, and only one in fourteen inhabitants of the province of Madras was a Muslim.

The Tamil poet Bharati spoke more in terms of India and the world, while Radhakrishnan, from the Telugu country, referred more frequently to the contrast between the East and the West. Yet another Telugu Brahman, the editor of the nationalist *Swarajya* (Freedom) daily and a leading figure in Congress politics in Madras, also used the terms East and West in commenting on Tagore's ideas, but in a secular way, completely rejecting Tagore's theory. T. Prakasam was the only one of these four Madras intellectuals to have studied abroad; he spent some eight years in Edinburgh before returning home to enter politics and journalism. His fiery nationalism brought him into the Congress and its parliamentary wing, the Swarajya Party founded in 1923 by Chittaranjan Das and Motilal Nehru. In that same year, when it was first announced that Tagore would visit China, Prakasam's newspaper carried a report from its own correspondent there, who doubted that the poet would be well received, for "the political conditions are so unsettled, and the bandits so active all over China that the people will not listen to the author of *Gītānjali*. Besides the Chinese are downright materialists today, and Rabi Babu's idealism, which does not promise gold, opium, and concubines, is not likely to appeal to them." [48]

Prakasam himself was responsible for the most critical editorial to appear in the Indian press on the subject of the Bengali poet's message to

China. "It is Dr. Tagore's and our misfortune that the time is out of joint with his great gifts. Everywhere in the East, in China, in Egypt and in India, the outstanding fact to-day is the subversion of the people, in the land of their own birth, by the powerful influence of adventurers from the West," the editorial began. The Western powers had gained "a position of vantage from which the inherited somnambulist spirituality of the East has been powerless to dislodge them. That is why harassed countries are awakening today to a new sense of nationalhood [sic], of solid cohesive endeavour as the one avenue for redemption within their means." Tagore's idealism unfortunately came into direct collision with this nationalist upsurge:

> He does not want nationality, he wants a federation of Asiatic cultures. Organisation is anathema to him; he would have in its place the soul-satisfying spiritualism of the Orient. Science with its destructive potentiality is a menace; he would implant in its stead the sense of beauty in nature as a more fruitful source of creative vision. . . .
> All this is without doubt highly elevating and idealistic. But it begins with renaissance at the wrong end. . . . To a subject people whose nationhood is exposed to insult and challenge before it has a chance to develop, the comprehensive ambition of cultural federation with the powers of a whole continent is liable to come home with something of the rudeness of a taunt. We believe that such a federation can only be the perfection of nationalism and not its antithesis.[49]

Secular nationalism, embracing not merely the upper classes but also the uneducated working people, was what India needed, Prakasam's editorial concluded.

> The consolations of a restful abode for the soul in the great Hereafter might be well for those that are placed in comfort and luxury, but to the toilers and workers it is prone to prove a refuge for sluggishness. We want a virile philosophy, one that insists on strength and energetic action and precludes the 'love of humanity' as a luxury beyond the reach of the weak. Dr. Tagore would have us sacrifice the substance for the vision.[50]

While these four Madras Brahmans seemed to differ in their views of Tagore, India, and the East in about the same proportions as their Bengali contemporaries, taken as a group they seem somewhat more conservative politically.[51] Madras in the 1920's did in fact lag behind Bengal and Bombay in the tempo of its political life, and this had also been true throughout the nineteenth century.[52] For one brief span of years, however, a Madras-based religious movement with political implications powerfully affected the English-educated class in Bombay and the United Provinces (somewhat as Bengal's Brahmo Samaj movement had stimulated this same class in the 1860's and 1870's). This was the Theosophical Society, brought to India in 1879 by its founders, the Russian-born mystic Madame Blavatsky and the American lawyer, Colonel Olcott. In 1882 they fixed its world headquarters at Adyar, near the city of Madras.

The immediate welcome accorded this new movement from the West and its rapid spread across India marked a new stage in the growth of the Hindu-Western cultural synthesis which had earlier taken root in Bengal. An American visitor of 1884 summed up well the significance of the Theosophists' arrival:

> And it was an event whose importance we western people can hardly comprehend when there appeared from America this company of people who had abandoned every form of Christianity, taken up their abode in India to lead in the work of at once rehabilitating and revising these ancient systems, and pointed Hindus and Buddhists to their own scriptures and prophets as fountains of faith and hope. They naturally gained a hold on the hearts of these people, and in a few years moved and attracted them more than did the Christian missionaries in as many centuries.[53]

In 1891 the Theosophical movement in London gained its most powerful convert in Mrs. Annie Besant, the Irish-English champion of one unpopular cause after another. Theism, rationalism, atheism, birth-control, socialism, and feminism had successively won her eloquent support in the 1870's and 1880's. Now the occultism and mysticism of Theosophy drew her into the study of the ancient religions of India. To India she came in 1893 (immediately after a triumphant reception at the World Parliament of Religions in Chicago), adopted Indian dress, and at once took up the cause of Hinduism. "India's Mission to the World," one of her lectures, given in Calcutta to an admiring audience of several thousands, articulated much the same message that Vivekananda also began to expound in that year.[54]

The remarkable influence that Theosophy in general and Annie Besant in particular exerted on the intellectuals of India between 1900 and 1920 has yet to be fully studied or appreciated. In South Africa a young Indian lawyer named Mohandas Gandhi, who had met and admired her in London in 1891, kept her picture hanging on his wall. At Allahabad, in 1901, she initiated into Theosophy a thirteen-year-old Brahman boy, Jawaharlal Nehru, whose tutor was a Belgian-Irish Theosophist.[55] In 1917, years before either of these two men occupied the presidency of the Indian National Congress, she was elected to that office. What were the keys to her success as a leader of Indian opinion in the opening decades of this century? Her forceful personality was one. The fact that she was an elderly woman was another ("the Mother of Modern India," some called her). Her adroitness and persistence as a public speaker, writer, editor, and organizer certainly helped. But the main key was probably the fact that she, a member of the ruling race, sincerely espoused two causes dear to most English-speaking Hindus: the cause of reformed, but still orthodox Hinduism, and the cause of India's freedom, to be achieved through an evolutionary process of constitutional change.

BOMBAY: GANDHI AND SAVARKAR

This fusion of Hindu religious with Western political ideals was not original with Annie Besant. It had been gaining popularity in Bengal since the 1860's, and in Western India since the 1880's. Naturally, it took different forms at different times among different groups, under the influence of different historical memories and different geographical situations. Thus, in the great Bombay Presidency, which covered the western coast of the subcontinent from Sind (now in West Pakistan) to Goa, modern nationalism first emerged among the small Parsi (originally Persian) Zoroastrian community in Bombay City, then among the Chitpavan Brahmans of Maharashtra (in the eastern and southern part of the Presidency), and only later among the Hindu and Jain population of Gujarat (located north of Bombay City). As in eastern India, this sequence followed the penetration of British rule and the diffusion of English education, but in western India religion was growing more rather than less important in politics during the opening decades of the twentieth century. By the 1920's two distinct schools of religious nationalism had come to the fore, one based on the Vaishnava and Jain ethos prevailing in Gujarat, the other on the more militant Hinduism associated with the eighteenth-century Maratha Empire in Maharashtra.

Mohandas K. Gandhi, whose life was ended by a Maharashtrian Brahman assassin in 1948, dominated the nationalist movement not only in Bombay but in all India during the 1920's and 1930's. Little research has been done on the intellectual influences affecting him during his formative years, but some tentative generalizations will be advanced here, if only to explain the gulf separating Gandhi's mental world from that of his greatest Bengali contemporary, Rabindranath Tagore. The first step is to see Gandhi against the cultural and historical background of his native Gujarat.

The region now inhabited by speakers of Gujarati has since prehistoric times been a thriving center of trade between ports on the shores of the Arabian Sea, Persian Gulf, and Red Sea and the hinterland of North and Central India. Excellent harbors at the mouths of several navigable rivers have been in use since before 2000 B.C.[56] Because of this traditional emphasis on commerce, which the British connection further stimulated, the merchant class has long dominated Gujarati society. Easily accessible by sea, Gujarat has been relatively inaccessible by land from the north and northwest. These two facts, along with the region's commercial emphasis, seem to have encouraged an unusual freedom and variety in social and religious matters. Historically, neither Brahmanical Hindu nor Sunni Islamic orthodoxy has been very strong. Jainism (from its very beginnings popular among the merchant class) was dominant for a time before the fourteenth-century Muslim conquest, and Jains and Vaishnava Hindus have continued to intermarry down to recent times.

The roots of Gandhi's religious nationalism lay in the Rajput political and the Vaishnava and Jain religious traditions which were especially strong in his home region, the Kathiawad peninsula. His father and grandfather had served as prime ministers for several of the Rajput rulers in this isolated peninsula, an area so unimportant strategically that the British never bothered to rule directly over its more than two hundred small princedoms. The Gandhis (the name means "perfumer") were Banias and by the late nineteenth century were adherents of the Vaishnava minority rather than the Jain majority of the Kathiawad Banias.[57] As Gandhi points out in his autobiography, "Jainism was strong in Gujarat, and its influence was felt everywhere and on all occasions." [58] Gandhi's own piety and asceticism, and his strict insistence on nonviolence and truthfulness suggest a Jain core to his thought, often expressed in Vaishnava terms.[59]

Mohandas was the youngest and brightest of the three Gandhi boys. He was seventeen when their father died. Determined to maintain the family's honor, he was advised by a Brahman friend of his late father to go to London to study law, as this would prepare him for a career as a prime minister to one of Gujarat's many princes. He resolved to follow this advice, but his devoutly religious mother refused her consent until he had vowed before her spiritual adviser, a Jain monk of their same Modh Bania subcaste, that in London he would not touch meat, wine, or women.[60] Thus, having determined to reach a particular goal, Gandhi adopted Jain ascetic practices to help him reach it — a pattern which marked his unique political style throughout his life.

Jain influences on Gandhi's thinking increased in the stressful months he endured after his return from England in 1891. He had kept his vows, but his mother had died, and he found himself treated as an outcaste by his subcaste fellows for having defied their ban on his supposedly defiling voyage to London. A Jain family took him in, and one of its members, the leading Jain reformer of his day, gave him religious guidance. For a time he shared his meals with another young Jain, Virchand Gandhi, then secretary of the Jain Association of India and in 1893 Jainism's official spokesman at the World Parliament of Religions in Chicago.[61]

By 1893 Mohandas Gandhi must have felt frustrated by the discovery that his studies abroad had not improved his chances of becoming a prime minister. He failed to establish himself as a lawyer in Bombay City, and in his native Kathiawad tightening British control was depriving independently minded Indians of political influence. Once again foreign travel seemed to offer a way forward. A Muslim firm in the Indian community of Natal in South Africa needed a lawyer, and Gandhi jumped at the chance. Almost at once he became the community's political leader (one might say its de facto prime minister), and initiated a twenty-one-year campaign to remove the indignities and inequities imposed on it by the dominant White South Africans.

Within two years of his arrival in South Africa, Gandhi had worked out the basic premises on which he subsequently based his entire life's work as a political leader and moral reformer. Two basic spheres, the political and the ethical, were interlinked from the beginning of his remarkable career, as they had been in the career of his own father and in the lives of the liberal statesmen of the day — leaders like Gladstone and Naoroji (the Parsi member of Parliament), whom he regarded as ideal men. But Gandhi faced in the rough frontier country of Natal and the Transvaal a radically different political situation than obtained in Britain or India at the time, and to meet that situation he developed a radical system of ideas and methods. Trained in the law, and accustomed in both India and England to equal treatment under the law, he encountered in South Africa a society where differences in skin color were given precedence over both the letter and the spirit of the law. In the first weeks of his stay, one White South African threw him out of a railway compartment, another kicked and beat him for refusing to give up his seat in a mail coach, and a hotel keeper made it clear that his presence as a "colored man" was embarrassing. What most aroused Gandhi were not these personal insults but the successive moves by the dominant White community to disenfranchise the Indian settlers and reduce them to an inferior legal status.[62] At first Gandhi resisted these moves by drawing up petitions. When these failed, he grew more and more convinced that his real enemy was not the White community, but their modern, materialistic civilization.

His friends in England and his reading in South Africa gave Gandhi considerable encouragement in adopting this stand against modern Western civilization. As a student in London he had been a devoted member of the Vegetarian Society, a small circle which included such eccentrics (by Victorian standards) as George Bernard Shaw, Annie Besant, Edward Carpenter, Henry Salt, and Edwin Arnold. Carpenter, an advocate of the simple life, asexuality, and Eastern wisdom, had written a popular tract, *Civilization — Its Cause and Cure,* which Gandhi admired. Another vegetarian, Edward Maitland (also a sometime Theosophist) directly influenced Gandhi in South Africa with the letters and books he sent him from England, and in 1894 Gandhi announced himself in the newspapers of Natal as the local agent for the publications of Maitland's Esoteric Christian Union, recommending them to "anyone of your readers who has found the present-day materialism and all its splendour to be insufficient for the needs of his soul." [63]

Another important influence, the teachings of Jesus, had already delighted Gandhi when he read the New Testament in London, and

Tolstoy's presentation of them in *The Gospels in Brief* and *The Kingdom of God is Within You* stirred him again in South Africa. His English friends there worked and prayed for his conversion. He read all the books they gave him, and even attended a three-day revivalist meeting, without being persuaded. Nevertheless, he found it hard to answer their criticisms of Hindu beliefs and practices, and for a time experienced a serious "mental churning," an inner crisis that paralleled his outer struggle against the injustices being done to the Indian community. In his characteristically methodical way, he wrote to a number of religious leaders in India for advice. Only the answers of his Jain friend in Bombay, Raychand Mehta, gave the peace of mind he sought.[64]

Raychand's letter of October 20, 1894, expounded in simple language the Jain teaching of the soul and matter as two distinct and eternal substances that combine in various ways in living creatures. The true nature of the soul being perfect and complete consciousness, and that of matter being lifelessness and nescience, the soul strives to free itself from the matter that surrounds it and obscures its self-knowledge. Liberation (*moksha*) from the material body comes gradually as the soul realizes its true nature, ceases to notice pleasure or pain, and brings all thought, speech, and action under its control.[65] But the progress of the soul toward liberation is arduous, requiring constant vigilance, austerity, and the observance of four main disciplines: truthfulness (because lying obscures consciousness); noninjury (*ahimsā*), (because violence uses matter to harm or destroy life and so dims the soul's awareness of other souls and of its own nonmaterial nature); chastity (because the sex act arouses consciousness-obscuring passion and destroys countless living spermatozoa, which would otherwise be transmuted into psychic energy); and poverty (possessions misleading the soul into identifying itself with the body).[66]

Although it was to take him some years to conform his life to these disciplines, Gandhi seems to have accepted Raychand's teachings without difficulty. He was particularly relieved to be told that there was no need for him to consider converting to another religion. Since he had been born into a Hindu family, Raychand noted, this must have been due to the influence of his activities in previous incarnations: therefore he should remain a Hindu. In any case, religion was not a matter of outward forms or creeds, Gandhi concluded in reflecting on Raychand's advice:

Religion is the quality of one's soul, and exists among men in visible or invisible forms. . . . Religion is that discipline of spiritual self-perfection through which we are able to know our own selves. This means we should adopt this discipline from wherever we may find it. It may be found in India, or Europe, or Arabia.[67]

Raychand's teaching of the nature of the soul and its striving for liberation gave Gandhi a religious certitude that enabled him gradually to transform the Indian community's struggle against White racism from a political fight to a spiritual one. By 1909 he had worked out a comprehensive theory of civilization to fit this South African situation. True civilization, he declared in his Gujarati manifesto *Hind Swarāj* (Indian home rule), consisted in "attaining mastery over ourselves and our passions. So doing, we know ourselves. . . . If this definition be correct, then, India, as so many writers have shown, has nothing to learn from anybody else, and this is as it should be," for "the tendency of Indian civilization is to elevate the moral being, that of the Western civilization is to propagate immorality." Europeans, Gandhi said, "appear to be half mad. They lack real physical strength or courage. They keep up their energy by intoxication. They can hardly be happy in solitude. Women, who should be the queens of households, wander in the streets, or they slave away in factories. . . . This civilization is such that one has only to be patient and it will be self-destroyed. According to the teaching of Mahomed this would be considered a Satanic civilization." [68]

It followed from this diagnosis that Indians must shun the civilization of the British and try to convert Britain to the true civilization, that of India. With this in mind, Gandhi drew a distinction between "Western" civilization and "modern" civilization. "It is not the British people who are ruling India," he insisted, but it is modern civilization, through its railways, telegraph, telephone, and almost every invention which has been claimed to be a triumph of civilization." Remove modern civilization, and India and Britain could live at peace, and both would be happier. "East and West can only meet," Gandhi argued, "when the West has thrown overboard modern civilization, almost in its entirety." [69]

Answering the practical question "How should Indians resist British domination without using modern weapons?" Gandhi advanced his concept of *satyāgraha*. He coined this word himself, translating it as "truth force" or "soul force" — the Sanskrit *satya*, "the true, the real," and *āgrahah*, "firmness, determination," combining to suggest much the same idea as Lincoln's "firmness in the right, as God gives us to see the right." Two Indian traditions familiar to Gandhi since childhood appear to have entered into his *satyāgraha* ideal: the absolute fearlessness of the Rajput warrior, and the absolute truthfulness, harmlessness, and ruthless disregard for the body practiced by the Jain aspirant to liberation.[70] Faced with what he regarded as an unjust law, the practitioner of *satyāgraha* deliberately disobeys it and cheerfully suffers the punishment meted out by the courts of law, hoping by his "soul force" to convert the oppressor and so bring him to correct the injustice. Gandhi himself described *satyāgraha* in essentially Jain terms when he declared in 1908: "The only condition of a successful use of this force was a recognition of the existence of the soul as apart from the body and its permanent and superior nature." [71] By 1909 he was already certain that his method was an "infallible panacea" for all of India's ills, and that: "It is the only weapon that is suited to the genius of our people and our land, which is the nursery of the most ancient religions and has very little to learn from modern civilization — a civilization based on violence of the blackest type, largely a negation of the divine in man and which is rushing headlong to its own ruin." [72]

By his inspiring example and deft leadership, Gandhi gradually infused the spirit of *satyāgraha* into the Indian community in South Africa, and by 1914 had succeeded in winning significant concessions from the dominant White community. He returned to India in 1915 convinced that his principles and methods would prove equally effective against the British-run government there. One of the first things he did was to make contact with the man who six years later would offer the stoutest opposition to his political program — Rabindranath Tagore.

Gandhi had known of Debendranath Tagore as the great leader of the Brahmo Samaj movement long before he tried to meet the aging Maharshi in 1901, when the Congress session Gandhi was attending met in Calcutta. The eighty-four-year-old sage was too ill to grant interviews, but young Gandhi and his friends were invited to attend a service of the Brahmo Samaj in the Tagore mansion. Rabindranath was away at Santiniketan at the time, and his first contact with Gandhi came in 1913, when his friend C. F. Andrews impressed on him the importance of the Indian community's *satyāgraha* campaign, then reaching its climax in South Africa. When Andrews arrived in Natal to help Gandhi, he brought him a personal message of encouragement from the world-famous Bengali poet.

When Gandhi returned to India in 1915 and was still without a fixed abode, Tagore at Andrews' suggestion offered him and his followers the hospitality of Santiniketan. His letter of invitation addressed Gandhi as *Mahātmā*, Sanskrit for "great soul," the title which clung to him from then on.[73] After the artistic ceremony of welcome at Santiniketan, at which ancient Hindu rites were followed, Gandhi replied in words that sound remarkably Tagorean:

> We were received with great pomp in Bombay but there was nothing in it to make us happy. For there the western modes had been carefully imitated. We shall move to our goal in the manner of the east, not in the manner of the west, for we are of the east. We shall grow up in the beautiful manners and customs of India and, true to her spirit, make friends with nations having different ideals. Indeed through her oriental culture India will establish friendly relations with the eastern and the western worlds.[74]

Within five years Gandhi's combination of the extremist nationalists' religious rejection of Western influences with the moderate nationalists' abhorrence of violent methods proved so appealing to the politically active middle class that the older Congress leaders had to acknowledge him as the foremost leader of the nationalist movement. Tagore, however, was not convinced that Gandhi knew what he was doing, and in 1919 publicly warned him that *satyāgraha* was "a force which is not necessarily moral in itself; it can be used against truth as well as for it." [75] In 1920, not long after the poet sailed for Europe with a healing message of spiritual peace from India, Gandhi organized an all-India campaign of noncooperation against British institutions in India, from law courts and legislatures to English-language schools and shops selling British goods. This radical, completely nonviolent program caught the imagination of the younger nationalists, who thenceforth looked to Gandhi as their supreme commander.

Tagore at first hailed the news of Gandhi's nonviolent movement, and wrote to Andrews from Chicago: "It is in the fitness of things that Mahatma Gandhi, frail in body and devoid of all material resources, should call up the immense power of the meek that has been lying

waiting in the heart of the destitute and insulted humanity of India.
. . . We, the famished ragged ragamuffins of the East, are to win freedom for all humanity." His enthusiasm turned abruptly to dismay, however, when he learned that Gandhi was condemning modern Western
civilization in its entirety. "What irony of fate is this," he wrote
Andrews, "that I should be preaching co-operation of cultures on this
side of the sea just at the moment when the doctrine of non-co-operation
is preached on the other side?" Opposing Gandhi's conception of India
as too narrow, he concluded: "my own prayer is: let India stand for the
co-operation of all peoples of the world. . . . For it is the mind of Man,
in the East and the West, which is ever approaching Truth in her
different aspects from different angles of vision." [76]

Andrews had Tagore's letters published in India's leading English-
language monthly, the *Modern Review,* and Gandhi, stung by Tagore's
criticisms, at once replied with two articles in his own English-language
weekly, *Young India.* Diplomatically praising Tagore for "his poetic
interpretation of India's message to the world," he parried the poet's
charge that noncooperation was a negative idea. "It is as necessary to
reject untruth as it is to accept truth," he argued. "Non-co-operation with
evil is as much a duty as co-operation with good." Gandhi agreed completely with Tagore's concept of India's mission, but insisted that it
could be given substance only by an independent and awakened India:

> Let him deliver his message of peace to the world, and feel confident
> that India, through her Non-co-operation, will have exemplified his mes-
> sage. Non-co-operation is intended to give the very meaning to patriotism
> that the Poet is yearning after. An India prostrate at the feet of Europe
> can give no hope to humanity. An India awakened and free has a message
> of peace and good-will to a groaning world. Non-co-operation is designed
> to supply her with a platform from which she will preach the message. [77]

When Tagore returned to India from his triumphal European tour
in mid-July 1921, he tried to refrain from criticizing Gandhi, whose
movement was steadily increasing in fervor. Pressed by a reporter to
declare his attitude toward Gandhi, he replied: "I shall humbly try to be
his own follower by following the dictates of my conscience and giving
utterance to what I believe to be true." But the more he learned about
the aims and methods of the Noncooperation movement, the more difficult he found it to maintain his self-imposed silence, and a few weeks

after his return to Calcutta he spoke out in two public lectures. The first, "The Union of Cultures," stressed his international ideal, and obliquely censured the narrow nationalism he feared in Gandhi. The second, "The Call of Truth," focused on the deeper conflict between his view of truth as an immediately accessible state of harmony in which all men recognized their essential unity, and Gandhi's view that truth was a moral state only to be reached by the arduous process of negating everything immoral.[78]

Gandhi came to Calcutta a few days after Tagore's second lecture and called on the poet at his mansion to enlist his support, but without success. As they talked, a commotion arose outside. "Come and look over the edge of my verandah, Gandhiji," said Tagore. "Look down there and see what your non-violent followers are up to. They have stolen [English-made] cloth from the shops. . . . They've lit that bonfire in my courtyard and are now howling around it like a lot of demented dervishes. Is that your non-violence? Can you keep these emotions under a strict control with your non-violent principles? You know you can't." "Well," Gandhi countered, "if you can do nothing else for me you can at least . . . lead the nation and spin [handspun yarn]. . . ." "Poems I can spin, songs I can spin," Tagore rejoined, "but what a mess I would make, Gandhiji, of your precious cotton!" [79]

This dramatic clash between twentieth-century India's two greatest men may be regarded from several standpoints. Essentially they differed because one was a reformer bent on changing the world, the other a poet listening for harmonies inaudible to less finely tuned ears. Beyond these basic differences in vocation and temperament, each man looked at India and the world through the lenses of his own regional, caste, and family traditions. India in the eyes of a Kathiawad Bania, raised in conservative Jain-Vaishnava religious and Rajput political traditions, appeared a quite different India from that seen by a Bengali Brahman whose unorthodox family had pioneered in assimilating modern Western ideas and synthesizing them with Hindu religious and artistic traditions. Gandhi's image of India and the West also reflected a very different experience with individual Westerners. His treatment in a colonial outpost at the hands of South Africa's White supremacists had been as brutal as Tagore's welcome in the literary circles of Western civilization's leading metropolis had been exhilarating.

The ironic result of Tagore's opposition to Gandhi was that, while in

Japan and China he had come under heavy fire for praising the spiritual civilization of the East, in India (during the 1920's at least) he was as severely criticized for reminding his countrymen that they still had much to learn from the modern West. Nationalist hostility against him was greatest in his native Bengal. C. R. Das, who had his own reservations about Gandhi's ideas but was keeping them to himself in 1921, was said to have closed each busy day with a full-dress denunciation of Rabindranath.[80] The precipitous decline in the poet's popularity after he began opposing Gandhi can be traced in the changing reactions of his Calcutta audiences between 1921 and 1924. At his first lecture after his return from Europe and the United States in 1921, the crowd was so large that windows were broken by those in the corridors who tried to force their way into the packed auditorium: "as the poet entered the hall he was given a most enthusiastic ovation and [the] clapping of hands and cheering continued for some time." At his second lecture a fortnight later the audience was smaller, showed "a certain lack of enthusiasm," and "an air of concern seemed to sit on the face of many." A few months later, when he returned to Calcutta from Santiniketan to explain the ideals of his newly founded Visva-Bharati international university, his lecture was received in stony silence, for he had failed to make any mention of the nationalist movement. And in August 1924, only a few weeks after his return from China, when Tagore was asked to preside at a meeting at Calcutta University, "there was such a riot of noise, uproar and confusion from the very beginning that the poet was unable to proceed and had to leave in company with Mr. B. C. Pal" (who also had opposed the Noncooperation movement).[81]

Shortly after his meeting with Gandhi in Calcutta, Tagore withdrew to Santiniketan to inaugurate his Visva-Bharati university in December 1921. Toward the end of its statement of aims, as if commenting on Gandhi's Noncooperation movement, he called for "a true co-operation of East and West, the great achievements of these being mutually complementary and alike necessary for Universal Culture in its completeness." Gandhi held fast to his principles, though he too came into conflict with the bulk of India's nationalists when in February 1922 he suspended his great movement after some of his rural followers in the United Provinces had burned to death twenty-two policemen, thus violating his code of strict nonviolence. "The sudden suspension of our movement," wrote young Jawaharlal Nehru, "was resented . . . by almost all the prominent Congress leaders. . . . Our mounting hopes tumbled to the ground." [82]

Gandhi's patriotism was once again emblazoned on the public mind when in March 1922 he was arrested, tried, and sentenced for encouraging contempt and hatred toward the Government of India. Released in 1924, he abstained from active politics until the expiration of his six-year term in 1928 but kept up a running commentary on Indian affairs in the columns of *Young India*. When, for example, C. F. Andrews sent him a glowing report of Tagore's 1924 tour of China and Japan, Gandhi reprinted it with an approving comment on "the Poet's humanitarian and peacegiving mission." In 1927 he dismissed the idea of a cultural and business union between India and other Asian countries by observing: "I venture to suggest that the cultural union is being sufficiently attended to by our great Poet and the business union by the great commercial firms." [83]

While Gandhi was remarking on Tagore's activities, the poet was commenting on the Mahatma's. He was so unfamiliar with the Jain premises on which Gandhi was reforming Hindu society, however, that in 1928 he ascribed Gandhi's asceticism to an improbably remote source: monastic Christianity as practiced in medieval Europe. Tagore implied this immediately after his impressive interview with Aurobindo at his Pondicherry retreat. Aurobindo, he wrote, was the true descendant of the Hindu sages to whom the eternal Word was revealed in the form of the Vedas:

> His face was radiant with an inner light and his serene presence made it evident to me that his soul was not crippled and cramped to the measure of some tyrannical doctrine, which takes delight in inflicting wounds upon life. He, I am sure, never had his lessons from the Christian monks of the ascetic Europe, revelling in the pride of that self-immolation which is a twin-sister of self-aggrandisement joined back to back facing opposite directions.
>
> I felt that the utterance of the ancient Hindu Rishi spoke from him of that equanimity which gives the human soul its freedom of entrance into the All. [84]

This passage reveals once more the mental distance between the modern Bengali and modern Kathiawadi reinterpretations of Hinduism, and of India herself: the Bengali vision dominated by the joyful equanimity of the Upanishads; the Kathiawadi image infused with the unconquerable will-power of Jain monasticism.

Tagore and Gandhi remained personal friends. They visited each other four times between 1925 and 1940, but the intellectual gulf between them was never bridged. In a generous appreciation written in 1938, Tagore said that he had learned to understand Gandhi as he would understand an artist, "not by the theories and fantasies of the creed he may profess, but by that expression in his practice which gives evidence to the uniqueness of his mind." Gandhi, "though an incorrigible idealist and given to referring all conduct to certain pet formulae of his own . . . is essentially a lover of men and not of mere ideas." Gandhi likewise dismissed their intellectual differences as meaningless by saying in 1945, during his last visit to Tagore's school: "I started with a disposition to detect a conflict between Gurudev and myself, but ended with the glorious discovery that there was none." These statements indicate the great good feeling that existed between the two men, but show also that neither had resolved the very real divergence between their ideas and methods revealed during their 1921 dispute.[85]

On one thing, however, the two leaders were agreed. As Tagore said many times and as Gandhi declared in 1921, India had "a message of peace and good-will to a groaning world." Gandhi reiterated this belief in the strongest terms in the last year of his life, while addressing the Inter-Asian Relations Conference convened in 1947 at Delhi by his disciple, Jawaharlal Nehru. In every vital point Gandhi's statement to the delegates from Asian countries echoed Tagore's message of Eastern spiritual revival, but reinforced it with the Mahatma's own zeal for nonviolent victory achieved through "soul-force":

> The message of the East, the message of Asia, is not to be learnt through European spectacles, not by imitating the vices of the West, its gunpowder and atom bomb. If you want to give a message of importance to the West it must be a message of love, it must be a message of truth. Asia has to conquer the West. You and I are the inheritors of a message of love. You can re-deliver that message now in this age of democracy, in the age of an awakening of the poorest of the poor. Then you will complete the conquest of the whole of the West. . . . The West is today pining for wisdom. It is despairing of [the] multiplication of atom bombs because such multiplication must destroy not merely all the West but the whole world. . . . It is up to you to deliver the whole world

and not merely Asia from wickedness and sin. That is the precious heritage which your teachers and my teachers have left for us.[86]

For Gandhi, no less than for Tagore, India was the heart of Asia. "If India falls, Asia dies," he declared at his daily prayer meeting four months before his assassination. India, he continued, "has aptly been called the nursery of many blended cultures and civilizations. Let India be and remain the hope of all the exploited races of the earth, whether in Asia, Africa or in any part of the world." [87]

Belief in the superiority of India's religious heritage, so prevalent among Hindu intellectuals of the time, could obviously take quite different forms in the minds of different thinkers in different parts of India. Within Gandhi's own province of Bombay, his nonviolent inter-pretation of Hinduism was vigorously repudiated by the passionate nationalist from the Marathi-speaking region of Maharashtra, Veer Damodar Savarkar. Savarkar was the leading spokesman (and president from 1938 to 1945) of the All-India Hindu Mahasabha, "the great association of Hindus," a militant political party, one of whose former members assassinated Gandhi in 1948.

The tension between Savarkar and Gandhi can be traced historically to the earlier tension between their respective heroes (both Maha-rashtrian Brahmans), the extremist Tilak and the moderate Gokhale.[88] Ideologically, the Gujarati and the Maharashtrian differed on two points: the use or nonuse of violent methods to achieve India's freedom; and the inclusion or noninclusion of India's Muslims in India's nationalist struggle. These differences, too, had roots in the pasts of their respective regions.

Maharashtra, "the great realm," was the homeland of the Maratha Empire, whose Hindu leaders successfully rebelled against the authority of the Mughal Empire in the seventeenth century, and nearly replaced it as the dominant power on the subcontinent in the eighteenth. The fighting spirit of the Marathas smoldered after the final defeat of their confederacy by the British in 1818, but it flared up again toward the close of the century. Maratha militancy showed itself especially in the nationalism of B. G. Tilak, who in 1907, with the assistance of Aurobindo and his Bengali followers, forced a split within the Congress between their new extremist wing and the older moderate wing. Tilak was jailed for seditious activity from 1908 to 1914, and became more moderate in his last years (he died in 1920); but the young revolutionary Savarkar, during and after his fourteen years in prison (1910–1924), formulated an explicitly Hindu religious nationalism on the basis of the Maratha tradition.

Savarkar's ideal was to unite all who felt India to be the homeland of their religion, be they Shaivas, Vaishnavas, Jains, Sikhs, or Buddhists. All these, he argued, should be called Hindus, since Hindu and India both derived from the same Sanskrit word *sindhu* (the land of) "the river." This inclusive definition would put an end to sectarian quarreling and make India a mighty nation:

> China alone of the present comity of nations is almost as richly gifted with the geographical, racial, cultural and numerical essentials as the Hindus are. Only in the possession of a common, a sacred and a perfect language, the Sanskrit, and a sanctified Motherland, we are so far [as] the essentials that contribute to national solidarity are concerned more fortunate.[89]

This image of India firmly excluded the Muslims, whose religion could never allow them to regard the subcontinent as their "holy land." It likewise excluded the rest of Asia and any attempt like Tagore's or Gandhi's to cover the whole continent with Hinduism's spiritual mantle. In Savarkar's view, such pan-Asian movements would distract Hindus from their main task of consolidating a strong national state in India. This task accomplished, their 300,000,000 people, "with India for their basis of operation, for their Fatherland, and for their Holyland, with such a history behind them, bound together by ties of a common blood and common culture, can dictate their terms to the whole world. A day will come when mankind will have to face the force." [90]

As it happened, neither Gandhi's nor Savarkar's religious ideal became the official policy of the Indian government established in 1947. That policy followed the secular principles on which the Indian National Congress had been based during its pre-Gandhian beginnings, from 1885 to 1920. Despite Gandhi's commanding position in the Congress, his "saintly style" in politics was always balanced, and eventually replaced, by the "modern style" followed by most of the Congress leaders,[91] who eschewed appeals to religious sentiment and yet emphasized the moral aspect of legal and political problems.

Foremost in the ranks of the secular Congressmen after C. R. Das's death were the North Indian leaders Motilal Nehru and his son Jawaharlal, irreverently called, together with Gandhi, "the Father, the Son, and the Holy Ghost" of Congress politics in the late 1920's. Jawaharlal Nehru's views of India, Asia, and Tagore's message are particularly interesting, not merely because he subsequently became independent India's first prime minister, but because his outlook dominated and molded the thought of so many others of his generation. As with Tagore, Gandhi, and other men of national stature, however, Nehru must be studied against the family and regional background from which he emerged.

HINDUSTAN: NEHRU

Hindustan — the Persian name for "the land of (the people of) the river," or "the land of the Hindus" has sometimes been used to denote the whole of India, at other times the whole of northern India. Its more limited meaning, traditionally used by inhabitants of Bengal, Bombay, and sometimes of the Punjab, refers to the vast and fertile plain bounded by the Himalayas on the north and watered by the upper Ganges and Jumna rivers.[92] Situated in the heartland of the subcontinent, Hindustan proper is dotted with cities and monuments cherished by both Hindus (such as the pilgrimage cities of Benares, Mathura, and Allahabad), and Muslims (such as the former Muslim capitals at Agra, Delhi, and Lucknow). By the time the British conquered most of it in the early nineteenth century, six centuries of Muslim rule over Hindustan had produced a blending of Hindu and Islamic cultures and a distinctive lingua franca, known as Hindustani, incorporating words drawn from both the Sanskrit and the Persian-Arabic vocabularies.

The history of the Nehru family illustrates the extent of this Hindu-Islamic synthesis in Hindustan, as well as its fragility under the impact of modern Western ideas and institutions. The Nehrus were Brahmans, originally from Kashmir, which since the Muslim conquest in the thirteenth century has been predominantly Muslim. In about 1716 a member of the family, famous for his Sanskrit and Persian learning, was invited to settle at Delhi by the Mughal Emperor Farukhsiyar. Despite the chaos into which Hindustan was plunged by the wars and invasions of the eighteenth century, the Nehrus kept up their tradition of learning, and when the new masters of the land arrived in the first decade of the nineteenth century they chose a Nehru, Jawaharlal's great-grandfather, to be their legal adviser at the court of their puppet, the powerless Emperor Shah Alam, now demoted to the rank of King of Delhi. Their knowledge of both Persian and English served the Nehrus well: the 1857 mutinies and civil uprising (which centered in Hindustan and hardly affected Bengal, Madras, or Bombay) wiped out their Delhi home, but they soon found legal work at Agra and other North Indian cities where their facility in English was a rare and valuable commodity.[93]

Jawaharlal's father Motilal was first taught Persian and Arabic, then studied in English at a British-run high school and at Muir College in Allahabad, the capital of the province at the time. Jawaharlal's education, however, both under British private tutors at home and during seven years in England from 1905 to 1912, was almost entirely in English, a fact characteristic of the new Hindu-British synthesis that emerged in late-nineteenth-century Hindustan to replace the earlier Hindu-Muslim one. Unlike the British-Hindu symbiosis already well-established in Bengal, the cultural synthesis represented by the Nehru family was entirely secular. So, naturally, was the form of nationalism which they embraced and propagated as leaders in the Indian National Congress, of which Motilal was elected president in 1919 and 1928, and Jawaharlal in 1929, 1936, and 1937. Both father and son accepted the program of nonviolent non-cooperation put forward by Gandhi in 1920, not because they agreed with its religious basis but because it offered a practical way to oppose and embarrass the government. Motilal's views were closest to those of C. R. Das, with whom he worked closely until Das's death in 1925. Jawaharlal felt on the one hand an emotional attachment to Gandhi, whom he called Bapu (father), and on the other, an intellectual tie with such leftist intellectuals as M. N. Roy, whom he met during his brief visit to Moscow in 1927 on the tenth anniversary of the Bolshevik Revolution. As time went on, he was increasingly attracted to Tagore as well, and particularly to his attempts to bring India into touch with all corners of the globe.[94]

Looking back on the entire sweep of Jawaharlal Nehru's remarkable career — first as general secretary of the Congress in the 1920's under his father's tutelage, then as Gandhi's understudy and heir apparent in the 1930's and early 1940's, and finally as prime minister of independent India from 1947 to 1964 — we see the centrality of international affairs in his thinking, often overshadowing his concern for the internal affairs of his country. He sought repeatedly to see India's problems in world terms —

reflecting perhaps the global preoccupations of the British upper class among whom he spent his formative years at Harrow, Trinity College, Cambridge, and the Inns of Court in London during seven years of heightening world tension just before World War I.

"Among the books that influenced me politically at Cambridge," Nehru noted in his *Autobiography*, "was Meredith Townsend's *Asia and Europe*." This collection of articles written in the last quarter of the nineteenth century abounded in such clichés as "the Asiatic mind" and in vast generalizations about "the East." Townsend was no more religious than Nehru; the Asiatic unity he posited was not of the cultural or spiritual type posited by Edwin Arnold, Keshub Chunder Sen, Okakura, or Tagore, but was essentially a bundle of political, racial, and creedal antipathies to the White European and to his own Christian civilization. Europe could never conquer or permanently rule Asia, Townsend argued, because of their "inherent differences." The resurgence of Asia, he predicted after the Japanese victories over the Czarist Empire, would be military and political, culminating in the expulsion of European rule from all parts of the continent. The young student from India must have relished one sentence in particular in Townsend's preface to the third edition of his influential book: "No one who has ever studied the question doubts that as there is a comity of Europe, so there is a comity of Asia, a disposition to believe that Asia belongs of right to the Asiatics, and that any event which brings that right nearer to realisation is to all Asiatics a pleasurable one." [95]

Nehru's lifelong pursuit of political ties with other Asian countries, and particularly with China, so closely parallels Tagore's pursuit of cultural contacts as to seem a secular and political extension of the Bengali poet's hope for the revival of Eastern civilization. Nehru first met with Chinese political leaders at the International Congress against Imperialism organized by Comintern leaders at Brussels in 1927. He was much feted as the head of the Indian delegation, and joined with the Chinese delegation in drafting and presenting a resolution recalling the ancient cultural ties between their two countries and urging a coordinated Sino-Indian struggle against British imperialism. [96]

Conversations with Tagore in the 1930's helped to deepen Nehru's attachment to the cause of Sino-Indian friendship. Nehru visited Santiniketan twice in the 1920's, and in 1934 decided to send his daughter

Indira there for her secondary school education, liking especially Tagore's freedom from the influence of orthodox British-directed education in India. When Tagore inaugurated his Hall of Chinese Studies (Cheena Bhavan) in 1937, Nehru promised to come but fell ill, and his daughter read out for him his message of warm support for the project.[97] Indira Nehru (now Indira Gandhi) did well under Tagore's guidance, went on to Oxford University, and eventually became India's first woman prime minister.

Nehru followed in the footsteps of Tagore — and M. N. Roy — by visiting China in the summer of 1939. Tagore had voyaged by sea, Roy by land, and Nehru flew. Like his predecessors, he went with a mission. The Indian National Congress had strongly supported the Government of China in its struggle to stave off Japan's attempted conquest. In 1938 it sent a medical unit to help the Chinese troops; Nehru's visit was a second demonstration of solidarity, and took place in response to the invitation of the Kuomintang government. Before leaving Calcutta for the flight to Chungking, China's wartime capital, Nehru called on Tagore, and the aged poet, now seventy-eight, gave the dashing Congress leader "his warm benedictions." [98]

Nehru's moods as he set out for China — his romantic nostalgia, his desire to elude the troubles of the present (his rival for Congress leadership, Bengal's militant Subhas Bose, had just been defeated in a tense showdown with Gandhi), and even his hesitation on the eve of his departure — call to mind the similar emotions which had stirred Tagore on the eve of his trip to China fifteen years earlier. "I chose to go," Nehru wrote after his two-week visit,

> because, while I hesitated, loving and comradely hands beckoned to me from China and distant memories of ages past urged me to go. The long perspective of history rose up before me, the agonies and triumphs of India and China, and the troubles of today "folded their tents like the Arabs and as silently stole away." The present will pass and merge into the future, and India will remain and China will remain, and the two will work together for their own good and the good of the world.[99]

When Tagore died in 1941 at the age of eighty, and Nehru wrote from his prison cell a tribute to his memory, once again the idea of China came to his mind:

I have met many big people in various parts of the world. But I have no doubt in my mind the two biggest . . . have been Gandhi and Tagore.

It amazes me that India in spite of her present condition (or is it because of it?) should produce these two mighty men in the course of one generation. And that also convinces me of the deep vitality of India and I am filled with hope, and the petty troubles and conflicts of the day seem very trivial and unimportant before this astonishing fact — the continuity of the idea that is India from long ages past to the present day. China affects me in the same way. India and China: how can they perish? [100]

As the prospect of India's independence grew closer, Nehru, already recognized as the Indian National Congress's spokesman on foreign affairs, articulated his plans for building a bloc of Asian nations. "We should like to be closely associated in a federation with our neighbors," he wrote in August 1940, " — China, Burma, Ceylon, Afghanistan, Persia. We are prepared to take risks and face dangers. We do not want the so-called protection of the British Army or Navy. We shall shift for ourselves." [101] In March 1947, with independence and partition only five months away, Nehru convened at Delhi the Asian Relations Conference. His inaugural address to the assembled delegates, written and read in an English more idiomatic than Tagore's, resounded with the idea of Asia's unity and greatness. "Asia, after a long period of quiescence, has suddenly become important again in world affairs," he began. Lauding "this dynamic Asia," "this mighty continent," Nehru noted India's special claim to link its varied cultures together:

Apart from the fact that India herself is emerging into freedom and independence, she is the natural centre and focal point of the many forces at work in Asia. Geography is a compelling factor, and geographically she is so situated as to be the meeting-point of Western and Northern and Eastern and South-East Asia. Because of this, the history of India is a long history of her relations with the other countries of Asia. Streams of culture have come into India from the West and the East and been absorbed in India. . . . At the same time, streams of culture have flowed from India to distant parts of Asia. If you would know India you have to go to Afghanistan and Western Asia, to Central Asia, to China and Japan and to the countries of South-East Asia. There you will find magnificent evidence of the vitality of India's culture which spread out and influenced vast numbers of people.[102]

We almost seem to hear Tagore himself in Nehru's concluding evocation of the ideal of resurgent and united Asia giving peace to a troubled world: "In this atomic age Asia will have to function effectively in the maintenance of peace. Indeed, there can be no peace unless Asia plays her part. . . . The whole spirit and outlook of Asia are peaceful, and the emergence of Asia in world affairs will be a powerful influence for world peace." [103]

This is not the place to recount the rise and fall of Nehru's hope for an India-centered comity of Asian nations. The key to its success would have to be the friendship and cooperation of India's two closest and most powerful neighbors, China and Pakistan. When Nehru died in May 1964, after seventeen years as prime minister and minister of external affairs, these two powers were joined in an entente against India, and Nehru's Asia policy lay in ruins.

Why independent India and Pakistan should have been on such bad terms since their creation in 1947 is a question inextricably connected with the whole tangled story of Hindu-Muslim politics in the decades before independence. Although this extraordinarily complex history can be analyzed from a number of viewpoints, the one most relevant here is the intellectual aspect, particularly the ideas about India, the East, and the West held by twentieth-century Hindu and Muslim intellectuals. Of these images in the minds of Hindu intellectuals of diverse regional backgrounds, and of diverse persuasions, both religious and secular, enough has now been said. The views of those Indian Muslim intellectuals who demanded, successfully, a partition of the subcontinent into Hindu and Muslim majority areas were most effectively expressed by their ideological hero, Sir Muhammad Iqbal of the Punjab.

PUNJAB: IQBAL

The historical, social, and educational situation of the Muslims of India was in many ways typified by their situation in the rich agricultural province in northwest India known as the Punjab ("five waters": the five rivers that flow across it before merging into the Indus). Historically, the Punjab was the second region of South Asia to come under Muslim rule (after Sind, at the mouth of the Indus, was conquered in the eighth century). From the eleventh century to the eighteenth, Muslims domi-

nated the political and cultural life of the province and came by con-
versions and natural increase to form half of its total population. The
Punjab suffered greatly from the civil wars and the Afghan and Persian
invasions which followed the collapse of the Mughal Empire, but by the
opening of the nineteenth century the rising Sikh power had restored
such unity to the province that in 1809 the British concluded with its
ruler a treaty of perpetual friendship. Forty years later, after two hard-
fought wars, the British took the Punjab from the Sikhs and set about
modernizing its administration and economy.

The Muslims, in the Punjab as elsewhere, benefited less by the spread
of the new economic and educational system that accompanied British
rule than did the more commercially minded Hindus and Sikhs. Whether
this was due to Qur'anic injunctions against usury, to resentment against
the British usurpers of their historic role as rulers of the country, to fear
that English education, especially in schools and colleges managed by
Christian missionaries, would diminish their sons' attachment to Islam,
or to other causes — are questions historians have yet to answer defini-
tively. The fact remains that in the Punjab as in Bengal the Muslim
community in the 1920's constituted the majority of the population but
were far behind the minority in the crucial realm of education. At a
time when the national average for literacy stood at 7.1 percent, only 2
percent of Punjab's 11,400,000 Muslims could read or write, as against
6.5 percent of its 6,600,000 Hindus and 5.9 percent of its 2,300,000
Sikhs.[104]

The Indian Muslims' "awakening," or "renaissance," when it finally
began in the last quarter of the nineteenth century, was motivated positively by the attractiveness of modern Western civilization and negatively
by awareness that the larger Hindu community, outnumbering the
Muslims three to one, had already moved well ahead of them in creating
the intellectual and economic sinews of what could become political
power when British rule eventually came to an end. The cradle of
Islamic modernism in India was Hindustan, where Muslim cultural
dominance lasted well into the nineteenth century. Some fifty years after
Rammohun Roy in Bengal began his reform of Hindu ethics and revitalization of Hindu religious thought, Sayyid Ahmad Khan in Hindustan launched a similar movement among India's Muslims. His chief
instrument was the Muhammadan Anglo-Oriental College, founded at
Aligarh with British encouragement in 1875, where both modern and

secular learning and Islamic studies were provided for. Within two decades the influence of the Aligarh movement began to affect the intellectual life of Punjab's educated Muslims, most significantly a young man named Muhammad Iqbal.

Iqbal, the foremost poet and philosopher of the Islamic revival in India, was like Jawaharlal Nehru a Kashmiri Brahman by descent. At about the same time the Nehrus left Kashmir for Delhi, Iqbal's paternal ancestors were converted to Islam by a Muslim saint and emigrated to Sialkot in the Punjab. Here Iqbal was born in 1876 of devoutly religious parents, and here he attended a Christian mission school and college, studying both English and Arabic. A wider world opened to him in 1895 when he went to Lahore to study, and later teach, Arabic and philosophy. His favorite professor at Government College was the English orientalist Thomas Arnold, who had previously taught for ten years at Aligarh and was an authority on Indian Islam. Arnold encouraged his brilliant pupil to pursue both his poetic and philosophical interests, and helped him to go to Cambridge for further study in philosophy.[105] Iqbal spent two years at Cambridge and several months in Germany, where he received a doctorate for his thesis on *The Development of Metaphysics in Persia*. The idealist psychology of his teachers James Ward and John McTaggart, and the writings of Hegel, Goethe, Nietzsche, Bergson, and Wordsworth stimulated Iqbal to reinterpret his Islamic heritage in a new spirit. (Nietzsche's attack on the Hellenized Christian tradition particularly appealed to him.) European post-Christian thought seems to have had a similar effect on Iqbal as on such modern Hindu thinkers as Radhakrishnan (also Christian-missionary educated); yet the direction in which he allowed this influence to move him was toward the roots of the Semitic rather than of the Aryan religious tradition. To recapture and revitalize the pristine spirit of Arabian Islam he rejected the Hellenic, Persian, and Indian elements superadded to it in medieval times as vigorously as Rammohun Roy had rejected medieval Hindu influences in his effort to return to the spirit of the Upanishads.

The Hindu thinker with whom Iqbal deserves the closest comparison is his equally great contemporary, Tagore. Both were poets of the first rank who also wrote and lectured on religious and political philosophy. Both were deeply concerned with identifying and revitalizing the essential core of the cultural heritages for which they acted as reinterpreters and spokesmen. Each believed in the possibility of a fruitful synthesis between Indian and modern European ideas, and each opposed both the xenophobic anti-Westernism and the superficial Westernization manifested by many of their countrymen and coreligionists. Tagore's poems were sung by all Bengali-speakers, whether Hindu or Muslim; Iqbal's verses were recited by Urdu- and Persian-speakers of both religions (Motilal Nehru loved to quote his incisive couplets). Today one is officially recognized as the national poet of Pakistan; the other has unofficially the equivalent status in India (and, to a degree, in East Pakistan). Parallels between their careers extended even to the recognition they earned abroad: Tagore was knighted in 1915, Iqbal in 1922. Iqbal wrote in Persian to reach a wider audience outside India; Tagore translated his poems into English for this same purpose.

Quite apart from these similarities in the form or structure of their careers, there is a close resemblance in the content of Tagore's and Iqbal's images of the West and its civilization. For Iqbal, as for Tagore, soulless materialism had corrupted Europe and rendered it unworthy:

> I tasted wine from the tavern of the West;
> Upon my life, I bought a headache.[106]

In an image remarkably similar to that in Tagore's 1900 "Sunset of the Century," Iqbal wrote of World War I: "That is not the rosy dawn of a new age on the horizon of the West, but a torrent of blood." [107] Like Tagore, he criticized the shortcomings of both West and East:

> Love is dead in the West, because thought has become irreligious.
> Reason is enslaved in the East due to incoherent ideas.[108]

Again like Tagore, Iqbal sought a synthesis of the best qualities of East and West:

> Westerners base their lives on practical intelligence,
> Easterners find the mystery of creation in love.
> But shrewdness needs love's power,
> And love needs shrewdness to give it firm foundations.
> When love and acumen work as one,
> They create the design for a new and better world.[109]

When Iqbal turned his gaze on India and Asia, however, he saw a picture quite different from Tagore's. For the Urdu and Persian poet of Lahore, the Muslim contribution to Indian and to Asian civilization loomed much larger than it did for the Bengali poet of Calcutta and Santiniketan. Before his sojourn in Europe, Iqbal had written poems exalting the comradeship of Hindus and Muslims in a united Indian nation, but after his return, and increasingly in the years after World War I when pan-Islamic sentiments captured the imagination of Indian Muslims, he wrote in this vein:

> Our essence is not bound to any place;
> The vigor of our wine is not contained
> In any bowl; Chinese and Indian
> Alike the shard that constitutes our jar,
> Turkish and Syrian alike the clay
> Forming our body; neither is our heart
> Of India, or Syria, or Rum [the Eastern Roman or Ottoman empires]
> Nor any fatherland do we profess
> Except Islam.[110]

One of his finest books of Persian verse, completed in 1922, bore the title *Payām-i mashriq* (The message of the East), but the message he propounded was that of a revitalized Islam giving its blessings to a tired West.

Iqbal's progression from the revitalization of his own heritage to a revitalized Asia was as natural as Tagore's; the results of these two extrapolations were of course radically different, because each derived from a different root. As early as 1909 Iqbal had declared: "The history of the Islamic people proves the secret truth — That thou [Muslim] art the guardian of the nations of Asia." [111] By 1930, speaking as president of the All-India Muslim League, he still urged his coreligionists to take the lead in solving Asia's problems, but told them they must first achieve:

> complete organization and unity of will and purpose in the Muslim community, both in your own interest as a community, and in the interest of India as a whole. The political bondage of India has been and is a source of infinite misery to the whole of Asia. It has suppressed the spirit of the East and wholly deprived her of that joy of self-expression which once made her the creator of a great and glorious culture. We have a duty towards India where we are destined to live and die. [And] we have a duty towards Asia, especially Muslim Asia.[112]

The unity of India's Muslims should produce a united nationalist movement, Iqbal argued, but if the Hindu majority would not concede certain safeguards to the Muslim minority, "our community may be called upon to adopt an independent line of action." This line of action, he suggested, would lead to "the formation of a consolidated North-West Indian Muslim State" in almost exactly the territory which seventeen years later became West Pakistan.[113] That the formation of a separate Muslim state would involve the bifurcation of the Punjab itself and the worst massacres in India's modern history did not enter into the poet-philosopher's vision of the future of his province.

Iqbal has exerted a remarkable influence on the thought of South Asia's Muslim intellectuals, not merely because of his occasional forays into the political sphere, and not alone because of his literary achievements, but because he performed to the satisfaction of many educated Muslims the task of reinterpreting and revitalizing their religious heritage in the light of modern Western thought — essentially the same task of cultural modernization which Tagore performed for Hindu religious philosophy and Gandhi for Hindu and Jain ethics. His contribution was all the more impressive for the disciplined and scholarly thought he brought to bear on religious problems, and it is significant that he was the only widely known thinker of modern South Asia to have undertaken graduate work in philosophy in Europe — not only in England but in Germany as well. In fact, India has produced no other thinker of comparable originality and influence who wrestled with eighteenth- and nineteenth-century German thought as Iqbal did. His closest counterpart elsewhere in Asia in this respect would be Nishida Kitarō, founder of the Kyoto school of Japanese philosophy. While Nishida concentrated on reinterpreting Buddhist ideas in the light of Western thought, Iqbal's attention was focused on Islam and on its confrontation with the modern West.

This preoccupation led Iqbal in the 1920's to write and deliver six lectures on *The Reconstruction of Religious Thought in Islam*. In this, his most complete and audacious statement of his religious philosophy, Iqbal confessed: "During the last five hundred years religious thought in Islam has been practically stationary. There was a time" — a phrase Tagore also liked to use, but with the time in mind when Buddhist India influenced East and Southeast Asia — "when European thought received inspiration from the world of Islam. The most remarkable phenomenon of modern history, however, is the enormous rapidity with which the world of Islam is spiritually moving towards the West. There is nothing wrong with this movement," Iqbal continued somewhat defensively, "for European culture, on its intellectual side, is only a further development of some of the most important phases of the culture of Islam." Again he recalls Tagore when he cautions: "Our only fear is that the dazzling exterior of European culture may arrest our movement and we may fail to reach the true inwardness of that culture." Not Westernization but modernization is our goal, he might have said with his Chinese contemporary Hu Shih; but he remained as unable as Hu was to deny the value of his classical heritage. Iqbal's paramount concern, it appears, was not to reach "the true inwardness" of Europe's culture, but, "to examine, in an independent spirit, what Europe has thought and how far the conclusions reached by her can help us in the revision and, if necessary, reconstruction of theological thought in Islam." [114]

It should not be surprising to learn that Iqbal made no published comment on Tagore's "message of the East" or on any of Tagore's ideas; for these two poet-philosophers, even though they seemed to see the same West, were inspired by radically different Easts — one Islamic, the other Hindu-Buddhist.[115] This divergence in outlook was accentuated by the physical distance between their two provinces, which had differed greatly in their political and cultural development. Bengal and the Punjab, lying a thousand miles apart at either end of the Indo-Gangetic plain, were respectively the first and the last major regions of the subcontinent to come under the sway of British power and modern Western civilization. Tagore first saw the Punjab when he was a boy of twelve, traveling with his father. In the 1880's, when he dreamed of hiking all the way from Calcutta to the Northwest Frontier, the Punjab was still a kind of frontier region, a land of opportunity for the Bengali professional men and civil servants whom Kipling was about to characterize in *Kim*. Not until 1935, after many travels within India and abroad, did Tagore return to the Punjab. In keeping with his ideal of harmonizing India's diverse regional and religious traditions, during his two-week visit to Lahore he called on Iqbal. The fact that it was the Bengali who came to see the Punjabi rather than the other way around (for Iqbal never visited Bengal) is symptomatic of their attitudes toward the unity of India's provinces.[116] On hearing of the Urdu poet's death in 1938, Tagore sent a generous message of appreciation: "The death of Sir Muhammad Iqbal creates a void in our literature that, like a mortal wound, will take a very long time to heal. India, whose place to-day in the world is too narrow, can ill afford to miss a poet whose poetry had such universal value." [117]

Iqbal's indifference to Tagore's message seems to have been typical of Muslim attitudes throughout India. The one Muslim writer in English who did comment on Tagore's concept of Eastern spiritual civilization did so skeptically, seeing it as a threat to the cause of Hindu-Muslim unity in India. Abdullah Yusuf Ali, educated at Bombay University, St. John's College, Cambridge, and Lincolns Inn, London, had retired in 1914 after nineteen years in the élite Indian Civil Service. He had written a number of books on Islamic and on medieval and modern Indian history by 1929, when he addressed the Royal Asiatic Society in London on "The Religion of Rabindranath Tagore." Very sympathetic to Tagore's religious outlook, Yusuf Ali nevertheless criticized the poet for encouraging that "class of mind, which dreams in ancient terms of the East, imagines that a spiritual outlook is the monopoly of a certain section of the East, and cannot conceive of spirituality as anything but foreign to the thought and mind of the 'materialistic West.'" Such an attitude, he warned, "is a barrier to a development of that universality which should bring the better minds of all nations together."

Turning to the national scene, Yusuf Ali pointed to the dangerous and widening rift between India's two largest religious communities, evidenced in the increasing number and intensity of Hindu-Muslim riots during the 1920's. Tagore's abstract religious ideas, he implied, were not helping to solve this critical problem:

> In India we have yet to work out a synthesis of the spiritual ideals of Muslims and Hindus, especially in their practical bearings on [the] everyday life of the people. That is our first need. Until we have created an understanding — a solid understanding that will endure and is based on the inner dictates of our own hearts — we cannot face the rest of the world without our claims being at once put out of court.[118]

These views were probably very close to those of the most respected secularist among the political leaders of India's Muslims, Muhammad Ali Jinnah. Like Yusuf Ali, Jinnah came from the Bombay Presidency, where Muslims were in the minority. Like Gandhi he came from a Kathiawadi family and studied law at the Inns of Court in London. Unlike Gandhi, Jinnah succeeded in the practice of law in Bombay City and kept his personal religious views to himself. And unlike either Gandhi, Tagore, or Iqbal, he had nothing to say about the spirituality of the East, however conceived. This did not mean he took no interest in India's relations with other parts of Asia, only that he saw these relations as problems of practical politics, not to be confused with sentimental or religious ties, whether to East, Southeast, or Southwest Asia.

INDIAN ATTITUDES TOWARD CHINA

India's two great internationalists of Hindu birth, Tagore and Nehru, looked to China in the 1920's and 1930's with genuine hope for closer ties, both cultural and political. Gandhi and Jinnah, on the other hand, being very practical politicians, paid almost no attention to China, and even when Chiang Kai-shek visited India in 1942, had conversations with him about India's political future, not China's. The internationalist Muslim Iqbal, however, took interest in the fact that China had a small Muslim population in its western provinces. On the rare occasions when he mentions China in his poetry, it is always this Muslim minority he has in mind:

We who know not the bonds of country
Resemble sight, which is one though it be the light of two eyes.
We belong to the Hijāz [Arabia] and China and Persia,
Yet we are the dew of one smiling dawn.
We are all under the spell of the eye of the cupbearer from Mecca.[119]

The historical relations between India and China thus appeared radically different to the Hindu poet Tagore and the Muslim poet Iqbal: the Muslim saw India and China linked by Islam, which bound them to a common center at Mecca, far to the west; the Hindu saw them linked by Buddhism, whose ancient homeland was India and whose heirs modern Hindus had begun to consider themselves.

For Indian intellectuals of whatever faith, however, China and Japan in the 1920's seemed as remote as the planet Mars today, and Tagore's voyages of discovery were hailed by many as great events inaugurating a new era of friendly relations. Some Muslims apart, Indians' images of China, as we have already seen evidenced in the comments of the Calcutta daily press, were very much the product of Tagore's own mind, his experiences, and his writings. He, after all, had been there, had gone as India's representative, had delivered India's message, and had come back with a rather optimistic report of his reception. Speaking to reporters on his return from China, Tagore had said: "Both the Chinese and the Japanese acknowledge that my visit was made at a very opportune time. . . . They were both very responsive." [120]

From this and other reports from members of the poet's party of their friendly reception in China the image of a great and spiritual nation to the northeast, almost another India, diffused itself throughout the Indian intelligentsia. In the southern city of Bangalore, the *Treasure Chest,* an English-language monthly for young people, commented enthusiastically:

> Tagore journeyed on a unique ministry of friendship to China. As his audiences in one city after another listened to him, they forgot that he was an Indian and they were Chinese. They remembered only that they had the same moral idealisms, the same spiritual hungers. And they felt an instinctive response to his challenge to keep, at all costs, their ancient spiritual culture.[121]

In western India the most popular and influential nationalist daily, the *Bombay Chronicle,* exuded an equal confidence in China's "spirituality," and in Japan's as well:

> The shock of post-war disillusionment has reacted with as much force on the heart of the Chinese and Japanese nations as it has on the heart of the Indian nation — and with almost exactly the same result, namely, the resurgence of the hidden bed of spiritual consciousness on which the life of each of these nations had been flowing all these centuries. Dr. Tagore has found in China and Japan the same response to the call of the Spirit that India has been giving since her new spiritual birth.[122]

Significantly, the editor of the *Bombay Chronicle* at this time was both an Englishman and a convert to Islam, Marmaduke Pickthall. We have seen how European intellectuals looked to India, Japan, and China for the spiritual satisfactions they could no longer find in their Greco-Roman and Judeo-Christian heritages, and encouraged Asian intellectuals to preserve and to make known to the Western world the cultural and religious achievements of their ancestors. Marmaduke Pickthall in Bombay, like Annie Besant, George Arundale, and James and Margaret Cousins (the Theosophical Society leaders) in Madras, Mme. Paul Richard ("The

Mother" of Aurobindo's religious community) in Pondicherry, and ex-judge John Woodroffe (an exponent of Shakta Hinduism) in Calcutta, carried on this tradition in the 1920's, making common cause with India's intellectuals in defending and propagating Indian ideas and ideals.[123] The Englishman closest to Tagore after Pearson's death in 1923 and Elmhirst's return to England in 1924 was C. F. Andrews. His account of the poet's China tour (which made it seem as if he had been there), like Pickthall's, put it in the best possible light:

> In China his visit was at first misinterpreted by one important section of the students. . . . Many of them had thrown aside all belief in God, as antiquated and out of fashion. They believed in armed force, as the only successful weapon in the modern world. . . . It was of deep interest to me personally to watch how the old sage, with his earnest face and gentle, fearless demeanour, won them over. . . . The fact that these young intellectuals have asked Mahatma Gandhi to come over, in succession to Tagore, shows that the poet's message has truly carried weight. For everyone in the East knows perfectly that on this central issue Tagore and Gandhi speak with the same voice, out of the heart of India.[124]

If India's intellectuals entertained a somewhat unrealistic picture of what was happening in the minds of their Chinese counterparts this was not only because of their nostalgia for the ancient period when Buddhist culture had linked their two countries, nor to the optimistic report Tagore gave them on his return, nor to the enthusiasm of Western converts for Indian spirituality. More fundamentally it was simply ignorance — of Chinese history, of current developments in China, but especially of the Chinese language — that permitted the romanticized view of India's great neighbor to be so widely held in this period. Ignorance and wishful thinking often go hand in hand. Gandhi, for example, in 1928 quoted with approval a reported interview in which Ku Hung-ming denounced machine-made cloth, as Gandhi did, because it created unemployment. Gandhi identified Ku as "one of the most prominent Chinese," when in fact Ku was regarded in China at the time as an eccentric old man with reactionary ideas.[125] In Tagore's case, his ignorance of the Chinese language led him to draw a false conclusion from the friendly way he had been received by English-speaking intellectuals in China, such as Hu Shih. Their personal warmth and courtesy did not at all mean that they agreed with his ideal of Eastern spiritual civilization.

At the deepest level of thought, even at a subconscious level for Tagore, sympathy with and an idealization of China and Japan welled up from the recurrent feelings of frustration and humiliation engendered in educated Indians by the continuing presence and power of their British rulers. Hence the fact that the presidents of the Indian National Congress in 1922, 1923, 1926, and 1927 called for the formation of a pan-Asian federation or league, and the fact that in 1928 the Congress voted to hold the first meeting of such a federation in India in 1930.[126] (The meeting was not actually held until 1947, on the eve of independence.) Such proposals were exercises in futility as long as the British controlled the Government of India and could refuse to grant exit or entry to whomsoever they chose. In the absence of direct political contacts with China or Japan, Tagore's lecture tours there provided a kind of substitute link on the symbolic level. By the same token, however, his rhetorical appeals to the cultural and spiritual unity of the East led many Indians — even the secularists — to idealize China, somewhat as European intellectuals had done a century and a half earlier. For Nehru, as for Voltaire, China's distance lent enchantment.

SUMMING UP

What educated Indians were thinking about the civilizations of "the East" and "the West" between the two world wars is harder to glean from their writings than are the equivalent thoughts of their Japanese and Chinese contemporaries. If only an Okakura or a Hsü Chih-mo had won the Nobel Prize and come to India to lecture at leading universities on the need to revive Asia's cultural unity, a number of Indian intellectuals might have reacted to this idea at the same time, providing future historians with the kind of published cross section of opinion that Tagore's lectures evoked in East Asia. The very fact that it was an Indian who won the prize in the West and did the lecturing in other parts of Asia tells much about the Indian intellectual scene. Because he was an Indian, by far the most respected literary figure in his country, and because he lived and worked in India for eighty years, what Tagore did and said carried infinitely greater weight there than in any foreign country he might visit for a few weeks or months.

Tagore's theory of Eastern spiritual civilization, too, held a natural, gravitational attraction for his educated countrymen because it had been born in India a century earlier out of the symbiotic relationship of Hindus and Europeans and was already widespread before he became its most eloquent exponent and overseas missionary. His masterful use of the English language, both abroad and within India, reflected and stimulated the continuing development of what by now had become a genuine synthesis of cultures. Indo-British civilization had created large, relatively modern port cities at Calcutta, Madras, Bombay, and Karachi, and had raised up there and in the interior several generations of English-speaking and Western-educated intellectuals and semi-intellectuals. It was this new class (new in some ways but drawn mainly from the high, traditionally literate, strata of the old society) that most admired Tagore and delighted in reading the English versions of his poems and essays. To members of this class, already partly deracinated by English-style education and urban surroundings, Tagore gave pride in a heritage they could call their own without disowning the modern Western culture they had absorbed so deeply. Consequently, both "Eastern spirituality" and "Western materialism" were theirs to enjoy, and the more they took of the latter, the more appreciative they tended to become of the generalized and undogmatic spirituality offered by their national poet.

Men and women of Bengal felt doubly proud of Tagore, for they knew the real poet, Rabindranath, who sang to them in their own mother tongue. Much as they might criticize his highly independent social or political views when he was in their midst, when he went abroad as India's cultural ambassador to the world they could not but take vicarious pleasure in his travels, his honors, and in the ideas he expressed on their behalf. Other Indians might look up to him as an ideal Indian, but Bengalis could love him as an incarnation of their province's creative and artistic genius. And, as a people inhabiting the easternmost major province in India, with a considerable Mongoloid strain in their genetic inheritance, Bengalis were closest to the Chinese and Japanese both geographically and racially. This gave them all the more reason to be grateful to Tagore for his efforts to link them with the easternmost lands of Asia.

Though it appears that the bulk of the Indian intelligentsia supported him (and ten out of the fifteen men quoted in this chapter approved of his Indo-Asian theory in one way or another), Tagore's advocates seem to have been more numerous in Bengal and in South India than elsewhere.[127] It is probably not coincidental that all three of the South

Indians who wrote so enthusiastically about his ideas were Brahmans. Madras Brahmans may have had special reasons for concurring so readily with the Bengali poet's belief in India's spiritual mission. His distrust of anti-British politics harmonized well with their attachment to the British-run administration in which they occupied the majority of the better-paid jobs. His articulation of Indian ideals as the basis for Asia's unity and the world's sanity seemed to accord well with their faith in a revitalized Hindu orthodoxy. And possibly the growing challenge to their social and political superiority from the rising non-Brahman castes predisposed some of them to respond favorably to Tagore in his role as champion of essentially Brahmanical religious ideas. Underlying all these attitudes was a conservative reluctance to abandon the Indo-British symbiosis that had operated successfully in the Madras Presidency since the 1750's — a symbiosis typified by Annie Besant's residence at Madras as world president of the Theosophical Society, and her election in 1917 as annual president of the Indian National Congress.

In Bengal, Madras, Bombay, the United Provinces, and the Punjab — in all five major provinces — by the middle 1920's this modern tradition of Indo-Western synthesis was in retreat before the advance of a new wave of influences coming from Great Britain: the ideas and institutions of modern nationalism. In each province, foreign nationalist ideas and institutions were selectively received and combined with indigenous traditions, producing distinctive regional nationalisms in each case. Different varieties of Hinduism, when impregnated with the nationalist seed, gave birth to a kind of Vaishnava-based nationalism in C. R. Das of Bengal, a Shaiva-based nationalism in Sumbramania Bharati of the Tamil country, and a Jain-based nationalism in Gujarat's Gandhi. Religion as the matrix for the shaping of nationalism in India also produced the diametrically opposed forms of pan-Hindu nationalism of Savarkar in Maharashtra and pan-Islamic nationalism of Iqbal in the Punjab. As the years passed, all these competing religious nationalisms combined or clashed, with Gandhi's eclipsing both Das's and Savarkar's in the 1920's and blending with the nonreligious nationalism of the Nehrus traditional to the Congress. The Congress coalition soon collided with the nationalism of the Muslim League, where a similar blending of Iqbal's religious and Jinnah's nonreligious Muslim nationalism took place in the 1930's. The net result was the withdrawal of British rule in 1947 and the break-up of British India into two nation-states, India and Pakistan.

Tagore's vision of a grand collaboration between the spiritual culture of the East and the material civilization of the West was pushed offstage by all these marchings and countermarchings, but Gandhi continued to lend it his blessings and Nehru tried to give it a secular political form after he became independent India's first prime minister. These leaders, and others such as C. R. Das and his successor in Bengal politics, Subhas Chandra Bose, regretted Tagore's aloofness from the nationalist movement in the 1920's (in the 1930's he was to lend it greater support). But the fact remained that there was no real incompatibility between Tagore's ideal of pan-Asian spiritual revival and the goals of the nationalists, for their political movement stood only to gain by an anti-Western cultural revival in all of Asia, especially if it would bring independent countries like Japan and China into some kind of alliance with India.

Politics aside, an over-all conspectus of the Indian intellectual landscape in the 1920's shows Tagore, Roy, and Gandhi representing three distinct schools of thought among those of Hindu descent who had been most affected by contact with modern Western ideas, with Nehru occupying an intermediate position within the triangle formed by these three. Tagore stood for the nineteenth-century Hindu-British symbiosis which originated in Bengal and either spread or else grew up independently in different regions as the result of similar conditions. This school accepted British political and commercial domination as beneficial to India, but asserted the superior value of Upanishadic Hindu thought, to which Europeans themselves were paying homage. Out of this symbiosis, which appealed most naturally to Brahmans, with their traditional assumption of religious superiority over the warrior-administrator Kshatriya and the commercial Vaishya caste groupings, there emerged the theory of Eastern spiritual civilization complementing Western materialistic civilization. Not surprisingly, the most active proponent of this theory after Tagore himself was the Telugu Brahman, Sarvepalli Radhakrishnan.

Gandhi represented and brought to its highest point a very different school of thought whose roots lay in the non-Brahman traditions of the region of India least affected by British political and commercial domination: the princely states of Rajputana and Kathiawad where Kshatriya values held sway in the political sphere and Jain-Vaishnava values in the religious sphere. Gandhi's political strivings conflicted with British power, both in South Africa and in India, and combined with his religious aspirations to produce the wholesale rejection of modern Western civilization which Tagore so deplored. In place of Tagore's ideal of a complementary balance between East and West, Gandhi proposed to expel the modern West and its civilization from India, and even to conquer it in its homeland by the worldwide triumph of Eastern spirituality.

The third school, that of M. N. Roy, might be said to represent the advance in the twentieth century of a newer wave of modern Western influence on India, that of the antireligious and staunchly materialist tradition of continental European Communism. His school of thought rejected the spiritual bases of both Tagore's and Gandhi's theories of Eastern civilization, and sought to achieve the triumph of that modern Western materialism which both Gandhi and Tagore so greatly feared.

Nehru represents to an amazing degree the fusion of elements from these three modern schools of thought. He has accurately described himself as "a queer mixture of East and West," [128] and this mixture was enhanced by the confluence of three streams of thought and culture in his family and in his native Hindustan: Brahman Hindu, Mughal Muslim, and modern British. Like his contemporary Roy, however, Nehru sloughed off the religious outlook on life that was so important to his elders, Gandhi and Tagore, and looked to the Soviet Union as a model for India's secular and material progress. Yet he shared Gandhi's passion for freedom and concern for the poor and Tagore's internationalism and desire to preserve and combine the best in both Indian and Western traditions.[129] The fact that he occupied a central ground amid the Tagore, Gandhi, and Roy schools of thought (as the United Provinces occupy the heartland midway between Bengal on the east, Bombay on the southwest, and the Punjab on the northwest sides of the subcontinent) greatly aided Nehru's rise to dominance over Indian politics by the middle decades of the twentieth century.

A fourth school of thought, represented by Iqbal, drew on the religious, cultural, and political traditions of Islam, and remained apart from, and latently hostile to, all three of these non-Muslim schools. The resurgence of Islam in modern India, so similar in form but so different in content from the resurgence of Hinduism which had preceded it by several decades, found in Iqbal a leader fully abreast of twentieth-century European (especially German) thought and able to reinterpret Islamic ideas in terms of the most modern philosophical idealism. Like Tagore, Iqbal wished to supply the world and the West with the spiritual vitality it seemed to lack, but the ancient tradition he wished to revitalize for this purpose was originally an Arabian rather than an Indian one, and the East of his historical imagination was the Muslim world rather than the Hindu-Buddhist world of Tagore.

Even this selective survey of images of East and West in the minds of Indian intellectuals at about the time of Tagore's East Asian missions reveals a range of viewpoints fully as diverse as those displayed by Japanese or Chinese intellectuals in this same period. Nevertheless, it is clear that Tagore's theory of East and West, which his own travels helped greatly to popularize, was most widely accepted among English-speaking Hindus, especially those in the coastal provinces where the Hindu-British symbiosis had long been operative. In these same provinces, and in the north Indian heartland of Hindustan, more politically minded intellectuals like Das, Gandhi, and Nehru wished to use Tagore's theory for nationalist purposes, but only the materialists Roy and Prakasam explicitly rejected it and its underlying foundation, "Indian spirituality." From the standpoint of a believing Punjab Muslim, however, whose exposure to modern European idealism had helped him to repudiate the Muslim-Hindu synthesis of Mughal times, the three main schools of thought that Hindus had taken up after themselves abandoning that medieval synthesis seemed alike inimitable to the resurgence of a revitalized Islam.[130]

EPILOGUE

Science progresses, not by constructing systems, but by finding fundamental explanations for particular events. The correct explanation of the minutest fact has limitless repercussions and it is possible, as the Hindu saying has it, "to show the infinite in a pea-hen's feather."

— Sylvain Lévi

TAKEN AS A WHOLE, THE VIEWS EXPRESSED by India's leading intellectuals in the 1920's show a much stronger belief in "the East" than was evident among Japan's intellectuals in 1916 or China's in 1924. Perhaps their pride in being Eastern was necessary to compensate India's most educated men for the humiliation they felt living as subjects of a Western power, Great Britain. A general pattern might be posited for intellectuals in all Asian societies: the greater the threat from the West to their sense of cultural and political integrity, the greater their psychological need to hold on to an idealized conception of the East as a counterweight to Western power and influence.

Nineteenth-century Russia provides some interesting parallels enabling us to broaden this hypothesis to embrace Eastern Europe as well. A century before the Bengali poet Tagore took his message to Japan and China, the Moscow philosopher Peter Chaadaev deplored the new school of Orientophiles in Russia who were saying: "Is the West, then, the homeland of knowledge and of all profound truths? That homeland, as everyone knows, is the Orient. . . . The old Orient is now in decline: well, are not we its natural heirs?"[1] Dostoevsky and Tolstoy also had moments of romanticizing Russia's "easternness," and even the most ardent of the Westerners in the nineteenth-century Slavophile-Westerner controversy, Alexander Herzen (died 1873) turned away from the West even while living in it as an exile and looked "with faith and hope to our native East, inwardly rejoicing that I am a Russian."[2]

Although contact with the West often generated defensive reactions of this kind, it could also lead to admiration and assimilation of Western ways, even among those who vehemently rejected Western political or cultural domination. Many Asian scholars, writers, politicians, and religious leaders recognized the advantages which might accrue to their societies by judiciously importing ideas and methods from the Western countries. The pragmatist philosopher Tanaka Ōdō and the exponent of representative government Yoshino Sakuzō come first to mind among Japan's men of a Westernizing persuasion. Tanaka's Chinese counterpart, Hu Shih, and Hu's friend, Communist Party Secretary Ch'en Tu-hsiu, were outstanding among young China's Westernizers, as were M. N. Roy and Jawaharlal Nehru in India.

A goodly number of Asian thinkers, however, took as their primary task the revitalization of ancient or medieval ideals which had somehow lost their earlier hold on the minds of their educated contemporaries. As Iqbal sought to infuse new life into Islam, so in their various ways Gandhi, Tagore, Aurobindo, and Radhakrishnan strove to revitalize Hinduism; Ku Hung-ming, Liang Sou-ming, and Chang Chün-mai worked to strengthen Confucian traditions; T'ai Hsü and Liang Ch'i-ch'ao, Buddhist traditions; Okakura and Noguchi, Japan's artistic heritage; and so on. All of these leaders were deeply concerned that the cultural achievements of their ancestors be not only preserved but propagated on a pan-Asian or even global scale.

This process of revitalizing earlier cultural traditions has been a central feature in the most creative periods of every human society, most notably in the period of European history now termed the Renaissance because of the rebirth then of ancient Greek and Roman traditions. At times intellectuals in China and India have seized upon this parallel between their revitalizing work and the earlier European experience by describing their endeavors under such rubrics as "the Chinese Renaissance," "the Hindu Renaissance," or even in regional terms as in the case of "the Bengal Renaissance." [3]

Analogies with the Europe of the fourteenth to sixteenth centuries are valid up to a certain point, but the motivations and tasks of Asia's twentieth-century "Renaissance men" were more complex and urgent than those of their European predecessors. Instead of enjoying a long period of gradual change in their ideas, the fruit of leisurely reading in books from a dead civilization, Asian intellectuals were confronted with an array of pressures and stimuli emanating from a living and powerful foreign civilization. Western military, political, and economic pressures were most intense in central, south, and southeast Asia, where Russia, Great Britain, France, the Netherlands, Portugal, Spain, and the United States established colonial governments. Even those societies which succeeded in maintaining their political independence — China, Japan, Thailand, and the Muslim countries of southwest Asia — faced serious threats to the integrity and continuity of their cultural traditions from the vitality and prestige of Western science, technology, and culture. The intensity of exogenous pressures, the pace of intellectual change, and the unprecedented variety of foreign stimuli to which they were exposed made the situation of Asia's intellectuals in the twentieth century considerably more trying than that of Europe's sixteenth-century thinkers.

The first men in each Asian society to try to cope with this emergency situation by studying seriously the civilization of the intruding Euramericans — men such as Rammohun Roy (1772?–1833) for Hindu India, King Mongkut (1804–1868) for Buddhist Siam, Sayyid Ahmad Khan (1817–1896) for Muslim India, Fukuzawa Yukichi (1835–1901) for Japan, and Yen Fu (1853–1921) for China — were relieved to discover that this "Western" civilization was not a monolithic whole, but a collection of many separable strands. All these thinkers, for example, and most of their successors, rejected Christian ideas about the nature of God, but many of them admired the moral teachings of Jesus. Another great tradition developed in the West, the humanistic scholarship of Orientalists at European and American universities, had a very strong appeal for Asian scholars and was of great use to those concerned with revitalizing the cultural traditions of their ancestors.

On a more personal level, Asian intellectuals were much encouraged by the Orientophilia of Western intellectuals who had become disillusioned with their own Judeo-Christian or Greco-Roman cultural heritages. Such Western allies as Colebrooke, Müller, Fenollosa, Nivedita, Besant, the Richards, Rolland, Keyserling, and Andrews (to mention only the most notable) contributed not a little to the élan of the Asian revitalists' activities. Gandhi, for instance, appended to his 1909 manifesto against modern Western civilization as supporting evidence eight "Testimonies by Eminent Men," four of them British, two German, and two French, and twenty books by "Some Authorities," six of which were by Tolstoy, two by Ruskin, two by Thoreau, and only one by a fellow-Indian.[4]

Quite often the most ardent revitalists were those who had spent the greatest number of years abroad and felt the greatest need to resolve the tensions and contradictions between the two cultures whose ideas they had absorbed. Gandhi had lived for three years in England and nearly twenty in South Africa; Aurobindo thirteen years in England; Ku Hung-ming thirteen years in Scotland and elsewhere in Europe; Chang Chün-mai about ten years in Japan, Germany, and England; Noguchi a dozen years in the United States and England. Similarly, many of the Westerners who encouraged them spent the better part of their lives in India or Japan or China, and even those who never saw Asia were usually men and women at odds with their own culture and in search of more exotic traditions as alternatives or supplements to their own. Working together, in Tokyo, in Boston, in Peking, or Paris, but most often in Calcutta and London, these Orientophiles formed an international community, a largely English-speaking confederation of rebels against the Westernization of the globe.

In their growing enthusiasm for the resurgence of Indian, Japanese, or Chinese cultural traditions, many members of this international fraternity were seized with the conviction that there existed a single entity they called Oriental, Eastern, or Asian civilization. Each Asian Orientophile, however, entertained a somewhat different notion of the essential features of this civilization, his image of the East consisting usually of an expanded version of those particular traditions he most wished to revitalize. Thus Okakura's "ideals of the East" were mainly those he derived from his study of Japan's artistic heritage (with its Chinese and Indian roots); T'ai Hsü's Eastern civilization was one school of Mahayana Buddhism writ large; Iqbal's was early Islamic civilization; Tagore's was based on his interpretation of the Upanishads — and so on.

All these conflicting theories seemed plausible as long as each Asian revitalist remained separate from the others and concentrated his attention on the contrast between his own version of Eastern (usually "spiritual") civilization and Western (usually "materialistic") civilization. But as scattered intellectuals grew increasingly vocal in proclaiming the universal validity of their reinterpreted cultural heritages, and as modern transportation and communication enabled them to enter into personal contact with one another and with their Western Orientalist and Orientophile allies, their mutually contradictory images of Eastern civilization began to collide. This unpleasant truth was first made apparent to Tagore as he attempted to rally to the support of his own particular message first Japan's intellectuals in 1916, then China's intellectuals in 1924. Despite these rebuffs, in the remaining years of his life he appealed twice more to Japan's revitalist intellectuals before finally recognizing the incompatibility of their views with his.

BRAHMAN AND SAMURAI — THE END OF AN ILLUSION

Tagore was in Peking when he received and accepted an invitation to revisit Japan; during his three weeks there in June 1924, he repeated in lectures at Osaka, Tokyo, and Kyoto the message he had first delivered in 1916. His visit happened to coincide with the tremendous wave of indignation which swept through Japan in reaction to the United States law banning any further Japanese immigration (already restricted by a "gentlemen's agreement").[5] Tagore joined in the protests, and told his audience at the University of Tokyo:

> Japan has now been severely insulted by another country. Not I alone, but all the people of India think that this is an insult to all Asian peoples. The materialistic civilization of the West, working hand in hand with its strong nationalism, has reached the height of unreasonableness. But the West will suffocate [from greed] after a short time, and will bow to the great and natural thought of the East.[6]

Two days later Tagore was the guest of honor at one of the strangest occasions in the history of Indo-Japanese relations — a banquet given by Tōyama Mitsuru and his associates, the leaders of the infamous Black Dragon, or Amur River, Society (Kokuryūkai), which had long used terrorism and assassinations to pressure cabinet ministers into expanding Japan's sphere of control on the Asian mainland. All was sweetness and light at the meeting, according to the innocent reporter who described the encounter of India's poet-sage with Japan's patron saint of political murder:

> These two venerable men stood still in silence for a moment. Then Mr. Tōyama bowed several times, after the Japanese manner of profound salutation, while the poet after the Hindu fashion held his hands joined together and kept his eyes closed all the while in prayer.
> It was the meeting of the Grand Old Man of Japan with one from India and solemn silence fell on the assembled multitude, as though

they had been present at an act of worship. The two countries of the East seemed to be cemented together in the bond of love by that ceremony.[7]

In thanking his hosts for their welcome, Tagore reminded them that on his previous visit, eight years ago, "I was very anxious for your future, I was nervous at the wholesale external imitation and at the lack of spirituality. To-day, there is an enormous difference. You have progressed in the way of the spirit considerably since I last was here, and this gives me exceedingly great joy." [8] Tagore was not necessarily thinking of the anti-American agitation at this point, although he did refer to it during this visit. His impression of Japan's greater spirituality was probably based not on this agitation, but on the deeper change in Tokyo's mood following the great earthquake and fire of September 1923 in which more than 130,000 people perished. This natural calamity, and the murder by the police of nine socialist and anarchist intellectuals during the ensuing period of martial law, helped to produce a shift toward "indigenous ethics" and "a more traditional line of thought," [9] which the American exclusion act only further encouraged. In any event, Tagore's restatement of his message of pan-Asian spiritual revival gave an additional fillip to the cause of those right-wing nationalists whose ultimate aims were the liberation of the Asian mainland from Western military, political, and cultural influence, and the establishment of what came to be called the Greater East Asian Co-prosperity Sphere.[10]

When Tagore met with Japan's ultranationalist leaders again on his final visits to Japan in 1929 he was no longer so sure that what they meant by "spirituality" was what he meant. Stopping off at Tokyo in late March en route to an international conference on education at Vancouver, he made several statements to the press reiterating his favorite themes:

> I have come to Japan three times, and I have a warm feeling that the hopes of Asia will be fulfilled. This is why I feel that my love for Japan is deepening more and more. At the same time, I sincerely hope that Japan will continue to develop the spiritual side of her life.[11]

> The Western world is losing much of its creative power. Japan has it still. It is a pity to find that the Japanese are doing so little to preserve their unique heritage and [are] following the Western model instead. What Japan should do to preserve her uniqueness is not allow it to be lost in the mire of Western civilization.[12]

After the Vancouver conference the Indian poet lost his passport and was rudely treated by the American consul to whom he applied for a visa. Deciding to cancel his various lecture engagements in the United States in protest against the treatment of Asians seeking entrance to that country, he sailed for Japan on a Japanese freighter and spent a busy month in Tokyo from May 10 to June 9.

Tagore's dramatic protest against American racial discrimination, fully reported in the Japanese press, made him more welcome than ever on his return to Tokyo, but he considered the incident closed and did not use it to buttress his theory of Asian unity. Instead he took the occasion to speak out against Japan's imperialist policies on the Asian mainland, especially in her colony Korea. Some Korean students had come to see him soon after his arrival, and he was so disturbed by their reports of Japanese actions in their country[13] that he devoted a portion of his last important lecture in Japan to this problem. Because of his "pride as an Asiatic" in Japan's emergence as a modern state, he was pained by her misuse of power within her own Asian empire. The discouraging news from Korea may also have forced him to admit for the first time that Asia did not yet possess the underlying unity which he had ascribed to it in his previous lectures. The very idea of the Asian mind, he now charged, and not unjustifiably, had been concocted by Westerners. His friend Okakura had pioneered in linking Japan with India, he reminded his audience, gathered under the auspices of the Indo-Japanese Association. If only such peaceful ties of culture and sympathy between their two countries could continue to grow, "then some day will be developed, not merely national culture, national minds, but a continental mind of Asia, greatly needed and long waiting to be revealed." [14]

With these words, Tagore made it clear that he had grown somewhat disenchanted with the way Japan was going about uniting Asia. He expressed himself even more sharply in his final confrontation with the patriarch of Japanese pan-Asianists, Tōyama Mitsuru. Tagore was spending his month in Tokyo as the guest of Ōkura Kunihiko, head of the trading company through which Tōyama had arranged to aid various Asian revolutionaries including China's Sun Yat-sen.[15] It was therefore convenient for Tōyama to call privately on Tagore at Ōkura's mansion to talk about Asian unity. They met again at a reception arranged by some members of the Japanese Foreign Office. By this time Tagore had been told by the Korean students about the strong-arm methods used in Korea, and he exploded at the arch-samurai: "You have been infected by the virus of European imperialism!" Chinese delegates from the Kuomintang government had also called on Tagore in Tokyo and he had not been pleased at what they reported either, for he told Tōyama and his associates they should be ashamed of their behavior in China. In particular he criticized them for refusing to attend the forthcoming ceremonies at Nanking, the new capital of the Nationalist government, where Sun Yat-sen's remains were to be transferred to their final resting place. Tōyama rose to reply to these charges: Tagore had been misinformed, he said. The government's policy was not the policy of the people; and the Tōyama group would indeed attend Sun's last rites in Nanking. His anger still not mollified, Tagore heatedly announced he would never visit Japan again.[16]

Japanese aggression in China in the next decade, progressing from the conquest of Manchuria in 1931 to the invasion of China proper in 1937, confirmed Tagore's worst fears. Yet his persistent belief that Japan's expansionism was no more than an imitation of European imperialism, and was in violation of Japan's true spirituality, is belied by the statements of many patriotic Japanese during this period. "Japanese spirit" (*Yamato tamashii*) was a favorite expression of those who sought to preserve the continuity of the nation's essence and to defend it against Western influences. Tagore's Tokyo host in 1929, the businessman Ōkura Kunihiko, wrote in 1933 that he was worried by the fact that:

since the Meiji Era we have been speedily and broadly submerged in the stream of western learning, education, politics, economics, and private life; so that though our faces are Japanese, our hearts have become intoxicated with the evil dregs of the West. Thus . . . we have completely forgotten our National Spirit. If there is no revival of self-consciousness, this will perhaps invite the greatest misfortune.[17]

This much Tagore had also said. But Ōkura's definition of the National Spirit boiled down to complete loyalty to the state and all its activities: "The Japanese Spirit consists in realizing the glory of being a subject of the Emperor, and in being plunged into the mighty life of the Empire, lost to all self-interest."[18] So also the official statement of national policy drawn up and published by the Ministry of Education in 1937 defined the national morality in terms of loyalty, patriotism, filial piety, social harmony, self-effacement, and the martial spirit.[19]

The great chasm separating Tagore's concept of Asian spiritual civilization and that of his Japanese friends came into full public view in 1938, when the poet Noguchi (prompted no doubt by government officials concerned about Japan's image in India) wrote to ask his support for Japan's war in China. Noguchi had consistently championed Tagore's ideas,[20] had met his fellow poet on each of his visits to Japan, and had visited him at Santiniketan in 1935.[21] Japan's war, Noguchi now insisted, was "the inevitable means, terrible though it is, for establishing a great new world in the Asiatic continent. It is the war of 'Asia for Asia.' " Her people were united, "each person of the country doing his own bit for the realization of idealism," and as a result of the war the Japanese had grown "spiritually strong and true." Tagore was not impressed, and had his secretary write and publish his reply, asserting that Noguchi's letter did not "harmonize with the spirit of Japan which I learned to admire in your writings and came to love through my personal contacts with you." He admitted that he believed "in the message of Asia, but I never dreamed that this message could be identified with deeds which might rejoice the heart of Tamerlane." Noguchi's conception of Asia, he charged, was "raised on a tower of skulls." Noguchi wrote again to defend Japan's actions in China, and introduced a new argument: that the war was to safeguard the "Japanese spirit that we cultivated for thousands of years" against the threat of Communism. If only China would show some sign of "repentance," he concluded, "we will then proceed together to the great work of reconstructing the new world in Asia." Tagore replied in bitter tones: "I suffer intensely, not only because the reports of Chinese suffering batter against my heart, but because I can no longer point out with pride the example of a great Japan." Tagore closed the correspondence by "wishing the Japanese people, whom I love, not success, but remorse." [22]

Thus ended Tagore's hope, first stirred by Okakura's visit to Calcutta in 1901–2 and quickened by Japan's victories over Russia in 1905, that this easternmost Asian country would lead the rest of the continent in regenerating what he believed to be the ancient spiritual civilization of the East. The light of hindsight now enables us to see that this hope rested on the false assumption that the concept of "spirituality" held the same meaning for Japan's intellectuals as for India's. In reality, those Japanese who extolled the power of "spirit" were usually thinking of the spirit of Bushido, the martial ethos of the samurai warrior class which had dominated their society until its class privileges had been abolished in the late nineteenth century. By contrast, when non-Muslim Indian intellectuals spoke of "spirit" they had in mind purely religious ideals (usually Brahmanical or Jain, sometimes with an admixture of Christian spirituality). The geographical extensions of these two sets of ideals beyond the borders of each country produced two sharply opposed forms of pan-Asianism: military in the case of Japan, religious in the case of Hindu India.

This contrast between the Hindu-Jain and the samurai concepts of spirituality appears especially significant when seen in relation to the contrasting tendencies evident in modern Indian and modern Japanese nationalisms, particularly in the 1930's. The hypothesis suggests itself that both the nonviolent form assumed by Indian nationalism under Gandhi and the violent form assumed by Japanese nationalism under the militarists resulted from the democratization or diffusion among the mass of the people in each society, of ideals and traditions previously cultivated only by an exclusive and hereditary élite within the society. In more general terms the hypothesis would be that the revitalization of ancient ideals was primarily an élite response to the threat of cultural Westernization, whereas their subsequent democratization was a popular phenomenon motivated by the need to respond to the threat of Western political imperialism.

In the Japanese case, the military character of the earlier, élite response is evident in that fact that the leaders who overthrew the Tokugawa system and set about transforming the country into a modern nation-state were younger samurai. One of these leaders, Ōkuma Shigenobu, who was prime minister when Tagore first visited Japan, credited their achievement in large part to the spread of samurai values among the population as a whole:

> When the samurai, upon the fall of feudalism in 1868, were divested of their privileges as a class, their spirit of Bushido not only did not perish, but permeated even other orders of the people, and, being subsequently blended with Western arts and sciences, the knowledge of which extended rapidly, has been largely instrumental in the growth of the empire.[23]

This same process took place in modern India as well, but starting from an altogether different cultural base (in Hindu Bengal) and proceeding under very dissimilar conditions (firmly established foreign rule). Eighteenth-century Bengali Hindu society, having long been under Muslim rule, contained in itself no important military class, and was instead dominated by a cultural élite drawn from three high castes, among whom the Brahmans were the most important. This Hindu élite generally welcomed the British and cooperated with them in the economic and administrative modernization of Northern India, but took little interest in military affairs, preferring the law above all other professions. While the British Indian system of jurisprudence deprived the Brahmans of the privileged position they had enjoyed under the old Hindu law codes, nevertheless their "spirit" of nonviolent moral and intellectual leadership did not perish, but permeated the non-Brahman middle classes, blended with the new knowledge being imported from the West, and prepared the way for Gandhi's transformation of the élitist Indian National Congress into a mass organization. Gandhi's technique of mass *satyāgraha* made possible the democratization both of the Brahmanical spirit and of the more extreme spirituality of revitalized Jainism.

NATIONALISM AND PAN-ASIANISM IN CHINA, INDIA, AND PAKISTAN

If this hypothesis — that at a certain stage in the development of nationalism in twentieth-century Asian societies élite traditions and values were diffused or democratized among the mass of the population — seems to hold true for India and Japan, at least in the 1930's, how useful is it as a tool for interpreting the development of Chinese nationalist ideologies during this same period? And how relevant is it to the dramatic changes in the Asian theater during the 1940's, 1950's and 1960's? Once again, Tagore's activities can be seen as a slender but significant thread weaving developments in South and East Asia into a single contextual web.

His experiences in the China of 1924 left Tagore in no doubt that the concept of "spirituality," however interpreted, was not a popular one at that time, and this discovery saved him from the sort of misunderstanding that persisted between him and Japan's proponents of pan-Asian spirituality until 1938. When he made his next contact with Chinese intellectuals, at Singapore in 1927 on his way to visit Java and Bali, he explicitly acknowledged that China's classical culture focused on political

EPILOGUE **323**

rather than religious problems. Lim Boon Keng, president of the University of Amoy but a native of Singapore, had asked him to write a preface for Lim's English translation of the classical Chinese elegy, *Li sao,* and Tagore wrote:

> The verses of this poem carry in them a lament, political in character, which makes vivid to us the background of a great people's mind, whose best aspiration was for building a stable basis of society founded upon the spirit of moral obligation. That the quest of a perfect social adjustment in righteousness was the most powerful and living impulse in the Chinese character has been proved by the Philosophy that China has treasured most for the guidance of her life, a philosophy which offers no stimulant of spiritual emotionalism, but is sanely practical, and sensitively mindful of the influence of human conduct upon its social surroundings.[24]

In 1929, when Tagore saw China for the second and last time, he had just about given up the hope that she could join India in revitalizing Eastern spiritual civilization. Stopping at Shanghai for two days on his voyage to Japan and Canada, he saw his friends Hsü Chih-mo, Hu Shih, and others, but he made no speeches. Given the political climate at the time, it was just as well, for the Shanghai District Kuomintang had reacted sharply to the news of his arrival and had sent a public petition to higher headquarters asking them to "stop and prevent any school or any public body from extending a welcome to the Indian poet-philosopher," inasmuch as his doctrines and principles "were just as dangerous and poisonous as those of Karl Marx." [25] It is not unlikely that the author of this denunciation was Tagore's old critic, Wu Chih-hui, for it contained the same emphasis on materialism for which Wu, one of the Shanghai Kuomintang's leading intellectuals, was famous: "Everyone in the country should strictly observe the San Min [Three People's] Principles of the late Dr. Sun Yat-sen in order to develop China in a more material way for the welfare of the Chinese people." [26]

Sun Yat-sen had died in 1925, but the Kuomintang army had in his name unified much of the country in its march north from Canton in 1926–27, during which the coalition with the Chinese Communist Party forged by Sun had split apart. By 1929, a military leader, General Chiang Kai-shek, had emerged as the head of the new national government. Recognizing the importance of ideology as the necessary cement to consolidate the "sheet of sand," as Sun had called China's hundreds of millions, Chiang tried to combine Sun's Three People's Principles (roughly equivalent to nationalism, democracy, and a socialist economy) with the time-tested Confucian principles of social harmony and political control. Radical Kuomintang revolutionaries like Wu Chih-hui were gradually pushed into the background, and more conservative intellectuals like Tai Chi-t'ao were given the task of propagating the new-old ideology. "Spiritual" values came back into favor, and with them the same theme of Asian spiritual unity that Tagore in his way and the Japanese pan-Asianists in theirs had propounded. The Chinese version, expounded monthly in the pages of the *Hsin Ya-hsi-ya* (New Asia) magazine, named Sun Yat-sen as the father of the Sinocentric Pan-Asian movement. The new magazine's opening manifesto thus exhorted its Chinese readers: "Everyone must work together energetically and as one man to build up the Three People's Principles China, to build up the Three People's Principles Asia!" [27]

In 1929 the Nationalist government, having moved its capital to Nanking, where the Ming dynasty had ruled until 1644, arranged to have Sun's remains transferred there from Peking as a symbol of the re-establishment of Chinese sovereignty after nearly three centuries of non-Chinese Manchu rule. The accompanying ceremonies were also made the occasion for the reassertion of China's traditional role as the dominant power in Eastern Asia — which was probably why Japan's pan-Asianists had at first refused to attend. In spite of the objections of the Kuomintang's Shanghai branch, Tagore was invited to the ceremonies in a belated effort to add both luster and Indian representation. The reburial was to take place on June 1, 1929, and on May 14 an important official of the Chinese legation in Tokyo called on the poet at his room in the Imperial Hotel and urged him to attend. They talked for two hours, but Tagore declined the invitation, saying he had already committed himself to lecturing in Japan. The Chinese are said to have pleaded that they "wanted the Poet in China, they had need of some one like the Poet, to guide them," but Tagore blandly replied: "I myself should be very happy if it were possible for me to come into contact with the young minds in your country, those which were open to conviction and not blinded by prejudices of party-politics." His parting advice to the delegation was to "let your people effectively decide to have a long period of settled government even if it is not the best government possible." [28]

The 1930's, the last decade of Tagore's life, saw a steady increase in the frequency and importance of contacts between India and China, with Tagore retaining the central position in Sino-Indian relations that he had assumed with his pioneering China trip in 1924. His guiding purpose remained cultural and educational, while the motives of the Nationalist government appear to have been primarily political. One Chinese intellectual, however, shared fully the Indian poet's objectives, and dedicated his entire career to the task of strengthening the frayed and faded strands linking the cultural worlds of India and China. T'an Yün-shan, previously a schoolmate of Mao Tse-tung, was still living in his native Hunan Province in 1924 when he read the newspaper reports of Tagore's lectures in China. By 1927 he had emigrated to Singapore, and there had his first meeting with the poet, who invited him to come to Santiniketan to study and teach. T'an agreed, spent three years there, three years in China, and returned to India in 1934, having founded at Nanking under government sponsorship the Sino-Indian Cultural Society.[29] Tagore was delighted with T'an's efforts, and together they established the Indian branch of this Society. Tagore then sent T'an back to China to raise funds and to gather books and works of art for the center of Chinese studies to be opened at Santiniketan. Tagore's message to the Chinese patrons of the Society stressed his desire for a firm basis of friendship between India and China:

> Friends,
>   I will not send you empty greetings from across the barriers of space and of indifference that have divided us for centuries. Let me fill my greetings with [the] hope that they but herald the time when our two peoples will come to understand each other more and add to each other's achievements.
>   There was a time when India and China stood very near, when they joined their hands and their hearts in one common homage to the spirit of Love and Renunciation. Today when the world is being divided into hostile camps, each ready to strangle the other, let us recall that spirit, which still lives among us and permeates our being, and prove in our relations that the forces of love and understanding are greater than those of hatred and aggrandisement.[30]

Missing from this message is any reference to Asia or the theme of Asian spiritual unity on which the poet had dwelt so frequently during his visit to China ten years earlier. But his insistence that the Chinese remain true to their own traditions expressed itself in the personal advice he gave to T'an before his return to China: "Don't forget my Chinese tea. And tell your young people that they should not blindly imitate the U.S.S.R. You have your own communism. You know, I have a great admiration for the U.S.S.R. But if you imitate blindly you will get no benefit but disadvantage." [31] Tagore did not realize that by 1934 the Chinese Communist Party had already purged itself of the direction from Moscow which had brought it to disaster in 1927, and had come under the peasant-oriented leadership of Mao Tse-tung. The support of the peasantry enabled it to use guerrilla tactics and to build an army which the Nationalist government, relying on city-based troops advised by German generals, found it impossible to destroy. Even as Tagore was penning his letter urging his friends in China to cultivate greater love and understanding, the Nationalist forces were waging their fifth and last campaign to exterminate their Communist brothers in their South China redout in Kiangsi Province. Like the preceding four this campaign failed, and the elusive Red Army marched and fought its way through the mountains of western China to establish a new base in Sian in the northwest, close to the U.S.S.R.

The Kuomintang government at Nanking, now threatened both by the Communist Party and its army within the country and from the Japanese forces occupying Manchuria, realized that it could not succeed in unifying and defending the country unless it could muster massive popular support. Its efforts to strengthen patriotic feeling took the form of appeals to Confucian values, and the ancient ideals of courageous loyalty and filial devotion were placed at the top of the list of twelve moral principles adopted in 1935 as the code all Kuomintang Party members were to follow.[32] In the concurrent "New Life" movement of 1934–1937, frequent mention was made of the loyal Chinese Confucian officials who saved the decadent Manchu dynasty from the formidable Taiping Rebellion in the middle of the nineteenth century.[33]

The Kuomintang attempt to create a nationalist ethos by revitalizing and diffusing among the population traditions of the old Confucian élite seems a close parallel in structure, but a strong contrast in content, to the Gandhian nationalist ethos in India and the ultranationalist ethos in Japan in this same decade. Unfortunately for the Chinese government, it was not given time to develop its Confucian-style nationalism, because the Japanese militarists, seeking to achieve by conquest their dream of freeing Asia from Western (and Soviet Russian) influence, launched in 1937 their invasion of China proper, captured Peking, Shanghai, Nanking, and Canton, and forced the Nationalist government to remove its capital to Chungking, deep in the interior.

In India, the news of the war created a strong sentiment critical of Japan's aggression, to which Tagore's letters to Noguchi gave eloquent expression. China's national resistance rose correspondingly in the estimation of India's nationalists, and the Indian National Congress in 1938 sent a team of five doctors to China to form a medical unit. The unit was attached to the Communist forces under Mao Tse-tung (with whom Chiang Kai-shek had been forced to make a common front against the Japanese), and Mao sent back a message of thanks to Nehru and the Indian people. Nehru visited Tagore in 1939 just before flying to Chungking to demonstrate Indian solidarity with the Chinese Nationalist and Communist struggle against Japan, and Tagore endorsed his mission, saying: "I feel proud that the new spirit of Asia will be represented through you and our best traditions of Indian Humanity will find their voice during your contacts with the people of China." [34]

How this "new spirit of Asia" differed from the old Tagore did not say, but presumably it excluded the military ethos of the "Japanese spirit" and perhaps included the humanistic Communist ideals both Tagore and Nehru had been told of during their visits to the U.S.S.R. (whose forces had also clashed with Japan's in their unpublicized 1939 war along the Mongolia-Manchuria border). What now remained of "Eastern civilization" in this Asian spirit was so attenuated as to be indistinguishable from the secular humanism of the Marxist and non-Marxist intellectuals of Europe and North America. Nevertheless, the image of "the East" still haunted Tagore's mind. In 1941, on his last birthday he declared his faith in Europe's civilization to be completely bankrupt but added:

> And yet I shall not commit the grievous sin of losing faith in Man. I would rather look forward to the opening of a new chapter of his history after the cataclysm is over and the atmosphere rendered clean with the spirit of service and sacrifice. Perhaps that dawn will come from this horizon, from the East where the sun rises. A day will come when unvanquished Man will retrace his path of conquest, despite all barriers, to win back his lost human heritage.[35]

In February 1942, six months after Tagore's life ended, the personal contact between Indian and Chinese leaders he had pioneered in fostering reached a climax in the visit to India of Generalissimo and Madame Chiang Kai-shek and their discussions with Gandhi, Jinnah, Nehru, and other Indian nationalists. Chiang was anxious to prevent an open break between the nationalists and their British rulers, for this would impair China's war effort, heavily dependent for supplies on the land and air routes coming "over the hump" from India to Chungking. Gandhi assured Chiang of India's sympathy with China in her armed struggle against the Japanese invaders, but explained that India's nonviolent struggle for independence from Britain took precedence over all other considerations and therefore precluded any immediate participation in the war.[36] When Churchill's government failed to meet the Indian demands, Gandhi declared a nationwide *satyāgraha* movement in August 1942 to force the British to "quit India," despite the fact that Japanese forces were poised for a possible invasion across the Burma frontier. The Government of India replied by jailing Gandhi and the entire leadership of the Congress for the duration of the war.

The political and military situation in Asia in 1942 thus demonstrates how the revitalization of Asian cultural traditions and their democratization in a fusion with the originally Western idea of nationalism could lead to sharp conflict among Asian nations, rather than to the kind of pan-Asian understanding Tagore and others had hoped to see established. Japan's leaders at the time were using the principles of Bushido, "Japanese spirit," and Asian solidarity in a desperate attempt to conquer China, Southeast Asia, and potentially even India, while China's nationalists fought back to preserve not only the cultural traditions of their land but also the time-honored principle of China's political unity, if not its hegemony over the entire East Asian area. Even in this hour of maximum danger in the face of Japanese aggression, the nationalist leaders of China and India saw their problems in such different terms that they were unable to agree on a common program of self-defense.

World War I and its aftermath had stimulated the rise of nationalisms in different parts of Asia and had popularized the idea of pan-Asian resistance to Western influence, in India and Japan particularly. World War II brought a further intensification of nationalism, but a concurrent deterioration in the idea of an Asia united on whatever basis — spiritual, cultural, military, political, or economic. Even the unity of India, which Tagore, Gandhi, and Nehru had assumed would continue after independence was gained from Britain, was dealt a mortal blow by the Muslim League's adoption in 1940 of the demand for a separate Muslim-majority state, on the theory that the Muslims of India constituted a separate nation from the Hindus.

This movement for a new nation, to be named Pakistan, "the land of the pure," once again illustrates how the revitalization and reinterpretation of ancient traditions by a small élite of scholars and poets (Muhammad Iqbal being the most influential) could lay the basis for a nationalist ideology easily absorbed by great numbers of people raised in the aura of these traditions. With the Congress leadership in prison during the war years, the Muslim League had little difficulty in organizing Muslim support for Iqbal's ideal of a revitalized Islamic polity. In the postwar elections of 1945–46 Muslim voters gave the League such overwhelming approval, and in 1946–47 Muslim-Sikh-Hindu riots reached such catastrophic proportions that the Congress and the departing British finally had to surrender their hopes for preserving a united India. Since their creation in 1947 the independent nation-states of Hindu-majority India and Muslim-majority Pakistan have twice gone to war over the status of Kashmir (in 1947–1949 and in 1965), and are still sharply divided over the issue of to which nation its Muslim-majority population rightly belongs.

China, too, became bitterly divided after the war, not along religious but along ideological lines. Demoralized by the long struggle against Japan, the nationalist administration and army proved no match for its Communist rivals in the civil war of 1945–1949, and removed to the offshore bastion of Taiwan. This "partition" of China between Communist and non-Communist regimes remains in effect (as do the parallel divisions of Germany, Korea, and Vietnam). In the 1950's the revitalized Chinese state established by the Chinese Communist Party came into conflict with India over the Tibetan frontier, the two giants going to war in 1962. Since then the Peoples' Republic of China and the Islamic Republic of Pakistan, both wishing to counterbalance India's preponderance of population and resources on the southern subcontinent, have drawn closer together in an entente which played a significant role in the India-Pakistan war of 1965.

In the 1960's the old refrain of pan-Asian solidarity against Western influence has been little heard in India or Japan, the two lands of its first adoption. Only in China does the doctrine survive in such forms as the often-heard hymn, "The East is Red." Sharpening competition with her northwestern neighbor, the Soviet Union, has lent a double meaning to this assertion of the "Redness" of "the East," rendering it a taunt aimed at both the "capitalist" West and the "revisionist" Soviets. How true another Maoist slogan will prove — "The east wind will prevail over the west wind" — time will tell. The history of other Asian societies suggests, however, that only in the early stages of their development do nationalism and pan-Asianism reinforce each other; at a later stage, as the practical demands of each particular nationalism and the territorial and ideological rivalries among national states become more intense, less and less is said about pan-continental combinations.

A POSTSCRIPT ON "MODERNIZATION" AND ITS AMBIGUITIES

The idea of "the East" is now all but extinct. The idea of "the West" is fast following it into limbo. That both are anachronisms is demonstrated by the postwar advance of Japan to superiority over most European countries in those scientific, technical, and economic achievements which used to be thought of as the essence of modern "Western" civilization. Japanese intellectuals were among the first to perceive that the term "Westernization" is no longer adequate to describing the realities of the closing third of the twentieth century, and have pioneered in developing the newer theory of "modernization." Based on the idea of progress inherited from the French Enlightenment through the German philosophical historians Hegel and Marx, the concept of modernization removes the center of innovation from a geographical plane, the compass point "West," and locates it in a linear sequence of changes through time, from the ever-receding "traditional" to the ever-arriving "modern."

While the modernization concept constructs a global framework within which innovations in technology and institutions may be described and compared, its extension to the realm of ideas and ideals can produce some weird and confusing paradoxes. Far from reducing the importance of tradition, technological improvements, by accelerating social change within societies and intensifying interaction with foreign cultures, can also heighten the desire to revitalize great ideas and symbols that provide living links with the past and a stronger sense of solidarity with the land and people of one's birth. The implication that "better" methods of production, transportation, and communication necessarily bring about "better" people is another non sequitur, one to which Tagore was particularly alert. "One must bear in mind that those who have the true modern spirit need not modernize, just as those who are truly brave are not braggarts," he noted in his *Nationalism* lectures. "True modernism is freedom of mind, not slavery of taste. It is independence of thought and action, not tutelage under European schoolmasters. It is science, but not its wrong application in life." [37]

Stripped of the colorful rhetoric about Eastern civilization in which he unfortunately clothed it, the message Tagore tried to bring his audiences in China, Japan, the United States, Europe, and even the Soviet Union was essentially a warning against the dehumanizing potentialities of unlimited technological modernization. On his last visit to Paris, in the spring of 1930, he summed up both the opportunities and the dangers inherent in modern civilization:

> The human world is made one, all the countries are losing their distance every day, their boundaries not offering the same resistance as they did in the past age. Politicians struggle to exploit this great fact and wrangle about establishing trade relationships. But my mission is to urge for a world-wide commerce of heart and mind, sympathy and understanding and never to allow this sublime opportunity to be sold in the slave markets for the cheap price of individual profits or to be shattered away by the unholy competition in mutual destructiveness.[38]

No man in his own lifetime had tried harder than Tagore to establish this "world-wide commerce of heart and mind," and historians reviewing his life will judge him more fairly by what he tried to do than by what he failed to achieve. As with every pioneer, his vision of the better world to come was so clear and strong that it blinded him to some of the specific realities of the world around him. Particularly when he turned his thoughts to East Asia, about which he had little solid knowledge, his simplistic image of the spiritual civilization of the Orient beclouded his perception of the full extent to which Japanese and Chinese intellectuals were giving, as he was, new life to ideas and ideals drawn from their ancient past, and were touching, as he was, "the mystic chords of memory" in the hearts of their countrymen, stirring them to greater pride in their common language, literature, arts, religions, philosophies, and social and political ideals.

As a Hindu, Tagore had an advantage over the intellectuals of Japan, China, and Muslim India in that leaders of his society had been the first in Asia to confront the problem of combining "modernization" (in the sense of adopting new inventions and institutions which can enlarge men's independence of their material and social environments) with the "revitalization" of those great ideals and traditions from past ages which enhance the individual's sense of purpose in life and show him ways to apply the energies liberated by technological innovations. Supported by this nineteenth-century Hindu tradition, Tagore took the initiative in contacting leading thinkers in other parts of Asia, seeking to join forces with them in revitalizing the best in all their cultural heritages. The gap between his culture — both in its classical form and in its modern transformation through interaction with European culture — and theirs was too wide for him to succeed immediately in understanding the ideals of his East Asian contemporaries, or in making his understandable to them.

What Tagore did accomplish was a first step toward a distant goal. His ultimate hope, he told an Anglo-American audience in Peking, was that "gradually world ideals will grow in strength until at last they have fulfilled their highest mission — the unification of mankind." [39] His unique contribution to this aim was to articulate and strive to exemplify in a modern setting the ancient Hindu ideal of man as identical with that eternal and universal Self who dwells in all men. "My religion," he explained to Albert Einstein during their 1930 conversation at Einstein's home near Berlin, "is in the reconciliation of the Super-Personal Man, the Universal human spirit, in my own individual being." [40] The manner by which he arrived at this reconciliation, however, insofar as it depended on achieving mutuality with other men, appears less Hindu than Judeo-Christian-Islamic, perhaps also Confucian — or simply as human, beyond all other categories.

The universality of his sympathies with his fellow men is indeed the hallmark of Tagore's mind in the closing years of his life. On his eightieth and last birthday, he chose to celebrate one event that had remained timeless in the storehouse of his memory: his meeting with China's men of letters and the affection they had shown him at the party

they had arranged in honor of his sixty-third birthday. Too weak to put
pen to paper, he dictated these lines:

> Once I went to the land of China.
> Those whom I had not met
> Put the mark of friendship on my forehead,
> Calling me their own.
>
> The garb of a stranger slipped from me unknowing.
> The inner man appeared who is eternal,
> Revealing a joyous relationship, unforeseen.
>
> A Chinese name I took, dressed in Chinese clothes.
> This I know in my mind:
> Wherever I find my friend, there I am born anew.[41]

NOTES

BIBLIOGRAPHY

SELECT GLOSSARY

INDEX

NOTES

Dedication. I have borrowed the quoted phrase from Ssu-yü Teng, John K. Fairbank, *et al., China's Response to the West: A Documentary Survey, 1839–1923* (Cambridge, Mass., 1954), p. 276, because it puts my purpose so well and because it places me in the company of those Chinese scholar-reformers who worked so strenuously to achieve and communicate this "deeper understanding."

Introduction

Epigraph. Rabindranath Tagore, *On Oriental Culture and Japan's Mission* (Tokyo, 1929), pp. 14–15.

1. For the changes produced in European thought by contact with Asia, see Donald F. Lach, *Asia in the Making of Europe*, Vol. 1 and its forthcoming sequels (Chicago, 1965–   ).

2. Sokichi Tsuda, *What is the Oriental Culture?*, tr. Yosataro Mori (Tokyo, 1955), makes a penetrating analysis of Japanese conceptions of "the Orient," and draws the firm conclusion (p. 96) that "Oriental culture does not exist as one culture." On the acceptance in Japan of European cartographic knowledge, see Hiroshi Nakamura, *East Asia in Old Maps* (Tokyo and Honolulu, 1963).

3. *Sources of the Japanese Tradition*, comp. Ryusaku Tsunoda, Wm. Theodore de Bary, and Donald Keene (New York, 1958), p. 607 and *passim*; Teng and Fairbank, pp. 50, 164. Chang probably derived his famous slogan of 1898 from the unpublished essays of 1860 by Feng Kei-fen.

4. Matthew Arnold, "Obermann Once More," *The Works of Matthew Arnold*, Vol. 1: *Poems* (London, 1903), p. 306.

5. Rudyard Kipling, "The Ballad of East and West," *Departmental Ditties and Ballads and Barrack Room Ballads* (London, 1916), Pt. 2, p. 11.

6. N. V. Sovani, "British Impact on India after 1850–1857," *Cahiers d'histoire mondiale*, 2.1:103–104 (1954).

Chapter One. The Making of a Modern Prophet

Epigraph. Translated, with the assistance of Amiya Chakravarty, from the Bengali original in Rabīndranāth Ṭhākur, *Sanchayitā* (A collection; Calcutta, 1931), pp. 788–789.

1. "Poet Rabindranath Returns Home Full of Hope: 'Asia Must Find Her Own Voice,'" *Forward* (Calcutta, July 18, 1924), p. 4.

2. Raghavan Iyer, ed., *The Glass Curtain between Asia and Europe. A Symposium on the Historical Encounters and the Changing Attitudes of the Peoples of the East and the West* (London, 1965), p. 7.

3. Edward Gibbon, *The History of the Decline and Fall of the Roman Empire* (London, 1881), I, 165, which is the opening page of Chapter II.

4. An authoritative study of these scholars and their institutions is David Kopf, *British Orientalism and the Bengal Renaissance. The Dynamics of Indian Modernization, 1772–1835* (Berkeley and Los Angeles, 1968). I am indebted to this source for the first reference in n. 22 below. Islamic legal and literary works were also translated at this time, but it is significant that in comparison with Hindu writings these aroused little interest in Europe.

5. Arthur Schopenhauer, *The World as Will and as Idea,* tr. B. B. Haldane and J. Kemp, 6th ed. (London, 1909), I, xiii.

6. Edgar Quinet, "La Renaissance orientale," *Genie des religions,* quoted on p. 18 of Raymond Schwab, *La renaissance orientale* (Paris, 1950), an admirable survey of the repercussions of Orientalist scholarship in the field of (especially French) literature. The German movement is surveyed in A. Leslie Willson, *A Mythical Image: The Ideal of India in German Romanticism* (Durham, 1964). A good example of a German who remained a devout Christian while feeling the attraction of ancient Indian thought is Christian von Bunsen, Prussian Ambassador to Great Britain, who wrote in 1813 while a student at Göttingen: "I remain firm and strive after my earliest purpose in life, more felt, perhaps, than already discerned — viz. to bring over into my own knowledge and into my own Fatherland the language and the spirit of the solemn and distant East. I would for the accomplishment of this object even quit Europe, in order to draw out of the ancient well that which I find not elsewhere." (F. Max Müller, "Bunsen," in his *Biographical Essays* [London, 1884], pp. 317–318.)

7. Rammohun Roy, "Translation of the Cena Upanishad . . . ," in *The English Works of Raja Rammohun Roy,* ed. Kalidas Nag and Debajyoti Burman (Calcutta, 1945), Pt. 2, p. 13.

8. These crucial developments have been studied in detail in A. F. Salahuddin Ahmed, *Social Ideas and Social Change in Bengal, 1818–1835* (Leiden, 1965). See, for example, p. 17: "While the Hindus had welcomed English rule with enthusiasm, the Muslims regarded it as a calamity. Their failure to adjust themselves to the new situation . . . brought about a sharp deterioration in their position."

9. Further on Rammohun Roy, see Sophia Dobson Collet, *The Life and Letters of Raja Rammohun Roy,* ed. Dilip Kumar Biswas and Prabhat Chandra Ganguli (Calcutta, 1962); also Stephen N. Hay, ed., *Dialogue Between a Theist and an Idolater (Brāhma pauttalik samvād): An 1820 Tract Probably by Rammohun Roy* (Calcutta, 1962); and Stephen N. Hay, "Western and Indigenous Elements in Modern Indian Thought: The Case of Rammohun Roy," in Marius B. Jansen, ed., *Changing Japanese Attitudes toward Modernization* (Princeton, 1965), pp. 311–328.

10. Rammohun Roy, "Introduction," *Translation of Several Principal Books, Passages, and Texts of the Ved[a]s and of Some Controversial Works on Brahmunical Theology,* 2nd ed. (London, 1832), p. viii.

11. Rabindranath Tagore, *The Religion of Man* (London, 1931) pp. 170–171. Accounts of the Tagore family can be found in Prabhātkumār Mukhopādhyāy̆, *Rabīndrajībanī o Rabīndrasāhitya-prabeśak* (The life of Rabindra, and an introduction to Rabindra literature). (Calcutta, B. E. 1340–1363 [1933–1956]), I, 1–19; and in the two best English-language biographies of Rabindranath: Edward Thompson, *Rabindranath Tagore, Poet and Dramatist*, 2nd rev. ed. (London, 1948), pp. 3–20; and Krishna Kripalani, *Rabindranath Tagore: A Biography* (New York, 1962).

12. James Wyburd Furrell, *The Tagore Family: A Memoir*, 2nd ed. (Calcutta, 1892), pp. 52–53. Blair Kling of the University of Illinois is preparing a full-length study of Dwarkanath Tagore.

13. *The Autobiography of Maharshi Debendranath Tagore*, tr. Satyendranath Tagore and Indira Devi (London, 1915), pp. 38, 75, 104.

14. Debendranath's religious ideas are set forth in his *Brāhmadharmah* (The religion of Brāhma), 10th ed. (Calcutta, B. E. 1356 [1949]), an original work which incorporates many passages from the Upanishads and later scriptures. The authorized translation is *Brahmo Dharma of Maharshi Debendranath Tagore*, tr. Hem Chandra Sarkar (Calcutta, 1928). For Debendranath's contacts with Rammohun Roy, see his *Autobiography*, pp. 54–56, and "Maharshi Debendranath Tagore: Reminiscences of Rammohun Roy," in *The Father of Modern India: Commemoration Volumes of the Rammohun Roy Centenary Celebrations, 1933* (Calcutta, 1935), Pt. 2, pp. 172–177.

15. Rabindranath Tagore, *My Reminiscences* (New York, 1927) pp. 67–70. The Bengali original, *Jībansmrti*, 2nd ed. (Calcutta, B.E. 1328 [1921–1922]), contains a fifteen-page appendix of useful explanatory notes.

16. Rabindranath Tagore, *Letters to a Friend*, ed. C. F. Andrews (London, 1928), p. 22. This passage appears to be Andrews' rendering of the remarks Rabindranath made during their conversation in London in September 1912.

17. R. Tagore, *Reminiscences*, pp. 25–30, 68.

18. *Ibid.*, p. 95.

19. *Ibid.*, p. 101.

20. *Ibid.*, p. 128.

21. Rabīndranāth Ṭhākur, "Bāṅgālīr āśā o nairāśya" (The hope and despair of the Bengalis), *Bhāratī* (The goddess of speech), 1.7:305. (B.E. Māgh 1284 [January–February 1878]). Thompson, p. 30, describes the essay as Rabindranath's without mentioning that it was published anonymously. Sajanīkānta Dās, *Rabīndranāth: Jīban o sāhitya* (Rabindranath: Life and literature; Calcutta, B.E. 1367 [1959–1960]), p. 236, lists the essay among Rabindranath's contributions to *Bhāratī* in B.E. 1284, and on pp. 190–192 tells how this identification was made. The article is also mentioned in P. C. Mahalanobis, ed., *Rabindranath Tagore's Visit to China* (*Visva-Bharati Bulletin*, No. 1, Pt. 2, Calcutta, 1925), p. 10.

22. W. B. Martin, "On the Character and Capacity of the Asiatics and Particularly of the Natives of Hindoostan," *Essays by the Students of the College of Fort William in Bengal* (Calcutta, 1802), p. 115.

23. Ram Doss (pseud. for Rammohun Roy), letter to the editor, *Bengal Hurkaru* (May 23, 1823), in *English Works of Raja Rammohun Roy*, Pt. 4, pp. 71-72, 72.

24. *Ibid.*

25. Keshub Chunder Sen, *Lectures in India* (Calcutta, 1954), pp. 25, 26. For an account of Keshub's life, see Prem Sunder Basu, *Life and Works of Brahmananda Keshav* (Calcutta, 1940)

26. K. C. Sen, pp. 134-135, 145, 326.

27. *Ibid.*, pp. 492, 494-497, 539, 543.

28. Rabindranath Tagore, Letter of Nov. 17, 1937, in *Navavidhan* (*The New Dispensation*), Vol. 1, No. 2 (1938), as quoted in Mukhopādhyāy, *Rabīndrajībanī*, I, 20.

29. Edwin Arnold, *The Light of Asia, or The Great Renunciation* (London, 1879), pp. ix-x. For a delightful and scholarly account of Arnold's career, see Brooks Wright, *Interpreter of Buddhism to the West: Sir Edwin Arnold* (New York, 1957). This edition unfortunately omits the documentation contained in Wright's "Sir Edwin Arnold: A Literary Biography of the Author of *The Light of Asia*" (Ph.D. thesis, Harvard University, 1951).

30. F. Max Müller, *India: What Can It Teach Us?* (London, 1883), p. 6. Müller had come to know Dwarkanath Tagore quite well during the latter's 1843 stay in Paris, where Müller was studying the Vedas. Müller later claimed, "there can be little doubt that his son Debendranath heard from his father that European scholars had begun in good earnest the study of the Veda, and that its halo of unapproachable sanctity would soon disappear." Müller, *Biographical Essays*, pp. 37, 40.

31. M. K. Gandhi, *An Autobiography, or The Story of My Experiments with Truth*, tr. Mahadev Desai, 2nd ed. (Ahmedabad, 1940), pp. 90-92.

32. P. C. Mozoomdar, *Sketches of a Tour around the World* (Calcutta, 1940). Mozoomdar nevertheless developed the idea that Jesus Christ was an Asian in his 1883 Boston lectures published as *The Oriental Christ* (Calcutta, 1933).

33. Swami Vivekananda, "The Work before Us," in *The Complete Works of Swami Vivekananda*, Mayavati Memorial ed. (Calcutta, 1922-1959), III, 277; Vivekananda, "Christ the Messenger," in his *Complete Works*, IV, 142. Mozoomdar's penultimate address to the World Parliament of Religions bore the significant title, "The World's Religious Debt to Asia" (in P. C. Mozoomdar, *Lectures in America and Other Papers* [Calcutta, 1955], pp. 15-29).

34. Vivekananda, "My Master," in his *Complete Works*, IV, 156. Vivekananda's reflections on the relationship of East and West are set forth in his posthumously published *The East and West* (Calcutta, 1955).

35. Rabindranath Tagore, "The Vision," recited by Tagore on *Hindusthan Record*, H. 782 (Calcutta, c. 1935); R. Tagore, *Reminiscences*, pp. 222, 218.

36. *Ibid.*, p. 219.

37. *Ibid.*, pp. 157-192; Rabīndranāth Thākur, *Ẏuropprabāsīr patra* (Let-

ters of a sojourner in Europe), in *Rabīndra-rachanābalī* (The writings of Rabindra; Calcutta, B.E. 1346–1355 [1939–1948]), I, 531–584; Prabhātkumār Mukhopādhyāy, *Rabīndrajībankathā* (The story of Rabindra's life; Calcutta, B.E. 1366 [1959]), pp. 25–26; and Kripalani; pp. 86–87. Although Rabindranath says in his *Reminiscences* (p. 47) that he was "delighted at the prospect" of returning home, the last paragraph of his last published letter from London reads: "So I am happy in this family circle. In the evening we amuse ourselves — sing songs, read books. And Ethel does not want to leave her Uncle Arthur's side for a minute." *Rabīndra-rachanābalī*, I, 584.

38. Tagore, *Reminiscences*, p. 204. See also Kripalani, pp. 98–99. Thompson, p. 34, without giving the source of his information (which may well have been Rabindranath himself, since he conversed with him on various occasions), tells us "the Maharshi, perhaps never very enthusiastic as to his future as a pleader, merely said, 'So you have come back. All right, you may stay.'"

39. Tagore, *Reminiscences*, pp. 101, 102, 178, 208, 210.

40. *Ibid.*, pp. 260, 263.

41. *Ibid.*, p. 262; Nagendranath Gupta, *Reflections and Reminiscences* (Bombay, 1947), p. 63.

42. My translation is modified from the translation in Rabindranath Tagore, *Our Universe*, tr. Indu Dutt (London, 1958), pp. 105, 106. The Bengali original, "Chabi" (A picture), was written at Allahabad in 1914 and has been reprinted in Ṭhākur, *Sanchayitā* (1946), pp. 534–538. Kadambari Devi's memory remained fresh in Rabindranath's mind even in his old age as Maitreyī Devi has shown in her *Maṃpute Rabīndranāth* (With Rabindranath at Mongpu) (Calcutta, B.E. 1364 [1958–1959]).

43. Tagore, *Our Universe*, pp. 104, 105.

44. Tagore, *Reminiscences*, p. 271.

45. Thompson, pp. 76–77. The Bengali original, "Duranta āśā" (Wild hopes), is reprinted in *Rabīndra-rachanābalī*, II, 197–201.

46. Tagore, *Reminiscences*, pp. 269, 270; Rabindranath Tagore, "The Voice of Humanity," in *Lectures and Addresses*, comp. Anthony X. Soares (London, 1950), p. 142.

47. Rabīndranāth Ṭhākur, "Yurop-yātrīr dāyāri'r khasrā" (Draft copy of *A diary of a traveler to Europe*), *Biśvabhāratī patrikā* (Visva-Bharati journal), No. 3: 155 ff., 159, 164 (B.E. Māgh-Chaitra 1356 [January–April 1950]).

48. Rabīndranāth Ṭhākur, "Yurop-yātrīr dāyāri" (Diary of a traveler to Europe), in *Rabīndra-rachanābalī*, I, 607.

49. *Ibid.*, p. 608.

50. Rathindranath Tagore, "Father As I Knew Him," *Visva-Bharati Quarterly*, 18.4:338 (February–April 1953).

51. Kripalani, pp. 184–85.

52. Rabīndranāth Ṭhākur, *Chhinna patra* (Torn letters), as translated in his *The Wayfaring Poet* (Calcutta, 1961), pp. 42–43.

53. Thompson, p. 100. For personal recollections of his father's life in East Bengal, see Rathindranath Tagore, *On the Edges of Time* (Calcutta, 1958), pp. 22–43.

54. Rabīndranāth Ṭhākur, "Prāchya o pāśchatya sabhyatā" (Eastern and Western civilization), *Rabīndra-rachanābalī*, IV, 416–424, 424.

55. Rabindranath Tagore, "The Sunset of the Century," in his *Nationalism* (New York, 1917), pp. 157–159. This English poem in five stanzas is a condensation rather than a direct translation, and is based on poems 64–68 of the Bengali collection *Naibedya*, in *Rabīndra-rachanābalī*, VIII, 51–54. As usual in his translations, Rabindranath made minor alterations, the most significant one here being the use of the English word "nation" for the Bengali *sabhyatā*, which is usually translated as "civilization."

56. Government of India, *Report of the Native Press: Bengal, 1900* (printed for official use only), July 7, 1900, translating from *Hitabādī* (Calcutta, June 29, 1900); Mukhopādhyāy, *Rabīndrajībanī*, I, 228, cites Rabindranath's own statement in a letter to his friend Shrishchandra Majumdar that he was engaged as literary editor for *Hitabādī* on its founding in 1891, and adds that his connection with the paper did not last more than three months. Brajendranāth Bandyopādhyāy, *Bāṃlā sāmayik-patra* (Bengali periodical publications), 2nd. rev. ed. (Calcutta, B.E. 1359 [1952–1953]), II, 61, says that the paper remained until 1907 the best Bengali newspaper of its time.

57. Rabīndranāth Ṭhākur, "Chīnemyāner chiṭhi" (Letters of a Chinaman), *Rabīndra-rachanābalī*, IV, 403. This review was first published in June–July 1902, in *Bangadarśan* (The vision of Bengal), which Rabindranath was then editing.

58. *Ibid.*, p. 405.

59. Goldsworthy Lowes Dickinson, *Letters from John Chinaman* (London, 1901). The American edition bore the title, *Letters from a Chinese Official: Being an Eastern View of Western Civilization* (New York, 1903). Rabindranath was not the only person taken in by Dickinson, for William Jennings Bryan took the trouble to write a reply, *Letters to a Chinese Official: Being a Western View of Eastern Civilization* (Lincoln, Neb., 1906). The story of how Dickinson came to write the letters is given in E. M. Forster, *Goldsworthy Lowes Dickinson* (New York, 1934), pp. 142 ff.

60. The best biography of Okakura in English is Yasuko Horioka, *The Life of Kakuzō, Author of "The Book of Tea,"* (Tokyo, 1963).

61. The fullest study of Fenollosa is Lawrence W. Chisholm, *Fenollosa: The Far East and American Culture* (New Haven and London, 1963).

62. Van Wyck Brooks, *Fenollosa and His Circle, with Other Essays in Biography* (New York, 1962), p. 24; Ernest Fenollosa, *East and West* (New York and Boston, 1893), p. 212.

63. *Ibid.*, p. v.

64. *Ibid.*, pp. v–vi; Ernest Fenollosa, "The Coming Fusion of East and West," *Harper's Monthly*, 98:122 (December 1898).

65. Horioka, pp. 36–38, states that Okakura was forced to resign because of his love affair with his superior's wife.

66. Lizelle Reymond, *Nivedita, fille de l'Inde* (Paris, 1945), p. 216; Romain Rolland, *Inde: Journal, 1915–1943* (Paris, 1951), p. 172, citing his interview with Miss Josephine MacLeod on May 16, 1927. (On p. 142 Rolland quotes this remark supposedly made by Vivekananda to Okakura after their first meeting: "You have nothing more to do with me. Here renunciation reigns. Go find Tagore. He is still in the midst of life." Rolland's source for this remark was Dhan Gopal Mukerji, who visited him on October 4, 1926; Mukerji must have obtained his information from someone else, since he was a mere child in 1901.) Vivekananda mentions Okakura, his invitation to Japan, and his travels in India, in nine different letters to Miss Josephine MacLeod and others between June 14, 1901, and April 21, 1902 (*Complete Works of Swami Vivekananda*, V, 161–164, 170, 173–178).

67. Sukumar Sen, "Some Early Influences in Tagore's Life," *Indo-Asian Culture*, 10.1:152 (July 1961), says that after the division of lands and his return to Calcutta, "city life became unbearable to him after a few weeks"; Mukhopādhyāy, *Rabīndrajībanī*, II, 27 ff. For a sketch of Brāhmabandhāb's life and work see B. Aminananda, *The Blade* (Calcutta, c. 1940).

68. Rai Govind Chandra, *Abanindranath Tagore* (Calcutta, 1951), p. 22, which seems to be based on Abanīndranāth Ṭhākur, *Jorāsānkor dhāre* (On the banks of the Jorasanko; Calcutta, B.E. 1351 [1945–1946]), p. 112. Nagendranath Gupta, p. 204, recalls meeting Nivedita "at the house of the American Consul-General in Calcutta in earnest conversation with Mr. Okakura"; Surendranath Tagore, "Kakuzo Okakura," *Visva-Bharati Quarterly*, new ser., 22:65, 72 (August 1936).

69. Rabindranath Tagore, "City and Village," *Kaizō* (Reconstruction), 6.7:106 (July 1924); Rabindranath Tagore, *On Oriental Culture and Japan's Mission* (Tokyo, 1929), pp. 1–2, 3, 6.

70. Kakuzō Okakura, *The Ideals of the East, With Special Reference to the Art of Japan* (London, 1903), p. 1.

71. *Ibid.*, pp. 223, 236, 240, 241, 244.

72. Vivekananda, "The Influence of Indian Spiritual Thought in England," in his *Complete Works*, III, 440–444; Chisholm, *Fenollosa*, p. 103.

73. S. Tagore, p. 68.

74. Okakura's manuscript is said by his biographer Horioka to have been published under the title, "The Awakening of the East," in *Okakura Tenshin zenshū* (Tokyo, 1939), Vol. 2. Material from it appears to have been incorporated in his *The Awakening of Japan* (New York, 1904). A portion of the manuscript, beginning with this quotation, is included in Okakura Kazuō, ed., *Risō no saiken* (The re-establishment of the ideal: Tokyo, 1938), pp. 1 ff.

75. Two independent sources tell us that Nivedita had some part in the composition of *The Ideals of the East*. Her biographer, who had access to many private papers and interviewed a number of her friends, informs us

(Reymond, p. 65) that Nivedita, "completely revised and rewrote" the manuscript, in an effort to appeal to Western readers and win their sympathy for India's nationalist struggle. Vivekananda's younger brother asserts that the manuscript, "was rewritten by the Sister, as she told the writer," and that it accordingly "contained the stamp of Swamiji's [Vivekananda's] ideology on Asia." Bhupendranath Datta, *Swami Vivekananda, Patriot-Prophet: A Study* (Calcutta, 1954), p. 117. None of Okakura's previous publications mention Asian ideals, so far as I can discover, whereas Nivedita's *Kali, the Mother* (London, 1900), refers on pp. 12, 16, 31, 49, 50, 51 and 60 to "Eastern," "Asiatic," or "Oriental" characteristics. Nivedita probably suggested to Okakura the title of his book as well, for her publisher had brought out in 1898 a book of poetry by Herbert Baynes under the title, *The Ideals of the East.* Baynes declared in his preface (p. vii), "to the Occident we look for Law, to the Orient for Light."

76. Nivedita of Ramakrishna-Vivekananda, "Introduction," in Okakura, *Ideals,* pp. xv–xxi.

77. Moni Bagchee, *Sister Nivedita* (Calcutta, 1956), pp. 97–108; Kripalani, pp. 208–209; Mukhopādhyāy̐, *Rabīndrajībanī,* II, 252–253. Rabindranath's personal tribute to Nivedita after her death is found in "Bhaginī Nibeditā" (Sister Nivedita), *Rabīndra-rachanābalī,* XVIII, 487–497, a portion of which appears in translation in Sister Nivedita, *Studies from an Eastern Home* (London, 1913), pp. xl–xliii. Rabindranath also contributed an introduction to her *The Web of Indian Life,* new ed. (London, 1918), pp. v–viii.

78. Mukhopādhyāy̐, *Rabīndrajībanī,* II, 426–427; Sano Jinnosuke, *Indō oyobi Indōjin* (India and the Indians, Tokyo, 1917), p. 2.

79. Interview with Mukul Dey, January 24, 1956; Rathindranath Tagore, *Edges of Time,* p. 76; Mukhopādhyāy̐, *Rabīndrajībanī,* II, 122 (my translation). Mukhopadhyay describes the poem as a translation from the Japanese, but in it the poet speaks as an Indian addressing Japan. Sano Jinnosuke, the judo teacher whom Okakura had sent to Santiniketan at Rabindranath's request, identifies the poem as Rabindranath's (and gives it in Japanese translation) in "Tagōru sensei to watakushi" (Master Tagore and I), in Kiyozawa Iwao, ed., *Meishi no Tagōru kan* (Views of famous men on Tagore; Tokyo, 1915), p. 278.

80. An excellent account of the initial phases of the antipartition agitation is given in John R. McLane, "The Development of Nationalist Ideas and Tactics and the Policies of the Government of India, 1897–1905" (Ph.D. thesis, School of Oriental and African Studies, University of London, 1961), pp. 331–430. Rabindranath's patriotic activities in this period are summarized in Praphullakumār Sarkār, *Jātīya āndolane Rabīndranāth* (Rabindranath in the national movement), 2nd ed. (Calcutta, B.E. 1354 [1947–1948]), pp. 32–82. For a lengthier treatment, with more quotations from Rabindranath's many essays of this period, see I. A. Tovstykh and A. I. Chicherov, "Problemy natsional'no-osvoboditel'nogo dvizheniia 1905–1908 gg. v Indii i ikh otrazhenie

v publitsistike Rabindranata Tagora" (Problems of the national-liberation movement of 1905–1908 in India and their treatment in the publicistic writings of Rabindranath Tagore), in *Rabindranat Tagor, k stoletiiu so dnia rozhdeniia, 1891–1961: Sbornik statei* (Rabindranath Tagore, for the centenary of his birth, 1861–1961: A collection of essays; Moscow, 1961), pp. 232–260.

81. Rabindranath Tagore, "Our Swadeshi Samaj," in his *Greater India*, (Madras, 1921), pp. 15–17, 30. The English article, like so many of Rabindranath's "translations," is actually a restatement in shorter form of the ideas contained in his Bengali work. The original lecture, delivered in August or September 1904, is "Svadeśī samāj," *Rabīndra-rachanābalī*, III, 526–558.

82. Tagore, *Greater India*, pp. 30–31.

83. Mukhopādhyāy̆, *Rabīndrajībankathā*, pp. 96–100; Thompson, p. 205 (erroneously dating this retirement in 1907). See also the account (correctly dating the retirement in 1908) given in V. Lesny, *Rabindranath Tagore, His Personality and Work*, tr. Guy McKeever Phillips (London, 1939), pp. 141–151.

84. Rabindranath Tagore, "East and West in Greater India," in his *Greater India*, pp. 82, 86–90, 100–101. The Bengali article on which this is based is "Purba o paschim" (East and West), originally printed in *Prabāsī* (B.E. Bhādra 1315 [August–September 1908]).

85. Undated letter in Bengali from Rabīndranāth Ṭhākur to Arabindamohan Basu, c. 1908, "Chiṭhipatra" (Letters), *Biśvabhāratī patrikā*, 12.1:1–2 (July–September 1955).

86. Thompson, p. 205, quoting from an article by Ajit Kumar Chakravarti, which Thompson erroneously says appeared in *Modern Review* for July 1917.

87. Mukhopādhyāy̆, *Rabīndrajībankathā*, p. 99.

88. Tagore's indebtedness to the devotional, or *bhakti*, school of medieval Hinduism, and to its continuing development by humble, itinerant mystic singers, the Bāuls, has been well demonstrated by Edward C. Dimock, Jr., in his "Rabindranath Tagore, 'The Greatest of the Bāuls of Bengal,'" *Journal of Asian Studies*, 19.1:33–51 (November 1959).

89. This fragment is given, without its source being specified, in ed. Amal Home, *Calcutta Municipal Gazette: Tagore Memorial Special Supplement* (Sept. 13, 1941), Pt. 1, p. 53. A careful analysis of several of Tagore's Bengali poems and the difficulties of translating them into English is given by the Bengali poet Buddhadeva Bose in his "Tagore in Translation," *Jadavpur Journal of Comparative Literature*, 3:22–40 (Calcutta, 1963).

90. Thompson, pp. 215–216, quoting Rabindranath's words during one of their private conversations.

91. Rabindranath Tagore, *My Boyhood Days* (Calcutta, 1943), p. 87.

92. Hermann Keyserling, *The Travel Diary of a Philosopher*, tr. J. Holroyd Reece (New York, 1926), I, 337–338; William Rothenstein, *Men and Memories* (New York, 1931–1940), II, 249; Rathindranath Tagore, *Edges of Time*,

p. 112. Keyserling (I, 338) remarks, "Rabindranath, the poet, impressed me like a guest from a higher, more spiritual world. Never perhaps have I seen so much spiritualised substance of soul condensed into one man."

93. S. Tagore, p. 72. For Okakura, the most memorable event in this second visit to India was the beginning of his friendship with a Bengali lady (apparently a member of the Tagore family), to whom he subsequently addressed a series of poignant letters. "Indeed we are all one," he once wrote her. "It would be an everlasting delight if we could meet on some cloud-capped hills and spend our lives writing about the unity of Asia and things that will bring the East into closer union." Kakuzo Okakura, "Letters to a Friend," *Visva-Bharati Quarterly*, 21.2:196–197 (Autumn 1955).

94. Mukhopādhyāy̐, *Rabīndrajībankathā*, p. 113; Rothenstein, II, 262; Kripalani, pp. 217–218.

95. W. B. Yeats, "Introduction," in Tagore, *Gitanjali* (Song Offerings) (London, 1957), pp. vii, xvii.

96. Richard Ellmann, *Yeats, the Man and the Masks* (New York, 1948), pp. 195–196.

97. Interview with Rathindranath Tagore, Jan. 21, 1960; Tagore, *On Oriental Culture*, pp. 8–10.

98. Okakura, "Letters," pp. 10, 21.

99. Thompson, p. 223, apparently citing his personal conversation with Tagore, which must have occurred some years later.

100. Rabindranath Tagore to Harriet Monroe, Dec. 31, 1913; manuscript in University of Chicago Library.

101. Bipin Chandra Pal, "Rabindra Nath and the Nobel Prize," *Hindu Review*, 2.6:408 (Calcutta, December 1913). Pal's translation of Rabindranath's remarks differs from the more polite version given (in Bengali) in "Rabindranath Tagore: A Chronicle of Eighty Years, 1861–1941," *Calcutta Municipal Gazette* (Sept. 13, 1941), Pt. 2, p. xxii.

Chapter Two. India's Messenger in Japan

Epigraph. Rabindranath Tagore, *The Message of India to Japan* (Tokyo, 1916), p. 14. This lecture was reprinted, with a few minor changes, as "Nationalism in Japan. I," in Tagore's *Nationalism*, pp. 65–87, to which version subsequent notes refer.

1. Letter from Tagore to C. F. Andrews (Santiniketan, Oct. 7, 1914), in Tagore, *Letters to a Friend*, p. 47.

2. The Viceroy, Lord Hardinge, used this phrase in his closing remarks after C. F. Andrews' lecture at Simla, the Indian government's summer capital. See C. F. Andrews, "Rabindranath Tagore," *Modern Review*, 14.1:35 (July 1913).

3. Rabindranath Tagore to William Rothenstein (Dec. 29, 1914). This and the other letters from Tagore to Rothenstein cited below are in the Houghton Library at Harvard University.

4. Gandhi, *Autobiography*, pp. 455, 464–466.

5. Tagore to Andrews (Calcutta, Feb. 18, 1915), as quoted in Tagore, *Letters to a Friend*, p. 55; Kiyozawa Iwao, ed., *Meishi no Tagōru kan* (How famous men regard Tagore; Tokyo, 1915), plate facing p. 355 reproducing Rabindranath's letter to Kimura Taiken, (Calcutta, Feb. 18, 1915). Kimura's own recollections of this period are given in Rev. Nikki Kimura, "My Memory about the Late Rash Behari Bose," in Radhanath Rath and Sabitri Prasanna Chatterjee, eds., *Rash Behari Basu: His Struggle for India's Independence* (Calcutta, 1963), pp. 38-40. Kimura says (p. 39) of Tagore: "I called on him at his Jorasanko home every day; sometimes several times in a day from my boarding house. . . . Next year [1915], he told me that he had long cherished a desire to go to Japan and that he would like to visit Japan by all means within one or two years. He requested me to accompany him to act as his interpreter and also asked me to make all necessary arrangements beforehand." Kimura's version of Tagore's reception in Japan (p. 40) is that "all [the] Japanese were completely fascinated by his profound lectures, which encouraged our people very much and led them to see the bright side of human lives."

6. Mukhopādhyāẏ, *Rabīndrajībankathā*, p. 134. It is not impossible that Kimura and Kawaguchi were inspired to write Rabindranath by the Japanese government, to whom they presumably reported on their respective visits to Tibet and Bengal. One staff member of Calcutta University, in a conversation with me in Calcutta in 1960, recalled that Kimura had the reputation of being a government spy. This seems probable on the basis of Kimura's own account. He was in India almost continuously from 1907 through 1931, and in 1931 was appointed by General Tojo "to act as adviser to the Japanese Army General Staff Office, and [Tojo] requested me to render every assistance to realize Indian Independence." (Nikki Kimura, pp. 38-41, 43.)

7. Tagore to Rothenstein (Bolpur [Santiniketan], Apr. 4, 1915); also quoted in Rothenstein, II, 300. Tagore to Rothenstein (Shil[e]ida, Nadia, July 22, 1915). Although this poem resembles several of the poems in Rabindranath's great cycle *Balākā* (A flight of swans), it is not included therein. An abridged version of this English poem is given as poem 8 in Rabindranath Tagore, "Fruit-Gathering," *Collected Poems and Plays of Rabindranath Tagore* (London, 1961), p. 179.

8. Tagore to Andrews (Shileida, July 16, 1915), quoted in Tagore, *Letters to a Friend*, p. 63; Tagore to Andrews (Srinagar, Oct. 12, 1915), quoted in *ibid.*, p. 72.

9. Thompson, pp. 246-247. Rabindranath gave a similar description of his situation and his feelings in December 1915: "I have done a great deal of writing lately and been generally successful in making myself fiercely hated by a large body of my countrymen. . . . The migratory impulse is in my wings now. I felt exactly this restlessness before leaving for Europe last time. Possibly it is some inner accumulation in me which wants bursting its pod to be scattered in the wind." (Tagore to Rothenstein, Calcutta, Dec. 10, 1915.)

10. Tagore, *Letters to a Friend*, pp. 57, 57-58; C. F. Andrews, "Rolland

and Tagore," in *Rolland and Tagore,* ed. Alex Aronson and Krishna Kripalani (Calcutta, 1945), pp. 10–11.

11. Rabīndranāth Ṭhākur to Rathindranāth Ṭhākur, in Rabīndranāth Ṭhākur, *Chiṭhipatra* (Letters; Calcutta, B.E. 1349–1367 [1942–1960]), II, 35; Rabīndranāth Ṭhākur to Srīmatī Mīrā Debī ([Santiniketan], B.E. Baisakh 1323 [Apr. 14, 1916]), *ibid.,* IV, 71. Both letters are cited in Mukhopādhyāẏ, *Rabīndrajībanī,* II, 410.

12. *Ibid.;* Rabīndranāth Ṭhākur, poem 45 in "Balākā," *Rabīndra-rachanābalī,* XII, 76, as translated in Rabindranath Tagore, *A Flight of Swans: Poems from Balākā,* tr. Aurobindo Bose (London, 1955), p. 78.

13. Mukhopādhyāẏ, *Rabīndrajībanī,* II, 419.

14. John W. Spellman, "The International Extensions of Political Conspiracy as Illustrated by the Ghadr Party," *Journal of Indian History,* 37.1:32 (April 1959).

15. Nikki Kimura, p. 39.

16. One of Ōkuma's biographers ascribes the defects in his China policy to the fact that, "although he was the most popular Prime Minister that Japan had ever seen he was not, owing to the political conditions of the time, in a position to act as he pleased." (Smimasa Idditti, *The Life of Marquis Shigenobu Okuma, A Maker of New Japan;* Tokyo, 1940, p. 388.)

17. Rabīndranāth Ṭhākur, *Jāpān-yātrī* (A traveler to Japan), 2nd ed. (Calcutta, B.E. 1334 [1927–1928]), pp. 49–51, 65. This has been translated by Shakuntala Rao Sastri and edited by Walter Donald Kring as *A Visit to Japan* (New York, 1961). Excerpts were also translated by Indira Devi Chowdhurani as "On the Way to Japan," in *Visva-Bharati Quarterly,* new ser., 4.2:95–106 (August–October 1938), and 4.3:186–198 (November 1938). *Jāpān yātrī* is also in *Rabīndra-rachanābalī,* XIX, 295–359.

18. *Tōkyō asahi shimbun* (May 30, 1916); Ṭhākur, *Jāpān-yātrī,* pp. 71–72.

19. *Tōkyō asahi shimbun* (June 2, 1916). This chance remark was regarded as especially significant by the editors of the volume published in honor of Rabindranath's visit, for they reproduced it in that volume's appendix, "Shisei Tagōru shi raichō ki" (A record of the visit to Japan of the teacher-saint Tagore), *Sei Tagōru* (Tagore the sage; Tokyo: Kyōiku gakujutsu kenkyūkai, 1916), p. 253.

20. "Nihon taizai chū no Tagōru shi" (Mr. Tagore's stay in Japan), *Nichi-In kyōkai kaihō* (Indo-Japan Association news; Tokyo, December 1916), pp. 112 ff.; interview with Mukul Dey; "Poet Tagore's Diary during His First Visit to Japan" (typed MS. in the possession of Mme. Kora Tomiko, Tokyo), p. 1.

21. *Ōsaka asahi shimbun* (June 3, 1916), as quoted in "India and Japan," *Modern Review,* 20.2:216 (August 1916).

22. *Ibid.,* pp. 216, 217; "Tagōru bummei o norou," *Tōkyō asahi shimbun,* June 2, 1916. The only newspaper to give the full English text of this lecture was the *Japan Chronicle* (June 2, 1916). *Tōkyō asahi shimbun* (June 3, 4, and 5) gave a complete Japanese translation.

23. Ṭhākur, *Jāpān-yātrī*, pp. 4, 24, 32, 49, 61, as tr. in *Visva-Bharati Quarterly*, new ser., 4.2: 96, 104 and 4.3: 187, 190, 193.

24. Ṭhākur, *Jāpān-yātrī*, p. 77, as tr. in *Visva-Bharati Quarterly*, 4.3:196. The translation ends at the middle of this letter. Ṭhākur, *Jāpān-yātrī*, pp. 76, 78, 79, 80–87.

25. *Ibid.*, p. 90.

26. *Nichi-In kyōkai kaihō*, under date June 5, 1916; *Sei Tagōru*, pp. 260–264.

27. *Ibid.*, pp. 264–265; "Poet Tagore's Diary," p. 2; Ṭhākur, *Jāpān-yātrī*, pp. 90–93.

28. *Sei Tagōru*, pp. 266 ff.; *Japan Times* (Tokyo; June 11, 1916).

29. Idditti, p. 396.

30. *Sei Tagōru*, p. 273.

31. *Ibid.*, p. 274; E. R. S., "India's Message to Japan. An Address at the University of Tokyo by Sir Rabindranath Tagore. Special Correspondence," *Outlook*, 113:856–858 (New York, Aug. 9, 1916).

32. *Tōkyō asahi shimbun* (June 12, 1916). According to the *Outlook's* special correspondent, Tagore "quickly retired at the close of his address," a fact that would suggest no Japanese translation followed the lecture, and would explain some of the bafflement expressed by Japanese intellectuals (see below, Chapter Three).

33. Tagore, *Nationalism*, pp. 66, 75, 78, 80, 85.

34. *Ibid.*, pp. 73, 76, 77.

35. *Ibid.*, pp. 82, 84, 84–85.

36. *Ibid.*, pp. 69, 71, 73–74, 75, 85, 86.

37. Rolland, *Inde*, p. 12. Rolland had read the excerpts of the lecture printed in *The Outlook*, 113:856–858 (Aug. 9, 1916).

38. *Tōkyō asahi shimbun* (June 14, 1916); "Poet Tagore's Diary," p. 3.

39. *Sei Tagōru*, pp. 280–281.

40. *Kobe Herald* of unspecified date, as quoted in "Rabindranath's Bengali Speech in Japan," *Modern Review*, 20.2:231–232 (August 1916); *Sei Tagōru*, frontispiece; *ibid.*, p. 281.

41. Rabīndranāth Ṭhākur to Rathīndranāth Ṭhākur (Tokyo, B.E. 31 Jyaishṭha, 1323 [June 13, 1916]), in Ṭhākur, *Chiṭhipatra*, II, 42–43.

42. *The Manchester Guardian* (July 20, 1916). This interview was later reproduced in *Modern Review*, 20.3:344–345 (September 1916), but was not mentioned or quoted in the Japanese newspapers, which were under wartime censorship.

43. *Manchester Guardian* (July 20, 1916).

44. *Japan Times* (June 15, 1916); Rabindranath Tagore, "Paradise, Being an Address Delivered by Rabindranath Tagore before Japanese Students in Tokyo," in William W. Pearson, *Shantiniketan, the Bolpur School of Rabindranath Tagore* (London, 1917), p. 102. Rabindranath's anger at seeing the children being made to do military drill in a government kindergarten school at Kobe was reported in *Methodist Recorder* (London), June 24, 1937,

and is quoted in Maitreyi Devi, *The Great Wanderer* (Calcutta, 1961), p. 38.

45. Ṭhākur, *Jāpān-yātrī*, pp. 102–105; Tagore, *Letters to a Friend*, p. 6.

46. Interview with Mukul Dey; interview with Yashiro Yukio (Tokyo, Feb. 8, 1955); Sasaki Nobutsuna, "Tagōru ou no inshō" (Impressions of Dr. Tagore), *Taiyō* (The sun), 32.10:128 (August 1916).

47. *Japan Weekly Chronicle* (Kobe; June 15, 1916); *Tōkyō asahi shimbun* (June 29, 1916); interview with Yashiro Yukio; interview with Mukul Dey.

48. "Poet Tagore's Diary," p. 4; Rabīndranāth Ṭhākur to Srīmati Mīrā Debī (Yokohama, 18 Āshāṛ 1323 [July 1, 1916]), *Chiṭhipatra*, IV, 74; *The Spirit of Japan: A Lecture by Sir Rabindranath Tagore Delivered for the Students of the Private Colleges of Tokyo and the Members of the Indo-Japanese Association, at the Keio Gijuku University* (Tokyo, 1916). This pamphlet went through four printings in July 1916. Its contents later appeared (with the omission of pp. 1–5) as "Nationalism in Japan. II," in Tagore, *Nationalism*, pp. 87–114.

49. Tagore, *Nationalism*, pp. 90, 91.

50. *Ibid.*, p. 92; Tagore, *Spirit of Japan*, pp. 3–4; Tagore, *Nationalism*, p. 92.

51. *Ibid.*, p. 99.

52. *Ibid.*, pp. 98, 101, 102, 97.

53. *Ibid.*, pp. 93–94.

54. *Ibid.*, p. 94.

55. *Ibid.*, pp. 106, 111.

56. *Ibid.*, p. 109.

57. *Ibid.*, pp. 107, 110.

58. *Ibid.*, pp. 111–112, except that the word "civilisation" in the original lecture was changed to "nationalism" in the New York version cited here.

59. *Ibid.*, p. 112.

60. Rolland, *Inde*, p. 19; Tagore, *Letters to a Friend*, p. 68.

61. *Ibid.*, p. 69; Tagore, "Nationalism in the West," in his *Nationalism*, pp. 38–39.

62. *Shin chō* (New tide; Tokyo, July 1916), frontispiece. Both the Bengali poem, in Rabindranath's own handwriting, and a Japanese translation are reproduced in this illustration.

63. Tagore, *Collected Poems and Plays*, p. 220.

64. *Tōkyō asahi shimbun* (July 13, 1916).

65. Takao Kenichi, "Tagōru ou o omou" (Thinking about Tagore), *Rikugō zasshi* (Universe magazine), 37.6:136–142 (June 1917); Akita Ujaku, "Sanjō no Tagōru" (On top of the hill with Tagore), *Waseda bungaku* (Waseda literature; July, 1916); Yoshida Genjirō, "Tagōru o otonau no ki" (A record of a visit to Tagore), *Rikugō zasshi*, 36.8:107 (August 1916).

66. Takao, p. 142.

67. Rabīndranāth Ṭhākur to Pramatha Chaudhuri (Yokohama, July 20, 1916), *Chiṭhipatra*, V, 215.

68. *Ibid.*

69. Tagore to Rothenstein (Yokohama, Aug. 2, 1916). Rabindranath develops much these same ideas at greater length in the closing portions of *Jāpān-yātrī*.

70. *Tōkyō asahi shimbun* (Aug. 3, 1916).

71. Interview with Yashiro Yukio.

72. My authority for the statement that such an offer was made at some time during Rabindranath's visit to Japan has asked me to withhold his identity.

73. *Nichi-nichi shimbun* (June 8, 1924); C. F. Andrews, "The Poet," in *The Golden Book of Tagore: A Homage to Rabindranath Tagore from India and the World in Celebration of his Seventieth Birthday*, ed. Ramananda Chatterjee (Calcutta, 1931), p. 26. Andrews, writing from memory, has both garbled the historical incident (correctly recounted in *Japan: The Official Guide*, ed. Tourist Industry Division, Ministry of Transportation, rev. ed. [Tokyo, 1954], p. 379) and misquoted the poem, the final version of which (not given here) is No. 186 in Tagore, *Stray Birds*, p. 55. This collection of 326 short reflections modeled vaguely on the haiku form (many of them written in guest and autograph books) was composed during Rabindranath's stay in Japan and is dedicated to his Yokohama host, T. Hara.

74. "Poet Tagore's Diary," p. 4; photograph album with dedication dated August 29, 1916, in archives of Rabindra Sadan, Santiniketan; interview with Mrs. Kora Tomiko (Tokyo, Jan. 20, 1955).

75. Rabīndranāth Thākur to Surendranāth Thākur, manuscript letter in Bengali of 11 Bhadra, B.E. 1323 (1916), quoted in Mukhopādhyāẏ, *Rabīndrajībanī*, II, 429. William W. Pearson, "To the Memory of Mr. K. Okakura," *Modern Review*, 20.5:541–542 (November 1916).

76. *Tōkyō asahi shimbun* (Sept. 2, 1916).

77. *Ibid.*

78. Thākur, *Jāpān-yātrī*, p. 114.

79. *Ibid.*, p. 115.

80. *Ibid.*, pp. 115–116.

81. *Ibid.*, p. 116.

82. Tagore, *Nationalism*, p. 53.

83. Kalidas Nag, "Tagore in Far Eastern Press," in Kalidas Nag, ed., *Tagore and China* (Calcutta, 1945), p. 45, quoting from a Peking newspaper account of Tagore's address to the Anglo-American Association on April 25, 1924.

84. "Tagore and His Critics," *Japan Weekly Chronicle* (Aug. 17, 1916).

85. L. B. Cholmondeley, "Rabindranath Tagore in Japan," *The East and the West*, 15.1:28 (London, January 1917). The article is dated Tokyo, Sept. 1, 1916.

86. Interview with Mukul Dey; "The Wild Reporter," *Japan Chronicle* (Sept. 29, 1921). My research assistant, Hagihara Nobutoshi, could find no reference to Tagore in *Tōkyō asahi shimbun* for January or February 1917. In all probability, Tagore paused about three weeks in Yokohama before

taking the train for Kobe to embark for India. He left San Francisco on January 21, 1917, and arrived in Calcutta 55 days later, on March 17. He would have spent at least 10 days on the Pacific, and 26 days between Kobe and Calcutta, if his ship followed the same schedule as the *Tosa Maru*.

87. *New York Times* (Feb. 28, 1918).

88. See Stephen N. Hay, "Rabindranath Tagore in America," *American Quarterly*, 14.3:45–53 (Fall 1962).

89. Sukumar Bhattacharya, "Lord Carmichael in Bengal. Proposal for his Recall," *Bengal Past and Present*, 79:69–70 (July–December 1960). The Government of India sent a telegram to the Tokyo Embassy to warn them about the Tagore party, particularly C. F. Andrews, terming him a "sentimental agitator."

Chapter Three. Japanese Views of Tagore's Message

Epigraph. Natsume Sōseki, "Gendai Nihon no bunka" (Contemporary Japanese culture), in *Natsume Sōseki zenshū* (Collected works of Natsume Sōseki; Tokyo, 1954), IV, 329–332.

1. *Sources of the Japanese Tradition*, p. 644. This excellent anthology also contains the text of Prince Shōtoku's seventeen-article constitution of 604, which embodies Buddhist and Confucian ideas.

2. Fukuzawa Yukichi, editorial in *Jiji shimpō*, reprinted in *Zoku Fukuzawa zenshū* (Continuation of Fukuzawa's works; Tokyo, 1933), I, 742–749, as translated in Robert S. Schwantes, "Christianity *versus* Science: A Conflict of Ideas in Meiji Japan," *Far Eastern Quarterly* 12.2:128 (February 1953).

3. Yoshikazu Kataoka, "Introduction," *Introduction to Contemporary Japanese Literature*, ed. Kokusai Bunka Shinkōkai (Tokyo, 1939), p. xvi.

4. Sobu Rokurō et al., tr., *Tagōru kessaku zenshū* (A complete collection of Tagore's masterpieces), 4th ed. (Tokyo, 1915); announcement in advertisement section of *Chūō kōron* (Central review; March 1915), p. 1; Sobu Rokurō, *Tagōru hyōden* (A critical biography of Tagore; Tokyo, 1915); Yoshida Genjirō, *Tagōru seija no seikatsu* (The life of the sage Tagore; Tokyo, 1915); Nakazawa Rinsen, *Tagōru to sei no jitsugen* (Tagore and the realization of life; Tokyo, 1915); Ebu Ōson, *Tagōru no shisō to shūkyō* (Tagore's thought and religion; Tokyo, 1915).

5. Kiyozawa, item 9.

6. *Ibid.*, pp. 291–292.

7. *Ibid.*, item 15.

8. I have mislaid the exact source of this quotation, which may have been in one of the 1915 issues of the *Nichi-In kyōkai kaihō*.

9. Kiyozawa, p. 6.

10. *Ibid.*, items 3, 5.

11. *Ibid.*, pp. 313, 317.

12. Forty-five comments were published in an article, "Tagōru no inshō to kansō" (Impressions of and reflections about Tagore), *Rikugō zasshi*, 36.7:90–115 (July 1916); and seven separate articles (cited individually

below) commenting on Tagore's ideas appeared in the same issue. Eighteen comments by free-lance writers and translators were published in "Ika ni Tagōru o miru ka" (How shall we regard Tagore?), *Shin chō*, 25.1:2–11 (July 1916). Nine comments were published in "Tagōru shi Teidai no kōen ni taisuru kansō" (Reflections on Mr. Tagore's lecture at Tokyo Imperial University), *Shin jin* (New man), 7.7:47–51 (July 1916); and two longer articles on the same subject appeared in this same issue. Various other periodicals carried separate articles (cited below) on Tagore's message in July 1916 and subsequent months.

13. Yone Noguchi, *The Spirit of Japanese Art* (London, 1915), p. 105. For Noguchi's admiration for English civilization, see *The Story of Yone Noguchi, Told by Himself* (Philadelphia, c. 1914), pp. 119 ff. Identifying with Japanese traditions was a personal problem for Noguchi as much as an artistic one, for during his eleven years in the United States and England he had married a Los Angeles girl and when he returned to Japan in 1904 he had her join him. Some of their feelings are suggested in *ibid.*, pp. 185 ff.

14. Noguchi Yonejirō, "Tagōru shi to kataru" (A talk with Tagore), *Bunshō sekai* (Literary world; July 1916), p. 205.

15. Yone Noguchi, "Tagore in Japan," *Modern Review*, 20.5:528–529 (November 1916).

16. Noguchi wrote a Whitmanesque poem in English praising Tagore in the weekly magazine *Far East* (Tokyo), 9.13:352 (June 24, 1916). A picture of Noguchi escorting Tagore through the Tokyo Central Station appears in *ibid.*, 9.3:298 (June 10, 1916).

17. Akita Ujaku, "Sanjō no Tagōru" (On top of the hill with Tagore), *Waseda bungaku* (July 1916).

18. Yoshida Genjirō, *Rikugō zasshi*, 36.2:108 (August 1916). Less impressed was Tanizaki Seiji, the younger brother of the famous novelist Tanizaki Junichirō. Tanizaki had also majored in English at Waseda, and later became professor and dean of his department. Asked for his comment, he wrote that he respected Tagore as "a clear and bright person," but preferred the painful sensitivity of a Leonardo da Vinci to "the holy man who [thinks he] can understand everything." (*Shin chō*, July 1916, p. 8.)

19. *Rikugō zasshi* (July 1916), pp. 101–102.

20. *Ibid.*, p. 94.

21. Edwin McClellan, "An Introduction to Sōseki," *Harvard Journal of Asiatic Studies* 22:152–162 (1959); *Story of Yone Noguchi*, pp. 128–129.

22. *Shin chō* (July 1916), p. 10.

23. Tatsuo Arima, *The Failure of Freedom: A Portrait of Modern Japanese Intellectuals* (Cambridge, Mass., 1969). Arima devotes one chapter to Arishima Takeo and another to the Shirakaba school, both mentioned below.

24. *Shin chō* (July 1916), p. 3. Another well-known but less important novelist of the period, Morita Sōhei, reacted in an identical manner to Tagore's visit. Considered a disciple of Sōseki and a member of the Haikai (or haiku: seventeen-syllable verse) school which stressed detachment and aes-

thetic pleasure in reaction to the harsh delineation of life in naturalistic writings, Morita had created a sensation in 1908 by recounting in his first novel the story of his attempted double suicide. Like Arishima, he had not read Tagore's works, regretted that the poet's reception in Japan had become "a pageant," and concluded: "I must wait with Tagore until this bad time passes; may it pass as soon as possible." (*Ibid.*, p. 10.)

25. Arishima was also a founder and member of this school.

26. *Ibid.*, p. 2.

27. *Ibid.*

28. Another admirer of Tolstoy and a much deeper student of Russian culture than Mushakōji was Noboru Shomu (b. 1878), a graduate of the Russian Orthodox Seminary in Tokyo in 1903, and subsequently a teacher of Russian there and at the Military Staff College. Noboru translated Tolstoy, Dostoevsky, and Kuprin from Russian into Japanese and wrote several histories of Russian literature. Like Arishima and Mushakōji, Noboru deplored the superficial and enthusiastic way Tagore was welcomed in Japan, and contrasted it to the lack of attention given the Russian poet Balmont on his recent visit. Of course Tagore had received the Nobel Prize and Balmont had not; Tagore was an Oriental and Balmont was not; Tagore was (so Noboru thought) a Buddhist, and Balmont was not. "But all these reasons are accidental and secondary ones. I think it is not the right way to welcome the great writers and poets of the world," he complained. Nevertheless, he professed to "respect deeply Tagore's thought and life, which are at one with nature, like the pious and humble attitude of the holy men of ancient times." In a second, separately published comment, Noboru praised Tagore as "the Tolstoy of India." (*Ibid.*, pp. 10–11; *Rikugō zasshi*, July 1916, p. 90.)

29. *Ibid.*, pp. 98, 98–99. Two other writers known as leaders of the naturalist movement in the 1905–1910 period commented on Tagore's lecture, one favorably and the other critically. Hasegawa Seiya, who by 1916 was mainly occupied as a publisher, wrote appreciatively: "Since saints and gentlemen are gradually becoming rarer these days, I think Mr. Tagore's visit has been [clarifying in its effect,] like throwing alum into muddy water." Possibly Hasegawa's sympathy was due to his familiarity with English literature, in which he had majored and which he had taught for a while at Waseda University. The other writer, Sōma Gyofū, also a graduate of Waseda's English literature department and also a publisher, had become interested in writing and publishing *waka* poetry. He commented caustically: "Somehow Tagore has come to Japan. I am reading articles about him in the daily papers. I picture to myself how all Tokyo is crowding around him. I wonder how that hermit can stand it in the midst of such a crowd. As for me, I cannot understand his way of living." (*Ibid.*, p. 96; *Shin chō*, July 1916, p. 5.)

30. Shūichi Katō, "Japanese Writers and Modernization," in Marius B. Jansen, ed., *Changing Japanese Attitudes toward Modernization* (Princeton, 1965), asserts (p. 427) that no events between 1867 and 1945 exerted a

greater influence on the Japanese intellectual world than the Russo-Japanese war and this incident, and (p. 430) that the executions "deepened the gap between the ruling political power and the politically conscious intellectuals."

31. *Shin chō* (July 1916), p. 5. Ogawa, an ex-Christian, had graduated from Waseda University at a time when it was considered a stronghold of naturalism. In 1916 he was best known as Japan's foremost writer of children's stories.

32. *Ibid.*, pp. 5, 7, 5; *Rikugō zasshi* (July 1916), p. 92.

33. [Kawahigashi] Hekigotō, "Tagōru no inshō" (Impressions of Tagore), *Nippon oyobi Nipponjin*, No. 685:135 (July 15, 1916). Kawahigashi was a pupil of Masaoka Shiki (d. 1902), founder of the movement to revive haiku, who also encouraged Sōseki to write in this traditional verse form.

34. Iwano Hōmei, "Nihon kodai shisō yori kindai no hyōshōshugi o ronzu" (Modern symbolism in the light of ancient Japanese thought); this passage is given as translated in *Japanese Literature in the Meiji Era*, comp. and ed. Yoshie Okazaki, tr. V. H. Viglielmo (Tokyo, 1955), p. 631. For an interesting and sympathetic appraisal of Hōmei see Yone Noguchi, *Spirit of Japanese Poetry* (New York, 1914), pp. 106–110.

35. As quoted in English translation in *Japan Magazine*, 7.6:368 (October 1916).

36. *Shin chō* (July 1916), p. 8.

37. *Rikugō zasshi* (July 1916), pp. 98, 111; Takeda Toyoshirō, "Tagōru ou ni taisuru kansō" (Impressions on seeing Dr. Tagore), *Waseko bungaku* (July 1916), pp. 295–296. Shimaji's life and work are summarized in Bruno Petzold, "Daito Shimaji (1875–1927): An Obituary," *Young East*, 3.4:105–124 (Sept. 8, 1927).

38. *Rikugō zasshi* (July 1916), pp. 110, 90. Itō named his community Muga-ai (Unselfish love).

39. Takakusu Junjirō, "Yo ga mitaru Tagōru," *Rikugō zasshi* (July 1916), pp. 29–33.

40. Masaharu Anesaki, "An Oriental Evaluation of Modern Civilization," in *Recent Gains in American Civilization, By a Group of Distinguished Critics of Contemporary Life*, ed. Kirby Page (New York, 1928), p. 356.

41. *Ibid.*

42. In his inaugural address at Harvard (delivered only months after Tagore's lectures there in February 1913), Anesaki announced that his task there would be "to persuade you, as students of man, of his life and mind, to study the Buddhico-Oriental culture," and went on to quote Okakura Kakuzō to support his claim that "Japanese civilization is a repository of all the elements of Oriental culture." Masaharu Anesaki, *The Professorship of Japanese Literature and Life at Harvard University: Its Scope and Work* (Cambridge, Mass., 1913), pp. 9, 10. A third Tokyo University scholar of Buddhism, Kimura Taiken, appointed lecturer in 1913, was also asked his opinion of Tagore. Like Takakusu and Anesaki, he did not commit himself one way or the other in his discussion of the Indian poet's ideas, asking only that his

countrymen study them systematically, neither overvaluing or undervaluing them. (Kimura Taiken, "Indo shisō to Tagōru" [Indian thought and Tagore], *Rikugō zasshi*, July 1916, p. 62.) If the neutral comments of Takakusu, Anesaki, and Kimura were actually written before Rabindranath's arrival in Japan (and this is a distinct possibility, since all three were published as articles in the special Tagore issue of the *Rikugō zasshi*), their noncommittal tone can be more readily explained, and these comments may be omitted from the tabulation of Japanese responses to Rabindranath's message. If the articles were in fact written before he spoke, then the complete silence of the three men after he had delivered his message would seem a damning, not with faint praise, but with no praise.

43. *Rikugō zasshi* (July 1916), p. 94.

44. Masaharu Anesaki, *History of Japanese Religion* (London, 1930), p. 400n, explains that this name was "derived from the Buddhist legend, that among thousands of lanterns dedicated to Buddha the one lantern brought by a poor woman outshone all others," an interesting parallel with Jesus' parable of the widow's mite.

45. *Rikugō zasshi* (July 1916), p. 112. Two teachers at Ōtani University, maintained by the Shinshū sect, commented on Tagore's visit. Ebu Ōson, the author of many books on Buddhism, satirized Iwano Hōmei's inability to grasp the real power in the thought of Tagore, and of India generally, comparing Hōmei to the child who reaches for the moon's reflection in the water thinking that it was the moon itself. Ōsumi Shun, however, avoided controversy entirely by praising Tagore's voice (which he had heard at Osaka) as "exactly like unforgettable music." (*Ibid.*, p. 98; *Shin chō*, July 1916, p. 8.)

46. See Charles R. Boxer, *The Christian Century in Japan, 1549–1650* (Berkeley, 1951).

47. This tendency is noted in Kyoson Tsuchida, *Contemporary Thought of Japan and China* (London, 1927), p. 19: "Japanese Christians who have any advanced views are now holding [molding] it in such a way as to Japanize it, *i.e.*, to vary it more or less in the direction of the Buddhistic style which has been Japan's manner of life through the long ages."

48. *Shin jin* (July 1916), p. 49. *Rikugō zasshi* had been one of Japan's most influential journals in the 1880's, but by 1916 its circulation had fallen to a mere 2000. (*The Christian Movement in the Japanese Empire*, ed. Edwin Taylor Inglehart [Tokyo, 1917], p. 127.) Uchigasaki had welcomed Tagore and Indian culture in the special issue of *Rikugō zasshi* for May 1915, and in his June 1916 issue (p. 155) had expressed his great hopes for the influence Tagore would exert on Japan.

49. Ukita Kazutami, "Tō zai bummei no daihyōsha, hikōka Sumisu to shisei Tagōru" (Leading representatives of Eastern and Western civilizations: The aviator Smith and the poet-sage Tagore), *Taiyō*, 22.19:12 (July 1, 1916).

50. This was not equally true for all Japanese Unitarians, however, for Kishimoto Nobuta, a graduate of Doshisha and of Harvard Divinity School,

who in 1916 was teaching philosophy and ethics at Waseda University (where Uchigasaki and Ukita were also on the faculty), felt that Tagore's outlook was "too Oriental . . . subjective, and pantheistic, and therefore is rather simple." He did agree with Rabindranath that the objective and active qualities in Western civilization should be synthesized with the subjective and meditative qualities of Eastern civilization, but asserted that Japan, rather than India, was best fitted to create this synthesis: "Being Oriental, and at the same time objective, is it not our Japanese national mission to harmonise the East and the West?" he wrote. (*Rikugō zasshi*, July 1916, p. 90.)

51. Ebina's formative years are analyzed in Fred Notehelfer, "Ebina Danjō: A Christian Samurai of the Meiji Period," *Papers on Japan*, 2:13–36 (Harvard University, East Asian Research Center, 1963). For discussions of Ebina's theological position, see Hideo Kishimoto, comp., *Japanese Religion in the Meiji Era*, ed. and tr. John F. Howes (Tokyo, 1956), pp. 273–276; and Charles W. Inglehart, *A Century of Protestant Christianity in Japan* (Rutland, Vt. and Tokyo, 1959), pp. 111–112, 251.

52. Ebina Danjō, "Shijin Tagōru no bummei hihyō o yomu" (On reading the poet Tagore's criticism of civilization), *Shin jin* (July 1916), pp. 20, 23–25.

53. Further examples of this tendency are two minor Christian intellectuals, perhaps followers of Ebina, who expressed themselves in terms similar to his in the pages of the July 1916 *Shin jin*), the monthly Ebina had founded and edited. Tominaga Tokuma wrote (*ibid.*, p. 50): "I regret that Tagore's ideas are too crude for modern thought, for he touches so seldom on the problems which the men of today want to try to solve. . . . I wanted him to say clearly that it is a fundamental fact that the Japanese have accepted Western civilization and made it their own. . . . But personally I do not need to distinguish between East and West. I think that if both Occidentals and Orientals seek the way of humanity and contribute to it, this will be enough." And Ojima Shinji (*ibid.*, pp. 50–51) berated the Indian poet because "he roundly condemns the materialistic civilization which appears in politics, science, technology and war, and he more or less ignores the spiritual civilization which appears in religion, morality, and the arts. As a man from the ruined country of India, he has a mind which resists Europe and America. So there is a plaintive note in his voice, and he cannot avoid being somewhat prejudiced." Ojima concluded with a jibe and an exhortation: "He is indeed a skillful poet; I wish he were also a skillful thinker. Look at the living Christ in order to be a fair critic of Western civilization. True progress and the true life do not depend only on meditation in the forest."

54. *Ibid.*, pp. 49–50.

55. McClellan, p. 153.

56. It was no coincidence that thirty years later, after the defeat of Japanese militarism, the two writers whose works were most in demand in Japan were Natsume Sōseki and Abe Jirō. (Donald Keene, "Literary and Intellectual Currents in Postwar Japan and Their International Implications," in Hugh

Borton *et al., Japan between East and West* [New York, 1957], pp. 156–157.)

57. *Rikugō zasshi* (July 1916), p. 96.

58. *Ibid.*, p. 110.

59. Gino K. Piovesana, S.J., *Recent Japanese Philosophical Thought, 1862–1962: A Survey* (Tokyo, 1963), p. 50. Von Koeber's advanced age (he was 68 in 1916) must also have impressed his Japanese students. Von Koeber was teaching the following courses at Tokyo University in 1913: Introduction to Philosophy, Kant, History of Christianity, Schopenhauer, Lessing's *Nathan der Weise,* and readings in Homer, Aeschylus, Virgil, and Ovid. (Tsunezo Kishiname, *The Development of Philosophy in Japan* [Princeton, 1915], pp. 22–23.)

60. *Sei Tagōru,* p. 75. The anonymous compilers of the volume (and Kaneko may well have been one of them) arrived at an identical conclusion in their closing essay: "He will never create a new philosophy; he is a poet." (*Ibid.*, p. 339.) The title of this volume, and the fact that none of the eleven essays (all appreciative) made any reference to Tagore's lectures in Japan — even though translations of all three were included, together with a detailed itinerary of the first two weeks of his visit — suggest that most if not all of the essays were ready for the press before the poet arrived.

61. *Rikugō zasshi* (July 1916), p. 92.

62. Tsuchida, p. 73.

63. Compare the similar confluence of German idealism and Chinese Neo-Confucianism in the writings of the Chinese philosopher and sometime-politician, Chang Chün-mai, mentioned in Chapters Four, Five, and Six below. Chang studied in Japan, at Waseda University, in the years before 1914, and could have been influenced by Inoue's writings.

64. Interview with Maruyama Masao (Bermuda, Jan. 26, 1962).

65. Inoue Tetsujirō, "Tagōru no kōen ni tsuite" (Concerning Tagore's lecture), *Rikugō zasshi* (July 1916), p. 27.

66. *Shin jin* (July 1916), pp. 48–49. Inoue's senior colleagues on the Textbook Investigation Council, and his predecessor as president of the Imperial Education Society, Sawayanagi Masatarō, probably shared these views, but contented himself with remarking, "there are many points in his lecture at the university with which I cannot agree." (*Rikugō zasshi,* July 1916, p. 91.) Sawayanagi had been president of both Tohoku and Kyoto Imperial universities before his retirement, and was known as a supporter of the autonomy of universities from government control.

67. Tsuchida, p. 69.

68. *Rikugō zasshi* (July 1916), p. 91.

69. Yoshino Sakuzō, "Kensei no hongi o toite sono yūshū no bi o motarasu no michi o ronzu," *Chūō kōron,* 31.1:17–125 (January 1916). For a translation of most of the article see *Sources of the Japanese Tradition,* pp. 725–746.

70. *Shin jin* (July 1916), p. 51.

71. The fact that Yoshino was a Christian may be related to his strong preference for democratic government of the Anglo-American kind.

72. Tsuchida, pp. 155, 158. The quotations are taken from Tsuchida's summary of Tanaka's views.

73. Tanaka Ōdō, "Tagōru shi ni ataete shi no Nihon kan o ronzu" (I discuss Mr. Tagore's views of Japan), *Chūō kōron*, 31.9:32, 36 (September 1916).

74. Tanaka Ōdō, "Tagōru wa kita so shite satta," *Shin kōron* (New opinion), 31.10:14 (October 1916).

75. *Ibid.*, pp. 14, 16–17.

76. Tanimoto Tomi, "Tagōru wa shijin no mi Indojin no mi" (Tagore as a poet and as an Indian), *Rikugō zasshi* 36.7:36–37 (July 1916).

77. Tanimoto Tomi, "Tagōru no betsuji" (Tagore's parting words), *Rikugō zasshi*, 36.10:38–40 (October 1916).

78. *Ibid.*, p. 40.

79. Quoted as translated in Yoshi S. Kuno, *Japanese Expansion on the Asiatic Continent* (Berkeley, 1937–1940), I, 320.

80. Marius B. Jansen, *The Japanese and Sun Yat-sen* (Cambridge, Mass., 1954); Hugh Byas, *Government by Assassination* (New York, 1942), pp. 188–189. Bose managed to escape from India by boarding a ship in Calcutta and posing as Raja P. N. Tagore, a distant relative of the poet. After the danger of extradition had passed, Tōyama arranged Bose's marriage to the daughter of a follower of his, a baker, and Bose spent the rest of his life in Tokyo as a restaurateur in Shinjuku. (Radhanath Rath and Sabitra Prasanna Chatterjee, eds., *Rash Behari Basu: His Struggle for India's Independence* [Calcutta, 1963], pp. xxxiv, 39, 27 ff.).

81. "Great Asianism: Its Meaning," *New East*, 1.3:98 (August 1917).

82. "A Japanese Appreciation of Sir Rabindranath Tagore," *Modern Review*, 20.3:343 (September 1916), citing *Herald of Asia*.

83. Zumoto revived the *Herald of Asia* in 1931 as the title of a series of pamphlets defending Japan's occupation of Manchuria.

84. Soejima Yasoroku, "Indo no gendai oyobi shōrai," (The present and future of India), *Chūō kōron*, 31.8:137–138 (July 1916).

85. "Tōzai namboku" (East, West, South, North), *Nippon oyobi Nipponjin* No. 681:6 (May 15, 1916); "Tagōru o mukau" (Tagore has come), *ibid.*, No. 682: 80 (June 1, 1916).

86. Ōsumi Chōfū, "Tagōru to bonkyōkai" (Tagore and the Brāhmo Samāj), *ibid.*, No. 683:101 (June 15, 1916).

87. *Ibid.*, No. 688:6 (Sept. 15, 1916).

88. *Rikugō zasshi* (July 1916), p. 94. In 1915 Mitsui had castigated Tagore's thought as "an escape from reality."

89. *Ibid.*, pp. 97–98.

90. *Ibid.*, p. 93. Nagai had studied in England and the United States from 1906 to 1909, and was for a time editor of the nationalist periodical *Shin Nippon* (New Japan).

91. *Rikugō zasshi* (July 1916), p. 112; *Shin jin* (July 1916), p. 49. The Japanese phrase Kanokogi uses for "beautiful flower of a lost country" is a

mellifluous one: "Horobiru kuniri no uruwashiki hana." Kanokogi had graduated in 1904 from the Japanese Naval Engineering School, served in the Russo-Japanese War, resigned his commission, and then studied philosophy in the United States and Europe, where he married a Miss Cornelia. In later life he became an exponent of Japanocentric pan-Asianism, wrote a book on "the philosophy of the Japanese spirit," and was sent to China to "re-educate" the Chinese during World War II. He ended his days in Japan during the American occupation restricted to his home as a Class A war criminal.

92. These nine were Yoshida, Iwano, Ojima, Sugiura, Inoue, Tanaka, Nagai, one Arikawa Jisuke (who did not attain sufficient distinction to be mentioned in a Japanese biographical dictionary), and Kayahara Kazan. Kayahara was a famous writer on political, social, and philosophical problems. He had been a journalist for twenty years, six of which were spent in the United States, Europe, North Africa, China, and Korea. His article, "It is Great Britain and America which Lead to the Suicide of the Japanese People," *Far East*, 8.185:68–69 (Oct. 9, 1915) and 8.186:93–94 (Oct. 16, 1915), which advocated joining Germany's side in the war and carving out a new empire in Australia and New Zealand, created a considerable stir. On the night that Tagore arrived in Tokyo, the American aviator Art Smith performed a daring night flight over Tokyo; Kayahara went to see Smith rather than Tagore, and summarized his preference between the two saying: "Tagore is the symbol of the ruined country, India, . . . just as Smith is the symbol of the principles of science . . . and the material side of life. . . . Count Ōkuma talks glibly about the harmony that exists between Eastern and Western civilizations, but how can Tagore and Smith be harmonized?" (*Shin chō*, July 1916, p. 8.)

93. *Rikugō zasshi* (July 1916), p. 109. Hirasawa was deeply moved when he saw Tagore in the Tokyo University auditorium: "A saint stood in a great, wide cathedral and my heart went out to him."

94. "Notes," *Modern Review*, 20.2:232 (August 1916). The letter is presented here after the opening words: " 'A Japanese' writes to a paper published in Japan."

95. *Rikugō zasshi* (July 1916), p. 91.

96. In view of the large number of intellectuals who commented on Tagore's message in 1916, only the more important ones in the fields of literature, religion, and philosophy have been quoted here, with the addition of comments on India or pan-Asianism. The remaining comments repeat the points made by the more distinguished intellectuals, with about the same proportion of favorable, neutral, and negative views expressed. One article worth special notice is Takao, "Tagōru ou o omou." Takao was a student of philosophy at Waseda at the time, and was so keenly interested in Tagore that he went to see him five times during his stay in Japan. He seems to have approved of Tagore's idealist philosophy, for he told him at one of their interviews: "In order to meet the needs of modern Japan, young thinkers want to proceed from the enjoyment of materialism and naturalism to enjoying the

spiritual side of life, as Bergson, Eucken, and you have done." Takao's article is interesting because of his analysis of Rabindranath's failure to impress the Japanese. One factor was language: "In the beginning Tagore had great hope and respect for Japan, but gradually became disillusioned, not because of his personal experiences in Japan, but because of the English language." Not only did his ignorance of Japanese limit his contacts with Japan's intellectuals, but the committee set up to welcome him, Takao believed, was controlled by the British, who were reported to have told officials of the Japanese government that Tagore was "a dangerous man." When Takao asked a member of the Hara household, whose guest the poet was in Yokohama, whether this was true, he was told only that "many foreign visitors come to see him, but not many Japanese." All of this incidental intelligence led Takao to conclude: "Japanese critics could not study Tagore very closely, so that the studies of and criticisms of him are based only on his works — which are rather small in number and do not express his ideas very well — and on some impressions based on his appearances at public meetings. This attitude is insincere and irresponsible, and these studies are not done in good faith."

97. Leo Tolstoy, *Anna Karenina*, tr. Constance Garnett (New York, 1939), I, 10.

98. *Tōkyō asahi shimbun* (June 13, 1916); *ibid.* (July 3, 1916).

99. "Tagore," *Japan Magazine*, 7.4:250–251 (August 1916), citing an editorial of unspecified date in *Yorozu chōhō* (Universal news).

100. For example, the war then going on between England and Germany, the two countries from which modern Japan had absorbed the most, produced a heightening of this tension, which was to abate with the victory of the Allies but reappear in the 1930's with the rise of Fascism and Nazism.

Chapter Four. Western Encouragement for "The Message of the East"

Epigraph. Paul Richard, "Creators of New Asia," *Asian Review*, 1.2:172 (1920).

1. See Hay, "Tagore in America." Rabindranath used the phrase "the message of the East" during the interview he gave to Gertrude Stevenson, published in the Boston *Journal* (Dec. 2, 1916).

2. *Yale Daily News* (Dec. 7, 1916).

3. Letter from Tagore to Rothenstein (July 6, 1917).

4. Tagore to Rothenstein (June 1, 1918).

5. See Hay, "Tagore in America," pp. 450–452.

6. Kripalani, p. 263, quoting Tagore's letter to Pearson of February 28, 1918. Pearson had stayed on in Japan after their 1916 visit there, then visited China. He was arrested there for allegedly anti-British activities, repatriated to England, and there met Tagore at the dockside when the latter arrived from India in June 1920.

7. Kripalani, p. 270, writes: "The period, 1917–1919, hectic with political and educational activities, was comparatively sterile in new literary creations."

8. Rolland, *Inde*, pp. 48–49, under the heading "27 janvier 1924 — Visite de Paul Richard et de son fils."

9. Ṭhākur, *Chiṭhipatra*, II, 55–56.

10. Paul Richard, *To the Nations: From the French of Paul Richard, with an Introduction by Rabindranath Tagore*, tr. Aurobindo Ghose, 2nd ed. (Madras, 1921), pp. 56, 80, xv–xvi. Tagore wrote this introduction on January 17, 1917, just before he sailed homeward from San Francisco.

11. See Mukhopādhyāy̆, *Rabīndrajībankathā*, pp. 142–143.

12. Rabindranath Tagore, *The Centre of Indian Culture* (Calcutta, 1951), pp. 28, 26, 15, 34, 33.

13. *Ibid.*, p. 31.

14. Rolland to Tagore (Apr. 10, 1919), in *Rolland and Tagore*, pp. 19–20. Rolland's original French letters, and French translations of Tagore's replies, are in *Rabindranath Tagore et Romain Rolland: Lettres et autres écrits*, ed. Madeleine Rolland (Paris, 1961). Rolland had earlier expressed this same sentiment in his reply of March 18, 1917, to a letter from the young Bengali writer Amiya Chakravarty (later Tagore's secretary): "Je sense, depuis quelques années, le besoin urgent de rapprocher l'esprit de l'Europe de celui de l'Asie. Ni l'un ni l'autre ne se suffit, à soi seul. Ce sont les deux hémisphères de la pensée. Il faut les réunir. Que ce soit la grande mission de l'age qui va venir! Si j'étais plus jeune, je m'y vouerais tout entier. Je me contente de la joie de goûter par avance la plénitude de la civilisation future, qui réalisera l'union des deux moitiés de l'âme humaine. J'admire votre Rabindra Nath Tagore, parce que je sense un peu en lui déjà vibrer cette harmonie." (*Sabuj patra* (Green leaf), 4.6–7:421, Aśvin-Kārtik, B.E. 1324 [September–November 1917].) Rolland's closing sentence evinces the same thirst for the wisdom of India as Schopenhauer, Bunsen, and other Europeans felt a century earlier: "Puissent mes yeux un jour boire (comme mon esprit) cette lumière de l'Inde, que je vois à travers vos lignes, lorsque vous décrivez la nature qui vous entoure."

15. *Rolland and Tagore*, pp. 25–26. I have made one correction in this translation, based on the French original in *Rabindranath Tagore et Romain Rolland*, pp. 27–28.

16. *Ibid.*, p. 30.

17. Martin Buber, comp., *Reden und Gleichnisse des Tschuang-tse* 4th ed. (Leipzig, 1921) p. 82. Buber later repudiated the ideas he expressed in this work.

18. Alex Aronson, *Rabindranath through Western Eyes* (Allahabad, 1943), p. 13 (emphasis mine). Aronson's work is based on the press clippings on file at Rabindra Sadan, Santiniketan.

19. Rathindranath Tagore, *Edges of Time*, p. 127.

20. Kripalani, p. 269, notes that the ostensible purpose of the trip was to obtain for Visva-Bharati both publicity and material support, "but the necessity was welcome because of an inner and personal need." "Tagore now had

an additional incentive or excuse to travel. He needed it. He was restless. The world's adulation was like an intoxicant; he wanted more of it."

21. Aronson, *Western Eyes,* p. 54, says: "In May 1921 Rabindranath's birthday was celebrated all over Europe," but goes on to point out that in France this was less true than in Germany; and Rolland, *Inde,* p. 23, writes that his anniversary "passes unnoticed in France."

22. Aronson, p. 66, translating a passage in Hermann Keyserling, ed., *Der Weg zur Vollendung,* Vol. 2 (Darmstadt, 1921).

23. Tagore to C. F. Andrews, from Berlin (May 28, 1921), in Tagore, *Letters to a Friend,* p. 171.

24. Tagore to Andrews (July 6, 1921), from SS. *Morea,* in *ibid.,* p. 176. Rathindranath Tagore, *Edges of Time,* p. 126, confirms this personal worship by Europeans: "In central and northern Europe, the people simply worshipped the ground he trod upon. In crowded meetings and railway stations we got used to the sight of people jostling each other to approach Father in order to touch the hem of his robe." In a lecture in Karachi some months later Rabindranath declared: "When I went to the Continent last with this message [that nationalism is equal to cannibalism], I was received in a manner you would consider incredible. For fear of being charged with vanity, both personal and national, I did not send any accounts of the receptions. In me they saw once more the Wisdom of the East and welcomed my doctrine and my preaching." (Tagore, "The Prophet's Voice," *Sind Observer,* Karachi, Mar. 22, 1923.)

25. Tagore, *Letters to a Friend,* pp. 124, 128, 134, 169.

26. Rabindranath Tagore, *Creative Unity* (London, 1922), pp. 174, 175. This evolution in Rabindranath's conception of his university seems to have taken place not long after his arrival in Europe. On December 17 he wrote from New York to Andrews: "When I left you I was labouring under the delusion that my mission was to build an Indian University in which Indian cultures would be represented in all their variety. But when I came to the continental Europe and fully realised that I had been accepted by the Western people as one of themselves I realised that my mission was the mission of the present age. It was to make the meeting of the East and West fruitful in truth." This portion of the letter is omitted from Tagore, *Letters to a Friend,* pp. 105–107, but is quoted in *Modern Review* 30.12:647 (December 1921).

27. Rolland to Tagore (Apr. 22, 1921) from Paris, in *Rolland and Tagore,* p. 28; Rolland, *Inde,* p. 18, entry for April 19, 1921. The original reads: "Malgré sa charmante politesse, on voit qu'il est parfaitement convaincu de la supériorité morale et intellectuelle de l'Asie — surtout de l'Inde — sur l'Europe." Rolland, *Inde,* p. 17, gives an interesting vignette of Rabindranath as he appeared on this day, at their first meeting. "He is in Hindu costume, with a high cap of black velvet, and a long, beige-colored robe. He is very handsome — almost too handsome — tall, a fine regular figure, pure Aryan, but of that warm skin-color which brings golden sunlight to life, luminous

brown eyes, in the shadow of beautiful eyelashes, a straight nose, a mouth smiling under a white moustache, a silky beard with three points, the middle one still black between the two other white ones. His whole countenance beams with an abundant and tranquil joy, which translates itself in all that he says." Of the inner man he remarked some days later (*Inde*, p. 23): "Beneath the harmonious calm which I immediately perceived, there are also sadnesses held in check, a view of men unobstructed by illusions, and a virile intelligence which firmly stands up to all battles — even though his soul makes it a rule never to let itself be troubled."

28. Tagore, *Letters to a Friend*, pp. 123, 132 (Mar. 5, 1921, from Chicago), 180–181 (July 9, from SS. *Morea*).

29. *Ibid.*, p. 185 (July 13, from SS. *Morea*).

30. Tagore to Andrews, in Rabindranath Tagore, *Letters from Abroad* (all to C. F. Andrews; Madras, 1924), p. 132. This phrase is omitted from the text later included in Tagore, *Letters to a Friend*, p. 171.

31. The gradual evolution of Tagore's educational ideals, based on his own writings in Bengali and English, is given in Himangshu Bhushan Mukherjee, *Education for Fullness: A Study of the Educational Thought and Experiment of Rabindranath Tagore* (Bombay and London, 1962). For the development of Visva-Bharati, see esp. pp. 87–98 and 185–203.

32. "Visva-Bharati," *Modern Review*, 31.1:124 (January 1922). This initial statement was soon modified, leaving out the ungrounded assertion that cultural currents had flowed into India from as far to the east as Japan, and emphasizing the need for "patient study and research" in order to bring together "the different cultures of the East on the basis of their underlying unity." The list of Eastern civilizations to be studied did not include Confucian, Taoist, or Shinto traditions; the terminology used in describing the Supreme Being as Shantam, Shivam, Advaitam indicates the central place of Hindu traditions in the thinking of Visva-Bharati's founder. ("Visva-Bharati. Founder-President: Rabindranath Tagore. Memorandum of Association," *Visva-Bharati Quarterly*, Vol. 1, No. 1, inside of back cover, April 1923, and subsequent issues.)

33. Rathindranath Tagore, *Edges of Time*, pp. 144, 146–147. For a biographical sketch of Lévi, and a bibliography of his writings to that date, see Kalidas Nag, "Sylvain Lévi and the Science of Indology," *Modern Review*, 30.6:670–676 (December 1921).

34. Sylvain Lévi, "Abel Bergaigne et l'Indianisme," *Revue politique et littéraire*, 40:269 (1890). Sylvain Lévi's life work of revealing what he called "Greater India" is surveyed in the presentation volume, *Memorial Sylvain Lévi*, ed. Louis Renou (Paris, 1937). See especially his statement of purposes in the contribution by Frederic Lefevre, "Une heure avec M. Sylvain Lévi," p. 421.

35. Sylvain Lévi, "Eastern Humanism: An Address Delivered in the University of Dacca on February 4th, 1922," in his *l'Inde et le monde* (Paris, 1928), pp. 174, 173.

36. See William W. Pearson, "From Kyoto to Peking," *Modern Review*, 31.1:41–44 (January 1922).

37. "Presidential Address of Mr. C. F. Andrews at the Bihari Students' Conference," *Modern Review*, 28.5:560 (November 1920).

38. Leonard Elmhirst, "Personal Memories of Tagore," in *Rabindranath Tagore: A Centenary Volume*, p. 13.

39. *Ibid.*, p. 17; letter to the author from Leonard K. Elmhirst (Oct. 21, 1968).

40. A masterful treatment of this period is Chow Tse-tsung, *The May Fourth Movement: Intellectual Revolution in Modern China* (Cambridge, Mass., 1960). Both the intellectual and political revolutions are summarized in John K. Fairbank, Edwin O. Reischauer, and Albert M. Craig, *East Asia: The Modern Transformation* (Boston, 1965), chap. 8. For an interesting comparison between those Chinese students who went to Japan and those who went to the United States and England, see Y. C. Wang, "Intellectuals and Society in China, 1860–1949," *Comparative Studies in Society and History*, 3.4:395–426 (July 1961).

41. (Ch'en) Tu-hsiu, "Ching-kao ch'ing-nien" (A respectful warning to our young people), *Hsin ch'ing-nien* (New youth), 1.1:4 (Sept. 15, 1915); Hu Shih, "Introduction," *The Development of the Logical Method in Ancient China* (Shanghai, 1922), p. 7. Surprisingly little research has been done on Ch'en's career. The commonly accepted statement, for instance, that Ch'en spent three years in France from 1907 to 1910 has never been substantiated.

42. Liang Ch'i-ch'ao, *Ou-yü hsin-ying lu chieh-lu* (Record of impressions of a European tour), in his *Yin-ping-shih ho-chi, chuan-chi* (Collected writings from the ice-drinker's studio, special collection) (Shanghai, 1936), Vol. 5, Pt. 2, p. 15, approximately as translated in Wen-han Kiang, *The Chinese Student Movement* (New York, 1948), p. 42.

43. Liang Ch'i-ch'ao, *Ou-yü hsin ying lu chieh-lu*, pp. 36, 37–38 (translation mine). For a major study of Liang's ideas, see Joseph R. Levenson, *Liang Ch'i-ch'ao and the Mind of Modern China* (Cambridge, Mass., 1953).

44. On the origins of the Chiang-hsüeh she, see Chow Tse-tung, pp. 192–193; also Richard Wilhelm, "Intellectual Movements in Modern China," *Chinese Social and Political Science Review*, 8.2:123 (April 1924). Liang's associate, Chang Chün-mai, informed one of its guest lecturers that its funds came from "wealthy Chinese scholars and bankers with assistance from the government." (Hans Driesch, *Lebenserrinerungen* [Basel, 1951], p. 167.)

45. Mukherjee, *Education for Fullness*, p. 201.

46. Bertrand Russell, *The Problem of China* (New York, 1922), pp. 14, 12. For details of Russell's visit to China, see Chow Tse-tung, pp. 192, 232–239. When Russell arrived in Peking, Liang delivered an address of welcome, as he later did when Tagore arrived. (Levenson, p. 191.) Russell later confessed — in view of China's history after his visit — that his assessment was wrong, and the more pessimistic one of his friend Joseph Conrad right. See his *Portraits from Memory* (New York, 1956), p. 90.

47. Russell, *The Problem of China*, pp. 208, 14, 215.

48. *Rudolf Eucken: His Life, Work, and Travels, by Himself*, tr. Joseph McCabe (London, 1921), p. 179; Hans A. E. Driesch and Margarete Driesch, *Fern-Ost, als Gäste Jungchinas* (Leipzig, 1925), p. 223; interview with Chiang Fu-ts'ung (the secretary of the Peking Lecture Association), Taipei, Apr. 8, 1955. Driesch was not the first German scholar to lecture in China. Count Hermann Keyserling had spoken at the International Institute of China in Shanghai in 1912 on "The East and the West and their Search for the Common Truth," later translated into Chinese and Japanese and first published in German in 1913. For the German text see Hermann Keyserling, *Philosophie als Kunst*, 2nd ed. (Darmstadt, 1922), pp. 101–127. Keyserling concluded his lecture with "the earnest hope that the new era in China — no matter how much it may seem to be an era of Westernization — may in truth signify a reawakening of the old, classical spirit."

49. Rudolf Eucken and Carsun Chang, *Das Lebensproblem in China und in Europa* (Leipzig, 1922). Chang's preface, p. v, reads: "The foundations of morality and custom have grown unstable in China as well. How far can the old be preserved, how far must European culture be accepted? This is the most important question for the Chinese intellectual world. I had the honor of discussing this problem often with Privy Councillor Eucken, whose philosophy is highly esteemed in East Asia. This incited him to outline an ethic within which the attempt would be made to synthesize European and Chinese culture. As a basis for this I would like most respectfully to submit for Privy Councillor Eucken's inspection the following essay setting forth the development of ethics in China."

50. It is interesting that Driesch's itinerary in China was much the same as Tagore's: in Peking he frequently visited the grounds of the Imperial Palace (although he did not meet the ex-emperor), and gave a lecture on Buddhist influence on German thought at a meeting at the Temple of the Origin of the Law (Fa yüan ssu). Driesch and Tagore visited the same provincial capitals in Central and North China, but neither went to Canton. (Driesch, *Fern-ost, passim.*) For Chang's address of welcome, emphasizing the need for a meeting of East and West, see *Ostasiatische Rundschau*, 4.2:19–20 (Hamburg, Feb. 15, 1923). Chang's farewell speech on June 15, 1923 (at the Navy Club in Peking, with Liang Ch'i-ch'ao as the chief host), is mentioned in Driesch, *Fern-ost*, p. 223; and Driesch's reply, "Die Einheit von Westen und Osten," is in *ibid.*, pp. 301–307. After his return to Germany, Driesch wrote a short article on the need for China's youth to retain their traditional values: "Alt- und Jung-China," *Ostasiatische Rundschau*, 5.3:33–35 (March 1924). His academic lectures in China were published in English translation as *The Crisis in Psychology* (Princeton, 1925), dedicated "To My Friends in the Far East, in Particular Dr. Carsun Chang and Mr. Ch'ü Shi Ying, M.A."

51. Chang Chün-mai, "Jen-sheng-kuan" (View of life), in *K'o-hsüeh yü jen-sheng-kuan* (Science and view of life; Shanghai, 1923), I, 9–10.

52. Chang and Ting each wrote three essays, Hu and Wu two. For a summary of the arguments advanced, see Alfred von Forke, *Geschichte der neueren chinesischen Philosophie* (Hamburg, 1938), pp. 647 ff; Chow Tse-tsung, pp. 333–337; and D. W. Y. Kwok, *Scientism in Chinese Thought, 1900–1950* (New Haven and London, 1965), pp. 135–60. Chow's estimate of the final outcome agrees with that in Wen-han Kiang, p. 74: "The net result of the polemic . . . re-enforced the supremacy of science in the minds of the Chinese students." An excellent scholar of this period concurs in this judgment: "Despite these illustrious names marshalled on his side [Liang Ch'i-ch'ao and the German-trained philosopher Chang Tung-sun], Chang Chün-mai was against the majority opinion: a fact quite symptomatic of the spirit of the times and the growing vogue of positivism." (O. Brière, *Fifty Years of Chinese Philosophy, 1898–1950* [London, 1956], p. 30).

53. L. K. Elmhirst, "Some Impressions of China (April 1923)," *Visva-Bharati Quarterly*, 1.3:211–220 (October 1923). One of Elmhirst's lectures was illustrated with a motion picture on "Tagore and the International University." (*North China Star*, Peking, May 5, 1923.); Chi Che (Cheng Chen-to), "T'ai-ko-erh lai-Hua ti chi-shih" (A record of Tagore's visit to China), *Hsiao-shuo yüeh-pao* (Short story monthly), Vol. 15, No. 4 (April 1924), "Welcome Tagore" supplement, p. 1; cablegram from F. C. Tsiang, secretary of the Lecture Association, c/o Sung Po Library (cable address of Liang Ch'i-ch'ao), to Rabindranath Tagore (June 6, 1923), MS. in Rabindra Sadan archives.

54. Hsü Chih-mo, "T'ai-ko-erh," *Ch'en-pao fu-k'an* (Morning news supplement; May 19, 1924). p. 1, recounting Tagore's remarks to Hsü about his feelings before the trip. Hsü continued: "He really felt very hesitant, and therefore he postponed his trip. However, he told us that when the winter was over and the spring wind blew (the Indian spring is earlier than the Chinese) he could not help feeling an inner impulse. Facing the blowing grass and flowers he involuntarily gave up his obligations, and these surroundings liberated his ability to blend his song with the song of the newly-arrived sparrows, to sing joyfully, opening his shirt to the tender south wind. At this time he read our letter urging him to come to China. Our young men's earnest wish to have him come gave this old man courage. He then decided to come eastward. He said to himself: 'While my body is not yet dead and my heart is still able to feel, I should not miss this last and unique opportunity. In my youth I made up my mind to make this pilgrimage, and if in the lonely, quiet hours of the sunset of my life I might regret not having done so, why should I not choose to fulfill my heartfelt wish to be a pilgrim in the late afternoon before the sky grows dark?' Therefore he decided to come eastward, disregarding the advice of his friends and relatives, the warning of his doctors, his old age and bad health, and his responsibilities in his own country."

55. Tagore to Rothenstein, from Colombo, Ceylon (Oct. 20, 1922). The

original has "keep him reminding," which I have replaced with "keep reminding him."

56. *Ibid.*

57. Tagore to Rothenstein, undated (late 1923?). There seems to be no evidence that Rabindranath was really ill, although he did suffer from nervous tension on occasion. His son informs us that after his operation in 1913 "he enjoyed perfect health for many years until old age." (Rathindranath Tagore, *Edges of Time*, p. 182.)

58. Rolland, *Inde*, pp. 41, 38, entries of September 1923.

59. As quoted, with no original source given, in Hira Lal Seth, *Tagore on China and Japan* (Lahore, c. 1943), pp. 18, 20. A French translation of the letter in Rolland, *Inde*, pp. 51, 52, gives as the date of writing Feb. 21, 1924.

60. The Bombay textile millionaire, G. D. Birla, a strong supporter of Gandhi, contributed 11,000 rupees to cover the expenses of the Bengali group. (Mahalanobis, *Tagore's Visit*, Pt. 1 [1924], p. 1; interview with Leonard K. Elmhirst, Totnes, June 30, 1956.)

61. Nag, *Tagore and China*, p. 34.

Chapter Five. "The Representative of Asia" Visits China

Epigraph. Tagore probably gave this poem to Mei at their last meeting on May 20. This version is my English translation of the French translation quoted in *Politique de Pekin,* 11.21:503 (Peking, May 25, 1924).

1. Nag, *Tagore and China*, pp. 37-38. Nag's source is evidently the *Rangoon Mail* for the period during or just after the party's stay in Rangoon from March 24 to 27, 1924. For a slightly fuller reporting of this talk, apparently from the same source, see "Dr. Tagore's Message to China," *Chinese Students' Monthly,* 19.7:5-6 (Ann Arbor, May 1924).

2. Leonard Elmhirst, "Personal Memories," p. 21.

3. Rabindranath Tagore, "Civilisation and Progress," *Talks in China: Lectures Delivered in April and May, 1924* (Calcutta, 1925), pp. 136, 141-142. I have found no record that this lecture was ever given; probably it was the fifth, sixth, or seventh of those prepared for the Peking series, of which only four were read. "Satyam," the last chapter in *ibid.,* was added to the book to fill out its length; Amiya Chakravarty and others compiled it by translating into English some of Tagore's Bengali sermons delivered earlier at Santiniketan. (Letter to the author from Amiya Chakravarty, Sept. 24, 1961.) Tagore dedicated the book "To my friend Susima (Tsemou Hsu [Hsü Chih-mo]), to whose kind offices I owe my introduction to the great people of China." No subsequent edition of this volume has been published; an earlier edition was printed in 1924 but withheld at Tagore's request. Tagore then edited this printed text, omitting some passages and replacing with general titles the specific headings identifying many of the talks. Leonard K. Elmhirst kindly allowed me to consult his copy of this earlier edition in order to establish the date and place of those talks which could not be otherwise

identified. Most of the talks were taken down by Elmhirst as they were delivered, since Tagore usually spoke extemporaneously; others were based on versions printed in China in English-language newspapers. The unpublished edition is cited below as "Talks," the published edition as *Talks*.

4. Photograph of letter from Sun Yat-sen to Rabindranath Tagore (Apr. 7, 1924), in Yang Yün-yüan, "Sheng-p'ing jeh-ai Chung-kuo ti T'ai-ko-erh" (Tagore, who warmly loved China during his lifetime), *Ch'uan-chi wen-hsüeh* (Biographical literature), 7.6:36 (Taipei, December 1965). I am indebted to Dr. David Roy for bringing this letter to my attention.

5. *South China Morning Post* (May 1, 1924); letter from L. K. Elmhirst to Rathindranath Tagore (May 4, 1924), in Rabindra Sadan archives.

6. For the military and political situation in China in 1924, see Chien-nung Li, *The Political History of China, 1840–1928*, tr. and ed. Ssu-yu Teng and Jeremy Ingalls (New York, 1956), Chap. 14.

7. Nag, *Tagore and China*, p. 39.

8. Bengali letter of April 14, 1924, quoted in English translation in *ibid.*, p. 40.

9. Photographs and a summary of the welcome at the dock are found in Chi Che (Cheng Chen-to), *Huan-ying T'ai-ko-erh hsien-sheng! Welcome to Mr. Tagore!* (Shanghai, c. May 1, 1924). This 21-page booklet is bound with *Hsiao-shuo yüeh-pao* (Shanghai), as a supplement to the issue of Vol. 15, No. 4 (April 1924), in the file held by Harvard-Yenching Library. According to Elmhirst's diary for April 12, 1924, the Sikhs, led by H. P. Sastri, the spokesman for the Indian community, all gave cries of "Gandhiji ki jai!" (Long live Gandhi).

10. "T'ai-ko-erh chih lai-Hua kan-hsiang t'an" (Talking with Tagore about his impressions on arriving in China), *Shen pao* (Shanghai, Apr. 14, 1924), p. 14.

11. *Ibid.*

12. Elmhirst Diary (Apr. 12, 1924).

13. K[shitimohan Sen? Kalidas Nag?]., "Rabindranath Tagore's Visva-Bharati Mission," *Modern Review*, 36.3:288 (September 1924).

14. "Rabindranath to Chinese Students," *Visva-Bharati Quarterly*, 2.2:198 (July 1924).

15. Tagore, *Talks*, pp. 57–59.

16. *Ibid.*, pp. 59–60; Nag, *Tagore and China*, p. 41; Tagore, *Talks*, p. 60.

17. Elmhirst diary for April 12, 1924; K., pp. 288–289.

18. *China Press* (Shanghai, Apr. 20, 1924); Tagore, *Talks*, pp. 62–65.

19. Elmhirst diary (Apr. 15, 1924); K., p. 289; Mahalanobis, *Tagore's Visit*, Pt. 1, p. 20, quoting Tagore's (Bengali) letter of Apr. 14, 1924.

20. *China Press* (Apr. 20, 1924); Chi Che, *Huan-ying*, pp. 11–14. For a French translation see Léon Wieger, S.J., comp., "Visite de Sir R. Tagore," in *Nationalisme, xénophobie, anti-christianisme* (Hsien-hsien, Chihli, 1924), pp. 72–73. I am grateful to Joseph R. Levenson for pointing out to me this important source.

21. Chi Che, *Huan-ying*, p. 14.
22. K., p. 288; Elmhirst diary (Apr. 15, 1924); *China Press* (Apr. 20, 1924). See also *Shen pao* (Apr. 19, 1924).
23. Elmhirst, "Personal Memories," p. 20.
24. Letter from L. K. Elmhirst to Rathindranath Tagore (May 4, 1924); only slightly reworded, this letter appears in Mahalanobis, *Tagore's Visit*, Pt. 2, pp. 11–12. Nag, *Tagore and China*, p. 43, and K., p. 290 give similar but not identical reports of this interview.
25. Elmhirst diary (Apr. 20, 1924); Nag, p. 43; K., p. 290.
26. *Central China Post* (Hankow, May 16, 1924); Elmhirst diary (Apr. 20, 1924); K., p. 291.
27. Tagore, "Talks," p. 26; *ibid.*, pp. 80–81, 82, 85–86, 85. Elmhirst recorded in his diary that this was the best speech he ever heard Tagore give; he also noted that Tagore believed only forty of the three thousand in the audience had understood him. One of the students has described how reluctant the poet was to leave the pavilion on campus where he meditated for thirty minutes and then talked with a group of students who had been watching him from afar. "My heart is like you young people at every moment," he told them. "Therefore I am always a young man and like to play with young people. I would like to be young forever." Tung Feng-ming, "T'ai-ko-erh chih [shih] tsai Nan-ching" (Mr. Tagore at Nanking), *Ch'en-pao fu-k'an* (Morning news literary supplement; Peking, Apr. 26, 1924), pp. 3–4.
28. Nag, *Tagore and China*, p. 52; K., pp. 290–291; the photograph on p. 290 is captioned "The President of the Lotus Convent at Tsinanfu," but I am told by Holmes Welch, an authority on Chinese Buddhism, that the woman's dress and hairdo show her to be a lay woman, probably the head of a *lien-shih*, or club of lay women who observe vegetarianism and other meritorious practices.
29. *North China Herald* (May 3, 1924); K., p. 291; Mahalanobis, *Tagore's Visit*, Pt. 2, p. 21, quoting Elmhirst's letter of April 24, 1924.
30. *China Press* (May 7, 1924).
31. For a detailed description of the people of Peking, their social organization and economic activities in the warlord period, see Sidney D. Gamble, assisted by John Stewart Burgess, *Peking: A Social Survey* (New York, 1921). Peking's population in 1924 was about 1,000,000, as compared with Shanghai's nearly 2,500,000. In addition to the usual tourist guidebooks, the most illuminating and detailed work on the historical monuments of Peking and their condition in the 1920's is Juliet Bredon, *Peking: A Historical and Intimate Description of Its Chief Places of Interest*, 2nd rev. ed. (Shanghai, 1922). A recent and richly illustrated work is Lin Yutang, *Imperial Peking: Seven Centuries of China* (New York, 1961).
32. K., pp. 291–292; *China Press* (May 7, 1924). The one American in Tagore's party, the nurse at his village uplift center, gives six pages in her autobiography to this China trip, and of this incident she writes: "With bandits expected to hop aboard any moment, as we neared Peiping, the train

journey proved exhilarating. Soldiers on guard slept in the corridor and a special engine threw its searchlight along the track. There was never a sign of a bandit by night, but any quantity of tourists invaded the compartment by day. A countrywoman of mine leaned over, fingering my cape of camel's hair. 'Did he give it to you?' she whispered audibly, pointing to the Poet. 'Tell her,' he replied for himself, 'I killed for you my last and favourite camel.' " (Gretchen Green, *The Whole World and Company* [New York, 1936], p. 84.)

33. *China Illustrated Review* (Tientsin, Apr. 24, 1924); Nag, *Tagore and China*, p. 44; *North China Herald* (May 3, 1924), quotes a *Far Eastern Times* report that over two hundred students of Nankai University in Tientsin (founded and led by Liang Ch'i-ch'ao's friend Chang Po-lin) and Tsing Hua College near Peking, came to welcome Tagore.

34. Mahalanobis, *Tagore's Visit*, Pt. 2, p. 17; Ben G. Kline, "New Philosophy of Living Needed, Poet Says," April 25 dispatch from Peking, in *Trans-Pacific* (Tokyo, May 10, 1924), p. 12; Mahalanobis, *Tagore's Visit*, Pt. 2, p. 18; Nag, *Tagore and China*, pp. 45, 46.

35. Bredon, pp. 92–93, thus describes the hall (the Tzu kuang ko): "From the marble of its balustrades to the pointed eaves that trim it like a rich valance, the whole structure was cleverly calculated to impress the envoys before they entered the presence of Majesty. Pausing at the foot of the broad steps that form a dignified approach, even the casual visitor to-day is thrilled." For the names of some of the Chinese present, see K., p. 292.

36. Liang Ch'i-ch'ao, "Yin-tu yü Chung-kuo wen-hua chih ch'in-shu ti kuan-hsi" (The brotherly relations between the Indian and Chinese cultures), in his *Yin-ping-shih ho-chi, wen-chi*, Pt. 41, pp. 36–46. The English translation quoted here was probably done by Hsü Chih-mo; it was published as the "Introduction" to Tagore, *Talks*, and as "China's Debt to India," in *Visva-Bharati Quarterly*, 2.3:251–261 (October 1924).

37. Tagore, "Talks," p. 33; Tagore, *Talks*, p. 66. For the Indian view of Jesus, see above, pp. 21–22.

38. Tagore, *Talks*, pp. 66–69; K., p. 293.

39. *Chiao-yü ts'ung-k'an*, 5.2:5; Mahalanobis, *Tagore's Visit*, Pt. 2, p. 24; Tagore, *Talks*, p. 74.

40. *Ibid.*, pp. 73–74, 76–77. The quotation, evidently Tagore's own translation, he attributes (p. 75) to "the great ones of my people," that is, the authors of the Upanishads.

41. *Fo-hua hsin-ch'ing-nien* (Buddhist youth), 2.2:5 (Peking, 1924).

42. "T'ai-ko-erh yü Fo-hua hsin-ch'ing-nien hui" (Tagore and the Young Men's Buddhist Association), *Fo-hua hsin-ch'ing-nien*, 2.2:2, 3–4.

43. Nag, *Tagore and China*, p. 53; Mahalanobis, *Tagore's Visit*, Pt. 2, pp. 35–36; K., p. 294; Nag, *Tagore and China*, p. 54, quoting in English translation a Bengali letter written by Nandalal Bose.

44. *New York Times* (May 1, 1924); interview with Chiang Fu-ts'ung; Mahalanobis, *Tagore's Visit*, Pt. 2, pp. 35–36; K., p. 294; Green, p. 185. The

visit is also mentioned in Reginald F. Johnston, *Twilight in the Forbidden City* (London, 1934), p. 347, with a photograph of Tagore and P'u-i facing p. 348. According to his account, Johnston initiated the invitation: "I was anxious that Tagore should not leave Peking without catching a glimpse of the courteous and dignified China that has never failed to rouse the homage of foreign visitors" and was proud to have introduced Tagore to Cheng Hsiao-hsü (Su-k'an), a distinguished poet and calligraphist devoted to the ex-emperor. Johnston (who was probably the Westerner who had told Tagore the previous day that China was the most suitable country to prove the value of spiritual civilization) further remarks: "I felt glad to have brought together, under imperial auspices, the foremost poets of two great countries once closely linked together by bonds of spiritual kinship."

45. "At the Scholar's Dinner, Peking: Mr. Lin's Opening Speech," in Tagore, "Talks," p. 59.

46. Tagore, *Talks,* pp. 34, 36, 43, 40; letter to the author from Leonard K. Elmhirst (Aug. 8, 1955).

47. *China Illustrated Review* (May 3, 1924); K., p. 295; *Hsü Chih-mo nien-p'u* (A chronology of the life of Hsü Chih-mo), comp. Ch'en Ts'ung-chou (Shanghai?, 1949), p. 38, places the lecture at the Altar of Heaven, and Tagore, "Talks," p. 43, at the Temple of Earth, but all other sources locate it at the Altar of Agriculture, which is also the most suitable of the three places for such a gathering; *ibid.;* Tagore, *Talks,* pp. 69, 70; Wieger, p. 78. Either on this day or the previous one Tagore visited the nearby Altar of Heaven and the beautiful Temple of the Good Year, known among foreigners by the name of the area comprising both, the Temple of Heaven. Gretchen Green describes the colorful scene: "Today the Poet was beauty himself, standing at the top of the Temple of Heaven wearing a gift robe, yellow with black scroll embroidery, after the fashion of Confucius. Hundreds of Chinese in coloured satins flocked up and down the steps; in the encircling gardens bloomed peonies and lilacs, fragrant in the sun of spring."

48. Interview with Kalidas Nag (Nov. 17, 1955); Tung Feng-ming, p. 4; interview with T'ao Chen-yü (a primary school student in Nanking who with his schoolmates was invited to attend the lecture), April 9, 1955; Leonard K. Elmhirst, private diary for 1924, entry for April 17; *China Illustrated Review* (May 3, 1924).

49. K., pp. 295–296; interview with Chang P'eng-ch'un (dean at Tsing Hua, 1923–1926), Hong Kong, Aug. 2, 1956. The Western scholars were Baron von Stäal Holstein, professor of Sanskrit at Peking University, and Reginald Johnston. Tagore also enjoyed talking with Richard Wilhelm in Peking. Green, p. 188, reports that "a Chinese artist journeyed three hundred miles to give Tagore a book of chrysanthemums he had drawn in a hundred ways."

50. Elmhirst diary (Apr. 29 and May 1, 1924); Tagore, *Talks,* p. 87; "Talks," p. 49; *Talks,* pp. 87–88.

51. *Talks,* p. 88; "Talks," p. 49; *Talks,* pp. 88, 90, 92, 90, 91, 91–92, 92–93.

A slightly different reporting of this talk is given in *China Illustrated Review* (May 10, 1924), pp. 7–9.

52. Interview with Wu Kan, a student at Tsing Hua in 1924 (Taipei, Apr. 12, 1955); K., p. 297; Elmhirst diary (May 4, 1924). Some of the questions were written out at Tagore's request; see "Rabindranath's Answers to Questions by the Students of Tsing Hua College," *Visva-Bharati Quarterly*, 2.2:295–298 (October 1924).

53. Elmhirst diary (May 6, 1924).

54. Mahalanobis, *Tagore's Visit*, Pt. 2, 33–34; Tagore, *Talks*, pp. 95–97, 101–105; Nag, *Tagore and China*, p. 48. Tagore had also spoken on his educational ideals to the students and teachers of the Chinese Women's College in Shanghai, on April 17 (Elmhirst diary) or 18 (K., p. 290), and this talk is perhaps incorporated in the chapter entitled "To Teachers," in Tagore, *Talks*, pp. 95–105.

55. Mahalanobis, *Tagore's Visit*, Pt. 2, p. 34.

56. My retranslation into English from the French translation in *Politique de Pekin*, 11.21:503 (May 25, 1924).

57. Nag, *Tagore and China*, p. 48.

58. Interviews with Hu Shih (New York, Oct. 13, 1954), Chiang fu-ts'ung, Li Tsung-t'ung (Taipei, Apr. 13, 1955), and Ch'en Yüan (London, June 21, 1956). Three of these men were members of the Crescent Moon Club (Hsin-yüeh p'ai), made up of returned students from England and the United States. Hsü Chih-mo was the club's most active member, and its meetings were usually held in his house.

59. K., pp. 298–299; Liang Ch'i-ch'ao, "T'ai-ko-erh ti Chung-kuo ming, Chu Chen-tan" (Tagore's Chinese name, Chu Chen-tan), in his *Yin-ping shih ho-chi, wen-chi*, Pt. 41, pp. 47–48.

60. Hu Shih, "Pariṇāmana," a poem in Chinese and English, with an accompanying birthday message to Rabindranath Tagore (May 8, 1924). MSS. in Rabindra Sadan archives.

61. K., p. 299; Mahalanobis, *Tagore's Visit*, Pt. 2, pp. 40–41; *Politique de Pekin*, 11.19:453 (May 11, 1924); interview with Chang Hsin-hai (who played the prince), (New York, Oct. 14, 1954). On Mei, see A. C. Scott, *Mei Lan-fang, Leader of the Pear Garden* (Hong Kong, 1959); Tagore's meeting with Mei is briefly mentioned on p. 105. Green, p. 186, seems to exaggerate in saying that the function lasted "well into the morning."

62. *North China Star* (Peking, May 10?, 1924); *Far Eastern Times* (May 10, 1924).

63. Tagore, *Talks*, pp. 23–24.

64. *Ibid.*, pp. 24, 31, 31–32, 33.

65. Interview with Hu Shih (Oct. 13, 1954); "T'ai-ko-erh chih erh-tz'u yen-chiang" (Tagore's second lecture), *Shen-pao* (May 13, 1924), p. 10, which notes that Hsü did not translate Hu's warning into English; *Politique de Pekin*, 11.20:478 (May 18, 1924).

66. Tagore, "The Rule of the Giant," *Visva-Bharati Quarterly*, 4.2:99, 103,

112, 111–112 (July 1926). Apparently Tagore kept the two lectures merged in this published text, but used the title of the second only.

67. "T'ai-ko-erh chih erh-tz'u yen-chiang"; interview with Hu Shih (Oct. 13, 1954); Hu Shih to Rabindranath Tagore (May 11, 1924), MS. in Rabindra Sadan archives.

68. Richard Wilhelm, "Aus Zeit und Leben: Abschied von China," *Pekinger Abende*, 2.4:5 (July 1924), writes, after mentioning the pamphlets: "Die Sache wäre nun ohne grösseres Aufsehen vorbeigegangen. Besonnenere Führer der Jugend, wie Hu Shih, griffen ein und warnten vor Unhöflichkeit gegen Gäste, dem schlimmsten Fehler gebildeter Menschen. Allein Tagore wurde durch japanische Freunde von diesen Vorgängen unterrichtet."

69. The original being unobtainable, this translation is based on Wieger, pp. 78–80, a French translation of the Chinese text as published in the Peking press on May 1, 1924. (*China Illustrated Review*, May 3, 1924.) This text was apparently signed by "a group of Peking students" (Wieger, p. 78), and was the one circulated at the Altar of Agriculture on April 28. The leaflet found in the True Light Theater on May 10, either identical or similar in content, was entitled "Sung T'ai-ko-erh" (Farewell, Tagore), and was described in *Shen-pao* (May 13, 1924) as having been signed with the pseudonym Po Hai (Gulf of Chihli). An abbreviated translation of the text cited here, described as "a typical statement of opposition to Tagore," is given in a dispatch from Ben G. Kline, a staff correspondent, in *Trans-Pacific* (June 7, 1924).

70. Interview with Chien Yu-wen (Hong Kong, May 6, 1955).

71. Four sources give slightly different accounts of Tagore's emotional state at this point. Leonard Elmhirst (letter to the author, Oct. 21, 1968) writes: "What he was really terrified of was involvement in a political situation, all the competing threads of which he could not grasp, so that he knew beforehand he would be made a fool of . . . So now he took flight from a situation his Chinese friends would not explain to him. He had answers to all the complaints but was never allowed to meet the complainers." Kalidas Nag (interview of Jan. 2, 1956) recalls that Tagore's mind was upset by the crosscurrents of controversy flowing around him and that he consequently did not feel well. A semi-official publication of Peking's French community reported that, "Despite the intervention of Dr. Hu Shih, Sir Tagore, faced with these impertinent displays [of opposition], chose to cancel his series of lectures on the pretext of his state of health, and retired to the [Western] Hills. (*Politique de Pekin*, 11.20:478 [May 18, 1924].) Richard Wilhelm, who was in personal contact with the poet in Peking, declared that "the suddenness of the impression made [presumably by the pamphlet] on his sensitive poetic temperament was so strong that he had a complete nervous breakdown." (Wilhelm, "Abschied," p. 5.) The breakdown, if it occurred, was not so complete as to prevent Tagore from lecturing the following morning and fulfilling another engagement the day after.

72. "T'ai-ko-erh tsai ching tsui-hou chih chiang-yen" (Tagore's last speech

in the capital), *Shen pao* (May 15, 1924), p. 7; the *Far Eastern Times* (May 10, 1924), had observed concerning the May 9 lecture, "it was a pity that the gathering was not much larger"; Rabindranath Tagore, "Judgment," *Visva-Bharati Quarterly*, 3.3:195, 205, 205–206, 207, 208 (October 1925).

73. *Central China Post* (May 17, 1924) quoting a May 12 Chung Mei dispatch from Peking; a similar report was carried in *China Weekly Review* (May 24, 1924).

74. *North China Standard* (May 13, 1924); Kshitimohan Sen to Rathindranath Tagore (May 13, 1924), MS. in Rabindra Sadan archives.

75. "T'ai-ko-erh chiang yu Su-o" (Tagore will visit Soviet Russia), *Shen pao* (May 17, 1924), p. 7. The Tagore-Karakhan interview was not reported in any of the accounts of the tour written by members of Tagore's party, probably because the Government of India was quite worried about the possible influence of Communist propaganda on Indian nationalism and was at that very moment arraigning suspected Indian Communists on charges of conspiracy to overthrow the government.

76. *Ibid.*

77. *Ibid.*; Elmhirst diary (May 13, 1924). The visit to Moscow did not take place until 1930.

78. *Japan Chronicle* (May 17, 1924), quoting May 14 Kokusai dispatch from Peking.

79. Mahalanobis, *Tagore's Visit*, Pt. 2, p. 42; Bredon, p. 356, describes the springs and the marble-lined baths built by K'ang Hsi as lying "under the lee of a stone-freckled hill with the picturesque ruins of three old temples silhouetted against the sky-line." Tangshan is also not far from the Ming Tombs and the Great Wall.

80. Elmhirst diary (May 18, 1924). The dinner was probably held on May 17.

81. K., pp. 299–300; "To a Surprise Gathering of Students in the National University, Peking," in Tagore, "Talks," p. 134; *Talks*, pp. 79, 78, 79.

82. Interview with Li Tsung-t'ung; interview with Chiang Meng-lin (Taipei, Apr. 1, 1955).

83. K., pp. 299–300; Tagore, *Talks*, pp. 106, 107–108.

84. *Ibid.*, pp. 109, 106, 113, 112–113.

85. *Ibid.*, pp. 113–114.

86. "Talks," pp. 155–157.

87. "T'ai-ko-erh kuan-yü Fo-chiao chih t'an-hua" (Tagore's conversation about Buddhism), *Shen pao* (May 20, 1924), p. 7. This delegation represented the Peking Buddhist Research and Teaching Society (Pei-ching Fo-chiao chiang-hsi hui).

88. "The International Institute of China: Annual Report of the Director, Dr. Gilbert Reid," *Far Eastern Times* (Peking, Apr. 25, 1924; Committee of Religions and Religious Societies (chairman, Gilbert Reid) to Rabindranath Tagore (May 1924), MS. in Rabindra Sadan archives; Mahalanobis, *Tagore's Visit*, Pt. 2, p. 44; Elmhirst diary (May 19, 1924). The new religious groups

listed in the letter of invitation were the Association for Promotion of Goodness (Wu shan she), the Universal Swastika Society, the Society of Moral Enlightenment, and the Peking Tao Yuan (Source of the Tao). At some point during his stay in Peking, Tagore received a letter of welcome from the Moral Teaching Society (probably identical with the Society of Moral Enlightenment just mentioned) proclaiming his aim identical with that of its founder, Tuan Cheng-yuan: "According to Mr. Tuan, the present confusion of the world is not due to the development of materialism of the West. But it is due to the wrong application of this materialism. Therefore he says that spiritualism and materialism should go hand in hand. But he wishes to see that spiritualism be treated as the principal and materialism as its assistant." (MS. in Rabindra Sadan archives.)

89. Tagore, *Talks*, p. 43; Mahalanobis, *Tagore's Visit*, Pt. 2, p. 44; *Talks*, pp. 43-44, 45-52, 53, 54-55.

90. K., p. 300; *China Weekly Review*, 28.14:492 (May 31, 1924); interview with Ch'en Yüan.

91. Telegram from Shansi Provincial Education Association to Tagore (May 20, 1924), MS. in Rabindra Sadan archives; see Donald G. Gillin, "Portrait of a Warlord: Yen Hsi-shan in Shansi Province, 1911-1930," *Journal of Asian Studies*; 19.3:289-306, 296 (May 1960). During his 1923 visit to China, Elmhirst had visited Yen Hsi-shan and found him favorably disposed to the idea of having Tagore as his guest. (Interview with Elmhirst.)

92. "Conversation between Rabindranath Tagore and Governor Yen, of Shansi, China," *Visva-Bharati Quarterly*, 2.3:293, 294 (October 1924); Nag, *Tagore and China* p. 63; K. p. 300; interview with Elmhirst.

93. According to the *North China Herald* (June 7, 1924), this meeting was sponsored by twenty-three different organizations and the audience totaled five thousand, which if so would make it one of Tagore's largest in China.

94. Tagore, "City and Village," in *Visva-Bharati Quarterly*, 2.3:221, 225 (October 1924). This talk is not included in Tagore, *Talks* and is referred to only vaguely in Mahalanobis, *Tagore's Visit*. A report of May 22 in the *North China Herald* (June 7, 1924) tells us: "The theme of Dr. Tagore on this occasion was village as contrasted with city life. He pleaded for the conservation of village habits, customs and standards of living, opposing the rush of population to the cities." The text quoted here may well be a more finished version of the talk, since he gave it again at the University of Tokyo on June 9.

95. See Jean Chesneaux, *Le mouvement ouvrier chinois de 1910 à 1927* (Paris, The Hague, 1962), p. 318; James Bissett Pratt, *The Pilgrimage of Buddhism and a Buddhist Pilgrimage* (New York, 1928), pp. 386-388. In an article on "labour agitation," datelined Wuchang, May 31, the *North China Herald* (June 7, 1924) noted that "its leaders appear to be mostly students and teachers in the schools . . . but the leaders of the movement have been arrested in Wuchang by agents of Wu Pei-fu and taken to Loyang, where five of them have already been executed."

96. Wang Hung-wen, "T'ai-ko-erh tsai Han-k'ou fu teh chung-hsüeh-hsiao chih chiang-yen" (Tagore's lecture at the Supporting Virtue Middle School), *Ch'en-pao fu-k'an* (June 21, 1924).

97. Interview with Nag (Nov. 17, 1955); interview with Chang Chün-mai (Washington, Oct. 12, 1954). In confirmation of Nag's eyewitness report, we find in *Shen-pao* (May 27, 1924), p. 4, a telegraphed dispatch from Hankow with this concluding sentence: "Wen T'ai i Hua-jen ch'ang fa fan-tui ch'uan-tan, yü jen p'o lao-sao" ([Some of the] Chinese listening to Tagore frequently distributed opposition handbills and told people they were very unhappy with him).

98. *North China Herald* (June 21, 1924); Tagore, *Talks,* pp. 74, 74–75, 74, 76, 77.

99. *North China Herald* (June 21, 1924). It is curious that this same weekly newspaper published on June 7, 1924 (p. 373) an entirely different account of this same Wuchang speech, estimating the audience at three to four thousand and asserting there was "no sign of the opposition manifested in other places." Perhaps the June 21 account was meant as a reply to that published June 7, for it was dated June 8 and was written by someone at Wuchang who had been on the scene when Tagore lectured there. In contrast to the June 7 report that "the appearance and personality of Tagore made a great impression," the June 21 account was headed: "Tagore's Failure with Young China. The Man who Preaches Spiritual Power and Control Has no Hearing from the China set on Material Progress and Physical Domination."

100. *China Press* (May 29, 1924); Tagore, "Talks," pp. 97–101; Nag, *Tagore and China,* pp. 41–42; K., pp. 289–290, 301; "Tagore's Message," *Chinese Recorder,* 55.7:476 (July 1924).

101. Tagore, *Talks,* p. 119; "Talks," p. 100.

102. *Talks,* p. 116; "Talks," p. 98; *Talks,* p. 117.

103. *Talks,* pp. 119–120.

104. Hsü Chih-mo, postscript to "Kao-pieh tz'u" (Parting words), *Hsiao-shuo yüeh-pao,* 15.6:4 (June 1924).

105. Interview with Nag (Nov. 17, 1955); K., p. 301. For Tagore's speech to the Parsi community, on the theme of the importance of the individual, see the two-column report in *North China Herald* (June 21, 1924), p. 477.

106. Wieger, p. 83; *Shanghai Times* (July 11, 1924).

Chapter Six. Chinese Views of Tagore's Message

Epigraph. Richard Wilhelm, "Abschied," p. 5. I am grateful to Hellmut Wilhelm for bringing this source to my attention, and for lending me his personal file of *Pekinger Abende.*

1. Rolland, *Inde,* p. 78. Elmhirst wrote an optimistic report of the tour on June 8, 1924, and spoke briefly of "a certain opposition which, enlightened as to the facts on which it had been misinformed, made its apology and retired from the scene." (L. K. Elmhirst, "Rabindranath Tagore's Visit to China," *Modern Review,* 36.2:164–165 (August 1924).

2. N. H. Pitman, "Education," *China Year Book, 1925–1926,* ed. H. G. W. Woodhead (Tientsin, 1925), p. 228. Woodhead was also editor of the *Peking and Tientsin Times,* a British-owned newspaper.

3. "Tagore's Message." The editors devoted two of their three paragraphs to the final Peking meeting arranged by another missionary, Dr. Gilbert Reid, and noted with satisfaction that at this "unique gathering the spiritual training of the soul was placed first." (*Chinese Recorder,* 55.7:477.) A different strand of missionary opinion was expressed in an article by Rachel Brooks, "The Spiritualism of the Orient versus the Materialism of the Occident," *ibid.,* 55.8:495–505 (August 1924). Without referring to Tagore, Miss Brooks (who left China in June 1924, after three years' service with the Y.W.C.A.) refuted the theory that the East was spiritual and the West materialistic.

4. Tsuchida, p. 210.

5. *Trans-Pacific* (June 7, 1924), quoting Peking dispatch from Ben G. Kline.

6. Letter from Dr. Henry Hodgson, in *Japan Weekly Chronicle* (n.d.), as quoted in *Modern Review,* 36.3:349 (September 1924).

7. "Sciences and Institutions," *China Journal of Science and Arts,* 3.1:120 (January 1925); *Peking and Tientsin Times* (Tientsin, Dec. 6, 1924). There is a possibility that this anonymous letter, signed "Impressed but not Converted," was written by a Chinese intellectual, but the fact that it was sent to this British daily and the fluency of the author's English style suggest that the writer was an American or Englishman familiar with the Chinese intellectual world in Peking — perhaps the Rev. Dr. Gilbert Reid.

8. Wilhelm, "Abschied," p. 5. Wilhelm explains Tagore's failure in these terms (my translation): "If we inquire into the deeper causes of this failure —for the tactless deeds [of the opposition] are, in the last analysis, only accidental by-products of a process with its own internal necessity — they appear to me to lie in the fact that Tagore erred in his appraisal of the intellectual climate in China. He thought [that he found] prevailing among the youth of China moods similar to his own, and wished to come to awaken and gather together the most sacred possessions he and they held in common. But such blissful islands of old culture no longer exist. China today is no longer a power, but a place where power is contended for. It stands in the midst of the intellectual contention among the most diverse views of life."

9. Wieger, pp. 66, 83.

10. *Peking Daily News* (Apr. 26, 1924), as quoted in Mahalanobis, *Tagore's Visit,* Pt. 2, p. 20.

11. *North China Standard* (n.d.), as translated in *Trans-Pacific* (May 17, 1924), p. 10.

12. "The Inspiration of Tagore," *North China Star* (Tientsin, May 3, 1924). This was seen in the newspaper cuttings in the Rabindra Sadan archives. Unfortunately only the introduction, but not the editorial itself, has been preserved there.

13. *She-hui jih-pao* (n.d.), as translated in *Trans-Pacific* (May 17, 1924), p. 11. Where "crazy" appears in that translation, I have inserted "absurd."

14. *Ta wen pao* (n.d.), as translated in *North China Standard* (Apr. 25, 1924), and as rendered grammatically correct by me.

15. *Ibid.*

16. Ch'en T'ing-jui, "Ching-shen wen-ming yü wu-chih wen-ming" (Spiritual civilization and material civilization), *Shen pao* (Apr. 29, 1924), p. 3. Although a contributed article, this was printed in the editorial section and clearly was intended to represent *Shen pao's* stand on Tagore's message. *Shen pao* also carried short comments from contributors in a section toward the end of each issue, headed *Ts'a-lu* (Miscellany), one of which, from a writer signing himself Keng Kuang ("dazzling light"), defended Tagore against his leftist critics. "We should try to grasp his theory, not just pick out one part," the author argued. Since the political chaos and social deterioration in China was partly due to everyone's concentration on material needs, Tagore's speeches advocating spirituality "are the right medicine for us today. As for the opinion that there is no such thing as Oriental culture in the world, this is self-depreciation, and I am afraid that even the Westerners will agree with this opinion." ("Ching-kao fan-tui T'ai-ko-erh-che" [Serious statement to those who oppose Tagore], *Shen pao* [May 13, 1924], p. 17.)

17. The translations in article form and the essays on Tagore before his arrival are listed in *Chung-wen tsa-chih so-yin* (Index to Chinese periodicals), comp. Ling-nan ta-hsüeh t'u-shu-kuan (Lingnan University Library; Canton, 1935), pp. 462–464; and in *Wen-hsüeh lun-wen so-yin* (Index to literary essays; Peiping, 1932–1936), I, 241–242. Only those essays published before his arrival which concerned his ideas are mentioned in the following pages, with the exception of those by three minor intellectuals, which are noted here. Chou Yüeh-jan, co-founder with the classical scholar Chang T'ai-yen of the Society for the Study of Ancient Asia (Ya-chou ku-hsüeh hui), described the "admiring faith" in Tagore he had gained from reading his works and talking about him with Indian friends, and urged his countrymen to study his writings carefully, for "otherwise we will not be able to grasp his thought at all." (Chou Yüeh-jan, "Chi wo li-liang" [Give me strength], *Hsiao-shuo yüeh-pao*, 14.9:1–3 [September 1923].) Wang T'ung-chao, associated with the Peking Lecture Association and charged by it with drawing up Tagore's itinerary, exulted: "Now we await the light of 'love' which Tagore is bringing to us from his Indian forest, carrying it in person to our sinking, dispirited midst. We must not greet this world-famous poet-philosopher with routine courtesy, rather we must truly understand his philosophy of life, which is limitless vitality and creative love." (Wang T'ung-chao, "T'ai-ko-erh ti ssu-hsiang chi ch'i shih-ko ti piao-hsiang" [Tagore's thought and its expression in poetry and song], *ibid.*, p. 15.) Thirdly, Wang Hsi-ho, a teacher in Shanghai, asked by the country's most important general magazine to introduce a special section on Tagore, replied by characterizing him as "a pioneer of the Eastern spirit." The essence of his thought was "harmony between man and the universe —

in other words, the search for the life of the spirit." Perhaps feeling that his article was a bit vague, Wang promised that "when Tagore comes to China, and I am able to hear his speeches, and can also get more ideas from studying his works, I shall write another essay to correct the errors in this one." (Wang Hsi-ho, "T'ai-ko-erh hsüeh-shuo kai-kuan" [An outline of Tagore's theory], *Tung-fang tsa-chih* [Eastern miscellany], 20.14:73, 90 [July 25, 1923].) In fact, neither Wang nor any other intellectual who wrote favorably about Tagore's ideas before he arrived made any comments on them after he had delivered his lectures in China — an indication that they found his general spirituality uplifting when taken in the diluted form of translations from his writings, but difficult to swallow in the concentrated form in which he presented it in his lectures to Chinese audiences.

18. Cheng Chen-to, "Huan-ying T'ai-ko-erh" (Welcome, Tagore), *Hsiao-shuo yüeh-pao*, 14.9:4 (September 1923). The Literary Studies Association (Wen-hsüeh yen-chiu hui), founded by Chou Tso-jen, Shen Yen-ping (Mao Tun), and others in Peking in 1921, soon had a membership of 172 important writers. From 1923 its hegemony over the movement to create a new literature was challenged by the Creation Society (Ch'uang-tsao she), led by Kuo Mo-jo and others. For a short history of the Literary Studies Association, see William Ayers, "The Society for Literary Studies, 1921–1930," *Papers on China*, 7:34–79 (Harvard University, East Asian Research Center, 1953).

19. Chi Che, *Huan-ying T'ai-ko-erh hsien-sheng!*, p. 2.

20. T'ai-ko-erh (Tagore), "I-ko wen-hsüeh ko-ming-chia ti kung-chuang," tr. Hsü Chih-mo, *Hsiao-shuo yüeh-pao*, Vol. 15, No. 6 (June 1924). The other three talks published in this monthly, and also translated by Hsü, were "Ti-i-tz'u ti t'an-hua" (First talk [in China]) "Kao-pieh tzu" (Parting words) — both in *ibid.*, Vol. 15, No. 8 (August 1924) — and "Ch'ing-Hua yen-chiang" (Lecture at Tsing Hua College), *ibid.*, Vol. 15, No. 10 (October 1924).

21. [Cheng Chen-to], "Kuo-nei wen-t'an hsiao-hsi" (News items on Chinese literature), *ibid.*, Vol. 15, No. 6 (June 1924).

22. In the very first issue published after he took over editorship of the Short Story Monthly from Shen Yen-ping, Cheng published in it some of his own translations of Tagore's poetry, and in the next issue inserted a special section of articles on the Indian poet, including the first installment of his own biography of Tagore. (See *ibid.*, Vol. 13, Nos. 1 and 2 [January and February 1922].) Cheng's biography was published in one volume as *T'ai-ko-erh chuan* (A life of Tagore; Shanghai, 1926); it contains no reference to Tagore's message to China or its reception by China's intellectuals.

23. Hsü Chih-mo, "T'ai-ko-erh lai-Hua ti ch'üeh-ch'i" (The exact date of Tagore's arrival in China), *Hsiao-shuo yüeh-pao*, Vol. 14, No. 10 (October 1923).

24. "Tagore's Visit to China," *Indian Review*, 25.3:206 (March 1924); *Servant* (Calcutta, Feb. 19, 1924). The former gives the full quotation without identifying the writer; the latter quotes only the first sentence and identi-

fies it as part of a letter to Tagore from Hsu Tse-mon [Hsü Chih-mo] on behalf of the Peking Lecture Association. Hsü was greatly concerned over the fact that Tagore did not arrive as promptly as had been expected; a telegram from the Indian poet reassured the Lecture Association that he hoped to come in October 1923. October arrived, but it brought no word from Tagore. C. F. Andrews did write to say that the poet had contracted dengue fever and would be delayed still further. By this time a rumor had begun to spread that the invited lecturer had pocketed his check for $1000 and did not intend to come at all! Then on October 21 Hsü received a letter in which Tagore explained that with the approach of cold weather in Peking he thought it better to postpone his visit until the following spring, adding that "many Chinese friends have written letters welcoming me." (Hsü, "T'ai-ko-erh lai-Hua.") Hsü's excitement at the prospect of Tagore's arrival is vividly conveyed in his ecstatic article, "T'ai-shan jih-ch'u" (Sunrise on Mount T'ai), *Hsiao-shuo yüeh-pao*, Vol. 14, No. 9 (September 1923), in which he compared the coming of the poet-sage of the East with the rising of the sun.

25. Hsü Chih-mo, "T'ai-ko-erh tsui-chin hsiao-hsi" (Latest news of Tagore), *Ch'en-pao fu-k'an* (Apr. 19, 1924), pp. 3–4; Elmhirst diary for April–May 1924.

26. Hsü Chih-mo, "Ch'ü pa!" (Go away!), *ibid.* (June 17, 1924), p. 2, as translated in Kai-yu Hsu, tr. and ed., *Twentieth Century Chinese Poetry: An Anthology* (Garden City, 1963), p. 83.

27. Hsü Chih-mo, "T'ai-ko-erh" (Tagore), *Ch'en-pao fu-k'an* (May 19, 1924), pp. 1–2. Hsü was speaking on this occasion to the audience just before Tagore gave his third and last lecture in the series he had come to deliver.

28. *Ibid.* For a full-length portrait of Hsü and his work, see the forthcoming book by Cyril Birch of the University of California, Berkeley. Hsü's cosmopolitan and Westerncentric attitude is also evident in, among other writings, his article (in English), "Art and Life," *Ch'uang-tsao* (Creation), 2.1:1–15 (August 1927), in which he bemoans the Confucian stress on ethics and its detrimental effects on the imagination, and urges his countrymen to take the Hellenic age and Italian Renaissance as models of times when art molded life, and life was seen as a whole.

29. Hsü Chih-mo, postscript to "Kao pieh-tzu," pp. 4, 5.

30. For sketches of Wen's career and samplings of his poetry, see Kai-yu Hsu, *Chinese Poetry*, pp. 47–68, and Kai-yü Hsü, "The Life and Poetry of Wen I-to," *Harvard Journal of Asiatic Studies*, 21:134–79 (December 1958).

31. Wen I-to, "T'ai-kuo-erh p'i-p'ing" (A criticism of Tagore), *Shih-shih hsin-pao, wen-hsüeh* (Shanghai *Times*, literary supplement; Dec. 3, 1923), reprinted in *Wen I-to ch'üan-chi* (Collected works of Wen I-to; Shanghai, 1948), Vol. 3, Pt. 1, p. 278.

32. *Ibid.,* p. 279.

33. Wen I-to, "Nü-shen chih ti-fang se-ts'ai" (Local color in [Kuo Mo-jo's] "The Goddess"), *ibid.,* pp. 195–201.

34. Another member of this select group of English-speaking intellectuals,

Wang Wen-hsien, a University of London graduate and dean of studies at Tsing Hua College, expressed his disappointment with Tagore's philosophizing: "When a poet poetises, he is invulnerable to mere logical criticism. Against mysticism, against poetical inflatus, cold human reason is abjectly defenseless, impotent and futile. . . . We have made unsuccessful attempts to read his poetry and have found his mysticism more than a match for our patience." Despite this difficulty, Wang appreciated Tagore's lecture at Tsing Hua and was grateful that the poet "came down to our level, the level of the matter-of-fact sons of Han." Wang stated openly what Hsü Chih-mo had implied: that Tagore was not peculiarly Indian at all, but was rather "very much of a cosmopolitan in intellect, part of a world heritage." (J. Wong-Quincey [Wang Wen-hsien], "A Criticism of Tagore's Tsing Hua Speech," *China Illustrated Review* [Tientsin, May 10, 1924], pp. 8, 9.)

35. Chou Tso-jen, " 'Ta-jen chih wei-hai' chi ch'i t'a" ("The danger of the giant" and so on), *Yü-t'ien ti shu* (Book for a rainy day), 2nd ed. (Shanghai, 1935), pp. 125, 127.

36. Chou Tso-jen, "Chi-nan tao chung chih san" (Three [essays] on the road to Tsinan), *ibid.*, p. 235.

37. *Lu Hsün jih-chi* (Diary of Lu Hsün; Peking, 1959), I, 486.

38. Lu Hsün, "Lao tiao-tzu i-ching ch'ang-wan" (The old song has been sung long enough), in *Lu Hsün hsüan-chi* (Selected works of Lu Hsün; Peking, 1952), p. 666, as translated in Chow Tse-tsung, p. 282. This essay was delivered as a speech in Hong Kong on February 19, 1927. See also the more famous passage in Lu Hsün's "The Diary of a Madman" in which the hero, reading a book of Chinese history, finds in it the words "Benevolence, Righteousness, Truth, Virtue" on each page, but on looking closely between the lines discovers everywhere the same two words: "Eat men!" For summaries and evaluations of the writings of Lu Hsün, and of Shen Yen-ping (Mao Tun) and Kuo Mo-jo, see C. T. Hsia, *A History of Modern Chinese Fiction, 1917–1957* (New Haven, 1961).

39. Shen Yen-ping, "Tui-yü T'ai-ko-erh to hsi-wang" (What we expect of Tagore), *Min-kuo jih-pao, chüeh-wu* (Republic daily, Awakening supplement), (Shanghai, Apr. 14, 1924). As I do not have access to the original, my translation is compounded from Wieger's French translation and from the Chinese excerpts given in *Wu-ssu shih-ch'i chi-k'an chieh-shao* (An introduction to periodicals of the May Fourth period; Peking, 1958–1959), I, 217.

40. Shen Yen-ping, "Tu T'ai-shih yen-chiang hou ti kan-hsiang" (My impressions after reading reports of Mr. Tagore's lectures), *Min-kuo jih-pao, chüeh-wu* (May or June 1924), as quoted in French translation in Wieger, pp. 80–81.

41. Wieger, p. 81.

42. The concept of a "third age of humanity" does not appear in the version of the lecture given in Tagore, *Talks*, but is mentioned as one of six points in that lecture in the summary given in Wieger, p. 78.

43. Shen Yen-ping, "Tu T'ai-shih," p. 82.

44. Kuo Mo-jo, "T'ai-ko-erh lai-Hua ti wo-chien" (My view of Tagore's visit to China), *Ch'uang-tsao chou-pao* (Creation weekly), No. 23:3–4 (Oct. 14, 1923). Kuo also alludes briefly to this early enthusiasm for Tagore in his autobiographical *Ch'uang-tsao shih-nien* (Ten years of the Creation Society; Chungking, 1943), p. 42. For a close examination of these years of Kuo's life see David Tod Roy, "Kuo Mo-jo: The Pre-Marxist Phase (1892–1924)," *Papers on China*, 12:69–146 (1958), and the same author's forthcoming book, "Kuo Mo-jo: The Early Years."

45. Kuo Mo-jo, "T'ai-ko-erh," p. 5.

46. *Ibid.*, p. 6.

47. Kuo Mo-jo, "Chih Ch'eng Fang-wu shu" (A letter to Ch'eng Fang-wu), in *Chung-kuo hsin wen-hsüeh ta-hsi* (Comprehensive outline of modern Chinese literature), vol. 6., *San-wen, i-chi* (Essays, first series; Shanghai, 1935), pp. 220, 227. For the opening and closing parts of the quotation I have used the translation in Hsia, p. 98.

48. Kuo Mo-jo, "Chih Ch'eng Fang-wu shu," p. 227.

49. To estimate the influence which Tagore's writings exerted on the development of Chinese literature is beyond the scope of this study. His use of free verse or prose poem style in rendering his metrical Bengali poetry into English did become popular among young Chinese poets, among whom Hsieh Ping-hsin is often mentioned as an admirer of Tagore. (She was studying at Wellesley at the time of his visit to China, and did not comment then on his possible influence on her countrymen.) Even Ch'en Tu-hsiu, who so roundly belabored Tagore and his ideas in 1924, printed in the second issue of his amazingly popular monthly, New Youth, his own translations of several Tagore prose poems (*Hsin ch'ing-nien*, Oct. 15, 1915). But there is nothing peculiarly Indian about the free verse form. It is clear, on the other hand, that those Chinese writers who reacted most sympathetically to Tagore were not the defenders of classical forms and themes but the avant-garde romantics steeped in the literary traditions of nineteenth- and twentieth-century England and America.

50. Interview with Chang P'eng-chün. A photograph of the two sages taken on that occasion, showing rather dour expressions on both their faces, is reproduced as a frontispiece in *Hsiao-shuo yüeh-pao*, Vol. 15, No. 6 (June 1924).

51. *Shanghai Mercury* (May 30, 1924). See also Francis Borrey, *Un sage chinois: Kou Hong Ming: Notes biographiques* (Paris, 1930), pp. 65–73, for a summary of the letter and of Ku's subsequent remarks to Borrey concerning his conversation with Tagore. For example, on pp. 69–70: "Whoever says 'Oriental civilization' expresses the idea of mystery and darkness, coupled with pompous splendor. This is the civilization of India, of Persia. In Chinese civilization, there are neither mysteries nor darkness." An anonymous writer to North China's leading English-language newspaper five months later made the doubtful claim that Ku's letter "went a long way to kill the movement" in favor of Tagore's ideas. (*Peking and Tientsin Times*, Dec. 6, 1924.)

52. *Shanghai Mercury* (May 30, 1924).

53. *Ibid.*

54. Ku Hung-ming, *The Story of a Chinese Oxford Movement* (Shanghai, 1912), p. 3. It is said that while a student in Edinburgh, Ku became Western-ized to the extent of cutting off his queue as proof of his love for a Scottish girl who spurned him all the same. To the end of his life he spoke and wrote better English than Chinese. (Interview with Chang Hsin-hai.)

55. See Johnston, *passim*. On pp. 345–347 he speaks admiringly of Ku's loyalty to the old regime and describes his "awe-stricken speechlessness" on meeting the ex-emperor in 1924. Johnston and the ex-emperor are depicted in the delightfully written book of Henry McAleavy, *A Dream of Tartary: The Origins and Misfortunes of Henry P'u Yi* (London, 1963). For other European appreciations of Ku Hung-ming, see Alfons Pacquet, "Vorwort," in Ku Hung-ming, *Chinas Verteidigung gegen europäische Ideen* (Jena, 1911), pp. xi–xiv; Keyserling, *Travel Diary*, II, 92, 97, 106; and Richard Wilhelm, *The Soul of China*, tr. J. Holroyd Reece (New York, 1928), p. 94.

56. Ku Hung-ming, *The Spirit of the Chinese People*, 2nd rev. ed. (Peking, 1922), p. 151; 1st ed. (Peking, 1915), p. 17.

57. Liang Sou-ming, *Tung-hsi wen-hua chi ch'i che-hsüeh* (Eastern and Western civilizations and their philosophies; Shanghai, 1922). By 1926 seven "editions" (printings) had been published to meet the continuing demand for Liang's book.

58. *Ibid.*, 7th ed., pp. 199, 202.

59. *Ibid.*, pp. 186–187.

60. Kalidas Nag, private diary for April–May 1924, as read aloud to me during our interview Nov. 17, 1955.

61. Liang Sou-ming, *Chung-kuo min-tsu tzu-chiu yün-tung chih tsui-hou chüeh-wu* (The final awakening of the Chinese People's Self-Salvation Move-ment), 3rd ed. (Shanghai, 1936), p. 12; as translated in Lyman P. Van Slyke, "Liang Sou-ming and the Rural Reconstruction Movement," *Journal of Asian Studies*, 18.4:458 (August 1959).

62. Liang Ch'i-ch'ao, *Intellectual Trends in the Ch'ing Period*, Immanuel C. Y. Hsü tr. (Cambridge, Mass., 1959), pp. 123–124. In pursuance of this interest in Buddhism (which makes an interesting contrast with Liang Sou-ming's turning away from Buddhism in this same period), Liang Ch'i-ch'ao wrote a lengthy history of Chinese Buddhism in the next few years. On Liang's intellectual development in the Republican period, see Levenson, pp. 193–219; also Forke, pp. 598–617. Forke notes (p. 650) that "not a few [Chinese scholars] have gone over to Buddhism and seek to reconcile it with Confucianism."

63. *Ibid.*, p. 124.

64. Liang Chi-chao, "Introduction," in Tagore, *Talks*, p. 1. In the Chinese original ("In-tu yü Chung-kuo wen-hua," p. 36), Liang uses the expression "Fo-hsüeh-chia," which is less of a commitment than is implied by the Eng-lish phrase, "a Buddhist."

65. Liang, "Introduction," in Tagore, *Talks*, pp. 6, 21, 18.

66. Fo (Hsü Fo-ssu), "T'ai-ko-erh yü k'o-hsüeh" (Tagore and science), *K'o-hsüeh* (Science), 9.3:245, 246. This number is dated March 1924, but it must have been issued later, for Hsü began his article by observing (p. 244): "Since the poet Tagore came to China, intellectual circles have suddenly come alive, the whole nation is full of welcomers, thousands of people fill the streets, and his opponents also are ready to attack him with swords and arrows, as though encountering a great enemy." The storm around Tagore had "nearly filled the country like the wind and the rain," Hsü noted, "but the mass of society, who understand little and who blindly follow others, have already been fascinated by a variety of colors, and don't know how to make up their minds." It is interesting that China's leading scientist, Ting Wen-chiang, a member of Liang Ch'i-ch'ao's circle (he was present at several of the receptions for Tagore) did not criticize Tagore, and that the one man of science who commented in print on Tagore's message was much more sympathetic toward it than most of the philosophical, literary, and political leaders mentioned here. Wang Ch'ung-yu, an American-trained engineer who had been a member of the Chinese delegation to the Washington Conference of 1921–22, was in 1924 head of the technical department of the Lin Ho Kon Mining Company in Peking, but he also had humanistic interests, for in an English lecture in 1925 on "Chinese Pictorial Art, An Essay on Its Interpretation," he began: "The declamatory utterance of Tagore in his recent public lectures in Peking, against the materialistic tendency of Western civilization as compared with Asian civilization is both fortunate and unfortunate; fortunate in that he re-emphasized the spiritual meaning of Asian civilization, unfortunate in that he failed to see the inner unity of the two major civilizations. Indeed there is no sharp line to divide the two, for they can be likened to two members of a long and intergrading series, very distinct in their isolated and extreme expression, but completely connected.' As I conceive it, they are complementary one to another and are conjointly necessary for the development and betterment of the human race. Civilization as a whole would become lopsided if one were overemphasized and the other be-littled. A well-balanced ideal civilization in the future will be possible only when contributions from the two civilizations, Oriental and Occidental, interact properly." (*China Journal of Science and Arts*, 3.1:4 [January 1925].)

67. Liang, "Introduction," in Tagore, *Talks*, p. 20.

68. T'ai Hsü, "Hsi-wang lao-shih-jen ti T'ai-ko-erh pien wei Fo-hua ti hsin-ch'ing-nien" (I wish the old poet Tagore would become transformed into a new Buddhist youth), *Fo-hua hsin-ch'ing-nien* (New Buddhist youth), 2.2:4–6 (Peking and Shanghai, 1924).

69. T'ai Hsü, "Tung-yang wen-hua yü hsi-yang wen-hua" (Eastern and Western civilizations), *Hsüeh heng* (The critical review), No. 32:5–6 (Nanking, August 1924).

70. T'ai Hsü, "Ching-kao kung-ch'an-tang" (Warning to the Communist Party), *Fo-hua hsin-ch'ing-nien*, 2.2:26 (1924). For more information on

T'ai Hsü, his movement, and the general state of Buddhism in China in 1924, see Pratt, pp. 305 ff.; see also Holmes Welch, *The Practice of Buddhism in China* (Cambridge, Mass., 1967), and his *The Buddhist Revival in China* (Cambridge, Mass., 1968).

71. Interview with Hu Shih (Aug. 3, 1956).

72. *Shen pao* (May 31, 1924).

73. *Ibid.*

74. See above, Chapter Five, last section.

75. Carsun Chang, *China and Gandhian India* (Calcutta, 1956), pp. 263, 271–316.

76. Carsun Chang, *The Development of Neo-Confucian Thought* (New York, 1962), II, 433, 452.

77. In my interview with him Dr. Chang recollected that Tagore had nothing definite to say in China except "spirit," did not know China very well, and left no impression on China's intellectuals. Chang's young assistant, Ch'ü Shih-ying, trained at Columbia, was especially interested in Tagore's philosophy of education, and published two articles on the Indian poet: "T'ai-ko-erh ti jen-sheng-kuan yü shih-chieh-kuan" (Tagore's view of life and the world), *Hsiao-shuo yüeh-pao*, Vol. 13, No. 2, item 2 in special section, "T'ai-ko-erh yen-chiu" (Tagore studies; February 1922); and "T'ai-ko-erh ti kuo-chi ta-hsüeh" (Tagore's international university), *Tung-fang tsa-chih*, 21.10:64–73. It is curious that although this number is dated May 25, 1924, Ch'ü makes no mention of Tagore's visit or message to China. Probably the article was written before his arrival. It does support Tagore's general emphasis on idealism as against utilitarianism and materialism.

78. Hu Shih, *Development of the Logical Method*, pp. 7, 8, 9.

79. Chow Tse-tsung, pp. 317–320.

80. Hu Shih, *The Chinese Renaissance: The Haskell Lectures, 1933* (Chicago, 1934), pp. ix–x.

81. *Politique de Pekin*, 11.18:478–479 (May 18, 1924); *Shen pao* (May 15, 1924), p. 17. In the fuller form of the statement given in *Shen pao*, Hu denied the allegation that Tagore was invited to China to bolster the cause of metaphysics, pointing out that the science-metaphysics debate began with Ting Wen-chiang's reply to Chang in mid-April, which was just about the time the decision to invite Tagore was being decided upon.

82. Hu Shih actually discussed these ideas privately with Tagore (interview with Hu Shih, Aug. 3, 1956), and first stated them publicly in a speech in Chinese delivered in 1925. He developed them more fully in his essay of June 6, 1926, "Wo-men tui-yü hsi-yang chin-tai wen-ming ti t'ai-tu" (Our attitude toward modern Western civilization), in *Hu Shih wen-ts'un san-chi* (Writings of Hu Shih, third collection), 5th ed. (Shanghai, 1946), I, 3–22. He rewrote this essay in English at the request of the American historian, Charles Beard. The quotation given here is from that essay, "The Civilizations of the East and the West," in Charles A. Beard, ed., *Whither Mankind* (New York, 1928), pp. 25, 40–41.

83. Wu Chih-hui, "Chen yang-pa-ku-hua chih li-hsüeh" (A warning to foreign-formalized Neo-Confucianism), in *Wu Chih-hui hsien-sheng wen-ts'ui* (Selected essays of Mr. Wu Chih-hui; Shanghai, 1928), III, 321. This essay was actually directed against Chang Chün-mai's defense of Neo-Confucianism in the 1923 controversy on science and metaphysics. A selection from Wu's writings has recently been published by the Kuomintang in commemoration of the centenary of his birth: *Wu Chih-hui hsien-sheng hsüan-chi* (An anthology of Wu Chih-hui's writings; Taipei, 1964).

84. Wu Chih-hui, "Wan-kao T'ai-ko-erh" (Courteous advice to Tagore), *Wu Chih-hui hsien-sheng wen-ts'ui*, I, 292, 293, 294, 295.

85. *Ibid.*, p. 296.

86. Wu Chih-hui, "Huang-hui sheng-chung ti T'ai-ko-erh," *ibid.*, I, 296–297. Wu's two articles first appeared in *Min-kuo jih-pao chüeh-wu* (published in Shanghai and an organ of the Kuomintang) on April 18 and 24 respectively, 1924. It was perhaps not a coincidence that Wu was in Shanghai just before Tagore returned there from Peking, and gave a speech to a women's organization denouncing spiritual civilization. (*Shen-pao*, May 26, 1924, p. 14.)

87. A recent history, O. Edmund Clubb's *Twentieth Century China* (New York and London, 1964), p. 123, has pictured the political situation in about 1924 in these words: "The raw materials for a revolution were present in China. The domination of the corrupt, ineffective, and unimaginative central government at Peking by a succession of rival warlords had resulted in maladministration of the country's political affairs and almost complete neglect of national economic problems. Bad government at Peking had led to worse government in the countryside. Every petty military satrap was doing his utmost to squeeze more wealth, as well as endless manpower, from the peasantry for the support of his swollen ambitions. Foreign imports, enjoying that 'freedom of commercial opportunity' provided by the five percent import duty fixed by treaty, exacerbated the economic distress of the agricultural villages. The Chinese peasantry was more restless than at any time since the Taiping Rebellion. Banditry, always a warning sign of trouble in Chinese politics, was growing. The process of political disintegration had reached an acute stage."

88. *China Press* (Shanghai, Apr. 13, 1924).

89. *China Express and Telegraph* (London, June 19, 1924), quoting a Reuters dispatch datelined Peking, April 22, 1924.

90. *China Weekly Review* (Shanghai, May 17, 1924), p. 430. Other newspapers reported that an attempt had been made to secure a building in the grounds of the president's palace as Tagore's residence, but this request by unidentified "students' bodies" had been denied on the principle that this part of the palace had not yet been opened to the public. (*Daily Mail* [Bombay, Apr. 24, 1924]; *South China Morning Post* [Hong Kong, Apr. 17, 1924]; *Trans-Pacific* [May 17, 1924], quoting a dispatch by Ben G. Kline datelined Peking, May 3, 1924.) This studied indifference to the Indian poet contrasts

markedly with the official reception and banquet tendered the German philosopher Driesch, Tagore's predecessor in the series of foreign lecturers in Peking. (Driesch, *Lebenserinnerungen*, p. 177.)

91. Sun Yat-sen, "Pan-Asianism," in his *The Vital Problem of China* (Taipei, 1953), p. 162.

92. *Ibid.*, p. 167.

93. Sun Yat-sen, "Nationalism: Lecture 6," in his *San Min Chu I: The Three Principles of the People,* tr. Frank W. Price, ed. L. T. Chen (Shanghai, 1929), p. 136.

94. *Ibid.*, pp. 123–124, 126 ff., 148, 147–148.

95. Interview with Leonard K. Elmhirst; Nag, *Tagore and China*, p. 51 (the Kuomintang officer's name is given here as Li Tong Cong); letter from Leonard K. Elmhirst to Rathindranath Tagore (May 4, 1924), in Rabindra Sadan archives. In addition to these visits from personal emissaries, Tagore also received a telegram from Sun on April 19, inviting him to be Sun's guest in Canton. Tagore replied that he hoped to be in Canton in early June. (*China Press*, Apr. 20, 1924.)

96. Sun Yat-sen, "Pan-Asianism," p. 171.

97. Sun's social conservatism may be related to the fact that, like Ku Hung-ming, he spent so many years of his life abroad. As in the case of many other Asian intellectuals (Aurobindo Ghose in India and Yone Noguchi in Japan are other examples), distance from his homeland may have lent a certain enchantment to a social system which intellectuals who stayed at home often viewed as in need of drastic overhauling. Read, for example, Sun's hopeful remarks on clan loyalties as the basis for national unity in China ("Nationalism: Lecture 5"), p. 114; "If this worthy clan sentiment could be expanded, we might develop nationalism out of clanism. If we are to recover our lost nationalism, we must have some kind of group unity, large group unity. An easy and successful way to bring about the unity of a large group is to build upon the foundation of small united groups, and the small groups we can build upon in China are the clan groups and also the family groups." Unfortunately, Sun did not realize that the attention devoted to family ties by members of the Kuomintang government between 1927 and 1949 would prove a major source of its weakness and unpopularity.

98. An excellent way to trace the development of this symbiosis, and its abrupt termination in 1927, would be to examine the pages (which do not seem to be available outside of mainland China) of the daily *Min-kuo jih-pao, chüeh-wu.* In the complete listing of contents of *Chüeh-wu* included in *Wu-ssu shih ch'i chi-k'an chieh-shao,* I, 702–707 we find twelve articles concerning Tagore for the period March 30 through June 1, 1924, of which the two by Shen Yen-ping and one anonymous one, apparently by Ch'en Tu-hsiu, are given in French translation in Wieger, and the one by Wu Chih-hui was reprinted in *Wu Chih-hui wen-ts'ui,* I, 292–294.

99. For a sketch of Ch'en's intellectual development, see Benjamin I.

Schwartz, "Ch'en Tu-hsiu and the Acceptance of the Modern West," *Journal of the History of Ideas*, 12:61–74 (January 1951).

100. Ch'en Tu-hsiu, "Ching-kao ch'ing-nien," p. 4.

101. Ch'en Tu-hsiu, "Wo-men wei shen-mo huan-ying T'ai-ko-erh" (Why do we welcome Tagore?), *Chung-kuo ch'ing-nien*, No. 2:15 (Oct. 27, 1923).

102. Cheng Han [Ch'en Tu-hsiu], "Huan-ying T'ai-ko-erh" (Welcome to Tagore), *ibid.*, No. 26:12–15 (Apr. 12, 1924); French translation in Wieger, pp. 67–69.

103. "Fan-tui T'ai-ko-erh," *Chüeh-wu* (Apr. 13, 1924); French translation in Wieger, pp. 69–72.

104. Shih An [Ch'en Tu-hsiu], "T'ai-ko-erh yü tung-fang wen-hua," *Chung-kuo ch'ing-nien*, No. 27:1–2 (Apr. 18, 1924); French translation in Wieger, pp. 73–75. This issue was entitled *T'ai-ko-erh t'e-hao* (Special Tagore number), and contained three other articles mentioned below in notes 113, 137, and 140. The issue was published one day earlier than usual, apparently to be ready for distribution to the audience at Tagore's major Shanghai address at the Commercial Press auditorium on April 18.

105. For the text of the five-point broadside, see Chapter Five. The exact authorship of the Peking broadside cannot be established on the basis of the evidence available at this writing. See the reports mentioned in Chapter Five, n. 69 above, one attributing the broadside to "a group of Peking students," the other to a single author using the pseudonym Po Hai. It may be that two or more different leaflets were distributed to Tagore's listeners, some coming directly from Shanghai, others being Peking revisions of a Shanghai original. Alternatively, the same text may have been printed with different kinds of identification.

106. [Ch'en] Tu-hsiu, "Ts'un-t'ieh" (The dagger), *Hsiang-tao* (Guide weekly), No. 62:496 (Apr. 23, 1924).

107. Interview with Kalidas Nag (Nov. 17, 1955); interview with Chiang Mon-lin; Chou Tso-jen, " 'Ta-jen chih wei-hai,' " p. 128.

108. [Ch'en] Tu-hsiu, "Ts'un-t'ieh," *Hsiang-tao*, No. 64:516 (May 7, 1924).

109. *Ibid.*, No. 67:539 (May 28, 1924).

110. *Ibid.*, No. 63:506 (Apr. 30, 1924).

111. Ch'ü Ch'iu-pai, "T'ai-ko-erh ti kuo-chia kuan-nien yü tung-fang" (Tagore's concept of the nation-state and the East), *ibid.*, No. 61:488–489 (Apr. 16, 1924).

112. *Ibid.*, pp. 489, 490.

113. [Ch'ü] Ch'iu-pai, "Kuo-ch'ü ti jen T'ai-ko-erh" (Tagore, the has-been), *Chung-kuo ch'ing-nien*, No. 27:2–3 (Apr. 18, 1924).

114. *Forward* (Calcutta, July 18, 1924).

115. Elmhirst diary for April 1924. Elmhirst elaborated on this theme in his short article, "Tagore and China," in Nag, *Tagore and China*, p. 62: "Tagore used to say before we left India that it was vitally necessary for

Indians to try and discover the aspirations of modern China. He refused to visit ancient buildings not because he was not interested in them, but because time was short and he had brought a team of Indian specialists with him, an artist, a Sanskrit scholar and a historian to study every aspect of China's past. Meanwhile he determined to devote all his energy to trying to meet and fathom the mind and aspirations of modern China, of her students, her professors, her writers, her living painters, actors, singers and musicians."

116. [Lin] Jui-t'ang, "Wo ti li-hsiang chi shih-hsien ti T'ai-ko-erh hsien-sheng" (The Mr. Tagore of my ideal and in reality), *Ch'en-pao fu-k'an* (May 12, 1924), pp. 2–3. The anonymous writer to the *Peking and Tientsin Times* (Dec. 6, 1924), signing himself "Impressed but not converted," remarked that Tagore had shown special attention to the fair sex during his stay in Peking: "He was very fond of some of the exquisite Chinese women he met and a chosen few were almost inseparable from him during his visit."

117. "Rabindranath's Answers."

118. Lu Mou-te, "Ko-jen tui-yü T'ai-ko-erh chih kan-hsiang" (My personal opinion of Tagore), *Ch'en-pao fu-k'an* (June 3, 1924), p. 4. Not all Tsing Hua students viewed Tagore in so favorable a light. One of them recalled that he and his fellows were curious about his exotic dress and poetic way of life, but did not take his ideas seriously, in fact, were rather cynical about them; ideas like his were found in the Buddhist scriptures and the Chinese classics, whereas the students were generally dissatisfied with traditional values, wanted something new, and for this reason were most interested in the modern West. (Interview with Wu Kan, April 12, 1955.) The estimate of the then dean of Tsing Hua strikes a balance between these two views. In his opinion, a small sprinkling of students greatly appreciated Tagore, the large mass did not seem to be touched by him, and a small group was definitely opposed to his ideas. (Interview with Chang P'eng-chün.)

119. Yüan Lieh-ch'eng, "Wo tui-yü T'ai-ko-erh lai-Hua chih kan-yen" (My word of thanks to Tagore for coming to China), *Fo-hua hsin-ch'ing-nien*, 2.2:24, 25–26 (1924).

120. Liu Ling-hua, "Wo-men chiu-ching wei shen-mo yao huan-ying T'ai-ko-erh" (Why then do we wish to welcome Tagore?), *ibid.*, p. 4. This is possibly the same person as the Liu Yen Hon whose poem composed on the occasion of Tagore's visit is in *The Golden Book of Tagore: A Homage to Rabindranath Tagore from India and the World in Celebration of His Seventieth Birthday,* ed. Ramananda Chatterjee (Calcutta, 1931).

121. Tung Feng-ming, pp. 3–4.

122. *Ibid.*

123. *Hsüeh heng*, Vol. 1, No. 1 (January 1922), and each successive issue. See also Chow Tse-tsung, p. 282, and Tsi C. Wang, *The Youth Movement in China* (New York, 1927), pp. 150–152. Two men, who as students heard Tagore lecture at the National Southeastern University, said years later that he made no impression on them and their fellows. One described him as "a dreamer of the old civilization of the Orient" which had already disap-

peared; the other recalled that the students were somewhat disappointed when they realized that he did not oppose imperialism, but were not greatly disappointed because they had not expected a great deal. (Interviews with T'ao Chun-yü and with Kuo T'ing-i, Taipei, Apr. 5, 1955.)

124. Feng Yu-lan, "Yü Yin-tu T'ai-ko-erh t'an-hua" (A talk with the Indian Tagore), *Hsin ch'ao* (New tide), Vol. 3, No. 1 (Winter 1920–1921), as reprinted in Liang Sou-ming, *Tung-hsi wen-hua*, appendix, pp. 59–60.

125. *Ibid.*, p. 61.

126. For an English summary of the letter, which forms an interesting example of the Western encouragement for Asian cultural revitalization discussed in Chapter Four above, see Derk Bodde, *Tolstoy and China* (Princeton, 1950), pp. 50–57. Tolstoy's letter was published in Russian and in German and French translations, on which Bodde gives details.

127. Feng Yu-lan, "Yü Yin-tu," p. 63. This paragraph was reprinted in the editorial welcoming Tagore which was the only comment on his ideas published in China's leading fortnightly, The Eastern Miscellany (Ch'ien K'ua, "Huan-ying T'ai-ko-erh" [Welcome, Tagore], *Tung-fang tsa-chih*, 21.6:1 [Mar. 25, 1924]). The Eastern Miscellany's total silence after the Indian poet began lecturing in China suggests that its editors were less than enthusiastic about his message to China, which failed to repeat this exhortation to study science.

128. Feng Yu-lan, "Yü In-tu," pp. 64–65.

129. Fung took his doctorate at Columbia in 1923 with a thesis on "A Comparative Study of Life Ideals," and in 1924 was professor of philosophy and dean of the department of liberal arts at Chung Chow University, Kaifeng, in his native Honan. For a summary of Fung's own philosophy see his *Short History of Chinese Philosophy*, ed. and tr. Derk Bodde (New York, 1962), p. 335: "From the statement: 'Something exists,' I have . . . been able in my *Hsin li-hsüeh* [New metaphysics; Changsha, 1939] to deduce all the metaphysical ideas of Chinese philosophy and to integrate them into a clear and systematic whole. The book was favorably received because in it critics seemed to feel that the structure of Chinese philosophy was more clearly stated than hitherto. *It was considered as representing a revival of Chinese philosophy, which was taken as the symbol of a revival of the Chinese nation.*" (Italics mine.)

130. P'eng Chi-hsiang, "T'ai-ko-erh-chih ssu-hsiang chi ch'i p'i-p'ing" (A presentation and criticism of Tagore's thought), *Hsin min-kuo* (New republic), 1.6:1 (June 1924).

131. *Ibid.*, pp. 8–9.

132. *A Chinese Testament: The Autobiography of Tan Shih-hua, As Told to S. Tretiakov*, tr. anon. from the Russian (New York, 1934), p. 281. For excerpts from contemporary Chinese sources on leftism among the students in 1924, see Wieger, *Nationalisme*, esp. sections 11 ("Affaires russes"), 12 ("Feu Lenine"), 13 ("Agitation anti-impérialiste"), and 16 ("Socialisme, Communisme").

133. Richard Wilhelm, "Aus Zeit und Leben: Eine interessante Statistik," *Pekinger Abende,* 2.3:1–6 (April 1924). This article summarizes the results of the poll, administered by an unnamed private source to persons at the university ("[es] wurden von privater seite Fragebogen an die Besucher ausgegeben"). The written questions were answered by 1007 individuals, of whom 752 were identified as teachers or students (including 47 women students), 22 as administrative personnel, 11 as soldiers or policemen, 8 as tradesmen and 7 as workers, but 207 reamined unidentified as to profession. Total enrollment at the National Peking University in 1924–25 (according to *China Year Book,* 1925–26, p. 252a), was 1920, and the faculty numbered 199. This question of how to save China was a biased one, for the only other alternatives offered were "control by foreigners," chosen by 19, and "militarism," chosen by 10. The remaining 253 expressed no opinion.

134. *Ibid.*

135. *Ibid.* The next most popular were Marshall Tuan Chi-Jui, leader of the defeated Anfu clique, 45; Hu Chih, 45; Liang Ch'i-ch'ao, 29; and Marshall Wu P'ei-fu, the warlord then controlling Peking, 27.

136. Opinions on the radical political student movement were: approval, 232; conditional agreement, 190; opposition, 286. (*Ibid.*)

137. I Hsiang, "T'ai-ko-erh lai-Hua-hou ti Chung-kuo ch'ing-nien" (China's youth after Tagore's arrival in China), *Chung-kuo ch'ing-nien,* No. 27: 15 (Apr. 18, 1924); French tr. in Wieger, p. 75.

138. [Han]Lin-fu, "Fei Liang Cho-ju [Liang Ch'i-ch'ao] ti 'Yin-tu yü Chung-kuo wen-hua chih ch'in-shu ti kuan-hsi'" (Against Liang Ch'i-ch'ao's 'Brotherly relations between the Indian and Chinese cultures'), *Cheng-chih sheng-huo chou-pao* (Peking, April 1924).

139. Edgar Snow, *Red Star over China* (New York, 1938), pp. 142–143.

140. [Shen] Tse-min, "T'ai-ko-erh yü Chung-kuo ch'ing-nien" (Tagore and China's youth), *Chung-kuo ch'ing-nien,* No. 27:5–13 (Apr. 18, 1924); French tr. in Wieger, pp. 76–78. Shen was the younger brother of Shen Yen-ping.

141. *Ibid.* Shen Tse-min later wrote a second essay, "P'ing 'Jen-lei ti-san-chi chih shih-chieh'" (I criticize "The Third Age of Humanity" [Kropotkin's theme, mentioned in Tagore's Altar of Agriculture talk]), *Chung-kuo ch'ing-nien,* No. 31:4–11 (May 17, 1924).

142. [Shen] Tse-min, in *ibid.* (Apr. 18, 1924); *Chüeh-wu* (Apr. 13, 1924).

143. Hsü Chih-mo, "T'ai-ko-erh lai-Hua" (Tagore comes to China), *Hsiao-shuo yüeh-pao,* 14.9:2 (September 1923).

144. Ch'ü Ch'iu-pai, "T'ai-ko-erh ti kuo-chia kuan-nien," p. 487.

145. Wilhelm, "Abschied," p. 4. The coolie's words as Wilhelm reports them in his German translation were "Das ist der Heiland des Westens."

146. For an excellent outline of the rise and fall of Buddhism in China, see Arthur F. Wright, *Buddhism in Chinese History* (Stanford, 1959).

147. Chiang Monlin, *Tides from the West: A Chinese Autobiography* (New Haven, 1947), p. 239. Chiang, like Hu Shih and Fung Yu-lan, took

his Ph.D. in philosophy under John Dewey at Columbia. Fung Yu-lan (*Short History*, p. 189) has pictured two basically Sinocentric attitudes toward India holding sway in China since the arrival of Buddhism: "The introduction of Buddhism seems to have given many Chinese the realization that civilized people other than the Chinese existed, but traditionally there have been two kinds of opinion regarding India. Those Chinese who opposed Buddhism believed that the Indians were simply another tribe of barbarians. Those who believed in Buddhism, on the other hand, regarded India as the "pure land of the West." Their praise of India was that of a realm transcending this world. Hence even the introduction of Buddhism, despite its enormous effect upon Chinese life, did not change the belief of the Chinese that they were the only civilized people in the *human* world."

148. Hu Shih, "The Indianization of China: A Case Study in Cultural Borrowing," in *Independence, Convergence, and Borrowing in Institutions, Thought, and Art* (Cambridge, Mass., 1937), pp. 240, 247.

149. Liang Ch'i-ch'ao, *Ou-yü shin-ying lu chieh-lu,* as translated in *Sources of Chinese Tradition,* comp. Wm. Theodore de Bary, Wing-tsit Chan, and Burton Watson (New York, 1960), p. 848. The "special characteristic" Liang refers to here is the unification of the ideal and the practical, which he also sees as characteristic of modern Western pragmatism and evolutionism, and hence the wave of the future.

Chapter Seven. Indian Images of East and West

Epigraph. Toward Freedom: The Autobiography of Jawaharlal Nehru (New York, 1941), pp. 274–275.

1. *Census of India, 1921* (Calcutta, 1923–24), Vol. 1, Pt. 2, p. 72; *Census of India, 1931* (Delhi, 1933), Vol. 1, Pt. 1, pp. 339–341.

2. On the growth of the regional languages, see Suniti Kumar Chatterjee, *Languages and Literatures in Modern India* (Calcutta, 1963).

3. *Census of India, 1921,* Vol. 1, Pt. 2, pp. 72–79.

4. [Aurobindo Ghose], "The Asiatic Role," in *Bande Mataram,* weekly ed. (Apr. 12, 1908), as identified and reprinted in *Bande Mataram and Indian Nationalism,* ed. Haridas Mukherjee and Uma Mukherjee (Calcutta, 1957), pp. 66, 65, 66.

5. Rabindranath Tagore, "Aurobindo Ghosh," *Modern Review,* 44.1:60 (July 1928).

6. "Rabindranath has imported many things from the West. That no doubt has added to the rich variety and wealth of Bengali literature but has not helped to develop and preserve Bengal's individual culture and its national genius. Under no circumstances should we suffer ourselves to be led by the glamour of the West." (Quoted from *Nārāyaṇa* [a name of the god Vishnu], in Hemendranath Das Gupta, *Deshbandhu Chittaranjan Das* [Delhi, 1960], p. 25.)

7. C. R. Das, "Bengal and the Bengalees," Presidential address to the

Bengal Provincial Conference (April 1917), in the English translation approved by Das, as reprinted in *Deshabandhu Chitta Ranjan: Brief Survey of Life and Work. Provincial Conference Speeches. Congress Speeches* (Calcutta, preface 1926), pp. 19-20, 40. Das repeated this rebuke to Tagore in his presidential address to the Indian National Congress in 1921, which he was unable to deliver because of his arrest in that year. See *ibid.*, pp. 129-130, 151.

8. C. R. Das, "Presidential Address, Thirty-Seventh Sessions of The Indian National Congress, Held at Gaya in December 1922," reprinted in Prithwis Chandra Ray, *Life and Times of C. R. Das* (London, 1927), pp. 273-274.

9. "Asia Must Find Her Own Voice," *Forward* (Calcutta, July 19, 1924). For Tagore's remarks on landing, see *ibid.* (July 18, 1924). *Forward* was the official organ of the Swarajya party, which Das and Motilal Nehru formed as a wing of the Congress in 1923.

10. "Asiatic Federation," *Amrita Bazar Patrika* (Calcutta, July 19, 1924), p. 4. I have corrected several errors in grammar, spelling, and punctuation in the passages quoted here.

11. For the development of this rift, see John Broomfield, *Elite Conflict in a Plural Society: Twentieth-Century Bengal* (Berkeley and Los Angeles: University of California Press, 1968).

12. *Census of India, 1921*, Vol. 1, Pt. 2, p. 77.

13. Nazrul Islam, "Āmār kaiphiyat" (Answer to complaints by friends), tr. Mizanur Rahman in his *Nazrul Islam* (Dacca, 1955), p. 93.

14. Nazrul Islam, "Allah is My Lord: No Fear for Me," tr. Mizanur Rahman in his *Nazrul Islam*, p. 81.

15. "An Asiatic Union," *New Empire* (June 10, 1924); "Arrival in Calcutta," *Bengalee* (July 18, 1924); "Hero Comes," *New Servant* (Dec. 20, 1926).

16. Jadunath Sarkar, *India Through the Ages: A Survey of the Growth of Indian Life and Thought*, 4th ed., (Calcutta, 1951), pp. 82, 83.

17. *Ibid.*, pp. 74, 76; "Hearty Send-Off to Rabindra Nath," *Forward* (July 7, 1927).

18. These reports, written in Bengali, were first published in various newspapers and periodicals, then in a series of thirteen volumes under the general title *Vartamān jagat* (The contemporary world; Calcutta, 1914-1935).

19. Benoy Kumar Sarkar, *Chinese Religion Through Hindu Eyes: A Study in the Tendencies of Asiatic Mentality* (Shanghai, 1916), p. xi; Benoy Kumar Sarkar, *The Futurism of Young Asia and Other Essays on the Relations Between the East and the West* (Berlin, 1922), pp. 154, 176. I have corrected the quotation on p. 154, which gives 1912 as the date of the Nobel Prize.

20. B. Sarkar, *Chinese Religion*, pp. 301, 229, 276, 279.

21. Kedarnath Chatterjee, "Benoy Sarkar As I Saw Him," in Haridas Mukherjee, *Benoy Kumar Sarkar: A Study* (Calcutta, 1953), p. 75; B. Sarkar, "Preface," *Chinese Religion*, pp. xv-xvi; "Publisher's Preface," in Benoy Ku-

mar Sarkar, *The Beginning of Hindu Culture as World-Power*, A.D. 300–600 (Shanghai, 1916), pp. i–ii.

22. Benoy Kumar Sarkar, "Rabindranath and World-Forces," in *Golden Book of Tagore*, p. 323. For other comments by Sarkar on Tagore, see Nagendra Nath Chaudhury, "Pragmatism and Pioneering in Benoy Sarkar's Sociology and Economics," in Banesvar Das, ed., *The Social and Economic Ideas of Benoy Sarkar* (Calcutta, 1940), pp. 561–563.

23. For a recent examination of Roy's role at this meeting, see John P. Haithcox, "The Roy-Lenin Debate on Colonial Policy: A New Interpretation," *Journal of Asian Studies* 23.1:93–101 (November 1963).

24. "Poet and Private Property," as quoted in *Advocate* (Bombay, May 24, 1925), apparently a reprinting from an unnamed European publication.

25. *Ibid.*

26. Robert C. North and Xenia J. Eudin, *M. N. Roy's Mission to China: The Communist-Kuomintang Split of 1927* (Berkeley and Los Angeles, 1963), pp. 113–114. The quotation is their translation from Ts'ai Ho-s[h]en, "Istoriia opportunizma v kommunisticheskoi partii Kitaia," *Problemy Kitaia*, 1:55 (1929).

27. M. N. Roy, *India's Message (Fragments of a Prisoner's Diary*, Vol. 2) 2nd ed. (Calcutta, 1950), pp. 191, vii.

28. *Ibid.*, p. x. For Roy's materialist reinterpretation of Indian philosophy, see his *Materialism: Outline of the History of Scientific Thought*, 2nd rev. ed. (Calcutta, 1951).

29. *British Parliamentary Papers*, XXI (*Reports of Commissioners, etc.*, Vol. 11), "Royal Commission on the Public Services," (Cmd. 7293, 1914), pp. 103–104. I am grateful to Eugene Irschick for bringing this data to my attention.

30. K. S. Ramaswami Sastri, *Vita Sua* (Madras, [1948]), pp. 21–22.

31. K. S. Ramaswami Sastri, *Sir Rabindranath Tagore: His Life, Personality, and Genius* (Madras, 1916), pp. 163–164.

32. K. S. Ramaswami Sastri, *Rabindranath Tagore: Poet, Patriot, Philosopher* (Srirangam, 1924), pp. 46, 47, 68–69.

33. *Ibid.*, p. 46.

34. Sastri, *Sir Rabindranath*, pp. 494, 496.

35. Sastri, *Rabindranath Tagore*, pp. 239, 243, 244, 243.

36. *Ibid.*, pp. 247, 57, 96.

37. Sankara Sastri, said to be the head English master in the Madras Government College, opposed Rammohun Roy's views in a letter to the *Madras Courier* in December 1816, and Rammohun replied with a short tract entitled *A Defence of Hindoo Theism in Reply to the Attack of an Advocate for Idolatry at Madras* (Calcutta, 1817), reprinted in *English Works of Raja Rammohun Roy*, Pt. 2, pp. 81–93.

38. "A rough distribution of Vaishnavites and Saivites in the [Madras] Presidency would be that the Telugu region prefers Vaishnavism, the Tamil,

Shaivism, and the West Coast recognizes neither. The spirit of Vaishnavism increases as one goes north." *Census of India, 1931,* Vol. 14, *Madras,* Pt. 1, *Report* (Madras and Calcutta, 1932), p. 322.

39. "Between the stern philosophy of Sankara with its rigorous logic of negation and the ascetic ethic of inaction, and the human philosophy of Rabindranath Tagore, it is war to the knife," wrote S. Radhakrishnan in *The Philosophy of Rabindranath Tagore* (London, 1918), p. 114. K. S. Ramaswami Sastri replied to this thrust six years later: "I cannot but say about this that the view is vitiated by base errors as regards the nature and content of Sankara's thought. Professor Radhakrishnan is full of admiration for Tagore's philosophy. I do not yield to him in this respect. Tagore is the greatest of the modern revealers of the elements of truth and beauty and sweetness in life. But we cannot give him more than his due place amidst the *durbar* [court assembly] of Indian thought." (*Rabindranath Tagore,* pp. 244–245.)

40. S. Radhakrishnan, *My Search for Truth,* 2nd Indian ed. (Agra, 1956), pp. 5, 9. For biographical details see D. S. Sarma, "Introduction: Professor S. Radhakrishnan," in S. Radhakrishnan, *Great Indians* (Bombay, 1949), pp. 7–13. It would be interesting to compare Radhakrishnan's career as a lecturer on Indian spirituality in foreign lands in the years just before and after World War II with Tagore's similar activity in the years before and after World War I. On Radhakrishnan's Christian schooling and its impress on his subsequent thought, see Otto Wolff, *Radhakrishnan* (Goettingen, 1962).

41. Radhakrishnan, *Philosophy of Tagore,* pp. vii–viii, 196.

42. *Ibid.,* pp. 256, 278, 279, 281.

43. S. Radhakrishnan, "Rabindranath Tagore," in his *East and West in Religion* (London, 1933), p. 133.

44. S. Radhakrishnan, *Eastern Religions and Western Thought* (Oxford, 1939), p. 176 and *passim.* Note also p. 186: "Buddha and Jesus are the earlier and later Hindu and Jewish representatives of the same upheaval of the human soul, whose typical expression we have in the Upanisads."

45. *Ibid.,* p. 259. Also like Tagore, but twenty years later, Radhakrishnan visited China and delivered lectures on Indian and Chinese culture. Because of wartime conditions, however, his visit in 1944 was limited to Chungking and lasted only two weeks. A revised version of some of his fourteen lectures there was published as S. Radhakrishnan, *India and China: Lectures Delivered in China in May 1944* (Bombay, 1947). His principal lecture, "China and India," incorporates many themes in Tagore's talks to China, and concludes (*ibid.,* pp. 45–46): "You have been, for ages, pacifist by disposition. . . . I am certain that you will do nothing to impair the precious heritage, that you will never lose faith in the efficacy of moral values and fall a prey to militarism and say, 'Evil, be thou my good.' For that would be the greatest defeat for China. It is for the East to give to the world a new hope in the hour of its greatest need.

46. Subrahmanya Bharati, *Agni and Other Poems, Translations, and Essays* (Madras, n.d.), Pt. 2, pp. 47–48. These essays were probably first written in Tamil and published in the original in the newspaper *Swadeshmitran* (Friend of freedom). Bharati's patriotic songs abound in reference to Hindu deities and symbols. For examples, see S. Prema, tr. *Bharati in English Verse* (Madras, 1958).

47. In other moods, the Tamil poet could take an even more parochial stand toward the rest of India. In 1919, not long after concluding his ten-year exile, Bharati heard that Tagore had come to South India and was staying at Madura. Bharati went to the school where one of his admirers was teaching, dragged him out of his class-room and harangued him in this amusing dialogue:

BHARATI: "How can the visitor to Tamil Nad [the land of the Tamils] go away without seeing me? Despatch a telegram at once."

DISCIPLE: "To what address?"

BHARATI: "Tush: Tagore, Madura will reach him like a bird in flight."

DISCIPLE: "Alright, but what is the message to be sent?"

BHARATI: " 'Tamil Nad's poet-laureate wishes to meet you!' Despatch it at once."

DISCIPLE: "What exactly is your idea in seeking an interview with Tagore?"

BHARATI: "I shall tell him: 'You are the poet of Bengal: I am the poet of Tamil Nad. Let a meeting be convened at the Victoria-Edward Hall in Madura. Let both of us sing and let the audience judge.' The verdict is a foregone conclusion: for my songs will be pronounced superior to his. Then Tagore will have no choice but to surrender the Nobel prize to me! I shall demand it as of right." . . . [Bharati here rhapsodized on the beauty of the Tamil language.]

DISCIPLE: "I agree that Tamil is no whit inferior to Bengali. Still, you must forgive me if I say that Tagore has become a world-poet, since the whole world has come to know him and praise him."

BHARATI: "As if I can't win such fame. You miserable faint-heart! Don't you see that it is to win world-fame that I am devising this challenge to Tagore?"

(P. Mahadevan, *Subramania Bharati, Patriot and Poet* [Madras, 1957], pp. 107–108.)

48. *Swarajya* (Madras, Nov. 11, 1923).

49. *Ibid.* (July 17, 1924).

50. *Ibid.* In a possible reference to Subramania Bharati, Prakasam's editorial added: "When poets mingle in politics, the more human among them are wont to move with the current of national impulse and the more ambitious to philosophise from a distance. Dr. Tagore is evidently one of the latter."

51. South Indian approbation for Tagore's general outlook could be documented at some length. Two further examples may suffice. One of the poet's most fervent admirers in Madras was a Christian, John J. Cornelius. His *Rabindranath Tagore, India's Schoolmaster* (Madras, 1930), based on his Ph.D. dissertation at Columbia's Teachers College, wholeheartedly endorsed

Tagore's plan for "the meeting of East and West," in these words (p. 3): "The spiritual idealism of the East needs the practical knowledge of the West; likewise the intellect of the West probably has need of the soul of the East to give modern civilization the beauty of completeness." Using a distinction possibly acquired from Columbia Professor Carlton J. Hayes, Cornelius emphasized (p. 50) that Tagore upheld "cultural nationalism" and condemned "political nationalism."

The name of V. K. Krishna Menon, many years later India's ambassador at the United Nations, also appears in an early South Indian publication praising Tagore's ideas. Menon was credited by T. S. Ganesa Iyer, his schoolmate at the Maharajah's Collegiate High School in Mysore, with giving him the idea of reading as a paper to their Literary Union the pamphlet he published as *Some Impressions about Sir Rabindranath Tagore and His Works* (Madras, 1921). Iyer approved of Tagore's warning that the East should not imitate the West, and agreed that the relation between the two should be a complementary one.

52. For a thorough study of Madras political life during the 1920's and of its larger contexts, see Eugene F. Irschick, *Politics and Social Conflict in South India, 1916–1929* (Berkeley, 1968).

53. Moncure Daniel Conway, *My Pilgrimage to the Wise Men of the East* (London, 1906), p. 204. The principal doctrines of the Theosophists are given in H. P. Blavatsky, *The Key to Theosophy,* 3rd rev. ed. (London, 1893).

54. Arthur H. Nethercot, *The Last Four Lives of Annie Besant* (Chicago, 1963), p. 22. See also Nethercot's companion volume, *The First Five Lives of Annie Besant* (Chicago, 1960). An important contemporary, W. T. Stead, contributed a useful short biography, *Annie Besant: A Character Sketch* (London, 1891; reprinted at Adyar, Madras, 1946).

55. Joseph J. Doke, *M. K. Gandhi, An Indian Patriot in South Africa* (Varanasi, 1956), p. 8; Jawaharlal Nehru, *An Autobiography* (London, 1936), pp. 14–16.

56. Mortimer Wheeler, *Civilizations of the Indus Valley and Beyond* (London, 1966), pp. 34, 68.

57. The Bombay Gazetteer of 1884 showed Jain Banias outnumbering Vaishnava ones by a ratio of three to two, both in Gujarat as a whole (334,000 to 213,000) and in Kathiawad (96,150 to 63,400). (*Gazetteer of the Bombay Presidency,* Vol. 9, Pt. 1: *Gujarat Population* [Bombay, 1884], p. 70; *ibid.,* Vol. 8: *Kathiawar,* p. 147.)

58. Gandhi, *Autobiography,* pp. 33–34.

59. This admittedly novel interpretation is substantiated in my article, "Jain Influences on Gandhi's Early Thought," read as a paper at the 17th International Congress of Orientalists, Ann Arbor, Mich., to be published in Sibnarayan Ray, ed., *Gandhi and Gandhism* (Melbourne, 1969). Relations between Jains and Vaishnavas in Gujarat have long been so close as to make the two communities almost indistinguishable (much to the dismay of the British census officials). Thus the *Census of India, 1901,* Vol. 1: *General*

Report (Calcutta, 1904), p. 368, observed: "In some parts, e.g., in Central India, the Jains are said to admit no connection with Hindus at all, but elsewhere, as in Baroda, they are equally anxious to be regarded as a Hindu sect and not as members of a separate religious body." The *Census of India, 1921,* Vol. 8: *Bombay Presidency,* Pt. 1 (Bombay, 1923), p. 68, noted somewhat plaintively: "In the case of Jainism it is doubtful whether any student of comparative religion could possibly class Jainism as a sect of Hinduism. Yet it is a fact that many Jains regard themselves and are regarded as Hindus." Gandhi himself took this view of the matter, declaring in an article, "I do not regard Jainism or Buddhism as separate from Hinduism." (M. K. Gandhi, "Why I am a Hindu," *Young India* [Oct. 20, 1927], reprinted in his *Hindu Dharma* [Ahmedabad, Navajivan Publishing House, 1950], p. 6.)

60. Gandhi, *Autobiography,* pp. 52–56. Gandhi's early years are recounted in some detail in Pyarelal [Nair], *Mahatma Gandhi: The Early Phase,* Vol. 1 (Ahmedabad, 1965). Of special value in this work is the information on pp. 213–214 that Gandhi's mother was raised in the Pranāmī sect, and the discussions of the ideas of Edward Maitland (pp. 321–327), and Raychand Mehta (pp. 327–331), two men who greatly helped Gandhi in his spiritual crisis of 1893–1895.

61. *Ibid.,* pp. 111–115, 119. The Jain reformer was Rajchandra (or Raychand) Mehta; his career and aims are summarized in J. N. Farquhar, *Modern Religious Movements in India* (New York, 1918), pp. 327–328. For further references on Raychand and Virchand, see Hay, "Jain Influences." It is significant that Gandhi gives no indication in his *Autobiography* that these two close friends were Jains.

62. Gandhi, *Autobiography,* pp. 140–150, 173–175.

63. *Ibid.,* pp. 67, 79–84; Stephen Winsten, *Salt and His Circle* (London, 1951); *The Collected Works of Mahatma Gandhi,* Vol. 1 (1884–1896) (Delhi, 1958), pp. 139–141, 165–169, 140.

64. Gandhi, *Autobiography,* pp. 92, 169–172; Mahātmā Gāndhījī, "Srīmad Rājchandranāñ smaraṇo" (Reminiscences of Shrimad Rajchandra), in *Mahātmā Gāndhījī ane Srīmad Rājchandra* (Ahmedabad, [1936–37]), p. 9.

65. "Mahātmā Gāndhījīe puchhāvelā praśnonā Srīmad Rājchandre āpelā javābo" (Shrimad Rajchandra's own answers to the questions asked by Mahatma Gandhi), in *ibid.,* pp. 23 ff.

66. This summary of Jain teachings is drawn from various modern writings on Jainism, notably the works of Virchand Gandhi, the booklet by Herbert Warren, *Jainism, In Western Garb, As a Solution to Life's Great Problems, Chiefly from Notes of Talks and Lectures by Virchand R. Gandhi* (Madras, 1912); Jagmanderlal Jaini, *Outlines of Jainism* (Cambridge, England, 1916); and Mrs. Sinclair Stevenson, *The Heart of Jainism* (Oxford, 1915). Raychand's letter contains only a partial exposition of the Jain teachings, but Gandhi must have learned more about them from his many conversations with Raychand in Bombay in 1892–1893, and perhaps when he revisited Bombay in 1896. Gandhi ascribes his adoption of the vow of chastity

(*brahmacharya*) in 1906 to the influence of Raychand's teachings (*Auto-biography*, pp. 252–256, 401). Shortly after learning from Gandhi that he had been satisfied by the answers to his questions, Raychand composed a long poem condensing his teachings, at the end of which his pupil exclaimed with delight, "you have shown me the separateness of the self [from the body] like the sword in its sheath." See *The Atma-siddhi* (*or the Self-Realisation*) *of Shrimad Rajchandra*, tr. with an introduction and notes by J. L. Jaini, 2nd ed. (Ahmedabad, 1960), p. 97 and *passim*. Raychand's other works (not yet translated from the Gujarati) are collected in *Śrīmad Rājchandra*, ed. Mansukhlal Ravjibhai Mehta (Bombay, Samvat 1992 [1935–1936]).

67. Gāndhījī, "Śrīmad Rājchandranāñ smaraṇo," pp. 19–20.

68. M. K. Gandhi, *Hind Swaraj, or Indian Home Rule*, 3rd ed. (Madras, c. 1921), pp. 55, 58, 25, 26.

69. M. K. Gandhi, "A Confession of Faith" (a letter to a friend written in 1909), in *Speeches and Writings of Mahatma Gandhi*, pp. 1041, 1042. Gandhi never moved from this basic position, and reiterated it in his prefaces to the 1921 and 1938 reprintings of *Hind Swaraj*.

70. Gandhi, *Hind Swaraj*, pp. 85–87, lists four virtues required of passive resisters: chastity, poverty, truthfulness (nonviolence is not mentioned, perhaps being considered a quality that would follow automatically from these cardinal virtues), and fearlessness.

71. M. K. Gandhi, in an address delivered to an audience of Europeans at the Germiston (Transvaal) Literary and Debating Society, in *Speeches and Writings of Mahatma Gandhi*, p. 166. The Jains' belief in the "permanent and superior nature" of the soul is shown in their doctrine that the liberated *jīva* rises to the top of the universe to float there, completely independent, for all eternity — in contrast to the Hindu belief that the *ātman* merges into the Absolute as a drop of water is absorbed into the ocean.

72. These are Gandhi's concluding words in a message addressed to the 1909 session of the Indian National Congress. (He was replying to a cabled request from the Congress.) His message was published in the *Indian Review* (Madras), in December 1909, and reprinted in *Speeches and Writings of Mahatma Gandhi*, pp. 182–184.

73. Benarsidas Chaturvedi and Marjorie Sykes, *Charles Freer Andrews: A Narrative* (New York, 1950), pp. 90–93; C. F. Andrews, "The Poet," pp. 23–24.

74. Nirmalchandra Chattopadhyaya, "Mahatma Gandhi at Rabindranath's Santiniketan," in *Gandhi Memorial Peace Number*, ed. Kshitis Roy (Santiniketan, 1949), p. 327, translating from the report in *Tattvabodhini patrikā* (Śaka Chaitra 1836 [March–April 1915]).

75. Tagore to Gandhi (Apr. 12, 1919), in *Indian Daily News* (Apr. 16, 1919), as quoted in *Tagore and Gandhi Argue*, comp. Jag Parvesh Chander (Lahore, 1945), p. 11.

76. Tagore to C. F. Andrews (Mar. 2, 5, and 13, 1921), in Tagore, *Letters to a Friend*, pp. 127–128, 128, 132, 135, 136.

77. M. K. Gandhi, "The Poet's Anxiety," *Young India* (June 1, 1921), reprinted in Gandhi, *Young India, 1919–1922,* 2nd ed. (Madras, 1924), pp. 608, 611, 612–613. Gandhi wrote a second article in this same issue of *Young India,* answering Tagore's charge that by boycotting English education Gandhi was turning India into an intellectual prison. Gandhi's brilliant phrase is now inscribed over the entrance to the National Library in Calcutta: "I want the cultures of all lands to be blown about my house as freely as possible. But I refuse to be blown off my feet by any." (*Ibid.,* p. 460.)

78. *Amrita Bazar Patrika* (July 26, 1921); Rabindranath Tagore, "The Union of Cultures," *Modern Review,* 30.5:533–542 (November 1921); Rabindranath Tagore, "The Call of Truth," *ibid.,* 30.4:423–433 (October 1921). After Tagore's second lecture was published, Gandhi replied with an editorial restating his position and defending his hand-spinning program as the best solution to the problem of India's poverty. (M. K. Gandhi, "The Great Sentinel," *Young India* [Oct. 13, 1921], reprinted in *Young India, 1919–1922,* 2nd ed. [Madras, 1924], pp. 668–675.)

79. Elmhirst, "Personal Memories," p. 15.

80. Thompson, p. 261, citing an unidentified private conversation.

81. *Amrita Bazar Patrika* (Aug. 16, 1921); *Servant* (Sept. 2, 1921); interview with Elmhrist; *Amrita Bazar Patrika* (Aug. 17, 1924). A slightly different version of this last incident was given in C. R. Das's *Forward* (Aug. 15, 1924), according to which Tagore "received a tremendous ovation from the assembled crowd," but neither he nor B. C. Pal was able to gain a hearing. When Das's lieutenant Subhas Chandra Bose (during World War II the leader of the Indian National Army under Japanese sponsorship) rose to speak, however, "scarcely had he opened his mouth when the gathering was lulled to complete silence and quiet and Sj. Bose was accorded a patient and respectful hearing." *Forward* failed to mention what the *Amrita Bazar Patrika* called this "insult to Sir Rabindra Nath."

82. "Visva-Bharati," p. 124; Nehru, *Autobiography,* p. 80.

83. *Young India,* 6.30:243 (July 24, 1924), also quoted in *Modern Review,* 36.2:218 (August 1924); *Young India* (Jan. 6, 1927), also quoted in Mahatma Gandhi, *Young India, 1927–1928* (Madras, 1935), p. 5. Although a visionary in many of his ideas, Gandhi was also a very practical man, and he had scouted the idea of Asiatic federation before. In 1924, in the wake of Tagore's return from China, a group of nineteen Bengali leaders had called for such a federation as part of a four-point program, and Gandhi replied: "And the final proposal to organise a federation of all the Asiatic races in the immediate future demonstrates the present impossibility of the programme." (*Amrita Bazar patrika,* July 23, 1924.)

84. Tagore, "Aurobindo Ghosh," p. 60.

85. Rabindranath Tagore, "Gandhi the Man," in *Gandhi Memorial Peace Number,* pp. 11, 12; Chattopadhyaya, p. 336.

86. Mahatma Gandhi, "The Message of Asia," *United Asia,* 1.1:3 (Bombay, May–June 1948).

87. This statement of Sept. 22, 1947 was printed in Gandhi's weekly *Harijan* (Child of God; Oct. 5, 1947), and is also quoted in Pyarelal [Nair], *Mahatma Gandhi: The Last Phase* (Ahmedabad, 1958), II, 453.

88. These two leaders are compared and their conflicting careers summarized in Stanley A. Wolpert, *Tilak and Gokhale: Revolution and Reform in the Making of Modern India* (Berkeley and Los Angeles, 1962).

89. V. D. Savarkar, *Hindutva*, 2nd ed. (Poona, 1962), pp. 113–114.

90. *Ibid.*, p. 117.

91. I owe this distinction to W. H. Morris-Jones, "India's Political Idioms," in C. H. Philips, ed., *Politics and Society in India* (London, 1963), pp. 133–154.

92. Both broad and limited meanings are given in John T. Platts, *A Dictionary of Urdū, Classical Hindī, and English* (London, preface 1884), p. 1236, under *hind*: "India, Hindustān (properly restricted to the Upper provinces, between Banāras and the Satlaj."

93. The history of the Nehru family is summarized in B. R. Nanda, *The Nehrus: Motilal and Jawaharlal* (London, 1962; New York, 1963).

94. Nehru wrote in 1931: "Nationalism, specially when it urges us to fight for freedom, is noble and life-giving. But often it becomes a narrow creed, and limits and encompasses its votaries and makes them forget the many-sidedness of life. But Rabindranath Tagore has given to our nationalism the outlook of internationalism and has enriched it with art and music and the magic of his words, so that it has become a full-blooded emblem of India's awakened spirit." (*Golden Book of Tagore,* p. 183.) On the centenary of Tagore's birth, Nehru wrote: "In my later years, my attraction to Tagore grew. I felt a great deal of kinship with his thought and with his general outlook on life." ("Introduction," in *Rabindranath Tagore: A Centenary Volume, 1861–1961,* p. xv.)

95. Meredith Townsend, *Asia and Europe,* 3rd ed. (London, 1905), *passim* and pp. xxi, xviii.

96. Nehru, *Toward Freedom,* pp. 123–26; Franz Borkenau, *Der europäische Kommunismus* (Munich, 1952), p. 56; *Pravda* (Feb. 4, 1927). The resolution's first and third paragraphs sound a Tagorean note: "For more than three thousand years the people of India and China were united by the most intimate cultural ties. From the days of Buddha to the end of the Mughal period and the beginning of British domination in India this friendly intercourse continued uninterrupted. . . . With the strengthening of British imperialism, India was cut off more and more from intercourse with China, and in their cultural and intellectual isolation, the Indian people have now become completely ignorant of China." (Jawaharlal Nehru, "Report on the International Congress against Imperialism held at Brussels," *The Indian National Congress,* 1927 [Madras, 1928], pp. 61 ff., as reprinted in Bimla Prasad, *The Origins of Indian Foreign Policy: The Indian National Congress and World Affairs, 1885–1947* [Calcutta, 1960], p. 272.)

97. Nehru called the opening ceremony: "great in memories of the long

past that it invokes, great also in the promise of future comradeship and the forging of new links to bring China and India nearer to each other. . . . We have traded in ideas, in art, in culture, and grown richer in our own inheritance by the other's offering. The political subjection came to both of us in varying forms, and stagnation and decay, and at the same time new forces and ideas from the West to wake us out of our torpor. We have been struggling to find a new equilibrium, to rid ourselves of the forces that throttle us, to give expression to the new life that already pulsates through our veins. The whole world seeks that new equilibrium, but the forces of darkness are strong and in the name of Fascism and Imperialism and their allies seek to crush the spirit of man. . . . But the spirit of man is not easily crushed. . . . It will triumph afresh. China and India, sister nations from the dawn of history, with their long tradition of culture and peaceful development of ideas, have to play a leading part in this world drama, in which they themselves are so deeply involved." (Message read by Indira Gandhi on April 14, 1937, as quoted in Tan Yun-shan, *Twenty Years of the Visva-Bharati Cheena-Bhavana, 1937–1957* [Santiniketan, 1957], p. 16.)

98. See Prasad, pp. 126–128; Kalidas Nag, *New Asia* (Calcutta, 1947), p. 25.

99. Jawaharlal Nehru, *China, Spain and the War: Essays and Writings* (Allahabad, 1940), pp. 21 ff., as quoted in Prasad, p. 128.

100. Kripalani, p. 399, quoting Nehru's letter to Kripalani of Aug. 27, 1941.

101. Nehru, *Autobiography*, p. 384. This statement is also reproduced in Jawaharlal Nehru, *The Unity of India: Collected Writings, 1937–1940* (London, 1941), p. 389.

102. "Jawaharlal Nehru's Inaugural Address to the Asian Relations Conference, New Delhi, March 23, 1947," as reprinted in Prasad, pp. 311, 312, 314.

103. *Ibid.,* p. 316.

104. *Census of India, 1921,* Vol. 1, Pt. 2, pp. 72, 78.

105. Iqbal was at Trinity College from 1905 to 1907, the same college at which Nehru studied from 1907 to 1910.

106. Muḥammad Iqbāl, *Armughān-i Hidjāz* (Gift from the Hidjaz; Lahore, 1948), p. 63, mainly as translated in Mazheruddin Siddiqi, *The Image of the West in Iqbāl* (Lahore, 1956), p. 64.

107. Quoted in *Poems from Iqbal,* tr. V. G. Kiernan (London, 1955), p. xxiii.

108. Muḥammad Iqbāl, *Żarb-i Kalīm* (The rod of Moses), 7th ed. (Lahore, 1947), p. 81, as translated in Siddiqi, p. 69.

109. Muḥammad Iqbāl, *Jāvīdnāme,* 2nd ed. (Lahore, 1947), p. 71. I wish to thank Mr. Manoutchehr Mohandessi for cotranslating this passage with me.

110. Muhammad Iqbal, *The Mysteries of Selflessness,* tr. Arthur J. Arberry (London, 1955), p. 29.

111. This unidentified poem of Iqbal is quoted as translated in A. Anwar

Beg, *The Poet of the East: The Life and Work of Dr. Shaikh Sir Muhammad Iqbal, the Poet-Philosopher* (Lahore, 1939), p. 41.

112. "Presidential Address Delivered at the Annual Session of the All-India Muslim League at Allahabad on the 29th December, 1930." *Speeches and Statements of Iqbal,* comp. "Shamloo," 2nd rev. ed. (Lahore, 1948), p. 34.

113. *Ibid.,* pp. 35, 12. To put in perspective the statements of Iqbal and of later Muslim proponents of a separate Muslim-majority state, it should be noted that the basic idea had already been proposed in 1924 by the Punjab Hindu leader Lala Lajpat Rai, one of the staunchest of nationalists and a member simultaneously of the Congress and the Hindu Mahasabha. Lajpat Rai was also prominent in the Arya Samaj, which had its headquarters and its main strength in the Punjab. Muslim fears of Hindu domination were aggravated by the aggressive spirit of the Arya Samaj, especially in the 1920's. After a brief visit to Japan, Lajpat Rai declared in a 1916 article his firm belief that India, China, and Japan were united by similarities in religion, social outlook, and art. (Lajpat Rai, "Is Not the East a Unity As Compared with the West?" *Modern Review,* 20.6:582–591 [December 1916].)

114. Mohammad Iqbal, *The Reconstruction of Religious Thought in Islam* (originally delivered as lectures in English, at Madras, Mysore, and Aligarh in 1927; Lahore, 1954), pp. 7, 8.

115. Numerous quotations could be adduced from Iqbal's writings on Islam as the essence of the East. See, for example, his poems, "Eastern Nations," and "An Eastern League of Nations," in *Żarb-i kalīm,* one of his last books of Urdu verse, as translated in *Poems from Iqbal,* pp. 66, 74. In the course of a significant exchange between Iqbal and Nehru in 1933 the former suggested a triangular relationship between Islam, East, and West: "All I can say is that, lying midway between Asia and Europe and being a synthesis of Eastern and Western outlooks on life, Islam ought to act as a kind of intermediary between the East and the West." (*Speeches and Statements of Iqbal,* p. 143.) For Nehru's reply, which demarcates the intellectual gulf between him and Iqbal, see Jawaharlal Nehru, *Recent Essays and Writings on the Future of India, Communalism, and Other Subjects* (Allahabad, 1934), pp. 60–69.

116. Tagore's visit to Lahore is described in Mukhopādhyāẏ, *Rabīndrajī-banī,* IV, 4, but his call on Iqbal is curiously enough omitted from this account. The visit is mentioned in Muḥammad Iqbāl *Iqbālnāme,* ed. Shaikh Muhammad Ata (Lahore, n.d.), I, 287, according to Annemarie Schimmel, *Gabriel's Wing: A Study into the Religious Ideas of Sir Muhammad Iqbal* (Leiden, 1963), p. 58n.

117. Quoted, from an unidentified original source, in Beg, pp. 92–93.

118. A. Yusuf Ali, "The Religion of Rabindranath Tagore," *Islamic Culture* (Hyderabad, 4.1:114–129, January 1930).

119. Iqbal, *The Secrets of the Self* (*Asrar-i-Khudi*), tr. Reynolds A. Nicholson (Lahore, 1944), p. 33.

120. *Forward* (July 18, 1924).

121. *Treasure Chest,* as quoted in *Modern Review,* 36.4:453 (October 1924).

122. Editorial in *Bombay Chronicle,* as quoted in *Forward* (Calcutta, July 19, 1924). The *Bombay Chronicle* at this time had a circulation of 12,000, the highest figure for an Indian-managed newspaper in that city. Second to it, with 8,000 circulation, came the *Bombay Daily Mail,* edited by a Ceylonese of Dutch descent, Frederic Holsinger. (*Report on Native Newspapers Published in the Bombay Presidency, for the Week Ending 5th January 1924* [Bombay, 1924], p. 1.) The *Bombay Daily Mail* commented on June 18, 1924: "Dr. Tagore's visit to China appears to have been a complete success. . . . It is evident that the citizens of the Imperial capital were able to appreciate thoroughly the greatness of the Indian poet." This judgment seems to have been based on the editorial, "Tagore's Visit," signed "From a Chinese Contributor," in the Japanese-edited daily, *North China Standard* (Peking, Apr. 25, 1924).

123. These Indianized Europeans exerted a considerable and as yet little-studied influence on English-speaking Indian intellectuals. For a biography of Pickthall, see Anne M. H. Fremantle, *Loyal Enemy* (London, 1938). See also Nethercot, *First Five Lives of Annie Besant,* and his *Last Four Lives of Annie Besant;* and James H. Cousins and Margaret E. Cousins, *We Two Together* (Madras, 1950). Aurobindo Ghose, in the preface to his *The Renaissance in India,* 3rd ed. (Calcutta, 1946; first published in his magazine, *Arya,* in August–November 1918), acknowledged that he had written this book in "appreciation of Mr. James H. Cousins' book of the same name." Cousins, in turn, may have taken his book's title from C. F. Andrews, *The Renaissance in India* (London, 1912). For Sir John Woodroffe's theory of Eastern spiritual civilization, see his *Is India Civilized? Essays on Indian Culture,* 3rd ed. (Madras, 1922; 1st ed. 1918).

124. *Bombay Daily Mail* (July 31, 1928), quoting the *Manchester Guardian.* Andrews had not been with Tagore in China, but had met him in Hong Kong on his way back to India. (Chaturvedi and Sykes, p. 199.)

125. M. K. Gandhi, "A Parallel from China," *Young India* (Feb. 9, 1928); reprinted in his *Young India, 1927–1928,* p. 604.

126. Prasad, pp. 78–84. For more detailed accounts of the annual Congress sessions see *Indian Annual Register,* ed. H. N. Mitra and N. N. Mitra (Calcutta) for these years (published as *Indian Quarterly Register,* 1924–1929).

127. A number of minor writers from Bengal and South India not dealt with here who commented on Tagore's ideas are quoted in Stephen N. Hay, "India's Prophet in East Asia: Tagore's Message of Pan-Asian Spiritual Revival and Its Reception in Japan and China, 1916–1929" (Ph.D. thesis, Harvard, 1957), pp. 33–49. See also *Books about Rabindranath Tagore,* comp. Pulinbehari Sen (Calcutta, April 1947). A comprehensive bibliography of writings on Tagore is being compiled by the Sahitya Akademi (Academy of literature), New Delhi.

The superior spirituality of India and the East in general and of Hinduism in particular over modern Western civilization was such a favorite theme of Indian writers of Hindu background that many books on it were published in the period from World War I to about 1950. Some representative titles are: U. P. Krishnamacharya (a Madras Brahman), *The Wisdom of the East* (Benares, first published as a periodical, Vol. 1, Nos. 1–5 being dated August [?]–December 1914); Harendranath Maitra, *Hinduism: The World-Ideal* (London, 1916); T. L. Vaswani (a Sindhi Hindu), *The Secret of Asia: Essays on the Spirit of Asian Culture* (Madras, c. 1920); Anilbaran Ray (a Bengali disciple of Aurobindo Ghose), *India's Mission in the World* (Calcutta, c. 1930); M. K. Acharya (President of Madras Varnashram Swarajya Sangha, and Member of Legislative Assembly, 1924–1930), *India's Higher Call* (Madras, 1934); N. Lakshmanan (a journalist then living in Coimbatore, South India), *India, The Fountain of Peace: A Sourcebook of Leadership for the New Era* (Coimbatore, 1937); Nolini Kanta Gupta, *The Malady of the Century and Other Essays* (Madras, 1943); Maharaj Rana Sir Udaibhan Singhji (of Dholpur), *Eastern Light of Sanātan Culture* (Calcutta, 1946); G. K. Datta (a Bengali follower of Dr. Shyama Prasad Mukherjee, the founder of the Jan Sangh Party), *Road to Peace* (Calcutta, preface 1949).

The views of the distinguished historian and critic of Indian and Indonesian art, Dr. Ananda Kentish Coomaraswamy, may also be recalled here, although he was not an Indian. The son of an English Unitarian mother and a Ceylonese judge of Tamil descent, Coomaraswamy was educated at the University College, London as a mineralogist. Disturbed by the Westernization of Ceylon after he settled there, he founded the Ceylon Social Reform Society. Turning his attention to the preservation and elucidation of Asia's artistic heritage, he joined the circle of the Tagore family in Calcutta in the first decade of this century, became an assistant to E. B. Havell, principal of the Government School of Art in Calcutta, and became Okakura's successor as curator of the Oriental collection at the Museum of Fine Arts, Boston. Coomaraswamy, a far better scholar than Tagore or Aurobindo, voiced the same sentiments on Asia's spirituality as they in his collection of essays, *The Dance of Shiva* (New York, 1924; 2nd ed., Bombay, 1948). Romain Rolland contributed a forward to this volume. I am indebted for this information to the excellent unpublished paper by Mary Carmen Lynn (Department of History, University of Chicago), "Sources of Modern Aesthetic Discourse in Bengal."

128. Nehru, *Autobiography,* p. 353.

129. Nehru wrote of Tagore in the early 1940's: "More than any other Indian, he has helped to bring into harmony the ideals of the east and the west, and broadened the bases of Indian nationalism. He has been India's internationalist par excellence, believing and working for international cooperation, taking India's message to other countries and bringing their message to his own people." (Jawaharlal Nehru, *The Discovery of India* [London, 1951], p. 318.)

130. Iqbal and the leaders of other movements in twentieth-century Muslim thought in India, as they expressed themselves mainly in publications in Urdu, are treated in the superb analysis by F. Rahman, "Muslim Modernism in the Indo-Pakistan Sub-continent," *Bulletin of the School of Oriental and African Studies,* 21.1:82–99 (London, 1958). The nature and decline of the Muslim-Hindu synthesis have been treated in the pioneering study by Heinrich Goetz, *The Crisis of Indian Civilization in the Eighteenth and Early Nineteenth Centuries* (Calcutta, 1939).

Epilogue

Epigraph. Frederic Lefevre, "Une heure avec M. Sylvain Lévi," in *Memorial Sylvain Lévi,* ed. Louis Renou. (Paris, 1937), p. 431.

1. Peter Chaadaev, *Oeuvres choisies de Pierre Tchadaief,* ed. P. Gagarin (Paris, 1862), pp. 139–140.

2. B. H. Sumner, *A Short History of Russia* (New York, 1949), p. 309.

3. See Hu Shih, *The Chinese Renaissance;* D. S. Sarma, *The Renaissance of Hinduism in the Nineteenth and Twentieth Centuries* (Benares, 1944); Amit Sen (pseud. of Sushabhusan Sarkar), *Notes on the Bengal Renaissance,* 2nd ed. (Calcutta, 1957); *Studies in the Bengal Renaissance,* ed. Atulchandra Gupta (Jadavpur, 1958); and Kopf, *British Orientalism and the Bengal Renaissance.*

4. Gandhi, *Hind Swaraj* (3rd ed.), "Appendices," pp. i–v.

5. A contemporary observer, the Harvard-educated Tsurumi Yusuke, noted that the law "excluding Japanese immigration made a tremendous impression on the thinking part of the nation. The disappointment with the West drove them to turn to their old schools of thought for enlightenment. Orientalism received a new stimulus." (*Present Day Japan* [New York, 1926], pp. 47–48.)

6. *Nichi-nichi shimbun* (Daily news; Tokyo, June 11, 1924).

7. C. F. Andrews, "India in the Far East," *Young India,* 6.30:242–243 (July 24, 1924), paraphrasing and quoting "a very beautiful account of the poet's visit there" which had just reached Hong Kong from Tokyo. The author of the report was probably L. K. Elmhirst. Either he or Andrews sent the report to the *South China Morning Post* (Hong Kong), which reproduced it in full on June 25, 1924.

8. *Nichi-nichi shimbun* (June 15, 1924).

9. Tsurumi, p. 47. See also the evidence mentioned in Richard Storry, *The Double Patriots: A Study of Japanese Nationalism* (Boston, 1957), p. 25.

10. In contrast to 1916, Tagore's 1924 visit and lectures occasioned little comment among Japan's intellectuals. The only significant article was Tanaka Ōdō, "Haruka ni Tagōru shi yosete Ajiya dōmei no shisō ronzu" (I discuss with Tagore, who lives far away, the idea of an Asian league), *Chūō kōron,* 39.12:4–47 (December 1924). Tanaka repeated his 1916 critique of Tagore's concept of spiritual civilization, but he agreed with the suggestion mooted by Tagore that an Asian league was needed to defend Asian cultures against the West. In Tanaka's opinion, the nation most qualified to lead such a

league, because of its greater experience with modern civilization, was Japan. For a bibliography of books, periodical articles, and newspaper comments on Tagore's 1924 and 1929 visits to Japan, see *Apollon*, 1.1:123–134 (May 1958). Details of these visits are given in Hay, "India's Prophet," pp. 118–153.

11. *Tōkyō asahi shimbun* (Mar. 28, 1929).

12. *Osaka Mainichi and Tokyo Nichi-nichi* (Osaka, Mar. 29, 1929).

13. Interview with Apurva Kumar Chanda (a member of the Indian Educational Service who was Tagore's companion and secretary on this trip), in Calcutta, Dec. 1, 1959.

14. Tagore, *On Oriental Culture*, pp. 14–15, 12.

15. Interview with A. K. Chanda; Jansen, pp. 71, 75, 159, 161, 196.

16. Interview with A. K. Chanda. Tōyama's attendance at the ceremonies in Nanking is described in Jansen, pp. 1–3. One other incident during this final stay in Japan marked the widening gap between Tagore's Asianism and that of Japan's ultranationalists. The fanatic followers of Tachibana Kosaburo invited him to visit their headquarters at Mito, sixty miles north of Tokyo. When he declined, one of them vowed to commit hara-kiri if he did not come, and the perplexed poet gave in. (Interview with Mrs. Kora Tomiko, Tagore's interpreter on this as on his 1916 and 1924 visits.) Tagore had no stomach for the Tachibana fanatics, and returned from Mito on the same day he arrived (May 17), having lectured on feminism to a group of high school girls. Tachibana's ideals nevertheless resembled Tagore's at several points: the evil of cities growing fat at the expense of the farmers (see Tagore's lecture, "City and Village"); the bankruptcy of Western civilization, and the hope of creating a pan-Asian league. On Tachibana, see Storry, pp. 98, 100, 108, 119–120.

17. Kunihiko Ōkura, *My Thoughts,* tr. Iwao Matsuhara and E. T. Inglehart (Yokohama, 1935), p. 149.

18. *Ibid.,* p. 173.

19. *Kokutai no hongi: Cardinal Principles of the National Entity of Japan,* tr. John Owen Gauntlett, ed. Robert King Hall (Cambridge, Mass., 1949).

20. Noguchi Yonejirō, *Indo no shijin* (The Indian poet; Tokyo, 1926), the only biography of Tagore published after 1916, contains this statement (pp. 33–34): "Japan is now in a crisis . . . In trying to overcome this crisis, Tagore's teachings offer us many suggestions. I do not agree with him completely, but I do believe that almost all of his opinions can help us in saving contemporary Japan."

21. See Noguchi Yonejirō, *Indo wa kataru* (India speaks; Tokyo, 1936), pp. 58–66; and Yone Noguchi, *The Ganges Calls Me* (Tokyo, 1938), which contains an appendix, "Reception at Santiniketan."

22. *Poet to Poet* (Calcutta: Visva-Bharati, 1939), reprinted as *Tagore-Noguchi Correspondence* (Cleveland, 1942). The two letters from Tagore to Noguchi were actually written by his secretaries (according to their statements to me in personal interviews), but are in full accord with his views.

The first letter, dated Sept. 1, 1938, was the work of Amiya Chakravarty, the second, dated simply October 1938, was the work of Krishna Kripalani.

23. Shigenobu Ōkuma, "Summary of the History of Japan," in Shigenobu Ōkuma, ed., *Fifty Years of New Japan* (London, 1910), I, 41. This persistence and expansion of the samurai ethos was even hailed by Japan's leading internationalist, the Christian educator Inazō Nitobe, in his famous *Bushido, The Soul of Japan* (New York, 1905), pp. 188–189: "What won the battles on the Yalu, in Corea and Manchuria, were the ghosts of our fathers, guiding our hands and beating in our hearts. They are not dead, these ghosts, the spirits of our warlike ancestors. To those who have eyes to see, they are clearly visible. Scratch a Japanese of the most advanced ideas, and he will show a samurai." Nitobe married an American Quaker girl and in later life served for some years as a member of the secretariat of the League of Nations.

24. "Dr. R. Tagore's Preface," in Ch'ü Yüan, *The Li Sao: An Elegy on Encountering Sorrows,* tr. Lim Boon Keng (Shanghai, 1929), p. xxiii.

25. *Shen pao* (Mar. 20, 1929); *North China Star* (Mar. 26, 1929).

26. *North China Star* (Mar. 26, 1929).

27. *Hsin Ya-hsi-ya,* 1.1:i (Nanking, October 1930). Tai Chi-t'ao has an article in almost every issue. This periodical seems to have ceased publication in 1936, by which time Japan's pan-Asian movement was making much faster headway than China's. The magazine' title tends to confirm the supposition that it was started as a means of countering Japanese pan-Asian propaganda in China; Tōyama's Kokuryūkai had published from 1921 to 1923 an English-language monthly, *New Asia,* with Paul Richard as one of its editors.

28. P. C. Mahalanobis, "Tagore's Visit to Canada and Japan," *Visva-Bharati Quarterly,* 7.1:159, 160, 163 (April–July 1929). Evidently Tagore learned at this interview of the Japanese pan-Asianists' refusal to attend this ceremony.

29. Tan Yun-shan, *Twenty Years,* pp. 18–19. While in China, T'an had talked with Tai Chi-t'ao, as well as with the Buddhist leaders T'ai Hsü and Ou-yang Ching-wu.

30. Letter from Rabindranath Tagore addressed "To my Chinese Friends," dated Santiniketan, Apr. 18, 1934, as given in Tan Yun-shan, *Twenty Years,* p. 36.

31. Tan Yun-shan, "My Dedication to Gurudeva Tagore: written on the First Anniversary of his Death," in V. G. Nair, *Professor Tan Yun-shan and Cultural Relations between India and China* (Madras, 1958), p. 9.

32. "The Kuomintang," in *China Handbook, 1937–1945,* comp. Chinese Ministry of Information, rev. ed. (New York, 1947), pp. 38–39.

33. This use of nineteenth-century precedent is ably surveyed in Mary C. Wright, "From Revolution to Restoration: The Transformation of Kuomintang Ideology," *Far Eastern Quarterly,* 14.4:515–532 (August 1955).

34. Quoted in G. D. Khanolkar, *The Lute and the Plough: A Life of Rabindranath Tagore* (Bombay, 1963), p. 349.

35. Rabindranath Tagore, *Crisis in Civilization,* rev. ed. (Calcutta, 1950), pp. 17–18.

36. The Gandhi-Chiang meeting is described in Maulana Abul Kalam Azad, *India Wins Freedom. An Autobiographical Narrative* (Bombay, 1959), p. 45; also in a letter from Mahadev Desai (Gandhi's chief secretary) to Ghanshyamdas D. Birla, July 16, 1942, quoted in G. D. Birla, *In the Shadow of the Mahatma: A Personal Memoir,* 2nd ed. (Calcutta, 1955), p. 218. Desai objected to the publicity the Chinese gave the meeting and concluded: "The whole thing leaves a most unpleasant taste in the mouth. The visit ought not to have taken place. But it is well that Bapu [Gandhi] was face to face with that 'inscrutable' man, as he always calls him." Gandhi's message of June 14, 1942, to Chiang is quoted in D. G. Tendulkar, *Mahatma: Life of Mohandas Karamchand Gandhi* (Bombay, 1951–1954), VI, 141–144.

37. Tagore, *Nationalism,* p. 75.

38. Rabindranath Tagore, Holograph message dated May 3, 1930, reproduced in *Indo-Asian Culture* (Calcutta), 10.1:115 (July 1961).

39. Rabindranath Tagore, Address to the Anglo-American Association in Peking, quoted in Mahalanobis, *Tagore's Visit,* Pt. 2, p. 18.

40. Tagore, *Religion of Man,* p. 225.

41. As translated in Shakti Das Gupta, *Tagore's Asian Outlook* (Calcutta, 1961), p. 68.

BIBLIOGRAPHICAL NOTE

From among the many varieties of sources used in this study certain kinds stand out as especially useful. These are, in approximate order of their importance: the writings of the men and women whose ideas form the subject of this book; biographies or entries in biographical dictionaries; newspaper and periodical articles; interviews; manuscript letters and diaries; books surveying all or part of the intellectual histories of modern Japan, China, and India; and such reference works as bibliographies, library catalogs, yearbooks, guide books, and census reports.

Most of the sources yielding information on the intellectuals of the India-Pakistan area are in English, for most of them published more in that language than in their mother tongues during the first half of this century. The poets (Tagore, Iqbal, Bharati, Nazrul) are exceptions. Two general surveys of modern South Asian thought proved most helpful when I began this study: J. N. Farquhar's *Modern Religious Movements in India,* and D. S. Sarma's *Studies in the Renaissance of Hinduism in the Nineteenth and Twentieth Centuries.* On Tagore, I have used the standard edition of his Bengali works, *Rabīndra-rachanābalī,* and have found two bibliographies by Pulinbehari Sen most useful: *Books about Rabindranath Tagore,* and his "Bibliography" of Tagore's political essays, in Sachin Sen, *The Political Thought of Tagore.* Among the biographies of Tagore, the most generally useful has been that by Krishna Kripalani.

Japanese thought currents in the period preceding Tagore's encounter with Japan's intellectuals are intelligently surveyed in *Japanese Religion in the Meiji Era,* edited by Hideo Kishimoto and translated and adapted by John F. Howes, and in *Japanese Thought in the Meiji Era,* edited by Masaaki Kōsaka and translated and adapted by David Abosch. Two excellent works covering the Taisho period are Kyoson Tsuchida, *Contemporary Thought of Japan and China,* and Gino K. Piovesana, *Recent Japanese Philosophical Thought, 1862–1962: A Survey.* The Kokusai Bunka Shinkokai's *Introduction to Contemporary Japanese Literature* provides much information on the leading writers and literary currents of the period 1902–1935, and A. Morgan Young's *Japan under Taisho Tenno, 1912–1926* and *Imperial Japan, 1926–1938,* are uniquely valuable for political history. Biographical data on Japan's intellectuals and leading figures is given in the massive *Japan Biographical Encyclopedia & Who's Who,* but the earlier annual *Who's Who in Japan* and the ten-volume *Dai jimmei jiten* contain even more detailed entries.

My introduction to modern Chinese thought began with the rich anthology

China's Response to the West: A Documentary Survey, 1839–1923, edited by Ssu-yü Teng and John K. Fairbank. Most useful for twentieth-century thought were O. Brière. *Fifty Years of Chinese Philosophy, 1898–1950*, Wing-tsit Chan, *Religious Trends in Modern China*, Wen-han Kiang, *The Chinese Student Movement*, and Chow Tse-tsung's masterful *The May Fourth Movement: Intellectual Revolution in Modern China*. For biographical data I have made use of the China Weekly Review's *Who's Who in China* series and the usually reliable *Who's Who in Modern China*, edited by Max Perleberg. Three reference works guided me to articles in Chinese periodicals: *Chung-wen tsa-chih so-yin, Chung-kuo hsin wen-hsüeh ta-hsi* (especially vol. 10, *Shih-liao, so-yin*), and *Chung-kuo hsien-tai ch'u-pan shih-liao*. John King Fairbank and Kwang-Ching Liu, *Modern China: A Bibliographical Guide to Chinese Works, 1898–1937*, introduced me to other sources, as did my co-translators from Chinese, C. M. Ch'en, Lin Yu-sheng, and Cheng Chung-ying.

As the bibliography shows, much important material came from periodical articles. Most useful for the Indian scene was the *Modern Review*. For items by and about Tagore, his *Visva-Bharati Quarterly* was a major source. For the Japanese scene, the *Rikugō zasshi, Shin jin, Shin chō*, and *Asian Review* were the periodicals most used. For China, *Tung-fang tsa-chih, Hsiao-shuo yüeh-pao*, and *Ch'en-pao fu-k'an* were richest in articles and editorial comments. Newspapers of all three countries yielded a large amount of significant detail, most notably the *Tōkyō asahi shimbun*, the Shanghai *Shen pao*, and the Calcutta *Amrita Bazar Patrika*.

BIBLIOGRAPHY

Acharya, M. K. *India's Higher Call*. Madras: Huxley Press, 1934.

Advocate. Bombay, 1925.

Ahmed, A. F. Salahuddin. *Social Ideas and Social Change in Bengal, 1818–1835*. Leiden: E. J. Brill, 1965.

Akita Ujaku 秋田雨雀. "Sanjō no Tagōru" 山上のタゴール (On top of the hill with Tagore); *Waseda bungaku* 早稲田文學 (Waseda literature; July 1916).

Ali, A. Yusuf. "The Religion of Rabindranath Tagore," *Islamic Culture*, 4.1:114–129 (Hyderabad, Deccan, January 1930).

Aminananda, B. *The Blade*. Calcutta: Roy and Son, c. 1940.

Amrita Bazar Patrika. Calcutta, 1916, 1921, 1924.

Andrews, C. F. *The Renaissance in India*. London: United Council for Missionary Education, 1912

——— "Rabindranath Tagore," *Modern Review*, 14.1:35 (July 1913).

——— "India in the Far East," *Young India*, 6.30:242–243 (July 24, 1924).

——— "The Poet," in *The Golden Book of Tagore*, pp. 23–26.

——— "Rolland and Tagore," in *Rolland and Tagore*, pp. 7–15.

Anesaki, Masaharu. *The Professorship of Japanese Literature and Life at Harvard University: Its Scope and Work*. Cambridge, Mass., 1913.

——— "An Oriental Evaluation of Modern Civilization," in *Recent Gains in American Civilization, By a Group of Distinguished Critics of Contemporary Life*, ed. Kirby Page. New York: Harcourt, Brace and Co., 1928.

——— *History of Japanese Religion*. London: Kegan Paul, Trench, Trubner, 1930.

Arima, Tatsuo. *The Failure of Freedom: A Portrait of Modern Japanese Intellectuals*. Cambridge, Mass.: Harvard University Press, 1969.

Arnold, Edwin. *The Light of Asia, or The Great Renunciation*. London: Trübner and Co., 1879.

Arnold, Matthew. "Obermann Once More," in *The Works of Matthew Arnold*, Vol. 1: *Poems*. London: Macmillan and Co., 1903.

Aronson, Alex. *Rabindranath through Western Eyes*. Allahabad: Kitabistan, 1943.

Asano Akira 淺野晃. *Okakura Tenshin ronkō* 岡倉天心論考 (A study of Okakura Tenshin). Tokyo, 1939.

Atma-siddhi (or The Self-Realisation) of Shrimad Rajchandra, The, with an introduction and notes by J. L. Jaini. Ahmedabad: Shrimad Rajchandra Gyan Pracharak Trust, 1923; 2nd ed., 1960.

Ayers, William. "The Society for Literary Studies, 1921–1930," *Papers on China*, 7:34–79. Harvard University, East Asian Research Center, 1953.

Azad, Maulana Abul Kalam. *India Wins Freedom: An Autobiographical Narrative*. Bombay: Orient Longmans, 1959.

Aziz Ahmed. *Studies in Islamic Culture in the Indian Environment*. Oxford: Clarendon Press, 1964.

———— *Islamic Modernism in India and Pakistan, 1857–1964*. London: Oxford University Press, under the auspices of the Royal Institute of International Affairs, 1967.

Bagchee, Moni. *Sister Nivedita*. Calcutta: Presidency Library, 1956.

Bandyopādhyāẏ, Brajendranāth. *Bāmlā samāyik-patra* (Bengali periodical publications). 2nd rev. ed.; 2 vols.; Calcutta: Bangīẏa-sāhitya-parishat, B.E. 1359 (1952–1953).

Basu, Prem Sunder. *Life and Works of Brahmananda Keshav*. Calcutta: Navavidhan Publications Committee, 1940.

Baynes, Herbert. *The Ideals of the East*. London: Swan Sonnenschein and Co., 1898.

Beg, A. Anwar. *The Poet of the East: The Life and Work of Dr. Shaikh Sir Muhammad Iqbal, the Poet-Philosopher*. Lahore: Qaumi Kutub Khana, 1939.

Bengalee. Calcutta, 1924.

Bharati, Subrahmanya. *Agni and Other Poems, Translations, and Essays*. Madras, n.d.

Bhattacharya, Sukumar. "Lord Carmichael in Bengal: Proposal for His Recall," *Bengal Past and Present*, 79: 67–70 (July-December 1960).

Birla, G. D. *In the Shadow of the Mahatma: A Personal Memoir*. 2nd ed.; Calcutta: Orient Longmans, 1955.

Blavatsky, H. P. *The Key to Theosophy*. 3rd rev. ed.; London: Theosophical Publishing Society, 1893.

Bodde, Derk. *Tolstoy and China*. Princeton: Princeton University Press, 1950.

Bombay Daily Mail. Bombay, 1924.

Books about Rabindranath Tagore, comp. Pulinbihari Sen. Calcutta: Visva-Bharati Quarterly, April 1947.

Borkenau, Franz. *Der europäische Kommunismus*. Munich, 1952.

Borrey, Francis. *Un sage chinois, Kou Hong Ming: Notes biographiques*. Paris: Marcel Rivière, 1930.

Bose, Buddhadeva. "Tagore in Translation," *Jadavpur Journal of Comparative Literature*, 3:22–40 (Calcutta, 1963).

Boxer, Charles R. *The Christian Century in Japan, 1549–1650*. Berkeley: University of California Press, 1951.

Brahmo Dharma of Maharshi Debendranath Tagore, tr. Hem Chandra Sarkar. Calcutta: H. C. Sarkar, 1928.

Bredon, Juliet. *Peking: A Historical and Intimate Description of Its Chief Places of Interest*. 2nd rev. ed.; Shanghai: Kelly and Walsh, 1922.

Brière, O. *Fifty Years of Chinese Philosophy, 1898–1950*. London: George Allen and Unwin, 1956.

British Parliamentary Papers, XXI (*Reports of Commissioners, etc.*, Vol. 11), "Royal Commission on the Public Services" (Cmd. 7293, 1914).

Brooks, Rachel. "The Spiritualism of the Orient vs. the Materialism of the Occident," *Chinese Recorder*, 55.8:495–505 (August 1924).

Brooks, Van Wyck. *Fenollosa and His Circle, with Other Essays in Biography*. New York: E. P. Dutton, 1962.

Broomfield, John. *Elite Conflict in a Plural Society: Twentieth-Century Bengal*. Berkeley and Los Angeles: University of California Press, 1968.

Bryan, William Jennings. *Letters to a Chinese Official: Being a Western View of Eastern Civilization*. Lincoln, Neb.: Commoner Publishing Co., 1906.

Buber, Martin, comp. *Reden und Gleichnisse des Tschuang-tse*. 4th ed.; Leipzig: Insel-Verlag, 1921.

Byas, Hugh. *Government by Assassination*. New York: Alfred A. Knopf, 1942.

Calcutta Municipal Gazette: Tagore Memorial Special Supplement, ed. Amal Home. Calcutta, Sept. 13, 1941.

Census of India, 1901, Vol. 1: *General Report*. Calcutta: Superintendent of Government Printing, 1904.

Census of India, 1921, Vol. 1, Pt. 2. Calcutta: Superintendent of Government Printing, 1923–1924.

Census of India, 1921, Vol. 8: *Bombay Presidency*, Pt. 1. Bombay, Government Central Press, 1923.

Census of India, 1931, Vol. 1, Pt. 1. Delhi: Manager of Publications, 1933.

Census of India, 1931, Vol. 14: *Madras*, Pt. 1, *Report*. Madras and Calcutta: Government of India Central Publication Branch, 1932.

Central China Post. Hankow, 1924.

Chakravarty, Amiya. Letter to the author. Boston, Sept. 24, 1961.

Chan, Wing-tsit. *Religious Trends in Modern China*. New York: Columbia University Press, 1953.

Chandra, Rai Govind. *Abanindranath Tagore*. Calcutta: Thacker, Spink, 1951.

Chang, Carsun (Chang Chün-mai). Address of welcome to Professor Hans Driesch, in *Ostasiatische Rundschau*, 4.2:19–20 (Hamburg, Feb. 15, 1923).

——— *China and Gandhian India*. Calcutta: Book Co., 1956.

——— *The Development of Neo-Confucian Thought*. 2 vols.; New York: Bookman

Associates, 1962.

Chang Chün-mai 張君勱. "Jen-sheng-kuan" 人生觀 (View of life); in *K'o-hsüeh yü jen-sheng-kuan* 科學與人生觀 (Science and view of life), I, 1–13. 2 vols.; Shanghai: Ya-tung t'u-shu-kuan, 1923.

Chatterjee, Kedarnath. "Benoy Sarkar As I Saw Him," in Haridas Muk-herjee, *Benoy Kumar Sarkar: A Study*. Calcutta: Das Gupta and Co., 1953.

Chatterjee, Suniti Kumar. *Languages and Literatures in Modern India*. Calcutta: Bengal Publishers, 1963.

Chattopadhyaya, Nirmalchandra. "Mahatma Gandhi at Rabindranath's Santiniketan," in *Gandhi Memorial Peace Number*, pp. 319–336.

Chaturvedi, Benarsidas and Marjorie Sykes. *Charles Freer Andrews: A Narra-tive*. New York: Harper and Bros., 1950.

Chaudhury, Nagendra Nath. "Pragmatism and Pioneering in Benoy Sarkar's Sociology and Economics," in Banesvar Das, ed., *The Social and Econo-mic Ideas of Benoy Sarkar*. Calcutta: Chuckervertty Chatterjee and Co., 1940.

Ch'en T'ing-jui 陳廷瑞. "Ching-shen wen-ming yü wu-chih wen-ming" 精神文明與物質文明 (Spiritual civilization and material civilization); *Shen pao* (Apr. 29, 1924).

Ch'en Tu-hsiu 陳獨秀. "Ching-kao ch'ing-nien" 敬告青年 (A respectful warning to our young people); *Hsin ch'ing-nien* 新青年 (New youth), 1.1:4 (Sept. 15, 1915).

—— "Wo-men wei shen-mo huan-ying T'ai-ko-erh" 我們爲什麼歡迎太戈爾 (Why do we welcome Tagore?); *Chung-kuo ch'ing-nien* 中國青年 (China's youth), No. 2:15 (Oct. 27, 1923).

—— "Ts'un-t'ieh" 寸鐵 (The dagger); *Hsiang-tao* 嚮導 (Guide weekly), Nos. 62–64, 67 (April-May 1924).

—— See also Cheng Han and Shih An.

Cheng Chen-to 鄭振鐸. "Huan-ying T'ai-ko-erh" 歡迎太戈爾 (Welcome, Tagore); *Hsiao-shuo yüeh-pao* 小說月報 (Short story monthly), 14.9:4 (September 1923).

—— "Kuo-nei wen-t'an hsiao-hsi" 國內文壇消息 (News items on Chinese literature); *Hsiao-shuo yüeh-pao*, 15.6:1 (June 1924).

—— *T'ai-ko-erh chuan* 太戈爾傳 (A life of Tagore). Shanghai: Shang-wu yin-shu-kuan, 1926.

—— See also Chi Che.

Cheng Han 正广 (Ch'en Tu-hsiu). "Huan-ying T'ai-ko-erh" 歡迎太戈爾 (Welcome to Tagore); *Chung-kuo ch'ing-nien*, No. 26:12–15 (Apr. 12, 1924).

Chesneaux, Jean. *Le mouvement ouvrier chinois de 1910 à 1927*. Paris: Mouton,

1962.

Chi Che 記者 (Cheng Chen-to). "T'ai-ko-erh lai-Hua ti chi-shih" 太戈爾來華的記事 (A record of Tagore's visit to China); *Hsiao-shuo yüeh-pao*, Vol. 15, No. 4 (April 1924).

———— *Huan-ying T'ai-ko-erh hsien-sheng!* 歡迎太戈爾先生 (Welcome to Mr. Tagore!). Shanghai: Hsiao-shuo yüeh-pao, May 1, 1924.

Chiang, Monlin. *Tides from the West: A Chinese Autobiography.* New Haven: Yale University Press, 1947.

Ch'ien K'ua 掔瓠. "Huan-ying T'ai-ko-erh" 歡迎太戈爾 (Welcome, Tagore); *Tung-fang tsa-chih* 東方雜誌 (Eastern miscellany), 21.6:1 (Mar. 25, 1924).

China Express and Telegraph. London, 1924.

China Handbook, 1937–1945, comp. Chinese Ministry of Information. Rev. ed.; New York: Macmillan Co., 1947.

China Illustrated Review. Tientsin, 1924.

China Journal of Science and Arts. Shanghai, 1925.

China Press. Shanghai, 1924.

China Weekly Review. Shanghai, 1924.

Chinese Students' Monthly. Ann Arbor, 1924.

Chisholm, Lawrence W. *Fenollosa: The Far East and American Culture.* New Haven: Yale University Press, 1963.

Cholmondeley, L. B. "Rabindranath Tagore in Japan," *The East and the West*, 15.1:28 (London, January 1917).

Chou Tso-jen 周作人. " 'Ta-jen chih wei-hai' chi ch'i t'a" 「大人之危害」及其他 ("The Danger of the Giant" and so on); in his *Yü-t'ien ti shu* 雨天的書 (Book for a rainy day), pp. 125–128. 2nd ed.; Shanghai, 1935.

———— "Chi-nan tao chung chih san" 齊南道中之三 (Three [essays] on the road to Tsinan); in his *Yü-t'ien ti shu*, pp. 231–235.

Chou Yüeh-jan 周越然. "Chi wo li-liang" 給我力量 (Give me strength); *Hsiao-shuo yüeh-pao*, 14.9:1–3 (September 1923).

Chow Tse-tsung. *The May Fourth Movement: Intellectual Revolution in Modern China.* Cambridge, Mass.: Harvard University Press, 1960.

Christian Movement in the Japanese Empire, The, ed. Edwin Taylor Inglehart. Tokyo: Conference of Federated Missions, Japan, 1917.

Chung-kuo hsien-tai ch'u-pan shih-liao 中國現代出版史料 (Historical data on modern Chinese publishing). Peking: Chung-hua shu-chü, 1954– .

Chung-wen tsa-chih so-yin 中文雜誌索引 (Index to Chinese periodicals), comp. Ling-nan ta-hsüeh t'u-shu-kuan 嶺南大學圖書館. Canton, 1935.

Chūō kōron 中央公論 (Central review). Tokyo, 1915–1929.

Ch'ü Ch'iu-pai 瞿秋白. "T'ai-ko-erh ti kuo-chia kuan-nien yü tung-fang" 太戈爾的國家觀念與東方 (Tagore's concept of the nation-state and the

East); *Hsiang-tao*, No. 61:487–490 (Apr. 16, 1924).

———— "Kuo-ch'ü ti jen—T'ai-ko-erh" 過去的人＝太戈爾 (Tagore the has-been); *Chung-kuo ch'ing-nien*, No. 27:2–3 (Apr. 18, 1924).

Ch'ü Shih-ying 瞿世英. "T'ai-ko-erh ti jen-sheng-kuan yü shih-chieh-kuan" 太戈爾的人生觀與世界觀 (Tagore's view of life and the world); *Hsiao-shuo yüeh-pao*, Vol. 13, No. 2 (February 1922), in the special section, "T'ai-ko-erh yen-chiu" 太戈爾研究 (Tagore studies).

———— "T'ai-ko-erh chih kuo-chi ta-hsüeh" 太戈爾之國際大學 (Tagore's international university); *Tung-fang tsa-chih*, 21.10:64–73 (May 25, 1924).

Clubb, O. Edmund. *Twentieth Century China*. New York: Columbia University Press, 1964.

Collet, Sophia Dobson. *The Life and Letters of Raja Rammohun Roy*, ed. Dilip Kumar Biswas and Prabhat Chandra Ganguli. 3rd rev. ed.; Calcutta: Sadharan Brahmo Samaj, 1962.

Conway, Moncure Daniel. *My Pilgrimage to the Wise Men of the East*. London: Archibald Constable, 1906.

Coomaraswamy, Ananda Kentish. *The Dance of Shiva*. New York: Sunwise Turn, 1924; 2nd ed., Bombay: Asia Publishing House, 1948.

Cornelius, John J. *Rabindranath Tagore, India's Schoolmaster*. Madras: Methodist Publishing House, 1930.

Cousins, James H. and Margaret E. Cousins. *We Two Together*. Madras: Ganesh, 1950.

Dai jimmei jiten 大人名辭典 (Comprehensive encyclopedia of famous men). 10 vols.; Tokyo: Heibon-sha, 1953–1955.

Daily Mail. Bombay, 1924.

Das, C. R. "Bengal and the Bengalees," in *Deshabandu Chitta Ranjan: Brief Survey of Life and Work. Provincial Conference Speeches. Congress Speeches*. Calcutta: Rajan Sen and B. K. Sen, preface 1926.

———— "Presidential Address, Thirty-Seventh Sessions of the Indian National Congress, Held at Gaya in December 1922," in Prithwis Chandra Ray, *Life and Times of C. R. Das*. London: Oxford University Press, 1927.

Dās, Sajanīkānta. *Rabīndranāth: Jīban o sāhitya* (Rabindranath: Life and literature). Calcutta: Śatābdī grantha-bhaban, B.E. 1367 (1959–1960).

Das Gupta, Hemendranath. *Deshbandhu Chittaranjan Das*. Delhi: Publications Division, Government of India, 1960.

Das Gupta, Shakti. *Tagore's Asian Outlook*. Calcutta: Nava Bharati, 1961.

Datta, Bhupendranath. *Swami Vivekananda, Patriot-Prophet: A Study*. Calcutta: Navabharat Publishers, 1954.

Datta, G. K. *Road to Peace*. Calcutta: Sri Guru Library, preface 1949.

Devī, Maitreyī. *Mampute Rabīndranāth* (With Rabindranath at Mongpu). Calcutta: Prajñā Prakāśanī, B.E. 1364 (1958–1959).

——— *The Great Wanderer*. Calcutta: Grantham, 1961.

Dickinson, Goldsworthy Lowes. *Letters from John Chinaman*. London: R. Brimley Johnson, 1901. Republished as *Letters from a Chinese Official: Being an Eastern View of Western Civilization*, New York: McLure, Phillips, 1903.

Dimock, Edward C., Jr. "Rabindranath Tagore, 'The Greatest of the Bāuls of Bengal,'" *Journal of Asian Studies*, 19.1: 33–51 (November 1959).

Doke, Joseph J. *M. K. Gandhi, An Indian Patriot in South Africa*. Varanasi: Akhil Bharat Sarva Seva Sangh Prakashan, 1956.

Doss, Ram (pseud. of Rammohun Roy). Letter to the editor, in *Bengal Hurkaru* (May 23, 1823).

Driesch, Hans A. E. "Alt- und Jung-China," *Ostasiatische Rundschau*, 5.3:33–55 (Hamburg, March 1924).

——— *The Crisis in Psychology*. Princeton: Princeton University Press, 1925.

——— *Lebenserrinerungen*. Basel: Ernst Reinhardt Verlag, 1951.

——— and Margarete Driesch. *Fern-Ost, als Gäste Jungchinas*. Leipzig: Brockhaus, 1925.

Ebina Danjō 海老名彈正. "Shijin Tagōru no bummei hihyō o yomu" 詩人タゴールの文明批評を讀む (On reading the poet Tagore's criticism of civilization); *Shin-jin*, 17.7:20–36 (July 1916).

Ebu Ōson 江部鴨村. *Tagōru no shisō to shūkyō* タゴールの思想と宗教 (Tagore's thought and religion). Tokyo, 1915.

Ellman, Richard. *Yeats, The Man and the Masks*. New York: Macmillan Co., 1948.

Elmhirst, Leonard K. "Tagore and the International University," *North China Star* (Peking, May 5, 1923).

——— "Some Impressions of China, April 1923," *Visva-Bharati Quarterly*, 1.3:211–220 (October 1923).

——— Private diary for 1924, as read aloud during personal interviews with the author, June 30 and 31, 1956.

——— "Rabindranath Tagore's Visit to China," *Modern Review*, 36.2:164–165 (August 1924).

——— Letter to Stephen N. Hay, Aug. 8, 1955.

——— "Personal Memories of Tagore," in *Rabindranath Tagore: A Centenary Volume, 1861–1961*, pp. 12–26.

Eucken, Rudolf. *Rudolf Eucken: His Life, Work, and Travels, by Himself*, tr. Joseph McCabe. London: T. Fisher Unwin, 1921.

————— and Carsun Chang. *Das Lebensproblem in China und in Europa.* Leipzig: Quelle & Meyer, 1922.

Fairbank, John K., ed. *Chinese Thought and Institutions.* Chicago: University of Chicago Press, 1957.

————— and Kwang-Ching Liu. *Modern China: A Bibliographical Guide to Chinese Works, 1898–1937.* Cambridge, Mass.: Harvard University Press, 1950.

—————, Edwin O. Reischauer, and Albert M. Craig. *East Asia: The Modern Transformation.* Boston: Houghton Mifflin Co., 1966.

"Fan-tui T'ai-ko-erh" 反對太戈爾 (Oppose Tagore!); *Chüeh-wu* 覺悟(Awakening; Apr. 13, 1924).

Far Eastern Times. Peking, 1924.

Farquhar, J. N. *Modern Religious Movements in India.* New York: Macmillan Co., 1918.

Feng Yu-lan 馮友蘭. "Yü Yin-tu T'ai-ko-erh t'an-hua" 與印度太戈爾談話 (A talk with the Indian, Tagore); *Hsin ch'ao* 新潮 (New tide), Vol. 3, No. 1 (Winter, 1920–1921). Reprinted in Liang Sou-ming, *Tung-hsi wen-hua chi ch'i che-hsüeh*, Appendix, pp. 59–66.

————— *Hsin li-hsüeh* 新理學 (New metaphysics). Changsha: Shang-wu yin-shu kuan, 1939.

————— See also Fung Yu-lan.

Fenollosa, Ernest. *East and West.* New York, Boston: T. Y. Crowell, 1893.

————— "The Coming Fusion of East and West," *Harper's Monthly*, 98:122 (December 1898).

Fo-hua hsin-ch'ing-nien 佛化新青年 (Buddhist youth). Peking, 1924.

Forke, Alfred von. *Geschichte der neueren chinesischen Philosophie.* Hamburg: Friederichsen, De Gruyter & Co., 1938.

Forster, E. M. *Goldsworthy Lowes Dickinson.* New York: Harcourt, Brace and Co., 1934.

Forward. Calcutta, 1924, 1927.

Fremantle, Anne M. H. *Loyal Enemy.* London: Hutchinson [1938].

Fukuzawa Yukichi 福澤諭吉. Editorial in *Jiji shimpō* 時事新報 (The times); reprinted in *Zoku Fukuzawa zenshū* 續福澤全集 (Continuation of Fukuzawa's works), I, 742–749 (Tokyo, 1933).

Fung, Yu-lan (Feng Yu-lan). *A Short History of Chinese Philosophy*, ed. and tr. Derk Bodde. New York: Macmillan Co., 1962.

Furrell, James Wyburd. *The Tagore Family: A Memoir.* 2nd ed.; Calcutta, privately published, 1892.

Gamble, Sidney D., assisted by John Stewart Burgess. *Peking: A Social Survey.*

New York: George H. Doran, 1921.

Gandhi, M. K. (Mahatma Gandhi). *Hind Swaraj, or Indian Home Rule*. 3rd ed.; Madras: G. A. Natesan, c. 1921; 1st ed., 1909.

———— "The Poet's Anxiety," *Young India* (Ahmedabad, June 1, 1921). Reprinted in M. K. Gandhi, *Young India, 1919–1922*, 2nd ed. (Madras: S. Ganesan, 1924).

———— "The Great Sentinel," *Young India* (Oct. 13, 1921). Reprinted in M. K. Gandhi, *Young India, 1919–1922*, 2nd ed. (Madras: S. Ganesan, 1924).

———— "A Parallel from China," *Young India* (Feb. 9, 1928). Reprinted in M. K. Gandhi, *Young India, 1927–1928*, pp. 604–605.

———— *Speeches and Writings of Mahatma Gandhi*. 4th ed.; Madras: G. A. Natesan, 1933.

———— *Young India, 1927–1928*. Madras: S. Ganesan, 1935.

———— *Mahātma Gāndhījī ane Srīmad Rājchandra*. Ahmedabad: Ozā Āyurvedik Pharmasī, preface Samvāt 1993 (1936–1937).

———— *An Autobiography, or The Story of My Experiments with Truth*, tr. Mahadev Desai. 2nd ed.; Ahmedabad: Navajivan Publishing House, 1940.

———— "The Message of Asia," *United Asia*, 1.1:3 (Bombay, May-June 1948).

———— "Why I Am a Hindu," *Young India* (Oct. 20, 1927). Reprinted in his *Hindu Dharma* (Ahmedabad: Navajivan Publishing House, 1950).

———— *The Collected Works of Mahatma Gandhi*, Vol. 1: *1884–1896*. Delhi: The Publications Division, Ministry of Information and Broadcasting, Government of India, 1958.

Gandhi Memorial Peace Number, ed. Kshitis Roy. Special issue of *Visva-Bharati Quarterly*; Santiniketan, 1949.

Gazetteer of the Bombay Presidency, Vol. 8: *Kathiawar;* Vol. 9, Pt. 1: *Gujarat Population*. Bombay: Government Central Press, 1884.

Ghose, Aurobindo. Preface to his *The Renaissance in India*. 3rd ed.; Calcutta: Arya Publishing House, 1946.

———— "The Asiatic Role," in *Bande Mataram*, weekly ed. (Apr. 12, 1908). Reprinted, with author identified, in *Bande Mataram and Indian Nationalism*, ed. Haridas Mukherjee and Uma Mukherjee (Calcutta: Firma K. L. Mukhopadhyay, 1957).

Gillin, Donald G. "Portrait of a Warlord: Yen Hsi-shan in Shansi Province, 1911–1930," *Journal of Asian Studies*, 19.3: 289–306 (May 1960).

Goetz, Heinrich. *The Crisis of Indian Civilization in the Eighteenth and Early Nineteenth Centuries* (Calcutta University Readership Lectures). Calcutta: University of Calcutta, 1939.

Golden Book of Tagore, The: A Homage to Rabindranath Tagore from India and the World in Celebration of His Seventieth Birthday, ed. Ramananda

Chatterjee. Calcutta: Golden Book Committee, 1931.

Green, Gretchen. *The Whole World and Company.* New York: John Day, 1936.

Gupta, Nagendranath. *Reflections and Reminiscences.* Bombay: Hind Kitabs, 1947.

Gupta, Nolini Kanta. *The Malady of the Century and Other Essays.* Madras: Sri Aurobindo Library, 1943.

Haithcox, John P. "The Roy-Lenin Debate on Colonial Policy: A New Interpretation," *Journal of Asian Studies,* 23.1: 93–101 (November 1963).

[Han] Lin-fu 韓麟符. "Fei Liang Cho-ju [Liang Ch'i-ch'ao] ti 'Yin-tu yü Chung-kuo wen-hua chih ch'in-shu ti kuan-hsi' " 非梁卓如的「印度與中國文化之親屬的關係」 (Against Liang Ch'i-ch'ao's "Brotherly relations between the Indian and Chinese cultures"); *Cheng-chih sheng-huo chou-pao* 政治生活週報 (Political and economic weekly; Peking, April 1924).

Harijan. Ahmedabad, 1947.

Hay, Stephen N. "India's Prophet in East Asia: Tagore's Message of Pan-Asian Spiritual Revival and Its Reception in Japan and China, 1916–1929." Ph.D. thesis; Harvard University, 1957.

———— "Rabindranath Tagore in America," *American Quarterly,* 14.3: 439–463 (Fall 1962).

———— "Western and Indigenous Elements in Modern Indian Thought: The Case of Rammohun Roy," in Marius B. Jansen, ed., *Changing Japanese Attitudes toward Modernization,* pp. 311–328. Princeton University Press, 1965.

———— "Jain Influences on Gandhi's Early Thought," in Sibnarayan Ray, ed., *Gandhi and Gandhism.* University of Melbourne Press, 1969.

————, ed. *Dialogue Between a Theist and an Idolater (Brāhma pauttalik samvād): An 1820 Tract Probably by Rammohun Roy.* Calcutta: Firma K. L. Mukhopadhyay, 1962.

Horioka, Yasuko. *The Life of Kakuzō, Author of "The Book of Tea."* Tokyo: Hokuseido Press, 1963.

Hsia, C. T. *A History of Modern Chinese Fiction, 1917–1957.* New Haven: Yale University Press, 1961.

Hsin Ya-hsi-ya 新亞細亞 (New Asia). Nanking, 1930.

Hsü Chih-mo 徐志摩. "T'ai-ko-erh lai-Hua" 太戈爾來華 (Tagore comes to China); *Hsiao-shuo yüeh-pao,* 14.9:2 (September 1923).

———— "T'ai-shan jih-ch'u" 泰山日出 (Sunrise on Mt. T'ai); *Hsiao-shuo yüeh-pao,* 14.9:1 (September 1923).

———— "T'ai-ko-erh lai-Hua ti ch'üeh-ch'i" 太戈爾來華的確期 (The exact date of Tagore's arrival in China); *Hsiao-shuo yüeh-pao*, 14.10:1 (October 1923).

————— "T'ai-ko-erh tsui-chin hsiao-hsi" 太戈爾最近消息 (Latest news of Tagore); *Ch'en-pao fu-k'an* 晨報副刊 (Morning news literary supplement; Apr. 19, 1924), pp. 3–4.

————— "T'ai-ko-erh" 太戈爾; *Ch'en-pao fu-k'an* (May 19, 1924), p. 1.

————— "Kao-pieh tz'u" 告別辭 (Parting words); *Hsiao-shuo yüeh-pao*, 15.6:4 (June 1924).

————— "Art and Life," *Ch'uang-tsao* 創造 (Creation), 2.1:1–15 (August 1927).

————— "Ch'ü pa!" 去罷 (Go away!), in *Ch'en-pao fu-k'an* (June 17, 1924), p. 2; tr. in Kai-yü Hsü, tr. and ed., *Twentieth Century Chinese Poetry: An Anthology*, p. 83.

Hsü Chih-mo nien-p'u 徐志摩年譜 (A chronology of the life of Hsü Chih-mo), comp. Ch'en Ts'ung-chou 陳從周. Shanghai, 1949.

[Hsü] Fo[-ssu]. "T'ai-ko-erh yü k'o-hsüeh" 太戈爾與科學 (Tagore and science); *K'o-hsüeh* 科學 (Science), 9.3: 244–246 (March 1924).

Hsü, Kai-yü, "The Life and Poetry of Wen I-to," *Harvard Journal of Asiatic Studies*, 21:134–179 (December 1958).

—————, tr. and ed. *Twentieth Century Chinese Poetry: An Anthology*. Garden City, N.Y.: Doubleday, 1963.

Hu Shih 胡適. *The Development of the Logical Method in Ancient China*. Shanghai: Oriental Book Co., 1922.

————— "The Civilizations of the East and the West," in Charles A. Beard, ed., *Whither Mankind*, pp. 25–41. New York: Longmans, Green, 1928.

————— *The Chinese Renaissance: The Haskell Lectures, 1933*. University of Chicago Press, 1934.

————— "The Indianization of China: A Case Study in Cultural Borrowing," in *Independence, Convergence, and Borrowing in Institutions, Thought, and Art* (Harvard Tercentenary Publications), pp. 240–247. Cambridge, Mass.: Harvard University Press, 1937.

————— "Wo-men tui-yü hsi-yang chin-tai wen-ming ti t'ai-tu" 我們對於西洋近代文明的態度 (Our attitude toward modern Western civilization); in *Hu Shih wen-ts'un san-chi* 胡適文存三集 (Writings of Hu Shih, third collection), I, 3–22. 5th ed.; 4 vols.; Shanghai: Ya-tung t'u-shu-kuan, 1946.

I Hsiang 亦湘. "T'ai-ko-erh lai-Hua-hou ti Chung-kuo ch'ing-nien" 太戈爾來華後的中國青年 (China's youth after Tagore's arrival in China); *Chung-kuo ch'ing-nien*, No. 27:15 (Apr. 18, 1924).

Idditti, Smimasa. *The Life of Marquis Shigenobu Okuma, A Maker of New Japan*. Tokyo: Hokuseido Press, 1940.

India, Government of. *Report of the Native Press: Bengal, 1900.* Printed in Calcutta for official use only, 1900.

Indian Annual Register, ed. H. N. and N. N. Mitra. Calcutta: The Annual Register Office, 1918–1947; published as *Indian Quarterly Register,* 1924–1928.

Indian Daily News. Calcutta, 1919.

Indian Review. Madras, 1924.

Inglehart, Charles W. *A Century of Protestant Christianity in Japan.* Rutland, Vt. and Tokyo: Charles E. Tuttle, 1959.

Inoue Tetsujirō 井上哲次郎. "Tagōru no kōen ni tsuite" タゴールの講演に就いて (Concerning Tagore's lecture); *Rikugō zasshi,* 37.6:27–28 (July 1916).

Interviews Granted to the Author by the Following Contemporaries of Tagore and His Critics:

Chakravarty, Amiya. Boston, September 1954 and August 1961.

Chanda, Apurva Kumar. Calcutta, Dec. 1, 1959.

Chang Chün-mai (Carsun Chang) 張君勱. Washington, D.C., Dec. 12, 1954.

Chang Hsin-hai 張星海. New York, Oct. 14, 1954.

Chang P'eng-ch'un 張彭春. Hong Kong, Aug. 2, 1956.

Ch'en Yüan 陳源. London, June 21, 1956.

Chiang Fu-ts'ung 蔣復聰. Taipei, Apr. 8, 1955.

Chiang Meng-lin (Monlin Chiang) 蔣夢麟. Taipei, Apr. 1, 1955.

Chien Yu-wen 簡又文. Kowloon, May 6, 1955.

Das, Taraknath. New York, Oct. 15, 1954.

Dey, Mukul. Santiniketan, Jan. 24, 1956.

Elmhirst, Leonard K. Totnes, Devon, June 30, 1956.

Hu Shih 胡適. New York, Oct. 13, 1954 and Aug. 3, 1956.

Kripalani, Krishna. New Delhi, June 1960.

Kōra Tomiko (Mrs. 高良富子). Tokyo, Jan. 20, 1955.

Kuo T'ing-i 郭廷以. Taipei, Apr. 5, 1955.

Li Tsung-t'ung 李宗侗. Taipei, Apr. 13, 1955.

Maruyama Masao 丸山正雄. Bermuda, Jan. 26, 1962.

Nag, Kalidas. Calcutta, Nov. 17, 1955 and Jan. 2, 1956.

Ōkura Kunihiko 大倉邦彦. Tokyo, Feb. 10, 1955.

Sen, Pulinbehari. Calcutta, Jan. 1960.

Shen Kang-po 沈剛伯. Taipei, Apr. 12, 1955.

Spear, Percival. London, June 6, 1956.

T'ao Chen-yü 陶振譽. Taipei, Apr. 9, 1955.

Vetch, Henri. Hong Kong, June 19, 1955.

Wu Kan 吳幹. Taipei, Apr. 12, 1955.

Yashiro Yukio 矢代幸雄. Tokyo, Feb. 8, 1955.

Iqbāl, Muḥammad. *Iqbālnāme* (The illustrious Iqbal), ed. Shaikh Muhammad Ata. 2 vols.; Lahore, n.d.

———— *The Secrets of the Self (Asrar-i-Khudi)*, tr. Reynold A. Nicholson. Rev. ed.; Lahore: Muhammad Ashraf, 1944.

———— *Jāvīdnāme*. 2nd ed.; Lahore: Shaikh Mubarak Ali, 1947.

———— *Ẓarb-i Kalīm* (The rod of Moses). 7th ed.; Lahore: Shaikh Mubarak Ali, 1947.

———— *Armughān-i Hidjāz* (Gift from the Hidjāz). Lahore: Shaikh Mubarak Ali, 1948.

———— *Speeches and Statements of Iqbal*, comp. "Shamloo." 2nd rev. ed.; Lahore: Al-Manar Academy, 1948.

———— *The Reconstruction of Religious Thought in Islam*. Lahore: Javid Iqbal, 1954.

———— *The Mysteries of Selflessness*, tr. Arthur J. Arberry (Wisdom of the East Series). London: John Murray, 1955.

———— *Pilgrimage of Eternity: Being an English Translation of Dr. Sir Muhammad Iqbal's "Javid Nama,"* tr. Shaikh Mahmud Ahmad. Lahore: Institute of Islamic Culture, 1961.

Irschick, Eugene F. *Politics and Social Conflict in South India, 1916–1929*. Berkeley and Los Angeles: University of California Press, 1968.

Iwano Hōmei 岩野泡鳴. "Nihon kodai shisō yori kindai no hyōshōshugi o ronzu" 日本古代思想より近代の表象主義を論ず (Modern symbolism in the light of ancient Japanese thought); tr. in *Japanese Literature in the Meiji Era*.

Iyer, Raghavan, ed. *The Glass Curtain between Asia and Europe: A Symposium on the Historical Encounters and the Changing Attitudes of the Peoples of the East and the West*. London: Oxford University Press, 1965.

Iyer, T. S. Ganesa. *Some Impressions about Sir Rabindranath Tagore and His Works*. Madras, 1921.

Jaini, Jagmanderlal. *Outlines of Jainism*. Cambridge, Eng.: Cambridge University Press, 1916.

Jansen, Marius B. *The Japanese and Sun Yat-sen*. Cambridge, Mass.: Harvard University Press, 1954.

Japan: The Official Guide, ed. Tourist Industry Division, Ministry of Transportation. Rev. ed.; Tokyo: Japan Travel Bureau, 1954.

Japan Biographical Encyclopedia and Who's Who. 3rd ed.; Tokyo: Rengo Press, 1965.

Japan Chronicle. Kobe, 1921, 1924.

Japan Magazine. Tokyo, 1916.

Japan Times. Tokyo, 1916.

Japan Weekly Chronicle. Kobe, 1916.

Japanese Literature in the Meiji Era, ed. Yoshie Okazaki, tr. and adapted by V. H. Viglielmo. Tokyo: Ōbunsha, 1955.

Japanese Thought in the Meiji Era, ed. Masaaki Kosaka, tr. and adapted by David Abosch. Tokyo: Pan-Pacific Press, 1958.

Johnston, Reginald F. *Twilight in the Forbidden City.* London: Victor Gollancz, 1934.

K. (Kshitimohan Sen? Kalidas Nag?). "Rabindranath Tagore's Visva-Bharati Mission," *Modern Review*, Vol. 36, No. 3 (September 1924).

Kataoka, Yoshikazu. Introduction to *Introduction to Contemporary Japanese Literature.* Tokyo: Kokusai bunka shinkokai, 1939.

Katō, Shūichi. "Japanese Writers and Modernization," in Marius B. Jansen, ed., *Changing Japanese Attitudes toward Modernization.* Princeton University Press, 1965.

[Kawahigashi] Hekigotō 河東碧梧桐 "Tagōru no inshō" タゴールの印象 (Impressions of Tagore); *Nippon oyobi Nipponjin*, No. 685:135 (July 15, 1916).

Kayahara, Kazan. "It is Great Britain and America Which Lead to the Suicide of the Japanese People," *Far East*, 8.185: 68–69 (Oct. 9, 1915), and 8.186: 93–94 (Oct. 16, 1915).

Keene, Donald. "Literary and Intellectual Currents in Postwar Japan and Their International Implications," in Hugh Borton et al., *Japan between East and West.* New York: Harper and Bros., 1957.

Keng Kuang 耿光 (pseud). "Ching-kao fan-tui T'ai-ko-erh che" 敬告反對太戈爾者 (Serious statement to those who oppose Tagore); *Shen pao* (May 13, 1924).

Keyserling, Hermann. *Philosophie als Kunst.* 2nd ed.; Darmstadt: Otto Reichl Verlag, 1922.

——— *The Travel Diary of a Philosopher*, tr. J. Holroyd Reece. 2 vols.; New York: Harcourt, Brace, 1926.

———, ed. *Der Weg zur Vollendung.* Darmstadt, 1920– .

Khanolkar, G.D. *The Lute and the Plough. A Life of Rabindranath Tagore.* Bombay: Book Centre Private Ltd., 1963.

Kiang, Wen-han. *The Chinese Student Movement.* New York: King's Crown Press, 1948.

Kimura, Nikki. "My Memory about the Late Rash Behari Bose," in Radhanath Rath and Sabitri Prasanna Chatterjee, eds., *Rash Behari Basu: His Struggle for India's Independence*, pp. 38–43. Calcutta: Biplabi Mahanayak Rash Behari Basu Smarak Samity, 1963.

Kimura Taiken 木村泰賢. "Indo shisō to Tagōru" 印度思想とタゴール (Indian thought and Tagore); *Rikugō zasshi*, 36.7:40–43 (July 1916).

Kipling, Rudyard. "The Ballad of East and West," *Departmental Ditties and Ballads and Barrack Room Ballads*, Pt. 2. London: Review of Reviews, 1916.

Kishimoto, Hideo, comp. *Japanese Religion in the Meiji Era*, ed. and tr. John F. Howes. Tokyo: Ōbunsha, 1956.

Kishiname, Tsunezo. *The Development of Philosophy in Japan*. Princeton University Press, 1915.

Kiyozawa Iwao 清澤巖, ed. *Meishi no Tagōru kan* 名士のタゴール觀 (How famous men regard Tagore). Tokyo, 1915.

Kline, Ben G. "New Philosophy of Living Needed, Poet Says," *Trans-Pacific* (Tokyo, May 10, 1924), p. 12.

Kokutai no hongi: Cardinal Principles of the National Entity of Japan, tr. John Owen Gauntlett, ed. Robert King Hall. Cambridge, Mass.: Harvard University Press, 1949.

Kopf, David. *British Orientalism and the Bengal Renaissance: The Dynamics of Indian Modernization, 1773–1835*. Berkeley and Los Angeles: University of California Press, 1969.

Kripalani, Krishna. *Rabindranath Tagore: A Biography*. New York: Grove Press, 1962.

Krishnamacharya, U. P. *The Wisdom of the East*. Benares, published as a periodical, Vol. 1, Nos. 1–5 dated August (?)-December 1914.

Ku, Hung-ming. *The Story of a Chinese Oxford Movement*. Shanghai: Shanghai Mercury, 1912; 1st ed., 1910.

—— *The Spirit of the Chinese People*. Peking: Peking Daily News, 1915; 2nd rev. ed., Peking: Commercial Press, 1922.

Kuno, Yoshi S. *Japanese Expansion on the Asiatic Continent*. 2 vols.; Berkeley: University of California Press, 1937 and 1940.

Kuo Mo-jo 郭沫若. "T'ai-ko-erh lai-Hua ti wo-chien" 太戈爾來華的我見 (My view of Tagore's visit to China); *Ch'uang-tsao chou-pao* 創造週報 (Creation weekly), No. 23:3–4 (Oct. 14, 1923).

—— "Chih Ch'eng Fang-wu shu" 致成仿吾書 (A letter to Ch'eng Fang-wu); in *Chung-kuo hsin wen-hsüeh ta-hsi* 中國新文學大系 (Comprehensive outline of modern Chinese literature), Vol. 6: *San-wen, i-chi* 散文一集 (Essays, first series). Shanghai, Liang-yu t'u-shu kung-ssu, 1935.

—— *Ch'uang-tsao shih-nien* 創造十年 (Ten years of the Creation Society). Chungking: Chung-ch'ing tso-chia, 1943.

Kwok, D.W.Y. *Scientism in Chinese Thought, 1900–1950*. New Haven: Yale University Press, 1965.

Lach, Donald F. *Asia in the Making of Europe,* Vol. 1. University of Chicago Press, 1965.

Lakshmanan, N. *India, the Fountain of Peace: A Sourcebook of Leadership for the New Era.* Coimbatore: N. Lakshmanan, 1937.

Lefevre, Frederic. "Une heure avec M. Sylvain Lévi," in *Memorial Sylvain Lévi.*

Lesny, V. *Rabindranath Tagore, His Personality and Work,* tr. Guy McKeever Phillips. London: George Allen and Unwin, 1939.

Levenson, Joseph R. *Liang Ch'i-ch'ao and the Mind of Modern China* (Harvard Historical Monographs, Vol. 26). Cambridge, Mass.: Harvard University Press, 1953.

Lévi, Sylvain. "Abel Bergaigne et l'Indianisme," *Revue politique et littéraire,* 40:269 (1890).

———— "Eastern Humanism: An Address Delivered in the University of Dacca on February 4th, 1922," in his *L'Inde et le monde.* Paris: Librairie Ancienne Honoré Champion, 1928.

———— "Greater India," in *Memorial Sylvain Lévi.*

Li, Chien-nung. *The Political History of China, 1840–1928,* tr. and ed. Ssu-yu Teng and Jeremy Ingalls. New York: Van Nostrand, 1956.

Liang Ch'i-ch'ao 梁啓超. *Yin-ping-shih ho-chi* 飲冰室合集 (Collected writings from the Ice-drinker's Studio). Shanghai: Chung-hua hsu-chü, 1936. *Chuan-chi* 專集 (Special collection), 24 vols. in 45 pts.; *Wen-chi* 文集 (Literary collection), 16 vols. in 45 pts.

———— *Ou-yü hsin-ying lu chieh-lu* 歐遊心影錄節錄 (Record of impressions of a European tour); in his *Yin-ping-shih ho-chi, Chuan-chi,* Vol. 5, Pt. 2.

———— "Yin-tu yü Chung-kuo wen-hua chih ch'in-shu ti kuan-hsi" 印度與中國文化之親屬的關係 (The brotherly relations between the Indian and Chinese cultures); in his *Ying-ping-shih ho-chi, Wen-chi,* Pt. 41, pp. 36–46.

———— "T'ai-ko-erh ti Chung-kuo ming, Chu Chen-tan" 太戈爾的中國名＝竺震旦 (Tagore's Chinese name, Chu Chen-tan); in his *Yin-ping shih ho-chi, Wen-chi,* Pt. 41, pp. 47–48.

———— *Intellectual Trends in the Ch'ing Period,* tr. Immanuel C.Y. Hsü. Cambridge, Mass.: Harvard University Press, 1959.

Liang Sou-ming 梁漱溟. *Tung-hsi wen-hua chi ch'i che-hsüeh* 東西文化及其哲學 (Eastern and Western civilizations and their philosophies). Shanghai: Commercial Press, 1922.

———— *Chung-kuo min-tsu tzu-chiu yün-tung chih tsui-hou chüeh-wu* 中國民族自救運動之最後覺悟 (The final awakening of the Chinese People's Self-Salvation Movement). 3rd ed.; Shanghai: Chung-hua shu-chü, 1936.

Lin Yutang. *Imperial Peking: Seven Centuries of China.* New York: Crown Publishers, 1961.

Ling-hua 靈華. "Wo-men chiu-ching wei-shen-ma yao huan-ying T'ai-ku-erh" 我們究竟爲什麽要歡迎泰谷爾 (Why then do we wish to welcome Tagore?); *Fo-hua hsin-ch'ing-nien*, 2.2:4ff. (1924).

[Lin] Jui-t'ang 林瑞棠. "Wo ti li-hsiang chi shih-hsien ti T'ai-ko-erh hsien-sheng" 我的理想及實現的太戈爾先生 (The Mr. Tagore of my ideal and in reality); *Ch'en-pao fu-k'an* (May 12, 1924).

Lu Hsün 魯迅. "Lao tiao-tzu i-ching ch'ang-wan" 老調子已經唱完 (The old song has been sung long enough); in *Lu Hsün hsüan-chi* 魯迅選集 (Selected works of Lu Hsün), pp. 666ff. Peking, 1952.

Lu Hsün jih-chi 魯迅日記 (Diary of Lu Hsün). 2 vols.; Peking: Pei-ching wen-hsüeh ch'u-pan-she, 1959.

Lu Mou-te 陸懋德. "Ko-jen tui-yü T'ai-ko-erh chih kan-hsiang" 個人對於太戈爾之感想 (My personal opinion of Tagore); *Ch'en-pao fu-k'an* (June 3, 1924).

McAleavy, Henry. *A Dream of Tartary: The Origins and Misfortunes of Henry P'u Yi*. London: George Allen and Unwin, 1963.

McClellan, Edwin. "An Introduction to Sōseki," *Harvard Journal of Asiatic Studies*, 22: 152–162 (1959).

McLane, John R. "The Development of Nationalist Ideas and Tactics and the Policies of the Government of India, 1897–1905." Ph.D. thesis; School of Oriental and African Studies, University of London, 1961.

Mahadevan, P. *Subramania Bharati, Patriot and Poet*. Madras: Atri Publishers, 1957.

Mahalanobis, P. C. "Rabindranath Tagore's Visit to Canada and Japan," *Visva-Bharati Quarterly*, 7.1:114ff. (April-July 1929).

——— *Rabindranath Tagore's Visit to China (Visva-Bharati Bulletin*, No. 1). Published in 2 parts: Pt. 1, Calcutta, 1924; Pt. 2, Calcutta, 1925.

Maitra, Harendranath. *Hinduism: The World-Ideal*. London: Cecil Palmer and Hayward, 1916.

Manchester Guardian, The. 1916.

Martin, W. B. "On the Character and Capacity of the Asiatics and Particu-larly of the Natives of Hindoostan," in *Essays by the Students of the College of Fort William in Bengal*. Calcutta: Company Press, 1802.

Memorial Sylvain Lévi, ed. Louis Renou. Paris: Paul Hartmann, 1937.

Methodist Recorder. London, 1937.

Modern Review. Calcutta, 1913, 1916, 1921–1930.

Morris-Jones, W. H. "India's Political Idioms," in C. H. Philips, ed., *Politics and Society in India*. London: George Allen and Unwin, 1963.

Mozoomdar, P. C. *The Oriental Christ*. Calcutta: Navavidhan Publication

Committee, 1933.

────── *Sketches of a Tour Around the World*. Calcutta: Navavidhan Publication Committee, 1940.

────── "The World's Religious Debt to Asia," in his *Lectures in America and Other Papers*. Calcutta: Navavidhan Publication Committee, 1955.

Mukherjee, Himangshu Bhushan. *Education for Fullness: A Study of the Educational Thought and Experiment of Rabindranath Tagore*. Bombay: Asia Publishing House, 1962.

Mukhopadhyay, Prabhatkumar. *Rabīndrajībanī o Rabīndrasāhityaprabeśak* (The life of Rabindra, and an introduction to Rabindra literature). 4 vols.; Calcutta: Biśvabhāratī, B.E. 1340–1363 (1933–1956).

────── *Rabīndrajībankathā* (The story of Rabindra's life). Calcutta: Biśvabhāratī, B.E. 1366 (1959).

Müller, F. Max. *India: What Can It Teach Us?* London: Longmans, Green, 1883.

────── *Biographical Essays*. London: Longmans, Green, 1884.

Nag, Kalidas. "Sylvain Lévi and the Science of Indology," *Modern Review*, 30.6: 670–676 (December 1921).

────── Private diary for 1924, as read aloud during personal interviews with the author, Nov. 17, 1955, and Jan. 2, 1956.

────── *New Asia*. Calcutta: Prajna Bharati, 1947.

──────, ed. *Tagore and China*. Calcutta: Pranabeshchandra Sinha, 1945.

Nakamura, Hajime. *Ways of Thinking of East Asian Peoples*. Honolulu: East-West Center Press, 1965.

Nakamura, Hiroshi. *East Asia in Old Maps*. Tokyo: Center for East Asian Cultural Studies; and Honolulu: East-West Center Press, 1963.

Nakazawa Rinsen 中澤臨川. *Tagōru to sei no jitsugen* タゴールと生の實現 (Tagore and the realization of life). Tokyo, 1915.

Nanda, B. R. *The Nehrus: Motilal and Jawaharlal*. London: George Allen and Unwin, 1962; New York: John Day Co., 1963.

Natsume Sōseki 夏目漱石. "Gendai Nihon no bunka" 現代日本の文化 (Contemporary Japanese culture); in *Natsume Sōseki zenshū* 夏目漱石全集 (Collected works of Natsume Sōseki), IV, 323–334. Tokyo: Sōgeisha, 1954.

Nehru, Jawaharlal. "Report on the International Congress against Imperialism Held at Brussels," in *The Indian National Congress, 1927*. Madras: All-India Congress Committee, 1928.

────── *Recent Essays and Writings on the Future of India, Communalism, and Other Subjects*. Allahabad: Kitabistan, 1934.

────── *An Autobiography*. London: John Lane, The Bodley Head, 1936. Also published as *Toward Freedom: The Autobiography of Jawaharlal Nehru*. New York: John Day, 1941.

—— *China, Spain, and the War: Essays and Writings*. Allahabad: Kitabistan, 1940.

—— *The Unity of India: Collected Writings, 1937–1940*. London: Drummond, 1941.

—— *The Discovery of India*. London: Meridian Books, 1951.

—— "Introduction," in *Rabindranath Tagore: A Centenary Volume, 1861–1961*, pp. xiii-xvi.

Nethercot, Arthur H. *The First Five Lives of Annie Besant*. Chicago: University of Chicago Press, 1960.

—— *The Last Four Lives of Annie Besant*. Chicago: University of Chicago Press, 1963.

New Asia. Tokyo, 1921–1923.

New Empire. Calcutta, 1924.

New Servant. Calcutta, 1926.

New York Times. 1918, 1924.

Nichi-In kyōkai kaihō 日印協會會報 (Journal of the Indo-Japanese Association). Tokyo, 1915–1916, 1924.

Nichi-nichi shimbun 日々新聞 (Daily news). Tokyo, 1924.

"Nihon taizai chū no Tagōru shi" 日本滞在中のタゴール氏 (Mr. Tagore's stay in Japan); *Nichi-In kyōkai kaihō* (December 1916), pp. 112ff.

Nippon oyobi Nipponjin 日本及日本人 (Japan and the Japanese). Tokyo, 1915–1916.

Nitobe, Inazo. *Bushido, The Soul of Japan*. New York: G.P. Putnam's Sons, 1905.

Nivedita, Sister (Margaret Noble). *Kali, the Mother*. London: Swan Sonnenschein and Co., 1900.

—— *Studies from an Eastern Home*. London: Longmans, Green and Co., 1913.

—— *The Web of Indian Life*. New ed.; London: Longmans, Green and Co., 1918.

Noguchi, Yone (Noguchi Yonejirō 野口米次郎). *Spirit of Japanese Poetry*. New York: E. P. Dutton, 1914.

—— *The Story of Yone Noguchi, Told by Himself*. Philadelphia: George W. Jacobs, c. 1914.

—— *The Spirit of Japanese Art* (The Wisdom of the East Series). London: John Murray, 1915.

—— "Tagōru shi to kataru" タゴール氏と語る (A talk with Tagore); *Bunshō sekai* 文章世界 (Literary world; July 1916).

—— "Tagore in Japan," *Modern Review*, 20.5:528–529 (November 1916).

—— *Indo no shijin* 印度の詩人 (The Indian poet). Tokyo, 1926.

———— *Indo wa kataru* 印度は語る (India speaks). Tokyo, 1936.

———— *The Ganges Calls Me*. Tokyo, 1938.

North China Herald. Peking, 1924.

North China Standard. Peking, 1924.

North China Star. Tientsin, 1924, 1929.

North, Robert C. and Xenia J. Eudin. *M. N. Roy's Mission to China: The Communist-Kuomintang Split of 1927*. Berkeley and Los Angeles: University of California Press, 1963.

Notehelfer, Fred. "Ebina Danjō: A Christian Samurai of the Meiji Period," *Papers on Japan*, 2:1–56. Harvard University, East Asian Research Center, 1963.

Okakura Kakuzō 岡倉覺三. *The Ideals of the East, With Special Reference to the Art of Japan*. London: John Murray, 1903.

———— *The Awakening of Japan*. New York: Century Co., 1904.

———— "The Awakening of the East," in *Okakura Tenshin zenshū* 岡倉天心全集 (Complete works of Okakura Tenshin [Kakuzō]), Vol. 2. Tokyo: Rikugeisha, 1939.

———— "Letters to a Friend," *Visva-Bharati Quarterly*, 21.2:196ff. (Autumn 1955).

Okakura Kazuo 岡倉一夫, ed. *Risō no saiken* 理想の再建 (The re-establishment of the ideal). Tokyo: Kawade Shobō, 1938.

Ōkuma, Shigenobu. "Summary of the History of Japan," in Shigenobu Ōkuma, ed., *Fifty Years of New Japan*. 2 vols.; London, 1910.

Ōkura, Kunihiko. *My Thoughts*, tr. Iwao Matsuhara and E. T. Inglehart. Yokohama, published by the author, 1935.

Osaka Mainichi and Tokyo Nichi-nichi. Osaka, 1929.

Ōsumi Chōfū 大住嘯風. "Tagōru to bonkyōkai" タゴールと梵教会 (Tagore and the Brahmo Samaj); *Nippon oyobi Nipponjin*, 683:101 (June 15, 1916).

Ōta Saburō 太田三郎, comp. "Nihon ni okeru Tagōru bunken" 日本における タゴール文献 (Literature on Tagore in Japan); *Aporon* アポロン (*Apollon*), 1.1:120–135 (May 1958).

Outlook. New York, 1916.

Pacquet, Alfons. "Vorwort," in Ku Hung-ming, *Chinas Verteidigung gegen europäische Ideen*. Jena: Eugen Diederichs, 1911.

Pal, Bipin Chandra. "Rabindra Nath and the Nobel Prize," *Hindu Review*, 2.6:408 (Calcutta, December 1913).

Pearson, William W. "To the Memory of Mr. K. Okakura," *Modern Review*, 20.5:541–542 (November 1916).

——— *Shantiniketan, the Bolpur School of Rabindranath Tagore.* London: Macmillan and Co., 1917.

——— "From Kyoto to Peking," *Modern Review*, 31.1:41–44 (January 1922).

Peking Daily News. Peking, 1924.

Peking and Tientsin Times. Tientsin, 1924.

P'eng Chi-hsiang 彭基相. "T'ai-ko-erh ti ssu-hsiang chi ch'i p'i-p'ing" 太戈爾底思想及其批評 (A presentation and criticism of Tagore's thought); *Hsin min-kuo* 新民國 (New republic), 1.6:1ff. (June 1924).

Petzold, Bruno. "Daito Shimaji (1875–1927): An Obituary," *Young East*, 3.4:105–124 (Sept. 8, 1927).

Piovesana, Gino K., S.J. *Recent Japanese Philosophical Thought, 1862–1962: A Survey.* Tokyo: Enderle Bookstore, 1963.

Pitman, N. H. "Education," in *China Year Book, 1925–1926*, ed. H. G. W. Woodhead, pp. 227–260. Tientsin, 1925.

Platts, John T. *A Dictionary of Urdū, Classical Hindī, and English.* London: Sampson Law, Marston and Co., preface 1884.

Po Hai 渤海 (pseud). "Sung T'ai-ko-erh" 送太戈爾 (Farewell, Tagore); *Shen pao* (May 13, 1924).

Poems from Iqbal, tr. V. G. Kiernan (Wisdom of the East Series). London: John Murray, 1955.

"Poet Tagore's Diary during His First Visit to Japan." Typed manuscript in the possession of Mme. Kōra Tomiko, Tokyo.

Politique de Pékin. Peking, 1924.

Prasad, Bimla. *The Origins of Indian Foreign Policy: The Indian National Congress and World Affairs, 1885–1947.* Calcutta: Bookland, 1960.

Pratt, James Bissett. *The Pilgrimage of Buddhism and a Buddhist Pilgrimage.* New York: Macmillan Co., 1928.

Pravda. Moscow, 1927.

Prema, S., tr. *Bharati in English Verse.* Madras: Higginbothams, 1958.

Pyarelal [Nair]. *Mahatma Gandhi: The Last Phase.* 2 vols.; Ahmedabad: Navajivan Publishing House, 1958.

——— *Mahatma Gandhi: The Early Phase*, Vol. 1. Ahmedabad: Navajivan Publishing House, 1965.

Rabindra Sadan Archives, deposited at Santiniketan.

Cablegram from F. C. Tsiang (Chiang Fu-ts'ung) secretary of the Lecture Association, Sung Po Library, Peking, to Rabindranath Tagore. June 6, 1923.

Letter from Committee of Religions and Religious Societies (Chairman, Gilbert Reid) to Rabindranath Tagore. May 1924.

Letter from Moral Teaching Society, Peking, to Rabindranath

Tagore. May 1924?

Liu, F. C. "A Welcome Speech to Dr. Rabindranath Tagore," delivered in Taiyüan. May 1924.

Letter from L. K. Elmhirst to Rathindranath Tagore. May 4, 1924.

Hu Shih. "Pariṇāmana." A poem in Chinese and English, with an accompanying birthday message to Rabindranath Tagore; May 8, 1924.

Letter from Lin Jui-t'ang to Rabindranath Tagore. May 10, 1924.

Telegram from the Shansi Provincial Education Association to Rabindranath Tagore. May 20, 1924.

Rabindranath Tagore: A Centenary Volume, 1861–1961. New Delhi: Sahitya Akademi, 1961.

Rabindranath Tagore et Romain Rolland: Lettres et autres écrits, ed. Madeleine Rolland (Cahiers Romain Rolland, No. 12). Paris: Éditions Albin Michel, 1961.

"Rabindranath's Answers to Questions by the Students of Tsing Hua College," *Visva-Bharati Quarterly,* 2.2:295–298 (October 1924).

Radhakrishnan, S. *The Philosophy of Rabindranath Tagore.* London: Macmillan and Co., 1918.

—— "Rabindranath Tagore," in his *East and West in Religion,* pp. 129–143. London: George Allen and Unwin, 1933.

—— *Eastern Religions and Western Thought.* Oxford: Clarendon Press, 1939.

—— *India and China: Lectures Delivered in China in May 1944.* Bombay: Hind Kitabs, 1947.

—— *My Search for Truth.* 2nd Indian ed.; Agra: Shiva Lal Agarwala, 1956.

Rahman, F. "Muslim Modernism in the Indo-Pakistan Subcontinent," *Bulletin of the School of Oriental and African Studies,* 21.1:82–99 (London, 1958).

Rahman, Mizanur. *Nazrul Islam.* Dacca: Pakistan Cooperative Book Society, 1955.

Rai, Lajpat. "Is Not the East a Unity As Compared with the West?" *Modern Review,* 20.6:582–591 (December 1916).

Rath, Radhanath and Sabitra Prasanna Chatterjee, eds. *Rash Behari Basu: His Struggle for India's Independence.* Calcutta: Biplabi Mahanayak Rash Behari Basu Smarak Samity, 1963.

Ray, Anilbaran. *India's Mission in the World.* Calcutta: Hindu Mission, c. 1930.

Reischauer, Edwin O. and John K. Fairbank. *East Asia: The Great Tradition.* Boston: Houghton Mifflin Co., 1964.

Report on Native Newspapers Published in the Bombay Presidency, 1924. Bombay: Government of Bombay, 1924.

Reymond, Lizelle. *Nivedita, fille de l'Inde.* Paris: Editions Victor Attinger, 1945.

Richard, Paul. *To the Nations: From the French of Paul Richard, with an Introduction by Rabindranath Tagore*, tr. [Aurobindo Ghose]. New York: J. B. Pond, 1917; 2nd ed., Madras: Ganesh and Co., 1921.

——— "Creators of New Asia," *Asian Review*, 1.2:172 (1920).

Rikugō zasshi 六合雜誌 (Universe magazine). Tokyo, 1915–1916.

Rolland and Tagore, ed. Alex Aronson and Krishna Kripalani, tr. Indira Devi Chaudhurani and Alex Aronson. Calcutta: Visva-Bharati, 1945.

Rolland, Romain. Letter to Amiya Chakravarty, Mar. 18, 1917, in *Sabuj patra* (Green leaf), 4.6–7:421 (Aśvin-Kārtik, B.E. 1324 [A.D. 1917]).

——— *Inde: Journal, 1915–1943*. Paris: Editions Vineta, 1951.

Rothenstein, William. *Men and Memories*. 3 vols.; New York: Coward-McCann, 1931–1940.

Roy, David Tod. "Kuo Mo-jo: The Pre-Marxist Phase, 1892–1924," *Papers on China*, 12:69–146 (1958).

——— "Kuo Mo-jo: The Early Years." To be published by Harvard University Press.

Roy, M. N. *Materialism and Spiritualism: Presidential Address to the Third Session of the Madras Presidency Radical Youths' Conference, 25 July 1937*. Bombay: Satya Mitra Press, 1937.

——— *India's Message (Fragments of a Prisoner's Diary*, Vol. 2). 2nd ed.; Calcutta: Renaissance Publishers, 1950.

——— *Materialism: Outline of the History of Scientific Thought*. 2nd rev. ed.; Calcutta: Renaissance Publishers, 1951.

Roy, Rammohun. *A Defence of Hindoo Theism in Reply to the Attack of an Advocate for Idolatry at Madras*. Calcutta, 1817; reprinted in *The English Works of Raja Rammohun Roy*, Pt. 2.

——— "Introduction," *Translation of Several Principal Books, Passages, and Texts of the Ved[a]s and of Some Controversial Works on Brahmunical Theology*. 2nd ed.; London: Parbury, Allen and Co., 1832.

——— *The English Works of Raja Rammohun Roy*, ed. Kalidas Nag and Debajyoti Burman. Calcutta: Sadharan Brahmo Samaj, 1945.

Russell, Bertrand. *The Problem of China*. New York: Century Co., 1922.

——— *Portraits from Memory*. New York: Simon and Schuster, 1956.

Sano Jinnosuke 佐野甚之助. "Tagōru sensei to watakushi" タゴール先生と私 (Master Tagore and I); in Kiyozawa Iwao, ed., *Meishi no Tagōru kan*.

——— *Indo oyobi Indojin* 印度及印度人 (India and the Indians). Tokyo, 1917.

Sarkār, Binay (Benoy) Kumār. *Vartamān jagat* (The contemporary world). 13 vols.; Calcutta, 1914–1935.

——— *Chinese Religion Through Hindu Eyes: A Study in the Tendencies of Asiatic Mentality*. Shanghai: Commercial Press, 1916.

——— *The Beginning of Hindu Culture as World-Power, A.D. 300–600.* Shanghai: Commercial Press, 1916.

——— *The Futurism of Young Asia and Other Essays on the Relations between the East and the West.* Berlin: Julius Springer, 1922.

——— "Rabindranath and World-Forces," in *The Golden Book of Tagore.*

Sarkar, Jadunath. *India Through the Ages: A Survey of the Growth of Indian Life and Thought* (Sir William Meyer Lectures, Madras University, 1928). 4th ed.; Calcutta: M. C. Sarkar and Sons, 1951.

Sarkār, Praphullakumār. *Jātīya āndolane Rabīndranāth* (Rabindranath in the national movement). 2nd ed.; Calcutta: Anand-Hindusthān Prakā-śanī, B.E. 1354 (1947–1948).

Sarma, D. S. *Studies in the Renaissance of Hinduism in the Nineteenth and Twentieth Centuries.* Benares: Benares Hindu University, 1944.

——— "Introduction: Professor S. Radhakrishnan," in S. Radhakrishnan, *Great Indians.* Bombay: Hind Kitabs, 1949.

Sasaki Nobutsuna 佐佐木信綱. "Tagōru ou no inshō" ターゴル翁の印象 (Impressions of Dr. Tagore); *Taiyō* 太陽 (The sun), 32.10:128 (August 1916).

Sastri, K. S. Ramaswami. *Sir Rabindranath Tagore: His Life, Personality, and Genius.* Madras: Ganesh and Co., 1916.

——— *Rabindranath Tagore: Poet, Patriot, Philosopher.* Srirangam: Sri Vani Vilas Press, 1924.

——— *Vita Sua.* Published by the author; Madras, 1948.

Savarkar, V. D. *Hindutva.* 2nd ed.; Poona: V. G. Ketkar, 1962.

Schimmel, Annemarie. *Gabriel's Wing: A Study into the Religious Ideas of Sir Muhammad Iqbal.* Leiden: E. J. Brill, 1963.

Schopenhauer, Arthur. *The World As Will and As Idea,* tr. B.B. Haldane and J. Kemp. 6th ed.; 3 vols.; London: Kegan Paul, Trench, Trübner, 1909.

Schwab, Raymond. *La renaissance orientale.* Paris: Payot, 1950.

Schwantes, Robert S. "Christianity *versus* Science: A Conflict of Ideas in Meiji Japan," *Far Eastern Quarterly,* 12.2:128 (February 1953).

Schwartz, Benjamin I. "Ch'en Tu-hsiu and the Acceptance of the Modern West," *Journal of the History of Ideas,* 12:61–74 (January 1951).

——— "The Intellectual History of China: Preliminary Reflections," in John K. Fairbank, ed., *Chinese Thought and Institutions,* pp. 15–30.

Scott, A. C. *Mei Lan-fang, Leader of the Pear Garden.* Hong Kong University Press, 1959.

Sei Tagōru 聖タゴール (Tagore the sage). Tokyo: Kyōiku gakujutsu kenkyūkai, 1916.

Sen, Amit (pseud. of Sushabhusan Sarkar). *Notes on the Bengal Renaissance.*

2nd ed.; Calcutta: National Book Agency, 1957.

Sen, Keshub Chunder. *Lectures in India*. Calcutta: Navavidhan Publication Committee, 1954.

Sen, Pulinbehari. *Books about Rabindranath Tagore*. Santiniketan: Visva-Bharati, 1957; reprinted from *Visva-Bharati Quarterly* (Spring 1957).

———— "Bibliography," in Sachin Sen, *The Political Thought of Tagore*, pp. 335–360. Calcutta: General Printers and Publishers, 1947.

———— and Jaganindra Bhaumik. "Works of Rabindranath Tagore: A Bibliography," in *Rabindranath Tagore: A Centenary Volume*, pp. 504–519.

———— and Subhendu Mukhopadhyaya. *Rabindranath Tagore: Contributions and Translations Published in Periodicals*. Santiniketan: Visva-Bharati, 1961; reprinted from *Visva-Bharati News* (1961).

Sen, Sukumar. "Some Early Influences in Tagore's Life," *Indo-Asian Culture*, 10.1:152 (July 1961).

Servant. Calcutta, 1921, 1924.

Seth, Hira Lal. *Tagore on China and Japan*. Lahore: Tagore Memorial Publications, c. 1943.

Shanghai Mercury. Shanghai, 1924.

Shanghai Times. Shanghai, 1924.

Shen pao 申報. Shanghai, April-June 1924, March 1929.

Shen Tse-min 沈澤民. "T'ai-ko-erh yü Chung-kuo ch'ing-nien" 太戈爾與中國青年 (Tagore and China's youth); *Chung-kuo ch'ing-nien*, No. 27:5–13 (Apr. 18, 1924).

———— "P'ing 'Jen-lei ti-san-chi chih shih-chieh' " 評「人類第三紀之世界」 (I criticize "The Third Age of Humanity"); *Chung-kuo ch'ing-nien*, No. 31: 4–11 (May 17, 1924).

Shen Yen-ping 沈雁冰. "Tui-yü T'ai-ko-erh ti hsi-wang" 對於太戈爾的希望 (What we expect of Tagore); *Min-kuo jih-pao, Chüeh-wu* 民國日報覺悟 (Republic daily, Awakening supplement; Shanghai, Apr. 14, 1924).

———— "Tu T'ai-shih yen-chiang hou ti kan-hsiang" 讀太氏演講後的感想 (My impressions after reading reports of Mr. Tagore's lectures); *Min-kuo jih-pao, Chüeh-wu* (May or June 1924). French tr. in Leon Wieger, "Visite de Sir R. Tagore," pp. 80–81.

Shih An 實菴 (Ch'en Tu-hsiu). "T'ai-ko-erh yü tung-fang wen-hua" 太戈爾與東方文化; *Chung-kuo ch'ing-nien*, No. 27:1–2 (Apr. 18, 1924).

Shin chō 新潮 (New tide). Tokyo, 1916.

Shin jin 新人 (New man). Tokyo, 1916.

Siddiqi, Mazheruddin. *The Image of the West in Iqbāl*. Lahore: Bazm-i-Iqbal, 1956.

Singhji, Maharaj Rana Sir Udaibhan. *Eastern Light of Sanātan Culture*. Calcutta: Thacker, Spink, 1946.

Snow, Edgar. *Red Star over China*. New York: Random House, 1938.

Sobu Rokurō 蘇武綠郎. *Tagōru hyōden* タゴール評傳 (A critical biography of Tagore). Tokyo, 1915.

——— et al., trs. *Tagōru kessaku zenshū* タゴール傑作全集 (A complete collection of Tagore's masterpieces). 4th ed.; Tokyo, 1915.

Soejima Yasoroku 副島八十六. "Indo no gendai oyobi shōrai" 印度の現代及 將來 (The present and future of India); *Chūō kōron*, 31.8:137–138 (July 1916).

Sources of Chinese Tradition, comp. William Theodore de Bary, Wing-tsit Chan, and Burton Watson. New York: Columbia University Press, 1960.

Sources of the Japanese Tradition, comp. Tsunoda Ryusaku, William Theodore de Bary, and Donald Keene. New York: Columbia University Press, 1958.

South China Morning Post. Hong Kong, April-June 1924.

Sovani, N. V. "British Impact on India after 1850–1857," *Cahiers d'histoire mondiale*, 2.1:103–104 (1954).

Spellman, John W. "The International Extensions of Political Conspiracy As Illustrated by the Ghadr Party," *Journal of Indian History*, 37.1:32 (April 1959).

Srīmad Rājchandra, ed. Mansukhlal Ravjibhai Mehta. 2 vols.; Bombay: Hemchand Tokarshi Mehta, Samvāt 1992 (1935–1936).

Stead, W. T. *Annie Besant: A Character Sketch*. London: 1891; reprinted, Adyar, Madras: Theosophical Publishing House, 1946.

Stevenson, Mrs. Sinclair. *The Heart of Jainism*. Humphrey Milford, Oxford University Press, 1915.

Storry, Richard. *The Double Patriots: A Study of Japanese Nationalism*. Boston: Houghton Mifflin Co., 1957.

Studies in the Bengal Renaissance, ed. Atulchandra Gupta. Jadavpur, West Bengal: National Council of Education, Bengal, 1958.

Sumner, B. H. *A Short History of Russia*. Rev. ed.; New York: Harcourt, Brace, 1949.

Sun Yat-sen. "Nationalism: Lectures 5 and 6," in his *San Min Chu I: The Three Principles of the People*, tr. Frank W. Price, ed. L. T. Chen. Shanghai: Commercial Press, 1929.

——— "Pan-Asianism," in his *The Vital Problem of China*. Taipei: China Cultural Service, 1953.

Swadeshmitran (Friend of the country). Madras, 1916.

Swarajya. Madras, 1923–1924.

Tagore, Abanindranath, see Abanīndranāth Ṭhākur.

Tagore and Gandhi Argue, comp. Jag Parvesh Chander. Lahore: Indian Printing

Works, 1945.

Tagore, Debendranath (Debendranāth Ṭhākur). *The Autobiography of Maharshi Debendranath Tagore*, tr. Satyendranath Tagore and Indira Devi. London: Macmillan and Co., 1915.

—— "Maharshi Debendranath Tagore: Reminiscences of Rammohun Roy," in *The Father of Modern India: Commemoration Volume of the Rammohun Roy Centenary Celebrations, 1933.* Calcutta: Rammohun Roy Centenary Committee, 1935.

—— *Brāhmadharmaḥ* (The religion of Brāhma). 10th ed.; Calcutta: Sādhāran Brāhmasamāj, B.E. 1356 (1949).

Tagore, Rabindranath (Rabīndranāth Ṭhākur). "Bāngālīr āśā o nairāśya" (The hope and despair of the Bengalis); *Bhāratī* (The goddess of speech), 1.7:305 (B.E. Māgh 1284 [January-February 1878]).

—— Letters to William Rothenstein: Dec. 29, 1914; Apr. 4, 1915; July 22, 1915; Dec. 10, 1915; Aug. 2, 1916; July 6, 1917; June 1, 1918; Oct. 20, 1922; undated, possibly late 1923. Deposited in Houghton Library, Harvard University.

—— *Stray Birds*. New York: Macmillan Co., 1916.

—— *The Spirit of Japan: A Lecture by Sir Rabindranath Tagore Delivered for the Students of the Private Colleges of Tokyo and the Members of the Indo-Japanese Association, at the Keio Gijuku University.* Tokyo: Indo-Japanese Association, 1916.

—— *The Message of India to Japan.* Imperial University of Tokyo, 1916.

—— *Nationalism.* New York: Macmillan Co., 1917.

—— "Paradise, Being an Address Delivered by Rabindranath Tagore before Japanese Students in Tokyo," in W. W. Pearson, *Shantiniketan, The Bolpur School of Rabindranath Tagore*, pp. 99–104.

—— "The Call of Truth," *Modern Review*, 30.4:423–433 (October 1921).

—— *Greater India.* Madras: S. Ganesan, 1921.

—— "The Union of Cultures," *Modern Review*, 30.5:533–542 (November 1921).

—— *Jībansmṛti* (My reminiscences). 2nd ed.; Calcutta: Biśvabhāratī, B.E. 1328 (1921–1922).

—— *Creative Unity.* London: Macmillan and Co., 1922.

—— "The Prophet's Voice," *Sind Observer* (Karachi, Mar. 22, 1923).

—— *Letters from Abroad.* Madras: S. Ganesan, 1924.

—— "City and Village," *Kaizō* 改造 (Reconstruction), 6.7:95–106 (July 1924); reprinted in *Visva-Bharati Quarterly*, 2.3:215–227 (October 1924).

—— "Talks in China." Calcutta, 1924; printed but withheld from publication.

——— *Talks in China: Lectures Delivered in April and May 1924.* Calcutta: Visva-Bharati Bookshop, 1925.

——— "I-ko wen-hsüeh ko-ming-chia ti kung-chuang"一個文學革命家的供狀 (Confessions of a literary revolutionist), tr. Hsü Chih-mo; *Hsiao-shuo yüeh-pao*, Vol. 15, No. 6 (June 1924).

——— "Ti-i-tz'u ti t'an-hua" 第一次的談話 (First talk [in China]), tr. Hsü Chih-mo; *Hsiao-shuo yüeh-pao*, Vol. 15, No. 8 (August 1924).

——— "Ch'ing-hua yen-chiang" 清華演講 (Lecture at Tsing Hua College), tr. Hsü Chih-mo; *Hsiao-shuo yüeh-pao*, Vol. 15, No. 10 (October 1924).

——— "Judgment," *Visva-Bharati Quarterly*, 3.3: 195–208 (October 1925).

——— "The Rule of the Giant," *Visva-Bharati Quarterly*, 4.2: 99–112 (July 1926).

——— *My Reminiscences.* New York: Macmillan Co., 1927.

——— *Jāpān-yātrī* (A traveler to Japan). 2nd ed.; Calcutta: Biśvabhāratī granthālaẏ, B.E. 1334 (1927–1928).

——— *Letters to a Friend,* ed. C. F. Andrews. London: Allen and Unwin, 1928.

——— "Aurobindo Ghosh," *Modern Review,* 44.1: 60 (July 1928).

——— "Dr. R. Tagore's Preface," in Ch'ü Yüan, *The Li Sao: An Elegy on Encountering Sorrows,* tr. Lim Boon Keng, pp. xxiii-xxiv. Shanghai: Commercial Press, 1929.

——— *On Oriental Culture and Japan's Mission.* Tokyo: Indo-Japanese Association, 1929.

——— *Sanchayitā* (A collection). Calcutta: Biśvabhāratī, 1931; 6th ed., 1946.

——— *The Religion of Man.* London: George Allen and Unwin, 1931.

——— "The Vision," *Hindusthan Records,* H. 782. Calcutta: H.M.V. Syndicate, c. 1935.

——— Letter of November 17, 1937, in *Navavidhan* (The new dispensation): *Keshub Chandra Centenary Number,* Vol. 1, No. 2 (1938).

——— "On the Way to Japan," *Visva-Bharati Quarterly,* new ser., 4.2:95–106 (August-October 1938); *ibid.,* 4.3:186–198 (November 1938). Tr. from his *Jāpān-yātrī* by Indira Devi Chowdhurani.

——— *Rabīndra-rachanābalī* (The writings of Rabindra), 26 vols.; Calcutta: Biśvābhāratī, B.E. 1346–1355 (1939–1948).

——— *Chiṭhipatra* (Letters). 7 vols.; Calcutta: Biśvabhāratī granthālaẏ, B.E. 1349–1367 (1942–1960).

——— *My Boyhood Days.* Calcutta: Visva-Bharati, 1943.

——— "Gandhi the Man," in *Gandhi Memorial Peace Number,* pp. 10–13.

——— "The Voice of Humanity," in *Lectures and Addresses,* comp. Anthony X. Soares. Indian ed.; London: Macmillan and Co., 1950.

——— "Ÿurop-yātrīr ḍāẏāri'r khasṛā" (Draft copy of *A diary of a traveler to Europe*); *Biśvabhāratī patrikā* (Visva-Bharati journal), No. 3:155ff.

(B.E. Māgh-Chaitra, 1356 [January-April 1950]).

———— *The Centre of Indian Culture*. Calcutta: Visva-Bharati Bookshop, 1951.

———— "Chiṭhipatra" (Letters); *Biśvabhāratī patrikā*, 12.1:1–2 (July-September 1955).

———— *A Flight of Swans: Poems from Balākā*, tr. Aurobindo Bose (Wisdom of the East Series). London: John Murray, 1955.

———— *Our Universe*, tr. Indu Dutt. London: Meridian, 1958.

———— Holograph message dated May 1930, in *Indo-Asian Culture*, 10.1:115 (July 1961).

———— *Chhinna patra* (Torn letters), as tr. in his *The Wayfaring Poet*. Calcutta: Dunlop Rubber Co., 1961.

———— "Fruit-Gathering," in *Collected Poems and Plays of Rabindranath Tagore*. London: Macmillan and Co., 1961.

———— *A Visit to Japan*, tr. Shakuntala Rao Sastri, ed. Walter Donald Kring. New York: East West Institute, 1961.

———— and Yone Noguchi. *Poet to Poet*. Calcutta: Visva-Bharati, 1939.

Tagore-Noguchi Correspondence. Cleveland: Foreign Affairs Council, 1942.

Tagore, Rathindranath. "Father As I Knew Him," *Visva-Bharati Quarterly*, 18.4: 338 (February-April 1953).

———— *On the Edges of Time*. Calcutta: Orient Longmans, 1958.

Tagore, Surendranath. "Kakuzo Okakura," *Visva-Bharati Quarterly*, new ser., 2.2:65–72 (August 1936).

"Tagore's Message," *Chinese Recorder: Journal of the Christian Movement in China*, 5.7: 478 (July 1924). Shanghai: Presbyterian Mission Press.

T'ai Hsü 太虛. "Hsi-wang lao-shih-jen ti T'ai-ko-erh pien-wei Fo-hua ti hsin-ch'ing-nien" 希望老詩人的太戈爾變爲佛化的新青年 (I wish the old poet Tagore would become transformed into a new Buddhist youth): *Fo-hua hsin-ch'ing-nien*, 2.2:4–6 (Peking and Shanghai, 1924).

———— "Ching-kao kung-ch'an-tang" 警告共產黨 (Warning to the Communist party); *Fo-hua hsin-ch'ing-nien*, 2.2:26 (1924).

———— "Tung-yang wen-hua yü hsi-yang wen-hua" 東洋文化與西洋文化 (Eastern and Western civilizations); *Hsüeh heng* 學衡 (The critical review), No. 32:5–6 (Nanking, August 1924).

"T'ai-ko-erh chiang yu Su-o" 太戈爾將遊蘇俄 (Tagore will visit Soviet Russia); *Shen pao* (May 17, 1924).

"T'ai-ko-erh chih erh-tz'u yen-chiang" 太戈爾之二次演講 (Tagore's second lecture); *Shen pao* (May 13, 1924).

"T'ai-ko-erh chih lai-Hua kan-hsiang t'an" 太戈爾之來華感想談 (Talking with Tagore about his impressions on arriving in China); *Shen pao* (Apr. 14, 1924).

"T'ai-ko-erh kuan-yü Fo-chiao chih t'an-hua" 太戈爾關於佛教之談話 (Tagore's conversation about Buddhism); *Shen pao* (May 20, 1924).

"T'ai-ko-erh tsai ching tsui-hou chih chiang-yen" 太戈爾在京最後之講演 (Tagore's last speech in the capital); *Shen pao* (May 15, 1924).

Takakusu Junjirō 高楠順次郎. "Yo ga mitaru Tagōru" 余が見たるタゴール (I look at Tagore); *Rikugō zasshi*, 36.7:29–33 (July 1916).

Takao Kenichi 高尾謙一. "Tagōru ou o omou" タゴール翁を想ふ (Thinking about Tagore); *Rikugō zasshi*, 37.6:137–142 (June 1917).

Takeda Toyoshirō 武田豊四郎. "Tagōru ou ni taisuru kansō" タゴール翁に對する感想 (Impressions on seeing Dr. Tagore); *Waseda bungaku* (July 1916), pp. 295–296.

———— "Tagōru o otonau no ki" タゴールを訪ふの記 (A record of Tagore's visit); *Rikugō zasshi*, 36.8:107 (August 1916).

Tan Shih-hua. *A Chinese Testament: The Autobiography of Tan Shih-hua, As Told to S. Tretiakov*, tr. anon. from the Russian. New York: Simon and Schuster, 1934.

Tan, Yun-shan. *Twenty Years of the Visva-Bharati Cheena-Bhavana, 1937–1957.* Santiniketan: The Sino-Indian Cultural Society of India, 1957.

———— "My Dedication to Gurudeva Tagore: Written on the First Anniversary of his Death," in V. G. Nair, *Professor Tan Yun-shan and Cultural Relations between India and China.* Madras: Indo-Asian Publications, 1958.

Tanaka Ōdō 田中王堂. "Tagōru shi ni ataete shi no Nihon kan o ronzu" タゴール氏に與へて氏の日本觀を論ず (I discuss Mr. Tagore's views of Japan); *Chūō kōron*, 31.9: 17–38 (September 1916).

———— "Tagōru wa kita so shite satta" タゴールは來たそして去った (Tagore came and then left); *Shin kōron* 新公論 (New opinion), 31.10:12–21 (October 1916).

———— "Haruka ni Tagōru shi yosete Ajiya dōmei no shisō ronzu" 遙かにタゴール氏寄せて亞細亞同盟の思想論ず (I discuss with Tagore, who lives far away, the idea of an Asian league); *Chūō kōron*, 39.12:4–47 (December 1924).

Tanimoto Tomi 谷本富. "Tagōru wa shijin no mi Indojin no mi" タゴールは詩人のみ，インド人のみ (Tagore as a poet and as an Indian); *Rikugō zasshi*, 36.7:36–37 (July 1916).

———— "Tagōru no betsuji" タゴールの別辞 (Tagore's parting words); *Rikugō zasshi*, 36.10:38–40 (October 1916).

Tendulkar, D. G. *Mahatma: Life of Mohandas Karamchand Gandhi.* 8 vols.; Bombay: Vithalbhari K. Javeri and D. G. Tendulkar, 1951–1954.

Teng, Ssu-yü and John K. Fairbank. *China's Response to the West: A Documentary Survey, 1839–1923.* Cambridge, Mass.: Harvard University Press, 1954.

Thākur, Abanīndranāth. *Jorāsānkor dhāre* (On the banks of the Jorasanko) Calcutta: Biśvabhāratī granthālaẏ, B.E. 1351 (1945–1946).

Thākur, Debendranāth, see Debendranath Tagore.

Thākur, Rabīndranāth, see Rabindranath Tagore.

Thompson, Edward. *Rabindranath Tagore, Poet and Dramatist.* 2nd rev. ed.; London: Oxford University Press, 1948.

Tōkyō asahi shimbun 東京朝日新聞. 1916–1917, 1924, 1929.

Tolstoy, Leo. *Anna Karenina*, tr. Constance Garnett. 2 vols.; New York: Random House, 1939.

Tovstykh, I. A. and A. I. Chicherov. "Problemy natsional'no-osvoboditel'-nogo dvizheniia 1905–1908 gg. v. Indii i ikh otrazhenie v publitsistike Rabindranata Tagor" (Problems of the National-Liberation Movement of 1905–1908 in India and their treatment in the publicistic writings of Rabindranath Tagore); in *Rabindranat Tagor, k stoletiiu so dnia rozhdeniia, 1861–1961: Sbornik statei* (Rabindranath Tagore, for the centenary of his birth, 1861–1961: A collection of essays). Moscow: Izdatel'stvo vostochnoi literatury, 1961.

Townsend, Meredith. *Asia and Europe.* 3rd ed.; London: Archibald Constable and Co., 1905.

Trans-Pacific. Tokyo, 1924.

Tsuchida, Kyoson. *Contemporary Thought of Japan and China.* London: Williams and Norgate, 1927.

Tsuda, Sokichi. *What Is the Oriental Culture?* tr. Yosataro Mori. Tokyo: Hokuseido Press, 1955.

Tsurumi, Yusuke. *Present Day Japan.* New York: Columbia University Press, 1926.

Tung Feng-ming 董鳳鳴. "T'ai-ko-erh chih tsai Nan-ching" 太戈爾之在南京 (Mr. Tagore at Nanking); *Ch'en-pao fu-k'an* (Apr. 26, 1924).

Ukita Kazutami 浮田和民. "Tō zai bummei no daihyōsha, hikōka Sumisu to shisei Tagōru" 東西文明の代表者，飛行家スミスと詩聖タゴール (Leading representatives of Eastern and Western civilizations: The aviator Smith and the poet-sage Tagore); *Taiyō*, 22.19: 12 (July 1, 1916).

Van Slyke, Lyman B. "Liang Sou-ming and The Rural Reconstruction Movement," *Journal of Asian Studies*, 18.4:457–474 (August 1959).

Vaswani, T. L. *The Secret of Asia: Essays on the Spirit of Asian Culture.* Madras: Ganesh, c. 1920.

"Visva-Bharati," *Modern Review*, 31.1:124 (January 1922).

Vivekananda, Swami. "The Work before Us," in *The Complete Works of Swami Vivekananda*, III, 269–284. Mayavati Memorial ed.; 8 vols.;

Calcutta: Advaita Ashrama, 1922–1959.

———— "The Influence of Indian Spiritual Thought in England," in *The Complete Works of Swami Vivekananda*, III, 440–444.

———— "Christ the Messenger," in *The Complete Works of Swami Vivekananda*, IV, 138–153.

———— "My Master," in *The Complete Works of Swami Vivekananda*, IV, 154–187.

———— *The East and West*. Calcutta: Advaita Ashrama, 1955.

Wang, Ch'ung-yu. "Chinese Pictorial Art: An Essay on Its Interpretation," *China Journal of Science and Arts*, 3.1:4ff. (January 1925).

Wang Hsi-ho 王希和. "T'ai-ko-erh hsüeh-shuo kai-kuan" 太戈爾學說概觀 (An outline of Tagore's theory); *Tung-fang tsa-chih*, 20.14:73–90 (July 25, 1923).

Wang Hung-wen 王鴻文. "T'ai-ko-erh tsai Han-k'ou Fu-teh chung-hsüeh-hsiao chih chiang-yen" 泰戈爾在漢口輔德中學校之講演 (Tagore's lecture at the Supporting Virtue Middle School); *Ch'en-pao fu-k'an* (June 21, 1924).

Wang, Tsi C. *The Youth Movement in China*. New York: New Republic, 1927.

Wang T'ung-chao 王統照. "T'ai-ko-erh ti ssu-hsiang chi ch'i shih-ko ti piao-hsiang" 太戈爾的思想及其詩歌的表象 (Tagore's thought and its expression in poetry and song); *Hsiao-shuo yüeh-pao*, Vol. 14, No. 9 (September 1923).

Wang, Y. C. "Intellectuals and Society in China, 1860–1949," *Comparative Studies in Society and History*, 3.4: 395–426 (July 1961).

Warren, Herbert. *Jainism In Western Garb, As a Solution to Life's Great Problems, Chiefly from Notes of Talks and Lectures by Virchand R. Gandhi*. Madras: Thompson and Co., 1912.

Welch, Holmes H. *The Practice of Buddhism in China*. Cambridge, Mass.: Harvard University Press, 1967.

———— *The Buddhist Revival in China*. Cambridge, Mass.: Harvard University Press, 1968.

Wen-hsüeh lun-wen so-yin 文學論文索引 (Index to literary essays). 3 vols.; Peiping: Chung-hua t'u-hsu-kuan li-hui, 1932–1936.

Wen I-to 聞一多. "T'ai-kuo-erh p'i-p'ing" 泰果爾批評 (A criticism of Tagore); *Shih-shih hsin-pao, wen-hsüeh* 時事新報文學 (Shanghai times, literary supplement; Dec. 3, 1923). Reprinted in *Wen I-to ch'üan-chi* 聞一多全集 (Collected works of Wen I-to), 4 vols. (Shanghai: K'ai-ming shu-tien, 1948), Vol. 3, Pt. 1, pp. 275–279.

———— "Nü-shen chih ti-fang se-ts'ai" 女神之地方色彩 (Local color in "The Goddess"); in *Wen I-to ch'üan-chi*, Vol. 3, Pt. 1, pp. 195–201.

Wheeler, Mortimer. *Civilizations of the Indus Valley and Beyond*. London: Thames and Hudson, 1966.

Who's Who in China. 3rd ed.; Shanghai: China Weekly Review, 1925.

Who's Who in Japan, 1916, ed. Ishikawa Yasujiro. 5th ed.; Tokyo, 1916.

Who's Who in Modern China, ed. Max Perleberg. Hong Kong: Ye Olde Printerie, 1954.

Wieger, Léon, S. J., comp. "Visite de Sir R. Tagore," in *Nationalisme, xénophobie, anti-christianisme (La Chine moderne*, Vol. 5), pp. 66–83. Hsien-hsien, Chihli: Imprimerie de Hsien-hsien, 1924.

Wilhelm, Richard. "Intellectual Movements in Modern China," *Chinese Social and Political Science Review*, 8.2: 110–124 (April 1924).

———— "Aus Zeit und Leben: Eine interessante Statistik," *Pekinger Abende*, 2.3:1–6 (April 1924).

———— "Aus Zeit und Leben: Abschied von China," *Pekinger Abende*, 2.4: 4–5 (July 1924).

———— *The Soul of China*, tr. J. Holroyd Reece. New York: Harcourt, Brace, 1928.

Willson, A. Leslie. *A Mythical Image: The Ideal of India in German Romanticism*. Durham: Duke University Press, 1964.

Winsten, Stephen. *Salt and His Circle*. London: Hutchinson and Co., 1951.

Wolff, Otto. *Radhakrishnan* (Kleine Vandenhoeck-Reihe, No. 124). Goettigen: Vandenhoeck & Ruprecht [1962].

Wolpert, Stanley A. *Tilak and Gokhale: Revolution and Reform in the Making of Modern India*. Berkeley and Los Angeles: University of California Press, 1962.

Wong-Quincey, J. (Wang Wen-hsien). "A Criticism of Tagore's Tsing Hua Speech," *China Illustrated Review* (Tientsin, May 10, 1924), pp. 8–9.

Woodroffe, Sir John. *Is India Civilized? Essays on Indian Culture*. 3rd ed.; Madras: Ganesh, 1922; 1st ed., 1918.

Wright, Arthur F. *Buddhism in Chinese History*. Stanford University Press, 1959.

Wright, Brooks. "Sir Edwin Arnold: A Literary Biography of the Author of *The Light of Asia*." Ph.D. thesis; Harvard University, 1951.

———— *Interpreter of Buddhism to the West: Sir Edwin Arnold*. New York: Bookman Associates, 1957.

Wright, Mary C. "From Revolution to Restoration: The Transformation of Kuomintang Ideology," *Far Eastern Quarterly*, 14.4: 515–532 (August 1955).

Wu Chih-hui 吳稚暉. "Wan-kao T'ai-ko-erh" 婉告太戈爾 (Courteous advice to Tagore); in *Wu Chih-hui hsien-sheng wen-ts'ui* 吳稚暉先生文粹 (Complete essays of Mr. Wu Chih-hui), I, 292–296. 4 vols.; Shanghai: Ch'üan-min shu-chü, 1928.

————— "Chen yang-pa-ku-hua chih li-hsüeh" 箴洋八股化之理學 (A warning to foreign-formalized Neo-Confucianism); in *Wu Chih-hui hsien-sheng wen-ts'ui*, III, 315–322.

————— "Huang-hui sheng-chung ti T'ai-ko-erh" 皇會聲中的太戈爾 (Tagore in the midst of the noise of the monarchist movement); in *Wu Chih-hui hsien-sheng wen-ts'ui*, I, 296–298.

————— *Wu Chih-hui hsien-sheng hsüan-chi* 吳稚暉先生選集 (An anthology of Wu Chih-hui's writings). 2 vols.; Taipei: Chung-kuo Kuo-min-tang, 1964.

Wu-ssu shih-ch'i chi-k'an chieh-shao 五四時期季刊介紹 (An introduction to periodicals of the May Fourth period). 3 vols.; Peking: Jen-min ch'u-pan she, 1958–1959.

Yale Daily News. New Haven, 1916.

Yang Yun-yüan 楊允元. "Sheng-p'ing jeh-ai Chung-kuo ti T'ai-ko-erh" 生平熱愛中國的太戈爾 (Tagore, who warmly loved China during his lifetime); *Ch'uan-chi wen-hsüeh* 傳記文學 (Biographical literature), 7.6:36 (Taipei, December 1965).

Yeats, W. B. "Introduction," in Rabindranath Tagore, *Gitanjali* (Song offerings), pp. vii–xxii. London: Macmillan and Co., 1957.

Yoshida Genjirō 吉田絃二郎. *Tagōru seija no seikatsu* タゴール聖者の生活 (The life of the sage Tagore). Tokyo, 1915.

————— "Tagōru o otonau no ki" タゴールを訪ふの記 (Record of a visit to Tagore); *Rikugō zasshi*, 36.8:107–108 (August 1916).

Yoshino Sakuzō 吉野作造. "Kensei no hongi o totte sono yūshū no bi o motarasu no michi o ronzu" 憲政の本義を取ってその有終の美を齎すの道を論ず (On the meaning of constitutional government and the means by which it can be perfected); *Chūō kōron*, 31.1:17–125 (January 1916).

Young India. Ahmedabad, 1921, 1924, 1927.

Yüan Lieh-ch'eng 袁烈成. "Wo tui-yü T'ai-ko-erh lai-Hua chih kan-yen" 我對於太哥爾來華之感言 (My word of thanks to Tagore for coming to China); *Fo-hua hsin-ch'ing-nien*, 2.2:24–26 (1924).

For Chinese-Japanese characters of the names of persons whose writings are cited in the Notes, see the Bibliography.

SELECT GLOSSARY

Abe Jirō　阿部次郎
Anesaki Masaharu　姉崎正治
Arishima Takeo　有島武郎

bummei kaika　文明開化

Chang Chih-tung　張之洞
Chang T'ai-yen　章太炎
cheng-li kuo-ku　整理國故
Chiang-hsüeh she　講學社
Chiang Kai-shek　蔣介石
Ch'i Hsieh-yüan　齊燮元
Chou Yüeh-jan　周越然
Chu Chen-tan　竺震旦
Ch'uang-tsao she　創造社
Chung-kuo　中國
Ch'ü Shih-ying　瞿世英

Ema Nagashi　江馬修

Fan Yüan-lien　范源濂

goyō　御用

haiku　俳句
Hasegawa Seiya　長谷川誠也
Heki Mokusen　日置默仙
Hirasawa Tetsuo　平澤哲雄
Hishida Shunsō　菱田春草
horobiru　亡びる
Hsieh Ping-hsin　謝冰心
Hsin-yüeh　新月
Hsüeh-heng　學衡
hung-t'ou ah-san　紅頭阿三

Ikuta Chōkō　生田長江

Itō Shōshin　伊藤證信
Ittō-en　一燈緣

Jih-pen　日本

Kamitsukasa Shōken　上司小劍
Kaneko Umaji　金子馬治
Kanokogi Kazunobu　鹿子木員信
Katō Asadori　加藤朝鳥
Katō Kazuo　加藤一夫
Kawaguchi Ekkai　川口慧海
Kayahara Kazan　茅原華山
Keng Kuang　耿光
Kihira Masayoshi　紀平正義
Kimura Taiken　木村泰賢
Kishimoto Nobuta　岸本能武太
kōdō　皇道
Kokuryūkai　黑龍會
kokutai　國體
Ku Hung-ming　辜鴻銘
Kuroiwa Shūroku　黑岩周六
Kuruma Takudō　來馬琢道
Kuwaki Genyoku　桑木嚴翼

Lim Boon Keng　林文慶
Lin Ch'ang-min　林長民

Mao Tse-tung　毛澤東
Mao Tun　茅盾
Maruyama Kanji　丸山幹治
Masaoka Shiki　正岡子規
Mei Lan-fang　梅蘭芳
Mitsui Kōshi　三井甲之
Mori Ōgai　森鷗外
Morita Sōhei　森田草平

muga-ai 無我愛

Mushakōji Saneatsu 武者小路實篤

Nagai Kafū 永井荷風
Nagai Ryūtarō 永井柳太郎
Naitō Arō 内藤濯
Nihon bijutsuin 日本美術院
Nishida Kitarō 西田幾多郎
Nishida Tenkō 西田天香
Noboru Shomu 昇曙夢

Ogawa Mimei 小川未明
Okakura Yoshisaburō 岡倉由三郎
Ojima Shinji 尾島眞治
Ōkuma Shigenobu 大隈重信
Ōkura Kunihiko 大倉邦彦
Ōsumi Shun 大住舜

Pei-ching Fo-chia chiang-hsi hui
北京佛家講習會
P'u-i 溥儀

Saitō Takeshi 齋藤勇
Sakuma Shōzan 佐久間象山
san-min chu-i 三民主義
Satō Kiyoshi 佐藤清
Sawayanagi Masatarō 澤柳政太郎
She-hui jih-pao 社會日報
Shin Bukkyō 新佛教
Shin Nihonshugi 新日本主義
Shirakaba-ha 白樺派
Sōma Gyofū 相馬御風
Sugiura Sadajirō 杉浦貞二郎

Sun Yat-sen 孫逸仙

ta-t'ung 大同
Ta-wen pao 大文報
Tai Chi-t'ao 戴季陶
Takashima Beihō 高島米峯
Tanizaki Seiji 谷崎精二
T'an Yüan-shan 譚雲山
Ting Wen-chiang 丁文江
Tominaga Tokuma 富永徳磨
Tōyama Mitsuru 頭山滿
Toyoshima Yoshio 豐島與志雄
Tōzai namboku 東西南北
Ts'ai Yüan-p'ei 蔡元培
Ts'ao K'un 曹錕

Uchigasaki Sakusaburō 内ヶ崎作三郎
Uchimura Kanzō 内村鑑三

waka 和歌
Wang Hsi-ho 王希和
Wang T'ung-chao 王統照
Watanabe Kaikyoku 渡邊海旭
Watsuji Tetsurō 和辻哲郎
Wu P'ei-fu 吳佩孚

Ya-chou Ku-hsüeh hui 亞州古學會
Yen Hsi-shan 閻錫山
Yokoyama Taikan 横山大觀
Yorozu chōhō 萬朝報
Yosano Akiko 與謝野晶子

Zumoto Motosada 頭本元貞

INDEX

Abe Jirō, 104, 105, 111, 357n.56; his *Santarō no nikki*, 104

Activism, 103; Chinese Communists advocate, 226, 230; in Western life, 235

Administrative classes, bureaucrats, officials: of China, 4, 8, 9, 10, 171, 191, 222, 225, 248; of Japan, 9, 111, 120, 121–122; of India, 13, 20, 248, 250, 251, 265. *See also* Brahmans; Confucianism; Samurai

Adyar, 274

Aeschylus, 358n.59

Aestheticism, 203; of Creation Society, 203; Tagore valued for his, 233–234

Afghan: rulers, 15; wars, 264; invasion of Punjab, 296

Afghanistan, 248, 294

Africa, 1, 2, 288; Western imperialism in, 33, 112. *See also* South Africa

Africans (White South Africans), 277, 278, 281, 284

Africanus, Leo, 48

Aglen (President, Anglo-American Association, Peking), 229

Agnosticism, 212

Agra, 290, 291

Ahimsā 279. *See also* Non-violence

Ahmad Khan, Sayyid, 296, 314

Ahmedabad, 247

Akita Ujaku, 74, 89

Alexander (of Macedon), 13

Alexandria, 13

Aligarh, 296, 297

Alipore Bomb Conspiracy Case (1908), 253

Allahabad, 275, 290, 291

Altar of Agriculture (Peking), 162, 163, 372n.47, 374n.69

Altar of Heaven (Peking), 372n.47

Amritsar Massacre, 130

Amsterdam, 80

Anarchism: in Japan, 85, 94, 98, 317; in China, 218, 225

Andrews, C. F.: Tagore's letters to, 52, 54, 131, 132, 283, 339n.16, 363n.24, 363 n.26; links Gandhi and Tagore, 53, 281–282; encourages Tagore to visit Japan, 55; accompanies Tagore to Japan, 56; on Tagore's tour of Japan, 72, 286, 351n.73; on India-China relations, 135; on Tagore's tour of China, 286, 305, 381n.24; in Hong Kong with Tagore, 405n.124

Anesaki Masaharu, 62, 98, 99, 100, 103, 111, 123, 356n.42

Anglo-American: Association (Peking), 79, 156, 162, 221, 229; 332; thought, 108, 140, 141; traditions, 123; literature, 198; influences on Chinese students, 231, 233

Anglo-Japanese Alliance, 58, 81

Anhwei, 153, 221

Anna Karenina (of Leo Tolstoy), 120

Anti-American agitation in Japan, 316, 317

Anti-British: espionage, by Bengali revolutionaries, 56; feeling in Japan, 81; agitation in India, 251, 308; activities of Pearson, 361n.6

Anti-Western: attitudes of Tagore, Iqbal, 298; cultural revival in Asia, 309

Arabia, 256, 280, 303, 311

Arabian Nights, 184

Arabian Sea, 276

Arabic language, 290, 291, 297

Arabs, 1, 293

Arikawa Jisuke, 360n.92

Arishima Takeo, 91, 353n.23, 354n.28; translation of *Leaves of Grass*, 91

Aristocracy, 261–262

Arnold, (Sir) Edwin, 23, 24, 278, 292, 340n.29; *Light of Asia*, 23

Arnold, Matthew, 6, 206, 207

Arnold, Thomas, 297

Aronson, Alex, 130

HARVARD EAST ASIAN SERIES

22. *After Imperialism: The Search for a New Order in the Far East, 1921–1931.* By Akira Iriye.
23. *Foundations of Constitutional Government in Modern Japan, 1868–1900.* By George Akita.
24. *Political Thought in Early Meiji Japan, 1868–1889.* By Joseph Pittau, S.J.
25. *China's Struggle for Naval Development, 1839–1895.* By John L. Rawlinson.
26. *The Practice of Buddhism in China, 1900–1950.* By Holmes Welch.
27. *Li Ta-chao and the Origins of Chinese Marxism.* By Maurice Meisner.
28. *Pa Chin and His Writings: Chinese Youth Between the Two Revolutions.* By Olga Lang
29. *Literary Dissent in Communist China.* By Merle Goldman.
30. *Politics in the Tokugawa Bakufu, 1600–1843.* By Conrad Totman.
31. *Hara Kei in the Politics of Compromise, 1905–1915.* By Tetsuo Najita.
32. *The Chinese World Order: Traditional China's Foreign Relations.* Edited by John K. Fairbank.
33. *The Buddhist Revival in China.* By Holmes Welch.
34. *Traditional Medicine in Modern China: Science, Nationalism, and the Tensions of Cultural Change.* By Ralph C. Croizier.
35. *Party Rivalry and Political Change in Taishō Japan.* By Peter Duus.
36. *The Rhetoric of Empire: American China Policy, 1895–1901.* By Marilyn B. Young.
37. *Radical Nationalist in Japan: Kita Ikki, 1883–1937.* By George M. Wilson.
38. *While China Faced West: American Reformers in Nationalist China, 1928–1937.* By James C. Thomson Jr.
39. *The Failure of Freedom: A Portrait of Modern Japanese Intellectuals.* By Tatsuo Arima.
40. *Asian Ideas of East and West: Tagore and His Critics in Japan, China, and India.* By Stephen N. Hay.